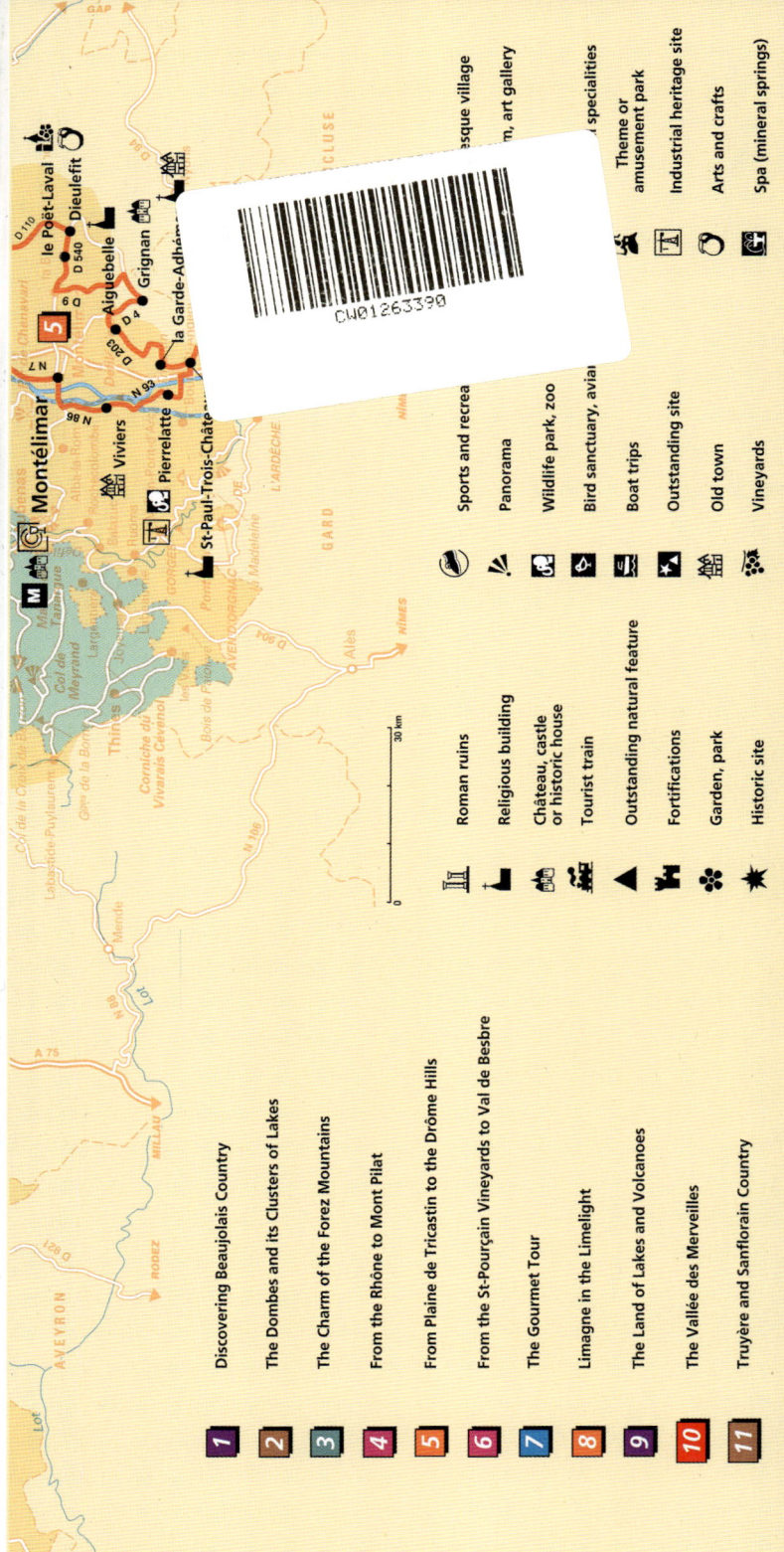

THEGREENGUIDE
Auvergne Rhone Valley

Rooftops of Vieux Lyon with Primatiale St-Jean © J. Elliott/robertharding/Getty Images

THEGREENGUIDE **AUVERGNE RHONE VALLEY**

Editorial Director	Cynthia Clayton Ochterbeck
Editor	Sophie Friedman
Principal Writer	Emily Monaco, Terry Marsh
Production Manager	Natasha George
Cartography	Peter Wrenn
Picture Editor	Yoshimi Kanazawa
Interior Design	Chris Bell
Cover Design	Chris Bell, Christelle Le Déan
Layout	Natasha George

Contact Us

Michelin Travel and Lifestyle North America
One Parkway South
Greenville, SC 29615
USA
travel.lifestyle@us.michelin.com

Michelin Travel Partner
Hannay House
39 Clarendon Road
Watford, Herts WD17 1JA
UK
01923 205240
travelpubsales@uk.michelin.com
www.viamichelin.co.uk

Special Sales

For information regarding bulk sales, customized editions and premium sales, please contact us at:
travel.lifestyle@us.michelin.com

Note to the reader Addresses, phone numbers, opening hours and prices published in this guide are accurate at the time of press. We welcome corrections and suggestions that may assist us in preparing the next edition. While every effort is made to ensure that all information printed in this guide is correct and up-to-date, Michelin Travel Partner accepts no liability for any direct, indirect or consequential losses howsoever caused so far as such can be excluded by law.

HOW TO USE THIS GUIDE

PLANNING YOUR TRIP

The blue-tabbed PLANNING YOUR TRIP section gives you **ideas for your trip** and **practical information** to help you organise it. You'll find tours, practical information, a host of outdoor activities, a calendar of events, information on shopping, sightseeing, kids' activities and more.

INTRODUCTION

The orange-tabbed INTRODUCTION section starts by exploring **The Region Today**. The **History** section spans from prehistory to the present day, including information about famous local figures. **Architecture** covers everything from religious and military buildings to traditional rural housing, while the **Literature** section examines writers from the Auvergne. The final section delves into **Nature**.

DISCOVERING

The green-tabbed DISCOVERING section features Principal Sights by region, featuring the most interesting local **Sights**, **Walking Tours**, nearby **Excursions**, and detailed **Driving Tours**. Admission prices shown are normally for a single adult.

ADDRESSES

We've selected from the best hotels, restaurants, cafés, shops, nightlife and entertainment to fit all budgets. See the Legend on the cover flap for an explanation of the price categories. See the back of the guide for an index of hotels and restaurants.

Sidebars

Throughout the guide you will find blue, orange and green-coloured text boxes with lively anecdotes, detailed history and background information.

A Bit of Advice

Green advice boxes found in this guide contain practical tips and handy information relevant to your visit or a sight in the Discovering section.

STAR RATINGS★★★

Michelin has given star ratings for more than 100 years. If you're pressed for time, we recommend you visit the ★★★ or ★★ sights first:

- ★★★ Worth a special journey
- ★★   Worth a detour
- ★   Interesting

MAPS

- Regional Driving Tours map.
- Region maps.
- Maps for major cities and towns.
- Local tour maps.

All maps in this guide are oriented north, unless otherwise indicated by a directional arrow. The term "Local Map" refers to a map within the chapter or Tourism Region. A complete list of the maps found in the guide appears at the back of this book.

© Christian Guy/hemis.fr

INTRODUCTION TO AUVERGNE RHÔNE VALLEY

The Region Today   **52**
21C Auvergne and the Rhône valley ...52
Government 54
Economy............................54
Food and Drink......................57

History   **59**

Architecture   **67**
Roman Architecture in the
Rhône valley 67
Religious Architecture 68
Military Architecture 74
Civil Architecture....................76
Industrial Architecture...............76
Spa Resort Architecture.............77
Traditional Rural Housing 78

Literature   **81**

Nature   **82**
Rhône valley 82
Auvergne 84
Auvergne's Mineral Springs 85
Flora and Fauna 89

PLANNING YOUR TRIP

Michelin Driving Tours   **12**
Local Drives..........................12
Regional Drives 13

When and Where To Go   **17**
When to Go 17
Themed Tours.......................17
Tourist Trains........................19
River and Canal Cruising 19
Nature Parks and Reserves...........20

What to See and Do   **21**
Outdoor Fun 21
Activities for Kids....................27
Spas and Mineral Springs 27
Shopping 28
Books...............................29
Films 29

Calendar of Events   **30**

Know Before You Go   **32**
Useful Websites 32
Tourist Offices.......................32
International Visitors 33
Accessibility.........................35

Getting There and Getting Around   **36**
By Plane 36
By Ship 36
By Train............................ 36
By Coach/Bus 37
By Car 37

Where to Stay and Eat   **39**
Where to Stay 39
Where to Eat 40

Useful Words and Phrases   **42**
Basic Information   **45**

DISCOVERING AUVERGNE RHÔNE VALLEY

Clermont-Ferrand and Monts Dôme   **94**
Clermont-Ferrand 96
Volvic..............................114
Monts Dôme 117
Lac d'Aydat 124

Monts Dore, Artense and Cézallier   **127**
St-Nectaire.........................129
Massif du Sancy 133
Le Mont-Dore 143
Besse-et-Saint-Anastaise 139
La Bourboule 149
Bort-les-Orgues and l'Artense.......153
Monts du Cézallier 156
Condat 160

Aurillac, Châtaigneraie and Monts du Cantal   **162**
Aurillac 165
Les Monts du Cantal................171

CONTENTS

Vic-sur-Cère	177
Murat	180
Salers	182
Riom-ès-Montagnes	185
Mauriac	188
Saint-Cernin	190

St-Flour, Sanflorain and Margeride du Cantal — 192
St-Flour	194
Gorges de la Truyère	198
Ruynes-en-Margeride	202

Velay and Brivadois — 203
Le Puy-en-Velay	205
Brioude	215
Lavaudieu	220
Saugues	222
Le Monastier-sur-Gazeille	224

Thiers and the Livradois-Forez — 228
Parc Naturel Régional Livradois-Forez	230
Thiers	231
Ambert	238
La Chaise-Dieu	242

Val d'Allier and Alagnon — 245
Issoire	247
Vic-le-Comte	252
Billom	254
Massiac	256

Limagne, Pays des Combrailles and Gorges de la Sioule — 258
Riom	260
Châtel-Guyon	266
Aigueperse	267
Gorges de la Sioule	269

Bourbonnais — 273
Moulins	276
Bourbon-l'Archambault	282
Souvigny	284
Montluçon	286
Forêt de Tronçais	289
Vichy	293
Lapalisse	301
Charroux	304
Montagne Bourbonnaise	306

Lyon — 309
Vieux Lyon	318
Fourvière Hill	324
La Presqu'île and its Squares	328
La Croix-Rousse	335
Left Bank	340
Outskirts	344

Bresse and the Dombes — 350
Bourg-en-Bresse	352
La Dombes	358
Pérouges	362

Beaujolais and the Monts du Lyonnais — 365
Villefranche-sur-Saône	367
Beaujolais	370
Monts du Lyonnais	377

Roannais and Le Forez — 379
Roanne	381
St-Germain-Laval	386
Feurs	388
Monts du Forez	390
Montbrison	394
St-Bonnet-le-Château	396

St-Étienne and Le Pilat — 399
St-Étienne	401
Monistrol-sur-Loire	409
Le Pilat	410

Ardèche — 414
Annonay	419
Tournon-sur-Rhône	422
Vallée de l'Eyrieux	424
St-Agrève	428
Yssingeaux	429
Privas	430
Vals-les-Bains	432
Aubenas	437
Les Vans	439
Gorges de l'Ardèche	442
Aven d'Orgnac	448
Bourg-St-Andéol	450
Viviers	452

Drôme Provençale and the Préalpes Drômoises — 456
Montélimar	458
Grignan	461
Valréas	464
Crest	464

Valentinois and the Lower Dauphiné — 466
Valence	468
Romans-sur-Isère	472
St-Antoine-l'Abbaye	476
La Côte-St-André	479
Lac de Paladru	480
Crémieu	482
Vienne	486

Index	**494**
Maps and Plans	**507**
Map Legend	**508**
Companion Publications	**509**

Welcome to Auvergne Rhône Valley

Very much at the heart of France, the Auvergne is a largely rural landscape, with 25 percent woodland, 45 percent grassland, 20 percent put to arable use, and only 10 percent given to urbanisation, mainly centred on the city of Clermont-Ferrand. The Rhône valley is long and wide and an important through route for transport. The valley boasts a host of different cultures and is dominated by Lyon, France's second most major city.

AUVERGNE

CLERMONT-FERRAND AND MONTS DÔME *(pp94–126)*

Backed by the impressive volcanic uplift of the Monts Dôme, Clermont-Ferrand is the natural capital of the Auvergne. The city has a bright and bustling atmosphere.

MONT-DORE, ARTENSE AND CÉZALLIER *(pp127–161)*

In a magnificent setting below the Puy de Sancy, the spa resort of Mont-Dore lies in the upper reaches of the Dordogne. Artense is a granite plateau bordered by the foothills of the Mont-Dore. Straddling Puy-de-Dôme and Cantal, Cézallier is a characterful region of plateaux and mountains.

AURILLAC, CHÂTAIGNERAIE AND MONTS DU CANTAL *(pp162–191)*

Aurillac is the business and tourist capital of Upper Auvergne, a modern town built around a network of ancient streets and alleys. The verdant Monts du Cantal feature the most beautiful landscapes in the Auvergne and cover a vast region formed by the largest volcano in France.

ST-FLOUR, SANFLORAIN AND MARGERIDE DU CANTAL *(pp192–202)*

St-Flour, isolated from the rest of the Auvergne by high mountains, is very much immune to external influence, although Sanflorain and Margeride embrace Languedoc-infuenced cultures and traditions.

VELAY AND BRIVADOIS *(pp203–227)*

Surrounded by the iconic volcanic forms of the region, Velay is often considered to be a sub-province of old Languedoc; its most striking attraction is Puy's cathedral. Centred around Brioude, the rurality continues in Brivadois, a place of small plains bordering Puy-de-Dôme and Cantal.

THIERS AND THE LIVRADOIS-FOREZ *(pp228–244)*

The Pays de Thiers – the eponymous town famed for its cutlery – and Livradois-Forez form one of the largest regional parks in France, varied in beauty and natural environment.

VAL D'ALLIER AND ALAGNON *(pp245–257)*

The valleys of Allier and Alagnon boast an exceptional historic and architectural heritage. The lively rivers and magnificent countryside beg to be explored by boat and on foot.

LIMAGNE, PAYS DES COMBRAILLES AND GORGES DE LA SIOULE *(pp258–272)*

Given largely to cereal production, the Limagne lies at the edge of the Massif Central. The Sioule is a tributary of the Allier renowned for the deep-cut gorges in its upper reaches. Combrailles covers almost 100 communities, representing an economic, cultural and social balance.

BOURBONNAIS (pp273–308)

Set amid high mountains, the Bourbonnais once performed a defensive role. Today it is a popular centre for golf, walking, cycling, horse riding and other adventure sports.

DRÔME ARDÈCHE

LYON (pp309–349)

The "City of Light" is magnificent at every level, from its architectural and cultural heritage to its contemporary wealth and renown. Situated at the confluence of the Rhône and the Saône, Lyon is a World Heritage Site.

BRESSE AND THE DOMBES (pp350–364)

Bresse, famed for its chickens, extends north from the Dombes, into a region where heath and coppice alternate with farmland and marshes. The undulating plateau of La Dombes is characterised by an impervious surface of clay creating over a thousand lakes offering opportunities to fish for carp, pike and tench.

BEAUJOLAIS AND THE MONTS DU LYONNAIS (pp365–378)

The attractive mountainous region of the Monts du Lyonnais is famed for chestnut groves, with vineyards and orchards in the low-lying valleys. The renown of the Beaujolais wines extends far beyond the borders of France.

ROANNAIS AND LE FOREZ (pp379–398)

The character of the Roanne region is heavily influenced by a long tradition of textile activity and crafts, but, like the Monts du Forez, it also offers a wide range of scenery and eerie landscapes.

Boutières Cross, Mont Mézenc, the Ardèche

© Emilie Chaix/Photononstop

ST-ÉTIENNE AND LE PILAT (pp399–413)

Le Pilat has an especially rich and diverse heritage and has been a regional park since 1974. St-Étienne, by contrast, thrived for many years on coal mining, before developing as a bicycle manufacturing city.

THE ARDECHE (pp414–455)

Rising to an altitude of 1 753m, Mont-Menzec lies to the east of Massif Central and is bordered to the west by the Monts du Velay, a region of plateaux networked by deep valleys. The Ardèche is known for its beautiful gorges and caves.

DRÔME PROVENÇALE AND THE PRÉALPES DRÔMOISES (pp456–465)

The Drôme is the gateway to Provence, and it shows. While this area belongs to the Rhône-Alpes, everything from olives to nougat evoke the atmosphere of the South of France..

VALENTINOIS AND THE LOWER DAUPHINÉ (pp466–493)

The Valentinois is a small alluvial plain along the banks of the Rhône that gradually takes on more southern landscapes as one proceeds through it. The same is true of le Bas-Dauphiné, a setting of hilly outcrops and basalt plateaus.

*Snowshoeing in Col de Serres,
Impradine valley, Puy Mary in the background,
Parc naturel régional des volcans d'Auvergne*
© Christian Guy/hemis.fr

PLANNING YOUR TRIP

PLANNING YOUR TRIP

Michelin Driving Tours

LOCAL DRIVES

The following is a selection of the Driving Tours in the Discovering section:

- **A mini tour of the volcanoes**
  See CLERMONT-FERRAND. A half-day tour of the volcanoes around Clermont-Ferrand. 35km/21mi. Visit the Plateau de Gergovie and the spectacular Puy de Dôme.

- **Northern slopes of the Sancy Range**
  See MASSIF DU SANCY. From Le Mont-Dore. 85km/53mi, round trip – allow a full day. One of the most picturesque areas in the Auvergne.

- **Alpine Pastures of Le Cézallier**
  See CONDAT. From the Rhue Gorge to gentiane country. 80km/50mi – allow one day. Waterfalls, gorges, wildflowers.

- **Monts du Cantal**
  See MONTS DU CANTAL. The Route du Lioran from Aurillac. 55km/34mi – half a day. This agreeable drive makes the most of the Cère and Alagnon valleys.

- **The Puy Mountain range**
  See MONTS DÔME. 120km/75mi – allow a full day. Visit the volcanoes and byways of the Monts Dôme.

- **The Monts de Forez**
  See THIERS. A full day tour in the Parc Naturel Régional Livradois-Forez. From Thiers via the Col de Béal – vineyards, chateaux and rugged scenery.

- **Approaching the Livradois**
  See ISSOIRE. 45km/28mi round trip – 2h. Issoire, the Château de Parentignat and beyond.

- **The Dauphiné d'Auvergne**
  See ISSOIRE. 60km/37mi – half a day. SW of Issoire between the Cézallier and the Allier valleys.

- **Discover Terra Volcana and Les Combrailles**
  See RIOM. From Riom, a round trip of 75km/47mi – allow half a day. Gorges, lakes and chateaux.

- **Limagne Bourbonnaise**
  See ST POURÇAIN-SUR-SIOULE. 75km/47mi – allow half a day. Visit medieval villages, manor houses and Romanesque churches.

- **La Bresse**
  See BOURG-EN-BRESSE. A round trip of 104km/65mi – a full day. Explore the small towns surrounding Bourg-en-Bresse and sample the best chicken you are ever likely to taste.

- **The Dombes lakes**
  See LA DOMBES. A round trip of 99km/61mi from Villars-les-Dombes – a full day. Myriad lakes and waterways.

- **Beaujolais vineyards**
  See BEAUJOLAIS. Villefranche-sur-Saône to St-Amour-Bellevue. 98km/61mi – half a day+. The road climbs through the vineyards of Beaujolais and crosses a granite escarpment before descending to the Saône.

- **Monts du Lyonnais**
  See MONTS DU LYONNAIS. From Lyon to St Étienne. 128km/80mi – allow a full day. Explore the hills to the southwest of Lyon.

- **Explore Le Pilat**
  See LE PILAT. From St Étienne to Condrieu. 89km/56mi – half a day. An agreeable way to discover the delights of the Parc Naturel Régional du Pilat.

- **Discover Lauze country**
  See LE MONASTIER-SUR-GAZELLE. Lac d'Issarlès to the Loire's source, and rural architecture.

- **Ardeche Gorge Panoramic Route**
  See GORGES DE L'ARDECHE. 38km/24mi starting from Vallon-Pont-d'Arc – half a day.

- **The Hills of Drôme**
  See CREST. 82km/52mi – 3hrs. Explore the gently sloping hills and discover pretty views and "perched" villages.

- **The Land of Stone Roofs**
  See CRÉMIEU. A tour of the Île Crémieu. 70km/43.5mi – half a day+. Cliffs, lakes, standing stones and country houses.

MICHELIN DRIVING TOURS

REGIONAL DRIVES
See the Driving Tours map on the inside back cover.

1 BEAUJOLAIS COUNTRY
Round tour of 129km/80mi leaving from Villefranche-sur-Saône.
This tour of the sun-drenched slopes of Beaujolais naturally starts from Villefranche-sur-Saône, seen by many as the capital of the famous Beaujolais *appellation*.
The former walled city of Belleville is now an important wine-making centre, but it has kept many vestiges of its 12C church. Corcelles Château boasts a fine 17C vat whose aromas will make your head spin. The "Hameau Duboeuf" and its "station" set up in Romanèche-Thorins form a small museum that pays tribute to the noble traditions that have governed the art of wine-making throughout the centuries, and the adjoining safari park will delight young children.
In Beaujolais, each vineyard has developed its own peculiarities: the Fleurie grapes yield a young, lively wine, whereas the Villié-Morgon bottles are usually for laying down. A great many *crus* can be found in Beaujeu, a town wholly devoted to the commerce of wine. After pausing to admire the stunning panorama stretching from Mont Brouilly to the Saône plain, pay a visit to the Salles-Arbuissonnas-en-Beaujolais Priory, dating back to the 10C.
The two châteaux of Montmelas-St-Sorlin and Jarnioux are your next stops, leading to the quaint village of Oingt, perched on a hillside and crowned by a golden tower.
Driving through the Bagnols vineyards, you reach Châtillon and its 12C stronghold. In St-Jean-des-Vignes, the Museum of Geology explains the origins of the topography that characterises the Beaujolais region and that has produced its unique *terroir*. The tour ends with the village of Chazay-d'Arzergues, from where you can return to Villefranche via Anse.

Château de Montmelas and the Beaujolais vineyards, Montmelas-St-Sorlin
© Lionel Lourdel/Photononstop

2 THE DOMBES AND ITS CLUSTERS OF LAKES
Round tour of 155km/96.5mi leaving from Lyon.
Leaving from Lyon, a city that has successfully taken up the challenges of modern life while preserving its historical legacy, this tour is a charming nature trail dotted with ancient monuments. Stop to admire the medieval towers of Rochetaillée Château and then press on to Ars, famous for its bishop who was canonised in 1925 and who is the patron saint of all parish bishops. After visiting Ambérieux-en-Dombes, another town with religious associations awaits you: Châtillon-sur-Chalaronne, where St Vincent de Paul founded the first brotherhood of charity and where you can visit the Apothicairerie. The tour then takes you to the Romanesque church in St-Paul-de-Varax and the 19C Notre-Dame-des-Dombes abbey, which was instrumental in draining the surrounding plains.
The bird sanctuary in Villars-les-Dombes is the perfect spot for a family outing, and the brick castle in Le Montellier is an impressive sight indeed.
The hilltop village of Pérouges, circled by ancient ramparts and crossed by winding streets, is often used as a backdrop for historical films. Finally, after a halt in Montluel, you can return to the city of Lyon and its many attractions.

13

PLANNING YOUR TRIP

St-Haon-le-Châtel

3 THE CHARM OF THE FOREZ MOUNTAINS
Round tour of 200km/124mi leaving from Roanne.

The region, generally referred to as Forez, comprises a range of mountains, a series of plains, a natural park and a web of meandering roads. This tour begins in Roanne, a Roman city today known for its textile and food-processing industries. After a short drive through vineyards that produce a lively rosé wine, you reach pretty Ambierle with its old Cluniac priory, Flamboyant Gothic church and museum devoted to traditional costumes and lore. The fortified village of St-Haon-le-Châtel features some interesting Renaissance houses and the nearby Tache Dam, which dominates the local vineyards, and is the starting point for charming country walks across the Monts de la Madeleine. Driving down the Gorges Roannaises de la Loire, you come to St-Maurice-sur-Loire, where the church apse boasts remarkable 13C frescoes and the keep commands a fine panorama of the gorges. Also steeped in history are the two towns of St-Germain-Laval and Pommiers and their intricate network of cobbled alleys. After visiting the Château de Boën and its wine museum, drop by the fortress in Sail-sous-Couzan and feast your eyes on the Forez plain. Château de la Bastie-d'Urfé was once the residence of the famed writer Honoré d'Urfé, whose romantic novel *L'Astrée* set a new literary trend in early-17C France. A more austere atmosphere permeates the 14C church in Champdieu and the old convent of Montbrison, dominated by its 18C dome and circled by stone ramparts. Although the living quarters within the castle were destroyed by a fire in the 18C, Montrond-les-Bains is a pleasant fortified city whose spa is ideal for treating diabetes and other disorders. After a breath of fresh air, strolling through the bird sanctuary at the Écopôle du Forez, explore the medieval hamlet of Villerest, with its a curious museum retracing the history of fire and its domestic uses through the ages. The Loire gorges cutting across the rocky plains lead you back to Roanne, where the tour can be nicely concluded with a boat ride.

4 FROM THE RHÔNE TO MONT PILAT
Round tour of 170km/105.6mi leaving from St-Étienne.

The tour begins in St-Étienne, a city with deep-rooted traditions that has nevertheless kept abreast of the times, and houses an admirable Museum of Modern Art. Your journey then takes you to St-Chamond, the site of a factory producing armoured vehicles, followed by Rive-de-Gier and St-Genis-Laval. You approach Lyon via the antique city of Oullins. As for the modern metropolis, frequently dubbed France's second capital, it offers a host of museums, cafés, restaurants and historical monuments. Further on, you reach Vienne, yet another Roman city, whose Jazz Festival enjoys a prestigious reputation. At your next stop, Condrieu, take a seat on the sunny quays and sip a glass of *viognier*, the local white wine, as you watch boats gliding into port. After visiting Pélussin and its museum, do not miss the stunning vista afforded by the Crêt de l'Œillon, extending over the Rhône valley and Crêt de la Perdrix.

MICHELIN DRIVING TOURS

For a sweeping panorama, try the viewing table on the Pics du Mézenc. If weather conditions are favourable, why not tackle one of the skiing slopes at Le Bessat or venture down the formidable gully appropriately named "Chasm of Hell"? Round off the tour with a pleasant drive back to St-Étienne and a visit to the famous confectioner Weiss, whose chocolates will literally melt in your mouth.

5 FROM PLAINE DE TRICASTIN TO THE DRÔME HILLS
Round tour of 210km/130mi leaving from Montélimar.
The starting point of this tour is Montélimar, world famous for its delicious nougat with almonds. The former episcopal town of Viviers leads to the Plaine du Tricastin, where Pierrelatte, encircled by three mountainous ranges, is home to a nuclear power plant, not to mention a crocodile farm. In St-Paul-Trois-Châteaux, make a point of visiting the cathedral and the Maison de la Truffe. For a change of scene, after admiring the church in St-Restitut, take time to check out the wine cellars at Le Cellier des Dauphins. History lovers will appreciate the White Penitents' Chapel in La Garde-Adhémar and the abbey church at Notre-Dame-d'Aiguebelle. You'll then drive through a series of charming villages, including La Bégude-de-Mézenc, Le Poët-Laval (a medieval gem housing a former commandery) and Dieulefit (a bustling city dedicated to local arts and crafts). After leaving Soyons, you head for the Saoû forest at the foot of a sheer cliff face offering pleasantly shaded walks. Or you may prefer to seek refuge in the keep at Crest. Finally, your drive back to nougat country introduces you to the picturesque towns of Marsanne and Mirmande.

6 ST-POURÇAIN VINEYARDS TO VAL DE BESBRE
Round tour of 160km/99.5mi leaving from St-Pourçain.
The vineyards around St-Pourçain yield a lively, fragrant white wine, which it is your duty to taste…in moderation! More academic visitors will enjoy studying the numerous medieval frescoes that enliven the tiny churches dotted around St-Pourçain; the murals at Le Saulcet deserve special mention. After your exertions at the sports and leisure park in Le Pal, follow the course of the River Besbre, which guides you first to Thoury and its pink-sandstone castle, then to Jaligny and its Renaissance château, and finally to Lapalisse, a popular place among anglers for its waters teeming with trout and carp.

7 THE GOURMET TOUR
Round tour of 250km/155mi leaving from Ambert.
This tour pays tribute to Fourme d'Ambert, a deliciously smooth blue cheese made with cow's milk that is typical of the region. Made around Ambert and on the Forez heights, this delicacy is made in tall cylinders and sold in round slabs. Less well-known than Roquefort, it is also more subtle and nuttier. The nearby town of Thiers is the country's leading knife manufacturer, and you will be ideally equipped to carve a generous slice of cheese and savour it along the banks of the River Dore.

Mirmande, Drôme provençale
© Lionel Montico/hemis.fr

PLANNING YOUR TRIP

8 LIMAGNE IN THE LIMELIGHT
Round tour of 250km/155mi leaving from Clermont-Ferrand.

After leaving Clermont-Ferrand, the bustling yet discreet capital of the Auvergne, you will encounter the curious lava flows of Volvic stone, where the famous mineral water has its source. Your next stop is Billom, where a pleasant climate combines with a fine morning mist and a soft light reminiscent of the great Impressionist works. This stunning landscape is enhanced by the golden sunflower fields contrasting with the earthy plains, overshadowed by the volcanic range looming above the horizon.

9 THE LAND OF LAKES AND VOLCANOES
Round tour of 415km/258mi leaving from Le Mont-Dore.

Whatever your reasons for visiting the Auvergne, you can but succumb to the charm of Puy de Sancy, the highest peak towering above central France. The Dore mountain range and Pays des Couzes form a natural setting of outstanding beauty, enclosing a cluster of deep blue lakes with shimmering waters (Guéry, Servière, Aydat, Godivelle, Chambon). The surrounding villages too are worthy of note: Montpeyroux and its colony of artists and craftsmen; St-Nectaire, where the local cow's milk cheese is matured on a bed of rye; Besse and its Alpine skiing resort; and lastly Orcival, graced with a fine Romanesque basilica.

10 THE VALLÉE DES MERVEILLES
Round tour of 335km/208mi leaving from Brioude.

Before setting out on this tour, pay a visit to the Basilique St-Julien in Brioude and admire the intricate carvings adorning the Romanesque east end. Following the peaceful, lazy meanderings of the Sénouire, you discover the abbeys of Lavaudieu and La Chaise-Dieu, where the chancel houses early splendid 16C tapestries from Brussels and Arras.

The Allier, on the other hand, is an impetuous river whose waters swell between Monistrol and Lavoûte-Chilhac. While more adventurous tourists may engage in a spot of canoeing or rafting, ramblers and cyclists can pause to admire the Romanesque church of Chanteuges and the flower-decked streets in St-Arcons.

The pretty painted churches dotted around the Haut-Allier region have earned it the name of "Vallée des Merveilles" (Valley of Wonders). As you continue on the tour, you come upon Le Puy-en-Velay, one of the most extraordinary and unforgettable sites in France, sitting like a crown atop the landscape it dominates.

11 TRUYÈRE AND SANFLORAIN COUNTRY
Round tour of 270km/168mi leaving from St-Flour.

St-Flour, the starting-point of the tour, is perched on a basaltic plateau that faces south. You will be charmed by the landscapes around Les Margerides and by the chaotic course of the Truyère, which has carved sharp chasms between the Cantal and Aveyron rivers, at the northwest border of the regional natural parc of Aubrac. After reaching Pierrefort and tucking into a tasty *aligot* consisting of mashed potatoes seasoned with garlic and Cantal cheese, you can pay a visit to the spa resort of Chaudes-Aigues. From the fine medieval castle of Pesteils, perched on its rocky outcrop, drive up to Plomb du Cantal, the highest summit of the range, where you will be greeted by a calm, soothing atmosphere and a sweeping expanse of lush countryside.

WHEN AND WHERE TO GO

When and Where To Go

WHEN TO GO

The region covered by this guide presents a great variety of climatic conditions in all seasons. Spring weather is unpredictable: there may be heavy snowfall at higher altitudes while the valleys are fragrant with fruit blossom. In late spring, the Auvergne is outstandingly beautiful, as melting snow swells the rivers. The summer months are generally sunny and warm. The Ardèche gorges are especially popular in July and August, particularly for boating.

Along the Rhône, the weather in autumn is usually mild, but in other regions (like the Cévennes) heavy rain is likely. The colours in the Puys, Livradois and Dombes regions are especially vibrant at this time of year. Winter brings snow to the high peaks, where it can cover the ground for several months, closing off mountain passes to traffic. The wind in the region of the volcanoes of Auvergne can be intense. But south of Valence and in the southern part of the Cantal region, the climate is milder, and winter skies are usually clear thanks to winds blowing up from the Mediterranean.

The city of Lyon seems to have a climate all its own: summers are hot and sticky, and in the winter a mist seems to hang overhead all day. Spring and autumn are the best times to visit the city, as the weather is usually clearer then.

WEATHER FORECAST

For **Météo-France** (national weather bureau, www.meteo.fr) reports in French, dial 3250, then select from the recorded choices (€2.99 per call + network provider's charge). Information about the weather can be downloaded to mobile phones from http://mobile.meteofrance.com.

For **departmental forecasts** dial 08 92 68 02… followed by the number of the *département*: Ain 01; Allier 03; Ardèche 04; Cantal 15; Drôme 26; Haute-Loire 43; Isère 38; Loire 42; Puy-de-Dôme 63; Rhône 69.

Mountain weather forecast:
3250 (select 4); for information about snow cover and avalanche risk, 08 92 68 10 20.

Weather forecast for microlights and light aircraft 08 92 68 10 14. Information is also available on www.meteo.fr.

THEMED TOURS
HISTORY

Routes Historiques are signposted local itineraries following an architectural and historical theme, accompanied by an explanatory booklet available from local tourist offices.

The **Route Historique des Châteaux d'Auvergne** takes in a selection of the best castles in the region: imposing ruined fortresses as well as elegant manor houses; some of these house exhibitions, organise concerts and sports events; others offer bed-and-breakfast accommodation or are open late in the evening to enable visitors to appreciate their fascinating atmosphere. There are six itineraries: Bourbonnais, Limagnes, Volcans, Livradois-Forez, Montagnes Cantaliennes and Haute-Loire.
Association de la Route Historique des Châteaux d'Auvergne: Comité Régional de Développement Touristique d'Auvergne, 7 allée Pierre de Fermat, 63178 Aubière. 04 73 29 29 84; route-chateaux-auvergne.org

On the way to Santiago de Compostela – Pilgrims on their way to pay homage to the relics of St James have come through the Auvergne since the Middle Ages. Two itineraries converge on Le Puy-en-Velay: one from Lyon via

17

PLANNING YOUR TRIP

St-Ferréol and Monistrol-sur-Loire, the other from Cluny via Pommiers and Montbrison. Beyond Le Puy, the *via podiensis* (GR 65) leads to Roncevaux and the Spanish border (28 days on foot).

ARCHITECTURAL HERITAGE

Viaducts – The introduction of railways in this mountainous region meant the construction of several impressive viaducts spanning the Truyère, the Sioule, the Allier and the Besbre rivers. Six of these are now listed among the region's historic monuments: Garabit and Barajol (Cantal), La Récoumène (Haute-Loire), Les Fades (Puy-de-Dôme) and Neuvial and Rouzat (Allier).

TRADITIONS AND NATURE

The **Route des Jardins du Massif Central** links 22 botanical gardens dedicated to the preservation and promotion of the Massif Central's vegetation.

Association des Jardins du Massif central, Le Jardin pour la Terre, Terre Neyre, 63220 Arlanc. ✆04 73 65 00 71.

The **Route des Métiers en Livradois-Forez** winds its way across the Parc naturel regional du Livradois-Forez, linking authentic workshops where ancient crafts are perpetuated. These include Maison des Couteliers (cutlers' workshop) in Thiers, Maison du Verre (glass workshop) in Puy-Guillaume, Moulin Richard-de-Bas (traditional mill) and Musée de la Fourme (cheese museum) in Ambert.

Parc naturel regional du Livradois-Forez, Maison du Parc, 63880 Saint-Gervais-sous-Meymont ✆04 73 95 57 57; http://www.routedesmetiers.fr.

The **Route des Villes d'Eaux** links the region's numerous spas.

La Route des Villes d'Eaux, 8 avenue Anatole-France, 63130 Royat ✆04 73 34 72 80; www.villesdeaux.com.

The **Route des Fromages** is a gourmet tour of the main farming areas producing the best cheeses the Auvergne has to offer: Saint-Nectaire, Fourme d'Ambert, Bleu d'Auvergne, Cantal and Salers.

Association des fromages AOP d'Auvergne, 9 allée Pierre de Fermat, 63170 Aubière. ✆04 71 48 66 15; www.fromages-aop-auvergne.com.

WINE-TASTING

Côtes d'Auvergne (Puy-de-Dôme) – Some 1 240ha produce five different wines: Madargue, Châteaugay and Chanturgue north of Clermont-Ferrand, Corent and Boudes south of Clermont-Ferrand.
The Fédération Viticole du Puy-de-Dôme, place de la Mairie, 63340 Boudes ✆04 73 96 49 00, proposes a **Route des Vins** divided into three itineraries exploring the Riomois, Clermontois and Lembronnais areas.

Saint-Pourçain (Allier) – This is one of the oldest wine-growing areas in France; destroyed by phylloxera at the end of the 19C, the vines have been gradually replanted and the vineyards now cover 600ha.

Office de Tourisme, 29 Rue Marcelin Berthelot, 03500 Saint-Pourcain-sur-Sioule. ✆04 70 45 32 73; www.payssaintpourcinois.fr.

The following centres provide information about wine-growing in the Rhône valley:

- **Beaujolais** – Le Pays Beaujolais (bookings of tours and accommodation, guides/interpreters), contact – Maison du Tourisme, 96 rue de la Sous-Préfecture, 69400 Villefranche-sur-Saône. ✆04 74 07 27 40; www.villefranche-beaujolais.fr.
- **Côtes-du-Rhône** – You can browse at www.vins-rhone.com, or to obtain a list of cellars, wine-tour itineraries etc. contact: –Maison des Vins des Côtes du Rhône et de la Vallée du Rhône 485 avenue des Lots, 26600 Tain-l'Hermitage.

WHEN AND WHERE TO GO

📞 04 75 07 88 81.
www.vins-rhone.com
– Maison des Vins d'Avignon, 6 rue des Trois-Faucons, 84024 Avignon.
📞 04 90 27 24 00.

TOURIST TRAINS
These offer the opportunity to discover some spectacular scenery, away from busy modern routes. Contacts include:

Train de l'Ardèche
Gare de Tournon St-Jean, Route du Grand Pont, 07 300 St-Jean de Muzols. 📞 04 75 06 07 00; http://trainardeche.fr. Three viaducts, two tunnels and spectacular views.

Chemin de Fer Touristique du Haut-Rhône Montalieu Vercieu. 📞 04 78 81 84 30; www.cft-hr.com. 1-hour steam-train journey between Montalieu and the Pont de Sault-Brenaz.

Les Voies Ferrées du Velay contact relevant Office de Tourisme – see https://velay-express.fr. Several daily trips among the stations of Raucoules, Tence, Le Chambon-sur-Lignon et Saint-Agrève.

Chemin de Fer Touristique d'Anse
560 route de Saint Bernard, BP 10046, 69480 Anse. 📞 04 74 60 26 16 (tourist office); www.cftanse.fr – runs from Easter to the last Sunday in October on Sundays, holidays (also Saturdays from June to September) in the afternoon.

Train Touristique des Monts du Lyonnais 5 place de la Gare, 69610 Sainte Foy l'Argentière. 📞 06 07 27 88 42; http://train-touristique-monts-lyonnais.com. Exhibition of railway stock in Ste-Foy-l'Argentière station (end of the line). In addition, a steam train runs on Sundays from June to September.

Véloraill du Sud Ardèche Nivet, 07580 Saint-Jeanle-Centenier. 📞 07 68 30 63 47. 5 viaducts and 1 tunnel through the hills of Ardèche.

Les Trains de la Découverte du Livradois-Forez – La Gare, Place Jean-Berne, 63600 Ambert. Several possibilities along the Dore valley between Ambert and La Chaise-Dieu. AGRIVAP "train touristique".
📞 04 73 82 43 88; www.agrivap.fr.

Chemin de Fer du Haut Forez – La Gare, Estiraveilles 42380. Connects Estivareilles and La Chaise-Dieu.
📞 04 77 50 82 03.
www.cheminferhautforez.com.

Train Touristique des Gorges de l'Allier – Magnificent unspoilt landscapes unfold on this journey between Langeac and Langogne. The train runs through 53 tunnels and negotiates steep slopes and tricky bends. 📞 04 71 77 70 17; www.langogne.com/train.htm.

Autorail Touristique Gentiane Express – A fine journey through the summer pastures of the famous Salers cattle, from Bort-les-Orgues to Lugarde via Riom-ès-Montagne and the Barajol viaduct. Daily in July and August, Sundays and holidays from mid April to September. Office du Tourisme de Bort-les-Orgues (📞 05 55 96 02 49), or Office du tourisme du Pays Gentiane, Riom-ès-Montagnes. (📞 04 71 78 07 37).

RIVER AND CANAL CRUISING
SELF-SKIPPERED HOLIDAYS
Boats can be hired in Port-sur-Saône, Gray, St-Jean-de-Losne and Roanne to explore the Saône and the Rhône from Corre to Port-St-Louis-du-Rhône. The main harbours on the way are Lyon, Les Roches-de-Condrieu and Valence l'Épervière; a basic service is available in St-Germain-au-Mont-d'Or, Tournon-sur-Rhône, Viviers and Avignon. In the Lyon region, a series of mooring places along the Saône enables visitors to enjoy the surrounding area. Information is available from **Bureau de la Plaisance**, 2 rue de la Quarantaine, 69321 Lyon Cedex 05
📞 04 72 56 59 28.

PLANNING YOUR TRIP

The stretch of canal between Roanne and Briennon offers a pleasant journey with several locks along the way; contact **Marins d'Eau Douce**, Port de Plaisance, 42720 Briennon. ✆04 77 69 92 92. www.lesmarinsdeaudouce.fr.

CRUISES

Les Bateaux Lyonnais offer cruises and boat trips along the Rhône and Saône rivers; information and bookings, 13 bis quai Rambaud, 69002 Lyon ✆04 78 42 96 81; www.lesbateauxlyonnais.com.

Information can also be obtained from Avignon Tourist Office (✆04 32 74 32 74; www.avignon-tourisme.com).

NATURE PARKS AND RESERVES

PARKS

The region described in this guide includes five regional nature parks:

- **Parc Naturel Régional des Volcans d'Auvergne** (see *Parc Naturel Régional des VOLCANS D'AUVERGNE*). Château Montlosier 63970 Aydat. ✆04 73 65 64 00; www.parcdesvolcans.fr.

- **Parc Naturel Régional Livradois-Forez** (see *Monts du FOREZ*). Maison du Parc, 63880 St-Gervais-sous-Meymont. ✆04 73 95 57 57; www.parc-livradois-forez.org.

- **Parc Naturel Regional du Pilat** (see *Le PILAT*). Maison du Parc, Moulin de Virieu, 2 rue Benaÿ, 42410 Pélussin. ✆04 74 87 52 01; www.parc-naturel-pilat.fr.

- **Parc Naturel Régional des Monts d'Ardèche** (see *AUBENAS*). Domaine de Rochemure, 07380 Jaujac ✆04 75 36 38 60; www.parc-monts-ardeche.fr.

- **Parc Naturel Regional de l'Aubrac** (see *CHAUDES-AIGUES*). Place d'Aubrac, 12470 Aubrac. ✆05 65 48 19 11 www.parc-naturel-aubrac.fr

NATURE RESERVES AND NATURE-DISCOVERY CENTRES

The following organise activities on the theme of nature:

- **Vallée de Chaudefour**, Maison de la Réserve Naturelle de la Vallée de Chaudefour, Parc Naturel Regional des Volcans d'Auvergne, 63790 Chambon-sur-Lac. ✆04 73 88 68 80; www.parcdesvolcans.fr – guided tours (dogs are not allowed, even on a lead).

- **Sagnes de la Godivelle**, Montlosier, 63970 Aydat. ✆04 73 65 64 26, or 04 73 71 78 12 (during Jul-Aug, last two weekends in Jun and first two weekends in Sept).

- **Val d'Allier**, Outings are organised by the Ligue pour la Protection des Oiseaux. Espace Nature du Val d'Allier, 8 boulevard de Nomazy, 03000 Moulins ✆04 73 36 39 79; www.lpo-auvergne.org.

- **Centre permanent d'Initiatives pour l'Environnement d'Auvergne**, Château Saint-Étienne, 15000, Aurillac. ✆04 71 48 49 09; www.cpie15.com.

- **Office National des Forêts**, Direction territoriale Auvergne-Rhône-Alpes, 143, rue Pierre Corneille, 69406 Lyon. ✆04 72 60 11 90; www.onf.fr/auvrhal. Rambles through Tronçais forest.

- **Espace Nature du Val d'Allier**, see address above.

What to See and Do

OUTDOOR FUN

AERIAL VIEWS
Hot-air balloons
Contact local tourist offices, or:
- **France Montgolfières**, 4 bis rue du Saussis, 21140 Semur-en-Auxois. ☏03 80 97 38 61; www.franceballoons.com.

- **Objectif: Vols en Montgolfière**, 12, rue des Blés, 37150 Bléré. ☏02 47 57 19 77; www.objectif-ciel-montgolfiere.com.

- **Airshow Montgolfières**, place du 19 mars, 63840 Viverols. ☏07 86 41 57 45. www.airshow.fr.

- **Auvergne Montgolfières**, La Petite Plage, 63790 Lac Chambon. ☏04 73 88 40 00; www.auvergne-montgolfiere.com.

- **Voler avec les Oiseaux**, Aérodrome de Coltines, 15170 Coltines. ☏04 71 62 39 02; www.voleraveclesoiseaux.com.

- **Montgolfière Club du Velay**, Pouzols, 43200 St-Jeures. ☏04 71 65 47 89; www.montgolfiere-club-velay.com.

- **Les Montgolfières d'Annonay**, 20 rue Henri Guironnet, 07102 Annonay. ☏04 75 67 57 56; www.lesmontgolfieresdannonay.fr.

- **Annonay Berceau de l'Aérostation**, Mairie d'Annonay, 07100 Annonay. ☏06 89 50 21 95; www.annonay-aerostation.com.

- **Montgolfières & Cie** 41 Grande Rue, 07290 Quintenas. ☏04 75 34 41 14; www.montgolfieres-cie.com.

- **Montgolfière en Velay**, 7 rue Saint Benoît, 43750 Vals près Le-Puy-en-Velay. ☏06 06 83 43 43; www.montgolfiere-en-velay.fr.

Light aircraft and gliders
- **Aéroclub d'Auvergne**, Rue Youri Gagarine, 63100 Clermont-Ferrand. ☏04 73 92 00 56; www.aeroclubauvergne.fr.

- **Aéro-club Pierre-Herbaud**, Aérodrome d'Issoire, 63500 Le Broc. ☏04 73 89 16 62; www.aeroclub-issoire.fr.

- **Aéro-club du Livradois**, Le Poyet, 63600 Ambert. ☏04 73 82 01 64; http://aeroclub-ambert.fr.

Helicopters
- **Héli Volcan**, Aéroport de Clermont-Ferrand, 63510 Aulnat. ☏04 73 55 03 60; www.helivolcan.com.

- **Auvergne Giro Passion**, Aérodrome des Coltines, 15170 Coltines. ☏06 62 22 44 63; www.auvergne-giro-passion.com

Microlights
- **Aéro-club Combrailles**, École de pilotage, 63640 St-Priest-des-Champs. ☏04 73 86 84 52.

- **Azur Passion**, Aérodrome de Coltines, 15170 Coltines. ☏06 62 81 03 31; www.azur-passion-ulm.fr.

- **ULM Delta Dôme**, 63200 Riom. ☏06 87 48 66 29 www.delta-dome.com.

Hang-gliding and paragliding
The Auvergne mountains and the Massif du Mézenc in the Ardèche offer exceptional opportunities to practise hang-gliding and paragliding.

PLANNING YOUR TRIP

Cycling in Aubenas

École Ailes Libres Auvergne Limousin, 63730 Les Martres de Veyre. ℘04 73 40 08 61. Departures are from the Camping de La Font Bleix.

Action Parapente, 1 Sommet du Puy de Dôme, 63870 Orcines. ℘06 75 94 61 06; www.action-parapente.fr.

Barbule, École Ardéchoise de Parapente, 07140 Les Vans ℘06 08 98 22 92. www.ecole-parapente-france.fr.

CYCLING AND MOUNTAIN BIKING

Tourist offices should be able to provide lists of local companies that hire bicycles and mountain bikes *(vélos tout terrain,* or VTT) and suggested routes. Some SNCF railway stations organise bike rentals, and mountain bikes can be hired in season from information points within the Pilat park. A leaflet giving details is available from railway stations.

Useful Addresses
- **Fédération Française de Cyclotourisme**, 12 rue Louis-Bertrand, 94200 Ivry-sur-Seine ℘01 56 20 88 88. www.ffct.org.
- **Fédération Française de Cyclisme,** Vélodrome National de Saint-Quentin-en-Yvelines, 1 rue Laurent Fignon, 78 180 Montigny le Bretonneux. ℘08 11 04 05 55. www.ffc.fr.
- **Viarhôna,** 8 rue Paul Montrochet, 69002 Lyon. ℘04 26 73 31 59. www.en.viarhona.com.

CAVING

Groupe Spéléologique Auvergnat, 62, rue Alexis-Piron, 63000 Clermont-Ferrand. ℘06 80 81 61 43. www.gsa63.fr.

Comité Départemental de Spéléologie en Ardèche, 130 Chemin du Cirque de Gens 07120 Chauzon. ℘06 37 12 85 40. www.cds07.fr.

FISHING

The abundance of rivers, streams and lakes provides anglers with many opportunities to catch salmon, trout, perch, tench or carp. Whatever the site, however, it is necessary to be affiliated to a fishing association and to abide by fishing regulations. Daily fishing permits are available in certain areas. Contact the local tourist office, local fishing federations or fishing tackle stores.

Useful Addresses
Fédération Nationale de la Pêche en France et de la protection du milieu aquatique, 17 rue Bergère, 75009 Paris. ℘01 48 24 96 00; www.federationpeche.fr.
- **Allier** – 8 rue de la Ronde, 03500 Saint-Pourçain-sur-Sioule. ℘04 70 47 51 55; www.federation-peche-allier.fr.
- **Ardèche** –16 avenue Paul Ribeyre, 07600 Vals-les-Bains. ℘04 75 37 09 68; www.peche-ardeche.com.
- **Cantal** – 14 allée du Vialenc, 15000 Aurillac. ℘04 71 48 19 25; www.cantal-peche.com.
- **Haute-Loire** – 32 rue Henri-Chas, Le Val-Vert, 43000 Le Puy-en-Velay. ℘04 71 09 09 44; www.pechehauteloire.fr.
- **Loire** – 6 allée de l'Europe, 42480 La Fouillouse. ℘04 77 02 20 00; www.federationpeche42.fr.

Fishing at Lac du Bouchet

© Hervé Lenain/hemis.fr

- **Puy-de-Dôme** – 14, allée des Eaux et Forêts, Site de Marmilhat Sud, 63370 Lempdes. ✆04 73 92 56 29; www.peche63.com. Its *Le Pêcheur du Puy-de-Dôme* includes a map of rivers and lakes.
- **Rhône** – 1 Allée du Levant, 69890 La Tour de Salvagny. ✆04 72 18 01 80. www.federation-peche-rhone.fr.

GOLF

For locations, addresses and telephone numbers of golf courses in France, consult the map *Golfs, Les Parcours Français* published by Éditions Plein-Sud based on *Michelin map 989*.

Fédération Française de Golf, 68 rue Anatole-France, 92309 Levallois-Perret Cedex ✆01 41 49 77 00. www.ffgolf.org.

WALKING

Exploring the region on foot is an enchanting way of discovering the landscape and the life of the countryside. Many long-distance footpaths *(Sentiers de Grande Randonnée* or "GR") cover the area described in this guide. Short-distance paths *(Sentiers de Petite Randonnée* or "PR") and medium-distance paths offer walks ranging from a few hours to a couple of days.

Useful Addresses

Fédération Française de la Randonnée Pédestre (*64 rue du Dessous des Berges, 75013 Paris .* ✆*01 44 89 93 90; www.ffrandonnee.fr*)
A collection of *Topo-Guides* showing routes, access points, accommodation and places of interest along footpaths throughout France is published by the federation; some of the guides have been translated into English and are available in bookshops in the region. You can also order the catalogue of publications online – see above.

- **Comité Départemental de Randonnée Pédestre de l'Allier**, OT Cusset, 03300 Cusset ✆06 81 33 73 29; ffrandonnee-allier.fr.
- **Comité Départemental de Randonnée Pédestre de l'Ardèche**, 23 bis Cours du Palais, B.P. 210, 07002 Privas. ✆04 75 30 57 38; www.ardeche-ffrandonnee.fr
- **Comité Départemental de Randonnée Pédestre du Cantal**, Maison des Sports, 15000 Aurillac. ✆04 71 63 75 29; rando.cantal.fr.
- **Comité Départemental de Randonnée Pédestre de la Drôme**, 71 Rue Pierre Latécoère, 26000 Valence. ✆04 75 75 47 83; https://drome.ffrandonnee.fr/
- **Comité Départemental de Randonnée Pédestre de Haute-Loire**, 21, rue Collège, 43000 Le Puy-en-Velay. ✆04 71 04 15 95; www.rando-hauteloire.fr.

Forêt de Saoû near Crest, Drôme

- **Comité Départemental de Randonnée Pédestre du Puy-de-Dôme**, Centre d'Affaires Auvergne, 15 Bis Rue du Pré La Reine, 63000 Clermont-Ferrand. ☏ 04 73 91 94 01; puy-de-dome.ffrandonnee.fr/.

Chamina, *5 rue Pierre-le-Vénérable, 63057 Clermont-Ferrand Cedex 1 t04 73 92 81 44; www.chamina.com*. This association promotes walking and mountain biking throughout the Massif Central region and the western slopes of the Rhône valley.

Cicerone Press in the UK (*www.cicerone.co.uk*) produce a number of walking guides to areas in and around the Auvergne.

Play It Safe

Safety first is the rule when it comes to exploring the mountains as a climber, skier or walker. The risks associated with avalanches, mudslides, falling rocks, bad weather, fog, glacially cold waters and the dangers of becoming lost or miscalculating distances should not be underestimated.

Avalanches occur naturally when the upper layer of snow is unstable, in particular after heavy snowfalls. They may be set off by the passage of numerous skiers or walkers over a precise spot. A scale of risk, from 1 to 5, has been developed and is posted daily at resorts and the base of walking trails. It is important to consult this *Bulletin Neige et Avalanche* (BNA) before setting off on any expeditions cross-country or *hors-piste*.

Lightning storms are often preceded by sudden gusts of wind and put climbers and walkers in danger. In the event, avoid high ground, and do not move along a ridge top; do not seek shelter under overhanging rocks, isolated trees in otherwise open areas, at the entrance to caves or other openings in the rocks, or in the proximity of metal fences or gates. A car is a good refuge.

KARTING

- **Speed2Max,** 160 av. Jean Mermoz, 63100 Clermont-Ferrand. ☏ 04 73 14 14 28; www.speed-2-max.fr.
- **Kartingliss,** 11 rue Louis-Blériot, 63800 Cournon-d'Auvergne. ☏ 04 73 84 27 41.
- **Karting Sarron,** 1 avenue Hector Berlioz, 63200 Riom. ☏ 04 73 64 61 61. www.circuit-sarron.com.

RIDING TOURS

For information about riding holidays, contact the **Comité National de Tourisme Équestre** *(9 boulevard Macdonald, 75019 Paris ☏ 01 53 26 15 50)* which publishes the handbook *Cheval Nature, l'Officiel du tourisme équestre en France* with details of selected riding stables and equestrian establishments in France.

WHAT TO SEE AND DO

Donkeys and Horse-drawn Caravans

A **walk with a donkey** is sure to amuse kids and adults alike! Contact the **Fédération Nationale Ânes et Randonnées** (FNAR) (www.ane-et-rando.com) or the **Comité Départemental du Tourisme** in Privas at 04 75 64 04 66, for the list of places where donkeys may be hired.

Horse-drawn caravans, complete with bunk beds and kitchen facilities, may be hired in some areas to follow a planned itinerary; contact the Parc naturel régional du Pilat 04 74 87 52 00 or local tourist offices.

At regional level, contact:
- **Comité Régionale de Tourisme Équestre d'Auvergne**, 4 rue des Trois Meules 42012 Saint-Etienne. 06 37 41 57 33; tourismequestre-auvergnerhonealpes.fr.
- **Comité Régionale de Tourisme Équestre Rhône-Alpes**, Parc du Cheval, Bât. Equipôle, Le Luizard, 01150 Chazey sur Ain. 04 37 90 53 29; www.tourismequestre-rhonealpes.com.

ROCK-CLIMBING

There are numerous opportunities to tackle cliff faces in the Auvergne region. Information can be obtained from the following:
- **Club Alpin Français Clermont-Auvergne**, 21 Rue Jean Richepin, 63000 Clermont-Ferrand. 04 73 90 81 62; www.clubalpin-clermontauvergne.fr.
- **Comité Départemental de la Fédération Française de la Montagne et de l'Escalade**, 22 ter, impasse Bonnabaud, 63000 Clermont-Ferrand. 04 73 29 24 71; www.ffme.fr.

In January and February, some winter sports resorts offer an introduction to ice climbing on frozen waterfalls:
- **Club Alpin Français du Haut-Cantal**, 1 ave. Fernand Brun, 15400 Riom-ès-Montagnes 04 71 78 14 63.
- **Le Mont-Dore**, Contact the Peloton de Gendarmerie de Montagne (mountain squad of the Gendarmerie Nationale), rue des Chasseurs Alpins, 63240 Le Mont-Dore. 04 73 65 04 06.

SKIING

The Auvergne region is well equipped for the practice of Alpine skiing with three important resorts: Mont-Dore (*see* MONT-DORE), Super-Besse (*see* BESSE-EN-CHANDESSE) and Super-Lioran (*see* LE LIORAN), where the **Ski Pass Massif Central** can be used. It is also ideal for cross-country skiing, as there is an extensive network of tracks spread over 12 main ski areas.

The Massif du Pilat and the high plateaux of the Ardèche are also suitable for cross-country skiing and ski touring. In addition, **summer skiing** and **sledging** are popular summer activities in Le Mont-Dore, Super-Besse and Picherande; information is available from tourist offices.

Via ferrata du Pont du diable, Thueyts, Parc naturel régional des monts d'Ardèche

Kayaking in the Upper Ardèche valley, Thueyts

© Bertrand Rieger/hemis.fr

Useful Websites
The regional tourist office site **www.auvergne-destination-volcans.com** has information on ski resorts and conditions. Another site for information and reservations is **www.france-montagnes.com**, including all the latest updates on snow conditions in French resorts (some sites also list available accommodation).
Sign up for a snow condition newsletter via **www.la-montagne-ardechoise.com**.

WATERSPORTS

Natural and artificial lakes offer a wide choice of possibilities for water sports including rowing, windsurfing, waterskiing, canoeing, kayaking, rafting and canyoning.

Canoeing and Kayaking
Discover the region from the swirling waters of the Ardèche, the Sornin or the Allier: information on suitable spots for canoeing from:
- **Fédération Française de Canoë-Kayak**, Route de Torcy, 77360 Vaires sur Marne. ✆01 45 11 08 50; www.ffck.org.

Rafting and Canyoning
Rafting is the easiest of these freshwater sports, since it involves going down rivers in inflatable craft steered by an instructor; special equipment is provided.

Canyoning is a technique for body-surfing down narrow gorges and over falls, as though on a giant waterslide. This sport requires protection: wear a wetsuit and a helmet.

Rowing
Club Aviron Vichy, 3 avenue de la Croix-St-Martin, 03200 Vichy. ✆04 70 32 36 52; http://clubavironvichy.e-monsite.com – leisure activities and competitions.

Useful Addresses
- **Club Nordique des Crêtes du Forez**, 3, rue de Goye 63600 Ambert. ✆04 79 70 35 04, www.cretesduforez.fr.
- **Domaine nordique Prat de Bouc Haute Planèze Cézens**
  Col de Prat de Bouc, 15300 Albepierre-Bredons.
  ✆04 71 23 26 39;
  www.pratdebouc-cantal.fr.
- **École de ski français de Super-Besse**, 1 ronde de Vassivière, 63610 Super-Besse.
  ✆04 73 79 61 75;
  www.esfsuperbesse.com.
- **Domaine Nordique en Aubrac**, Place d'Aubrac, 12470 Aubrac.
  ✆05 65 48 19 11;
  www.parc-naturel-aubrac.fr.

Snow-cover information –
The following provide up-to-date information about snow conditions in the various ski areas.
- **Club Nordique des Crêtes du Forez:** ✆04 79 70 35 04.
- **Super-Besse:** ✆04 73 79 60 03.
- **Zone Nordique du Mézenc:** ✆04 71 08 34 33.
- **Stations du Massif du Pilat:** ✆04 77 20 43 43.
- **Stations des Monts du Forez:** ✆04 77 24 83 11.

WHAT TO SEE AND DO

ACTIVITIES FOR KIDS

Sights of particular interest to children are indicated with a KIDS symbol (). The Auvergne region of France has a lot to offer children, from water parks such as the Parc Aquatique Les Trois Chênes in Ambert (*04 73 82 14 23*) to zoos, châteaux and museums. &see *also Tourist Trains and Eco-tourism*. The French are family-oriented, and it is not uncommon to see well-behaved children dining in restaurants. Most attractions, parks, museums and buildings offer reduced rates for children, with very young children often going free.

Useful Websites

Get ideas for your holiday with kids via **France for Families** (*www.franceforfamilies.com*), **Tots to Travel** (*www.totstotravel.co.uk*) and **Take the Family** (*www.takethefamily.com*).

When you get there

Many of the local tourist office websites have pages dedicated to what children can do, and it is useful to consult those for your destination. Also, upon arriving in France, consider checking with the local tourist office for information about festivals, concerts or celebrations.

SPAS AND MINERAL SPRINGS

SPAS OF THE AUVERGNE

There are dozens of spas in France, ranging from upmarket spa resort hotels to charming small spa villages dating to Ancient Roman times.
The Auvergne and Rhône valley are no exception. The thalassotherapy, balneotherapy and thermal spring centres of the Auvergne are renowned for their professional treatments, volcanic thermal spa waters and warm welcome.
Spas generally offer care adapted to treat specific ailments, taking advantage of the richness of the natural spring water. Visitors drink the water and bathe in it to reap these benefits. Spas may also offer other treatments like chocolate body wraps, black soap rubs, or hot stone massages.
Flowing out of the immense natural filter formed by the volcanoes of Auvergne, mineral springs have lent their waters and names to famous brands, including Volvic, Châteauneuf, Sainte-Marguerite, Mont-Dore, Vichy, Saint-Yorre and Arvie. Less well-known brands include La Cantaline, La Tessièroise, Renlaigue, Chateldon or Hydroxydase.

RESORTS

The region has many spa resorts:
Bourbon-l'Archambault✠
&see BOURBON-L'ARCHAMBAULT
La Bourboule✠
&see LA BOURBOULE
Châteauneuf-les-Bains
&see GORGES DE LA SIOULE
Châtel-Guyon
&see RIOM
Chaudes-Aigues
&see GORGES DE LA TRUYÈRE
Le Mont-Dore
&see LE MONT-DORE
Montrond-les-Bains
&see MONTBRISON
Néris-les-Bains✠
&see MONTLUÇON
Neyrac-les-Bains
&see VALS-LES-BAINS
Chamalières
&see CLERMONT-FERRAND
St-Laurent-les-Bains
&see ST-LAURENT-LES-BAINS
Vals-les-Bains
&see VALS-LES-BAINS
Vichy✠
&see VICHY

INFORMATION

You can obtain more information by contacting the following:
- **Chaîne Thermale du Soleil,**
  *01 42 65 24 24;
  www.chainethermale.fr.
- **La Medecine Thermale**,
  www.medecinethermale.fr.
- **Auvergne thermale**,
  *04 73 34 72 80;
  www.auvergnethermale.com.

27

Saturday market on Place François Mitterand, Vienne

SHOPPING

FAIRS AND MARKETS

Traditional fairs – These offer visitors an opportunity to witness long-standing local customs; the most colourful ones are listed below.

- **Besse:** 3rd Sat in January: pig fair
- **Tournon-sur-Rhône:** 29 August: onion fair
- **St-Sorlin-en-Valloire:** 1st Sat in September: foal fair
- **Mourjou:** second to last weekend in October: chestnut fair
- **Claveyson:** 11 November: truffle fair
- **Chénelette:** 11 November: goat and cattle fair
- **Thueyts:** 11 November: potato fair
- **Romans-sur-Isère:** from the last Sat in September to the 1st Sun in October: Dauphiné Fair

Markets – The market is an integral part of the French way of life and a vital component of the country's rich heritage. The most important fruit and vegetable market in the Rhône valley takes place in Pont-de-l'Isère daily except Sundays from May to September and on Mondays, Wednesdays and Fridays the rest of the year.
Other markets include:

- **Aubenas:** Sat morning
- **Bourg-de-Péage:** Thu morning
- **Hauterives:** Tue morning
- **Maringues:** Mon morning
- **Riom:** Sat morning
- **Romans-sur-Isère:** Tue, Fri and Sun mornings
- **Ruoms:** Fri morning
- **St-Donat-sur-l'Herbasse:** Mon morning
- **St-Rambert-d'Albon:** Fri morning
- **Tain-l'Hermitage:** Sat
- **Les Vans:** Sat morning; a traditional handicraft market livens up the town's historic centre between 6 and 10pm on Tue in July and August.
- **Valence:** Sat morning; farmer's market Tue 4–7:30pm
- **Villeneuve-de-Berg:** Wed morning; activities are organised on Tue evenings throughout July and during the first fortnight of August.

The excellent website – www.jours-de-marche.fr – lists more than 7 500, and admits to there being a great many more.

LOCAL SPECIALTIES

Beaujolais and **Côtes-du-Rhône** wines go well with local cheeses such as **Picodon**, made from goat's milk, or creamy, cow's milk **St-Marcellin**. In the Auvergne, meanwhile, a host of local wines pair wonderfully with the five AOP cheeses produced in the region: **Bleu d'Auvergne, Fourme d'Ambert, Salers, Cantal**, and **Saint-Nectaire**.
You may be tempted by a pair of fine **shoes** from Romans-sur-Isère, once the capital of the shoe industry, a **knife** from Thiers, a hand-painted **silk scarf** or tie from Lyon or even by woollen clothes from the local manufacture in **St-Pierreville**.
If you are looking for more ideas, visit the **Marché de la Création** (painting, sculpture, pottery…) which takes place in Lyon along quai Romain Rolland on Sunday mornings or the **Marché de l'Artisanat** (handicrafts) which takes place along quai Fulchiron, also on Sunday mornings.

WHAT TO SEE AND DO

BOOKS

Portrait of the Auvergne – Peter Gorham (Robert Hale, 1975). There are few places in France where past and present mingle so naturally. Yet the true wealth of the Auvergne remains in its countryside.

Summer Days in Auvergne – Herbert de Kantzow (Adamant Media Corporation, 2004). A descriptive account of the author's travels in France and the Auvergne, originally published in 1875.

Mourjou: The Life and Food of an Auvergne Village – Peter Graham, (Prospect Books, 2003). The author explores the traditions, folklore and gastronomy of the Auvergne, discovering the rhythms of its rustic life, the warmth of its people and their passion for food.

Auvergne and its People – Frances Marion Gosling (Elibron Classics, 2004). An idiosyncratic look at the lives of the people of the Auvergne; this reproduction issue is full of atmosphere and detail.

Speak the Culture – (Andrew Whittaker, Thorogood Publishing, 2008). A general guidebook that shows you where to go in France and what to say when you get there, reasoning that through exploring the people and their lifestyles you will achieve an intimate understanding of France and its people.

The Grand Traverse of the Massif Central – Alan Castle (Cicerone Press, 2010). A guide to biking or walking the 700km/435mi-long route that departs from Clermont-Ferrand. The guide is suitable for novices or experts, as some of the more challenging routes can be avoided.

Walking in the Auvergne: 42 Walks in Volcano Country – Rachel Crolla and Carl McKeating (Cicerone Press, 2013). Essential walker's guidebook that explores the tranquil Auvergne region.

FILMS

Each November, Aubenas plays host to the **Rencontres des Cinémas d'Europe** (www.maisonimage.eu). The **Auvergne Film Commission** unites directors making films in the beautiful landscapes of the Auvergne. Among these are:

7 years – (Bruno Todeschini, Valérie Donzelli and Cyril Troley, 2005). Vincent has just been sentenced to seven years in prison. The only intimacy left to him and his wife, Maïté, lies in the prison's visiting rooms. Twice a week, she picks up his laundry, washes it, irons it, and brings it back to him.

The Singer – (Cecile de France, Gérard Depardieu, Mathieu Amalric, 2005) Alain is a 50-year-old singer famous throughout Clermont-Ferrand. Singing was his whole life until he met Marion.

To be and to have – (Directed by Nicolas Philibert, 2002). Throughout France, there are still single-classroom schools uniting children of all ages with one teacher. Together, these little groups face the trials and tribulations of daily life, large and small. It is in one such school, somewhere in the Auvergne, that this film takes place.

Bon Voyage – (Isabelle Adjani, Virginie Ledoyen, Yvan Attal, Gregori Derangère, 2002). At the start of World War II, the fate of the free world hangs in the balance at the Hotel Splendide in Bordeaux. Cabinet members, journalists, physicists, and spies of all persuasions gather to escape the Nazi occupation of Paris.

L'Incroyable Histoire du facteur Cheval (Directed by Nils Tavernier, with Jacques Gamblin and Laetitia Casta, 2019) Based on a true story, this film tells the tale of postal worker Ferdinand Cheval, who designed and built a monumental sculpture called the Palais Idéal, still standing in Hauterives.

Calendar of Events

JANUARY
La Bourboule
La Sancy Blanche. ☎04 73 81 31 04 www.sancy.com.

Villefranche-sur-Saône
Fêtes des Conscrits "La Vague". www.loisirs-beaujolais.fr.

FEBRUARY
Le Mont Dore
Sancy Snow Jazz. ☎04 73 65 21 96 www.sancy-snowjazz.com.

Clermont-Ferrand
International Short Film Festival. ☎04 73 91 65 73; www.clermont-filmfest.com.

MARCH
Clermont-Ferrand
"Vidéoformes": International digital arts festival. www.videoformes.com.

Lyon
International Fair. ☎04 72 22 33 37; www.foiredelyon.com.

APRIL
Yssingeaux
Carnival.

Cournon-d'Auvergne
Festival Puy-de-Mômes for young people: theatre, puppets, dance, music. ☎04 73 69 90 40.

Pierrefort
Fête des Tersons Aubrac, beef festival 15 days before Easter. www.pays-saint-flour.fr.

MAY
Vichy
Une Saison en Eté: theatre, classical music, opera at the Vichy Opera House from May to October. ☎04 70 30 50 30. www.ville-vichy.fr.

Allanche
Fete de l'Estive. ☎04 71 20 48 43; www.allanche.fr.

Orcival
Torchlight procession and midnight mass. ☎04 73 65 81 49.

Clermont-Ferrand
Feast of Our Lady of the Port ending with a procession through the old town. ☎04 73 91 32 94.

Volvic
Volvic Volcanic Experience: Outdoor, cultural, and festive events. www.volvic-vvx.com.

Le Puy-en-Vélay
Puy de Lumières: light installations. (May weekends, Jul–Sep daily). www.puydelumieres.fr.

JUNE
Royat
Festival de Pyromélodie ☎04 73 29 50 80; www.royat.fr

Villefranche-sur-Saône
Midsummer Night: bonfires, singers, illuminations. ☎04 74 65 04 48.

Riom
Piano à Riom: Classical music festival. www.piano-a-riom.com

Châtel-Guyon
Jazz aux Sources jazz festival. www.jazz-aux-sources.com

Saint-Flour
Hautes Terres: festival of mountain culture. www.pays-saint-flour.fr

Massif du Sancy
Horizons: art installations in nature. www.horizons-sancy.com.

JULY
Forez
Classical concerts in churches and castles. ☎04 73 51 55 67.

Issoire
International Dance and Music Festival. ☎04 73 89 92 85. www.festival-issoire.fr.

Ambert
World Dance and Music Festival. www.festival-ambert.fr.

Royat
VOLCADIVA: concerts and recitals. ☎04 73 29 74 70; www.volcadiva.com.

Vollore
Concerts de Vollore: – classical music, jazz and "musique tzigane". ☎04 73 51 55 67. www.concertsdevollore.fr.

CALENDAR OF EVENTS

Gannat
World Cultures Festival.
☏ 04 70 90 12 67.
www.culturesdumonde.org

AUGUST
La Chaise-Dieu
Classic and Sacred Music Festival.
☏ 04 71 00 01 16.
www.chaise-dieu.com.
Aurillac
Street Theatre Festival. ☏ 04 71 45 47 45. www.aurillac.net.
Allanche
Largest secondhand market in Auvergne. ☏ 04 71 20 48 43.
St-Pourçain-sur-Sioule
Wine and Food Festival.
www.allier-auvergne-tourisme.fr.
Mont Brouilly
Wine producers' pilgrimage to Brouilly Chapel. ☏ 04 74 66 82 19.
Ambert
Fourmofolies festival. www.fourme-ambert.com.

SEPTEMBER
Ravel
Pottery market. ☏ 04 73 68 44 74.
Le Puy-en-Velay
Les Fêtes du Roi de l'Oiseau: Renaissance fair. ☏ 04 71 09 38 41. www.roideloiseau.com.
Valence
Valence en Gastronomie food festival.
valenceengastronomiefestival.fr

SEPTEMBER–DECEMBER
Beaujolais, Coteaux du Rhône and du Forez
Grape harvest and wine Festivals in the wine-growing regions.
Puy-de-Dôme
Les Automnales: theatre and music throughout the region.
☏ 04 73 42 23 29.
www.puydedome.com.

OCTOBER
Montbrison
Fourme Festival: flower-decked float procession. ☏ 04 77 96 18 18. www.fourme-de-montbrison.fr

SEPTEMBER: Fêtes du Roi de l'Oiseau, Le Puy-en-Velay

Mourjou
Chestnut Festival. ☏ 04 71 49 69 34 www.mourjou.com.
Clermont-Ferrand
International Jazz Festival.
☏ 09 82 47 01 97.

NOVEMBER
Le Puy-en-Velay
International Hot-Air Balloon Rally.
☏ 04 71 09 38 41.
www.ot-lepuyenvelay.fr.
Lyon
Festival of Baroque Music.
www.lesgrandsconcerts.com.
Beaujolais
Beaujolais Nouveau: release 3rd Thurs of Nov of primeur wine

DECEMBER
Lyon
Festival of Light. ☏ 04 72 10 30 30. www.fetedeslumieres.lyon.fr/en
Bresse
Glorieuses de Bresse, contest of Volailles de Bresse.
www.glorieusesdebresse.com.
Oingt
Crèches d'Oingt installation of over 100 crèches.
www.loisirs-beaujolais.fr.

Know Before You Go

USEFUL WEBSITES

http://uk.france.fr
The French Government Tourist Office site has practical information and links to more specific guidance, for American or Canadian travellers, for example. The site includes information on everything you need to know about visiting France.

www.ViaMichelin.com
This site has maps, tourist information, travel features, suggestions on hotels and restaurants, and a route planner for numerous locations in Europe. In addition, you can look up weather forecasts, traffic reports and service station location, particularly useful if you will be driving in France.

www.uk.ambafrance.org
www.franceintheus.org
The websites for the French Embassy in the UK and the USA provide a wealth of information and links to other French sites (regions, cities, ministries).

www.france-travel-guide.net
A practical website written by a Francophile travel writer. Includes essential information, as well as a wide range of regional and local content.

www.francethisway.com
An website containing a wide range of information about travelling in France.

http://drive-france.com
Keep up-to-date with the rules and regulations governing driving in France, including all the things you need to know about motoring laws.

TOURIST OFFICES

ABROAD

For information and assistance in planning a trip to France, travellers should apply to the official French Tourist Office in their own country:

Australia
French Tourist Bureau, 25 Bligh Street, Sydney, NSW 2000, Australia
☏(0)292 31 52 44;
http://au.france.fr.

Canada
Maison de la France, 1800 av. McGill College, Bureau 1010, Montreal, Quebec H3A 3J6, Canada
☏(514) 288 20 26; http://ca.france.fr.

South Africa
Block C, Morningside Close 222 Rivonia Road, MORNINGSIDE 2196 – JOHANNESBURG
☏00 27 (0)10 205 0201.

UK and Ireland
Lincoln House, 300 High Holborn, London WC1V 7JH.
☏0207 092 6600;
http://uk.france.fr.

USA
825 Third Avenue, New York, NY 10022, USA
☏(212) 745 0967;
http://us.france.fr.

IN THE AUVERGNE

Visitors will find more extensive information through the network of tourist offices. The details of local tourist offices, sometimes also called *syndicats d'initiative* in smaller towns, are listed after the symbol 🛈 in the introductions to individual sights.

REGIONAL TOURIST OFFICES:
Comité Régional du Tourisme (CRT)
- **Auvergne Rhône-Alpes Tourisme** – 11B quai Perrache, 69002 Lyon fr.auvergnerhonealpes-tourisme.com

- **Auvergne Rhône-Alpes Tourisme** – 59 blvd Léon Jouhaux, 63050 Clermont-Ferrand ℘04 73 29 49 49. www.inauvergnerhonealpes.com.

DEPARTMENTAL TOURIST OFFICES

- **Ain Tourisme (ADT)** – 34 rue du Général-Delestraint, CS90078, 01002 Bourg-en-Bresse. ℘04 74 32 31 30. www.ain-tourisme.com.

- **Allier (CDT)** – Château de Bellevue, 03402 Yzeure. ℘04 70 46 81 50. www.allier-tourisme.com.

- **Ardèche (ADT)** – Pôle Bésignoles, 6 route des Mines, 07000 Privas. ℘04 75 64 04 66. www.ardeche-guide.com.

- **Alpes Isère Tourisme** – Palais du Parlement, 4 place Saint-André, 38024 Grenoble. ℘04 76 54 34 36. www.isere-tourisme.com.

- **Cantal (CDT)** – 12, rue Marie Maurel, CS 80 007, 15013 Aurillac. ℘04 71 63 85 00. www.auvergne-destination-volcans.com.

- **Drôme (ADT)** – 8 rue Baudin, 26005 Valence. ℘04 75 82 19 26. www.ladrometourisme.com.

- **Loire (ADT)** – 22 rue Paul Petit, 42100 St-Étienne. ℘04 77 59 96 97. www.loiretourisme.com.

- **Rhône (CDT)** – 142 bis, avenue Maréchal de Saxe, 69003 Lyon. ℘04 72 56 70 40. www.rhonetourisme.com.

- **Haute-Loire (CDT)** – 1 place Monseignuer de Galard, 43000 Le Puy-en-Velay. ℘04 71 07 41 65. www.auvergne-experience.fr.

Montverdun, fortified priory of the Pic de Montverdun in the background, Loire

- **Puy-de-Dôme** – Conseil Départemental du Puy-de-Dôme, www.auvergne-destination-volcans.com.

Numerous towns and areas, labelled **Villes et Pays d'Art et d'Histoire** by the Ministry of Culture, are mentioned in this guide, including: Ardèche méridional, Beaujolais, Billom, Clermont-Ferrand, Dombes Saône Valley, the Forez, the Haut-Allier, Issoire, Lyon, Montluçon, Moulins, Paladru-Les-Trois-Vals Lake, Puy-en-Velay, Riom, Saint-Étienne, Saint-Flour, Valence-Romans and Vienne. They are particularly active in promoting their architectural and cultural heritage and offer tours by qualified guides as well as activities for 6- to 12-year-olds. More information is available from local tourist offices and from www.vpah.culture.fr.

INTERNATIONAL VISITORS
FOREIGN EMBASSIES AND CONSULATES

Embassies provide diplomatic help to their citizens abroad, while consulates are a local base in Paris and in other large cities for adminstrative formalities.

PLANNING YOUR TRIP

EMBASSIES AND CONSULATES IN FRANCE		
Australia	Embassy	4 rue Jean-Rey, 75015 Paris 01 40 59 33 00. www.france.embassy.gov.au
Canada	Embassy	130 rue du Faubourg Saint-Honoré, 75008 Paris 01 44 43 29 00. www.international.gc.ca
Ireland	Embassy	12 ave. Foch, 75116 Paris 01 44 17 67 00. www.embassyofireland.fr
New Zealand	Embassy	103, rue de Grenelle, 75007 Paris 01 45 01 43 43. www.mfat.govt.nz
South Africa	Embassy	59 quai d'Orsay, 75343 Paris 01 53 59 24 10. www.afriquesud.net
UK	Embassy	35 rue du Faubourg St-Honoré, 75383 Paris 01 44 51 31 00. www.gov.uk/world/france
	Consulate	16 rue d'Anjou, 75008 Paris 01 44 51 31 01 (visas). www.gov.uk/world/france.
USA	Embassy	2 avenue Gabriel, 75008 Paris 01 43 12 22 22. http://fr.usembassy.gov
	Consulate	2 rue St-Florentin, 75001 Paris 01 42 96 14 88. https://fr.usembassy.gov

ENTRY REQUIREMENTS

Passport – Nationals of countries within the European Union entering France need only a national identity card; in the case of the UK, this means your passport. Nationals of other countries must be in possession of a valid national **passport.**

🛑 *In case of loss or theft, report to your embassy or consulate and the local police.*

🛑 *You must carry your documents with you at all times; they can be checked anywhere.*

Visa – No **entry visa** is required for Canadian, US or Australian citizens travelling as tourists and staying less than 90 days, except for students planning to study in France. If you think you may need a visa, apply to your local French Consulate.

US citizens – General passport information is available by phone toll-free from USAGov (item 5 on the automated menu), 844-USA-GOV1. US passport forms can be downloaded from http://travel.state.gov.

CUSTOMS

In Britain, go to the Customs Office (UK) website (*www.hmrc.gov.uk*) for information on allowances, travel safety tips, and to consult and download documents and guides. There are no limits on the amount of duty and/or tax paid alcohol and tobacco that you can bring back into the UK as long as they are for your own use or gifts and are transported by you. If you are bringing in alcohol or tobacco goods and UK Customs have reason to suspect they may be for a commercial purpose, an officer may ask you questions and make checks.
Australians will find customs information at www.abf.gov.au; for **New Zealanders** Advice for Travellers is at www.customs.govt.nz.

HEALTH

First aid, medical advice and chemists' night service rota are available from chemists/drugstores *(pharmacies)* identified by the green cross sign. It is advisable to take out comprehensive travel insurance

KNOW BEFORE YOU GO

cover, as tourists receiving medical treatment in French hospitals or clinics have to pay for it themselves.
Nationals of non-EU countries should check with their insurance companies about policy limitations. Remember to keep all receipts.
British and Irish citizens, if not already in possession of an EHIC (European Health Insurance Card), should apply for one before travelling. The card entitles UK residents to reduced-cost medical treatment. Apply at UK post offices, call ✆0845 606 2030, or visit www.ehic.org.uk. Details of the healthcare available in France and how to claim reimbursement are published in the leaflet Health Advice for Travellers, available from post offices. All prescription drugs taken into France should be clearly labelled; it is recommended to carry a copy of prescriptions.
US and Canadian citizens can contact the International Association for Medical Assistance to Travellers (*www.iamat.org*).

ACCESSIBILITY ♿

The sights described in this guide that are easily accessible to people of reduced mobility are indicated by the ♿ symbol. However, this does not necessarily mean that there is full access across the whole sight; check websites for any restrictions.
On French TGV and Corail trains there are wheelchair spaces in 1st-class carriages available to holders of 2nd-class tickets. On Eurostar and Thalys, special rates are available for accompanying adults. All airports are equipped to receive physically disabled passengers. Disabled drivers may use the EU blue card for parking entitlements.
Many of France's historic buildings, including museums and hotels, have limited or no wheelchair access. Older hotels tend not to have lifts.
Tourism for All UK (*Pixel Mill, 44 Appleby Road, Kendal, Cumbria LA9 6ES.*

Lift at Lyon-St-Exupéry airport station

✆*0845 124 9971; www.tourismforall.org.uk*) publishes overseas information guides listing accommodation that they believe to be accessible but haven't inspected in person. Information about accessibility is available from French disability organisations such as **Association des Paralysés de France** (*17 bd. Auguste-Blanqui, 75013 Paris;* ✆*01 40 78 69 00;* ♿ *www.apf.asso.fr*). Useful information on transportation, holidaymaking, and sports associations for the disabled is available at www.disabilityrightsuk.org.

PETS

Recent regulations make it much easier to travel with pets between the UK and mainland Europe. Full details are available from the website of the **Department for Environment, Food and Rural Affairs** (*www.gov.uk/take-pet-abroad*).

35

PLANNING YOUR TRIP

Getting There and Getting Around

BY PLANE

It is very easy to arrange air travel to either of Paris' two airports (Roissy-Charles-de-Gaulle to the north, and Orly to the south). There are also regular flights from the UK to **Lyon-Saint-Exupéry** airport, which is linked to the city centre by a regular shuttle service. Contact airline companies and travel agents for details of package tour flights with a rail link-up or Fly-Drive schemes.

You can get from CDG airport into the centre of Paris by using the Roissybus, Airport Shuttle or by using a taxi, which is much more convenient, but expensive. There is an extra charge (posted in the taxi) for baggage; the extra charge for airport pick-up is on the meter; drivers are usually given a tip of 10–15%.

BY SHIP

There are competing **cross-Channel services** (passenger and car ferries) from the United Kingdom and Ireland. To choose the most suitable route between your port of arrival and your destination, use the Michelin Tourist and Motoring Atlas France, Michelin map 726 (which gives travel times and mileages) or Michelin maps from the 1:200 000 series (with the orange cover). For details apply to travel agencies or to:

- **Brittany Ferries** 0330 159 7000 (UK). www.brittanyferries.com. Services from Portsmouth, Poole, Plymouth and Cork to Caen, Le Havre, Cherbourg, Saint-Malo and Roscoff.
- **Condor Ferries** 0345 609 1024. www.condorferries.co.uk. Services from Poole and Portsmouth.
- **DFDS Seaways** operate Dover-Calais, Dover-Dunkirk and Newhaven-Dieppe routes.

(UK) 0871 574 7235 and 0800 917 1201. www.dfdsseaways.co.uk.
- **P&O Ferries** 0800 130 0030 (UK). www.poferries.com. Service between Dover and Calais.

BY TRAIN

Eurotunnel operates a 35-minute rail trip for passengers with a car through the Channel Tunnel between Folkestone and Calais 08705 35 35 35 (in the UK) or 08 10 63 03 04 (in France); www.eurotunnel.com.
Eurostar runs from **London** (St Pancras) to **Paris** (Gare du Nord) in under 3h (up to 20 times daily). In Paris it links to the high-speed rail network (TGV) which covers most of France. From Paris (Gare de l'Est), the French national railways **SNCF** (*www.sncf.fr*) operates an extensive service to the region.

Bookings and information
Oui.sncf (formerly Voyages-SNCF) is SNCF's online travel distributor in France (*https://en.oui.sncf*).
Citizens of non-European Economic Area countries must complete a landing card before arriving at Eurostar check-in. These cards can be found at dedicated desks in front of the check-in area and from Eurostar staff. Once you have filled in the card, please hand it to UK immigration staff.
France Rail Pass and **Eurail Pass** are travel passes which may be purchased by residents of countries outside the E.U. (*See www.raileurope-world.com and www.eurail.com*).
If you are a **European resident**, you can buy an individual country pass, if you are not a resident of the country where you plan to use it.
At the SNCF (French railways) site, **www.sncf.fr**, you can book ahead, pay with a credit card, and receive your ticket in the mail at home or on your smartphone.
There are numerous **discounts** available when you purchase your tickets in France, from 25–50 percent below the regular rate. They include discounts for using senior cards and youth cards, and seasonal promotions.

Train Panoramique des Dômes, Puy de Dôme

There are a limited number of discount seats available during peak travel times, and the best discounts are available for travel during off-peak periods.

Tickets for rail travel in France must be validated *(composté)* by using the (usually) automatic date-stamping machines at the platform entrance *(failure to do so may result in a fine)*. The French railway company SNCF operates a **telephone information, reservation and prepayment service in English** from 7am to 10pm (French time) ✆08 36 35 35 39.

BY COACH/BUS

Eurolines – www.eurolines.com has information about travelling by coach in Europe.

BY CAR

DRIVING IN FRANCE

The area covered in this guide is easily reached by main motorways and national routes. **Michelin map 726** indicates the main itineraries as well as alternate routes for avoiding heavy traffic during busy holiday periods. It also gives estimated travel times. **Michelin map 723** is a detailed atlas of French motorways, indicating tolls, rest areas and services along the route; it includes a table for calculating distances and times. The latest Michelin route-planning service is available at **www.ViaMichelin.com.** Travellers can calculate a precise route using such options as "shortest route", "route avoiding toll roads", "Michelin-recommended route" and also gain access to tourist information (hotels, restaurants, attractions). The service is available on a pay-per-route basis or by subscription.

The roads are very busy during holiday periods and, to avoid traffic congestion, it is worth considering taking to the secondary routes (signposted as *Bison Futé – itinéraires bis*). The motorway network includes rest areas *(aires de repos)* and petrol stations *(stations-service)*, usually with restaurant and shopping complexes attached, about every 40km/25mi.

DOCUMENTS

Driving Licence

Travellers from other European Union countries and North America can drive in France with a valid national or home-state **driving licence**.
An **international driving licence** is useful because the information on it appears in nine languages.

Registration papers

For the vehicle, it is necessary to have the registration papers (logbook) and an approved nationality plate.

Insurance

Many motoring organisations offer accident insurance and breakdown service schemes for members. Check with your insurance company with regard to coverage while abroad. Because French autoroutes are privately owned, European Breakdown Cover service does not extend to

PLANNING YOUR TRIP

breakdowns on the autoroute or its service areas – you must use the emergency telephones, or drive off the autoroute, if you can, before calling your breakdown service.

ROAD REGULATIONS

The minimum driving age is 18. Traffic drives on the right. All passengers must wear **seat belts**. Children under the age of 10 must ride in the back seat. Headlights must be switched on in poor visibility and at night; dipped headlights should be used at all times outside built-up areas. Use sidelights only when the vehicle is stationary. In the case of a breakdown, a **red warning triangle** or hazard warning lights are obligatory, as are **reflective safety jackets**, one for each passenger, and carried within the car. it is now compulsory to carry an in-car **breathalyser kit**, too; you can be fined if you do not. UK right-hand drive cars must use headlight adaptors.

In the absence of stop signs at intersections, cars must **give way to the right**. Traffic on main roads outside built-up areas (priority indicated by a yellow diamond sign) and on roundabouts has right of way. Vehicles must stop when the lights turn red at road junctions and may filter to the right only when indicated by an amber arrow.

The regulations on **drinking and driving** (limited to 0.50g/l) and **speeding** are strictly enforced – usually by an on-the-spot fine and/or confiscation of the vehicle.

Speed limits

Although subject to changes, speed limits are as follows:
- Toll motorways (autoroutes) **130kph/80mph** (110kph/68mph when raining);
- Dual carriageways and motor ways without tolls **110kph/68mph** (100kph/62mph when raining);
- Other roads **90kph/56mph** (80kph/50mph when raining) and in towns **50kph/31mph**;
- Outside lane on motorways during daylight, on level ground and with good visibility – minimum speed limit of 80kph/50mph.

Parking Regulations

In urban areas there are zones where parking is either restricted or subject to a fee; tickets should be obtained from the ticket machines (*horodateurs* – small change necessary) and displayed inside the windscreen on the driver's side; failure to display may result in a fine or towing. Other parking areas in town may require you to take a ticket when passing through a barrier. To exit, you must pay the parking fee (usually there is a machine located by the exit – *sortie*) and insert the paid-up card in another machine which will lift the exit gate.

In some towns, "blue zones" have been implemented. To park in a blue zone, you must place a parking disk (*disque de stationnement*) on your dashboard showing the time you arrived. You can obtain one at a service station.

Tolls

In France, most motorway sections are subject to a **toll** (*péage*). You can pay in cash or with a credit card.

Fuel

French service stations dispense:
- *sans plomb98* (super unleaded 98)
- *sans plomb95* (super unleaded 95)
- *diesel/gazole* (diesel, including premium diesel)
- *GPL* (LPG).

Prices are listed on signboards on the motorways, although it is usually cheaper to fill up before joining or after leaving the motorway.

The website www.prix-carburants.gouv.fr collects information on current fuel prices around the country.

WHERE TO STAY AND EAT

CAR RENTAL

There are car rental agencies at airports, railway stations and in all large towns throughout France. European cars have manual transmissions; automatic cars are available in larger cities only if an advance reservation is made. Drivers must be over 21; between ages 21–25, drivers are required to pay an extra daily fee; some companies allow drivers under 23 only if the reservation has been made through a travel agent.

Car hire and holders of UK driving licences

In 2015, changes to the UK Driving License came into force which mean that because details of fines, penalty points and restrictions are now only held electronically you are going to have to enable a car hire company to access your online driving record by means of a DVLA-issued pass code. Full details are available at www.gov.uk/view-driving-licence.

RENTAL CARS – RESERVATIONS	
Avis	www.avis.co.uk / www.avis.fr
Europcar	www.europcar.com
Budget France	www.budget.com
Hertz	www.hertz.com
SIXT	www.sixt.com

Where to Stay and Eat

WHERE TO STAY
FINDING A HOTEL

Turn to the **Addresses** within individual Sight descriptions for a selection and prices of typical places to stay (**Stay**) and eat (**Eat**). The key at the back of the guide explains the symbols and abbreviations used in these sections. Use the map of **Places to stay** *(overleaf)* to identify recommended places for overnight stops. To enhance your stay, hotel selections have been chosen for their location, comfort, value for the money, and in many cases, their charm, but it is not a comprehensive listing. Prices indicate the cost of a standard double room for two people in peak season. For an even greater selection, use the red-cover **Michelin Guide France**, with its well-known star-rating system and hundreds of establishments throughout France.

The **Michelin Charming Places to Stay** guide contains a selection of 1 000 hotels and guest houses at reasonable prices. Always be sure to book ahead, especially for stays during the high season.

A guide to good-value, family-run hotels, **Logis et Auberges de France**, is available from the French Tourist Office (www.tourisme.fr). The website gives a list of accommodation for each *département*, as well as links for making reservations and a list of tourist offices all over France.

Another resource, which publishes a catalogue listing holiday villas, apartments or chalets in each *département,* is the **French national family tourism network Clévacances** (*www.clevacances.com*). For good-value, family-run accommodation, try the **Logis** network (*www.logishotels.com*).

Relais & Châteaux (*www.relaischateaux.com*) provides information on booking in luxury hotels with character:
UK: ☏ 0203 519 1967
France: ☏ 01 76 49 39 39
Australia: ☏ 1300 121 341

PLANNING YOUR TRIP

New Zealand: ☎0800 540 008
USA: ☎1 800 735 2478
www.viamichelin.com covers hotels in France, including famous selections from the Michelin Guide as well as lower-priced chains.

Economy Chain Hotels

If you need a place to stop en route, these can be useful, as they are inexpensive and generally located near the main road. Breakfast is usually available, but there may not be a restaurant; rooms are small, with a TV and bathroom.
Central reservation numbers and websites (online booking is usually available):

- **Akena:** ☎08 10 220 280; www.hotels-akena.com
- **B&B:** ☎02 98 33 75 29; www.hotel-bb.com
- **Best Hôtel:** www.besthotel.fr
- **Campanile:** ☎08 92 23 48 12; www.campanile.com
- **Kyriad:** UK ☎0207 519 50 45; France ☎08 92 23 48 13; www.kyriad.com
- **Première Classe:** ☎08 92 23 48 14; www.premiereclasse.com
- **International Hotels Group:** ☎08 71 42 3 48 96; www.ihg.com
- **Best Western Hotels:** www.bestwestern.fr
- **Ibis and Accor Hotels:** UK ☎0871 663 0628; France ☎08 25 88 22 22; www.ibis.com

COTTAGES, BED AND BREAKFAST

The **Maison des Gîtes de France** lists self-catering cottages or apartments, or bed and breakfast accommodation (chambres d'hôtes) at a reasonable price (☎01 49 70 75 75; www.gites-de-france.com).

La Fédération des Stations Vertes
(BP 71698, 21016 Dijon ☎03 80 54 10 50; www.stationverte.com) lists some 600 country and mountain sites ideal for families.

There is also **Bed and Breakfast France** (12 rue des Tulipes, 85100 Les Sables d'Olonne; www.bedbreak.com). The **Fédération des Logis de France** offers hotel-restaurant packages geared to walking, fishing, biking, skiing, wine-tasting and enjoying nature (☎01 45 84 83 84 (English spoken); www.logishotels.com). The adventurous can consult **www.gites-refuges.com**, where you can download a guidebook, Gîtes d'étapes et refuges, listing some 4 000 shelters for walkers, mountaineers, rock-climbers, skiers, canoe/kayakers, etc.: 74 rue A. Perdreaux, 78140 Vélizy ☎01 34 65 11 89.

HOSTELS, CAMPING

To obtain an International Youth Hostel Federation card (no age requirement; senior card also available) contact the IYHF in your own country. An online booking service (www.hihostels.com), lets you reserve rooms up to six months ahead.
The two main youth hostel associations (auberges de jeunesse) in France are:

- **Ligue Française pour les Auberges de la Jeunesse**
  67 r. Vergniaud, Bâtiment K, 75013 Paris. ☎01 44 16 78 78. www.auberges-de-jeunesse.com/en.
- **Fédération Unie des Auberges de Jeunesse**
  27 r. Pajol, 75018 Paris. ☎01 44 89 87 27. www.fuaj.org.

There are numerous officially graded **campsites** with varying standards of facilities throughout the region. The **Michelin Camping France** guide lists a selection of campsites. The area is very popular with campers in the summer months, so it is wise to reserve in advance.

WHERE TO STAY AND EAT

WHERE TO EAT

Turn to the Addresses throughout the *Discovering* section for descriptions and prices of selected places to eat in the different locations covered in this guide. The Legend on the cover flap explains the symbols and abbreviations used in these sections. Use **The Michelin Guide France**, with its hundreds of establishments all over France, for an even greater choice. If you would like to experience a meal in a highly rated restaurant from the Red Guide, be sure to book ahead! In the countryside, restaurants usually serve lunch between noon and 2pm and dinner between 7.30pm and 10pm. It is not always easy to find something in between those two meal times, as the "non-stop" restaurant is a rarity in the provinces. However, a hungry traveller can usually get a sandwich in a café, and ordinary hot dishes may be available in a brasserie or café. Among places in the Auvergne region that have been awarded the special distinction of *site remarquable du goût* are Billom – for its particularly fine pink garlic; St-Nectaire – for its soft cheese made from cow's milk; Salers – for its firm cheese similar to Cantal *(www.sitesremarquablesdugout.com)*.

A TYPICAL FRENCH MENU

La Carte	**The Menu**
Entrées	**Starters**
Crudités	Raw vegetables
Terrine de lapin	Rabbit terrine (pâté)
Frisée aux lardons	Curly lettuce with diced bacon
Escargots	Snails
Salade au crottin de Chavignol	Goat's cheese salad
Potage	Soup, broth
Plats (Viandes)	**Main Courses (Meat)**
Bavette à l'échalote	Sirloin with shallots
Faux filet au poivre	Steak in a pepper sauce
Pavé de rumsteck	Thick rump steak
Côtelettes d'agneau	Lamb cutlets
Filet mignon de porc	Pork fillet
Blanquette de veau	Veal stew in a cream sauce
Plats (Poissons, Volaille)	**Main Courses (Fish, Fowl)**
Filets de sole	Sole fillets
Dorade aux herbes	Sea bream with herbs
Saumon grillé	Grilled salmon
Truite meunière	Trout fried in butter
Magret de canard	Breast fillet of duck
Poulet rôti	Roast chicken
Fromage	**Cheese**
Fromage de chèvre	Goat's cheese
Fromage maigre	Low-fat cheese
Fromage à pâte dure	Hard cheese
Fromage à pâte molle	Soft cheese
Fromage râpé	Grated cheese

PLANNING YOUR TRIP

Desserts
Tarte aux pommes
Crème caramel
Mousse au chocolat
Sorbet: trois parfums

Desserts
Apple tart
Custard with caramel sauce
Chocolate mousse
Sorbet: choose three flavours

Boissons
Bière
Eau minérale (gazeuse)
Une carafe d'eau
Vin rouge, vin blanc, rosé
Jus de fruit

Beverages
Beer
(Sparkling) mineral water
Tap water (no charge)
Red wine, white wine, rosé
Fruit juice

Menu Enfant
Jambon
Steak haché
Frites
Purée

Children's Menu
Ham
Minced beef
French fries
Mashed potatoes

Note: *Nos viandes sont garnies* translates as "meat dishes are served with vegetables". Well-done, medium, rare, "blue" = **bien cuit**, **à point**, **saignant**, **"bleu"**.

Useful Words and Phrases

Here are some French words you may see on local maps or road signs

Sights

	Translation
Abbey	Abbaye
Belfry	Beffroi
Chapel	Chapelle
Castle	Château
Cemetery	Cimetière
Cloisters	Cloître
Courtyard	Cour
Convent	Couvent
Lock (Canal)	Écluse
Church	Église
Fountain	Fontaine
Covered Market	Halle
Garden	Jardin
Town Hall	Mairie
House	Maison
Market	Marché
Monastery	Monastère
Windmill	Moulin
Museum	Musée
Park	Parc
Square	Place
Bridge	Pont
Port/Harbour	Port
Gateway	Porte
Quay	Quai
Ramparts	Remparts
Street	Rue
Statue	Statue
Tower	Tour

Natural Sites

	Translation
Chasm	Abîme
Swallow-Hole	Aven
Dam	Barrage
Viewpoint	Belvédère
Waterfall	Cascade
Pass	Col
Ledge	Corniche
Coast, Hillside	Côte
Forest	Forêt

USEFUL WORDS AND PHRASES

Cave	Grotte
Lake	Lac
Beach	Plage
River	Rivière
Stream	Ruisseau
Beacon	Signal
Spring	Source
Valley	Vallée

Shopping

	Translation
Bank	la banque
Baker's	la boulangerie
Big	grand
Bookshop	la librairie
Butcher's	la boucherie
Chemist's	la pharmacie
Closed	fermé
Cough syrup	du sirop pour la toux
Throat lozenges	des pastilles pour la gorge
Entrance	l'entrée
Exit	la sortie
Fishmonger's	la poissonnerie
Grocer's	l'épicerie
Open	ouvert
Post office	la poste
Shop	le magasin
Small	petit
Stamps	des timbres

On the Road

	Translation
Car park	le parking
Driving licence	le permis de conduire
(To the) east	(à l') est
Garage (for repairs)	le garage
(To the) left	(à) gauche
Motorway	l'autoroute
(To the) north	(au) nord
Petrol	l'essence
Petrol station	la station essence/ la station-service
(To the) right	(à) droite
(To the) south	(au) sud
Straight ahead	tout droit
Toll	le péage
Traffic lights	le feu tricolore
Tyre	le pneu
(To the) west	(à l') ouest

Travel

	Translation
Travel	voyager
Airport	l'aéroport
Credit card	la carte de crédit
Customs	la douane
Passport	le passeport
Platform	la voie
Railway station	la gare
Shuttle	la navette
Suitcase	la valise
Train ticket	le billet de train
Plane ticket	le billet d'avion
Wallet	la portefeuille

Time

	Translation
Today	aujourd'hui
Tomorrow	demain
Yesterday	hier
Winter	hiver
Spring	printemps
Summer	été
Autumn	automne
Week	la semaine
Monday	lundi
Tuesday	mardi
Wednesday	mercredi
Thursday	jeudi
Friday	vendredi
Saturday	samedi
Sunday	dimanche

Numbers

	Translation
0	zéro
1	un(e)
2	deux
3	trois
4	quatre
5	cinq
6	six
7	sept
8	huit
9	neuf
10	dix
11	onze
12	douze
13	treize

PLANNING YOUR TRIP

14	quatorze
15	quinze
16	seize
17	dix-sept
18	dix-huit
19	dix-neuf
20	vingt
30	trente
40	quarante
50	cinquante
60	soixante
70	soixante-dix
80	quatre-vingts
90	quatre-vingt-dix
100	cent
1000	mille

Here are a few French translations for things you might need to say:

USEFUL PHRASES

Hello/good morning Bonjour
Goodbye Au revoir
Thank you Merci
Excuse me Excusez-moi
Yes/no Oui/non
Sorry! Pardon!
Why? Pourquoi?
When? Quand?
Please S'il vous plaît
Do you speak English?
　Parlez-vous anglais?

I don't understand
　Je ne comprends pas
Please talk more slowly
　Parlez plus lentement, s'il vous plaît
Where is …? Où est…?
When does the … leave?
　À quelle heure part…?
When does the … arrive?
　À quelle heure arrive…?
When does the museum open?
　À quelle heure ouvre le musée?
When does the film/show start?
　À quelle heure commence le film/le spectacle?
When is breakfast served?
　À quelle heure sert-on le petit-déjeuner?
How much does it cost?
　Combien est-ce que ça coûte?
Where can I buy an English paper?
　Où puis-je acheter un journal en anglais?
Where is the nearest petrol station?
　Où se trouve la station-service la plus proche?
Where can I change travellers' cheques?
　Où puis-je échanger des cheques de voyages?
Where are the toilets?
　Où sont les toilettes?
Can I pay with a credit card?
　Est-ce que je peux payer avec ma carte bancaire?

Quai des Célestins, Lyon

© Camille Moirenc/hemis.fr

BASIC INFORMATION

Basic Information

BUSINESS HOURS

Most of the larger **shops** are open Mondays to Saturdays from 9am to 6.30 or 7.30pm. Smaller shops may close during the lunch hour. Food shops – grocers, wine merchants and bakeries – are generally open from 7am to 6.30 or 7.30pm; some open on Sunday mornings. Many food shops close between noon and 2pm and on Mondays. Bakery and pastry shops sometimes close on Wednesdays. Hypermarkets usually stay open without a break from 9am until 9pm, or even later; they may be open only in the mornings or not at all on Sundays. Although business hours vary from branch to branch, **banks** are usually open from 9am to noon and 2pm to 5pm and are closed either on Mondays or Saturdays. Banks close early on the day before a bank holiday. **Post offices** are generally open Mondays to Fridays from 8am to 7pm and Saturdays from 8am to noon. National **museums and art galleries** are closed on Tuesdays; municipal museums are generally closed on Mondays.

COMMUNICATIONS

PUBLIC TELEPHONES

Due to the widespread use of mobile phones, the number of **public telephones** in France is decreasing. Those that remain accept pre-paid phone cards *(télécartes)*, rather than coins. Some telephone booths accept credit cards (Visa, Mastercard/Eurocard). *Télécartes* (50 or 120 units) can be bought in post offices, branches of Orange, *bureaux de tabac* (cafés that sell cigarettes) and newsagents and can be used to make calls in France and abroad. Calls can be received at phone boxes where the blue bell sign is shown; the phone will not ring, so keep your eye on the little message screen.

National calls

French telephone numbers have ten digits. Paris and Paris region numbers begin with 01; 02 in northwest France; 03 in northeast France; 04 in southeast France and Corsica; 05 in southwest France.

International calls

To call France from abroad, dial the country code (+33) + 9-digit number (omit the initial 0). When calling abroad from France, dial 00, then dial the country code followed by the area code and number of your correspondent.

International Dialling Codes

Dial 00 before the country code (*see box*) minus the first 0, then the full number.

Australia	61
New Zealand	64
Canada	1
United Kingdom	44
Eire	353
United States	1

MOBILE PHONES

While in France, all visitors from other European countries should be able to use their mobile phone as normal. Visitors from other countries need to ensure before departure that their phone and service contract are compatible with the European system (GSM).

The three main mobile phone operators in France are SFR, Orange and Bouygues:
Orange www.orange.fr
Bouygues www.bouyguestelecom.fr
SFR www.sfr.fr

The EU abolished roaming charges in June 2017, as a result EU citizens won't be charged extra for calls. But for the foreseeable future the application of this decision in practice remains unclear. If necessary, consult your own provider.

PLANNING YOUR TRIP

La Ruche-Trianon, Clermont-Ferrand

INTERNET
All hotels and, especially in urban areas, many cafes, restaurants, and bars have free WiFi.

ELECTRICITY
In France the electric current is 220 volts. Circular two-pin plugs are the rule. Adapters and converters (for hairdryers, for example) should be bought before you leave home; they are on sale in most airports. If you have a rechargeable device (video camera, portable computer, battery recharger), read the instructions carefully or contact the manufacturer or retailer. Sometimes these items only require a plug adapter, in other cases you must use a voltage converter as well or risk ruining your device.

EMERGENCIES
European Emergency Call: 112
Fire *(Pompiers)*: 18
Paramedics (SAMU): 15
Police: 17

POST
Main post offices are open Monday to Friday 9am to 7pm and Saturday 9am to noon. However, many post offices, especially smaller ones, close at lunchtime between noon and 2pm, and some may close early in the afternoon. In short, opening hours vary widely. Stamps are also available from newsagents and tobacconists *(tabacs)*. Stamp collectors should ask for *timbres de collection* in any post office.

Postage via air mail:
UK: letter (20g) €1.30.
North America: letter (20g) €1.30
Australia and NZ: letter (20g) €1.30
A useful website for mailing information and prices is www.tarifs-de-la-poste.fr.

MONEY
The euro is the only currency accepted as a means of payment in France, as in the other European countries participating in the monetary union. It is divided into 100 cents or centimes. There are no restrictions on the amount of currency visitors can take into France. Visitors carrying a lot of cash are advised to complete a currency declaration form on arrival, because there are restrictions on currency export: if you are leaving the country with more than €10 000, you must declare the amount to customs.

BASIC INFORMATION

BANKS

Bank hours vary from branch to branch, but for typical hours ⓘ see *BUSINESS HOURS above*.

One of the most economical ways to obtain money in France is by using **ATM machines** to get cash directly from your bank account (with a debit card), or to use your credit card to get a cash advance. Be sure to remember your PIN number; you will need it to use cash dispensers and to pay with your card in shops, restaurants, etc. Code pads are numeric; use a telephone pad to translate a letter code into numbers. PIN numbers have 4 digits in France; enquire with the issuing company or bank if the code you usually use is longer.

CREDIT AND DEBIT CARDS

Visa is the most widely accepted credit card, followed by MasterCard; other cards (Diners Club, Plus, Cirrus, etc.) are also accepted in some cash machines. American Express is accepted primarily in premium establishments. Most places post signs indicating which cards they accept and the minimum amount you will need to spend to pay by card; if you don't see such a sign, ask before ordering or making a selection. Cards are widely accepted in shops, hypermarkets, hotels and restaurants, at tollbooths and in petrol stations. Before you leave home, check with the bank that issued your card for emergency replacement procedures. At the same time, inform the bank that you will be using your credit card abroad – it may prevent refusal of your card at cash desks. Carry your card number and its emergency phone numbers separately from your wallet and handbag; leave a copy of this information with someone you can easily reach.

ⓘ **If your card is lost or stolen** call the appropriate 24h hotlines listed on ***www.totallymoney.com/credit-cards/lost-stolen-credit-card***.

Better still: always carry with you the correct number to call for your particular credit cards. Report any loss or theft of credit cards or traveller's cheques to the local police, who will issue you with a certificate (useful proof to show the issuing company).

PRICES AND TIPPING

Since a service charge is automatically included in the price of meals and accommodation in France, any additional tipping is up to the visitor: generally small change, and usually not more than 5 percent. Taxi drivers and hairdressers are normally tipped 10–15 percent.

Tour guides and tour drivers should be tipped according to the service given: €2–5 would not be unusual.

Restaurants usually charge for meals in two ways: a fixed price menu with two or three courses and sometimes a small jug *(pichet)* of wine, or *à la carte*, the more expensive way, with each course ordered separately.

Cafés have very different prices, depending on where they are located. The price of a drink or a coffee is cheaper if you stand at the counter *(au comptoir)* than if you sit down *(en salle)*, and sometimes more expensive if you sit outdoors *(en terrasse)*.

VALUE ADDED TAX

There is a Value Added Tax in France *(TVA)* of 19.6% on almost every purchase (some foods and books are subject to a lower rate). However, non-European visitors who spend more than €175 (including VAT) in a single shop on the same day can get the VAT amount refunded. Usually, you fill out a form at the store, showing your passport. Upon leaving the country, you submit all forms to customs for approval (they may want to see the goods, so do not pack them in checked luggage). The refund is usually paid directly into your bank or credit card account, or it can be sent by mail. Big department stores that cater to tourists offer special services to help you; be sure to mention that you plan to seek a refund *(remboursement)* before you pay for goods (there is no refund for

PLANNING YOUR TRIP

tax on services). If you are visiting two or more countries within the European Union, you submit the forms only on departure from the last EU country. The refund is worthwhile for those visitors who would like to buy fashionwear, furniture or other fairly expensive items, but remember, the minimum amount must be spent in a single shop (though not necessarily on the same day). See https://www.economie.gouv.fr/particuliers/touristes-detaxe-achat.

PUBLIC HOLIDAYS

Public services, museums and other monuments may be closed or may vary their hours of admission on public holidays (see box). In addition to the usual school holidays at Christmas and in the spring and summer, there are long mid-term breaks in February and early November. In some regions, some shops and municipal museums may close or reduce their hours in the off-season (from late October to March or April).

1 January	New Year's Day *(Jour de l'An)*
24 April (2011) 8 April (2012)	Easter Day *(Pâques)*
1 May	May Day *(Fête du Travail)*
8 May	VE Day *(Anniversaire 1945)*
Thurs 40 days after Easter	Ascension Day *(Ascension)*
7th Sun-Mon after Easter	Whit Sunday and Monday *(Pentecôte)*
14 July	France's National Day *(Fête Nationale)*
15 August	Assumption *(Assomption)*
1 November	All Saints' Day *(Toussaint)*
11 November	Armistice Day *(Armistice 1918)*
25 December	Christmas Day *(Noël)*

DISCOUNTS

Almost all attractions offer discounted admission prices for children, seniors, students and (sometimes) family groups; many also offer discounts for advance booking online.
The ages that children's discounts apply to vary, but where these relate to Sights that are noted as specific attractions for children with the symbol, the price and age range for children are shown. Student discounts tend as a rule to be for French students only, on presentation of a student ID card.

TIME

France is 1hr ahead of Greenwich Mean Time (GMT). France goes on daylight-saving time from the last Sunday in March to the last Sunday in October. In France "am" and "pm" are not used, but the 24-hour clock is widely applied.

WHEN IT IS **NOON IN FRANCE**, IT IS	
3am	in Los Angeles
6am	in New York
11am	in Dublin
11am	in London
7pm	in Perth (6pm in summer)
9pm	in Sydney (8pm in summer)
11pm	in Auckland (10pm in summer)

SMOKING

In France, smoking is banned in public places such as offices, universities railway stations, restaurants, cafés, bars, nightclubs, casinos and some parks. In 2013, the ban was extended to e-cigarettes. Smoking is permitted on most outdoor terraces, even when terraces are sheltered.

CONVERSION TABLES

Weights and Measures

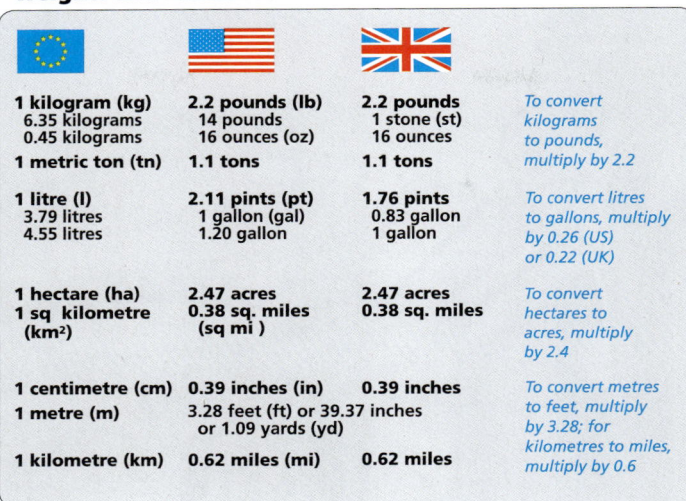

EU	US	UK	
1 kilogram (kg) 6.35 kilograms 0.45 kilograms **1 metric ton (tn)**	2.2 pounds (lb) 14 pounds 16 ounces (oz) 1.1 tons	2.2 pounds 1 stone (st) 16 ounces 1.1 tons	*To convert kilograms to pounds, multiply by 2.2*
1 litre (l) 3.79 litres 4.55 litres	2.11 pints (pt) 1 gallon (gal) 1.20 gallon	1.76 pints 0.83 gallon 1 gallon	*To convert litres to gallons, multiply by 0.26 (US) or 0.22 (UK)*
1 hectare (ha) **1 sq kilometre (km²)**	2.47 acres 0.38 sq. miles (sq mi)	2.47 acres 0.38 sq. miles	*To convert hectares to acres, multiply by 2.4*
1 centimetre (cm) **1 metre (m)**	0.39 inches (in) 3.28 feet (ft) or 39.37 inches or 1.09 yards (yd)	0.39 inches	*To convert metres to feet, multiply by 3.28; for kilometres to miles, multiply by 0.6*
1 kilometre (km)	0.62 miles (mi)	0.62 miles	

Clothing

Women

	EU	US	UK
Shoes	35	4	2½
	36	5	3½
	37	6	4½
	38	7	5½
	39	8	6½
	40	9	7½
	41	10	8½
Dresses & suits	36	6	8
	38	8	10
	40	10	12
	42	12	14
	44	14	16
	46	16	18
Blouses & sweaters	36	6	30
	38	8	32
	40	10	34
	42	12	36
	44	14	38
	46	16	40

Men

	EU	US	UK
Shoes	40	7½	7
	41	8½	8
	42	9½	9
	43	10½	10
	44	11½	11
	45	12½	12
	46	13½	13
Suits	46	36	36
	48	38	38
	50	40	40
	52	42	42
	54	44	44
	56	46	48
Shirts	37	14½	14½
	38	15	15
	39	15½	15½
	40	15¾	15¾
	41	16	16
	42	16½	16½

Sizes often vary depending on the designer. These equivalents are given for guidance only.

Speed

KPH	10	30	50	70	80	90	100	110	120	130
MPH	6	19	31	43	50	56	62	68	75	81

Temperature

Celsius (°C)	0°	5°	10°	15°	20°	25°	30°	40°	60°	80°	100°
Fahrenheit (°F)	32°	41°	50°	59°	68°	77°	86°	104°	140°	176°	212°

To convert Celsius into Fahrenheit, multiply °C by 9, divide by 5, and add 32.
To convert Fahrenheit into Celsius, subtract 32 from °F, multiply by 5, and divide by 9.

NB: Conversion factors on this page are approximate.

Arcade, Parc des Sources, Vichy
© Pierre Jacques/hemis.fr

INTRODUCTION TO AUVERGNE RHÔNE VALLEY

# The Region Today

21C AUVERGNE AND THE RHÔNE VALLEY

POPULATION AND PEOPLE

The Auvergne enjoys one of the lowest population densities in France; indeed, the *département* of Cantal would be virtually uninhabited were it not for the town of Aurillac.

The total population of the Auvergne is around 1.35 million, with a population density of just 50 per square kilometre. Moreover, the population of the Auvergne is declining, with more deaths annually than births. By contrast, the population around Lyon alone – around 2 million – exceeds the whole of the Auvergne, of which Lyon hosts just under half a million.

LANGUAGE

Like all the regions in France, the Auvergne has its own language, which has undergone continual development since the days of Antiquity. This means that the borders of the area in which the dialect of the Auvergne is spoken do not correspond to the historical and administrative borders of the province. *Auvergnat*, which is considered to be similar to North Occitan, is said to have developed from a Medio-Roman language used in the part of central France occupied by the Romans that gradually died out in the face of competition from *oïl*, the language of northern France. The dialect spoken in and around Aurillac is closer to the Guyennais dialect spoken in the south-west of France (Aquitaine), which was under English domination for a considerable time, but it has nevertheless been influenced by *Auvergnat*.

RELIGION

France enjoys freedom of religion as a constitutional right. However, a long history of conflict led the state to break its ties to the Catholic church in the 20C. No statistics are kept of religious leanings, but while many believe France to be staunchly Roman Catholic, there is contrary evidence suggesting that more than 50 percent of its people are either atheist or agnostic, with only 25 percent adhering to the Roman Catholic faith.

SPORT

Outdoor Adventure

With so much uninhabited countryside, it's easy to believe that the Auvergne was specifically designed for those who enjoy adventure in the outdoors.

Walking and mountain biking prevail almost everywhere in the region, while kayaking and a wide range of water sports are provided for on the Allier and Loire rivers and in the Ardèche gorges. Hang-gliding is a major sporting activity among the volcanic landscapes of the Auvergne, especially around the Puy-de-Dôme.

In winter the transformation is spectacular. Fully equipped downhill skiing resorts on the Puy de Sancy and the Plomb du Cantal allow visitors to take advantage of the fresh snow.

On your Bike

Cyclists have tons of choice in the region, with trails through the Ardèche including the 90km Dolce Via *(www.dolce-via.com)*, a gentle trail perfect for families. The ViaRhôna *(en.viarhona.com)* is a cycling route along the Rhône river from Lake Geneva to the Mediterranean Sea. The Auvergne is also hugely popular with motorcyclists, who have long had a soft spot for the region thanks to its openness. All-terrain motorcycles have a dedicated track at Clermont-Ferrand.

MEDIA

The Connexion

English language newspapers in France, other than imported UK newspapers, are virtually unheard of.

The Connexion is a monthly production targeting the expatriate community. Founded in 2002, *The Connexion* reports news stories of events in France and provides advice for expatriates living there. A free trial copy is available at www.connexionfrance.com.

THE REGION TODAY

Traditions in the Auvergne

Because of the isolated nature of much of the Auvergne countryside, many ancient traditions have survived; today, the utmost is being done to preserve the special character of this region and the cultural heritage.

Fêtes and Festivals

Many of the old customs are upheld on the most important occasions. Bonfires are still lit on the mountain tops to celebrate the summer solstice (Feast of St John), and local fêtes have kept up the tradition of the music and songs played to young girls by the young men of the village. There has also been a revival of country festivals to celebrate haymaking, cheesemaking, harvesting, etc.

Costume

Today every folk group has its own interpretation of traditional costume. The men wear the *biaude,* a voluminous dark blue smock over a pair of coarse black trousers, with a brightly coloured scarf, a wide-brimmed, black felt hat and the clogs or hob-nailed boots that are so vital when tapping out the dance rhythm. The women are dressed in long, multicoloured dresses with an embroidered apron and a headdress that varies depending on the region.

The Bourrée

This dance dates back a long time but it has been synonymous with the Auvergne since the 18C. The *bourrée* enacts the chasing of a coquettish young girl by an enterprising young man, whom she alternately runs away from and then beckons to.

Processions and Pilgrimages

Worship of the Virgin Mary has long been important in the Auvergne. Countless churches and chapels have been dedicated to her. Indeed, the statues of the Virgin Mary in the Auvergne are among the oldest in France.

Processions and pilgrimages in honour of the Blessed Virgin remain very much alive and are quite spectacular. The processions to Notre-Dame-du-Port (Clermont-Ferrand) or Orcival, and the pilgrimages to Mauriac and Thiézac in Cantal and to Marsat and Monton in Puy-de-Dôme are the most popular.

La Bourrée

INTRODUCTION TO AUVERGNE RHÔNE VALLEY

GOVERNMENT
Decision-making in France was once highly centralised. Each *département* was headed by a government-appointed prefect, in addition to a locally elected general council *(conseil général)*. But in 1982, the national government decided to decentralise authority by devolving a range of administrative and fiscal powers to local level. Regional councils were elected for the first time in 1986.

Administrative units with a local government consist of 34 967 communes, headed by a municipal council and a mayor, grouped in 96 *départements*, each headed by a *conseil général* and its president. The centre of administration of a *département* is called a *préfecture* (prefecture) or *chef-lieu de département*, which is usually geographically central to the départment.

The *conseil général* discusses and passes laws on matters that concern the department; it is administratively responsible for departmental employees and land and manages subsidised housing, public transport and school subsidies. It also contributes to public facilities. The council meets at least three times a year and elects its president for a term of three years. The presidident presides over its "permanent commission", usually up to 10 other departmental councillors. The *conseil général* has accrued new powers in the course of the political decentralisation that has occurred in France during the past 30 years.

Different levels of administration have different duties, and shared responsibility is common; for instance, in the field of education, *communes* run public elementary schools, while *départements* run public junior high schools and regions run public high schools. This only pertains to the building and upkeep of buildings; curricula and teaching personnel are supplied by the national Ministry of Education.

New French regions
In 2014, the French Parliament (the National Assembly and the Senate) passed a law that reduced the number of regions in Metropolitan France from 22 to 13. The new regions took effect on 1 January 2016. In the Auvergne, the *départements* are Allier, Cantal, Haute Loire and Puy-de-Dôme. These are now combined with Ain, Ardèche, Drôme, Isère, Loire, Rhône, Savoie, Haute-Savoie into the new region of Auvergne-Rhône-Alpes, the third largest region in metropolitan France.

ECONOMY
INDUSTRY
Industry in the region developed in the 16C with the introduction of silk-working around Lyon, paid for by the capital earned from fairs. Later, the coalfields in the area were a major factor leading to the expansion of industry. Once the seams had been worked out, the energy supply was provided by hydroelectric plants and, since the 1970s and 1980s, by nuclear power plants along the Rhône valley. Around Clermont-Ferrand, the major industry is tyre-making.

Metal-Working
After the gradual shut-down of the coal mines in the area around St-Étienne, the metal-working sector began to specialise in the production of steels, rare metals, fissile products for use in the nuclear industry, and smelting, a sector that benefits from the high demand for moulded components (boiler-making, pipes). The region along the Rhône ranks second to the Paris basin in the field of mechanical engineering (machine tools, precision engineering, car manufacture). Electrical and electronic engineering are well represented, with companies producing high-voltage equipment, communications equipment and domestic appliances. Until the 19C, tin and copper were the major materials used in the Auvergne.

Textiles
After the silk workers' revolts in 1831 and 1834 in the streets of Lyon, the textile industry relocated to villages, and manufacturers distributed the jobs (weaving and dyeing) to a rural workforce. This so-called outworker system still functions today. The importance of silk has decreased greatly in the face

Cattle in Les sucs de Meygal near Saint-Julien-Chapteui, Velay

of competition from man-made fibres, but the weaving of silky fabrics made of a combination of fibres and threads of all types has remained famous. The new products have remained faithful to the innovation and tasteful designs that won Lyon its reputation for silks.

The production and weaving of man-made textiles is carried out in Valence (nylon and polyester) and Roanne (viscose). The industry has many offshoots like dyeing and clothing manufacture (ready-to-wear, sportswear, lingerie, hosiery, curtains, net curtains, ribbons, elastic, lace).

Chemicals

A major chemical industry developed in Lyon in order to meet the needs of the textile industry. It was here that one of Europe's petrochemical centres was established.

In Feyzin, there is a large oil refinery, and the Institut Français du Pétrole has set up its largest research centre here. The region currently leads the field in certain areas of the chemical industry, notably fungicides, paint, varnish and, especially, pharmaceuticals.

Additional Industries

Other industrial activities in the region include tyre-making, food processing (dairy products, pork products, health foods), shoe-making, cabinetmaking, quarrying (Volvic) and mineral-water bottling (Vichy, Volvic) as well as the production of building materials, glass, wires, cables, leather, paper, jewellery, tobacco and enamelled lava (signposts, viewing tables). Thiers is one of France's major cutlery-making centres. Traditionally, industry in the Auvergne has centred around specialist crafts, with production frequently operating on a cottage-industry scale, such as copper-smithing (Cantal), lace-making (Velay) and paper-making (Livradois).

Administration offices (local authority and government offices, etc) and tourism also play an important part in the local economy; traditional industries (eg cheese-making) no longer do any more than "top it up".

Harnessing the Rhône

Important works upstream and downstream of Lyon, completed during the second half of the 20C, have offered this highly industrialised region the possibility of tapping the power resources of the mighty Rhône (16 billion kWh are produced yearly). At the same time, a series of canals provide a total of 330km/205mi of navigable waterways between Lyon and the sea.

AGRICULTURE

The Auvergne is first and foremost a rural area, in marked contrast to the Rhône valley, where industry predominates. Life on farms experienced profound change during the 20C, notably with the introduction of motor vehicles and the destruction of hedgerows, which ended the subdivision of properties into small fields.

INTRODUCTION TO AUVERGNE RHÔNE VALLEY

In many places, the traditional landscape of fields and narrow lanes lined with walnut trees has given way to one of wide, open fields.

Farmers, who are decreasing in number, have also had to comply with the milk quotas imposed on them by the EU; despite these difficulties, animal breeding and crop farming remain an important part of the economy of the region.

Stock Breeding

The high plateaux and mountains are popular with cattle breeders and, to a lesser extent, sheep farmers. The pastures on the slopes of the Dômes and Dore mountain ranges provide grazing land for the **Salers** breed of cattle (of which it is said that its fiery red coat turns pale if it leaves the basalt areas of Cantal), the French black-and-white Friesian, and the Montbéliarde.

Towards the middle of May the animals leave their byres and, for the five months of summer, live on the mountain pastures, which are now fenced so that there is no need for a herdsman to be in attendance. In days gone by, cowherds had a squat, low summer hut called a *buron*, built to withstand the wind.

The **fairs** give visitors an opportunity to enjoy the busiest moments of rural life. They are held in most of the centrally situated localities and in other places that lie in the heart of the stock-breeding areas. The largest fairs are held in late summer and in autumn.

Crops

In the Auvergne, wheat, barley and oats have traditionally been grown on the fertile black soil of the Limagnes. Today, sugar beet, tobacco, sunflowers and fodder or maize crops are also grown from selected strains of seeds.

At the southern end of the Rhône valley, the dampness and cold of maritime or continental climates gives way to the heat and radiant skies of the south of France – almond and olive trees and a few mulberry bushes can be seen in the countryside. The natural environment here is both crop- and farmer-friendly. The land is fertile and easy to irrigate; the soil is light and siliceous; well-sheltered corries and dales benefit from the spring sunshine.

Orchards

It was in 1880 that fruit production took over from wine, after the vineyards had been blighted by phylloxera. The long, fruit-producing season, made possible by careful selection of varieties and the differences in exposure or altitude, enable the orchards in the Rhône valley to produce one-third of all French fruit. Raspberries, redcurrants and blackcurrants are grown in Isère, sweet chestnuts in Ardèche. The region also grows cherries, apricots, apples and pears and, in particular, peaches: the fruit that has made the Eyrieux valley famous.

Vineyards

The vineyards in the Rhône valley, which were already popular in Roman times, underwent massive expansion after the crisis in the silkworm-breeding industry in the mid-19C. The best wines produced in the region are the **Côtes du Rhône**. Châteauneuf-du-Pape, St-Joseph, Crozes-Hermitage, Hermitage, Côte-Rôtie, Château-Grillet and Condrieu. These wines age well and have brought the area its reputation for excellence. With an annual output of 3.3 million hectolitres of *appellations contrôlées*, the Rhône valley vineyards account for 15 percent of the total French production of fine wines.

The vineyards stretch for 200km/124mi producing a variety of wines thanks to the **types of vines** selected: Marsanne and Viognier for the whites, Syrah and Grenache for the reds. The wines also vary depending on the different types of soil on which the vines are planted – the crumbly granite of the gorges, and the sands, pebbles or marl that predominate in alluvial plains. There are climatic differences in the basins and, the terraces that climb the hillsides between this area and the Alps face in different directions.

Further north, the vineyards of the **Beaujolais** – which are usually grouped

THE REGION TODAY

with those of neighbouring Burgundy in wine guides – produce wines which go very well indeed with the traditional cuisine of Lyon, where they are to be found in every local brasserie or *bouchon*. The third Thursday in November is a "red letter" day locally (and further afield, now that the reputation of Beaujolais wines has spread abroad!) as it marks *l'arrivée du beaujolais nouveau*, or the release for sale to the public of the latest Beaujolais vintage *(vin primeur)*. For further details on Beaujolais wines, see BEAUJOLAIS. The limestone hillsides to each side of the Limagnes used to be covered with vineyards. Nowadays, some of the wines fall within the all-enveloping name Côtes d'Auvergne, among them Châtaugay, Corent, Boudes and St-Pourçain.

FOOD AND DRINK
RHÔNE VALLEY

The Rhone valley is situated at the heart of various areas containing an outstanding wealth of local produce. Bresse is famous for its poultry; the Charolais area produces fantastic beef; the Dombes region abounds in game; the lakes of Savoy teem with fish; the Forez and Rhône valleys specialise in fruit and, of course, wine.

In the 19C silk workers ate, like their employers, in small family-run restaurants. The dishes served were based on cheap cuts of meat and offal, but the food was plentiful and tasty. Diners could eat sausages, potted pork, black sausage, pigs' trotters, veal knuckle and other slow-cooked meats.

The tradition of good food remains unchanged. Today, local **specialities** include spiced saveloy sausage with truffles and pistachio nuts, pigs' trotters and tails, artichoke with marrow bone jelly, pork brawn in vinaigrette, and gently stewed tripe. Other dishes include stuffed trout, fish in Burgundy wine and poultry cooked in stock with thin slivers of truffle inserted between the skin and the meat.

Forez

Hunting, shooting, fishing and stock-breeding provide the basic ingredients

Making Montélimar nougat

for local cuisine: crayfish and trout from the River Lignon, as well as poultry and meat of outstanding quality. Local dishes include pork pie, Feurs sausage or, in the autumn, game pâté; sometimes even woodcock.

Ardèche

Food here is rustic; this is the land of chestnuts and wild mushrooms such as St George's agaric and boletus. Among the stick-to-your-ribs specialities are partridge with cabbage, thrush with grapes, chicken cooked in a bladder, chicken with crayfish, goose and turkey with chestnuts, hare with *poivrade* (a highly seasoned sauce), and pork products. During the summer, the cherries, apricots, peaches, pears, plums and apples are among the finest found anywhere in France.

Lower Dauphiné

The Rhône valley area of Lower Dauphiné marks the transition between the Lyonnais area and Provence. This is the land of *gratin dauphinois*, veal with leeks, *pognes* (brioches, a sort of sweet bread) in Romans and Valence, cheese from St-Marcellin, Grignan-style braised beef and the inimitable Montélimar nougat.

AUVERGNE

The Auvergne, a rugged area of countryside, is not the place for complex, sophisticated cuisine; it specialises in family cooking – and plenty of it.

INTRODUCTION TO AUVERGNE RHÔNE VALLEY

The food in the Auvergne has traditionally been farm cooking, and as a result it has been accused of lacking any appreciable local specialities; this criticism is, happily, totally unfounded. The people of the Auvergne have taken great national specialities and adapted them to suit local taste so that, in the Auvergne, food is rich and sometimes heavy, but it is always extremely good.

Meat and Fish
Coq au vin (chicken stew) is delicious, especially when flavoured with a good wine. *Tripoux* from Aurillac, St-Flour and Chaudes-Aigues are wonderful, too. There is ham from Maurs, local sausages, trout from mountain streams, eels from the Dore and salmon from the Allier.

Vegetables
The *truffade* from Aurillac is a blend of fresh Tomme cheese and potatoes; puréed and seasoned with garlic in Chaudes-Aigues and Aubrac, it is called *aligot*. Potato paté, a light pastry browned in the oven with a lot of fresh cream and potatoes, is one of the specialities of the Montluçon and Gannat area. Morel mushrooms are cooked with cream and used to fill omelettes and stuff poultry. Peas from the Planèze and green lentils from Le Puy are well-known to gourmets.

Cheeses
This is one of the region's main specialities. The round, flat Saintt-Nectaire is a delight when well matured. There is also Fourme d'Ambert and Fourme de Montbrison, a blue cheese with an orange-tinted rind, as well as Bleu d'Auvergne, Cantal and Salers. While these are the best-known local cheeses, others include Murol, an orange-rinded variant of St-Nectaire, as well as the garlic-flavoured Gaperon, made on the plains and shaped like a rounded cone. Locally, the cheese usually known as Cantal is called Fourme, named after the wooden mould (or form) used to hold it together. This word gave the French language the word *formage* (forming) which later became *fromage* (cheese).

Wines
While the Auvergne's rich winemaking tradition suffered following phylloxera outbreaks, connoisseurs know the famous St-Pourçain, which can be left to age for up to four years, and Côtes d'Auvergne wines known since Roman times. The Auvergne is also known for a blossoming natural wine scene.
The most famous wine-growing areas are nevertheless found in the Rhône valley, where Beaujolais and Côtes du Rhône are produced. Thought to be the oldest in France, these vineyards were founded on vine stock introduced by the Greeks. They stretch along both banks of the river like a narrow ribbon, producing wines whose quality and balance are guaranteed by a skilful blend of varieties of grape. The reds should be consumed slightly cool, the whites well chilled. Château-Condrieu and Château-Grillet are among the greatest of all French white wines. If drunk young, they are a marvellous accompaniment to a crayfish gratin. Cornas was much appreciated by Charlemagne.
Further south, where the valley enters Provence, the vineyards produce the warm, friendly Châteauneuf-du-Pape, Gigondas, as well as the sweet, suave and flavoursome Muscat from Beaumes-de-Venise and, on the other bank of the Rhône, the rosés from Tavel and the reds and rosés from Lirac and Chusclan.

St-Nectaire

© Chris Dave/age fotostock

History

TIMELINE
BCE PREHISTORY

7500–2800	**Neolithic Era: Stone Age.** Volcanoes in the Puys range cease to erupt. Farmer stock-breeders settle in the Rhône valley and the Massif Central, leaving some 50 dolmens and 20 or more menhirs.
c.180–700	**Bronze Age.** Human settlements become denser and the Rhône valley is the major amber and tin route. The Celts settle in Gaul. The Helvians settle on the right bank of the Rhône, the Allobroges on the left and the Arverni in the Auvergne.

Prehistoric painting, Grotte Chauvet-Pont-d'Arc

Arverni domination of the Auvergne – The main expansion of the Celtic people occurred during the 5C BCE, probably as a result of the push southwards by Germanic tribes fleeing the rigorous climate of Northern Europe. Little is known about them; they had no written literature and were divided into different peoples in accordance with criteria that have remained mysterious. What *is* known is that the Celts in Gaul, like the **Allobroges** in Lugdunum (Lyon), were subject to the authority of the **Arverni** in the Massif Central. They traded with their own coinage. In order to ensure the submission of other peoples, their sovereigns acted as demagogues. King Luern, who reigned in the 2C, was famous for his gifts of gold. Rome, worried by his power, launched a campaign against his son, Bituit, who died in battle with Roman forces near Bollène in 121 BCE. The Roman legions settled in Vienne, the capital of the Allobroges. The Arverni monarchy was no more.
The great Celtic families took power and, thereafter, were forced to share it with the Aedui of Burgundy who were allied to Rome.

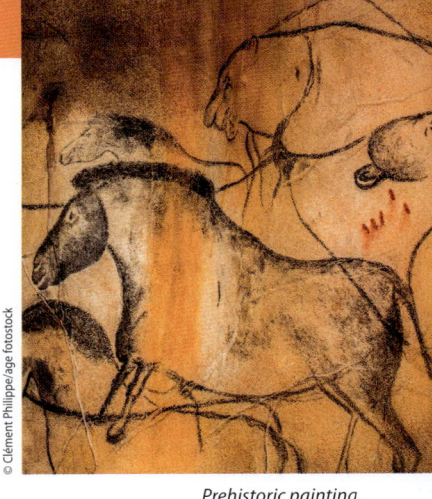

43	Lyon founded soon after Caesar's conquest of Gaul by one of his lieutenants, Munatius Plancus. Roman settlers arrive and build houses on the hillsides above the banks of the Saône.
27	Lyon, capital of the Gauls (Aquitaine, Lyon area, Belgium); the Rome and Augustus Altar is built on the hill at La Croix-Rousse.

CE

1C	Preachers come to spread the gospel in the Auvergne and the Rhône valley.
177	Marcus Aurelius instigates persecution. Christians are martyred in Lyon.
280	Emperor Probus removes the monopoly on sales of wine in Gaul previously enjoyed by the people of Lyon. This marks the start of Lyon's decline and, during the reign of Diocletian (284-305), the city is nothing more than the capital of the province.
406	After the invasion of the Vandals, the emperor introduces a federation of barbarian states in Gaul with the Visigoths

INTRODUCTION TO AUVERGNE RHÔNE VALLEY

in the Auvergne and the Burgundians on the left bank of the Rhône.

Sidonius Apollinaris stands up to the Visigoths – Sidonius Apollinaris was born in Lyon in AD 432 to a wealthy family of senators; later, his father-in-law, Avitus, was one of the last emperors of the Western world. Sidonius remained in Rome after the death of Avitus in AD 456 and wrote tributes to the emperors. His poetry pleased them, and when he returned to the Auvergne, he was elected Bishop of Clermont.

Euric, King of the Visigoths, who already owned a large part of Aquitaine, threatened the Auvergne. Sidonius headed the resistance and withstood a siege lasting several years in the walled town of Clermont. Eventually the province was transferred to the barbarians in exchange for Provence, and Sidonius went into exile. Twenty years later, the province passed into the hands of the Franks after the Battle of Vouillé.

5C-9C	Founding of the first abbeys – in Lyon, Vienne, Romans, in the Vivarais, the Lyonnais and the Velay.
761-767	Pepin the Short attempts to gain power over the noblemen of the Auvergne by means of military expeditions.
800	Charlemagne is crowned.
843	Treaty of Verdun. Charlemagne's empire is divided into three kingdoms (West, Central and East). The Auvergne is ruled by Charles the Bald (West Francia); the Rhône Valley by Lothair I (Lotharingia).
9C-10C	Power is actually held by the many castle owners, all of them difficult to control. Safe on their feudal mottes, they wage war against their neighbours, devastate the countryside, attack churches and pillage monasteries.
951	The first pilgrimage to Santiago de Compostela starts from Le Puy-en-Velay.
999	Gerbert, a former monk from Aurillac, is elected to the papacy as Sylvester II. He is the first French Pope, and he occupies the papal throne at the end of the first millennium.
1095	Pope Urban II preaches the First Crusade in Clermont. The wave of popular faith aroused by his call arrives just at the right time to channel the warring energies of the turbulent feudal lords. The Pope has a chance to gauge the vitality of the church in the Auvergne. The Gregorian Reform purges the parishes by removing the power of the layman. The influence of a few of the great monasteries begins to spread. The Counts of Albon, who come from Vienne, extend their territory; their lands, stretching from the Rhône to the Alps, become known as Dauphiné.

Royal intervention in the Auvergne – Divided between their position as vassals to the King of France and their allegiance to the Duke of Aquitaine, the great lords of the Auvergne failed to come to an agreement that would enable them to set up their own state. These feuding lords of mixed loyalties governed large estates with no clearly defined borders, which eventually enabled the sovereign to annex sections of the region little by little over the 12C and 13C; first Riom and the Limagne, then Montferrand and the area subsequently known as Dauphiné and finally Lower Auvergne.

13C-14C	The development of towns leads to the granting of

HISTORY

numerous municipal charters. Royal authority gains a foothold and is strengthened in Auvergne and the Rhône valley:

1210 Philip Augustus annexes the Auvergne to his kingdom.
1292 Nomination of a royal "guardian" in Lyon.
1307 The so-called "Philippine" conventions strengthen Philip the Fair's hold on Lyon.
1308 The Bishop of Viviers recognises royal sovereignty.
1349 Dauphiné is annexed to France as the States of Dauphiné.
1229 The Treaty of Paris ends the Albigensian Crusade and the influence of the counts of Toulouse in the Vivarais area.
1241-71 The Auvergne is part of the appanage with which Alphonse of Poitiers, St Louis' brother, is endowed. He dies childless, and the region is returned to the royal estate.
1262 Marriage of St Louis' son, Philip, to Isabella of Aragon in Clermont.
1337-1453 Hundred Years War.
1332 Birth in Chaudes-Aigues of the first village heating network of geothermal origin.
1348 The Black Death ravages France.
1360 The Auvergne becomes a duchy and is given to John the Good's son, Jean, Duc de Berry.
15C The first firearms are made in St-Étienne.
1416-25 The Auvergne and the Bourbonnais region are united for 100 years under the authority of the House of Bourbon.
1419 The first fairs in Lyon, instituted by the heir to the throne, the future Charles VII, make the town one of the largest warehouses in the world.
1450 Charles VII grants Lyon a monopoly on the sale of silk throughout the kingdom.

Auvergne, held in appanage by Jean de Berry – The sovereign's hold on the Auvergne took it out of the sphere of influence of Southern France. It was divided in two with the creation of a bailiwick in the mountainous region corresponding to Upper Auvergne.

While the Bourbons continued to increase their power with a barony that was raised to a duchy in 1327 (the Bourbonnais area), the Auvergne was granted in appanage to Jean, Duc de Berry in 1360.

War and epidemics combined with the heavy fiscal pressures imposed by a spendthrift lord. In order to circumvent the rules on land held in appanage, Jean de Berry transferred the Duchy of Auvergne to his son-in-law, the Duke of Bourbon, an action which the monarchy, by then in a weakened position, was obliged to accept formally in 1425. The Bourbons were then at the head of a huge feudal state which continued to exist until the Constable of Bourbon's treachery in 1527.

1473 The first book is printed in Lyon by Barthélemy Buyer.
1494 The start of the Italian Campaign. Charles VIII brings his court to Lyon.
1527 After the Constable of Bourbon's treachery, the Auvergne and the Bourbonnais region are confiscated by François I.
1528 The Reformation is preached in Annonay.
1536 A silk-making factory is opened in Lyon.
1562 Protestants led by Baron des Adrets ransack the Rhône valley and Forez area.
1572 After the St Bartholomew's Day Massacre, the Auvergne enters a period of chaos.

INTRODUCTION TO AUVERGNE RHÔNE VALLEY

Bloody battles are won in turn by the Huguenots, the royal army and members of the Catholic League.

1598 Promulgation of the Edict of Nantes which grants freedom of conscience to the Protestants, along with limited rights to hold church services, and gives them political equality.

The Reformation and the Wars of Religion – In 1525, the Reformation spread across the Cévennes and the Rhône valley, through the Vivarais area and along the Durance valley. The Auvergne, perhaps in part because of the mountainous lie of the land, was little concerned by the reformed religion, except in Issoire and the paper-making areas of Ambert and Aurillac.

The local people were attracted to Calvinist ideas, which allied with their taste for independence. The concepts were spread by craftsmen in the villages, carders and silk merchants travelling to Montpellier via Le Puy-en-Velay and Alès. The ideas were also spread by shoe-makers whose shops, like the tanneries, served as centres of propaganda. By 1550–60, the reformed religion had conquered the locality. Property belonging to the Catholic Church was sold and, by the end of the century, Mass was no longer being celebrated.

However, Catholics and Protestants were soon to engage in conflict. Eight wars, fought over a period of almost three decades, coincided with a time of political instability. Interspersed with ceasefires and edicts aimed at pacifying both sides, they never totally appeased the people's passion. In 1562 the murder of a group of Protestants in Champagne led to the Huguenot uprising, and Catholic resistance was led by the Parliament of Toulouse. The conflict was particularly bitter in the Dauphiné and Vivarais regions where the warring factions laid waste to entire towns and committed massacres.

The Baron des Adrets captured the main towns in Dauphiné, where he was the leader of the Huguenot movement, before moving on to decimate the Rhône valley with his troops and marching to the Forez area where he took Montbrison. After the tragic St Bartholomew's Day massacre (24th August 1572), the conflict took on a more political character and, paradoxically, led to forms of cooperation between Huguenots and Catholics in the face of royal authority and power.

Peace was not re-established until the Edict of Nantes was signed.

1629 Siege and destruction of Privas by the king's troops. Richelieu orders the dismantling of fortresses.
17C Counter-Reformation: founding of many convents.
1643 Accession of Louis XIV.
1685 Revocation of the Edict of Nantes. The dragoons sweep through the Vivarais area, tormenting and killing people.
1783 First public ascent by the Montgolfier brothers in a hot-air balloon.

Auvergne's finest hours – Although the aristocracy in the Auvergne was careful not to become involved in the Fronde Revolt against the monarchy, the king brought the hand of royal justice to bear on the region in order to ensure its submission for all time.

In September 1665, Louis XIV sent commissioners to the Auvergne, to provide a display of royal authority. The return to law and order included the repression of often tyrannical behaviour and excessive violence used by the local nobility to stamp out revolt among the country people. In the Auvergne, as elsewhere, rural uprisings had resulted from the constraints imposed by a central authority that had not yet acquired its finality. The Court heard 1 360 cases and passed 692 sentences, of which 450 were handed down by default, for the suspects had fled as soon as the first of the 23 executions was carried out. Thereafter, offenders were sentenced in their absence, and effigies were hung

HISTORY

in their place. This simulation of justice "without any spilling of blood" (**Esprit Fléchier**) nevertheless allowed for the return of a large amount of property and the destruction of castles that had been spared by Richelieu 40 years earlier.

The authority of the State and royal justice could be felt by all throughout France. The magistrates tried to remedy abuses of the system by drawing up regulations on statute labour, weights and measures.

The **Intendants** began to check the titles held by the nobility and laid the foundations for fiscal reform in order to share the burden of taxation more fairly.

1789	Start of the French Revolution. 14th July: capture of the Bastille Prison. France is subdivided into *départements*.
1790	The first town council is set up in Lyon.
1793	A Resistance movement is set up in Lyon to fight the Convention: the town is subject to vicious reprisals as a result. In the Auvergne, **Georges Couthon**, a member of the Committee of Public Salvation, orders the demolition of bell-towers on grounds of equality.
Early 19C	Mining begins in the coalfields around St-Étienne.
1804	The Jacquard loom is invented.
1820	Silk production becomes a boom industry in the Vivarais area.
1825	The Seguin brothers build the first suspension bridge over the Rhône.
1832	The St-Étienne-Lyon railway line is inaugurated. Barbier and Daubrée open a factory in Clermont and begin working with rubber; this is the pioneer of the future Michelin group.
1831-34	Silk workers revolt in Lyon.
1850	Pebrine, a disease that attacks silkworms, causes a crisis in the silk industry.
1855	The railway is extended as far as Clermont.
1870-71	The Fall of the Second Empire; the Third Republic is founded.
1880	Phylloxera destroys half of the vineyards in Ardèche. Orchards are planted in the Rhône and Eyrieux valleys.
1889	Phylloxera devastates the vineyards in the Limagne.
Late 19C	The chemical industry is set up in Lyon, and metal-working sees a period of expansion.
1895	The cinematograph is invented by the Lumière brothers in Lyon.

The birth of the cinematograph – In 1882, a photographer from Besançon named Antoine Lumière opened a workshop in a shed in Lyon and began to produce dry silver bromine plates to a formula that he had invented himself. Within four years he had sold over one million plates under the brand name *Étiquette bleue*.

The former photographer's two sons, Louis and Auguste **Lumière**, worked with their father on a new device; the equipment, invented in 1895 and exhibited in Lyon in June 1896, was to be known as the cinematograph.

The general public, after initial indifference, rushed to see the first 10 films – short farces whose humour has withstood the test of time.

The first film, *Workers Leaving the Lumière Factory* was followed by *The Arrival of a Train in the Station*, *The Gardener* (including the famous scene of the gardener being doused with water from the garden hose) and *Baby Food*.

1940	Vichy becomes the capital of occupied France.

The Vichy government – The armistice signed in Compiègne on 22 June 1940 marked the defeat of France by Nazi Germany. France was divided into two

INTRODUCTION TO AUVERGNE RHÔNE VALLEY

Famous Local Figures

Few regions in France have given the country so many scientists and engineers: the engineer Marc Seguin (steam boiler), the physicist André-Marie Ampère (electrodynamics), the physiologist Claude Bernard and cinematographers the Lumière brothers all hail from the region.

The Montgolfier brothers and the first flight – In the years before the French Revolution, brothers Joseph and Étienne de Montgolfier became famous by achieving the first flights in a hot-air balloon.
Tirelessly continuing research into a gas that was lighter than air, Joseph completed his first experiment with a taffeta envelope. His brother joined him in his research, and they launched their first aerostat on place des Cordeliers in Annonay on 4 June 1783. It was so successful that Louis XVI asked them to repeat it in his presence, and so it was that, on 19 September of that same year, the first "manned" flight took place in Versailles, under the control of Étienne and in the presence of the amazed royal family and Court. Attached beneath the balloon was a latticework cage containing the first passengers – a cockerel, a duck and a sheep. In just a few minutes, the **Réveillon** bearing the king's cipher on a blue background rose into the air and then came to rest in Vaucresson woods.

Lumière brothers

One month later, at the Château de la Muette in Paris, Marquis d'Arlandes and Pilâtre de Rozier completed the first human flight in a hot-air balloon.

Jacquard and the weaving loom – Jacquard was born in Lyon in 1752. His father, a small-time material manufacturer, employed his son to work the cords that operated the complicated machinery used to form the pattern in silk.
After his father's death, Jacquard tried to set up a fabric factory, but his lack of commercial experience and the experiments he undertook to try and perfect the weaving of the fabric left him financially ruined. He continued to work nights on the design of a new loom and on a machine to manufacture fishing nets. He registered his first patent in 1801. The officers of the Republic were looking for inventors, and so Jacquard was brought to Paris, where he earned a salary of 3 000 francs.
At the newly created **Conservatoire**, he perfected a machine invented by a man from Grenoble named Vaucanson. In 1804 Jacquard returned to Lyon

Jacquard loom, Soierie Saint-Georges, Lyon

HISTORY

to complete work on the loom with which his name has remained linked ever since. In place of the ropes and pedals that required the work of six people, Jacquard substituted a simple mechanism based on perforated cards laid on the loom to define the pattern. A single worker, in place of five in earlier times, could make the most complicated fabrics as easily as plain cloth. By decreasing the production costs, it would be possible to withstand foreign competition and increase sales. Manufacturers set an example and, in 1812, several Jacquard looms were brought into service in Lyon. The experiment worked so well that the name is still in use today.

Thimonnier, the unfortunate inventor of the sewing machine – Unlike Jacquard, Thimonnier did not have the good fortune to see his invention being used in his native country. His father was a dyer from Lyon who had fled the town and its upheavals during the French Revolution. In 1795 the family settled in Amplepuis where Thimonnier was apprenticed to a tailor. In 1822 he left the region to set up in business as a tailor near St-Étienne. Haunted by the idea of sewing clothes mechanically, and taking inspiration from the hooks used by embroiderers in the Lyonnais mountain range, he built a wooden and metal device that would produce chain stitch – the first sewing machine. To register a patent, the inventor entered a partnership with Auguste Ferrand, a teacher at the Miners' School in St-Étienne. An application was filed on 13 April 1830 in the names of both partners. Thimonnier then left St-Étienne for Paris, where the first mechanical sewing shop soon saw the light of day.

There, 80 sewing machines produced goods six times quicker than manual workers, arousing the hatred of Parisian tailors who feared that their profession was on the point of ruin.

On the night of 20 to 21 January 1831, 200 workers employed in the sewing and tailoring business ransacked the Parisian workshop. Thimonnier was ruined and he returned to Amplepuis where, in order to feed his large family, he again began work as a tailor. Thimonnier died at the age of 64 – without seeing the huge success enjoyed by the sewing machine.

Timeline

538-594 – **Gregory of Tours** (born in Clermont-Ferrand), churchman and historian.

938-1003 – **Gerbert d'Aurillac**, theologian and scholar who went on to become Pope Sylvester II.

1555-1623 – **Henri de La Tour d'Auvergne**, Marshal of France under Henri IV and Calvinist leader.

1623-1662 – **Blaise Pascal** (Clermont-Ferrand), academic, writer and philosopher (see LITERATURE).

1652-1719 – **Michel Rolle** (Ambert), mathematician and author of a treaty of algebra.

1757-1834 – **Marquis de La Fayette** (Chavaniac), general and politician

1851-1914 – **Fernand Forest** (Clermont-Ferrand), inventor (four-stroke engine).

1853-1929 – **André Messager** (Montluçon), composer.

1853-1931 and 1859-1940 – **André** and **Édouard Michelin** (Clermont-Ferrand), industrialists (rubber tyres and tourist publications).

1884-1932 – **Albert Londres** (Vichy), journalist and writer.

1911-1974 – **Georges Pompidou**, politician and President of the French Republic (1969–74).

b.1926 – **Valéry Giscard d'Estaing**, politician and President of the French Republic (1974–81).

INTRODUCTION TO AUVERGNE RHÔNE VALLEY

zones: the North was occupied, and the South was declared a free zone. Parliament, tolling the death knell of the Third Republic, vested all power in **Maréchal Pétain**, the victor of Verdun in 1916. The choice of a seat for the new government fell on the prosperous spa town of Vichy (see VICHY).

1942–44 Lyon is the centre of the French Resistance Movement.

1944 Battles are fought in the Rhône valley and in the Cantal (Mont Mouchet) as part of the liberation of France. The Germans blow up the bridges over the Rhône.

Lyon, a centre of the Resistance Movement – Lyon, a city in the southern zone, found itself near the demarcation line after the signing of the armistice in 1940. Countless Parisians sought refuge here, and initially it became the intellectual and patriotic heart of France. The city was one of the major centres for the printing of literature, posters and journals, many more popular with readers than the press that supported Vichy. Important Resistance actions were carried out in Lyon, but they were badly organised until the arrival of **Jean Moulin**, sent by General de Gaulle; the various groups then joined together in 1943 to form the *Mouvements Unis de la Résistance* (Unified Resistance Movements). Moulin set up an administrative structure for the Resistance, organising services that were common to all the networks and a secret army operating in the south of France and the Rhône valley.

1946 Start of the Fourth Republic.
1957 The Treaty of Rome leads to the setting up of the EEC.
1958 Birth of the Fifth Republic.
1969 Georges Pompidou, born in Cantal, is elected President of the Republic.
1972 The Auvergne and Rhône-Alpes regions are created.
1974 Valéry Giscard d'Estaing, Mayor of Chamalières (Puy-de-Dôme), elected President of the Republic.
1981 The first high-speed train service (TGV) runs between Paris and Lyon.
1986 **Superphénix**, Europe's first fast-breeder reactor to operate on an industrial scale, is brought into service in Creys-et-Pusignieu (Isère).
1989 Completion of the motorway link (A 71) between Clermont-Ferrand and Paris (Orléans).
1993 The EU introduces the Single Market.
1996 Lyon's hosting of the G7 summit confirms the city's international role.
2000 Clermont-Auvergne International Airport is inaugurated.
2002 Opening of **VULCANIA**. Located in the heart of the Puy range, Vulcania, the European Volcano Park, plunges you deep into the world of volcanoes and the Earth sciences.
2006 The 40th anniversary of La Chaise Dieu music festival, founded by Georges Cziffra in 1966.
2009 Olympique Lyonnais become French football ligue 1's most consecutive winners (2003-2009).
2014 Lyon's newest museum, the Musée des Confluences opens to wide acclaim.
2016 The Auvergne and Rhône-Alpes regions are combined into one new region.
2017 Emmanuel Macron is elected President of France, representing his "La République En Marche!" centrist political party. He beat the far-right National Front's Marine Le Pen.

Architecture

ROMAN ARCHITECTURE IN THE RHÔNE VALLEY

By the 1C, the region had become the starting point for the conquest of Germany, and Lyon was the capital of Gaul. In the 2C, major road building and town planning work was undertaken in Vienne and Lyon, then at the height of their power. However, the fires, pillaging and devastations by the Barbarians, coupled with the later destruction during the Middle Ages, destroyed the remains of the old civilisation.

From 1922 in Vienne and 1933 in Lyon, archaeologists began to uncover groups of buildings, in particular small theatres adjacent to smaller buildings or *odeons*. Some of the buildings are still being unearthed, and large areas have yet to be explored, in particular in St-Romain-en-Gal on the right bank of the Rhône, where part of a residential district has been uncovered.

Théâtre Romain, Vienne

THEATRES

These consisted of tiers of seats ending in a colonnade known as the **cavea**, an orchestra pit, a dais used by dignitaries and a raised stage *(scena)*. The actors performed in front of a wall with doors through which they made their entrances. Behind the wall, at the back of the stage, were the richly decorated actors' dressing rooms and the stores. Beyond that was a portico opening onto gardens, where the actors walked before entering the stage. Spectators could stroll there during intervals or take shelter from the rain.

TEMPLES

A closed sanctuary contained the effigy of a god or the emperor and an open vestibule. They were partially or totally surrounded by a colonnade. The Temple of Augustus and Livia in Vienne is one of the best preserved anywhere.

ROMAN BATHS

Roman baths were public and free of charge. They were not only public baths but also fitness centres, meeting places and a venue for games and entertainment. The Romans had acquired extensive knowledge concerning water supplies and heating: Water was brought to the baths by an aqueduct, stored in tanks, then piped through a system of lead and mortar ducts. Waste water was carried away through a sewage system. The water and rooms were heated by a system of hearths and hypocausts in the basement. The hot air obtained by the burning of coal and wood circulated through a conduit built into the walls. The buildings were vast, sumptuous and luxurious. There were columns and capitals decorated with vivid colours, mosaic facing on the walls, marble floors and wall coverings, richly coffered ceilings, and frescoes and statues like those found in the remains of the Roman baths in Ste-Colombe near Vienne.

AMPHITHEATRES

Shows were staged in the arena, usually oval in shape. There were fights between wild beasts or gladiators, and people sentenced to death were executed. Around the arena were tiers of seats for the audience. Lyon, the official centre for the worship of Rome in Gaul, had its own amphitheatre.

CIRCUS

The circus attracted crowds of people who enjoyed watching chariot racing. In the middle of the track was a long

INTRODUCTION TO AUVERGNE RHÔNE VALLEY

rectangular construction – the **spina** – marked at each end by huge, semi-circular stones. The horses and drivers wore the colours of the rival factions organising the competitions. Built partly of timber, the circus was, despite its impressive size, particularly vulnerable to destruction.

AQUEDUCTS

On the plateau to the south-west of Lyon stand well-preserved sections of aqueduct (Arches de Chaponost, *see LYON: Monts du Lyonnais*). Aqueducts were one of the essential features of any Roman town. The tall arches built to maintain the level of the pipes were monuments in their own right. Indeed, the aqueduct, more than any other construction, is a striking illustration of the building skills of the Romans, who attached great importance to the quality of the water supplied to their towns and cities.

DECORATIVE ARTS

The large, delicately coloured mosaics found in Lyon (circus games, Bacchus etc.) prove that mosaic-makers were particularly active in Lyon. The medallions that decorated the sides of vases were made by potters from Lyon and Vienne, who excelled in illustrations of scenes from mythology or everyday life.

RELIGIOUS ARCHITECTURE
THE ROMANESQUE PERIOD

There is no Romanesque School inherent to the Rhône valley, since the region, situated as it is at the junction of countless roads, was influenced by artists from Italy, Burgundy, Provence – and the Auvergne. In the Auvergne, on the other hand, the Romanesque School that developed is considered one of the most unusual in the history of the architecture of the Western world, giving the churches an air of similarity that is immediately apparent. It originated in the 11C. After the great invasions and the establishment of the Capetian kingdom, the Auvergne enjoyed a period of prosperity. The local people undertook land clearance, acquiring new areas of land and instigating new building projects. In the 11C this movement was amplified by the Gregorian Reform and the desire on the part of men of the Church for independence from lay authorities. Gradually, countless churches and chapels were built across the countryside and, even today, they reveal something of the soul of the Auvergne and its people, for they are all built with an economic use of resources and an immense simplicity. This is what gives the architecture its strength.

The churches in Clermont-Ferrand (Notre-Dame-du-Port), Issoire, Saint-Urcize, Orcival, St-Nectaire and St-Saturnin are just some of the finest examples of this Romanesque style in which the beauty is both austere and logical.

An Unusual School

The Romanesque school of the Auvergne developed in the 11C and 12C within the large diocese of Clermont. The churches, often small but always beautifully proportioned, give an impression of being much bigger than they actually are. Paul Bourget describes the appearance of these churches, powerful and rugged as those who created them: "Seen from the east end, especially with the tight semicircle of chapels huddled up against the mass of the main building, these churches give a striking impression of aplomb and unity."

Volcanic Building Materials

In Limagne, arkose, a yellowish metamorphic sandstone, was used until the 13C. Volcanic lava stone was first used for bonding beneath load-bearing arches, in the upper sections of buildings that did not support the weight of the vaulting, to which they added a touch of colour. In the 13C, improvements to the quality of tools made it possible to cut the hard blocks of lava stone, and developments in stone-cutting techniques made it the commonest building material available.

ARCHITECTURE

GREAT CHURCHES IN LOWER AUVERGNE

The layout of the churches slowly changed to meet new needs arising out of pilgrimages. The basic layout is the one seen in Clermont Cathedral, which was consecrated in 946 and was the first to have an ambulatory and radiating chapels. Today, all that remains is the crypt. Yet it took a period of trial and error (churches in Ennezat, Glaine-Montaigut) to achieve the perfection of the 12C buildings.

Exterior Features

West Front – Exposed to the elements and almost devoid of decoration, the west front – which includes a porch – forms a stark contrast to the east end because of its austerity. In some cases, it is topped by a central bell-tower and two side towers.

Bell-towers – Two-storey, traceried, octagonal bell-towers were a source of light, emerging from the mass of the building around the dome. They stood high above the chancel and ambulatory. In Auvergne, there are a large number of bell-cotes *(clocher à peigne)* – gable walls with openings in which the bells are hung in one or two tiers.

Side walls – The windows in the side aisles are built inside enormous load-bearing arches that support the walls. Beneath these arches, the stone often has a decorative role through its colour or layout. Above them is the line of the clerestory in which the windows are linked by arcading.

East end – The magnificent layout of the various levels at the east end is the most beautiful and most characteristic part of the Auvergne churches. This masterpiece of austerity counterbalances the thrust from the octagonal bell-tower. It stands like a carefully combined pyramid, giving an impression of harmony and security through the perfection of each of its elements and the regularity of the design.

Interior

The nave is often stark; the only decorative features are the capitals, and they are not immediately apparent because most of these buildings are very dark. Huge arches support the gallery and the weight of the bell-tower if it has been built above the west front.

Nave and vaulting – The wide naves lined with side aisles providing extra support were designed to cater for large numbers of pilgrims. Heavy Romanesque barrel vaulting replaced roof rafters which were too susceptible to fire and which, between the 5C and 11C, led to the loss of many churches.

Chancel – This part of the church was reserved for the clergy and the celebration of Mass. By raising it up a few steps and lowering the vaulting, perspective made it appear larger than it actually was. It was here that sculptors gave free rein to their talent, and the beautifully designed carved capitals in the chancel are often the finest in the church.
In large churches, the chancel included a straight bay. Behind it was a semicircle, around which tall columns, set out in such a way as to avoid blocking the light, extended into small raised arches forming a sort of crown.

Ambulatory – In large churches, an ambulatory extended beyond the side aisles and skirted the chancel. An even number of radiating chapels formed a crown around the ambulatory so that, on major feast days, several Masses could be celebrated simultaneously. The chapels were separated from each other by windows.

Transept and dome – The construction of the transept posed a difficult problem for architects; they had to design large ribbed vaulting capable of supporting the entire weight of the central bell-tower formed by the interpenetration of the vaulting in the nave and the arms of the transept.

INTRODUCTION TO AUVERGNE RHÔNE VALLEY

Religious Architecture

ORCIVAL – Notre-Dame Basilica (12C)

Most of the churches in Auvergne are in the Romanesque style, and belong to a school of design which developed in the 11C and 12C, which has a number of unique characteristics.

Relieving or **discharging arch:** an arch built over a lintel to distribute the weight of the load-bearing walls

Two-storey, **octagonal bell-tower**

Geminated bays: occur in pairs

Bays: occurring in groups of two, three, four, etc

Transept

Rounded hip roof covering the chevet

Gable-wall

Sloping hip roof

Semicircular bay

Apsidal chapel or radiating chapel

Modillion: a horizontal bracket or console; here the decorative scrolling recalls wood shavings

Cornice with checkerboard pattern

Buttress: masonry structure bonded to and projecting from the wall, which gives stability

Chevet: the graceful fall of tiered roofs is the most distinctive and attractive feature of churches in Auvergne

ARCHITECTURE

CLERMONT-FERRAND – Notre-Dame-du-Port Basilica (11C and 12C)

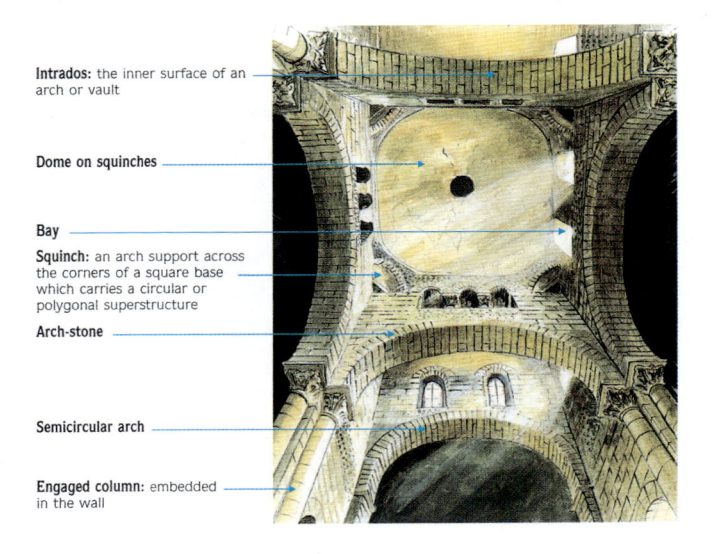

Intrados: the inner surface of an arch or vault

Dome on squinches

Bay

Squinch: an arch support across the corners of a square base which carries a circular or polygonal superstructure

Arch-stone

Semicircular arch

Engaged column: embedded in the wall

ISSOIRE – St-Austremoine Abbey (12C)

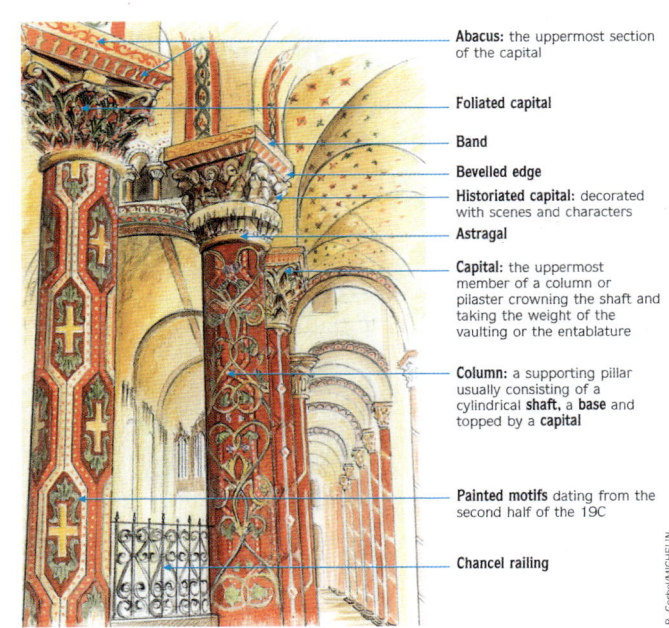

Abacus: the uppermost section of the capital

Foliated capital

Band

Bevelled edge

Historiated capital: decorated with scenes and characters

Astragal

Capital: the uppermost member of a column or pilaster crowning the shaft and taking the weight of the vaulting or the entablature

Column: a supporting pillar usually consisting of a cylindrical **shaft**, a **base** and topped by a **capital**

Painted motifs dating from the second half of the 19C

Chancel railing

71

INTRODUCTION TO AUVERGNE RHÔNE VALLEY

LE PUY-EN-VELAY – Doorway of St-Michel Chapel (12C)

Seeming to rise out of the rock below it, this chapel has been called the "eighth wonder of the world". Eastern influences are apparent in the polychrome motifs and geometric designs.

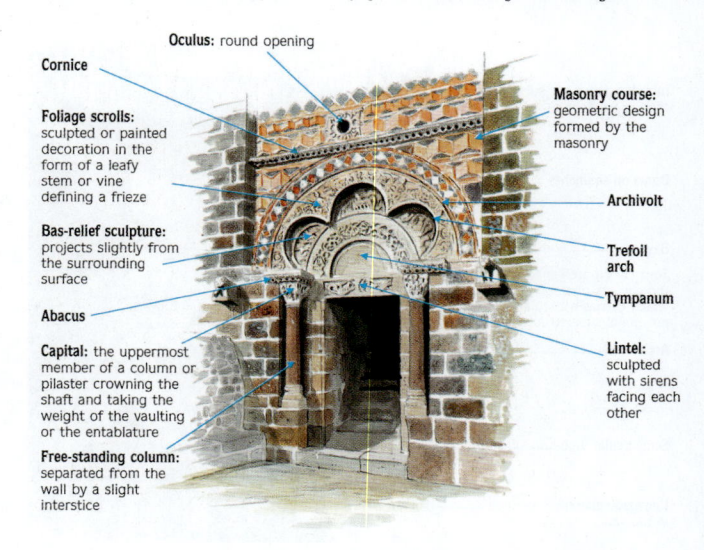

- **Cornice**
- **Oculus:** round opening
- **Foliage scrolls:** sculpted or painted decoration in the form of a leafy stem or vine defining a frieze
- **Bas-relief sculpture:** projects slightly from the surrounding surface
- **Abacus**
- **Capital:** the uppermost member of a column or pilaster crowning the shaft and taking the weight of the vaulting or the entablature
- **Free-standing column:** separated from the wall by a slight interstice
- **Masonry course:** geometric design formed by the masonry
- **Archivolt**
- **Trefoil arch**
- **Tympanum**
- **Lintel:** sculpted with sirens facing each other

CRUAS – Former Abbey (11C to 13C)

This beautiful abbey, typical of the Vivarais region, has managed to withstand the ravages of time. As research continues, new discoveries have brought to light architectural marvels from the Carolingian and Romanesque periods.

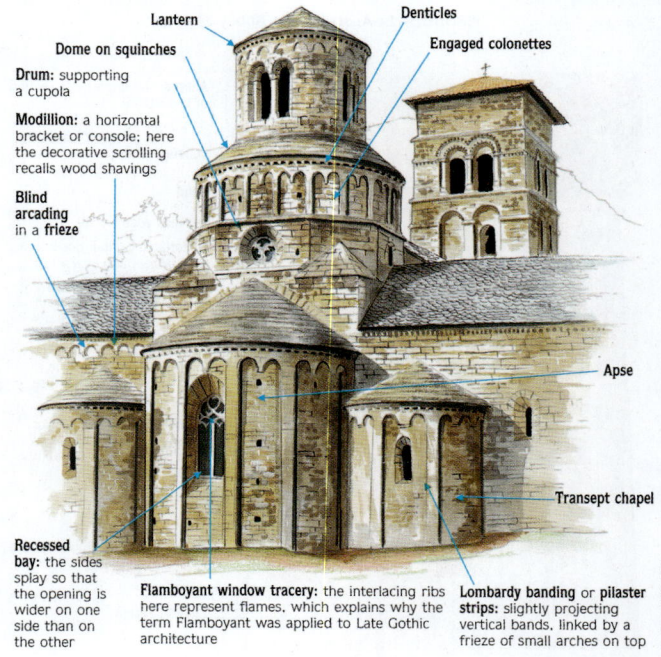

- **Lantern**
- **Dome on squinches**
- **Drum:** supporting a cupola
- **Modillion:** a horizontal bracket or console; here the decorative scrolling recalls wood shavings
- **Blind arcading** in a **frieze**
- **Denticles**
- **Engaged colonettes**
- **Apse**
- **Transept chapel**
- **Recessed bay:** the sides splay so that the opening is wider on one side than on the other
- **Flamboyant window tracery:** the interlacing ribs here represent flames, which explains why the term Flamboyant was applied to Late Gothic architecture
- **Lombardy banding** or **pilaster strips:** slightly projecting vertical bands, linked by a frieze of small arches on top

ARCHITECTURE

Crypt – Beneath the chancel in large churches, there is often a crypt laid out like the church above it. The chancel in the crypt, like the one in the upper church, is flanked by an ambulatory decorated with radiating chapels. The crypt never extends westwards beyond the transept.

Decorative Features

Capitals – Magnificently carved with fanciful scenes, most capitals are found around the chancel. Many artists introduced an entire portrait gallery: figures from Antiquity rub shoulders with eagles, mermaids, centaurs, minotaurs, telamones, snakes, genies, figures from the Orient, griffons and birds drinking out of a chalice. Beside them are the heroes of medieval epics, the founders of the Church, knights in armour dating from the period of the First Crusade and local saints.

Statues of the Virgin Mary in Majesty and statue-reliquaries – Worship of the Blessed Virgin Mary has always been an important part of religion in the Auvergne for, in Celtic countries, the Christian religion was grafted onto worship of a mother-goddess.

The Gothic Period

Gothic architecture originally came from the north, and it took some time to spread further south. It reached Lyon in the early 13C, but the Rhône valley has few of the great churches of which Northern France is so proud.

The Auvergne, strong in its own Romanesque School, resisted change for a long time. Not until the province had been conquered by Philip Augustus and the language of Northern France, *langue d'oïl,* was introduced in place of the Southern French *langue d'oc,* did the Rayonnant Gothic style gain a foothold on the rebellious region.

There were two main currents in the architectural style – Northern French Gothic and Languedoc Gothic.

Northern French Gothic

Clermont Cathedral, dating from the 13C and 14C, is only very vaguely reminiscent of the great buildings of the Paris basin. Not until the 19C was Gothic architecture introduced into its west front, with spires designed by the architect Viollet-le-Duc. Lava stone from Volvic, a building material that was too hard to be carved but that architects liked for its strength, resistance and permanence, gave the cathedral an austerity that even the sun cannot brighten. The roofs on the chapels and side aisles consist of stone slabs forming a terrace beneath the flying buttresses, a very unusual design that was totally unknown in the north of France.

The same stylistic movement can be seen in the Ste-Chapelle in Riom.

Languedoc Gothic

Characterised by a wide nave devoid of side aisles, side chapels inserted between the piers and the absence of flying buttresses, this was the most common style in the area. The abbey church at La Chaise-Dieu, a masterpiece of monastic architecture, is a fine example, as are other churches commissioned by the mendicant orders such as the Marthuret Church in Riom or Notre-Dame-des-Neiges in Aurillac.

Painting

A vast selection of medieval painting has been preserved within the Auvergne. The frescoes in the church of St-Julien in Brioude, for instance, date from the 12C; there is the 13C representation of the legend of St George in one of the ambulatory chapels in Clermont Cathedral, and the 14C Assumption and Coronation of the Virgin Mary in Billom. From the 15C are the Last Judgement in Issoire, St George Slaying the Dragon in Ébreuil, the Dance of Death in La Chaise-Dieu, and the frescoes in Ennezat. The triptych painted on wood by the Maître de Moulins is one of the last masterpieces of Gothic painting in France.

INTRODUCTION TO AUVERGNE RHÔNE VALLEY

Flemish Influence in Brou
In at least one case, northern European influence brought an architectural masterpiece to the region. The 16C Brou monastery in Bresse, commissioned by Margaret of Austria, is a a gem of the Flemish flamboyant gothic style. The rare architectural ensemble was built by Lous van Bodeghem, in association with a number of artists from Northern Europe, in memory of Margaret's late husband, Philibert II. Unique in France, the monastery possesses three cloisters and is home to a museum devoted in part to the life and legacy of Margaret.

MILITARY AND CIVIL ARCHITECTURE

Defensive Castles
During the days of the feudal system, the country was dotted with castles; by building fortresses, lords, viscounts and barons could display their power and authority as compared to that of the king. The resulting castles' outlines adapt to the shape of the rock beneath them. From the 13C, they were subject to successive attacks by Philip Augustus' troops. He conquered 120 of them from 1210 onwards, and many were destroyed both during the Hundred Years War and afterwards by villagers who, at enormous cost, succeeded in routing the mercenaries and captains who were using them as a source of building material for their own houses.

The Gentler Architecture of the Renaissance
The influence of the Italian Renaissance travelled to Northern France via the Rhône corridor, and in the 15C, it slowly penetrated the Auvergne. The fortresses were turned into charming residences in which ornamentation supplanted systems of defence, even if, in the Auvergne, the austerity of the lava stone remained intact. Numerous castles were bought up by gentlemen of the robe or members of the middle classes who had recently acquired wealth through trade.

Town Planning During the Classical Period
In Lyon, a new form of town planning can be seen mainly in the 17C Terreaux district around the town hall. In the 18C, a new concept of urban layout was introduced, based on speculation. The main feature of these areas is place Bellecour, laid out during the reign of Louis XIV and flanked by Louis XVI residences.

The 19C and the Architecture of the Auvergne Spas: a Fantasy World
In the spa towns of the 19C, "taking the waters" was not a new idea, but it was during this period that it became fashionable. Members of high society and those with power or money flocked to spa towns; their visits were an opportunity for socialising, and this governed the architectural style. In the centre of the town were the pump rooms, a veritable palace to which the architects paid particular attention; around them were the parks and springs built to resemble Ancient Greek or Roman temples. The casinos and the luxury hotels were decorated with an exuberance that was almost Baroque. In the streets of the town, troubadour-style castles stood next to Venetian palaces, and Henri IV residences rubbed shoulders with Art Nouveau mansions.

Centre Thermal des Dômes, Vichy

ARCHITECTURE

Military Architecture

TOURNEMIRE – Château d'Anjony (15C)

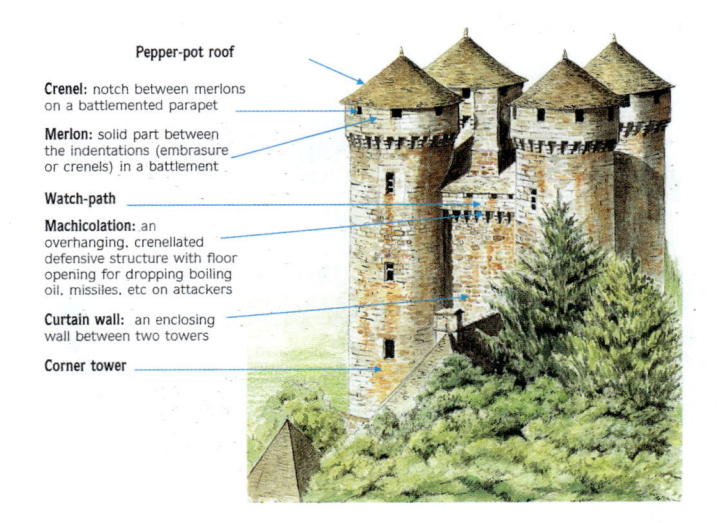

- **Pepper-pot roof**
- **Crenel:** notch between merlons on a battlemented parapet
- **Merlon:** solid part between the indentations (embrasure or crenels) in a battlement
- **Watch-path**
- **Machicolation:** an overhanging, crenellated defensive structure with floor opening for dropping boiling oil, missiles, etc on attackers
- **Curtain wall:** an enclosing wall between two towers
- **Corner tower**

ST-POURÇAIN-SUR-BESBRE
Fortified gate of Thoury Château (15C)

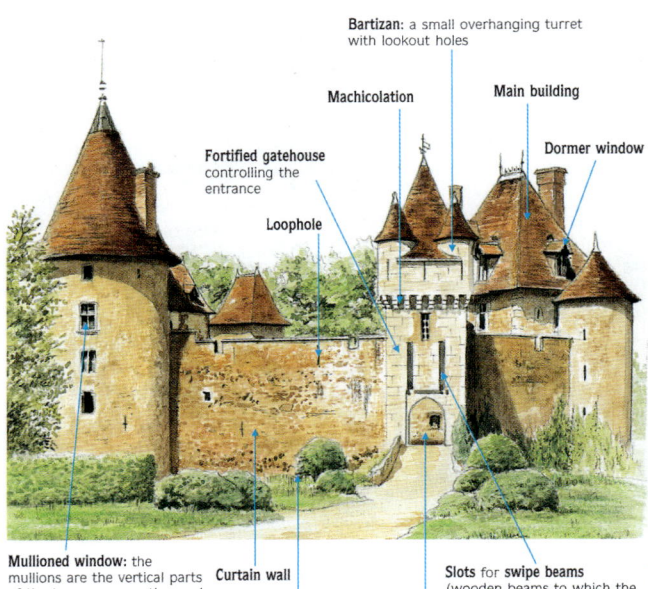

- **Bartizan:** a small overhanging turret with lookout holes
- **Machicolation**
- **Main building**
- **Fortified gatehouse** controlling the entrance
- **Dormer window**
- **Loophole**
- **Mullioned window:** the mullions are the vertical parts of the tracery, separating and supporting the window
- **Curtain wall**
- **Slots** for **swipe beams** (wooden beams to which the chains raising the drawbridge were attached)
- **Moat:** wide ditch filled with water, protecting the curtain wall and towers
- **Entrance gate**

R. Corbel/MICHELIN

INTRODUCTION TO AUVERGNE RHÔNE VALLEY

Civil Architecture

MARCY-L'ÉTOILE – Château de Lacroix-Laval (17C – 18C)

Renovated under the guidance of Soufflot in the 18C, this château was ransacked from cellar to attic during the French Revolution. It has since been restored several times, but has kept the classic façade typical of family manor houses in the 18C.

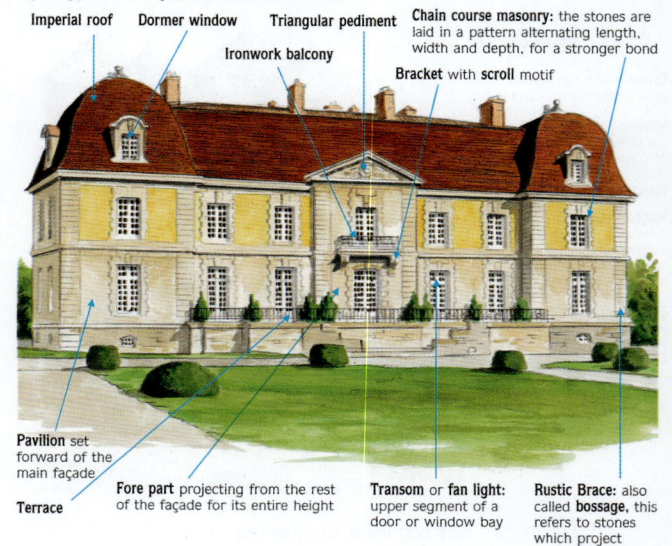

- **Imperial roof**
- **Dormer window**
- **Triangular pediment**
- **Ironwork balcony**
- **Chain course masonry:** the stones are laid in a pattern alternating length, width and depth, for a stronger bond
- **Bracket** with **scroll** motif
- **Pavilion** set forward of the main façade
- **Terrace**
- **Fore part** projecting from the rest of the façade for its entire height
- **Transom** or **fan light:** upper segment of a door or window bay
- **Rustic Brace:** also called **bossage**, this refers to stones which project beyond the mortar joint

Industrial Architecture

LYON – Halle Tony-Garnier (1914)

The covered market is a display of technical prowess: the 18000m^2/193 750sq ft area stands without interior pillars. Designed by local architect Tony Garnier, it now serves for cultural events and trade fairs, and remains a landmark of contemporary architecture.

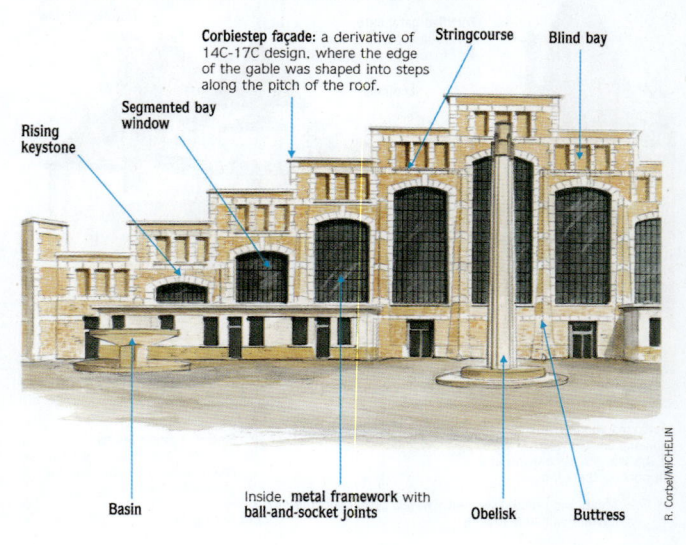

- **Corbiestep façade:** a derivative of 14C-17C design, where the edge of the gable was shaped into steps along the pitch of the roof.
- **Stringcourse**
- **Blind bay**
- **Segmented bay window**
- **Rising keystone**
- **Basin**
- Inside, **metal framework** with **ball-and-socket joints**
- **Obelisk**
- **Buttress**

ARCHITECTURE

Spa Resort Architecture

LE MONT-DORE – Caesar's spring gallery (1890 and 1935-38)

The design expresses the architectural eclecticism typical of spa towns. The inspiration can be traced to the Roman baths of Antiquity; the high ceilings and ornate decoration lend grandeur. The distinctive Romanesque style of Auvergne creates an atmosphere reminiscent of an opulent temple.

Transverse arch: semicircular, with **arch-stones** in an alternating white (limestone) and grey (andesite) pattern, typical of the Romanesque style in Auvergne

Cabochons in yellow glass

Entablature and **capitals** stucco moulding

Tympanum with **fresco** (Roman baths of Mont-Dore)

Coffered barrel vault

Colonnade of **engaged columns**

Claustra: a slab of stone or terracotta pierced in a geometric pattern, forming a bay

Aedicula: a niche in the form of a **tabernacle**, from which Caesar's spring flows

Floor laid with **tile** and **glass bricks**

Grand arcade with false transom (fan light)

R. Corbel/MICHELIN

INTRODUCTION TO AUVERGNE RHÔNE VALLEY

The history of this eclectic architecture, designed for enjoyment and pleasure, is the result of the intermingling of ideas from both the most fashionable urban architects of the day and locals inspired by a long tradition based on the Early Romanesque style and the volcanic and granite rocks available locally. Even the railway stations were not forgotten, since they provided the first impression for visitors who had just arrived. The result was a luxurious style full of exuberance constituting a dream world of exclusive resorts.

Lyon's Opera House, a Fine Example of 20C Architecture

Throughout the 19C and 20C, Lyon was considered an ideal place for architectural experiments. In 1825, new techniques allowed iron suspension bridges to be built over the Rhône. In 1896, the basilica on Fourvière hill was completed in a Byzantine-cum-medieval style.

In the 1970s, with a view to the launch of the high-speed train service which would bring Lyon to within 2hrs of Paris, a major development was begun in the La Part-Dieu district: a new business centre that was to take the city to the forefront of Europe's world of commerce. In 1993 the latest architectural feat was completed: **Jean Nouvel** was tasked with renovating the 1831 opera house. All that remains of the old building are the four walls and an old foyer decorated with gold leaf and stucco-work.

TRADITIONAL RURAL HOUSING

Over the centuries, changes in rural housing have kept pace with changes in agricultural work. Housing has also been subject to the influence of neighbouring regions and new building techniques.

AUVERGNE

Roofs

Owing to its geographical situation, the Auvergne is in contact with two different roofing styles: one, from Northern France, sees roofs built with a 45-degree slope and flat tiles; the more Mediterranean style boasts rounded tiles in a 30 degree slope. In the mountains, thatch is replaced by slate or corrugated iron. The most attractive roofs are those made of stone slabs called *lauzes,* which look like gigantic tortoise shells. They can only be mounted on a steeply sloping roof with a very strong set of rafters. On the plains, round tiles and rows of guttering are beginning to lose ground in favor of more stable, mass-produced tiles.

Housing in the Limagne

Houses with upper storeys, belonging to wine-growers or farmers, are commonplace in the old villages huddling on the hillsides. The ground floor is used for work (stables, cellars) and the upper floor is the family home, reached by an outside flight of steps leading to a balcony sheltered by a porch roof.

Housing in the Mountains

These sturdy buildings are constructed from large blocks of basalt. Heavy roofs extend below the top of the walls, and a single building contains both dwelling and byre side by side. They always face south and are sheltered from bad weather by the haybarn. Doors and windows are narrow, and roofs drop down to the ground at the rear of the building.

Housing in the Velay Area

Houses in this area are unusual as their walls are made of ashlar, with a grey or dark-red lava stone in volcanic areas, light-coloured granite in areas of older soil, and yellow arkose in areas of sedimentary rock. Stone blocks are cemented using a mortar often mixed with pozzolana, a reddish volcanic gravel. In the villages, a bell turret indicates the village hall *(assemblée)* or *"maison de la béate"*.

Shepherds' and Cowherds' Huts

A *buron* is a squat, stone-roofed temporary dwelling high up in the mountains, used by cowherds during periods of trans-humance. This was where the cheese and butter were made, which the *cantalès,* or master of the *buron,* sent down to the valleys. In the Livradois and Forez areas, and on the slopes of Mont Pilat, **"jasseries"** or mountain farms

ARCHITECTURE

From Beaujolais to Lower Vivarais

House in the Beaujolais region

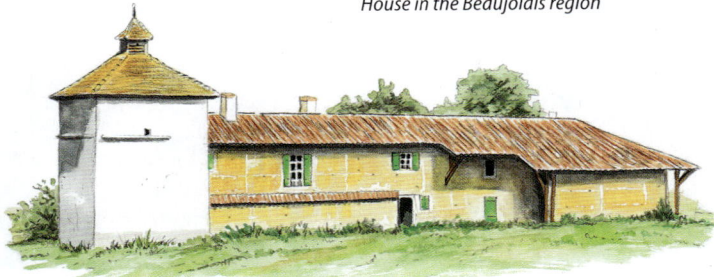

Farm and dovecote on Dombes plateau

Jasserie: summer farmstead in the Forez mountains

House in Lower Dauphiné

Farm in the Mézenc range

House in Lower Vivarais

INTRODUCTION TO AUVERGNE RHÔNE VALLEY

Bresse farm house, Musée de la Bresse, Saint-Cyr-sur-Menthon

were used during the summer months. Solidly built of stone with thatched roofs, they consist of a living room, a byre and a cheese cellar below.

RHÔNE VALLEY

Housing in the Forez and Lyonnais Areas

Houses in the Forez area are farmsteads enclosed by high walls around a central courtyard. In the Dombes area, the farmhouses are elongated and have an upper storey. External pebbledash protects the walls made of terracotta bricks or cob.

Housing in the Rhône Valley

On the **Valence and Montélimar plains**, walls often have no doors or windows on the north side to protect against the mistral wind. Additional protection is often provided by a row of thuyas, cypress and plane trees. The windowless external walls surrounding isolated farmsteads often make them look like fortresses.

Housing in Lower Dauphiné

Between Bourbe and Isère, pebbles or "**rolled stones**" were often used as a building material as they were commonplace in this area of moraine and alluvial deposits. The stones are assembled on a bed of mortar, the angle changing from one level to the next. In some area, like Morestel and Creys, **crow-stepped** or **corbie-stepped gabled roofing** has been imported from the Préalpes.

Housing in the Upper Vivarais

Along the Mézenc range and on the plateaux above the upper reaches of the Ardèche and Eyrieux, houses are low and squat with stone-slabbed roofs, seeming almost weighted by this shell designed to withstand bad weather.
On the St-Agrève plateau, granite farmhouses have an upper storey and bedrooms next to the hayloft.

Housing in the Lower Vivarais

Houses here have an upper storey and are built in a square, like southern French houses. The gently sloping roofs have half-round tiles. Between the top of the wall and the roof, a double or triple row of guttering is made with fragments of tiles mounted in mortar. The south-facing wall is often decorated with a trellis.

Fermes Bressanes

The typical farmhouse of Bresse is characterized by a long building of brick and wood opening towards the east. Roofs on the Savoyard side of the region tend to be gently sloped and built of channelled tiles; on the Burgundy side, slopes are steeper and tiles flatter. Beautiful Saracen chimneys appear on some of these buildings.

Literature

A FEW GREAT WRITERS FROM THE AUVERGNE

Local writers have brought fame to a few of the Auvergne's prelates, among them Sidonius Apollinaris, Gerbert (10C) and Massillon, who gave Louis XIV's funeral oration in the 18C. The Auvergne has also boasted poets such as Théodore de Banville (1823–91), who founded the Parnassian School of Poetry, and philosophers such as Pierre Teilhard de Chardin (1881–1955). In the 20C, Henri Pourrat and the chronicler Alexandre Vialatte both described their native land, each in his own style. Of all the Auvergnat authors, the best-known is Blaise Pascal, though Gregory of Tours, the medieval chronicler, is almost equally important.

Blaise Pascal

GREGORY OF TOURS

Born c. 583 in Clermont-Ferrand into a rich family of Senators, Gregory spent most of his life in Tours, of which he was appointed Bishop in 573. But he never forgot the place of his birth. His *History of the Franks,* which retraces the reigns of the Merovingian kings and their ancestors, is one of the main sources of historical information about the Auvergne during the Dark Ages.

BLAISE PASCAL

Pascal was born in Clermont-Ferrand in 1623. His mother died when he was three years old, and he was raised by his father, President of the Court of Aids (forerunner of the Customs & Excise) in Clermont. He retired to Port-Royal, which he was never again to leave, where he continued his writing. It was because his memory played tricks on him that he began noting his *Thoughts,* with a view to writing an *Apology of the Christian Religion.* Pascal died in 1662, at the age of 39.

EUGÈNE IONESCO

Eugen Ionescu (1909–94), playwright and dramatist, was born in Romania but grew up in France, and came to be one of the foremost playwrights of the Theatre of the Absurd. In addition to satirising the most banal situations, Ionesco depicts the loneliness of humans and the insignificance of our existence. Ionesco came to the theatre late, not writing his first play until 1948 (*La Cantatrice Chauve,* first performed in 1950 with the English title The Bald Soprano).

CONTEMPORARY WRITERS

Among the contemporary writers from the Auvergne, François Graveline rates highly. He is a journalist in Puy-de-Dôme, where he was born in 1959. He has written a number of titles on the countryside and the mountains, notably *Allier Simple* (2004), *La Profondeur des Sommets* (2003), *Couleur Massif Central* (2002) and *L'Invention du Massif Central* (1997). Patrick Cloux (born 1952 in the Auvergne) has written several books on the region and the pleasure of walking: *Un Cheval Deux Traits* (2006) and *Marcher à l'Estime* (1993). Local history books, as well as historical novels, are written by Anne Courtillé, including *Les Messieurs de Clermont.*

Some worthwhile titles have been written by visitors or scholars. Peter Graham's sensitive depiction of of *Mourjou: The Life and Food of an Auvergne Village,* ranks among the best, alongside Peter Gorham's *Portrait of the Auvergne* in Robert Hale's "Portrait" series.

Nature

The name **Auvergne** conjures up visions of a superb natural environment of outstanding beauty – a rugged landscape of mountain ranges and volcanoes, lakes and springs – in the heart of France. The area has been less accessible from the rest of France since time immemorial because of a lack of roads or railways. The **Rhône valley** is long and wide; its fast flowing river weaves its way through hills and mountains, plateaus and valleys, carving spectacular gorges, sinkholes and caves along its way. The valley separates the Massif Central and the Rhône-Alpes, and much of the fertile land is given over to vineyards and agriculture.

RHÔNE VALLEY
THE RHÔNE CORRIDOR

La Dombes – This clay plateau dotted with lakes ends in the fairly sheer "côtières" of the Saône to the west and the Rhône to the south. In the north, the plateau runs into Bresse.

The waters of the melting glacier in the Rhône valley dug shallow dips into the surface of the land and left moraines – accumulations of debris swept along by the glacier – on the edge of the dips. It is on these **poypes** or slight rises that the villages were built.

The **Dombes** is now a charming area of tranquil countryside, with lines of trees, countless birds and calm lakes reflecting the sky above.

Lower Dauphiné

The countryside in Lower Dauphiné is a succession of stony plateaus, plains and hills. The **Île Crémieu** is a limestone plateau separated from the Jura to the north by the Rhône and to the west by an unusual cliff. The water that infiltrated the soil created a series of caves, the best-known of which are the Grottes de la Balme.

The **Balmes area** west of Vienne is partially covered in vineyards. It consists of granite and shale hills separated from Mont Pilat by the Rhône. It extends into the **Terres Froides plateau,** which is slashed into strips by narrow valleys filled with fields of vegetables.

The **Bonnevaux and Chambaran plateaux** are vast expanses of woodland stretching south from Vienne and almost totally devoid of human habitation. The wide fertile **Bièvre and Valloire plains** specialise in cereal crops. They indicate the course once followed by the Isère, abandoned after the ice receded. The **Isère valley** itself opens out onto the Valence plateau; its well-cultivated terraces covered with walnut groves.

The Valence and Tricastin Areas

From Tain to the Donzère gorge, the Rhône valley widens to the east of the river, forming a patchwork of plains until it reaches the foothills of the Préalpes.

The **Valence plain** consists of a series of alluvial terraces built in steps. Its irrigated fields and its climate are a foretaste of the south of France and the Mediterranean. It was here that the "Tree of Gold", the mulberry, was first planted in the 17C and provided the local inhabitants with a reasonable living from the cultivation of silkworms. Nowadays, the many orchards have maintained the old-fashioned appearance of the countryside in which hedgerows abound.

The **Montélimar basin**, south of the Cruas gorge, is similar to but narrower than the Valence plain; olive trees grow on the south-facing slopes.

The **Tricastin area**, crossed by the Lauzon and the Lez, is a succession of arid hills covered with vineyards and olive trees. Its old villages perched on defensive sites form remarkable lookout posts.

THE EDGE OF THE MASSIF CENTRAL

The Massif Central ends to the east in a scarp slope high above the Rhône valley. It is a formidable precipice consisting of a mountain range that was broken down, raised up then overturned by the after-effects of Alpine folding. It

NATURE

has been severely eroded by the rivers, forming narrow gorges.

The Beaujolais Region

To the north, the upper Beaujolais is a mountainous zone of mainly granite soil. Tributaries of the Saône run down its steep slopes from west to east. The Lower Beaujolais, to the south, is formed of sedimentary soils. These soil types include a limestone that is almost ochre in colour and has earned the area the nickname 'Land of Golden Stone'. Economically, there is a clear demarcation of this region east to west, between the escarpment *(La Côte)* overlooking the Saône valley in the east, the wine-producing region, and the hills *(La Montagne)* or hinterland to the west, in which forests, crop-farming and industry predominate.

The Lyonnais Area

Set between the St-Étienne basin and the city of Lyon, the plateau is dotted with high grassy hills, pine forests, beech woods and orchards. The Mont-d'Or is a rugged area (highest peak: Mont Verdun, altitude 625m). The Lyonnais area owes its uniform appearance to the industries that have existed here for centuries. It ends with the Fourvière hill, the superb promontory that stands high above the confluence of the Saône and Rhône and the vast city of Lyon.

Forez and Roannais

In the **Forez mountains**, fields and meadows cover the slopes up to an altitude of 1 000m; above lie oases of beech and pine forest, providing raw material for sawmills. In summer, animals are taken up to graze on the scrubby mountain tops (on the land called the Hautes Chaumes) rising to the Pierre-sur-Haute moors. At the foot of the mountains is the water-logged Forez plain crossed by the River Loire. This is dotted with volcanic hillocks, where castle and church ruins are found.

The **Roanne basin** is a fertile rural area specialising in animal husbandry and is overlooked, to the west, by the vine-covered slopes of the Madeleine mountain range.

Mont Pilat and the St-Étienne Basin

Mont Pilat is a forest-clad pyramid with something of a mountainous air, rising above the surrounding dales. Its peaks are topped with granite boulders known as *chirats,* which form splendid observation platforms. The St-Étienne basin at the foot of the mountain follows the outline of the coalfield that stretches from the Loire to the Rhône and contains a string of factories, in stark contrast to the pastures on the slopes of Mont Pilat and the Lyonnais mountain range.

The Vivarais Area

This area forms the largest part of the eastern edge of the Massif Central. Huge basalt lava flows running down from the Velay area, shale ridges and widespread erosion make this a bizarre landscape of strange natural features.

The **Upper Vivarais** reaches from Mont Pilat and the Velay area to the Rhône valley. People here earn a living from cattle farming and cutting timber in the pine forests. Nearer the banks of the Rhône, there are fruit trees and vineyards. The **Vivarais Cévenol** (lying within the Cévennes range) runs from the Upper Allier valley to the Aubenas basin. To the west, the "uplands" are strongly characterised by volcanoes. They are covered in pine, beech and meadow. From Lablachère and Privas to the Rhône valley, the **Lower Vivarais** is a limestone area with a succession of basins and plateaux in which scrub, olive trees, almond trees, blackberry bushes and vines provide a foretaste of a more southerly environment. To the north it is separated from the **Upper Vivarais** by the Coiron plateau and its black basalt cliffs. The unusual features of the vast plains *(planèzes)* grazed by flocks of sheep are the **dikes** and **necks** (pinnacles), the most famous of which is in Rochemaure. The limestone Gras plateau forms a stretch of whitish stone, with swallowholes, deep narrow gullies and rocks shaped like ruined buildings.

INTRODUCTION TO AUVERGNE RHÔNE VALLEY

Mont Mézenc and conifer forest
© Ph. Bousseaud/Biosphoto

AUVERGNE
GRANITE AND VOLCANIC MOUNTAINS

In the region to the east, the climate is hard and the landscape rugged. From north to south, the **Madeleine** mountain range and the **Forez and Livradois areas** consist of valleys, rounded hilltops, forest plateaux and pastures on which flocks of sheep graze. The area is covered with forests that provide timber.

Further south, the **Velay area** is a succession of vast basalt plateaux lying at altitudes of more than 1 000m beneath skies that are a foretaste of the Riviera. Dotted across the countryside are **outcrops of rock** formed by lava. Crops are generally so rare that the basin around Le Puy, which is irrigated by the Loire, looks almost like an oasis. The mountains in the **Devès area** form one vast plateau where lava flows are covered with pasture and fields of barley or lentils. Along the watershed between the Loire and Allier basins are deep lakes in volcanic craters.

The *planèze* (sloping plateau) is dotted with cinder cones consisting of black or reddish ash often capped with pine trees. The **Margeride plateau** is gashed by deep valleys and its climate and vegetation are reminiscent of the Forez mountains.

Aubrac is high open plateau, punctuated by erratic blocks and herds, lakes bordered by paths and low walls, forests, pastures and "burons" (typical shepherds' shelters).

Limagnes

The *limagnes* are low-lying, fertile, sunny plains drained by the Dore and the Allier and its tributaries. The plains consist almost entirely of arable land. To the east are the "poor Limagnes" or "Varennes", a hilly area of marshes, woodland, fields of crops and lush pastures where alluvium has been washed down from the crystalline mountains of the Forez area. To the west, the soil in the so-called fertile Limagnes region is dark brown, almost black. It has been enriched by the mixture of decomposed lava and volcanic ash. This is very rich land, producing tobacco, wheat, sugar beet, vegetables, seed crops and fruit.

Volcanic Uplands

To the west, the **Dômes** and **Dore** mountain ranges and the mountains in the **Cézallier** and **Cantal** form a striking landscape of extinct volcanoes rising to an altitude of 1 885m at the highest peak, the Puy de Sancy. Around the Puy de Dôme, Puy Mary, Puy de Sancy, La Bourboule and St-Nectaire, forests, woods and pastures alternate with

NATURE

lakes and waterfalls. The **Artense,** which backs onto the Dore mountain range, is a rocky plateau worn away by glaciers; it now provides grazing land for sheep and cattle. The cultivated areas represent land that has been clawed back from the moors by the few people living there.

Bourbonnais

The scenery here is much like the people: calm and temperate. It marks the northern edge of the Massif Central, and the gently rolling countryside is covered with a patchwork of fields hemmed in by hedges that give the landscape a wooded appearance.

The Besbre, Cher and Aumance valleys are wide and well drained, forming open, fertile areas crossed by major road and rail links. It is here that the main towns are to be found. The St-Pourçain vineyards, the impressive Tronçais Forest and the conifers on the mountainsides in the Bourbonnais area add a touch of variety to a landscape that is otherwise dominated by grassland.

AUVERGNE'S MINERAL SPRINGS

Whether naturally carbonated or still, water is one of the main sources of wealth in the Auvergne, and it has been exploited here since ancient times. Puy-de-Dôme and the Vichy basin alone account for a third of French mineral springs. Volvic, the world-famous mineral water, is bottled at source in the Auvergne.

MINERAL SPRINGS

Substances or gases that have therapeutic properties are added naturally to the water as it flows underground. The adjective "**thermal**" is used more accurately to describe springs with water at a temperature of at least 35°C when it comes out of the ground: Vichy water, for instance has a temperature of 66°C and the water in Chaudes-Aigues rises to as much as 82°C.

RESURGENT SPRINGS

The water in these springs only flows at intervals, for example every eight hours. The column of water rising from the depths of the Earth is subjected, at some point along its course, to a very high increase in temperature. The steam produced at this point acquires sufficient pressure to project the upper part of the column of water above the surface of the ground. The projection is interrupted for as long as it takes to heat a second column, then the whole process begins again. This type of spring can be found in Bellerive, near Vichy.

Mineral spring (iron), Vallée de Chaudefour

INTRODUCTION TO AUVERGNE RHÔNE VALLEY

Chaîne des Puys, Puy Pariou in the foreground, Parc naturel régional des volcans d'Auvergne

The Volcanoes of the Auvergne

What makes the Auvergne so unusual is the presence of a large number of volcanoes which, although extinct, are a major feature of the landscape. They vary in appearance depending on their formation, type and age. Since 2018, the 80 volcanoes of the Chaîne des Puys and the Limagne plain were classed UNESCO World Heritage Sites.

Inverse composite volcanoes (Stromboli-type)
In the depths of the earth, magma is subjected to enormous pressure and infiltrates through cracks in the Earth's crust. When the pressure becomes too great, there is an explosion accompanied by a sudden eruption of incandescent matter. A huge column of gas, smoke and vapour rises into the sky, spreading out like a parasol, while the matter in fusion (spindle-shaped volcanic bombs, gas-swollen pozzolana looking like a very lightweight, dark reddish-coloured stone) falls back to earth and accumulates around the mouth of the volcano, gradually building up a **cinder cone**; at the top is a **crater.** The most typical can be seen on the Puy des Goules and the Pariou.

When the pressure inside the Earth's crust decreases and the matter thrown up by the eruption is more fluid, lava flows are created, running from the crater or down the mountainsides. Depending on the type of rock, these **lava flows** (cheires) may cool to form a fairly smooth surface or, alternatively, be rough and full of boulders. When the mass of lava is very thick, it contracts as it cools, breaking into prisms or columns (very much like organ pipes, hence their French name orgues) such as those in Bort-les-Orgues or Murat.

Sometimes a lava flow or an explosion carries away a piece of the volcanic cone, as it did in the Puy de Louchardière or the Puy de la Vache; in this case, the crater is described as **breached** and is shaped like a half-funnel. In the Pariou and the Puy de Dôme, a new cinder cone was formed inside the crater of an older volcano. This led to the formation of a **multiple volcanic complex.**

Volcanic domes (Mount Pelée-type composite volcano)
Sometimes, the volcanic eruption throws up a lava paste which solidifies upon contact with the ground. It then forms a dome with steep sides but has no crater at the summit. The Puy de Dôme is a good example of this type of volcano.

NATURE

Volcanoes with planèzes
When the Cantal volcano was active more than 9 million years ago, it would have been a formidable sight: it had a circumference of 60km/37mi and rose to an altitude of 3 000m. Formed by a succession of layers of lava and ash, it was dissected by erosion, which cut its sides into **planèzes** (sloping plateaus) with a tip pointing towards the centre of the volcano. The Dore mountain range, which is younger than the Cantal volcano (2–3.5 million years), also consists of successions of layers of lava and ash but the *planèzes* are less well developed.

Necks and dikes
Scattered across the Limagne in total disorder are volcanic systems which penetrated, and were consolidated within, a mass of sedimentary rock that has since been worn away. All that remain are a few spurs of rock called necks or ridges known as dikes, which no longer have their covering of soil. The Puy de Monton near Veyre, and Montrognon near Ceyrat, are typical necks. Montaudoux to the south of Royat is a good example of a dike.

Tables
Ancient lava flows originally spread out across the valleys, protecting the underlying soil from the erosion that cleared the area between rivers and caused an inversion relief. These lava flows now jut out above the surrounding countryside, forming tables like the Gergovie and Polignac plateaux.

Lahars
Volcanic eruptions are often accompanied by torrential rain and enormous emissions of water vapour. They then cause *lahars* (an Indonesian word) or flows of mud and boulders that move at astonishing speed, destroying everything in their path. The Pardines plateau near Issoire owes its existence to this type of phenomenon. South of Clermont-Ferrand, some of the small plateaux and hillocks in the Limagne area consist of rock formations created by underwater volcanic eruptions. Their "peppery" appearance is due to the mixing of lava and sediment from the bed of the lake.

Lakes of volcanic origin
The volcanoes have given the landscape a very particular relief and magnificent stretches of water that reflect the surrounding countryside. In some places, a lava flow closed off a valley, holding back the waters of a river; examples of this are the Aydat and Guéry lakes (the latter was also formed by the action of glaciers). In other places, a volcano erupted in the middle of a valley, blocking it with its cone, as was the case in Chambon and Montcineyre. Still elsewhere, subsidence caused by underground volcanic activity was filled with run-off water (Lake Chauvet). *Maars* are lakes formed in craters, such as Lake Servière and Lake Pavin. The latter is the region's deepest, at 92 meters.

The volcanoes of the Auvergne at present
The volcanoes are now well preserved depending on their age and the hardness of their rocks. The **Dômes** mountain range, with its 80 volcanoes that became extinct around 7 000 years ago, has a strikingly fresh-looking relief. The **Dore** mountain range is older and has a more fragmented appearance. The lava flows on Sancy, Aiguiller and Banne d'Ordanche are heaped up to a height of more than 1 000m, but water, snow and glaciers have worn away the sides. With its 60km/37mi circumference and altitude of 3 000m, the **Cantal volcano** was even more impressive in its day. The landscapes today are only a fraction of the original; it is difficult to imagine the initial size of the range.

INTRODUCTION TO AUVERGNE RHÔNE VALLEY

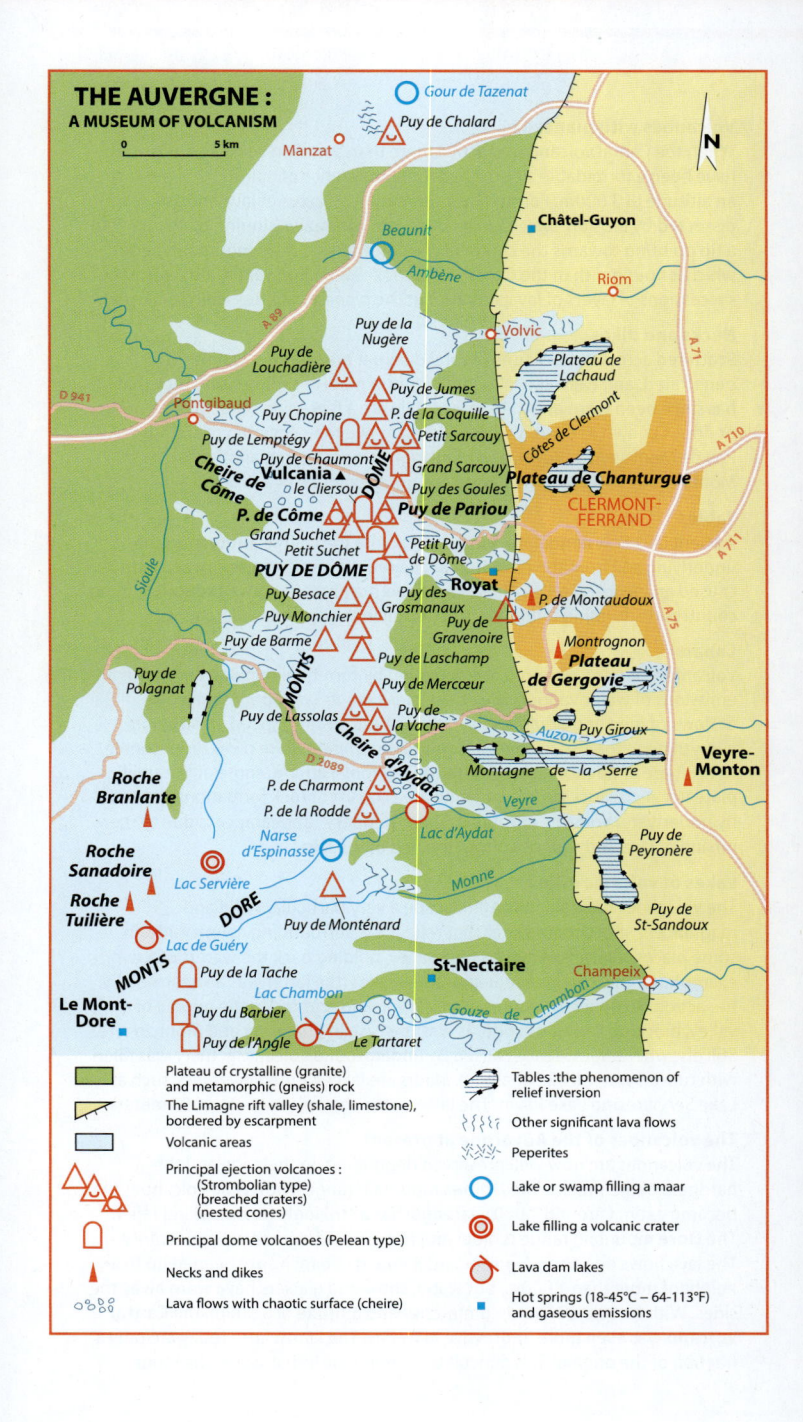

THE AUVERGNE: A MUSEUM OF VOLCANISM

0 — 5 km

Locations shown on map:

Gour de Tazenat, Puy de Chalard, Manzat, Beaunit, Ambène, Châtel-Guyon, Riom, Puy de la Nugère, Volvic, Plateau de Lachaud, Puy de Louchadière, Puy de Jumes, P. de la Coquille, Pontgibaud, Puy Chopine, Petit Sarcouy, Côtes de Clermont, Puy de Lemptégy, Grand Sarcouy, Plateau de Chanturgue, Puy de Chaumont, Puy des Goules, Vulcania, le Cliersou, Puy de Pariou, CLERMONT-FERRAND, Cheire de Côme, P. de Côme, MONTS DÔME, Grand Suchet, Petit Suchet, Petit Puy de Dôme, PUY DE DÔME, Puy Besace, Royat, P. de Montaudoux, Puy des Grosmanaux, Puy Monchier, Puy de Gravenoire, Puy de Barme, Puy de Laschamp, Montrognon, Plateau de Gergovie, Puy de Polagnat, Puy de Mercœur, Puy de Lassolas, Puy de la Vache, Cheire d'Aydat, Auzon, Puy Giroux, P. de Charmont, Montagne de la Serre, Veyre-Monton, P. de la Rodde, Lac d'Aydat, Veyre, Roche Branlante, Narse d'Espinasse, Monne, Puy de Peyronère, Roche Sanadoire, Lac Servière, Roche Tuilière, MONTS DORE, Puy de Monténard, Puy de St-Sandoux, Lac de Guéry, St-Nectaire, Champeix, Le Mont-Dore, Puy de la Tache, Lac Chambon, Gouze de Chambon, Puy du Barbier, Puy de l'Angle, Le Tartaret

Legend:

- Plateau of crystalline (granite) and metamorphic (gneiss) rock
- The Limagne rift valley (shale, limestone), bordered by escarpment
- Volcanic areas
- Principal ejection volcanoes: (Strombolian type) (breached craters) (nested cones)
- Principal dome volcanoes (Pelean type)
- Necks and dikes
- Lava flows with chaotic surface (cheire)
- Tables: the phenomenon of relief inversion
- Other significant lava flows
- Peperites
- Lake or swamp filling a maar
- Lake filling a volcanic crater
- Lava dam lakes
- Hot springs (18-45°C – 64-113°F) and gaseous emissions

NATURE

PROPERTIES OF THERMAL SPRINGS

Ordinary springs are created by water that seeps into permeable land and eventually meets an impermeable layer down which it runs. When the impermeable layer rises to the surface, the water follows suit.

When thermal water rises to the surface, it gives off a very low level of radioactivity which stimulates the human body. However, the water is very unstable and deteriorates as soon as it comes out of the ground, which is why it is important to take the water where it rises to the surface (and why spa towns were built). The composition of water varies depending on the type of rocks through which it passes, and different spa towns therefore have different specialties. People visit Vichy to treat disorders of the digestive system, Royat for heart and arterial diseases, Châtelguyon for intestinal problems, Le Mont-Dore for asthma, La Bourboule for respiratory diseases, and so on.

Spa towns declined in popularity after World War II, but are enjoying a revival. The medical aspect of "taking the waters" has been maintained, but people also come to keep fit, enjoy a round of golf, a day at the races, or a night at the opera.

MINERAL WATER, A BOOM INDUSTRY

The French drink more mineral water than any other country, and as water is one of the most difficult commodities to package, bottling has required the development of modern techniques. In towns like Volvic, the mineral water industry has encouraged employment, as the water is prized locally and abroad.

FLORA AND FAUNA
RHÔNE VALLEY

The Rhône valley is not only a major road and rail route and intersection of geographical areas, it also combines different natural environments, resulting in a variety of flora and fauna. Almost 3 000 species of plants, some 60 wild mammals and more than 200 birds have been observed in the forests, plains and lakes. The Pilat Regional Nature Park alone boasts some 90 species of bird.

Flora

In addition to the plants ordinarily found in the centre of France, the area also boasts mountain plants that have come down from the Alps and the Jura and Mediterranean plants that have spread from the south. Because of this, it is possible to find, in the mountains in the Forez for example, gentians, monkshood, or the superb martagon (or Turk's Cap) lily. This very rare but hardy annual grows to a height of 30–80cm or even sometimes more than 1.10m, with clusters of reddish-orange flowers spotted with black growing on a tall stem. On the lower plateaux and hillsides in the Saône and Rhône valleys, one might see evergreen oak, Montpellier aphyllantes, lavender or purple orchid growing on dry grasslands in April.

Fauna

Mediterranean species of fauna are found in the Rhône valley, including the tiny Provençal field mouse and the mouse-eared bat. Deer are adaptable creatures and can be found throughout the region in forested areas. The Rhône valley is a major point along migratory

Armeria maritima, Cantal mountains

© ANP PHOTO/age fotostock

routes followed by **birds** between Northern Europe and the Mediterranean. The banks of the Saône and Rhône are full of larks, buntings, quail, plovers and curlews. But it is the lakes of the **Dombes** that boast the largest variety. Birds from all over the world can be seen at the bird sanctuary in Villars-les-Dombes, where toucans and parrots rub shoulders with rare species such as the black-tailed godwit, or the endangered corncrake.

The largest freshwater fish
Before it was introduced into France in the second half of the 19C by fish farmers, the wels catfish, also known as the sheatfish, was found mainly in the waters of the Caspian Sea and the River Danube. Those living in the Rhône and Saône can, in rare cases, grow to a length of 3m and weigh some 100kg. Wels feed on bream, moorhens, ducks and rats; to kill its prey, the wels grabs their paws and drags them down to the river-bed until they drown. This aquatic monster is, however, short-sighted and dislikes the light, so it waits until nightfall before going on the prowl; it is therefore unlikely to be seen, except perhaps on a dinner plate, as it is becoming increasingly popular with fishermen.

Beavers of the Île du Beurre
The beaver is a hard-working animal, cutting, felling and nibbling branches of trees in order to build dams and dikes. These days, however, beavers have changed their habits: they no longer build lodges and instead live in burrows dug into the river banks. They are particularly fond of the Île du Beurre (in old French, *beurre* meant beaver). This island to the south of Lyon is the last place in France in which beavers live in the wild; because of this, it has been protected by a preservation order since 1988.

AUVERGNE
The Auvergne has a diverse landscape with extensive forest and peat bog. Each area has its own flora and fauna.

Vegetation at Different Altitudes
Forests in the Auvergne grow in specific tiers. The hillsides are covered with pedunculate oak on clay soil and sessile oak on better-drained ground. On the mountains there are beech and pine, although conifer predominates in cold, damp areas. The beech is the most common tree in the Auvergne and grows to a height of 30-40m after 150 to 300 years. It is easily recognisable for its smooth, grey bark and leaf colouring – red in winter and soft green in spring. Natural pine groves cover the driest hillsides, like those in Upper Loire.

The **moors** of the Margeride area often mark the abandonment of pastures or farmland. In fact, moorland precedes the stage at which land is overrun by forest. Ferns, calluna, gorse, myrtle and redcurrants grow here. Gradually, however, the forest takes over, with birch, hazelnut and pine the first trees to appear.

The **mountain pastures** above 1 000m provide a natural environment for species that have existed here for centuries, such as the three-coloured violet, the scented wild pansy, the red-purple saw-wort (used to produce a yellow dye), and globe flower. The gentian, a delightful yellow flower, is used to make the liqueur that bears its name; other species of gentian produce blue flowers. The **subalpine stage** of vegetation begins at altitudes over 1 400m. Plant life here varies depending on the exposure of the slopes. Calluna and myrtle grow on moorland, and ground-cover plants on grassland, rocks and scree. It is here, from May to July, that the spring anemone blooms, a rare plant with delicately indented leaves and flowers with huge white petals tinged with purple. Mountain arnica, a downy plant with yellow flowers, is used to make creams that prevent bruising. The blue carnation, with its unusual blue-green colour, can be seen in tufts only a few inches high on the peaks in the Dore and Cantal mountain ranges.

The Alps viewed from Crêt de l'Œillon, Parc naturel régional du Pilat

Peat Bogs

Peat bogs are natural environments created by an accumulation of organic matter in damp areas. A number of features lead to the formation of peat bogs, such as a break in a slope along the course of streams, or cold springs, as in the mountains of Cantal. They also tend to form on valley floors, along meanders and streams like those in the Upper Forez area, in the bases of volcanic craters, or over-deepening caused by glacial erosion as in the Margeride, Forez and Artense regions. *Maars* (lakes in the bottom of craters) can also be overrun by vegetation, as can be seen in the Devès range and the Velay.

Peat is formed from a range of spongy mosses, which ensure photosynthesis and retain up to 30 times their dry weight in water. Some of these bogs some are more than 5 000 years old and have developed unique flora and fauna. Carnivorous plants like the sundew and drosera, which suffer from nitrogen deficiency, have adapted to this environment. They capture small insects by secreting a sticky substance.

The Odyssey of the Salmon

Born in a river, salmon stay in the area where they are born for two years before letting the river carry them down to the sea tail-first: a period known as downstream migration. At this stage, its scales turn white, and certain salmon travel as far as Greenland. Here, they grow and acquire their more familiar pink colour thanks to the shrimp on which they feed. After two years, the salmon swim up the Loire to return to their spawning grounds in Allier or Upper Loire, in particular around Brioude, a famous paradise for salmon.

The trip can take several months, and when the fish arrive, they are exhausted and very thin, as they do not feed in the rivers.

Upon their arrival, the female salmon burrow into the gravel on the riverbed with their tails to lay their eggs. The males then cover the eggs with their milt. At this point, the salmon usually die, though some survive long enough to make the journey twice.

In the Auvergne, salmon are the subject of many anecdotal tales. One recounts how, at the turn of the 19C when the railway line was being built through the Allier gorge, workmen went on strike because they had nothing to eat – nothing, that is, but salmon!

REGIONAL NATURE PARKS

The Auvergne-Rhône Valley area includes five regional nature parks, described in the *Discovering* section of this guide (⊙ *see* AUBENAS, Monts du FOREZ, Le PILAT, CHAUDES-AIGUES *and Parc naturel regional des* VOLCANS D'AUVERGNE).

Grignan, Drôme Provençale
© Franck Guiziou/hemis.fr

DISCOVERING
AUVERGNE RHÔNE VALLEY

CLERMONT-FERRAND AND MONTS DÔME

Pushing gently at the gates of "outdoor heaven", the bright and busy city of Clermont-Ferrand enjoys a privileged position. The presence of such magnificent countryside at the very edge of town is a quality few French cities can boast. Nowhere does it seem that work, play and well-being so readily interplay as in the shadow of the Monts Dôme, and the opportunity to make the most of this explosive landscape is one that can be enjoyed by visitors and locals alike.

Highlights

1. Checking out the quaint streets of **Old Clermont** (p99)
2. Discovering the history of the vast **Gergovie plateau** and the Gallic Wars (p111)
3. Driving, walking, or taking the panoramic train to the summit of **Puy de Dôme** to enjoy the stunning view (p118)
4. Exploring a real volcano at the Volcan de Lemptégy (p122)
5. **Vulcania** theme park, for adults and children alike (p123)

Up in the Air

It would be a shame to visit this region and not somehow get to the top of the Puy de Dôme. But whether you get there by car or on foot, it is worth taking a parapente flight with one of the local experts. The range is magnificent no matter your viewpoint, but from the air, it really is something special.

Volcanic Landscape

The volcanic origins of the region to the west of Clermont-Ferrand have given way to the rolling green hills and valleys that define the area today. Photos far from do the landscapes justice, and behind every turn, a new one awaits. It's no surprise that the 80 volcanoes of the Puys and Limagne Fault became metropolitan France's first natural UNESCO World Heritage Site in 2018.

Taking the Water

The volcanic springs of Volvic mineral water were first tapped in 1922, but it took another 16 years before the first bottled water appeared on the market. Today, Volvic produces more than 1 billion bottles annually and exports to over 60 countries. This massive industry is the principal employer in the town of Volvic, which is also home to an information centre and underground quarry wth audio-visual installations open to the public tracing the history of the water and the volcanic region itself.

Vulcania, the Puy de Côme and the Pay Dôme in the background.

© Francis Cormon/hemis.fr/Getty Images

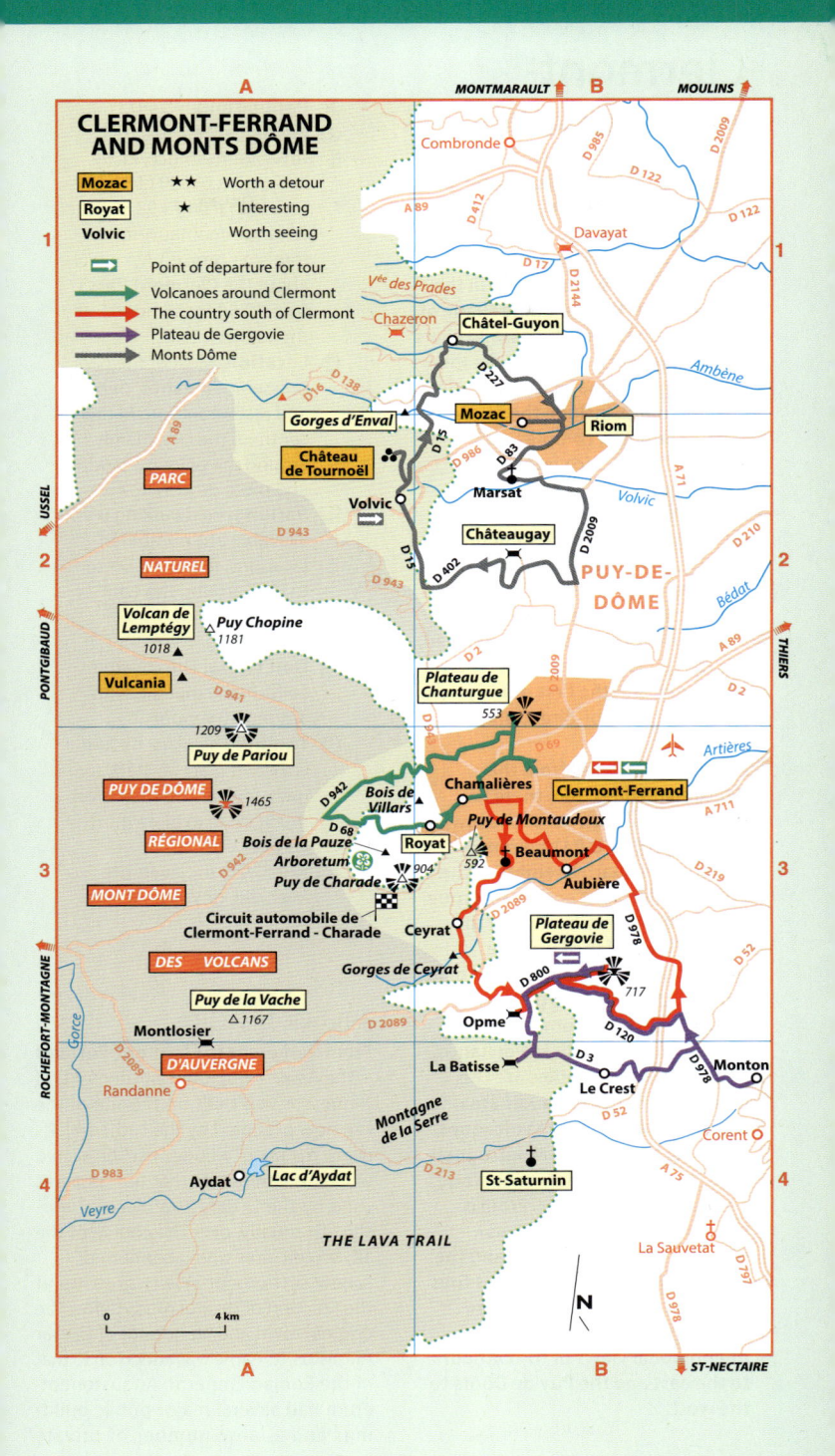

CLERMONT-FERRAND AND MONTS DÔME

Mozac ★★ Worth a detour
Royat ★ Interesting
Volvic   Worth seeing

⇨ Point of departure for tour
➙ Volcanoes around Clermont
➙ The country south of Clermont
➙ Plateau de Gergovie
➙ Monts Dôme

MONTMARAULT • MOULINS
Combronde • Davayat
Vée des Prades
Chazeron
Châtel-Guyon
Gorges d'Enval
Mozac — Riom
Château de Tournoël
Marsat
Volvic
Châteaugay
PUY-DE-DÔME

USSEL
PARC
NATUREL
Volcan de Lemptégy
Puy Chopine 1181
1018
Vulcania
PONTGIBAUD

1209
Puy de Pariou
PUY DE DÔME 1465
RÉGIONAL
MONT DÔME
D 68
Bois de Villars
Bois de la Pauze
Arboretum
Puy de Charade 904

Plateau de Chanturgue 553
Chamalières
Puy de Montaudoux
Clermont-Ferrand
Beaumont
Royat 592
Aubière
Circuit automobile de Clermont-Ferrand - Charade
Ceyrat
Plateau de Gergovie
717
Gorges de Ceyrat
DES VOLCANS
Puy de la Vache 1167
Montlosier
Opme
D 120
D 800
D 978
Monton
D'AUVERGNE
Randanne
La Batisse
Le Crest
Corent
Montagne de la Serre
Aydat Lac d'Aydat
St-Saturnin
La Sauvetat
THE LAVA TRAIL

ROCHEFORT-MONTAGNE
THIERS
0   4 km
N
ST-NECTAIRE

DISCOVERING CLERMONT-FERRAND AND MONTS DÔME

Clermont-Ferrand★★

Clermont-Ferrand is the natural capital of the Auvergne. The city centre is built on a slight rise, all that remains of a volcanic cone. The old houses built of volcanic rock in the "Black Town" huddle in the shade of the cathedral. Over the past 30 years or so, Clermont's urban landscape has undergone major changes. New developments include the **Jaude** (a vast shopping complex), the **St-Pierre** district (covered market), the **Fontgiève** district (law courts, residential buildings), and place du 1er-Mai (sculpture by Étienne Martin), all of which combine contemporary architecture with an older urban environment. In 2006, an urban tramway was inaugurated, the first phase in a transport revival of the city, and the first tram system in France to use bi-directional pneumatic tyres.

For visitors arriving from the Pontgibaud direction, there is a good general **view**★★ of the town from a **bend** on D 941A. From left to right, the nearby heights of the Côtes de Clermont and Chanturgue plateau give an indication of the original level of the Limagne plain prior to the major period of erosion. Opposite the platform lies the city itself, dominated by its black cathedral. In the distance, beyond the Allier valley, are the mountains of the Livradois area. To the right are the Comté volcanoes, Gergovie plateau and Montrognon rock. Avenue Thermale runs along a hilltop north of Royat. From it there are more superb **views**★ over the town of Clermont and the surrounding area. The rue des Gras has been a major thoroughfare since Roman times and affords phenomenal views of the cathedral to the east and the Puy de Dôme to the west.

▶ **Population:** 145 497.
Michelin Map: 326: F-8.
Info: Tourist office, Pl. de la Victoire, 63000 Clermont-Ferrand. 04 73 98 65 00. www.clermontauvergne tourisme.com. Ask about the **Clermont Pass** (€18.50 for 48 hours), at the tourist office.
Location: Most of the bars, brasseries, theatres, pubs and restaurants are in the centre of the city, mainly around the place de Jaude and place de la Victoire.
Parking: Paid parking is available at a number of locations. It is often better to park around the edge of the centre and walk in.
Don't Miss: The covered Saint-Pierre market, with around 40 vendors.
Timing: The place de Jaude is a good place to start, to get a feel for the city before going on to explore more widely.
Kids: Visit the Aventure Michelin, or Vulcania.

A BIT OF HISTORY

From Nemessos to Clermont-Ferrand – The Arverni oppidum (settlement) of Nemessos was built on the site of the rise now occupied by the cathedral. Its name, meaning "wooded rise" or "sacred wood", is a reminder that the spot was used by the Druids as a place of worship. Gradually, over the course of the 1C, Druidic rites were abandoned.

A new settlement slowly grew up at the junction of several roads below the original town and, in honour of Caesar Augustus, its name was added on to that of the Roman Emperor. Augustonemetum had several major public buildings and a large number of private

Rue des Gras, Puy de Dôme in the background

residences. An aqueduct brought water from the Villars valley to the summit of the rise where it was distributed to the various districts from a water tower.

At its height, in the 2C the town underwent fairly large-scale expansion, and its population rose to between 15 000 and 30 000 inhabitants. An ancient description indicates that it was "well-planted with vineyards, full of people, busy with traffic and trade and much given to pomp".

During the early Middle Ages, the town sank into decline. It suffered a number of destructive sieges at the hands of the Franks, the Saracens and the Vikings. It was in the 8C that the name "Clermont" was first applied to the fortress destroyed by Pepin the Short in 761.

In the 10C the town entered a period of economic revival. Bishop Étienne II had a new cathedral built, the population increased, the town grew beyond the old town walls and there were no less than 34 churches and chapels inside and outside the walls.

For centuries the episcopal town of Clermont was rivalled by Montferrand, the count's stronghold, and later by Riom, the seat of the Court of Appeal. Clermont finally won out, and, in 1630, Montferrand merged with its neighbour to form the conurbation known as Clermont-Ferrand.

Blaise Pascal, a man of genius – A few years earlier, the great writer and philosopher **Blaise Pascal** (1623–62) was born in Clermont. Pascal was not only very gifted in the arts, he was also a brilliant scientist with an enormous talent for mathematics and physics. When he was 12, it became obvious that he had outstanding natural ability in geometry. At the age of 16, he amazed the philosopher Descartes with an essay on conic sections. Two years later, he invented an early mechanical calculator. The "wheelbarrow" or "vinaigrette", a two-wheeled sedan chair, was also one of his inventions. It was Pascal, too, who had the idea of the "five *sous* coach service" travelling a fixed route and leaving at regular intervals. The coaches were an immediate success, and they paved the way for the Parisian omnibus service. It was Pascal again, with his brother-in-law Périer, who proved the weight of air following an experiment at Le Puy-en-Velay.

Tyre town – It is perhaps surprising that Clermont, situated in the heart of the Auvergne, far from the harbours through which rubber and cotton were imported and well away from the major wire-mills, became the leading centre of tyre production in France and, indeed, one of the industry's leading operators worldwide. The story behind this, however, is one of quite humble origins.

In the heyday of Romanticism, c. 1830, a former solicitor named Aristide Barbier, who had lost three-quarters of his personal fortune as a result of the difficult financial climate, set up in partnership

DISCOVERING CLERMONT-FERRAND AND MONTS DÔME

WHERE TO STAY	
Dav'Hôtel Jaude	①

WHERE TO EAT		
Bath's Restaurant	3	①
Chardonnay (Le)	1	②
Comptoir des Saveurs (Le)	2	③
Saint-Eutrope (Le)	5	④

with his cousin, Edouard Daubrée, a captain in the King's Light Cavalry who had resigned his commission in order to open a small farm machinery factory on the banks of the River Tiretaine. In order to amuse her children, Madame Daubrée, niece of the Scottish chemist **Charles Macintosh** (1766–1843) who had discovered that rubber dissolves in petroleum, made a few rubber balls as she had seen her uncle do. The balls proved so popular that Barbier and

PARIS-BORDEAUX 1895   1ÈRE VOITURE sur PNEUS MICHELIN

Daubrée began mass-producing them. Soon, the factory diversified its output to include other items made of rubber, such as hoses and belts. However, after a period of prosperity, it fell into decline. In 1886, Barbier's grandsons, the **Michelin brothers** (André and, later, Édouard), took over. These two creative geniuses were the first to apply scientific methods to industrial production. By meeting clients' real needs, carefully observing reality and constantly revising the knowledge and experience they had already acquired, they were able to create the first detachable bicycle tyre (1891). This development was followed by tyres for automobiles in 1895 and the low-pressure "Confort" tyre in 1923. In 1937 the "Métalic" tyre was introduced, with a steel carcass that made lorries a viable method of transport. In 1946 came the radial-ply tyre (marketed under the name "X" in 1949) which combined a radial carcass that overcame the problem of overheating and a triangular steel belt to ensure good road-holding. In 2006, pneumatic, bi-directional tyres were used, for the first time in France, on the city's new urban tramway system.

OLD CLERMONT★★

A leisurely stroll in the old district will take you through the narrow alleys laid out around the cathedral and place de la Victoire, featuring quaint, old-fashioned fountains and houses with lava stone courtyards.

Place de Jaude

The ancient origins of the name of this square remain a subject of controversy. Two Renaissance documents use the name *platea galli* – "rooster square", since in local dialect the word for cockerel is *jô* or *jau*. The square is therefore thought to have been a poultry market. Another explanation links the origin of the word *jaude* to the name of a suburb of Clermont, known in the Gallic language as *Vasso Galate*. While *wasso* or *vasso* is said to be the name of a Gallic divinity, *galate* is merely a local name which has evolved over the years into *galde* or *gialde* (10C), *jalde* (12C) and, finally, *jaude*.

Place de Jaude is bordered by trees and surrounded by department stores, cinemas and, on the south side, by the **Centre Jaude**, a vast shopping complex.

Église St-Pierre-les-Minimes

This vast domed church building in the Classical style has fine wood panelling in the chancel.

▶ Walk down avenue des États-Unis then turn right onto rue des Gras.

Rue des Gras

This road, a main thoroughfare since Roman times, is a popular shopping spot. A flight of steps used to lead from here right up to the cathedral. At No. 28, note the straight flight of steps, gallery and balcony dating from the 17C.

▶ Take the second street on the left.

Marché St-Pierre

This market is situated at the heart of an old district that has been renovated, and stands on the site of a Romanesque church. It is a bustling centre on which narrow, picturesque shopping streets such as rue de la Boucherie converge.

▶ Return to rue des Gras then, at place de la Bourse, turn left onto rue Ph.-Marcombes (north of the cathedral) which leads to place de la Poterne.

Fontaine d'Amboise★

This fountain erected in 1515 by Jacques d'Amboise, Bishop of Clermont, is a very fine piece of Renaissance architecture, carved in lava stone from Volvic. The basin is decorated with charming foliage in the Italian style. The central pyramid is adorned with small, naked figures with water pouring from their mouths.

Rue du Port

No. 21 *(right)* is a narrow old house with machicolations; on the right, at the corner of Rue Barnier, stands a 16C house with barbican. Note, on the left

DISCOVERING CLERMONT-FERRAND AND MONTS DÔME

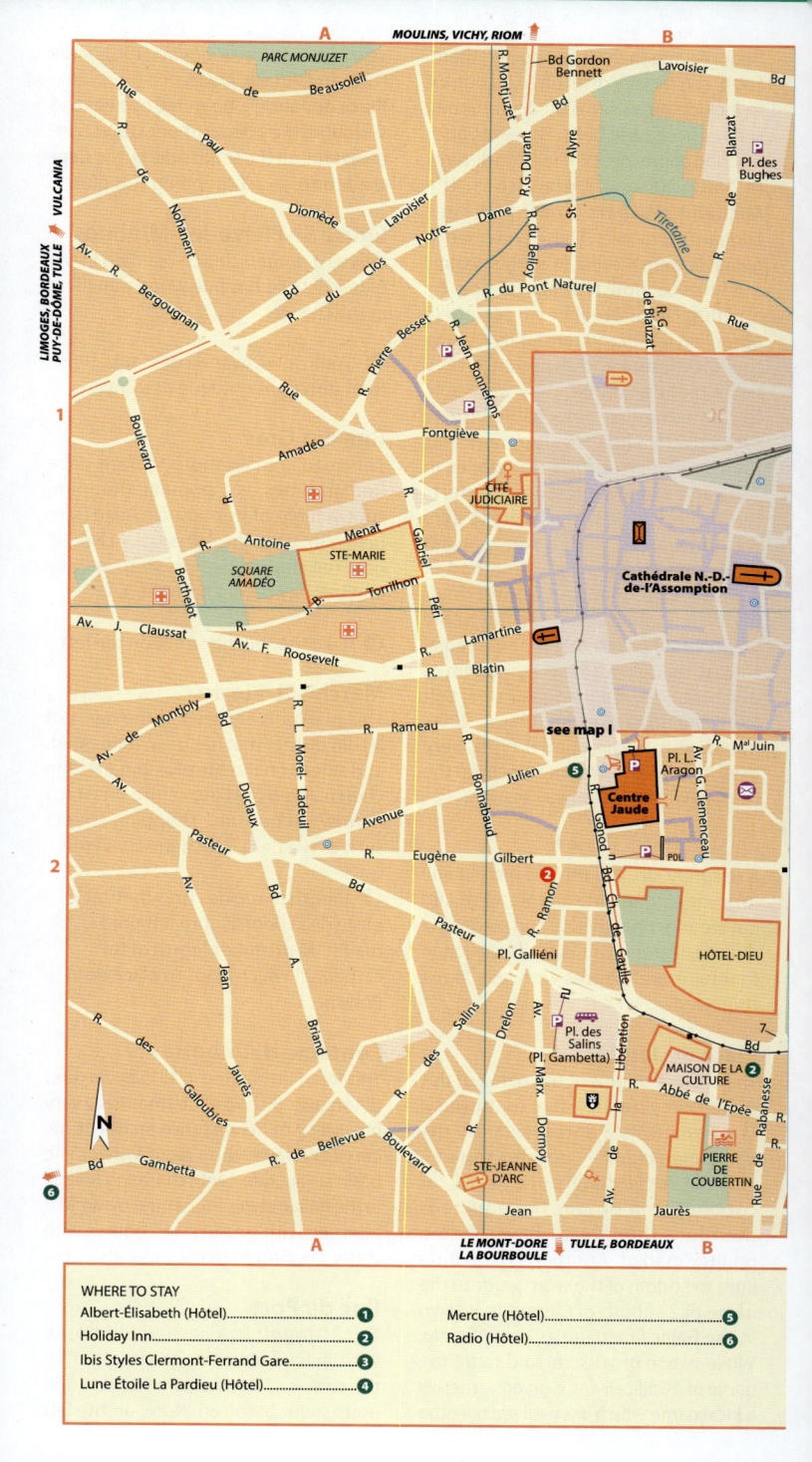

WHERE TO STAY	
Albert-Élisabeth (Hôtel)..........①	Mercure (Hôtel)..........⑤
Holiday Inn..........②	Radio (Hôtel)..........⑥
Ibis Styles Clermont-Ferrand Gare..........③	
Lune Étoile La Pardieu (Hôtel)..........④	

CLERMONT-FERRAND

CLERMONT-FERRAND
map II

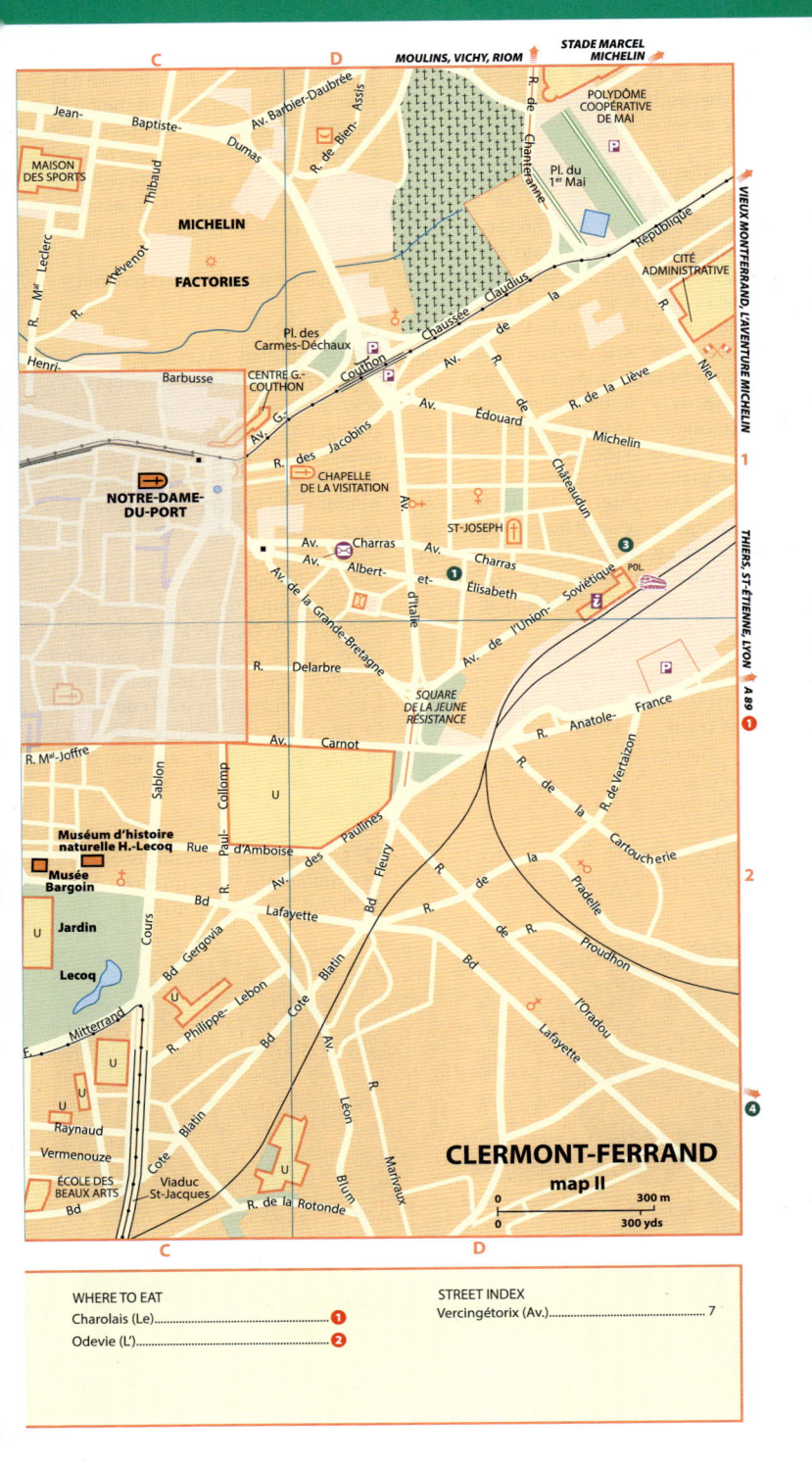

WHERE TO EAT
Charolais (Le) .... ❶
Odevie (L') .... ❷

STREET INDEX
Vercingétorix (Av.) 7

at No. 38, the superb carriage entrance of the residence built in the early 18C for the financier Montlosier.

Basilique Notre-Dame-du-Port★★

Founded in the 6C by Bishop St Avit and burned down by the Vikings, the church was rebuilt with outstanding stylistic unity in the 11C and 12C. The bell-towers and lava stone roof slabs that replaced the tiles are 19C additions. The edifice is now on UNESCO's World Heritage List. The east end, restored during the 19C, is a consummate example of Romanesque architecture in the Auvergne.

The plain, robust design of Romanesque architecture as developed in the Auvergne is apparent from the entrance. The raised **chancel**★★★, the most attractive part of the building, is strikingly beautiful. It is flanked by an ambulatory with four chapels.

Lighting is used to emphasize the details on the **capitals**★, which are among the most famous in the Auvergne.

The **crypt** dates from the 11C. Beneath the chancel, the "Underground", dear to the hearts of the local people, has the same layout as the east end.

▶ Leave the church by the steps down to place Notre-Dame-du-Port.

The bare, heavy west front forms a contrast with the remainder of the building; it is preceded by a 16C porch. The austerity and bareness of the old wall are tempered by a row of triple arches beneath the gable, itself consisting of a mosaic of multicoloured stonework.

▶ Follow rue du Port and turn left.

Rue Pascal

"The streets climb up between careworn façades where gateways open, yawning, onto damp courtyards. In the depths of the iron-coloured shadow is the turret of a spiral staircase, a decorated gallery, a doorway with a lintel shaped like the point of a shield." (Henri Pourrat)

The old house at No. 22 has bosses on the ground floor and a wrought-iron balcony. No. 4 is M de Chazerat's residence; he was the last Intendant of the Auvergne and his mansion is a fine late-18C building. The **oval courtyard,** broken up by Ionic pilasters designed in accordance with the principles of the Colossal Order, conveys an impression of majesty.

▶ Cross the tiny place du Terrail with its fountain (1664) and go down rue du Terrail. Turn right onto rue Fléchier,

Basilique Notre-Dame-du-Port

leading to rue des Grands-Jours which skirts the east end of the cathedral.

Place de la Victoire

In the centre is a monument commemorating the Crusades, and a fountain with a statue of Pope Urban II. From this now pedestrian square, there is a general view of the cathedral, and cafés and wine bars make it a popular evening spot for locals and visitors alike.

Rue des Chaussetiers

Shops and wine bars fill the vaulted ground floors of old houses, with an abundance of doors and arches. At No. 3, at the corner of rue Terrasse, is the **Maison de Savaron,** a mansion built in 1513. The **courtyard**★ contains a staircase turret linked to the main building by three floors of overhanging landings. The turret includes a superb carved doorway known as the "Door of the Wild Men". At No. 10, there is a Gothic doorway and mullioned windows. At the corner of rue des Petits-Gras are Romanesque arches (12C, the oldest examples of this style to be seen in vernacular buildings in Clermont).

Rue des Petits-Gras

At Nos. 4–6 (windows with grotesque masks), in the second of the two buildings beyond the courtyard, there is a monumental three-storey **staircase**★ supported by corbels and oblique basket-handled arches. The straight flights of steps and landings form a particularly fine example of 18C architecture.

Cathédrale Notre-Dame-de-l'Assomption★★

Mon–Sat 7.30am–noon, 2–6pm (7pm Jun–mid-Sept), Sun and public holidays 9am–noon, 3–8pm). 04 73 98 65 00; www.cathedrale-catholique-clermont.fr.

The design of this Gothic church, begun in 1248, was based on cathedrals in Île de France. Its sombre colour comes from the lavastone used in its construction; it is the only major cathedral to use it. Enter by the north door into the transept, beneath the Bayette Tower. Adja-

Place de la Victoire and the cathedral

© Luc Olivier/Photononstop

cent to the tower is the Guette Turret, once topped by a look-out post. The impression of lightness in the nave and, in particular, around the chancel shows the technical skills inherent in the Rayonnant Gothic style. The use of lava stone made it possible to reduce the width of the pillars, the arches of the vaulting, and the various sections of the openings. The scattering of the French fleur-de-lis motif and the towers of Castile visible on some of the windows would seem to suggest that they date from the days of St Louis; the King may have given them to the cathedral on the occasion of the marriage of his son (the future Philippe III) in the cathedral in 1262. Set in the gallery of the north transept arm is a clock with a **Jack o' the clock** (**1**) dating from the 16C (the mechanism is 17C and 18C).

Walk round the ambulatory.

Note, above the doorway flanked by foliage into the vestry (**2**), three paintings from 13C–15C.

(**3**) **Chapelle St-Georges** – Stained-glass window illustrating the life and martyrdom of the saint.

(**4**) **Chapelle St-Austremoine** –To the right, Austremoine's arrival in the Auvergne where he was the first bishop. In the centre is an illustration of his martyrdom; to the left, the miracles accomplished after his death.

DISCOVERING CLERMONT-FERRAND AND MONTS DÔME

CATHÉDRALE N.-D.-DE-L'ASSOMPTION

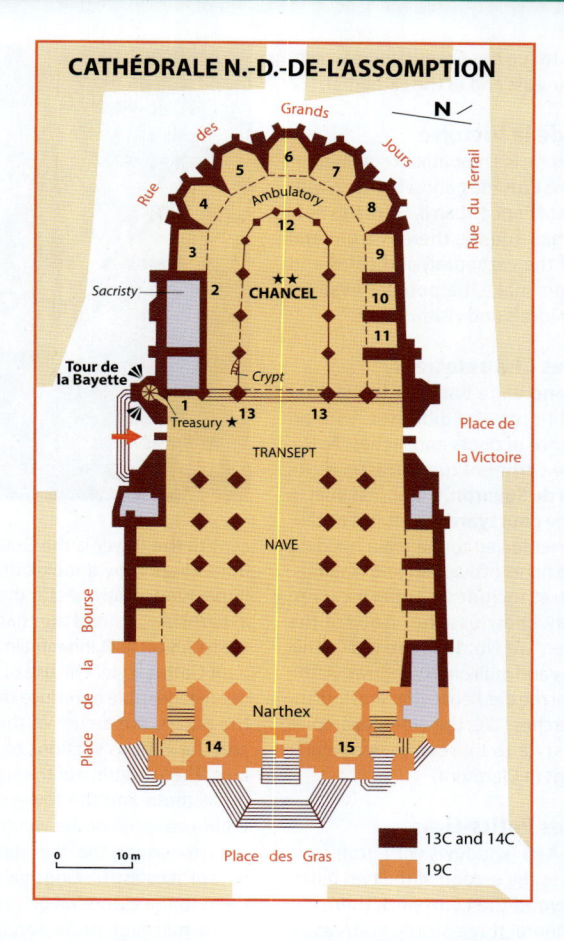

(5) Mary Magdalene windows – Stained glass illustrating the end of her life. 17C and 18C altar and Pietà. Statues of the Bishops of Clermont, St Arthème and St Alyre.

(6) Apsidal chapel – To the left is the life of John the Baptist; in the centre, the childhood of Christ and to the right the miracle worked by Theophilus.

(7) St Bonnet windows – St Bonnet was Bishop of Clermont in the 7C.

(8) Funeral chapel of the bishops – In the centre are 12C stained-glass windows from the former cathedral which illustrate the Life of Christ.

(9) Chapelle Ste-Marguerite – Altarpiece and Adoration of the Shepherds (17C).

(10) St Agatha windows.

(11) Chapelle St-Arthème – Endowed with an altarpiece which was rebuilt in 1840 using 17C statues. The **chancel**★★ is closed off by large but light arches. Above the triforium, the long 13C and 14C stained-glass windows (**12**) have a grisaille background and only one large figure per lancet. Set against the pillars in the transept are two statues of the Virgin Mary and St John (**13**); they were originally part of the rood screen which was demolished during the Revolution. At the west end of the inner north aisle note the 14C statue of Christ of the Last Judgement (**14**), once set against the tympanum of the north doorway. At the west end of the inner south aisle is

CLERMONT-FERRAND

a stained-glass window (1982) by Makaraviez illustrating the Apocalypse of St John (**15**).

OLD MONTFERRAND★★

Montferrand was founded by the counts of Auvergne who built a fortress on a rise that is now the site of place Marcel-Sembat, in order to counter the authority of the bishop, who was also Lord of Clermont. In the early 13C the town was rebuilt on the orders of a powerful woman named Countess Brayère and was turned into a bastide, a fortified hilltop town laid out to a strictly symmetrical geometric pattern. Montferrand was a commercial centre at the junction of several roads, and, in the 15C, the wealthy middle classes began to commission townhouses. The narrow plots of land made available by Countess Brayère's town plan, however, forced the architects to design houses that were deep rather than wide. Most of the houses were built with lava stone. Montferrand was so commercially successful that, in the 16C, the king set up law courts – known as the Cour des Aides – to try fiscal and criminal cases. The proximity of Clermont caused rivalry and jealousy between the two towns. Montferrand eventually went into decline. In 1962, work was undertaken to renovate the old town of Montferrand, a project that involved some 80 old townhouses and mansions. They have retrieved their original façades, decorated with carved heads, balustrades, staircase turrets, cornerstones and lava stone arches contrasting with the honey-coloured "Montferrand roughcast".

▷ Park in place de la Rodade.

Place de la Rodade

This square was once known as place de Belregard because of the view over the Puys range. In the centre stands the Four Seasons fountain made of lava stone.

▷ Enter the old town of Montferrand via rue de la Rodade.

Hôtel Regin
At No. 36.
This 15C and 16C town house belonged to a family of magistrates and is typical of the mansions built in Montferrand.

Hôtel Doyac
At No. 29.
Late-15C mansion built for Jean de Doyac, Royal Bailiff of Montferrand and Minister to Louis XI. Huge, imposing Gothic doorway.

Hôtel du Bailliage
At No. 20.
Bailiwick House is the former Consul's Residence. Its gargoyles and vaulted rooms are of interest.
After rue de la Rodade widens, a set of timbered houses with corbelling comes into view on the left, in the renovated district. Their rounded doorways are set out on high landings that show the original level of the roadway.

▷ Turn back; right on rue Marmillat.

Hôtel de la Porte
At No. 5.
In the courtyard of this mansion, also known as the Architect's House, there is a staircase turret decorated with a Renaissance sculpture from 1577.

▷ Turn right onto rue de la Cerisière.

Hôtel de la Faye des Forges
At No. 2.
A glass door protects a delightful inner door with a carved tympanum decorated with lions holding a phylactery. The house opposite has a double timber gallery, an unusual feature in Montferrand.

▷ Turn left along rue des Cordeliers onto rue Waldeck-Rousseau.

Rue Waldeck-Rousseau runs along the inside of the old ramparts, high above the road laid out along the moat, which was once liable to flooding by the Tiretaine.

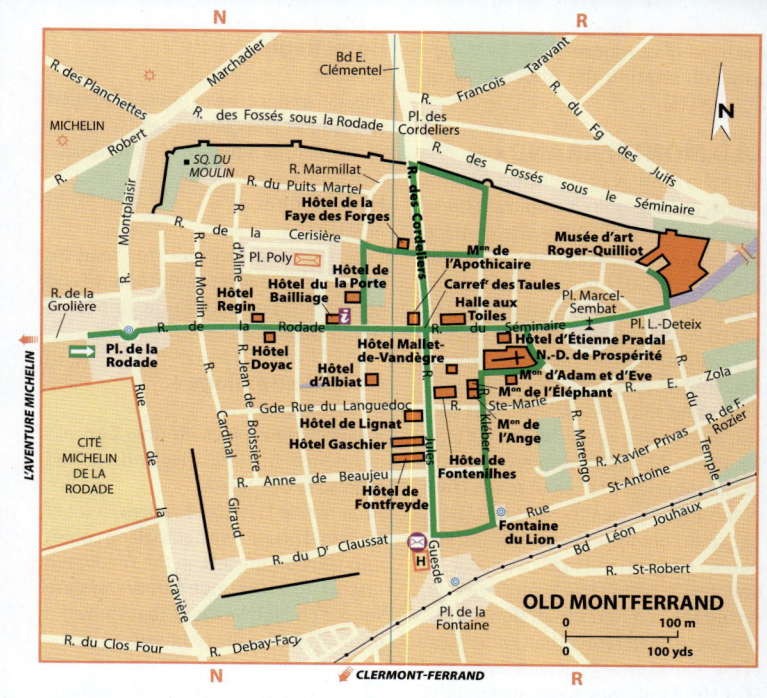

DISCOVERING CLERMONT-FERRAND AND MONTS DÔME

▶ Turn right onto Rue du Temple, back to Rue des Cordeliers.

Rue des Cordeliers
At No. 11.
Note the Renaissance ground floor flanked by pilasters and the delightful little inner courtyard.

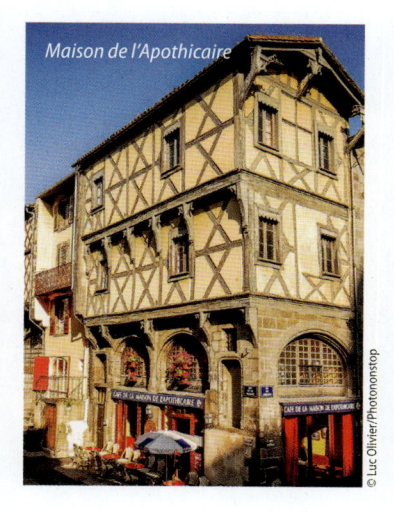

Maison de l'Apothicaire
© Luc Olivier/Photononstop

Carrefour des Taules
This is the central junction in the old town. Its name is a reminder that this was once a butchers' market.

Maison de l'Apothicaire
At No. 1 rue des Cordeliers.
The old Apothecary's House dates from the 15C and has two timbered upper storeys. At the top of the house, the brackets on either side of the gable are decorated with an apothecary and a patient awaiting his operation.

▶ Turn left onto rue du Séminaire.

Halle aux Toiles
At No. 3.
The old cloth market boasts a long balcony supporting a fine row of four basket-handled arches and corresponding side doors.

Hôtel d'Étienne Pradal
At No. 22.
The ground floor of this mansion has superb semicircular and basket-handled arches. Its "Montferrand roughcast" and

CLERMONT-FERRAND

Musée d'Art Roger-Quilliot

cornerstones made of lava stone are typical of the town's architecture.

Musée d'Art Roger-Quilliot★★

♿☉*Tue–Fri 10am-6pm, Sat–Sun and public holidays 10am-noon, 1-6pm).*
☉*1 Jan, 1 May, 1 Nov, 25 Dec.* ∞€5, no charge 1st Sunday in the month. ✆04 43 76 25 25. www.clermontmetropole.eu.

A change of use – The history of these premises reflects the history of Montferrand and Clermont, each in turn the seat of official bodies. The museum stands on the site of the Palais Vieux above the town walls. It was the seat of the royal bailiwick of the Cour des Aides of the Auvergne, the Limousin and the Marches; the monumental gateway built in the early 17C in front of the courtyard that precedes the chapel is all that remains of this building.
When Montferrand and Clermont were combined, the Cour des Aides moved to Clermont and the Ursuline Order of nuns took over and reconstructed the buildings. The site was turned into a seminary after the Revolution, then into a military hospital from 1914 to 1918, and into barracks for riot police and *gendarmerie*, before being transformed into a museum.
The buildings and their surroundings are a reflection of Montferrand. They constitute the old "Gateway of the Rising Sun" and open the historic centre of the town to its suburbs.

Église Notre-Dame-de-Prospérité

The west front still has its north tower, which was used as a watchtower. It is topped by a 16C lantern.

▶ Continue along rue Kléber.

Maison d'Adam et d'Eve

At No 4. In the courtyard on a balustrade is a 15C **bas-relief★** of Adam and Eve.

▶ Continue on rue Kléber.

Maison de l'Éléphant★

At No. 12.
A 13C Romanesque house. The great arches on the ground floor support the twin bay windows on the first floor.

Maison de l'Ange

At No. 14.
In the courtyard is a small, triangular tympanum above a doorway representing an angel carrying a coat of arms.

Fontaine du Lion

The fountain comes from a square of the same name. On the gable is a lion carrying the blazoned coat of arms of Montferrand.

▶ Turn right twice onto rue Jules-Guesde.

DISCOVERING CLERMONT-FERRAND AND MONTS DÔME

Hôtel de Fontfreyde
At No. 28.
In the courtyard of this 16th century mansion is a Madonna and Child on the Gothic doorway into the staircase turret. The balustrade on the gallery bears three fine Italianate medallions depicting Lucretia stabbing herself, torn between her husband and her seducer.

Hôtel Gaschier
At No. 20.
Three rows of galleries, one above the other, open onto the courtyard (15C–16C). The first floor is supported by superb pillars.

Hôtel de Lignat★
At No. 18.
The Lawyer's House dates from the 16C. Gracious mullioned windows open onto the street. An elegant door decorated with a garland of roses in the Italian Renaissance style leads to Grande-Rue-du-Languedoc.

Hôtel de Fontenilhes★
At No. 13.
The house, a fine residence dating from the late 16C, was built of lava stone from Volvic.

▶ Start walking along rue Notre-Dame.

Hôtel Mallet-de-Vandègre
At No. 2.
This building, with its austere courtyard, is said to have once been the women's prison.

▶ Cross carrefour des Taules, walk along rue de la Rodade and turn left onto rue du Dr-Balme.

At No. 5 is a Romanesque house with colonnettes and capitals on the front. At No. 11, there is a second **Hôtel d'Albiat** dating from the 16C.

ADDITIONAL SIGHTS

Musée Bargoin★
45 r. Ballainvilliers. ⓞTue–Sat 10am–noon, 1-5pm, Sun, 2–7pm. ⓞ1 Jan, 1 May, 1 Nov, 25 Dec. €5, no charge 1st Sunday in the month. ℘04 43 76 25 50. www.clermontmetropole.eu.
This museum houses a sizeable **prehistoric and Gallo-Roman archaeological collection**★ on the ground and basement floors, comprising artefacts discovered locally, particularly during recent excavations in the city of Clermont itself.
The Gallo-Roman period is the best represented, with a marvellous collection of statuettes of animals, men, women and children in white terracotta, pottery from Lezoux with fine examples dating from the 2C and vestiges of the great temple of Mercury built on the summit of the Puy-de-Dôme at the beginning of the Imperial era.
The **Carpet and Textiles** collection includes over 80 carpets from the Middle and Far East: Turkey, the Caucasus, Iran, Afghanistan, Tibet, China etc.

Hôtel Fonfreyde Centre Photographique
34 r. des Gras. ⓞTue–Sat 2–7pm. ⓞ1 Jan, 1 May, 1 Nov, 25 Dec. For each exhibition, a guided tour is arranged (no charge) on the 1st Sat and 1st Wed of the month at 4pm. ℘04 73 42 31 80.
This Renaissance mansion houses temporary photographic exhibitions and boasts a beautiful exterior staircase by which to reach the upper floors.

Muséum Henri-Lecoq
ⓞOct–Apr Mon–Sat 10am–noon, 2–5pm, Sun 2–5pm; May–Sept Tue–Sat 10am–noon, 2–6pm, Sun 2–6pm. ⓞPublic holidays. €5, no charge 1st Sunday in the month. ℘04 73 42 32 00.
This museum is named after the naturalist Henri Lecoq (1802–71) whose wide-ranging collections of stuffed animals, rocks and regional flora make this a natural history museum very much centred on the Auvergne.

Parks
The attractive **Jardin Lecoq** stretches right through the town centre. Near the lake is a 14C entrance brought over from the Château de Bien-Assis, built for the Duc de Berry and owned, in the 17C, by

CLERMONT-FERRAND

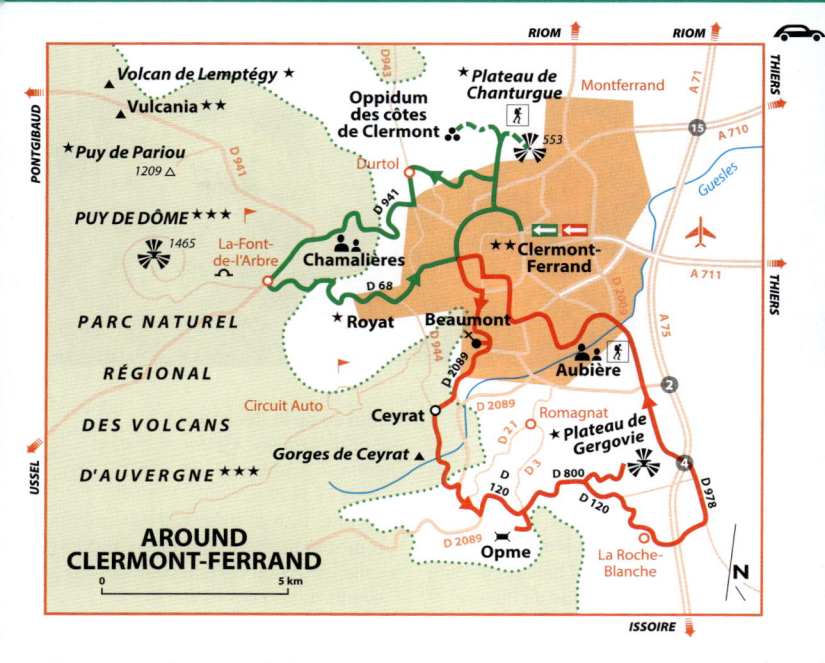

Florin Périer, Blaise Pascal's brother-in-law.

L'Aventure Michelin
32 rue du Clos-Four. Sept–Jun daily except Mon 10am–6pm; Jul–Aug daily 10am–7pm; 2 wks in Jan. €9.50 (children 7–18, €5.50). 04 73 98 60 60. www.laventuremichelin.com.

Tracing the history of the development of the eponymous company, the Michelin museum is a dream visit for any car fan, and is about so much more than the tyres for which it is famed. This is a history of the family, the evolution of transportation, tyres, modern media, marketing and much more, and all under the famed Michelin brand logo.

🚗 DRIVING TOURS

1 VOLCANOES AROUND CLERMONT
35km/21mi. Allow half a day.

Leave Clermont via place des Carmes-Déchaux and head N on boulevard J.-B. Dumas towards Limoges, then take rue de Blanzat on the right.

The road rises along the ravine separating the Côtes de Clermont from the Chanturgue plateau.

1.2km/0.8mi after the intersection with boulevard Charcot, turn right and drive on for 300m until you reach a junction.

A gravel path wends its way up towards the site, running along the edge of the ravine to the left *(1hr return)*.

Plateau de Chanturgue★
The Chanturgue plateau constitutes the remains of a vast volcanic table that erosion has worn down into several sections. In the bases of drystone walls, covered with stubble or concealed by the undergrowth, archaeologists have found the remains of what may have been Caesar's lesser encampment.

L'Oppidum des Côtes de Clermont
Follow the road to the start of a lane on the left, level with a right-hand turn

Village of Beaumont

and walk to the ridge of the Côtes de Clermont plateau (1h return).

History lovers will enjoy these ruins, the vestiges of a former stronghold.

▶ Go back towards Clermont and turn right onto boulevard Charcot, heading for Durtol. Go to avenue du Puy-de-Dôme (D 941A) via avenue de la Paix (D 941), then take côte de la Baraque.

Puy de Dôme★★★
see Monts DÔME.

▶ In La Font-de-l'Arbre, take D 68.

Royat – *see Excursions.*

Chamalières
Lying south-west of Clermont, Chamalières is an important residential and business centre and the headquarters for some of the tourist and spa amenities in Royat.

Église Notre-Dame
Of the five churches that once stood in Chamalières, only one remains. Its nave embraces an early building, dating from before 1000.

Moulin de la Saigne
Beyond the church take rue de la Coifferie and rue du Languedoc.
The swift currents of the River Tiretaine have always favoured the installation of water-wheels: there have been flour mills along the river since the 10C and papermills from the 15C.

Musée de la Résistance
7 pl. de Beaulieu. Mon–Sat 9am–noon, 2–5.30pm. Sun. €3. 04 73 31 28 42.
A collection of over 300 documents, reproductions, photographs and miscellaneous objects that bear witness to events during World War II.

▶ Cross place de Geretsried to no. 3 avenue de Fontmaure, within the Carrefour-Europe residential and shopping complex.

Galerie d'Art Contemporain
Tue–Sun 2–6pm. 04 73 30 97 22. www.amac-chamalieres.com.
Space is fairly limited in this Modern Art Gallery, but the exhibitions are interesting and they attract all the latest names in modern painting and sculpture.

▶ Take avenue de Royat, then rue Blatin to return to the town centre (place de Jaude).

Parc Bargoin – *see Excursions.*

2 THE COUNTRY SOUTH OF CLERMONT
45km/28mi. Allow half a day.

▶ Leave Clermont starting from place de Jaude and take rue Gonod to the S. Then take avenue de la Libération, which leads to N 89.

Église de Beaumont
The former wine-growing village of Beaumont developed around the **Église**

CLERMONT-FERRAND

The Battle of Gergovia

In the year 52 BCE, Caesar was carrying out his seventh military campaign in Gaul; he had just defeated the Gallic army in Bourges and the Gauls had retreated to the mountains of the Massif Central, pursued by six Roman legions. **Vercingétorix**, the leader of the Gallic coalition, had retreated to the Arverni's hillfort in Gergovia, which was defended by a drystone wall. Caesar captured the Roche-Blanche hill and set up a lesser encampment there, linking it to the main camp by a ditch along which he could move his troops. Caesar then ordered his troops to implement a diversionary movement by night, along the Bédat valley that skirted the Arverni's hillfort, to give Vercingétorix the idea that his army might be attacked from the rear.

The next day, three Roman legions moved from the main camp up to the lesser camp and, shortly after midday, launched an attack. Vercingétorix, however, was a good strategist and had concealed troops behind the Puy de la Mouchette who put up fierce resistance against the Romans. Furthermore, the Gauls on the plateau ran quickly back to the scene of the real battle and routed the Roman legions. The Gauls' success was short-lived, however: their chieftain was besieged in Alésia and finally surrendered to Caesar at the end of the summer.

St-Pierre. Founded in the 7C, the church was attached to a Benedictine convent until 1792.

Ceyrat
At the junction with the road to Boisséjour, on the left, you will notice the curious remains of a volcano.

▷ Continue heading S.

Gorges de Ceyrat
These high granite cliffs have been deeply eroded by the river.

▷ Go back to N 89 and turn right. After 250m, turn left onto D 120. Follow signs for Château d'Opme.

Château d'Opme
⊙ Easter–Oct, Sun and public holidays 2.30–6pm (mid-Jul–mid-Sept, daily except Tue, 2–7pm).
⊙ Nov–Easter. ℘ 04 73 87 59 35.
This old fortress (11C) stands high above a mountain pass which was once a Roman road from Clermont to Le Puy-en-Velay. It originally belonged to the counts of Auvergne and was converted into an elegant Renaissance château by Antoine de Ribeyre, Treasurer of France under Louis XIII. The upper terrace is laid out as a formal **French garden**★ around an ornamental basin with a fountain, the entire area shaded by two avenues of lime trees.

▷ Return to the intersection of D 3 and D 120 and turn right.

The road climbs up to the Gergovie plateau, offering pretty views of Clermont, the Puys mountain range and the Monts Dore in the distance.

Plateau de Gergovie★
see Excursions, below.

▷ Drive along D 120 to La Roche-Blanche then head for Clermont along D 978. Drive 2km/1.2mi along N 9 and turn left onto D 777 (avenue R.-Maerte); 1.5km/0.9mi further on, turn right onto D 69 (avenue J.-Noellet) to Aubière.

▷ Continue along D 69, then turn left onto boulevard Louis-Loucheur. A little further on, boulevard C.-Bernard will take you back to place de Jaude.

EXCURSIONS
PLATEAU DE GERGOVIE★
14km/8.6mi S of Clermont-Ferrand.
The Clermont landscape is dominated by this vast plateau, whose vaguely

111

DISCOVERING CLERMONT-FERRAND AND MONTS DÔME

trapezoid shape stands out clearly from the Limagne plain and Allier valley. From here, the view encompasses the entire Limagne de Clermont plain, the horizon enclosed by the Forez and Livradois mountains, and across the Allier valley, beyond which lie the Puys de la Comté.

Musée Archéologique de la Bataille de Gergovie★★

Wed–Sun 11am–6pm; Christmas and New Years Day, early Jan–end Feb. €8 (children 6–25, €5). 04 73 60 16 93. www.musee-gergovie.fr.

After several years of renovation, in 2019, a museum opened devoted to the historic last victory of Vercingétorix against Julius Caesar combines audiovisual, ethnographic, and interactive exhibits of Gérgovie through the ages, complete with a beautiful view over the plateau from enormous bay windows.

Château de la Batisse★

12km/7.5mi. Allow 2h. Leave the plateau de Gergovie and head for Opme, then drive towards Chanonat. At the entrance to the village, turn right for La Batisse. This **château** (*guided visits: Apr–Jun and mid-Sept–Oct by reservation; Jul–Aug Mon and Sun 3pm, 4.45pm, Tue–Fri 10.30am, 1/30pm, 3pm, 4.45pm. €8.50. 06 24 54 52 23. www.chateaudelabatisse.com*) built of pale stone exudes an atmosphere of tranquillity and gracious living which forms a stark contrast to the feudal fortresses of Auvergne. It is flanked by a pepper-pot tower and two corner towers crowned with red-tiled domes and lantern turrets, all that remain of the original 15C castle.

▶ Return to Chanonat and turn right onto D 3 for Le Crest.

Le Crest

This wine-growers' village at the very tip of the Serre mountain range has a 13C church. There is a fine **view★** from the old tower over the Gergovie and Limagne plateaux around Clermont.

▶ Go back down towards D 213 and A75, pass beneath them, and then take the small narrow road that climbs up around the Butte de Monton.

Monton

This village has its houses spread out over the southern slopes of a mound. Not far from Monton are a series of **troglodyte caves**, affording views of the surrounding countryside.

▶ Go back to Gergovie via La Roche-Blanche.

ROYAT

1km W of Clermont-Ferrand.
1 av. Auguste-Rouzaud, 63130 Royat.
04 73 29 74 70.

Royat is a large, elegant thermal spa terraced on the slopes of the Tiretaine valley. The Tiretaine flows from the granite plateau at the base of the Dômes mountain range; until it leaves Royat, it is a torrent. The bottom of its bed was filled with lava from the Petit Puy de Dôme, the waters then cut gorges in it.

The **waters** of Royat were exploited by the Romans, who built public baths here. Although the baths met with mixed success until the mid-19C, they have enjoyed popularity and fame ever since. A hydropathic establishment was built and the visit here by Empress Eugénie in 1862 launched Royat as a spa.

Parc Thermal

This spa garden, completed by the new English-style park through which flows the Tiretaine, contains the hydropathic establishment and the casino. The remains of the **Gallo-Roman public baths**, can be seen. One of the pools had mosaic-covered arches and marble-covered walls. Terracotta pipes brought the water into the pool in small, semicircular cascades.

▶ At the end of the park.

Grotte des Laveuses

The "Washerwomen's Cave" is on the banks of the Tiretaine. Several springs gush from the volcanic walls before flowing into the Tiretaine.

CLERMONT-FERRAND

Église St-Léger★
Built in the 11C, this fortified building deviates significantly from the churches of the Auvergne, it more resembles the churches of Provence. The bell tower is 19C.

Parc Bargoin
From Église St-Léger, follow avenue Jean-Jaurès then avenue A-France.
This is a well laid out park on hilly land, and a botanical garden. It is home to the largest maple in France (250 years old).

Walks
A map of the area on place Allard indicates a number of signposted trails for walkers leaving from Royat, including the **Bois de Villars**, **Puy de Montaudoux**, **Arboretum de Royat** and **Bois de la Pauze**, **Puy de Charade** and **Vallée de la Tiretaine**, and **Chemin des Crêtes**.

ADDRESSES

STAY

Hôtel Lune Étoile La Pardieu – *89 bd Gustave-Flaubert. ℘04 73 98 68 68. www.hotel-lune-etoile.com. 45 rooms.* Close to La Pardieu, and cubic in design; modern and functional.

Dav'Hôtel Jaude – *10 r. des Minimes. ℘04 73 93 31 49. www.davhotel.fr. 28 rooms.* This modern hotel within walking distance of the cathedral is located in a tranquil side street a few steps from the old quarter.

Hôtel Albert-Élisabeth – *37 av. Albert et Élisabeth. ℘04 73 92 47 41. www.hotel-albertelisabeth.com. 38 rooms.* A small hotel near the station.

Hôtel Radio – *43 av. P. et M. Curie. 63400 Chamalières. ℘04 73 30 87 83. www.hotel-radio.fr. Closed Jan and early Nov. 26 rooms. Restaurant – Closed Sat lunch, all day Sun, and Mon lunch).* Drawing its inspiration from the very beginnings of the radio era, this hotel has a 1930s decoration scheme.

Ibis Styles Clermont-Ferrand Gare – *53 av. de l'Union-Soviétique. ℘04 73 91 82 27. www.hotel-le-lafayette.com. Closed 24 Dec–4 Jan. 48 rooms.* Modern, comfortable hotel right at the station. Good value. hotel next to the station.

Holiday Inn – *59 bd F.-Mitterrand. ℘04 73 17 48 48. www.ihg.com. 94 rooms. Restaurant.* Modern hotel close by the botanic garden, with easy access to the town centre.

Mercure – *1 Avenue Julien. ℘04 63 66 21 00. www.mercure-clermint-ferrand-centre.com. 125 rooms.* Central chain hotel with good transport links; panoramic bar and fitness centre.

Royal St-Mart – *6 avenue de la Gare 63400 Royat ℘04 73 35 80 01. www.hotel-auvergne.com. 54 rooms. Restaurant.* 19th century hotel in the heart of Royat surrounded by lush gardens.

EAT

Le Chardonnay – *1 pl. Philippe-Marcombes. ℘04 73 26 79 95. www.lechardonnay.fr. Closed Sat lunch and Sun.* The generous bistro style and the easy-going ambience make for a very enjoyable meal.

Le Saint-Eutrope – *4 rue Saint-Eutrope. ℘04 73 34 30 41. www.sainteutrope.com. Closed Sat –Mon, Tue–Wed lunch.* The contemporary menu of modern French food and natural wine makes this a hip spot with great vibes.

Le Charolais – *77 r. Pré-la-Reine. ℘04 73 91 65 35. www.lecharolais.fr. Closed weekends and weekday evenings.* A favourite with meat-lovers; generous dishes at reasonable prices.

L'Odevie – *1 r. Eugène-Gilbert. ℘04 73 93 90 00. www.restaurantodevie.com. Closed Sun.* A few steps from the Place de Jaude; serves brasserie-style cuisine.

Le Comptoir des Saveurs – *5 r. Ste-Claire. ℘04 73 37 10 31. www.le-comptoir-des-saveurs.fr. Closed Tue–Wed evenings, all day Sun–Mon.* A kind of pick "n" mix approach to dining, chosing whatever takes your fancy.

Restaurant l'Ostal – *16 rue Claussmann, 63000 Clermont-Ferrand. ℘04 73 27 77 86. www.lostal-restaurant.fr. Closed Sat lunch, and all day Sun–Mon.* A gastronomic restaurant in the centre of Clermont. Modern setting, and relaxing if volcanic-influenced atmosphere.

Bath's Restaurant – *pl. Marché St-Pierre, 63000 Clermont-Ferrand. ℘04 73 31 23 22. Closed Sun, Mon and public*

DISCOVERING CLERMONT-FERRAND AND MONTS DÔME

holidays. Opulent dining brightened by contemporary art; good selection of wines by the glass.

TAKING A BREAK

Garden ici Café – *48 pl. de Jaude.* ☏*04 73 17 03 04. Daily 7.30am–1.30am.* Natives in the know frequent this large, chic and cosy café (formerly Le Suffren).

Les Goûters de Justine – *11 bis r. Pascal.* ☏*04 73 92 26 53. Mon–Fri noon–7pm, Sat 2.30–7pm.* This unique tea room reminds you of a charmingly chaotic antique shop.

The Salvation Jane Pub – *14 rue Terrasse.* ☏*04 73 25 39 50. www.pub-restaurant-clermontferrand.fr. Tue–Wed 6pm–1am; Thu–Fri 6pm–2am; Sat 5pm–2am.* A great hang-out for beer lovers. The kitchen is open Tue–Sat from 7–10.30pm; everything is home-cooked (Fait Maison), and uses the best local produce. If you like quizzes, come along on Thu when you'll find one in English (and French).

ON THE TOWN

Bars, brasseries, cinemas, *crêperies*, pubs, restaurants and tea rooms are where you'll find most of the lively goings-on in neighbourhoods downtown. Many of these are concentrated around the place de Jaude, near the cathedral at place de la Victoire, and at place Sugny, rue Fontgiève and place Gaillard.

International Jazz Festival – held in October, Jazz en Tête is a well established event for jazz enthusiasts. ☏*09 82 47 01 97; www.jazzentete.com.*

THEATRE AND ENTERTAINMENT

Contemporary concerts are held in the Coopérative de Mai www.lacoope.org

Classical music is generally performed in the Maison des Congrès.

Plays are staged at the Opéra Municipal or at the Maison des Congrès. La Maison du Tourisme houses a Massif Central wing and a Romanesque Art exhibit.

Le Zénith – *Plaine de la Sarliève 63800 Cournon d'Auvergne. Reservations on-line at www.fnac.com, or contact the Tourist office in Clermont.* The hall seats 8 500, and features pop stars and big entertainment spectaculars.

SHOPPING

Marché couvert-espace St-Pierre – *Pl. St-Pierre.* ☏*04 73 31 27 88. Mon-Sat 7am-7.30pm.* This covered food market features a few stands selling regional products… and chocolate!

Fromagerie Nivesse – *23 Pl. St-Pierre.* ☏*04 73 31 07 00. Tue-Fri 9am-7pm, Sat 0am-7:30pm.* This cheese shop just outside of the Marché Saint-Pierre is a great place to try some of Auvergne's famous cheeses, including the five it produces that bear the AOP.

Volvic

Volvic is built on the edge of the solidified lava flow from the Nugère volcano. The village is not only famous for the extremely pure water of its spring, filtered through thick layers of volcanic rock and now exported throughout the world, but also for the quarrying and processing of its lava.

A BIT OF HISTORY

Volvic lava – Andesite, extracted from open quarries, is both solid and light; this pale grey rock has been used as building stone since the 13C, and the fact that many buildings in the Auvergne

- ▶ **Population:** 4 573.
- **Michelin Map:** 326: F-7 – 14km/8.7mi N of Clermont-Ferand.
- **Info:** Pl. de l'Eglise, 63530 Volvic. ☏*04 4 73 33 28 31. www.terravolcana.com.*
- **Location:** Volvic is 14km/9mi N of Clermont Ferrand and 10km/6mi from Riom; it is reached using the D 986.
- **Timing:** Allow 2 hours.

VOLVIC

are black is due to atmospheric pollution and not to the stone's original colour. Volvic cemetery is full of extraordinary monuments cut from this stone.

The hardness of the lava and the fact that it can be enamelled at high temperatures have made it popular, for more than a century, for signs and plaques that have to stand up to the weather: clock faces, street signs, level gauges etc. As a result of its exceptional qualities, this rock was chosen by Michelin's road sign department to make enamelled lava corner-posts, signposts, wall plaques etc from 1920 to 1970. Andesite is also used to make apparatus used in the chemical industry because of its excellent resistance to acids.

SIGHTS
Church

This was part of the old priory of Mozac; its nave and façade were rebuilt during the 19C. The vast 12C chancel is surrounded by an ambulatory opening onto three radiating chapels; a beautiful wrought-iron grille, from the Romanesque period, closes the axial chapel. There are interesting historiated capitals. At the entrance to the chancel, on the left, note the 14C Virgin with a Bird.

Musée Municipal Marcel-Sahut

2 r. des Écoles. ⓞmid-May–Jun and Sept–early Nov Wed–Fri 2–6pm, Sat–Sun 10am–12.30pm, 2–6pm; Jul–Aug Wed–Sun 10am–noon, 2–6pm. ♿. ⓔ€3. ☏04 73 33 57 33.

The museum displays many works by Sahut, a native of this region, including charcoals, watercolours and paintings (View of Nantes, The Tumbler).

Grotte de la Pierre de Volvic

2 rte du Pont-Jany. ⓞearly Feb–Mar Tue–Thu 11am–1pm, 2–5pm; Apr–June daily 11am–6pm; Jul–Aug 10am–7pm; Sept daily 11am–1pm, 2–6pm; Oct daily except Sat 2–6pm. ⓞNov–early Feb. ⓔ€7.80; Chiildren 5–12 €6.30. ☏04 73 33 56 92. www.grotte-pierre-volvic.fr.

A former underground quarry has been used to create this centre focusing on lava and lava quarrying. Over the course of an hour-long visit, guests travel to the heart of a **lava flow★** from the Puy de la Nugère, while a soundtrack reproduces the noises heard during different phases of an eruption.

Volvic Springs

ⓞApr–Jun and Sept Mon–Fri 10am–12.15pm, 2–6pm, Sat–Sun and public holidays 2.30–6pm; Jul–Aug Mon–Fri 10am–6.45pm, Sat–Sun and public holidays 2–6.30pm; Oct Mon–Fri 2–6pm. ⓞNov–Mar, 1 May. ⓔNo charge. ☏04 73 64 51 24. www.volvic.fr.

In the **Information Centre**, discover a presentation of the hydrological characteristics of the Volvic area and of the bottling of its mineral water; there are also audiovisual shows about the Auvergne and its volcanoes. A network of footpaths provides visitors with walking opportunities (15min to 1h45).

🚗 DRIVING TOUR

MONTS DÔME
25km/15.5mi. Allow half a day.

▶ Leave Volvic N on D 15 towards Châtel-Guyon; left before the cemetery.

Château de Tournoël★

🌿 Guided tours only: Jul–Aug 10.30am–12.30pm, 2–6pm. ⓔ€9. ☏04 73 33 53 06. www.tournoel.com.

Tournoël Castle, on the crest of a rocky spur overlooking the whole of the Limagne, was owned by the counts of Auvergne, captured and almost entirely destroyed it in 1213. In the 14C, however, it was rebuilt by Hugues de la Roche, who widened the bases of the towers.

▶ Rejoin D 15; continue towards Enval.

Châtel-Guyon ✠
ⓘsee CHÂTELGUYON.

▶ Leave Châtel-Guyon SW on D 227.

Mozac★★ – ⓘsee RIOM.

DISCOVERING CLERMONT-FERRAND AND MONTS DÔME

Château de Tournoël

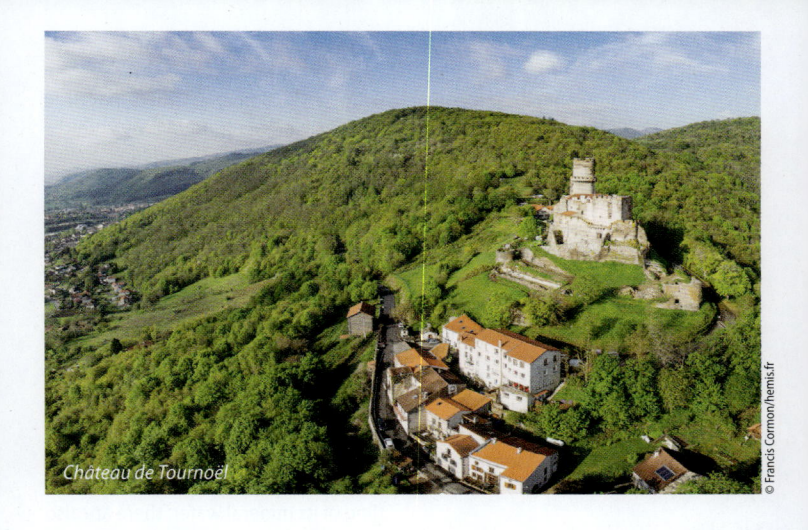

Riom★★ – see RIOM.

▶ Leave Riom to the SW on D 83.

Église de Marsat
Built in the 11C and 12C, the church consists of two heavily restored naves. It is known for its 12C Black Madonna.

▶ Leave Marsat on D 446, heading for Riom. It joins up with N 9 at the entrance to the town. Drive for 3km/1.9mi towards Clermont-Ferrand, then turn right onto D 402.

Châteaugay
The town is overlooked by the squat outline of its castle. Châteaugay was built in the 14C by Pierre de Giac, Chancellor of France, and its history is a tragic one. It was in the keep that the grandson of the Chancellor poisoned his wife, Jeanne de Giac, who had won over the heart of John the Fearless, Duke of Burgundy, before becoming one of his murderers' accomplices.

Keep★
For details, apply to the town hall.
The square keep built in lava stone is the most interesting part of the castle; it is almost the only one in the Auvergne to have remained intact. Richelieu did not include it in his demolition orders, and during the French Revolution, Couthon, a member of the National Convention, was unable to raze it to the ground.

ADDRESSES

STAY

Volvic Organic Resort – *rue du Pont Jany, 63530 Volvic.* ☎*04 22 96 20 99. www.volvic-organic.fr. 8 eco-lodges* Soak up the beautiful scenery at this charming ecotourism complex, where families, groups, and solo travelers are invited to partake in a wide variety of outdoor activities.

Hotel-Restaurant La Rose des Vents – *Luzet, 63530 Volvic.* ☎*04 73 33 50 70. www.hotel-volvic.com* This three-star hotel with swimming pool offers a panoramic view over the Puy de Dôme and the Limagne Plaine.

EAT

Le Commerce – *2 place de l'Eglise 63530 Volvic.* ☎*04 73 33 50 70. www.hotelducommerce-volvic.com. Tue-Sun lunch, Fri-Sat dinner, on reservation other nights.* This historic restaurant offers a revisited approach to classic regional dishes with local ingredients.

Monts Dôme ★★★

The range of volcanic cones known as the *Chaîne des Puys* or Dôme mountain range rises to the west of Clermont-Ferrand and stands high above the Limagne plain. Some 80 extinct volcanoes stretch in a line over a distance of 40km/25mi *(see INTRODUCTION: Volcanoes of the Auvergne).* **From the summit of the Puy de Dôme, the highest of the "cones" with an altitude of 1 465m, the view extends right across the range, providing a panorama of this extraordinary and magnificent landscape.**

- **Michelin Map:** 326: D-8 to E-9.
- **Location:** The most breathaking way of getting an idea of the landscape is to take the Apr–Sept shuttle service from Clermont-Ferrand railway station to the Puy de Dôme, or you can simply take the Panoramique des Dômes rack railway (*see below*).
- **Kids:** Vulcania theme park.

A BIT OF GEOLOGY

The Dôme mountain range has the youngest volcanoes in the Auvergne, which came into being in the Quaternary Era. The earliest human settlers may have witnessed their eruptions. The cones, which rise up from the plain in a long string, stand on a plateau of crystalline rocks 900–1 000m high. Most of the volcanoes rise by only 200–300m above this plateau, with the exception of the Puy de Dôme which rises to 500m above it.

These extinct volcanoes are not all the same shape. Several, such as the Puy de Dôme, are shaped like bells or domes; others contain a single or double crater, whereas a few have a breached crater. Areas of forest grew naturally, but much of it has been planted since the Count of Montlosier set the first example in the early 19C, showing that forests could be grown on land thought of as barren – he was initially taken for a fool. Long black lava flows known as *cheires* form heaps of rocks dotted with juniper and pines; they are scattered all across the plateau. One of these flows, created by the Puy de Lassolas and the Puy de la Vache, closed off the Veyre valley and created **Lac d'Aydat**.

PANORAMIQUE DES DÔMES

This rack railway is the easiest way of reaching the summit. Trains leave every 40 minutes (*9am–7pm*) during the season, every 20 minutes in summer, and every hour otherwise. The 15-minute trip provides 360°views of the volcanoes via panoramic windows on all sides. €12.40–€15.10 (return) in season, discounts in low and for children.
www.panoramiquedesdomes.fr.

VOLCANO WALK

1 LE PUY DE DÔME★★★

11km/7mi from Royat (see CLERMONT-FERRAND).

The ascent of the Puy de Dôme and the extraordinary panorama visible from the summit are quite unforgettable and best seen at sunset.

The Toll Road

In 1926, this road replaced the tracks used by the miniature steam train which had operated for about 20 years. The road, which is well designed, has a constant slope of 12 percent for about 4km/2.5mi. As it spirals around the Dôme, it offers a wonderful variety of views, becoming more extensive higher up. The first ascent on bicycle took place in 1891 in 28min; in 1913 a high-pow-

DISCOVERING CLERMONT-FERRAND AND MONTS DÔME

Puy de Dôme

Le Puy de Dôme★★★

This former volcano is the oldest, highest and most famous of the Dôme mountain range, of which it is the centre. It was only in 1751 that the volcanic origin of these mountains was recognised; until then, it was believed that they were part of gigantic fortifications built by the Romans.

Sacred Mountain – From the earliest times, the solitude of this Puy, which is so difficult to get to, has been awe-inspiring. The Gauls made it a sanctuary for their god Lug. The Romans replaced it with the cult of "Mercury of the Dome". They built a magnificent temple to him, the foundations of which were discovered in 1872 during construction of the first observatory. This temple and all of its treasures were destroyed by the Barbarian invasions.

According to popular superstition, the sorcerers of the Auvergne meet on the deserted mountaintop for blood-curdling midnight revels.

The weight of air – It was on the Puy de Dôme that **Blaise Pascal** carried out an experiment in 1648 that proved a theory about the weight of air. It had already been noted that mercury rises to about 76cm/30in in a tube in which a vacuum has been created. To explain this phenomenon, it was said that "nature hates vacuums". This axiom however did not satisfy Evangelista Torricelli; he put forward the hypothesis that it is the weight of the air that pushes the mercury up. Captivated by this idea, Pascal thought that, if this were the case, the weight of the air should be less at the top of a mountain. As Pascal was in Paris, he asked his brother-in-law to help. The latter chose a fine day, left a mercury barometer in Clermont and went with the Minimes Fathers to the top of the Puy de Dôme. He was overjoyed to see that the mercury rose 8.4cm/3.40in less than it did in Clermont. The theory was proven.

Puy-de-Dôme rather than Mont-Dore – In 1790, following the Revolution, administrative *départements* replaced the former provinces in France. There was talk of giving the name Mont-d'Or (Golden Mountain) – as Mont-Dore was then spelt – to the Lower Auvergne constituency, but the deputy for Clermont, Gaultier de Beauzat, was alarmed that such a wealthy sounding name would give the wrong impression to outsiders. He asked for the less compromising name of Puy-de-Dôme, and it was accepted.

MONTS DÔME

The Michelin Grand Prix

In 1908, when Henri Farman was making the first circular flight (1km/0.6mi) in the world, the Michelin brothers offered a Grand Prix of 100,000 francs to any aviator who could fly from Paris, with a 75kg passenger on board, to the top of the Puy de Dôme in less than 6 hours, skirting the cathedral of Clermont by 1 500m on their right.

Only three years later, on 7 March 1911, despite predictions that this feat could not possibly be achieved within less than a half a century, the aviator **Eugène Renaux**, with his passenger Senouque, successfully met the prescribed conditions in just 5hrs 11min.

---

ered car reached the summit for the first time, in just 11min.

Today, it is no longer possible to drive the toll road. From April to September, a shuttle operates from the centre of Clermont-Ferrand to the train station. For timetables, visit www.t2c.fr.

Ascent on Foot via the Chemin des Muletiers
Allow 45min for the ascent.

Park at the Ceyssat Pass in a forest of fir trees. It was up this winding path (35–40 percent slopes) that chariots pulled by five to eight tandem-driven horses transported materials needed to build the Roman temple and subsequently, in the 19C, the observatory.

The Summit
Reception and Information Centre
www.planetepuydedome.com.
This houses a display on volcanoes and exhibitions specifically on the Puy de Dôme and various other local sites.
The summit offers several dining options. At the main train station, a take-away stand offers sandwiches and drinks. At the summit, the 1911 (mid-Mar–Dec; 04 73 87 43 02) is a fine dining restaurant serving refined seasonal food and using local ingredients, and the Bousset is a bar and café with self-service facilities for lunch. A covered picnic area is also available with drink and snack machines.

Panorama★★★
To the north and south, over a distance of about 30km/19mi, can be seen the 100 or so extinct volcanoes forming the Dôme mountain range; a marvellous museum of volcanic shapes unique in France and perhaps in the world.

To the north can be clearly distinguished volcanoes of the same origin as the Puy de Dôme which resemble enormous craterless molehills: Petit Suchet, Clierzou and Sarcouy. The others are all cones of debris topped with craters: Petit Puy de Dôme or Nid de la Poule ("Hen's Nest"), Grand Suchet, Puy de Côme, Pariou and Louchadière.

The view extends over 11 *départements*, one-eighth of the total surface area of France. Visibility varies almost from one minute to the next. The puys may be covered with grass or heath, with fir-groves or hazel copses. The chain itself is uninhabited, as any rain which falls soaks into the volcanic rocks.

It is at sunset that the view is most spectacular. Fiery trails weave through the volcanic cones. The mountain throws its shadow to the east, covering first the Orcines plateau then suddenly reaching Clermont before gradually invading the plain: the extreme tip of its shadow goes right to Thiers.

A self-service restaurant, **La Table d'Epicure** *(10am–5pm),* can be found at the summit.

Temple of Mercury
No access.
This Temple to the God Mercury (now a ruin) was built by the Romans. Origi-

DISCOVERING CLERMONT-FERRAND AND MONTS DÔME

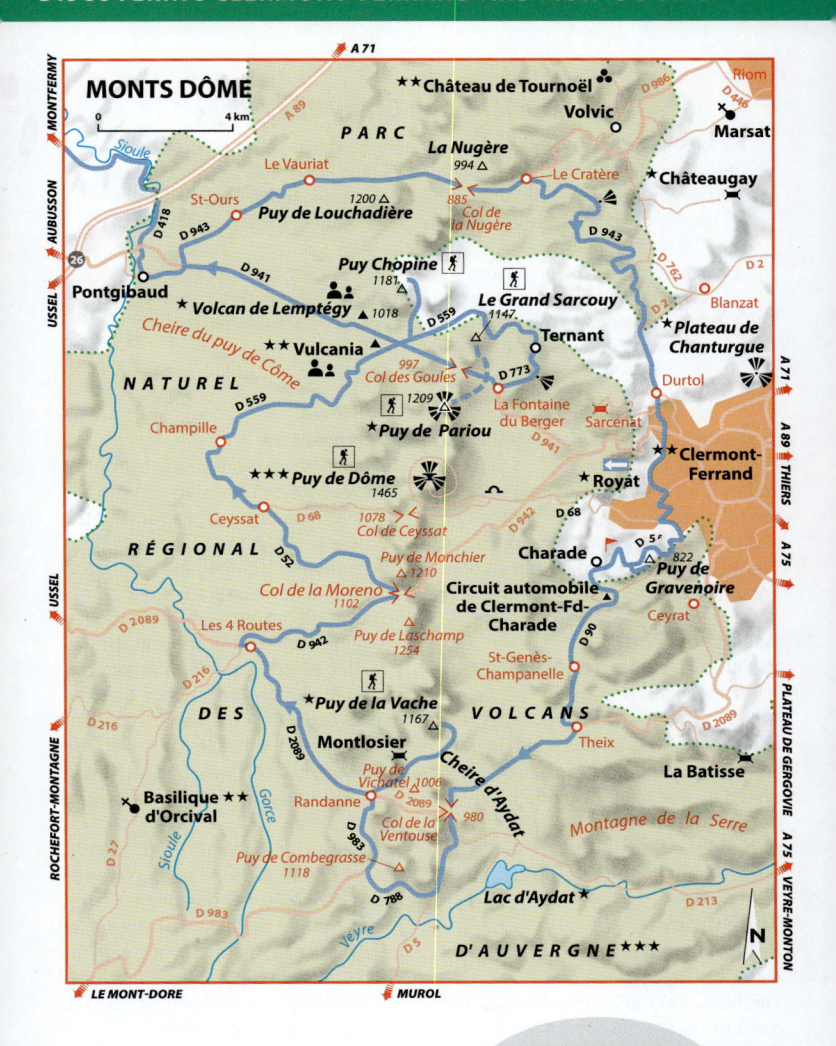

nally it was twice the size of the famous Maison Carrée (1C) in Nîmes; 50 sorts of marble were used to decorate it. The television transmitter stands on the original site of a monumental bronze statue of Mercury by the Greek sculptor Zenodorus. It was, according to Pliny the Elder, one of the marvels of the ancient world.

The path winds around the ruins and passes in front of the monument recalling Renaux's exploit.

DRIVING TOUR

2 PUYS MOUNTAINS★★★
120km/75mi round trip. Allow one day.

Royat★★
see CLERMONT-FERRAND.

▶ Leave Royat on D 941C SE then turn right onto D 5.

The road climbs above the plain until it reaches the granite base from which the volcanic cones rise.

MONTS DÔME

Puy de Gravenoire
There are pozzolana quarries here. This old volcano, now cloaked in pine forests, juts out from above the great Limagne fault. Its lava flowed down through the fault towards Royat and Beaumont, then the cone was formed from the materials thrown up during the eruption: ash, scoria and volcanic bombs.
At the top of the rise is the village of **Charade** at the foot of its own extinct volcano, the **Puy de Charade**.
The road then runs along the southern section of the **Clermont-Ferrand-Charade Racing Circuit**.
Follow the road through Thèdes and St-Genès-Champanelle and, in Theix, take N 89 which crosses the lava flow at Aydat.

Cheire d'Aydat
This is a lava flow 6km/4mi long and 1 200m wide. It was thrown up by the Lassolas and La Vache volcanoes, and cooled to form a heap of blackened scoria. The desolation of this volcanic landscape is softened to some extent by juniper bushes, broom, birch trees and, on the shores of Lake Aydat for which the lava flow forms a dam, a forest of pines and spruces planted in the second half of the 19C.

▶ Just beyond Col de la Ventouse, turn right onto D 5 towards Murol and right again along D 788.
At the junction turn right towards Randanne.

On the way to Randanne the road skirts the Puy de Combegrasse where the first gliding competition to be staged in France was held in 1922.

▶ From Randanne, D 5 leads to the Puy de la Vache.

Puy de la Vache
3km/1.9mi from Randanne (situated along N 89 between Clermont-Ferrand and Le Mont-Dore) on D 5.
🚶 *1h on foot there and back.*
This well-shaped volcano (alt 1 167m) offers, along with its neighbour, Puy de Lassolas, one of the most characteristic views of the Dôme chain.

Montlosier castle
The **Comte de Montlosier,** a returned émigré in the early 19C, wanted to demonstrate that it was possible to make a forest grow in places which had previously been considered barren; the experiment was carried out on his property. Initially considered to be a madman, he eventually gained recognition when the results of his efforts became tangible. His work was taken up and extended by the Forestry Department. The castle now houses the offices of the Parc Naturel Regional des Volcans d'Auvergne and organises exhibitions devoted to the region.
🚶 *The path leading to the breached crater of the Puy de la Vache (1hr on foot there and back) runs to the left off D 5. It follows the Cheire d'Aydat, a mass of solidified lava with a rough surface.*

The Volcano
The crater first spewed ash and slag, which formed the cone, then the lava mounted, filling the crater.
Under such enormous pressure the southern flank of the crater gave way, the volcano opened up and a real torrent of molten material poured out over the plateau, forming the present Cheire d'Aydat, 6km/3.7mi long which, by blocking off the Veyre valley, formed Lac d'Aydat.

▶ Return to Randanne and turn right on N 89.

Near the village of Recoleine, the road crosses a landscape dotted with volcanic rocks just breaking the surface of the ground. At the crossroads of Les Quatre-Routes, D 941A on the right runs up towards the Puys until it reaches Col de la Moreno between the Puy de Laschamp (south) and the Puy de Monchier (north), both of which are covered in forest.
From Col de la Moreno the route runs along D 52 northwards to Ceyssat and Champille, providing interesting views

DISCOVERING CLERMONT-FERRAND AND MONTS DÔME

of the numerous volcanic cones above the road.

The narrow D 559 (right) crosses the lava flow from the Puy de Côme, swathed in beech and conifer, then meets D 941B; turn right towards Col des Goules and La Fontaine du Berger.

This area is the site for the theme park **Vulcania★★**, which is devoted to volcanic activity in Auvergne (see below).

Le Grand Sarcouy

1h30 on foot there and back along a well-marked footpath leading off D 941B just after Col des Goules.

The Grand Sarcouy is still known as a "cauldron" because of its shape. In the south side of this gigantic mass of domite is a vast cavern.

Puy de Pariou★

Take D 941B W of Clermont; beyond Orcines, 500m after the Shepherd's Fountain (Fontaine du Berger), park beside the road. Take a path off to the left (1h30 on foot there and back). Visitors should know that the Puy de Pariou was used for military training. So it is forbidden to cross the firing range and the trenches. Visitors are advised not to pick up any projectile or suspect device lying on the ground.

Puy de Pariou is one of the most beautiful crater volcanoes in the Puys chain.

It consists of two volcanoes, one inside the other. Step over the side wall of the first crater, which produced the still visible lava stretching across the road near Orcines. From here it is possible to climb to the second, far more impressive crater, a regular funnel with a depth of 96m. From the edge of this crater there are views of the Dôme mountain range, in particular, to the west, beyond the Clierzou and the Puy de Côme with its two craters that fit perfectly inside one another; to the north, over the Puy Chopine, the Puy de Chaumont and, behind the Puy des Goules, the Sarcouy; to the south, over the Puy de Dôme.

Ternant

Just before reaching Ternant, when on a level with the great cross in the village, the road (D 773) provides superb views over Clermont and the Limagne plain.

Take the path on the right, 300m before the junction with D 941B.

Puy Chopine

2h on foot return.

In dry weather the path provides access to the volcanic cone's summit.

Carry on along D 559 to the junction with D 941B and turn right towards Pontgibaud.

Volcan de Lemptégy★★

31 route des Puys. mid Feb–early Nov, hours vary according to season; see website. €15.40 (Jul–Aug €15.90; Children 4–12 €612.40; On foot €11.20; Children 4–12 €9) . 04 73 62 23 25. www.auvergne-volcan.com.

This unique **open-topped volcano** is an old quarry hollowed out of a volcanic cone that now provides a unique pedagogic experience for visitors. Go down into the very centre either on foot or by train to see evidence of three successive phases of volcanic activity from 60,000 years ago. The visit ends with a 4D film inviting visitors to discover the birth of the volcano.

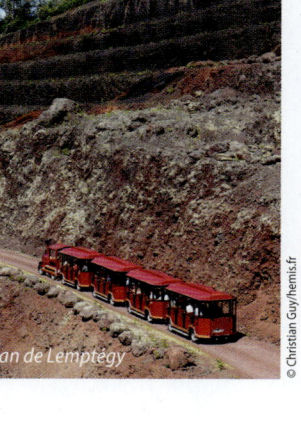

Volcan de Lemptégy
© Christian Guy/hemis.fr

Carry on along D 941B.

MONTS DÔME

Pontgibaud

This large peaceful village on the river was known in Gallo-Roman times for its silver-bearing lead mines. **Château Dauphin** (*guided tours: Easter–Oct Sun and public holidays 2–6pm; Jul-Aug daily except Mon 2–7pm. €6. ✆04 73 88 73 39; www.chateaudauphin.com*) is a lava stone fort which was built in the 12C.

Gorges and Site de Montfermy★

Leave Pontgibaud to the N on D 418 running alongside the Sioule gorges. In Montfermy, leave the car next to the bridge spanning the River Sioule.
Take the path skirting the left bank of the river, leading to a waterfall and the ruins of an old mill.
On leaving Pontgibaud, D 941 begins to climb the west side of the mountain range. Beyond St-Ours and Le Vauriat the road provides stunning views of the **Puy de Louchadière**, one of the main extinct volcanoes in the range, and has a breached crater 150m deep.
Further on, to the left, is the easily recognisable outline of the **Puy de la Nugère**. Beyond Col de La Nugère and Le Cratère the road winds down to the Limagne plain.

👥 PARC EUROPÉEN DU VOLCANISME VULCANIA★★

This gigantic theme park is devoted to the history of Auvergne and more specifically to its geological formation. Designed from plans by the architects **Hans Hollein** and **Philippe Tixier**, the park aims to spread knowledge about volcanoes and other Earth sciences, while contributing towards the protection of natural sites in Auvergne.

VISIT

15km/9.3mi W of Clermont-Ferrand along D 941B. ⓘ *Late Mar–early-Nov from 10am: check website for details. From €24.50.* ✆04 73 19 70 00. www.vulcania.com.
The range of attractions is constantly evolving, as new ideas surface. You might get the chance to witness a motion picture like Ouragan (Hurricane) shown on the big screen, or delve into an exhibit on earthquakes in France and around the world. Following the 2018 nomination of the Puys Volcanies and Limagne Fault as a UNESCO World Heritage Site, the park developed an outdoor exhibit called Large-Scale Nature that displays emblematic natural locations on a large scale. The **Rumbling Gallery**, which re-creates the conditions of an erupting volcano, complete with incandescent projections and formidable sound effects!

ADDRESSES

🛏 STAY

⊜⊜⊜ **Hotel le Pacifique** – *52 avenue de Paris 63200 Riom.* ✆04 73 33 71 00. www.hotel-le-pacifique-riom.com. *16 rooms.* This peaceful three-star establishment is right on the edge of the beautiful city of Riom.

🍴 EAT

⊜ **La Fourniale** – *Allée du Château, Recoleine, 63210 Nebouzat. 3km/1.8mi NW of Randanne via N 89.* ✆04 73 87 16 63. http://lafourniale.com. *Closed Mon–Tue Sept–Jun. Reservations required off-season.* Aficionados of authentic Auvergnat cuisine frequent this inn housed in an ex-sheepfold. The setting is as rustic as can be, with wood tables and a stone trough protruding from the wall.

⊜⊜ **Auberge de la Moreno** – *Col de la Moreno, 63122 St-Genès-Champanelle. At the intersection of D 941 and D 52, on the peak.* ✆04 73 87 16 46. *Closed first 2 wks of Jan and last 2 wks of Nov.* This small inn appeals to diners in search of authenticity, offering satisfying "100% regional" dishes.

DISCOVERING CLERMONT-FERRAND AND MONTS DÔME

Lac d'Aydat★

This lake, situated at an altitude of 825m, is a perfect example of a volcanic reservoir; its waters were retained by the Aydat lava flow (*see INTRODUCTION: Volcanoes of the Auvergne*). **The largest natural lake in Auvergne, it has been listed as a UNESCO World Heritage Site since 2018 thanks to its status as a tectonic hotspot. It is a tranquil destination ideal for boating and angling. Near the north bank is a small island called St-Sidoine in memory of the country house that Sidonius Apollinaris, Bishop of Clermont in the 5C, is said to have had built for himself.**

🚗 DRIVING TOUR

THE LAVA TRAIL
40km/37mi round trip. Allow 2h.

This round tour gives you the opportunity to admire Aydat Lake from several different viewpoints and to discover a variety of landscapes.

Aydat
The church has unusual buttresses in the shape of adjacent turrets.

▶ Leave Aydat on D 90 towards Sauteyras. Turn right towards Rouillas-Bas then left onto D 145. There are numerous views of the Serre mountain range (*see below*).

Nadaillat
A fine example of a village built of black lava stone.

▶ Leave Nadaillat to the E on D 96.

Montagne de la Serre
The long backbone of the Serre juts out like a promontory into the Limagne plain. It is a typical example of "inversion relief." Its unique location allows geologists insight into the order of events in the formation of this area over time.

- **Michelin Map:** 326: E-9.
- **Info:** Sauteyras, 63970 Lac d'Aydat. 04 73 79 37 69. www.tourism.mondarverne.com.
- **Location:** The most scenic approach is by the D 788, from Veyreras to Fohet.
- **Kids:** Swimming, accrobranch, pedaloes.
- **Timing:** Half a day should be enough.

▶ Continue N to St-Amant on D 96.

St-Amant-Tallende

This village and its shops form an attractive sight seen from the medieval bridge. Note the fortified house in the old town.

▶ Continue along D 8.

St-Saturnin★
This village in the Monne valley was the home of the barons of La Tour d'Auvergne who later became the counts of Auvergne. This is the family that produced Catherine de' Medici – daughter of Lorenzo de' Medici and Madeleine de La Tour d'Auvergne – who became Queen of France after marrying Henri II. St-Saturnin attracted a colony of painters and several writers, including novelist and critic **Paul Bourget** (1852-1935). The location of St-Saturnin near the Monts Dômes and the Couzes and Comté valleys, its picturesque streets, its castle and its little square with a charming 16C fountain, make this an attractive tourist destination.

Church★★
The church was built in the 12C and is very simple. Despite the lack of apsidal chapels, the **east end** is nonetheless quite attractive. The radiating transept chapels, the wide ambulatory around the semicircular chancel, and the powerful mass of the transept, which has the best-preserved octagonal bell-

LAC D'AYDAT

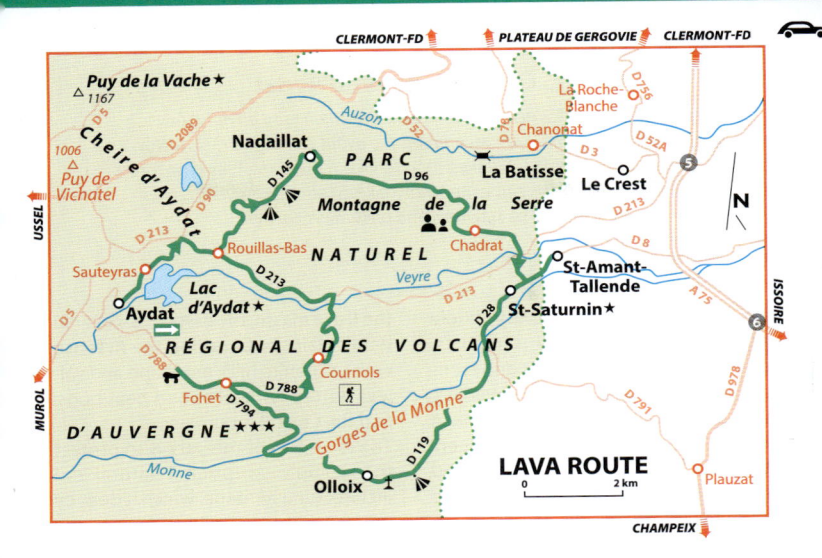

tower in the Auvergne, form a remarkable architectural whole. The external decoration is elaborate, with its strings of billet-moulding, its modillions and its set of arches, some of them remarkable just for the alternate colouring of their basalt and arkose archstones. In contrast to this lavish decoration, the side buttresses and simple end-wall of the west front are striking in their lack of ornamentation.

Inside, note the high barrel-vault of the nave, the galleries above the side aisles with their groined vaulting, the elevation of the transept crossing with its supporting diaphragm arches and the crypt resting on powerful pillars. Next to the church is the small 11C **Ste-Madeleine Chapel** fortified in the 14C.

Château Royal

Guided tours (50min): May–Sept. €7 (children 6–25, €5). . ℘04 73 39 39 64. www.chateaudesaintsaturnin.com.
This imposing fortress, which has undergone extensive restoration, is typical of

Church and the Château Royal, St-Saturnin

© Christian Guy/hemis.fr

125

DISCOVERING CLERMONT-FERRAND AND MONTS DÔME

Camping du lac d'Aydat

63970 Aydat – *2km/1.2mi NE of Aydat, take D 90 then road on right (near the lake). 04 73 79 38 09. www.camping-lac-aydat.com. Apr–early Nov. Reservation recommended. 150 sites; food service.* A pleasant, hilly pine forest is where you will find this campsite by the lake. Shaded sites, children's playground and a variety of activities and pastimes nearby.

the military architecture of the Middle Ages: triple curtain wall, ramparts, towers with machicolations and crenellations. The main part of the building, with a massive, late-15C roof, is flanked by two wings (14C and 15C). The keep, the watch-path (views of the village and its surroundings) and formal gardens are open to visitors.

▶ D 28 and D 119 go through an austere landscape of cropped grass dotted with rocks, but they provide some extensive views before reaching Olloix. Stop near the multilobed cross on the roadside to enjoy the panoramic view.

Olloix

This village consists of a string of old houses stretching out along the road. It was once the seat of a commandery of the Knights of St John of Jerusalem (Order of Malta) and one of its daughter-houses was the Knights Hospitallers' commandery in La Sauvetat. The **church** contains the tomb of Odon of Montaigu. The road down into the Monne gorge (D 794) provides a number of delightful views.

▶ Beyond Fohet, D 788 to the right of the calvary leads back to Aydat.

EXCURSION

Parc Naturel Régional des Volcans d'Auvergne★★★

This park is the largest of all France's regional nature parks; it encompasses 153 localities in the *départements* of Puy-de-Dôme and Cantal and has a resident population of 88 000. Five main natural regions make up the park: the **Dôme** mountain range of volcanic hills *(puys)*; the **Dore** massif, the vast grass-covered basalt plains of **Cézallier**; the **Artense** with its granite hills, moorland and valleys dotted with lakes and peat bogs; and the **Cantal** mountains.

The main aim of the park is to protect the region's exceptional natural and architectural heritage, which it does by running nature reserves and improving sites that have fallen into disrepair. It is also involved in boosting the local rural economy – based largely on agriculture and handicrafts – and developing tourism in the region (information centres, lodging for ramblers, marked footpaths and itineraries, cross-country skiing).

Maisons du Parc

There are eight excellent Maisons du Parc to inform visitors about activities within the park and present the local flora and fauna as well as typical local products: Maison des Fromages, Égliseneuve d'Entraigues; Maison du Buronnier, Belles-Aigues near Laveissière; Maison de la Pierre, Volvic; Maison de l'Eau et de la Pêche, Besse-en-Chandesse; Maison de la Faune, Murat; Maison des Fleurs d'Auvergne, Lac de Guéry; Maison des Tourbières, St-Alyre-ès-Montagne; La Chaumière de Granier, Thiézac.

Fauna and Flora

The region's varied flora includes 2 000 different species, like gentian, Alpine anemone, and bilberry valerian. The mountainous areas are the natural habitat of moufflon, chamois and marmot. Wild boar, roe deer, fox, marten and genet (rarer) live in forests. There are also numerous birds of prey including eagle owl, short-toed eagle, kite and goshawk.

MONTS DORE ARTENSE AND CÉZALLIER

The Dore mountains rank among the country's oldest winter sports resorts, forming a magnificent landscape dominated by the Puy de Sancy. This is a magical area, winter or summer. When the snows have gone, the region is a delight to explore at a leisurely pace, bright of face, loud with birdsong and endlessly enticing. Like much else hereabouts, the Dore and Cézallier ranges have volcanic origins, and this makes for exciting, convoluted scenery where the valleys are as distinctive as the peaks. Bounded by the Dordogne, and abutting the volcanic masses of the Dore, the Artense is a granite plateau once covered by huge glaciers that gave the region its unusual appearance.

Made in France

A dearth of good soil meant that in spite of charming woodland copses, little could be commercially produced in the Artense. But as the marshes that predominated were drained, the land became suitable for rearing the distinctive red Salers cattle alongside more familiar black and white Friesians. Together, these breeds produce the milk that goes into the lovely Cantal cheese and the tangy Bleu d'Auvergne.

Washed-rind **Saint-Nectaire cheese** has also been made in the Auvergne since the 17C. It is said to be named after the Marshall of Sennecterre who served it to Louis XIV. It is a pressed cheese made from cow's milk, with Holstein, Mont-béliarde and Salers being the preferred breeds. Saint-Nectaire is one of a select group of cheeses produced in France to have its own AOC status, awarded in 1979; it even has its own website: www.fromage-aoc-st-nectaire.com. It is one of five such cheeses in Auvergne, and producers of this and other AOC/AOP cheeses in Auvergne can be found along the Route des Fromages AOP d'Auvergne, which features 40 stops along 200 kilometres of road, where visitors can meet producers and sample their wares.

The plant gentian grows healthily on the hills slopes of Cantal and the Monts du Cézallier, where, since 1929, locals have been hand-picking roots to produce Gentiane Avèze as a way of supplementing their income. The drink is slightly bitter, quite strong and an acquired taste to be consumed in moderation. Elsewhere, verbena is used along with over 30 other plants to make the soothing but still distinctive Verveine du Velay.

Highlights

1. Learning how **Saint-Nectaire** cheese is made and matured, and sampling some (p130)
2. The panorama from the summit of the **Puy de Sancy** (p134)
3. Exploring the troglodytic houses in **Farges** (p146)
4. Joining a costumed visit of the **Château de Murol** (p131)
5. Driving the windswept volcanic plateaux of the **Monts du Cézallier** (p156)

Volcanoes and Glaciers

The Massif du Sancy and Le Mont-Dore, today at the centre of the Auvergne Volcanoes Natural Park, were fashioned by fire and ice more than 20 million years ago. The range is a spectacular destination for walkers, offering a mixture of gentle slopes, rugged crags and deep gorges. There are three peaks in excess of 1 800m, all with breathtaking views. The massif boasts over 650km/400mi of walking trails at all levels. This huge green area has numerous lakes, peat bogs, gorges and craters and endless peaceful paths.

Romanesque Legacy

The Romanesque period, from the end of the 10C into the 11C, was a time of extensive building throughout the Auvergne, more so than elsewhere in France. The region has over 250 Romanesque buildings, among the highest incidence in Europe. It is a unique heritage of considerable purity and unity.

MONTS DORE ARTENSE AND CÉZALLIER

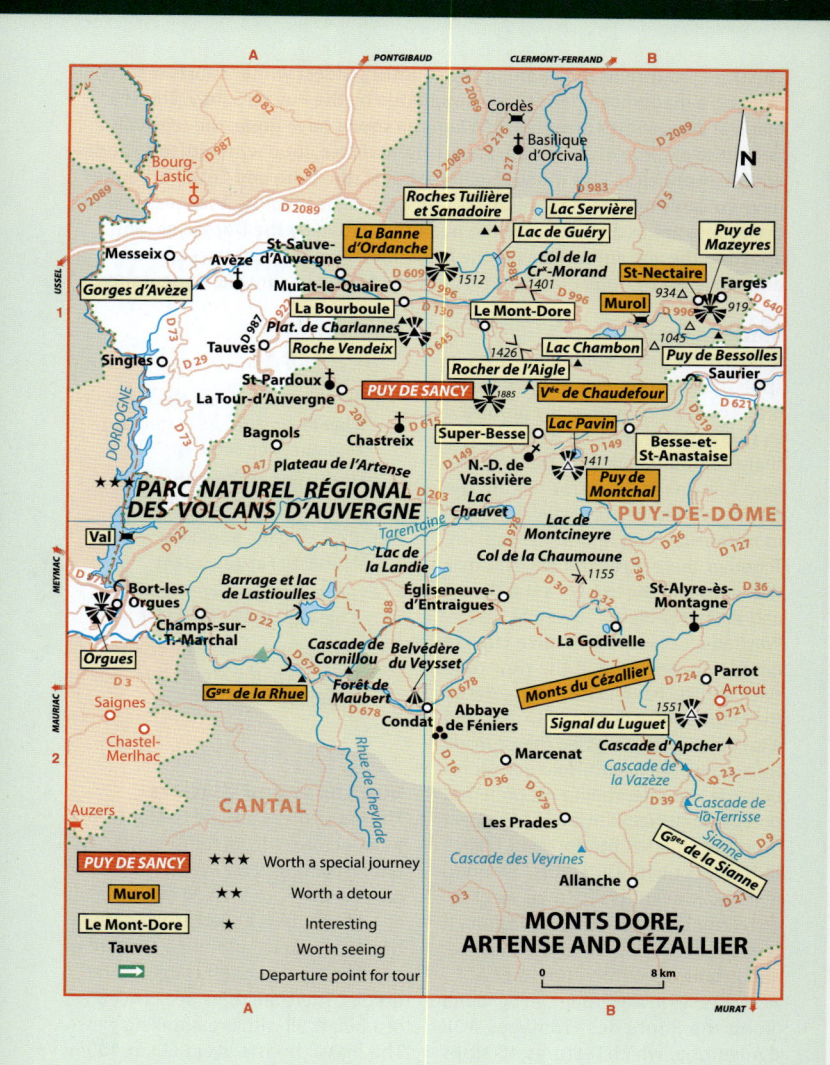

Five churches in particular are recognized locally for their architectural complexity and are thought to be based upon the former Romanesque cathedral of Clermont. These are the sister churches of Notre-Dame d'Orcival, Saint-Austremont d'Issoire, Saint-Saturnin, Notre-Dame du Port, and Saint-Nectaire.

Family Time

While family has always ranked high in importance in French culture, in recent years, holidays have become an even more essential time for extended families to unite. As a result, resorts throughout France, and especially in the Auvergne, with its wide open spaces, cater to family invasions in both winter and summer.

St-Nectaire ★★

Two villages are grouped together under this name: the former thermal spa of St-Nectaire-le-Bas (Lower St-Nectaire), which spreads out over 2km/1mi in a green valley, and the old village of St-Nectaire-le-Haut (Upper St-Nectaire) dominated by its church. In the Middle Ages, a Benedictine priory was established as an offshoot of La Chaise-Dieu Abbey; a castle, no trace of which remains, was also built on the hill. It was inhabited by the glorious St-Nectaire family whose most famous member was **Madeleine de St-Nectaire** – young, beautiful and virtuous, widowed early, always followed by 60 men on horseback. She sided with the Protestants in the Wars of Religion, defeated the king's lieutenant in Upper Auvergne and ended up killing him by her own hand. The name "Saint-Nectaire" is also given to a well-known local cheese, which has been produced for centuries in a well-defined area within the Cantal and Puy-de-Dôme *départements*.

- **Population:** 733.
- **Michelin Map:** 326: E-9 25km/15.5mi W of Issoire.
- **Info:** Les Grands Thermes, 63710 St-Nectaire. 04 73 88 50 86. www.stnectaire.com.
- **Location:** St-Nectaire lies 25km/15.5mi to the west of Issoire, on the D 996.
- **Timing:** A splendid and relaxing area; allow one or two days.

ST-NECTAIRE-LE-HAUT
Église St-Nectaire ★

This church, constructed around 1160, is typical of Romanesque architecture in the Auvergne; it occupies a very beautiful site near the Dore mountain range. It was built in honour of St Nectaire, the companion of St Austremoine. Monks from La Chaise-Dieu were the first priests in charge of it. This church is one of five sister churches in the area thought to be based on the former Romanesque cathedral of Clermont.

Église St-Nectaire

© Francis Cormon/hemis.fr

DISCOVERING MONTS DORE, ARTENSE AND CÉZALLIER

Grottes du Cornadore
mid-Feb–early July 10am–noon, 2–6pm; Jul–Aug 10am–7pm; Sept–early Nov 10am–noon, 2–6pm; Christmas–early Jan 10am–noon, 2–6pm. 6 Jan–8 Feb. Starts at €6.50 (€5 for children). 04 73 88 57 97. www.grottes-du-cornadore.com.

The Romans built public baths in these caves, where today visitors can discover the source of the spa water, its medical uses and petrifying properties. Guided visits leave every hour (and every half-hour in the high season).

Maison du Fromage
Feb–Jun and Sep-Oct 10am–noon, 2–6pm; early Jul and late Aug 9am–noon, 2–7pm; Jul–Aug 9am–7pm; Christmas–early Jan 10am–noon, 2–6pm, . Nov–Christmas, late Jan. €5.90 (discounts in low season and for kids). 04 73 88 57 96. www.maison-du-fromage.com.

A video (in French with English subtitles) explains the origin of farmhouse Saintt-Nectaire cheese, how it is made and matured. There is a demonstration cellar and a sampling at the end of the visit of two kinds of the cheese.

Fontaines Pétrifiantes★
All year from 9.30am, except mid-Nov–mid-Dec; consult website for current variable times. 25 Dec, 1 Jan. €6. 04 73 88 50 80. www.fontaines-petrifiantes.fr.

The water gushes forth at more than 50°C from volcanic faults. Since 1821, seven generations of the same family have developed the technique of petrification, turning it into a real art form. Visitors can discover the techniques by which locals have traditionally made petrified cameos and bas-reliefs, but also discover the more contemporary experimentation of the current generation.

Thermadore
4 avenue du Dr Roux. Tue, Fri, Sat 2:30–7:15pm; Wed 2:30–5:30pm; Sun 9:30am-12:30pm, 2:30–7:15pm. Open late Thur and all day Sun during school holidays. 25 Dec, 1 Jan, 1 May; Nov 18–Dec 1. €10.50; €7 for children. 04 73 78 83 47. www.thermadore.fr

Saint-Nectaire was once home to a thermal spa; today, the Thermadore wellness center has taken its place, with hammam, sauna, jacuzzi, heated pools, spa treatments, and activities for kids.

La Ferme Bellonte
3 rue du 10 août 1944. 25 Dec, 1 Jan, 1 May; Nov 18–Dec 1. 04 73 88 52 25.

Every day this working farm welcomes visitors to see how Saint-Nectaire cheese is made at no cost. Milking takes place at 6am and 3:15pm;

Fontaines Pétrifiantes

ST-NECTAIRE

Château de Murol

cheesemaking at 7:30am and 5:30pm. An on-site shop sells Saint-Nectaire and other local products.

WALKING TOURS

Puy de Châteauneuf

30min on foot there and back. Fairly steep climb. Follow the street climbing up from the north-east end of the church, then take a rocky path on the left.

The path leads to the top of the Puy (934m) from where there is an attractive view of the Dore mountain range. The side of the mountain is hollowed out by nine caves which, like the Jonas caves (see BESSE), were probably inhabited in prehistoric times, then used again in the Middle Ages.

Puy d'Éraigne

30min on foot there and back. Follow a rocky and very difficult path branching off to the left from the road to Sapchat, D 150.

From the summit there is a stunning vista of the Dore mountain range.

Cascade de Saillant

2km/1.2mi E of St-Nectaire-le-Bas.
see BESSE-ET-SAINT-ANASTAISE, The Couze valleys.

EXCURSIONS

Château de Murol★

Daily: Feb–Mar and Oct–mid-Nov 10am–6pm; Apr–Jun and Sept 10am–7pm; Jul–Aug 10am–8pm; mid-Nov–Jan 2–5pm (Christmas period 10am–5pm. 8–31 Jan, 14 Jul. €9.6 (child 10–17, €4.80); tariff varies according to type of visit. 04 73 88 82 50. www.murolchateau.com.

It was a descendant of the lords of Murol, Guillaume de Sam, an erudite baron and patron of the arts, who completed the

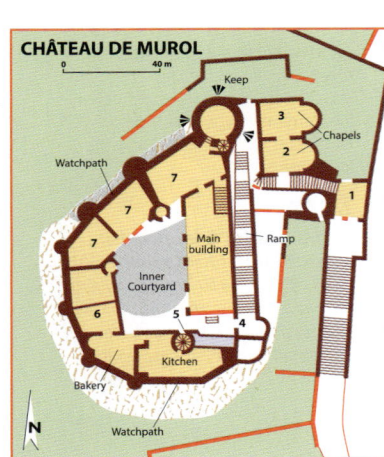

CHÂTEAU DE MUROL

0   40 m

Keep
Chapels
Watchpath
Main building
Ramp
Inner Courtyard
Kitchen
Bakery
Watchpath

131

original, inner fortress by building the keep, the second chapel and the eastern buildings. The castle, after passing into the hands of the powerful D'Estaing family in the 15C, was lavishly ornamented and, at the beginning of the following century, encircled by a huge curtain wall flanked with towers.

Murol emerged victorious from a siege during the time of the Catholic League. Peril having been averted, Jean d'Estaing foresook his vast abode and built the charming pavilion at the foot of the inner castle. Abandoned some time afterwards, Murol was spared by Richelieu because of the D'Estaing family's influence at court. After being used as a prison for some time, it became a robbers' hideout during the Revolution. During the 19C it fell into ruin and the inhabitants of the region came here looking for building stone.

Visitors pass through the outer curtain wall through a fortified gatehouse on the southside, passing the Murol tower on the right.

The Renaissance Pavilion (**1**) stands in the outer courtyard (the windows provide a nice view of the Capitaine tower). To the north is the inner castle (Château Central), its walls rising above a thick basalt base. Next to the keep, connected to a tower of smaller dimensions by a curtain wall, are the chapels. The first (**2**) was built in the 13C; the second (**3**) in the 15C, and though of greater proportions is less graceful. A stepped ramp leads up to an elegant door (**4**) decorated with the Murol and Gaspard d'Estaing coats of arms. In the inner courtyard, note the gallery once surmounted by the Knights' Hall followed by the guard-room.

Take the spiral stairway of the Chautignat tower up to the terrace from which there is a very beautiful **panorama★** of Murol, the Couze valley, Lake Chambon, the Dore mountain range and the Tartaret volcano. The watch-path leads to the Châtelaine tower (note the 16C door, **5**). Next come the kitchen, the bakery and its outbuildings (**6**). The adjacent rooms (**7**) were living quarters.

In the summer season, a great variety of activities and shows are on offer, such as jousting, blacksmith demonstrations, and more.

Beaune-le-Froid
8.2km/5mi via D996 and D145
While Saint-Nectaire lends its name to the famous local cheese, it's actually in nearby Beaune-le-Froid that you'll find many artisanal Saint-Nectaire cheesemakers, thanks in large part to the natural volcanic aging cellars that have existed here for centuries.

ADDRESSES

STAY

Régina – *43 Avenue du docteur Roux 63710 Saint Nectaire. ℘04 73 88 56 06. www.hotel-regina-saint-nectaire. com. Closed Nov-Jan. 17 rooms. Restaurant.* You can't miss the little tower that marks a corner of this hotel built in 1904. Swimming pool.

Villa Saint Hubert – Chambre d'Hôtes – *1 rue de l'Ancienne Poste 63710 Saint-Nectaire. ℘04 73 88 41 30. www.villasthubert.com. 4 rooms.* A villa dating to 1900 in the heart of the picturesque village.

Chambre d'Hôte Le Chastel Montaigu – *63320 Montaigut-le-Blanc. 10km/6mi E of St-Nectaire via D 996. ℘04 73 96 28 49. www.lechastelmontaigu. com. 5 rooms.* You'll sleep in the turret of this fortified medieval castle, in a delightful, beautifully furnished room.

Hôtel Mercure Saint Nectaire Spa et Bien-Etre – *26 avenue du Docteur Roux 63710. ℘04 73 88 57 00. www.hotel-bains-romains.com. 68 rooms.* This hotel has been renovated in a contemporary style and boasts a hammam, spa, and wonderful restaurant with upscale seasonal, local fare.

EAT

Auberge de l'Âne – *Les Arnats. 8km/4.8mi N of St-Nectaire via D 150 and D 643. ℘04 73 88 50 39. www.auberge-de-lane.com. Closed Oct and Mon–Tue except Jul–Aug. Reservations. required.* This country inn has been serving typical Auvergnat fare for 40 years. Plain and simple dining.

Super-Besse skiing area

Massif du Sancy ★★★

The Massif du Sancy, which forms part of the Dore mountain range, consists of a set of extinct volcanoes. It is one of the most attractive and appealing areas in the Auvergne, thanks to the dramatic power of its peaks, the depth of its valleys and the beauty of its waterfalls and its lakes. The highest peak in the range, Puy de Sancy, rises to an altitude of 1 885m and is the highest summit in central France.

- **Michelin Map:** 326: D-9.
- **Info:** Office du Tourisme du Mont-Dore, Av. de la Libération, 63240 Le Mont-Dore. ✆04 73 65 20 21. www.sancy.com.
- **Location:** Just 50km/30mi SW of Clermont Ferrand, within the Parc Naturel Régional Volcans d'Auvergne.
- **Don't Miss:** The Puy de Sancy panorama.
- **Timing:** Allow a full day for a driving tour of the area, and much longer to explore on foot.

A BIT OF HISTORY

Three huge volcanoes – The mighty system of volcanoes, of which the last remains form the Dore mountain range, evolved at the end of the Tertiary era. At its zenith, it covered an area three times larger than that of Vesuvius and consisted of three large cones in juxtaposition (Sancy, Banne d'Ordanche and Aiguiller) whose craters opened at an altitude of almost 2 500m. Today, volcanic lakes cover the landscape, which is also defined by forests of pine, spruce and beech. Lower down the slopes are valleys with meadows and hedgerows.

Rhinoceros in the Auvergne – Between the periods when the volcanoes were active, life returned to the Dore area. Footprints and bones found among the volcanic ash prove that laurel, bamboo and other plants, which are now found only in hotter climes, once grew on the slopes of the volcanoes, while rhinoceros, elephants and sabre-toothed tigers roamed the countryside.

Former glaciers –The great period of glaciation which spread across Europe at the beginning of the Quaternary Era covered the Dore mountain range with an ice cap more than 100m thick.
This considerable mass dug out corries and deep valleys, created the scarp slopes down which the waterfalls cascade, and threw into relief the most resistant sections of mountain, the peaks and enormous rocks that add to the picturesque beauty of the Dore mountain range.

Final throes – Decapitated and dismantled by the glaciers and by the surging meltwaters that accompanied the fusion of the ice flows, the central area of the range looked very much as it does today when the first human settlers arrived. It was then that a new volcanic upthrust occurred along the edges: secondary volcanoes erupted, closing off valleys with their cones and lava flows, gouging out craters and creating a number of lakes.

DRIVING TOURS

1 PUY DE SANCY★★★

Le Mont-Dore
see Le MONT-DORE.
From Le Mont-Dore, drive to the upper part of the winter resort (4km/2.5mi) in order to reach the **cable-car station**. After a 3min ride, allow 20min on foot to the summit.

Panorama★★★
Rising to an altitude of 1 885m, Puy de Sancy in the Dore mountain range is the highest peak in central France.

2 NORTHERN SLOPES ★★★
A round trip of 85km/53mi. It is also possible to start this trip from La BOURBOULE.

Le Mont-Dore
see Le MONT-DORE.

▶ Leave Le Mont-Dore N along D 983; 3km/1.9mi further on, turn right onto D 996.

Col de la Croix-Morand
Alt. 1 404m.
This pass is also known as **Col de Diane**, although the real pass of this name is set away from the road. It used to have a bad reputation, for according to a local saying: "The Col de la Croix-Morand claims one man every year."

▶ Return to D 983 and turn right (beware: in winter, this road is sometimes blocked by snow).

After driving through the forest, then through a valley with hillsides covered with basalt rock falls, the road reaches Lake Guéry (view of the Sancy massif).

Lac de Guéry★
The lake was formed by a basalt flow that closed off the end of the valley. The pastures are studded with black rocks, and the surrounding pine forests create a rather austere environment lightened in the springtime by great expanses of snow.

Centre Montagnard Cap Guéry
Col du Guéry, 63210 Orcival. Jun and Sept Wed–Fri noon–6pm, Sat–Sun 10am–6pm; Jul–Aug daily 10am–6pm; Christmas–Mar Sat–Sun 11am–4.30pm. €5.50– €8.50. 04 73 65 20 09. www.capguery.com.
Located at Col de Guéry, this centre belonging to the Parc Naturel Régional des Volcans d'Auvergne provides an introduction to the local flora. The Sentier nature Terra Alta is a unique, educational and unusual attraction for all ages.

Roches Tuilière et Sanadoire★
From Col de Guéry, there is a fine **view**★★ over the deep, wooded Chausse corrie from which the rocks of Tuilière and Sanadoire stand out.
To the left is **Tuilière rock**★, once the chimney of a ruined volcano. **Sanadoire rock**★ to the right is all that remains of a volcanic cone. Near the junction of

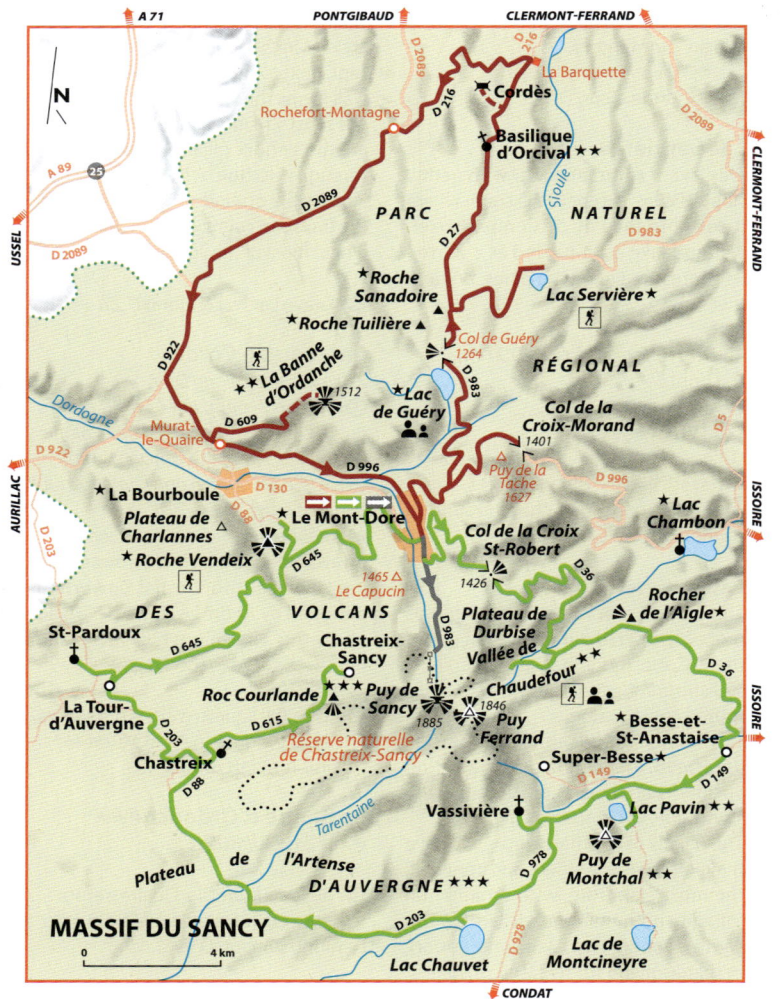

Tuilière and Sanadoire rocks

MASSIF DU SANCY

Orcival with Basilique Notre-Dame
© Gerard LABRIET/Getty Images

D27 and D983, a path off D983 leads to a rocky promontory.

▶ Continue along D 983.

Lac Servière★
This lake is a former crater with gently sloping sides, except to the south where it cuts into the Puy de Combe-Perret. A round lake as unruffled as a mirror, its shores are lined with pines, firs, and meadows.

▶ Turn back and follow D 27 on the right.

Orcival★★
Orcival, a small town in a cool valley watered by the River Sioulet, has a superb Romanesque church founded by monks from La Chaise-Dieu.

Basilique Notre-Dame★★
This grey mass of volcanic andesite was probably erected during the first half of the 12C and, judging by its remarkable stylistic unity, was the result of uninterrupted construction.

The very beautiful, although sparsely decorated, east end has four radiating apsidal chapels; one of these, on the south side, encompasses the crypt.

The panels of the three doors still have their Romanesque hinges and ironwork; the most elaborate, with ornamental foliage and human heads, are on the south door (known as St John's door). In thanksgiving for released prisoners, chains have been hung from the blind arcades in the southern part of the transept, next to the entrance. A high gable wall forms the west façade.

The most striking features of the interior are the slender pillars. Light disperses through the church through an increasing number of windows from the nave to the transept, culminating in the chancel where most of the light is concentrated.

▶ Leave Orcival N along D 27.

Château de Cordès
2.5km/1.5mi N along D 27.
⏱Jun, Sun 2–6pm; Jul–Aug 10am–noon, 2–6pm (👣Guided tours of the chateau at 11am, 2.30pm and 4pm). ≈€4 (€8 for garden and chateau in Jul and Aug only). ☏04 73 21 15 89. www.chateau-cordes-orcival.com.
An avenue lined with hedgerows enclosing two beautiful formal flowerbeds designed by André Le Nôtre (17C) leads up to this charming 13C–15C manor house, restored in the 17C.

▶ In La Baraquette turn left towards Rochefort-Montagne and Murat-le-Quaire. Turn left onto D 609.

La Banne d'Ordanche★★
see La BOURBOULE.

▶ Beyond Murat-le-Quaire, return either to La Bourboule on D 609 or to Le Mont-Dore on D 996.

MASSIF DU SANCY

In addition to the long-distance trails, marked with red and white stripes, and the local paths (Pays Balisé), marked in red and yellow, there are many other interesting footpaths.

3 THE SANCY RANGE★★
85km/53mi. Allow one day.

Some of the roads may be blocked by snow from November to April. The trip can also start from La BOURBOULE.

Le Mont-Dore✝✝
see Le MONT-DORE.

▶ Leave Le Mont-Dore E on D 983 and turn left onto D 36.

Col de la Croix-St-Robert
From the pass there is a superb **panoramic view★★** to the west over the Millevaches plateau, to the east over Lake Chambon, Murol plateau and castle and, in the distance, the mountains in the Forez and Livradois areas.
The road runs down beyond the pass towards Besse-et-Saint-Anastaise across the **Durbise plateau**. Bear in mind that the road is closed between November and April.

▶ Continue along D 36 and leave the car in the parking area at the entrance of the site.

Vallée de Chaudefour★★
This interesting valley was gouged out of the granite and lava by the glaciers of the Quaternary Era, which covered the slopes of the Dore mountain range, and by the River Couze which flowed through the area after the glaciers had melted.
The valley floor and lower slopes boast abundant plant life. Some of the upper slopes and peaks are gashed by ravines, others bristle with rocks which have been laid bare and carved into strange shapes by erosion.
Geology enthusiasts will discover many examples of volcanic rock, and there are numerous good climbs for those interested in mountaineering.

Viewpoint
From a small bridge spanning the Couze, a spring can be seen and there is a picturesque view over the valley floor forming a majestic amphitheatre. When facing Puy Ferrand, with the Roc de la Perdrix to the left and, opposite, the sharp pointed pyramid of the Aiguille standing out against its slopes.
To the right of Puy Ferrand stand some interesting rock formations, the Crête de Coq and the Dent de la Rancune.

▶ Return to the car park and continue along D 36.

Vallée de Chaudefour

© Don Whitebread/iStock

Rocher de l'Aigle★
From "Eagle's Rock" there is a striking view of the Chaudefour valley and the Dore mountain range.

▶ Keep driving along D 36.

Besse-et-St-Anastaise★
see BESSE-ET-ST-ANASTAISE.

▶ Leave Besse SW along D 149.

Lac Pavin★★
see BESSE-ET-ST-ANASTAISE.

▶ Return to D 978 and turn left.

Chapelle de Vassivière
During the summer, this 16C pilgramage chapel, standing in a beautiful rural setting, houses the statue of Our Lady of Vassivière.

▶ Turn round and then turn right onto D 978 towards La Tour-d'Auvergne.

Lac Chauvet
Lake Chauvet was formed by a series of volcanic eruptions that caused soil subsidence.

▶ Return to D 203 and turn left; 12km/7.5mi further on, turn right onto D 88.

Chastreix
The village of Chastreix is 7km from Chastreix-Sancy, known for winter sports. The church in the village is a fine building with a nave but no side aisles.

▶ Leave Chastreix N on D 615.

Roc Courlande
The road leads to the winter sports resort of Chastreix-Sancy then to Courlande rock on the west side of the Puy de Sancy.

▶ Turn back to rejoin D 203 and turn right.

La Tour-d'Auvergne
This is a small town in a delightful, rustic setting crisscrossed by streams forming waterfalls. It lies on a basalt plateau ending in prismatic columnar basalt rock that can be seen near the church. The marketplace laid out on the top of these prisms seems to be made of gigantic cobblestones.

▶ Continue NW along D 203.

Église de St-Pardoux
Interesting Gothic church still boasting 13C strap hinges on its doors and a fine gilt-wood altarpiece.

▶ Return to La Tour-d'Auvergne and drive NE on D 645.

Roche Vendeix★
see La BOURBOULE.

▶ Return either to La Bourboule by continuing along D 88 beyond Vendeix rock, or to Le Mont-Dore by turning right onto D 645.

ADDRESSES

STAY

Central Hôtel – *63113 Picherande. 5km/3mi W of Lac Chauvet via D 203.* ℘04 73 22 30 79. www.picherande-centralhotel.fr. *Restaurant for hotel guests only. 16 rooms.* Set right in the village, this family home built in 1930 has a rather outdated decor, but it is impeccably run. Simple, inexpensive meals. Bathrooms are shared, but at these prices a little inconvenience is to be expected. Family atmosphere.

Chambre d'Hôte Château de Voissieux – *63210 St-Bonnet-près-Orcival. 4km/2.4mi NE of Orcival via D 27 and D 556.* ℘04 73 65 81 02. *3 rooms.* Nestling in a park in the heart of the Auvergne countryside, a B&B in a 13C château built of volcanic stone.

Le Mont-Dore ⛄⛄

Le Mont-Dore stretches out along the banks of the upper reaches of the Dordogne in a magnificent corrie in the shadow of the Puy de Sancy; it is both a seasonal spa town from early April through early November and a remarkably well-equipped winter sports resort.

The ski area *(see below)* covers the north face of the Puy de Sancy and the slopes of Le Capucin. Paths that are waymarked in winter provide an opportunity to discover the unexpected beauty of the volcanic landscape under snow. In summer, the resort offers a wide range of leisure facilities and is an ideal base for ramblers or those touring by car.

THE SPA TOWN

The waters were used by the Gauls in swimming pools, the remains of which have been discovered beneath the Roman baths. The latter were a splendid sight and much larger than the present establishment.

It was not until Louis XIV's reign that the "Mont d'Or", as Mme de Sévigné wrote, regained its clientele – in spite of the fact that there was no road to the resort. The road was not built until the 18C, and the fashion for "taking the waters" emerged in the 19C.

- **Population:** 1 421.
- **Michelin Map:** 326: D-9 – 45km/28mi SW of Clermont-Ferrand.
- **Info:** Av. de la Libération, 63240 Le MONT-DORE ☎ 04 73 65 20 21. www.sancy.com.
- **Location:** Le Mont Dore lies 45km/28mi to the south-west of Clermont-Ferrand.
- **Don't Miss:** A ride in the ancient funicular.
- **Timing:** Half a day is sufficient to look around the spa town.

Établissement Thermal

The pump rooms were built between 1817 and 1823 and later extended and modernised. The most remarkable rooms are the **Hall des Sources**, the **Salle des Gaz Thermaux**, the **Galerie César**★ and the main foyer (**Salle des Pas Perdus**★) the arches of which bear delightful frescoes up to first floor level. Note the low height of the stairs constructed to ease the suffering of those with asthma.

Funiculaire du Capucin

© Hervé Lenain/hemis.fr

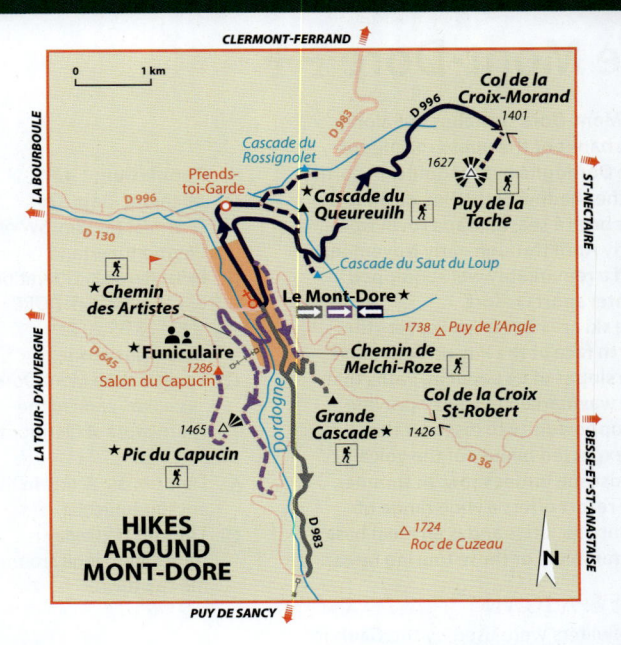

THE RESORT

Le Mont-Dore was one of the earliest winter resorts in France, dating from 1907. Situated south of the town, it takes advantage of the elaborate equipment and activities designed for visitors taking the waters (accommodation, skating rink, entertainment). During the winter season, activities include alpine skiing, monoskiing, snowboarding, cross-country skiing, snowshoeing and climbing frozen waterfalls.

Restaurants take second place to the pursuit of outdoor pleasure in Le Mont-Dore, but there are several places where you can enjoy regional dishes like *truffade* – potatoes with melted cheese – and the distinctive creamy *aligot*, a combination of cheese and potato purée.

Ski Area

Alpine ski runs can be found on the north slopes of the Puy de Sancy, which enjoy good snow cover. In winter, a free shuttle service operates between the town and the slopes. The **ski pass**, which can be bought in Le Mont-Dore, entitles holders to ski on the Super-Besse skiing area (*see BESSE-ET-SAINT-ANASTAISE*).

For **cross-country skiing**, there are marked tracks starting west of Le Mont-Dore (below Le Capucin).

NEAR THE RESORT

Chemin de Melchi-Roze
About 1h on foot.
This flat path overlooking the town is a delightful place for a stroll in the late afternoon or in cool weather.

Chemin des Artistes★
About 1h on foot along the path running down to the tennis courts.
This walk leads through the woods and offers attractive views of the resort. It is also possible to reach this path by taking the funicular to Le Capucin (*see below*).

Funiculaire du Capucin★
May–Jun and Sept Wed–Sun 10am–12.10pm, 2–5.40pm; Jul–Aug daily 10am–12.10pm, 2–6.40pm. €7 (adult return; child 5–11, €5.5) – combined ticket with téléphérique €10.50/€7.50. ☎04 73 65 01 25.
When this elegant 100 year-old funicular was inaugurated in 1898, it was electrically powered, although the resort itself was not yet enjoying the benefits of electricity. The funicular has two beau-

Puy de Sancy

tiful wooden carriages, which shuttle to the Salon du Capucin *(10min by funicular then 8min on foot)*.

Pic du Capucin★
1h walk from Salon du Capucin.
The path runs for some distance through woodland. From the summit of Le Capucin there is a particularly fine view of the Massif du Sancy.

TOWARDS COL DE LA CROIX-MORAND

Waterfalls
3km/2mi NE via Le Queureuilh and Prends-toi-Garde hamlets. About 3h on foot.
The most outstanding of the three cascades (Saut du Loup, Queureuilh and Rossignolet) is the **Queureuilh★** which drops down in a very attractive natural setting.

Puy de la Tache
5km/3mi E. 1h30 on foot there and back.
The road rises in a series of hairpin bends up to **Col de la Croix-Morand** where the landscape becomes increasingly rugged and bare. From here it is possible to walk to the summit of the Puy de la Tache.

TOWARDS PUY DE SANCY

Grande Cascade★
3.5km/2.2mi SE along D 36. About 1h30 on foot. Beware: the access path can be slippery.

At the waterfall's base, a footbridge leads to steps to the Plateau de Durbise.

Puy de Sancy★★★
Sancy station situated 4km/2.5mi along D 983. (see Massif du SANCY).
Rising to an altitude of 1 885m, Puy de Sancy is the highest peak in central France. It is part of an ancient stratovolcano that has now been dormant for over 220 000 years.
The valley to the north is the source of two streams, the *Dore* and the *Dogne*, which later combine to form the *Dordogne*.

Téléphérique du Sancy★
Sep 9am–noon, 1:30–5pm, last descent at 12:15pm and 5:15pm; mid-Oct–early Nov 9am–12:10pm, 1:30–5pm; Dec Sat–Sun 9am–5pm; other openings depending on snow conditions. €10.20 (adult return; child 5–11, €5.7)
This aerial tram was first inaugurated in 1962 and is now one of the most visited sites in the region, used frequently by skiiers in winter and hikers in summer. After a departure from 1 325 meters of altitude, follow a vertiginous journey to the top of the Puy de Sancy. A 20-minute walk from the arrival point, and you'll be rewarded with stunning 360° views over the Massif.

Téléphérique du Sancy, Le Mont-Dore ski area

© Béatrice Mollaret/Photononstop

ADDRESSES

STAY

Chambre d'Hôte La Closerie de Manou – Le Genestoux. *3km/1.8mi W of Mont-Dore via D 996, towards Murat-le-Quaire.* ☏04 73 65 26 81. www.lacloseriedemanou.com. *5 rooms.* Nestling in verdure, this 18C Auvergnat house is enchanting! Its cosy bedrooms are harmoniously and tastefully decorated.

Auberge du Lac de Guéry. *Lac de Guéry 63240 Le Mont-Dore.* ☏04 73 65 02 76. www.auberge-lac-guery.fr. *7 rooms.* This lakeside inn is a charming, friendly place to stay with delicious food and a cozy atmosphere.

EAT

Les Fées Mères – *21-23 rue Jean Moulin 63240 Mont-Dore.* ☏04 73 21 52 33. www.restaurant-lesfeesmeres.com. *Wed–Sat lunch and dinner; Sun lunch. Nov, Dec evenings and weekends.* Market-inspired cuisine featuring local produce.

Mon Clocher – *5 rue Maurice Sauvagnat.* ☏04 73 65 05 41. Mon Clocher is is ideally located in the heart of Mont-Dore's pedestrian and shopping zone between the church, the casino and the spa. The dining room's decor is countrified: old farming implements and shining copper pots.

Le Bougnat – *23 avenue Georges Clemenceau.* ☏04 73 65 28 19. *Closed mid-Nov–mid-Dec. Reservations required.* The furnishings chosen to decorate this old restored buron are faithful to tradition.

RECREATION

Given its altitude and location at the heart of all things mountainous and wintry, there is a strong temptation to look on Le Mont-Dore as just another playground for the ski-bound. But there's real focus on the pursuit of well-being at a more leisurely, less hazardous pace, whether it is a simple self-indulgent spa session or treatment for allergies, asthma, rheumatism and respiratory issues *(Thermes du Mont-Dore, 1 pl. du Panthéon; t04 73 65 05 10)*. A little more demanding, just, is the nine-hole golf course (2 162m) at Le Mont-Dore, with a 10-station driving range. In such a splendid location, it is impossible not to be distracted by the magnificent views of the Puy de Sancy *(Golf-Club du Mont-Dore, Rte de la Tour-d'Auvergne; t04 73 65 00 79; www.golfdumontdore.org; closed Dec–Mar)*. But where Le Mont-Dore scores heavily is in its various opportunities for walking. The town is surrounded by the most exquisite landscapes, across which paths and tracks offer a network of escape routes, and the chance to appreciate the natural beauty of the region in a healthy way.

Besse-et-Saint-Anastaise★

With its medieval and Renaissance houses and fortifications, Besse is a picturesque town worthy of its status as one of France's "Small Cities of Character".
The town is also the setting for a biological research centre specialising in the study of regional flora and fauna, which was set up by the Faculty of Science of Clermont-Ferrand University.

> **Population:** 1 560.
> **Michelin Map:** 326: E-9.
> **Info:** 13 Rue Notre Dame, 63610 Besse-et-Saint-Anastaise. ☏04 73 79 52 84. www.sancy.com.
> **Location:** Besse lies midway between Aurillac and Mauriac, in the south-west of Cantal.
> **Don't Miss:** A tour of the Old Town.
> **Timing:** Allow half a day.

OLD TOWN

Houses with picturesque corbelled turrets line the narrow streets of the old town.

Rue des Boucheries★

This is a quaint street with black houses made of lava stone. Note the 15C shops and **Queen Margot's House** (15C), on the corner with rue Mercière. According to local legend, Marguerite de Valois lived in this house. Its Gothic doorway, surmounted by a coat of arms, opens onto a beautiful spiral staircase.

Town Gate★

Corner of rue de l'Abbé and Le Petit Mèze.
In the 16C, this gate, which is protected by a barbican, was adapted to the use of fire arms. The belfry was added at a later date.

Château du Bailli

These remains of the outer town wall are visible from the road *(northwest)* behind the church.

Jardin Clos du Rempart

This medieval garden in the heart of town is home to a host of plants used for medicine or textiles.

Old town, Besse-et-Saint-Anastaise

ADDITIONAL SIGHTS
Musée du Ski
11 Rue de la Boucherie. 9am–noon, 2–6pm; the museum may be closed so check in advance. €4.50. 04 73 79 57 30. www.sancy.com.

This skiing museum is the first of its kind in France. Among the displays are 30 different pairs of skis, a 1925 bobsleigh, ski boots and shoes and a pair of 1910 skates. Prints and photographs show Besse at the turn of the 20C.

EXCURSIONS
Super-Besse✱
6km/3.7mi W.

Super-Besse is first and foremost promoted as a winter sports resort, but it is also popular in summer because of its quiet, peaceful surroundings.

There are a variety of chalets and holiday residences available. The vast, south-facing ski slopes are reached by ski lift; additional facilities include a skating rink and a swimming pool.

Ski Area
This resort, developed at the foot of Puy de la Perdrix, has south-facing ski slopes, drag-lifts, chair-lifts, and a gondola leading to 27 Alpine-ski runs (four black, nine red, nine blue, and five green). The ski pass sold on location gives access to the Mont-Dore skiing area (*see Le MONT-DORE*). In summer, the nearby lake can be used for swimming, canoeing and wind-surfing. The area is ideal for walking.

Tyrolienne Fantasticable★
€32.5. Children between 8 and 12 can ride with an adult at a discount; weight conditions apply. Reservations recommended. www.superbesse.sancy.com/offre/reservation-tyrolienne

It is in Super Besse that visitors can find France's longest zipline at 1 600m. The 1-2 minute ride affords breathtaking views over Super Besse.

Puy Ferrand
15min by cable-car, then 45min on foot there and back from Super-Besse.

The cable-car for Perdrix leaves from the Biche corrie and ends at the peak of Puy de la Perdrix. Follow the crest to the summit of Puy Ferrand, which offers a **view**★★ of the Dore mountain range, the lakes and Chaudefour valley.

Lac Pavin★★
4.5km/3mi SW of Besse. via D 149, which is a one-way road, joining up with D 978 from Besse to Condat, or via the "Fraux road" S of Besse which connects Besse to Pavin via a pasture-covered mountain.

The Fraux parking area offers a lovely **view**★ of the lake: an almost perfect circle at 800 meters in diameter, it is one of the most beautiful in Auvergne.

In the past, it was said that the old town of Besse was swallowed up by the lake as a divine punishment, and that throwing a stone into it would unleash terrific storms; this gave way to its name which comes from the Latin *pavens* meaning dreadful.

A gentle path offers a very pleasant stroll around the lake (about 45min on foot).

Puy de Montchal★★
The summit overlooking Lac Pavin offers a magnificent **panorama**★★ – to the northwest, the Dore mountain range; to the north, the Dômes mountain range clustered around Puy de Dôme; further to the east, the Couzes and Comté valleys; to the northeast and east, the Livradois and Forez mountains and to the southeast, in the far distance, the Chaise-Dieu plateau and Velay mountains.

Chapelle de Vassivière
8km/5mi SW on D 36 (see map p132) in the direction of La Tour-d'Auvergne. 3km/1.5mi after the crossroads separating lac Pavin from Super-Besse, take a minor road to the right.

This lovely 16C pilgrimage chapel stands amid a splendid pastoral setting southeast of Puy de Sancy.

BESSE-ET-SAINT-ANASTAISE

Lac de Montcineyre

8km/5mi SW along D 36. Skirt Lac de Bourdouze and, 1km/0.6mi further on, follow a path on the right (1km/0.6mi).
Crescent-shaped Montcineyre lake owes its existence to the wooded Puy Montcineyre, which dams the valley.
Follow the lake shore for a stunning view of the Sancy massif (*Massif de SANCY*).

DRIVING TOUR

THE COUZE VALLEYS
65km/40mi. Allow 1–2 days.

Leaving from Besse, take D 633, a charming corniche road offering interesting views of the Couze de Pavin valley and the Courgoul gorges. It becomes D619 after crossing Trossagne. Turn right onto the narrow road running above the Grottes de Jonas.

Grottes de Jonas
Daily Feb–early Nov at varying hours; call or check website for details. Dec–Jan. €8.5 (child 5–12 years, €6.5).
04 73 96 31 69. www.grottedejonas.fr.

The most rudimentary of these man-made caves carved out of the volcanic tufa were doubtless inhabited in prehistoric times. In the Middle Ages, a fortress and chapel were built within – its vaulting still bears traces of **frescoes** dating from 1100. The tower of the fortress contains a spiral staircase with 80 or so steps carved into the rock; it leads up to apartments laid out over several floors.

Return to Le Cheix and turn right onto D 978 then right again onto D 621.

Cheminée des Fées de Cotteuges
Before reaching the hamlet, turn right onto the Bedeaux track.
This path leads through a wood to an earth pillar standing among excavations. This interesting geological formation, known as the "**Fairy's Chimney**" is a clay column topped by a block of hard rock.
Beyond Cotteuges the road crosses one of the *cheires* (lava flows) that are a characteristic feature of this area. Further on, high above to the left of the road, stand a number of superb sheer-sided rocks.

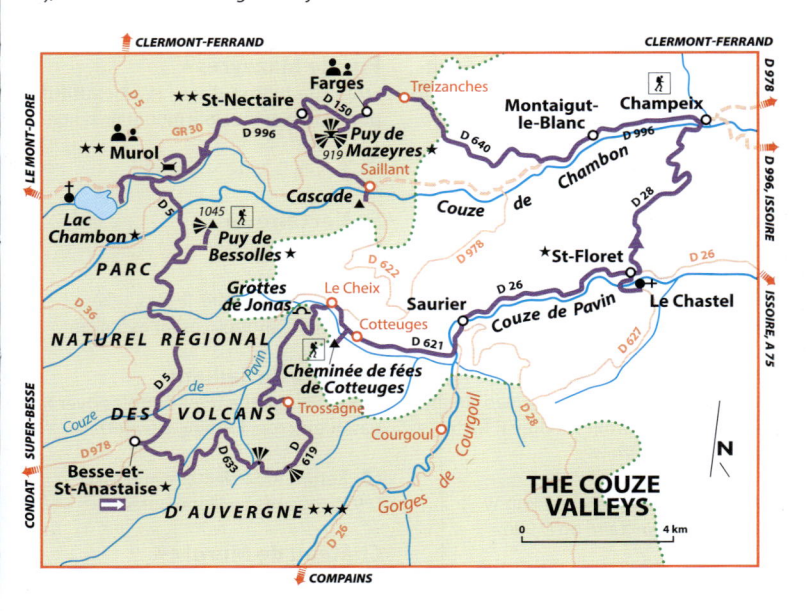

145

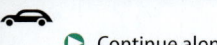

▶ Continue along D 621.

Saurier
This is an old fortified village. Left of the road crossing the River Couze there is an attractive view of the old bridge and its chapel. The valley narrows again and basalt rocks can be seen on the hillsides.

▶ Take D 26 towards Issoire.

St-Floret★
First of all, take a look at Chastel plateau, probably the original site of the village. The **Église du Chastel** is built on a promontory overlooking the Couze de Pavin. Near the church are the remains of a Merovingian graveyard (tombs dug into the rock, ossuary).

The **château**, located in the village of St-Floret itself, was built in the 13C and modified a century later. Large 14C **frescoes**★ depicting episodes from a tale of chivalry (Tristan) decorate the walls in the lower chamber.

▶ After the church, turn left onto D 28, which will take you to Champeix.

Champeix
This village stands between hillsides once carpeted with vineyards. The ruins of the old medieval castle, the "Marchidial", stand high above the village on a sheer-sided spur of rock.

Site du Marchidial
Can be reached on foot starting from the bridge; access by car: follow D 28 towards St-Floret; after 1km/0.6mi, turn right towards the college.

🚶 In the upper part of Champeix, this district owes its name to the markets and fairs which used to take place on the plateau during the Middle Ages. A narrow lane running east leads to the ruins of the former medieval fortress offering a fine view.

▶ Leave Champeix heading W towards St-Nectaire on D 996.

Montaigut-le-Blanc
The village lies in the shadow of its ruined castle. Its somewhat Mediterranean appearance – houses with flat roofs and rounded tiles, terraced vineyards, and fruit trees at the head of the valley – heralds the Limagne plateau.

▶ Carry on along D 996 for another mile or so. Turn right onto D 640. Just after Treizanches, turn left onto D 150.

Farges
This hamlet is home to an interesting group of **troglodytic houses** *(Les Mystères de Farges: guided visits (1h), every 20 min: May–Jun, Sep and school holidays 10am–noon, 2–5pm (Jul–Aug 10am–6pm); rest of year by appointment; €6.60. ☎04 73 88 52 25.)*, hollowed out of the white tufa that date from the Middle Ages. Visitors can also discover a Saint-Nectaire cheese aging cellar.

A little further on from Farges, a quarry comes into sight to the right of the road. The powdery white rock extracted here is pumice stone, evidence of the tremendous volcanic eruptions that shook this region millions of years ago.

▶ Carry on along D 150, then turn left.

Puy de Mazeyres★
From the hilltop, there is a beautiful **panorama** of the Dore mountain range.

▶ Rejoin D 150.

St-Nectaire★★
see ST-NECTAIRE.

▶ From St-Nectaire-le-Bas, take D 996 for Champeix, as far as Saillant.

Cascade de Saillant
In this village the river tumbles over a basalt outcrop, forming a waterfall.

▶ Return to St-Nectaire and take D 996 towards Le Mont-Dore.

Château de Murol★★
see CHATEAU DE MUROL.

BESSE-ET-SAINT-ANASTAISE

Lac Chambon

On leaving the castle, walk down to the village, cross the road and walk through a gate leading into the Parc Municipal.

Parc Municipal du Prélong
Once part of a private estate (the house now contains the Musée des Peintres de l'École de Murols), the park boasts a beautiful collection of azaleas, rhododendrons and camellias. The French-style garden has alleyways lined with box trees leading to the rose-garden, offering a striking contrast to the English-style park.
At the entrance stands the **Chaumière** (*daily 3–6pm*) which houses a small archaeological collection.

Musée des Peintres de l'École de Murols
Jun–Oct daily 10am–noon, 2.30–6.30pm; Nov–Apr Wed–Sun 10am–noon, 1.30–5.30pm; May Wed–Sun 10am–noon, 2.30–6.30pm. 1 Jan, 1 May, 14 Jul, 25 Dec, Nov–Dec. €4. 04 73 88 60 06. www.musee-murol.fr.
At the turn of the 20C, some 50 landscape painters found inspiration in and around the village. Gathered round Abbé Boudal, who was the initiator of this artistic movement, and Charenton, who was its leader, this group of artists was close to two contemporary trends: Impressionism and Fauvism. The permanent collection is displayed in several rooms, with another room reserved for temporary exhibitions.

Leave Murol on D 996, then turn left at the junction with D 5.

The road runs along the slopes of the Tartaret volcano.

Lac Chambon★★
The lake was formed by the Tartaret volcano, which erupted in the middle of the Couze valley and stemmed the flow of water. It is a vast but fairly shallow lake lying in a very attractive setting. It is dotted with tiny islands and has an extremely jagged shoreline, except on the north, and to the south-east where there is a large beach. In summer, this is a popular swimming spot; fishing and pedalos are also common seasonal activities here.
To the north of the lake is a slender rocky peak known as the **Saut de la Pucelle** (Maiden's Leap) which is all that remains of the ancient **Dent du Marais** volcano. The village of Chambon-sur-Lac lies at the end of the Couze de Chaudefour, in a mountainous area to the west of the lake, and consists of a group of houses huddling round the church.

Return to Murol and turn right onto D 5 towards Besse. After 2km/1.2mi turn right onto D 619, then after about 100m turn left.

147

Puy de Bessolles★

This peak is one of the best look-out points in the Couzes region, giving an impressive view of the Dore mountain range and Lake Chambon.

Follow the footpath signposted Plateau de Bessolles-Panorama. Allow 45min on foot there and back, and 2h to follow the footpath right round the plateau (signposted in yellow).

▶ Go back to Besse via D 5.

ADDRESSES

STAY

Hôtel Restaurant Mildiss – *Serre-Bas 63610 Besse-et-Saint-Anastaisie 04 73 79 10 10. www.mildiss.fr. 32 rooms.* This luxury mountain establishment offers unique, charming rooms with a minimalist, contemporary aesthetic. A spa with jacuzzi is on-site, and the restaurant's menu was developed in partnership with Michelin-starred chef Gilles Reinhardt.

Aaisa Chambres d'Hôtes – *2 rue du Marché 63610 Besse-et-Saint-Anastaisie 06 15 38 75 41. www.aaisa.eu. 6 rooms.* This 700-year-old house has been fully renovated to welcome five spacious rooms and one apartment.

Auberge de la Petite Ferme – *Le Faux 63610 Besse-et-Saint-Anastaisie 04 73 79 51 39. www.auberge-petite-ferme.com. 32 rooms.* Just 800m from the medieval heart of Besse, this charming hotel offers a cozy place to come home to after a day on the slopes. Whether warming in front of the fire or catching the last rays of sun on the terrace, you won't be disappointed.

Chambres d'hôtes 'Plus belle la vue' – *Trossagne, 63610 St-Pierre-Colamine. 7km/4.2mi NW of Besse via D 978 and D 619. 04 73 55 05 86. Closed Jan, Mon, Tue evening and Wed evening except school holidays. Reservations recommended.* The view from the terrace of this aptly named inn is breathtaking. Whether you dine al fresco in the summer or by the fireplace in the winter, local cuisine is the mainstay here, chosen à la carte or from one of the hearty fixed-price menus.

Ferme-Auberge La Voûte – *8 rue de la Mastre, 63320 Clémensat. 5km/3mi S of Champeix via D 28. 04 73 71 10 82. Open Sun lunch and Sat, evenings Jul–Aug except Sun and Mon. Reservations required.* A very popular farm-inn nestling in a small village. The vaulted dining room is often crowded with savvy diners enjoying fare from the farm, local recipes or savoury Auvergnat specialities (to be ordered ahead). Spacious, refurbished bedrooms.

EAT

Le Levant – *20 r. de l'Abbé-Blot, 63610 Besse-et-St-Anastaisie. 04 73 79 50 17. www.lelevant-besse.fr. Closed Sun eve and all day Mon.* How do you like your trout? With cabbage, wild mushrooms or lentils? Or would you prefer a different regional dish? There's plenty of choice here, served in a decor that seems to be firmly grounded in the 1970s.

Le Lac Pavin (Hotel-Restaurant) – *Au Lac Pavin. 4km/2.4mi W of Besse via D 149. 04 73 79 62 79. www.lac-pavin.com.* The fish – char, among others – served in this restaurant once lived in the alpine lake that you see from the dining room. The owner, who is also the chef, prepares simple dishes from fresh ingredients. A few modest rooms have views of the lake.

Hostellerie du Beffroy – *26 rue Abbé Blot, 63610 Besse-et-Saint-Anastaisie. 04 73 79 50 08. www.lebeffroy.com. Closed Mon and Tue (except in Jul–Aug), Wed lunch in Jul–Aug. Reservations required Sun. Restaurant.* This handsome 15C building in the village centre used to be the guardhouse. The gourmet fare is served in a charming dining room with white-draped tables and old wooden beams.

Le Buron du Col – *Col de la Croix Morand 63790 Chambon-sur-Lac. 04 73 22 14 25. www.buronducol.fr.* Typical mountain fare truffade is the mainstay of this auberge-restaurant at 1401 meters of altitude. A two-bedroom gîte is the perfect refuge for a family.

La Bourboule

La Bourboule, located at an altitude of 852m in the lush valley of the Upper Dordogne, enjoys a climate with few seasonal variations. This well-known spa and resort also offers many facilities for children. The town is situated at the confluence of the Dordogne which, at this point, is no more than a mountain stream 12km/7.5mi from its source, and the Vendeix, a tributary that also has its source in the Sancy range. The resort's pump rooms, casino, town hall and gardens line the banks of the two rivers, which are crossed by a dozen or so bridges and footbridges.

- **Population:** 1 894
- **Michelin Map:** 326: D-9.
- **Info:** 15 pl. de la République, 63150 La Bourboule. 04 73 65 57 71. www.sancy.com.
- **Location:** La Bourboule isn't especially large and the best way to get a feel for the place is on foot (see Walking Tour). The more energetic can walk up to La Banne d'Ordanche (1h return) for a splendid view over the valley and the town.
- **Parking:** Opposite the Parc Fenestre, on Ave. Agis Ledru.
- **Timing:** Take a ride in the little tourist train, and then explore the town on foot before wandering off up the valley sides.
- **Kids:** Parc Fenestre, a splendid wooded park with children's play area.

THE SPA RESORT

La Bourboule's first spa was opened in 1821. At the time, its cabins were closed off with serge curtains, revealing the bathers at the whim of the wind. The bathing water was used by several patients in turn, and water for the showers was pumped manually by an elderly peasant.

In 1854, Thénard the chemist discovered arsenic in the waters of La Bourboule, perfect, apparently, for the treatment of respiratory disorders. When the news spread, every house-owner in the town promptly began exploring his property in the hope of finding his own spring, and each person did his utmost to excavate faster and pump harder than his neighbour.

Today, the town's springs are managed by the Société Thermale de La Bourboule and the Compagnie des Eaux Minérales. There are two springs in La Bourboule – a hot spring at Choussy-Perrière (60°C/140°F), and a cold spring at Fenêstre (19°C/66°F). Their waters contain metalloid arsenic and are used to treat respiratory diseases and dermatoses using techniques such as inhalations, sprays and electro-sprays, baths and showers. Treatment is available in the **Grands Thermes** spa center.

The resort has all the facilities of a major spa town including tennis courts, stables, a swimming pool, an amusement park etc.

WALKING TOUR

A pleasant walk round the town will give you an opportunity to admire the Victorian-style architecture of the hotels and to understand how the city developed at the foot of the Roche des Fées. Near the church, a convincing pastiche of Romanesque art, you can see the **Maison Rozier** and its imposing balcony (Boulevard Georges-Clemenceau), the Grands Thermes, the former town hall, now a chocolate factory called the Marquise de Sévigné, and the casino, a listed, entirely renovated building.

👣 Parc Fenestre★

🕐 Apr–late Sept, but times vary; please check the website for details. ℘04 73 81 06 04. www.parcfenestre.com.

This splendid wooded park – partly planted with sequoias – is a charming place for outings and relaxation. The children's play area consists of wide expanses of lawn and outdoor games.

Roche des Fées

🚶 1h on foot there and back. Take the footpath from place G.-Lacoste.

This granite "Fairy Rock" rises some 50m above the spa and provides an attractive view of the town and its surroundings.

🚶 WALKING

1 TALES OF TOINETTE

10km/7mi N of La Bourboule.

▶ Leave the town on D 88.

Murat-le-Quaire

A rocky spur, once the site of a castle, marks the entrance to this village. There is a look-out point on the spur with a pretty view of the upper section of the Dordogne valley. Besides its role as a rural holiday destination, Murat-le-Quaire hosts a Bread Festival every other year (odd numbers) as part of its campaign to preserve local tradition.

▶ From the church, take D 609 towards La Banne d'Ordanche, as far as the school.

Scénomusée La Toinette et Julien★

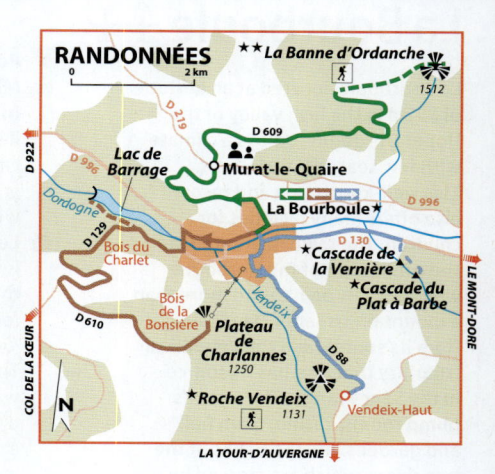

♿🕐 Daily: Jan–Mar and Oct–Nov 2–6pm; Apr–Jun and Sept 10am–noon, 2–6pm; Jul–Aug daily 10am–noon, 2–7pm. ⊘Mid Nov–20 Dec. ☛Toinette: €7.50; Julien: €5.70; combined ticket: €9.90. ℘04 73 81 12 28. www.toinette.com.

The museum contains an account of rural life through the seasons in the Dore mountain range region of the Auvergne during the 19C, presented through the eyes of a local woman of that period, Toinette Chaumard.

Beyond the belvedere lies the **Grange de Julien**, a barn where Toinette's young son returns from his travels and reflects on the future prospects of rural life in the area.

▶ Carry on along D 609 past a lake, then follow it uphill round a series of hairpin bends with pleasant views, to the end of the road.

La Banne d'Ordanche★★

🚶 From the car park a steep footpath leads uphill to a viewing table (1h). La Banne d'Ordanche (in the dialect of the Auvergne banne means "horn") rises from a grassy hillock. From the top of this basalt outcrop – the remains of the central chimney of an old volcano – there is a **wide view★★** of the Dordogne valley, the Puy de Sancy range, Puy de l'Angle, the Dômes mountain range and the Limousin.

2 TOUR OF WATERFALLS

3km/2mi. Allow 4h.

▶ Leave La Bourboule on D 130 along the Dordogne towards Le Mont-

150

La Banne d'Ordanche and the Cantal mountains

Dore. 1.5km/0.9mi after the swimming pool a track leads off opposite the Mont-Dore water company building (left of the road). Leave the car.

🚶 Take the GR 30 footpath to the right. Go past a farm and uphill into the forest. After a 15min walk, take a path to the right that cuts downhill.

Cascade de la Vernière★
The Vernière waterfall is formed by a large volcanic rock which obstructs the bed of the Cliergue.

▶ Return to the path and turn onto the track leading to the Plat à Barbe refreshment kiosk. Here it is possible to go down a stepped path (potentially dangerous) to a platform constructed opposite the Plat à Barbe waterfall.

Cascade du Plat à Barbe★
This waterfall owes its name (literally "shaving dish") to the dip worn in the rock by its waters.

③ THE BRIGAND'S DEN
4km/2.5mi trip. Allow 4h.

▶ Leave La Bourboule to the S on D 88 towards La Tour-d'Auvergne. 3.5km/2.3mi on past Parc Fenêstre, turn right and leave the car at Vendeix-Haut.

Roche Vendeix★
Access along a footpath off D 88 by an inn. 30min on foot there and back.
This rock of basalt carries the ruins of a castle which was re-fortified in the 14C by Aimerigot Marcheix, an infamous local brigand eventually caught by the king's men in 1390; he was taken to Paris and beheaded and quartered.

④ WOODLAND TO VALLEY
7km/4.5mi trip. Allow 1h.

▶ Leave La Bourboule to the W on D 129 towards La Tour-d'Auvergne via Col de la Sœur. About 500m after crossing the Dordogne, beyond a crossroads, leave the car and take a footpath branching off to the right.

Lac de Barrage
🚶 *30min on foot there and back.*
This delightful path runs through Charlet woods to the dam whose reservoir stretches for 1km/0.6mi along the Dordogne valley.

▶ Continue along D 129 and, 3km/1.9mi further on, turn left onto D 610.

Plateau de Charlannes
The beautiful Charlannes plateau is popular with spa patients for its restful scenery; it offers views of the Dore and Cantal mountains.

151

EXCURSIONS

St-Sauves-d'Auvergne
4km/2.5mi NW along D 996.
This village, situated on the north bank of the Dordogne, houses an interesting museum for children of all ages.

👥 Le Monde Merveilleux du Train et de la Miniature
🕐 *Jul–Aug daily 10am–noon, 2–6.30pm; mid-end-Jun and 1–mid-Sept daily 2.30–5.30pm.* ⊘*Oct–May.* ⊜*€7 (children €5).* ☎*04 73 65 54 61.*
This museum contains collections of toys and models (cars and lorries). There is a train diorama as well as the reconstruction of a typical village with miniatures depicting ancient crafts.

Le Mont-Dore ♨♨
⏵*See Le MONT-DORE.*

Tauves
A small village surrounded by lush pastures studded with houses roofed in the typical *lauze* tiles.

THE GORGES D'AVÈZE ★
60km/38mi round tour from Tauves. Allow 3h.

▶ Drive W out of Tauves along D 29.

Singles
This former miners' village has a pleasantly located church that overlooks the Burande and the Dordogne gorges.

▶ Return to "La Guinguette" (the paradise of anglers) and continue on D 73 until you reach Messeix.

Messeix
This little town was once famous for its coalmines. The Romanesque church here was altered in the Gothic period but has retained its attractive 13C entrance.

▶ Follow D 987 towards Tauves.\

Gorges d'Avèze★
This rocky gorge, situated on the border of the Puy-de-Dôme and of the Corrèze regions, offers breathtaking views of the upper section of the River Dordogne which has its source at the Puy de Sancy, some 30km/18.5mi east of the gorge.

Avèze
The church presents interesting furnishings (altarpieces, statues of St Roch and St Blaise). Nice panorama of the nearby gorges.

▶ Return to Tauves on D 987.
You can make a detour via St-Sauves (⏵*see above*) to admire its superb setting, a result of the glacial period.

ADDRESSES

🛏 STAY

⊜ **Hotel de l'Aviation** – *32 R. de Metz.* ☎*04 73 81 32 32. www.hotel-aviation.net. 41 rooms and 8 furnished apartrments.* The rooms in this gable-ended dwelling may be a bit outmoded, but they are neat and tidy. Simple cuisine. Indoor pool and fitness room.

⊜ **La Tour Pom'Pin** – *178 avenue d'Angleterre.* ☎*07 62 12 57 59. www.tourpompin.fr. 5 rooms.* This charming B&B features two suites and three rooms in a Belle Epoque mansion in La Bourboule. Several common spaces including a dining room, lounge, library, and terrace.

🍴 EAT

⊜⊜ **L'Amuse Bouche** – *15 rue des Frères Roziers.* ☎*04 73 21 68 85. www.restaurant-lamusebouche.fr.* 🕐 *Thur–Mon.* Local, seasonal products are done up right on this creative menu. The dining room evokes local tradition, with dark wood and old-fashioned tiling.

RECREATION

In summer, the **La-Bourboule-Charlannes** complex organises guided mountain-bike excursions, and there are also some 670km/416mi of waymarked paths for hiking. In winter the Charlannes plateau becomes a cross-country skiing area (58km/36mi of tracks).

Bort-les-Orgues and L'Artense

Set in the Dordogne valley, Bort owes its fame to the celebrated basalt columns which overlook it, as well as to its enormous dam. The town is an excellent starting point for exploring the granite plateau of the Artense, an area with much to commend a leisurely tour.

- **Population:** 2 967.
- **Michelin Map:** 330: Q-3.
- **Info:** Pl. Marmontel, 19110 Bort-les-Orgues. ℘05 55 96 02 49. www.tourisme-hautecorreze.fr.
- **Location:** Bort lies SW of Clermont-Ferrand along the A89.
- **Parking:** Limited parking areas in the centre of town.
- **Don't Miss:** The famous Orgues de Bort.

SIGHTS

Barrage de Bort★★

The dam's sheer size makes it a showcase of hydroelectric production. Its reservoir is partly filled by water from the Rhue, a tributary of the Dordogne. The road running along the top of the dam (390m long) overlooks the reservoir upstream dotted with **cruisers** (*May–Sept: boat trip (1h) Château de Val/Dordogne valley; Jul–mid-Sept: boat trip (1h) Bort Dam/Château de Val 11am, 2–5pm*). **A tourist itinerary** (*ask at the Tourist office: ℘05 55 96 02 49*) can be followed, starting from the foot of the dam on the west bank between the hamlet of Les Granges and Bort's tanning and leather works.

Church

The extremely simple architecture of Bort's church (12C and 15C) highlights a few fine works of art including modern stained-glass windows. A 17C priory stands by the church.

Cascade du Saut de la Saule

Leave Bort on D 922 towards Mauriac and turn left onto the road running up to the clinic. Follow the path across the Rhue, then turn left and follow the river. The path soon reaches a little gorge where pebbles caught by the waters have formed so-called "giant's cauldrons". Walk on to the outcrop beyond, which overlooks the Saut de la Saule; here the Rhue crosses a threshold of rock 5–6m high.

DRIVING TOURS

ORGUES DE BORT★

Round trip of 15km/9mi. Allow 2h.

This tour explores the volcanic valleys and granite plateaux along the boundaries of Cantal and Puy-de-Dôme.

A Convoluted Landscape

The Artense, a granite plateau south-west of the Dore mountain range, is cut across by the Tarentaine, a tributary of the Rhue which rises from Puy de Sancy. The plateau was once covered with vast glaciers that gave this region its highly unusual appearance of varied relief with peaks separated by small basins that are now lakes, peat bogs or marshy grasslands.

In a landscape typical of the Auvergne, the Artense is graced by charming copses, but the region was long known for the poverty of its soil. The marshes are gradually being drained, making it possible to breed red Salers cattle, more and more frequently sharing their pastures with black-and-white Friesians. Most of the milk produced by these cattle is used to make Cantal cheese and particularly the local blue cheese, **Bleu d'Auvergne**.

▶ Leave Bort on D 979 towards Limoges; then turn uphill on D 127.

As the road climbs, there is a beautiful view of the Rhue valley on the left.

▶ Just after the last houses in Chantery, park and turn right onto steps leading directly to the foot of the "Grottes des Orgues". These impressive columns extend for 2km/1mi and vary in height from 80–100m.

▶ Return to D 127 and, 2km/1.2mi further on, turn right onto a road that leads towards a television transmitter. Park and walk to a viewing table.

🚶 The vast **panorama**★★ extends over the Dordogne valley, the Artense and Cantal regions and the Dore mountains. To the south-west lies Lake Madic, relic of an earlier course of the Dordogne.

▶ Return to the car and follow D 127 for another 500m: here a path on the left leads to a rocky outcrop.

From here there is a panoramic view over Puy de Sancy, the mountains of Cantal, the Dordogne and its tributaries, the Monédières range and the Millevaches plateau.

L'ARTENSE
85km/53mi.

Between the Cantal and Puy-de-Dôme departments, the Artense is bounded on the west by the Dordogne, to the south and east by the Rhue, and to the north by the foothills of the Dore mountains.

▶ Leave Bort to the E on D 979. As it climbs the hillside, the road provides wonderful views of the columnar basalt around Bort.

Champs-sur-Tarentaine-Marchal
This holiday resort is huddled in a wooded valley near the confluence of the Rhue and Tarentaine.

▶ Leave Champs-sur-Tarentaine-Marchal N along D 49 towards Lanobre and turn immediately right onto D 22, a pretty road winding across the plateau.

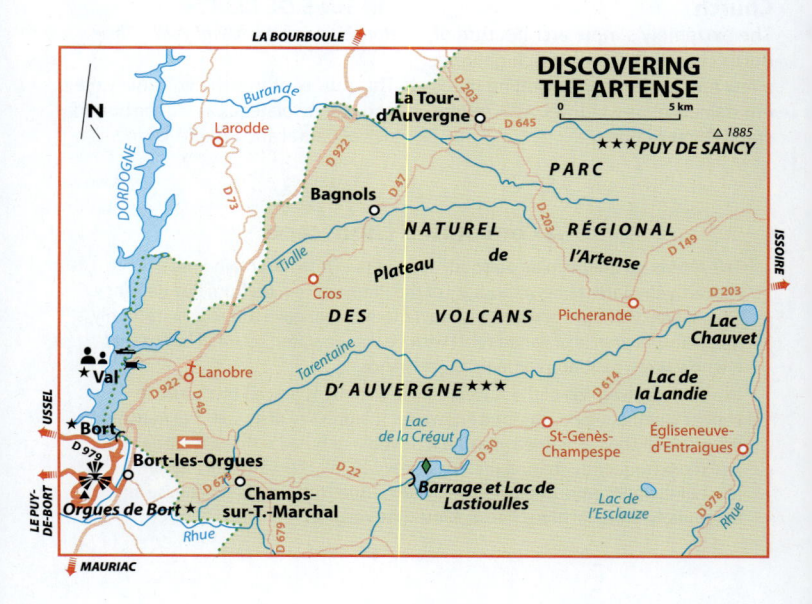

Château de Val

Barrage and Lac de Lastioulles
An outdoor leisure park has been laid out in pleasant **surroundings★★**, on the north side of the reservoir.
This crystalline lake boasts both fishing *(www.centredepechedelastioulles.com)* and other water activities *(www.lastioulles.fr).*

◯ Drive though St-Genès-Champespe and follow D 614 towards Issoire. As you come out of the village, take D 30 on the right.

Lac de la Landie
This lake is surrounded by peaceful meadows and woodlands.

◯ Rejoin D 614 then take D 203 on the right to Lac Chauvet.

Lac Chauvet
See Massif du SANCY.

La Tour-d'Auvergne
See Massif du SANCY.

◯ Drive SW out of La Tour-d'Auvergne along D 47.

The road to Bagnols passes the foot of the Pont de la Pierre waterfall.

Bagnols
This village lies in the undulating Tialle valley, a place of meadows and copses.

◯ Shortly after entering the Cantal département, turn left onto D 922.

Château de Val★
mid-Feb–mid-Mar, late Mar–Jun and Sept–Oct daily except Tue 10am–noon, 2–6pm;Jul–Aug daily 10am–12.30pm, 2–7pm. €6.5; Chlildren 6–12 €. 3.5. 04 71 40 30 20.
www.chateau-de-val.com.
Since the reservoir at Bort became functional, the presque-isle **setting★★** in which the 15C Château de Val stands is very picturesque. Each summer, artists and musicians take advantage of the magical setting for concerts and other shows. Its chapel devoted to Saint Blaise is well worth a visit.

◯ Turn back. At the crossroads take D 922 on the right to get back to Bort.

ADDRESSES

STAY
Camping Municipal de la Siauve – *15270 Lanobre, 3.5km/2.2mi N of Bort-les-Orgues via D 922 and secondary road. t04 71 40 31 85. www.camping-lac-siauve.fr. Open mid-Apr–mid-Sept. Reservations recommended. 220 sites.* Located on the edge of the lake in a beautiful natural environment, this is the perfect campsite for beach activities, fishing and sightseeing. Chalets and cabins for rent.

Le Rider – *Av. de la Gare. 05 55 96 00 47. www.lerider.fr. 17 rooms. Restaurant.* Meals are taken in a dining room-veranda with wrought-iron furniture and an original trompe-l'œil fresco of a country landscape.

Monts du Cézallier★

The Cézallier range is situated between the Dore mountain range and the mountains of Cantal; it consists of a succession of granite plateaux lying at an altitude of more than 1 200m, which were covered with a layer of basalt during the Tertiary Era.

> - **Michelin Map:** 326: E-10 to G-11.
> - **Location:** Lying south of Clermont-Ferrand, accessible by the A 75.
> - **Timing:** This is a region for leisurely exploration; allow as much time as you can, certainly a day to enjoy the tours.

A BIT OF HISTORY

The volcanoes from which the flows spread out all over the area have neither cones nor craters. Indeed, they scarcely even jut out from above the surrounding countryside, because the lava produced by the eruptions was very fluid and did not build up around the vents of the volcano. On the eastern side in particular, the plateaux are gashed by impressive valleys.

The Cézallier range is one vast area of pasture dotted with former shepherd's huts (*burons*) and a few villages with huge barns and byres as well as fountains made out of old drinking troughs. In the summer months, thousands of heads of cattle graze on the plateaux. The local people supplement their income by digging up gentian roots, used in the production of an alcoholic drink.

Despite its lack of hotels and places to stay, the Cézallier area is popular with those who enjoy wide open spaces, solitude and fresh air, and also with winter sports enthusiasts, especially cross-country skiers, since the lie of the land is ideal for this sport. Downhill skiing is also catered for, although facilities are, as yet, limited. The area is part of a regional park, the Parc Naturel Régional des Volcans d'Auvergne.

EXCURSION

Ardes-sur-Couze
41km/25mi E of Condat.
This old fortified town, once capital of the Duchy of Mercœur, has a 15C **church** in front of which there is a cross dating from the same period. Inside the church, the gilt-wood high altar (17C) features eight sculpture groups depicting the Passion. Near the chancel, a strange carved wooden bas-relief adorns the shrine of St Hubert. Opposite the pulpit, there is a 16C stone **Pietà**, and the chapel at the back of the church contains a 15C lectern.

The Parc Animalier d'Auvergne (*times vary, check website for details. Dec-Jan. €18–21 (child 3–9, €13.5–15). 04 73 71 82 86; www.parcanimalier-dauvergne.fr*), is a cross between a traditional zoo and a safari park. A great many animals of all types can be seen in relative freedom.

DRIVING TOURS

Two trips are described below; the first leads through the mountains, and the second follows the valley which plunges down to the River Alagnon to the east of the range.

1 ALPINE PASTURES
90km/56mi. About 5h.

Condat – *see CONDAT.*

> Leave Condat S on D 679 towards Allanche.

The road skirts a stretch of water that is a recent reconstruction of a lake originally built in the 12C by monks.

MONTS DU CÉZALLIER

Abbaye de Féniers

Abbaye de Féniers

The Cistercian abbey founded in the late 12C was rebuilt in 1686 and closed during the French Revolution. The buildings were partially destroyed by fire in 1872; only a few vestiges of the abbey, cloisters and church have survived.

▶ Turn right onto D 16.

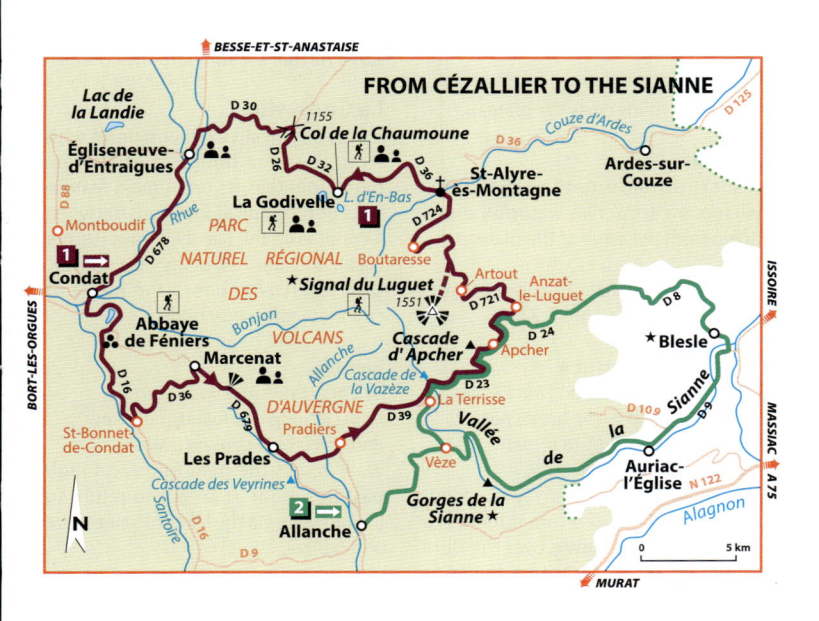

The road to St-Bonnet-de-Condat runs down into the Santoire valley and through a wooded gorge.

▶ In St-Bonnet-de-Condat; left on D 36.

FROM CÉZALLIER TO THE SIANNE

Village near La Godiville in winter

Marcenat
This is a modest winter sports resort which has also specialised in the production and selling of local cheese. Beyond Marcenat there are some superb views to the left of the road, over the Cézallier range.

Les Prades
Columnar basalt. From the summit, there is a delightful view of Landeyrat and the upper Allanche valley cutting into the planèze.

▶ Turn left off D 679 onto D 39 then D 23. Both roads cross the plateau.

Apcher
A short distance to the west of this village, an attractive waterfall drops down from the edge of the plateau.

▶ On leaving Anzat-le-Luguet, leave D 23 and turn left onto D 271.

Signal du Luguet★
🚶 1h30 on foot there and back from Parrot. Climb up to the summit across the meadows slightly to the left of the ski lift.
The wooded summit scarcely stands out above the plateaux. From it there is a vast **panoramic view**★ over the Dore mountain range and the mountains of Cantal.

▶ Continue along D 721 to Boutaresse then turn right onto D 724.

The road twists and turns through picturesque scenery.

St-Alyre-ès-Montagne
On a rise near the small village is the south-facing church overlooking superb countryside nestled in the shadow of Mount Gamet.

▶ Leave St-Alyre W along D 36; 3km/1.9mi further on, turn left onto D 32.

La Godivelle
This is a typical Cézallier hamlet with sturdy granite houses and a large, round fountain. Its other main feature is its geographical location, between a crater lake, the Lac d'En Haut (Upper Lake), and another, peaty lake, the Lac d'En Bas (Lower Lake), the haunt of countless migratory birds.

Ramble
🚶 3hr30 there and back, starting from La Godivelle; follow the yellow markings; keep dogs on a leash.
Walk across the peat bogs and high pastures as far as Jassy and return to La Godivelle via the lakes of Saint-Alyre and En-Bas.

MONTS DU CÉZALLIER

▶ Drive N out of La Godivelle along D 32, then 3km/1.9mi further on, turn right onto D 26.

Col de la Chaumoune
Near this mountain pass are several conifer plantations.

▶ Turn left onto D 30 and, 6km/3.7mi further on, turn left again onto D 978.

Égliseneuve-d'Entraigues
This small resort has a Romanesque church, but do not miss the regional Cheese Museum housed inside a barn. The **Maison des Fromages** explains the history and production of Saint-Nectaire, Cantal, Salers, Bleu d'Auvergne and Fourme d'Ambert.

▶ D 678 leads back to Condat along the lovely Rhue valley.

2 VALLÉE DE LA SIANNE
50km/31mi. About 1h30.

Allanche
Winter resort. The west end of the town still has remnants of its ramparts.

Rail-biking
Pedal away along disused tracks between Allanche and Lugarde.

▶ Head E from Allanche on D 9 towards Chavanon.

Between Allanche and Vèze, the road crosses the Cézallier's great alpine meadows and then, at the top of the rise, the mountains of Cantal come into view. The cliff road subsequently runs down to the **Gorges de la Sianne★**, providing some fine views of the ravine on the way. Beyond several gorges where huge boulders jut out from above both banks of the river, the valley widens out, becoming less sombre, and fruit trees appear.

Auriac-l'Église
This village is attractively situated to the right of the road.

▶ Turn right onto D 8.

Blesle★
See ST-FLOUR.

▶ Return to Allanche via the Bellan Valley, Anzat-le-Luguet and D 23, which will take you back to Vèze.

You can also pursue your route towards Massiac and the Alagnon gorges (see ST-FLOUR).

Allanche

Countryside near Condat, Massif de Sancy in the background
© Hervé Lenain/hemis.fr

Condat

This pleasant resort lies in the centre of a fertile basin into which flow the Rhue d'Égliseneuve, Bonjon and Santoire rivers.
The numerous slate-roofed villas standing on the sunlit slopes of the Rhue valley were almost all built by local people who went elsewhere to seek their fortune, many of them as linen-drapers.

- **Population:** 1 062.
- **Michelin Map:** 330: E-2, 32km/20mi SE of Bort-les-Orgues.
- **Info:** Place de la Mairie, 15190 Condat. ☎04 71 78 66 63.
- **Location:** At the heart of the Massif Central, SW of Clermont Ferrand.
- **Timing:** Take a leisurely half-day.

🚗 DRIVING TOUR

1 RHUE GORGE TO GENTIANE COUNTRY
80km/50mi. Allow one day.

▶ Leave Condat to the W.

The D 679 road follows the right bank of the Rhue. The road offers fine views of the gorge and Les Essarts lake-reservoir, then enters the lovely Maubert Forest planted with pine and beech. In the middle of the forest, the Gabacut, having dug numerous cauldrons into the rock, drops down in two small waterfalls.

Cascade de Cornillou
30min on foot return. 50m before the exit from the hamlet of Cornillou, turn left on a cart track.
🚶 Just before reaching a deserted barn, turn right onto an uphill track that soon runs along the shores of a small lake-cum-reservoir. Turn left across a small bridge; further on, an overgrown path leads to the top of the waterfall.

Gorges de la Rhue★★
Upstream from Embort, the river flows through a gorge with sides covered in greenery. The ravine widens out at the confluence of the two Rhues. Between Sarran and Champs, the road follows a dry valley where the Rhue flowed.

Champs-sur-Tarentaine-Marchal
see BORT-LES-ORGUES.

▶ Leave Champs E along D 679.

Bort-les-Orgues
see BORT-LES-ORGUES.

CONDAT

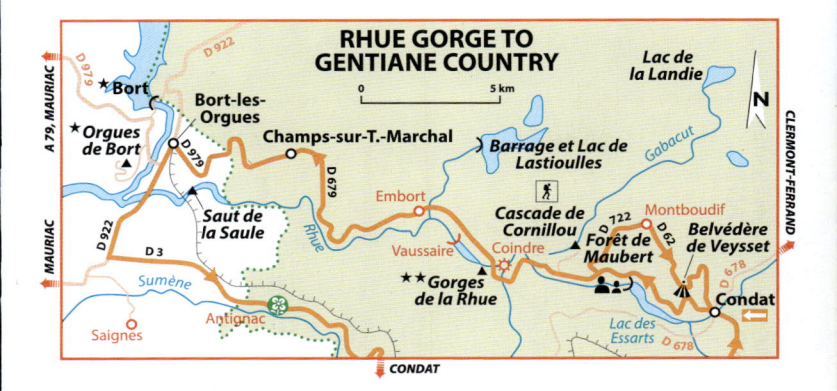

Leave Bort on D 922 in the direction of Mauriac and after 5km/3mi turn left onto D 3 to Riom ès Montagnes. The D 678 takes you back to Condat, following the opposite side of the Rhue.

2 CHEYLADE VALLEYS AND GENTIANE COUNTRY★★
see RIOM-ÈS-MONTAGNES.

3 BELVÉDÈRE DE VEYSSET AND FORÊT DE MAUBERT
20km/12.5mi. About 45min.

Leave Condat via the steep, winding D 62 N.

Belvédère de Veysset
The road leads to Montboudif, birthplace of Georges Pompidou (1911-74), President of the French Republic from 1969 to 1974. A **museum** (*daily mid Jun–mid Sept 10am–noon, 2–6pm; Apr–mid-Jun and mid-Sept–Oct Sat, Sun and public holidays 2–6pm. €4. 04 71 78 68 68; www.montboudif.fr*) is dedicated to his memory.

Turn left before the church onto D 622 and, a short distance further on, left again onto D 722.

Forêt de Maubert
The beautiful state-owned Maubert et Gaulis forest consists of landscaped woodland with a predominance of pines but also beech, lime and a few oaks. Many of the trees reach remarkable heights, and provide quality timber. In the heart of the forest, one beech tree reaches a height of 43m, with a girth of 3.1 metres. It is believed to be more than 200 years old, and is nicknamed the 'King of Maubert', a title previously enjoyed by a huge fir tree, which disappeared in 1930.

At the junction with D 679 follow it back to Condat.

The Rhues

A number of streams and rivers on the north side of Cantal bear the name Rhue. The largest of them, the Grande Rhue, flows into the Dordogne below Bort-les-Orgues after crossing a bar of rock known as the Saut de la Saule (*see BORT-LES-ORGUES*), but an underground drainage channel takes some of its water into the Bort reservoir. The Grande Rhue rises in the south of the Dore mountain range near the Biche corrie. Once its waters have been swollen by the Rhue de Cheylade that flows down from the mountains of Cantal, the Grande Rhue flows through very picturesque wooded gorges.

AURILLAC CHÂTAIGNERAIE AND MONTS DU CANTAL

163

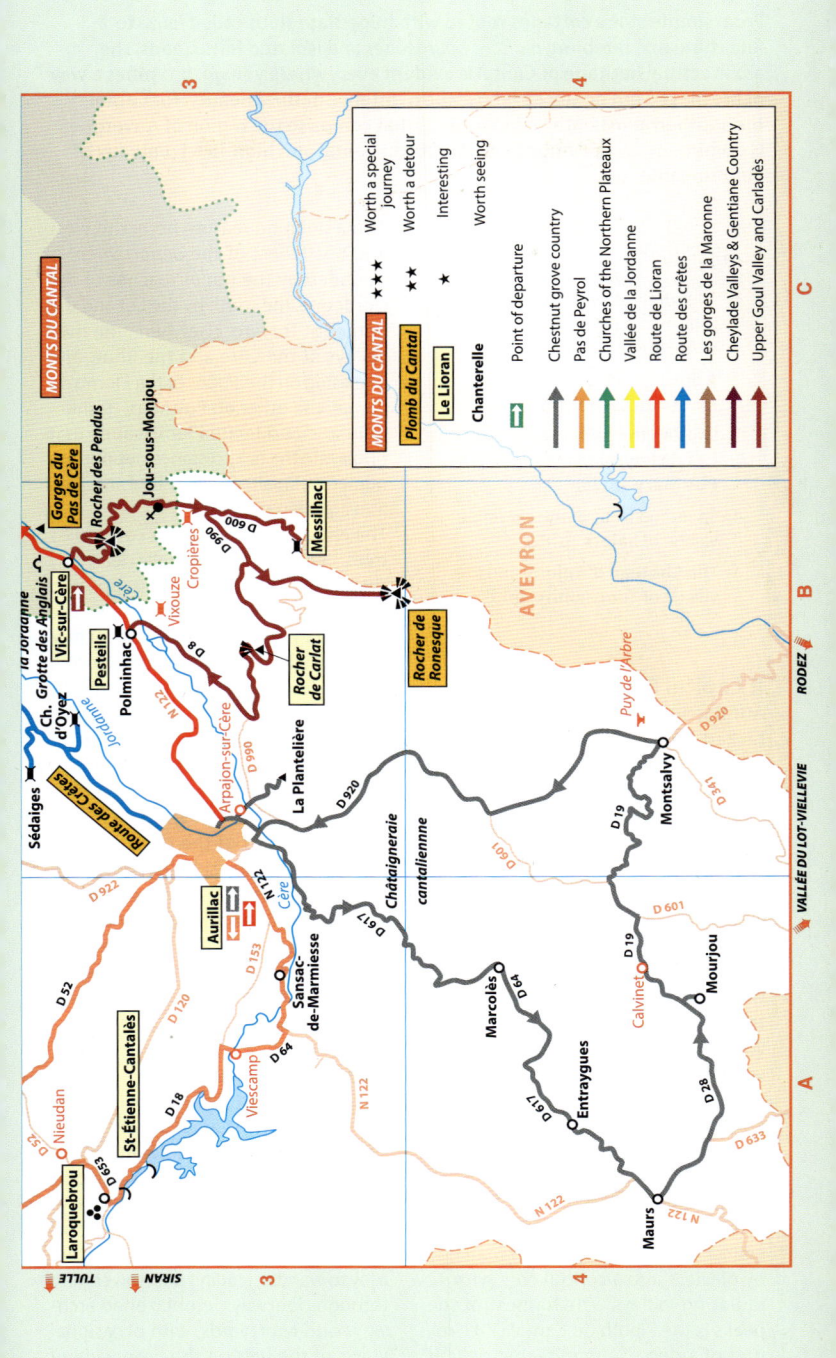

AURILLAC CHÂTAIGNERAIE AND MONTS DU CANTAL

From simple stone cottages roofed with huge slate slabs called *lauze* to fine châteaux, rambling *maisons bourgeoises* and isolated farmsteads, the architectural heritage of Cantal is evident everywhere you go. It typifies a way of life played out against a landscape of intense natural beauty, for Cantal, the southernmost of the *départements* that comprise the region of Auvergne, is dominated by the voluptuous Monts du Cantal and high-level plateaux of impermeable rock.

Highlights

1. A leisurely stroll around the Old Town *and Carmes District of* **Aurillac** (p167)
2. A driving tour of the stunning **Monts du Cantal** (p171)
3. Walking the paved path from **Pas de Peyrol** to the summit of **Puy Mary** (p175)
4. Spending a day in the charming village of **Salers** (p182)
5. The **Château d'Anjony** and the village of **Tournemire** (p191)

A Capital Place

Aurillac is a bright and modern city tacked onto an old town of narrow, twisting streets crammed with shops and cafés. In the district known as Carmes, south of the old town, the park on the place du Square is a shady niche of peace and quiet, its tiny pond populated by numerous carp and the odd terrapin. From here, it is a real pleasure to wander the adjacent streets of the old quarter wherein timber-framed houses topped with heavy *lauzes* gaze on a street scene that has changed little over the years. Were it not for Aurillac, Cantal would be virtually uninhabited.

Peaks and Pastureland

Lying within the Parc Naturel Régional des Volcans d'Auvergne, the green and wooded hills of the Monts du Cantal were formed as part of the largest extinct volcano in France, later moulded by glaciers into a central core with 12 radiating valleys. The highest of the peaks is the Plomb du Cantal (1 855m), part of a ring of summits that delimit the volcanic boundaries. Rivers are also a defining feature here: the west and northwest of the *département* is bounded by the upper reaches of the Dordogne, the south by the Lot and the gorges of Truyère. Elsewhere, the river valleys of the Cère and the Rhue – the one rising on the slopes of the Plomb du Cantal, the other on Puy Mary – fashion dramatic and fecund landscapes that ripple into the hazy distance, supporting numerous small settlements of antiquity and agrarian rusticity.

The entire region was once covered by trees, but they were gradually cleared by shepherds and have today disappeared from large tracts of countryside. The underlying strata support excellent pastureland where the landscape is dotted with *burons*: small, stone huts, originally used to produce cheese. Most today have been repurposed into museums or restaurants; only the buron de l'Algour is still used to make Salers Tradition.

The countryside is nevertheless covered with herds of the russet-coated Salers cattle, a sure sign that this is one of France's foremost dairy regions. At the end of May each year, after the last snows have melted, the cows are led to summer pastures in what is known as the *estives*, the occasion for festivals in the local villages.

Timeless Beauty

Two of the "Most Beautiful Villages in France" are in the Cantal département. One is Tournemire, with its huddle of cottages and towered Château d'Anjony; the other is Salers, a compact and architecturally well-preserved town of considerable antiquity. Its narrow streets are a joy to wander, leading past towers and through doorways, emblazoned archways and courtyards, with occasional views of the hills on the other side of the Maronne valley.

Aurillac ★

Aurillac, the business and tourist capital of Upper Auvergne, is a modern town that has sprung up around an old neighbourhood with narrow, winding streets. It's also one of France's sunniest cities.

A BIT OF HISTORY

Gerbert, the first French Pope (10C–11C) – Aurillac's Gallo-Roman origins were brought to light by the discovery of a 1C temple (rue Jacques-Prévert, reached from avenue Milhaud). In the 9C, St Gerald, Count of Auvergne, built an abbey, laying the foundations for the city's future prosperity; this abbey gave Christianity its first French Pope. Gerbert, a shepherd from the Aurillac area, attracted the attention of the monks of St-Géraud, who quickly taught this unusually bright student everything they knew. After completing his studies at the abbey, Gerbert left for Spain where he studied medicine and mathematics at the Moorish universities. He built the first pendulum clock, invented an astrolabe for sailors and improved the church organ. In AD 999 he became Pope under the name Sylvester II. He was the "Pope of the Millennium", who managed to impose the "Truce of God" – whereby hostilities were suspended on certain days and during certain seasons – on the feudal classes.

Gold-washers – According to Gerbert's contemporaries, his knowledge smacked of witchcraft. The gold flakes found in the River Jordanne were popularly ascribed to his spells.

▶ **Population:** 28 285.
🕭 **Michelin Map:** 330: C-5 – Local map see Monts du CANTAL.
Info: 7 due des Carmes, 15000 Aurillac. ☎04 71 48 46 58. www.iaurillac.com.
▶ **Location:** At the southern edge of Cantal, Aurillac is 156km/97mi SW of Clermont-Ferrand.
🅿 **Parking:** There are numerous parking places in the centre of town.
Don't Miss: A tour of the old town; plan from tourist office.
🕒 **Timing:** Allow half a day for a tour of the old town, or a full day if you want the bigger picture.

Aurillac by the Jordanne

© Bernard Jaubert/Getty Images

DISCOVERING AURILLAC, CHÂTAIGNERAIE & MONTS DU CANTAL

Église St-Géraud and Château St-Étienne

The gold industry was born, but remained fairly primitive: flakes of gold were collected by holding fleeces in the water to trap them.

Baron des Adrets (16C) – The people of Aurillac remained at odds with their lord, the abbot, but eventually managed to obtain administrative autonomy, as the consuls' residence (Maison Consulaire) proves.

The town was flourishing when it became involved in the Wars of Religion. In 1561, the governor ordered the slaughter of the large local Protestant population. They were avenged eight years later by the Baron des Adrets, a Protestant leader notorious for his brutality. His men began by swooping down on the monasteries on the outskirts of the town, burning or flaying the monks alive. On the night of 6 September 1569, the Huguenots blew up the town gate and burst their way in on the slumbering citizens, who were caught unawares and so put up minimal resistance.

From lace to umbrellas – Aubenas struggled to recover from these events for many years, until Colbert founded a laceworks that doubled as a gold and silver smithy. This entrepreneur also encouraged other industries, such as boiler-making and tanning, which have since declined.

Modern Aurillac's economy is based on agriculture and the manufacture of furniture, cheese, plastics and umbrellas.

WALKING TOUR

OLD TOWN
Place St-Géraud
The Romanesque façade with arcades and colonettes opposite the church entrance probably belonged to a pilgrims' hospice. The colonial house on the left dates from the late 15C.

Église St-Géraud
This old abbey church was founded in the late 9C by Count Gerald and became a stopover for pilgrims on their way to Santiago de Compostela.

▶ Walk down rue du Monastère and rue des Forgerons and turn right onto rue Victor-Hugo.

On reaching the 19C Hôtel de Ville, follow rue Vermenouze to place d'Aurinques. The **Chapelle d'Aurinques**, built at the end of the 16C in a tower in the city wall, was completed in the 19C.

▶ Follow rue de la Coste.

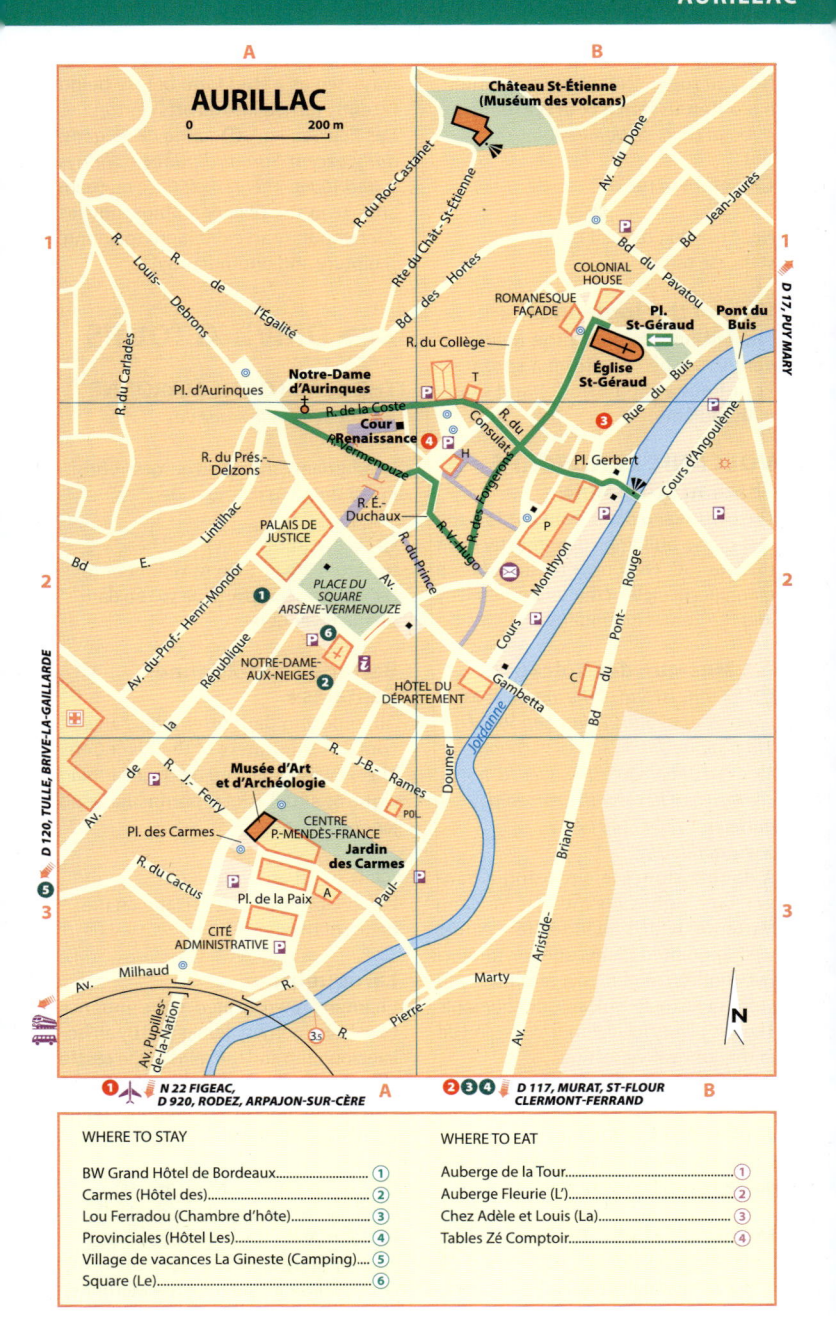

AURILLAC

WHERE TO STAY

- BW Grand Hôtel de Bordeaux ... (1)
- Carmes (Hôtel des) ... (2)
- Lou Ferradou (Chambre d'hôte) ... (3)
- Provinciales (Hôtel Les) ... (4)
- Village de vacances La Gineste (Camping) ... (5)
- Square (Le) ... (6)

WHERE TO EAT

- Auberge de la Tour ... (1)
- Auberge Fleurie (L') ... (2)
- Chez Adèle et Louis (La) ... (3)
- Tables Zé Comptoir ... (4)

DISCOVERING AURILLAC, CHÂTAIGNERAIE & MONTS DU CANTAL

No. 7 in rue de Noailles, on the right, has a **Renaissance courtyard** *(access through cours de Noailles)*.

▶ Return to rue de la Coste.

No. 4 rue du Consulat is notable for its staircase tower.

View of the Jordanne
The old houses along the River Jordanne can be seen from a spot near Pont Rouge (Red Bridge) and Cours d'Angoulême.

VOLCANIC LANDSCAPE
Château St-Étienne
The castle keep dates from the 13C; the rest of the buildings date mostly from the late 19C. The upper terrace offers a magnificent view of the Jordanne valley and the Cantal mountains.

Museum des Volcans★
Oct–Jun 1st Sun of the month 10am–noon; 2–6pm; Jun 21–late Sep Sun–Fri 11am–6pm; during school vacations Mon–Fri 2–6pm. €5 (under 18, no charge; joint ticket with archaeology museum). 04 7148 07 00. www.aurillac.fr.

A double staircase enclosing a banner 13m high leads into the Volcano Museum, which includes four large, well-appointed rooms offering interactive models, multimedia terminals and videos to explain volcanic phenomena. There is plenty for children to see and do in this innovative setting.

CARMES DISTRICT
Jardin des Carmes
Once part of a monastery, this pleasant garden gives access to an arts centre.

Musée d'Art et d'Archéologie
Centre Pierre Mendès France, 37 rue des Carmes. Same as Museum des Volcans. €5 (under 18, no charge; joint ticket with Museum des Volcans). 04 71 45 46 10. www.aurillac.fr.

The Art and Archaeology Museum is housed in the former Visitandines Convent (17C) which, after the Revolution, was used as a stud farm before being recently turned into an arts centre.

Les Écuries – *(during exhibitions, daily except Sun and public holidays 1.30-6.30pm; 04 71 45 46 08)*, a museum annexe in the former stables, houses contemporary art exhibitions (painting, sculpture and photography).

🚗 DRIVING TOURS

THE CÈRE TO THE MARONNE
100km/62mi. Allow one day.

Nearby dams, rivers and gorges; refreshing undulating countryside.

▶ Leave Aurillac on N 122 heading towards Figeac, then turn right onto D 64 to Viescamp and on to the dam on the River Cère.

Barrage de St-Étienne-Cantalès★
An imposing dam resembling a vault contains the waters of the River Cère. The view is enhanced by the charming sight of small islets, peninsulas and jagged coastlines.

▶ D 207, then D 7 lead to Laroquebrou, a pretty village on the banks of the Cère.

Laroquebrou
Charming town located at the entrance to the Cère gorges, dominated by an isolated outcrop and the ruins of the **castle** *(Jul–Aug only; call for opening hours. Sept–Jun. 04 71 46 00 48)*, once home to the Lords of Montal.

▶ Follow D 653, cutting across D 120 at Pont d'Orgon, then take D 2 for 15km/9mi. Turn right onto D 302 and continue until you reach the Enchanet dam spanning the Maronne, a tributary of the Dordogne.

Barrage d'Enchanet★
Its elegant silhouette is set against the backdrop of the Maronne gorges. D 61 offers a good overall view of the dam.

AURILLAC

▶ D 442 leads to St-Santin-Cantalès. Continue on D 52 and go back to Aurillac via St-Victor.

CHESTNUT GROVE COUNTRY
100km/62mi. Allow one day.
This round tour through "La Châtaigneraie Cantalienne" offers an interesting insight into local chestnut land, with long plateaux, luxuriant valleys and typical architecture.

▶ South of Aurillac, drive through Arpajon-sur-Cère and onto D 6 (2km/1.2mi).

Arpajon-sur-Cère – La Plantelière (Arboretum)
Dawn to dusk. 04 71 43 27 72. www.caba.fr.
Enjoy a pleasant stroll through gardens of different styles including the Devil's garden, the pond, the maple grove and the oak grove.

▶ Return to Arpajon-sur-Cère, turn right onto D 58 to the intersection with D 217, turn left and drive 12km/7.5mi; D 66 leads to Marcolès (3km/1.9mi).

Marcolès
In this restored medieval city, characteristic narrow lanes stem from rue Longue, closed off by an elegant 15C **porch**. West of the village, the D 64 leads to the **Rochers de Faulat** (1.5km/0.9mi) where several megaliths stand on a mound planted with oak trees.

▶ Take D 64, then D 217 and follow the banks of the River Rance.

Entraygues
This small village features a château typical of the area with its pepper-pot roofs.

▶ Go on driving until you reach Maurs.

Maurs
Maurs is situated to the south-west of the mountains in Cantal on a hill beside the River Rance and is the main town in the **La Châtaigneraie** area. The granite plateau is almost entirely covered with undulating moorland and gashed by green valleys where most of the local population lives.

In Maurs, which still has the circular layout dating to the days when it was a fortress, there is a definite air of Southern France; this is the start of the "Cantal Riviera" with its flowers and vineyards, explaining why Maurs has been dubbed the "Nice of Cantal".

By the late Middle Ages, Maurs had become one of the six "good towns" in Upper Auvergne and the seat of a provostship. It suffered during the Wars of Religion: captured and recaptured by the Huguenots in 1568 and 1583, it was pillaged and ransacked; in 1643 peasant rebels from the Rouergue sought refuge here and the King's troops were forced to intervene.

▶ Follow D 663 towards Decazeville then D 28 to Mourjou.

Mourjou
The pleasing **Maison de la Châtaigne** (*Apr–mid-Nov daily except Mon, 2–6pm (Jul–Aug daily 1.30–6.30pm); Oct during festival Sat–Sun 10am–6pm. €5 (child 6–12, €2.50). 04 71 49 98 00. www.maisondelachataigne.com*) traces the use of chestnuts through the ages in an imaginative and interesting display. Don't miss the 500-year-old chestnut tree.

▶ Follow D 28 to Calvinet, then take D 19 and drive 15km/9mi to Montsalvy.

Montsalvy
Nestling on the Plateau de la Châtaigneraie, this once-fortified town has kept several of its original gates. Near the church stand the **ruins** of the former abbey: the cloisters, the chapter-house, and the restored 14C refectory.

▶ Return to Aurillac on D 920.

DISCOVERING AURILLAC, CHÂTAIGNERAIE & MONTS DU CANTAL

ADDRESSES

STAY

Camping Village Vacances La Gineste – *La Gineste 15150 Arnac – 3km/2mi NW via D 61. ℘04 71 62 91 90. www.village-vacances-cantal.com.* At the end of a road, surrounded by nature, this camping site enjoys a prime location on a peninsula of the Enchanet lake.

Chambre d'Hôte Lou Ferradou – *At Caizac, 15130 St-Étienne-de-Carlat. ℘04 71 62 42 37. www.louferradou.com. 5 rooms.* Close to the Monts du Cantal, this old stone farmhouse offers smartly decorated rooms and a homey ambiance.

Hotel des Carmes – *20 r. Carmes, Aurillac. ℘04 71 48 01 69. www.hoteldescarmes.fr. Restaurant closed Dec 24 eve and Dec 25. 23 rooms.* Simple rooms, some with exposed beams, and one displaying the work of Danish painter Gorm Hansen. Swimming pool, sauna, and restaurant serving unfussy traditional cuisine.

Le Square – *15 pl. du Square, Aurillac. ℘04 71 48 24 72. http://hotel-le-square.com. 18 rooms. Restaurant.* Modern building near the old chapel. The rooms at the back are quieter.

Hôtel les Provinciales – *Pl. du Foirail, 15130 Arpajon-sur-Cère. ℘04 71 64 29 50. www.hotel-provinciales.com. 20 rooms. Restaurant closed Sat lunch (and dinner, in low-season) and all day Sun.* At the gateway of Aurillac, this hotel features 20 cosy, functional rooms. The "Félix Café" has a warm atmosphere and offers inventive, traditional cuisine prepared from fresh, local ingredients.

Best Western Grand Hotel de Bordeaux – *2 ave de la République. ℘04 71 48 01 84. www.hotel-de-bordeaux.fr. 36 rooms.* The best hotel in Aurillac, housed in a beautiful building dating from around 1850. Elegance, refinement and a warm welcome, and just a short distance from the centre of the town.

EAT

Chez Adèle et Louis – *3 r. du Buis. ℘09 51 70 10 13. Wed–Sat 10.30am–2pm, 6–10pm; Sun 10.30am–2pm.* This inviting, rustic eatery prides itself on its traditional Auvergnat cuisine and local wine and beers.

L'Auberge Fleurie – *Pl. du Barry, 15120 Montsalvy. 30km/20mi S of Aurillac. ℘04 71 49 20 02. www.auberge-fleurie.com. Closed Sun evenings and all day Mon except Jul–Aug.* A charming inn of some antiquity where the chef serves up tasty cuisine. Superb cellar, and if you want somewhere to stay, the inn has beautiful **colonial-style rooms**.

Table(s) Zé Komptoir – *10 Pl. de l'Hôtel de Ville. ℘04 71 48 78 13. www.tables-comptoir-aurillac.com. Open lunch and dinner daily.* Local cuisine with a strong accent on local producers and organic wines.

Auberge de la Tour – *Pl. de la Fontaine, 15220 Marcolès. ℘04 71 46 99 15. www.aubergedela-tour.com. Thur–Mon lunch and dinner.* This haute cuisine hotel and restaurant in a 17C stone building in the heart of the medieval village of Marcolès effortlessly blends local products and international influence.

SHOPPING

Distillerie Louis-Couderc – *14 r. Victor-Hugo. ℘04 71 48 01 50. www.distillerie-couderc.com. Tue–Sat 9.30am–noon, 2.30–7pm. Closed public holidays.* Founded in 1908, the Couderc distillery sells a wide variety of regional products made from gentian root, chestnut cream and berries.

Boutique Piganiol – *28 r. des Forgerons. ℘0471634260. www.piganiol.fr. Closed Sun. and public holidays.* Piganiol have been manufacturing umbrellas in Aurillac since 1884.

La Vitrine du Don – *10 r. des Frères 15000 Aurillac. ℘04 71 43 08 51. www.ledondufel.com. Tues–Sat 9.30am–noon, 2.30–6.30pm.* This airy boutique in Aurillac's pedestrian area is the urban antenna of the incredible Le Don du Fel centre for contemporay ceramics, a mere half-hour away in the neighbouring Aveyron. Here you'll find a fine collection of the salt-glazed stoneware that the Atkins family are famed for.

Les Monts du Cantal★★★

The mountains of Cantal, formed by the largest extinct volcano in France, embrace the most magnificent scenery in the Auvergne. Several of the peaks rise to more than 1 700m. Some, like the Puy Griou, are jagged; others, such as Puy Mary, are pyramid-shaped. The highest summit, the Plomb du Cantal, is rounded and soars to a height of 1 855m. From the mountain heartlands, deep, picturesque valleys fan out, providing easy access for visitors.

A BIT OF GEOGRAPHY

The Etna of the Auvergne – The volcano in Cantal reached an altitude of 3 000m and included a number of vents from which flowed either viscous lava that solidified into needles, or the more fluid lava that spread around the volcano over a 70km/44mi area.

Effects of erosion – Glaciers formed in Cantal during the Quaternary Era. Their slow but powerful action wore down the summit of the mountain, uncovering the lava plugs that filled the vents, digging out corries that later became the valleys, and giving the mountain range the appearance it has today.

Dairy industry – The entire range was once covered by forest. Gradually, land was cleared, and today it has disappeared in all but the entrance to a few valleys. Thanks to the basalt content of the lava, which produces a better quality pasture, Cantal has become best-known as a pastoral region.

DRIVING TOURS

1 ROUTE DU LIORAN★★
55km/34mi. About 4h.

This itinerary follows the Cère and Alagnon valleys.

- **Michelin Map:** 330 : D-3 to E-5.
- **Location:** This is very much walking country without any clearly defined centres of habitation.
- **Don't Miss:** The Puy Mary; not the highest, but a superb vantage point.
- **Timing:** Realistically, you will need to spend a few days here.

Aurillac★ –
see AURILLAC.

Leave Aurillac E along D 117, then the N 122.

The villages along the road have picturesque houses with hipped roofs that are typical of this area. The road then runs into the wide, attractive Cère valley.

Polminhac
The houses in the village huddle around the foot of Pesteils Castle.

Château de Pesteils –
see VIC-SUR-CÈRE.

Vic-sur-Cère★ –
see VIC-SUR-CÈRE.

Pas de Cère★★
45min on foot there and back.
The footpath leads off N 122, 3km/2mi upstream from Vic-sur-Cère.
The path crosses a small meadow then runs down through the woods to the Cère, which flows between high, narrow walls of rock.

Cascade de la Roucolle
From here, there is a wonderful view of the Roucolle waterfall and the Cère gorge.

Thiézac –
see VIC-SUR-CÈRE.

DISCOVERING AURILLAC, CHÂTAIGNERAIE & MONTS DU CANTAL

Cascade de Faillitoux
A small mountain road takes you through the hamlet of Lasmolineries; 1km later, you'll find the starting point of walking route GR400, an easy hike that will lead you to this stunning waterfall.

St-Jacques-des-Blats
This is an ideal centre for walking.

Col de Cère★
The D 67 skirting the Lioran road tunnel crosses the watershed separating the Dordogne basin, into which flows the Cère, and the Loire basin, into which flows the Alagnon. Just below the pass, the impressive pyramidal outline of Puy Griou can be seen in the distance to the left. Beyond the wide Cère valley is the narrow Alagnon valley, made darker by the pine forests lining it.

Le Lioran★
The winter and summer holiday resort of Le Lioran is encircled by the magnificent pine forests that cover the slopes of the Alagnon valley above meadows dotted with old shepherds' huts (*burons*, used for cheese-making).

Super-Lioran★
Accessible via Le Lioran (N side of tunnel). With the emphasis almost exclusively on winter sports, Super-Lioran, at a higher altitude than Le Lioran, is situated opposite the high grassy Font-d'Alagnon cor-

On Top of the World
Plomb du Cantal *(45 min there and back by cable-car and on foot from Super-Lioran)* is the highest peak in the Cantal range. From the summit there is a vast panoramic **view★★**. To the west, beyond the Cère valley, extend Cantal's great volcanic cones – Griou, Peyre-Arse, Mary, Violent and Chavaroche. A number of footpaths lead from the summit to the Puy Gros (view of the Cère valley at Thiézac) or to the Prat de Bouc via the Tombe du Père pass.

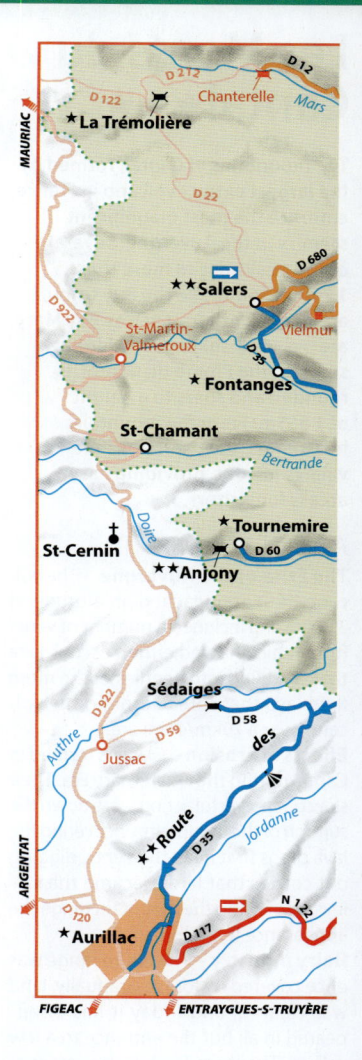

rie and closed off by pine woods. This modern winter sports resort stands in highly attractive surroundings. The resort is comprised of three separate sites: Font d'Alagnon, Font de Cère and Prairie des Sagnes.
Most of the ski runs are on the north and east-facing slopes of Plomb du Cantal.

Gorges de l'Alagnon★
3.5km/2.3mi NE towards Murat, then turn right (signpost) and follow a path 500m long down to the upper reaches of the river.

LES MONTS DU CANTAL

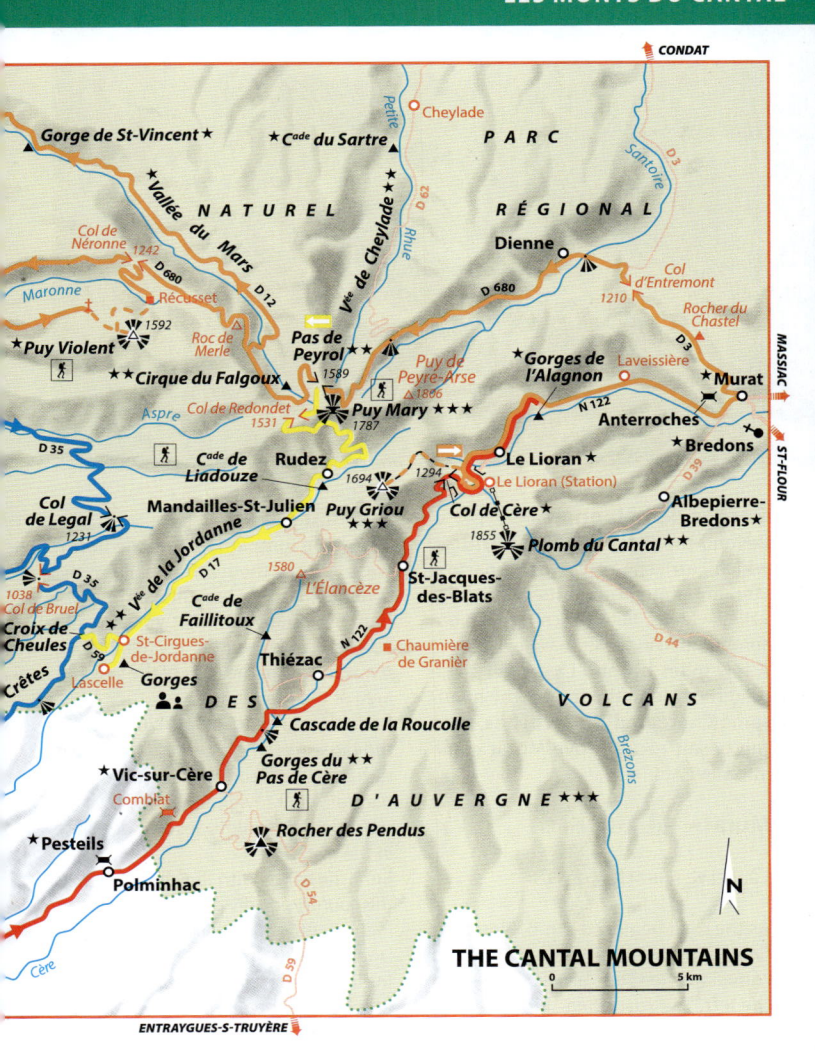

When the water level is low, it is possible to follow the river bed to the left over a distance of almost 200m. At the head of this very attractive ravine are piles of huge boulders.

2 PAS DE PEYROL★★

80km/50mi. Allow 6h.

This itinerary runs through "Puys" country along the Impradine, Mars and Maronne valleys. D 680, which crosses the Peyrol pass, is often blocked by snow from November to as late as June.

Puy Griou★★★

A strenuous walk. Begin by heading for the pastures in La Font d'Alagnon, then turn left through the woods to a holiday camp; there, bear right.

A clear path rises towards the alpine pastures of Col de Rombière (superb view★ over the Jordanne valley and the volcanic cones in Cantal) then turns left. To the summit, there is a strenuous climb over basalt rocks. From the top there is an exceptional view★★★ of the Puy Mary, the Puy de Peyre-Arse, and Plomb du Cantal barring the horizon to the north.

Peloton of the Tour de France riding to the Pas de Peyrol

© Razvan/iStock

Gorges de l'Alagnon★
Beyond the **Pierre-Taillade bridge,** which carries N 122 across a narrow stream fanning out in its course, the valley widens, but the scenery is more sombre than in the Cère valley.
A few miles beyond Laveissière, the road runs along the foot of the handsome **Château d'Anterroches**, then the basalt rocks above Murat come into view.

Murat★ – See MURAT.

▶ Leave Murat NW on D 3.

As the road begins to climb, Plomb du Cantal, Puy de Peyre-Arse and Puy Griou come into view, one after the other, to the left. The road then skirts the foot of Chastel rock and runs down from Entremont pass offering views of the Dore mountain range in the distance and Puy Mary on the left.
After **Dienne,** you turn into the Impradine valley as the road climbs up towards the Pas de Peyrol. Here, it clings to the sheer sides of Puy Mary and provides **views★★** over the Impradine and Rhue de Cheylade valleys, the Dore mountain range and the Cézallier area.

Pas de Peyrol★★
This is the highest mountain pass in the Massif Central. In the foreground, there is a view of the wooded Falgoux corrie overlooked by the Roc d'Auzière.

Puy Mary★★★
A steep footpath follows the northwest ridge of the mountain. From the summit, there is a breathtaking view of Cantal's gigantic extinct volcano and a superb view over the crystalline plateaux that form the base of the volcanic area of the Auvergne.
In the foreground is a striking view of the gigantic fan formed by the valleys radiating out from the centre of this natural water tower, separated by massive ridges with altitudes that decrease in the distance.
Rural life varies with the altitude across this countryside divided by deep corries. In the depths of the valleys near the villages are fields of crops and meadows. In the lesser exposed areas are birch woods followed by beeches halfway up the slopes and then conifers. At higher altitudes, alpine pastures are dotted with burons (the huts once lived in by shepherds during the summer) surrounded by ash trees. The drive down from Pas de Peyrol affords splendid views over the Mars valley.

Cirque du Falgoux★★
The Mars valley starts here, as the river gouges out a course for itself along the foot of Puy Mary.

▶ Head NW along D 12.

174

LES MONTS DU CANTAL

Vallée du Mars★
The road follows the valley, in which there is a striking contrast between the shaded slopes, covered in woodland but devoid of houses, and the sunny slopes carpeted with meadows and trees and dotted with houses. In the **Gorge de St-Vincent★** the valley narrows.
To the left of the road beyond the gorge is the Château de Chanterelle, a fortified residence dating from the 17C.

▶ Return to D 680 (or drive to Salers on D 212 – follow signs to Anglards – and D 22).

At the pass known as Col de Néronne, the road moves to the other side of the hill and overlooks the wide, glacial Maronne valley far below.

Puy Violent★
Walkers will enjoy Puy Violent, leaving from St-Paul-de-Salers.

▶ Go to Vielmur and turn left. Follow a narrow shepherd's lane which leads beyond the Croix des Vachers.

The walk to the top of the mountain (2h30 return) affords a lovely panorama, namely of the Maronne valley.

③ CREST ROAD★★
60km/38mi.

This itinerary takes over from the previous one and runs along the Aspre and Doire valleys. *The road up to Col de Legal is blocked by snow during the winter months, often until as late as April.*

Salers★★ – *see SALERS.*

▶ Leave Salers on D 35 E.

Running along the western slopes of Cantal's ancient volcano, the road crosses a few of the valleys that fan out from the heart of the range. It hairpins down into the Maronne valley then crosses the river and enters the Aspre valley. The traces left by the ancient glaciers that formed these valleys are obvious, even today. Huge boulders called erratics were carried there by the ice, now scattered along the hillsides.

Fontanges
To the right, at the entrance to the village, is a chapel dug into a mass of volcanic rock; entry is through a wrought-iron door set between colonnettes and archivolts. The castle, which now lies in ruins, once belonged to the family of Louis XIV's mistress.

▶ Continue on D 35 along the Aspre.

Col de Legal
From this pass there is a view into the distance over the Limousin plateau.

▶ At Col de Bruel turn right onto D 60 to Tournemire.

Tournemire – *see TOURNEMIRE.*

Château d'Anjony★★ – *see TOURNEMIRE.*

▶ Turn back and take D 35 to the right.

Beyond the Croix de Cheules, the D 35, which is called the **Route des Crêtes★★**, follows the long ridge that separates the Authre and Jordanne valleys. The journey provides some very attractive views.

▶ After 6km/4mi, turn right onto D 58 to Marmanhac.

Château de Sédaiges
Sédaiges, rebuilt in the 15C and modified in the 18C and 19C, is neo-Gothic. The furnishings and decor reflect the lifestyle of a 19C aristocratic family.

▶ Return to the Route des Crêtes, D 35.

Château d'Oyez
This 16C manor is a little-known architectural jewel with a large round tower at its northeast corner.

▶ Return to the Route des Crêtes, D 35.

DISCOVERING AURILLAC, CHÂTAIGNERAIE & MONTS DU CANTAL

Jordanne valley and the Cantal mountains

As the road slopes down towards Aurillac, the broad plain at the edge of the town can be seen stretching away, whereas to the left there is a magnificent view of the Jordanne valley.

Aurillac★ – see AURILLAC.

4 VALLÉE DE LA JORDANNE★★
25km/15mi

Pas de Peyrol★★ – see above.

▶ Leave the pass on D 17 S.

The cliffroad overlooks the superb Falgoux corrie, where the River Mars rises. Beyond Redondet pass, there is a view of Plomb du Cantal before the road runs into the Jordanne valley.

Rudez
Huddled together, the village houses cling to the mountain slopes in order to leave the valley floor free for pasture.

Vallée de la Jordanne★★
The slopes that flank this picturesque valley are lush and green, carpeted with meadows screened by clumps of trees. Here and there are a few rocky escarpments dotted with caves.

Gorges de la Jordanne★ –
Jun Mon–Fri 2–6pm, Sat–Sun 9.30am–7.30pm; Jul–Aug daily 9.30am–7.30pm; Sep Mon–Fri 2–6pm; Sat–Sun 10am–6pm. €4, €1.5 children 4–14.
Wooden bridges and passageways along 2km of this former fishermen's path and bridges allow you to explore these breathtaking gorges on foot.

Cascade de Liadouze
The waterfall drops over a threshold of rock into a narrow gorge.

Mandailles
This village, lying in picturesque surroundings, is the starting point of numerous rambles.

▶ Turn right onto D 59.

The road crosses the Jordanne then wends its way up the hillside.

Croix de Cheules
The crossroads marks the start of the Crest Road.

Vic-sur-Cère ★

The former spa town town of Vic in the Cère valley boasts picturesque houses clustered around the church.

A BIT OF HISTORY

The "mad monk" – In the 12C, Pierre de Vic, the youngest son of a local family forced to join the clergy. While still quite young, he was put in charge of a rich priory, and he turned it into a pleasure-dome, composing drinking songs and love ballads there. He gradually tired of his sedentary life and began to travel and sing ballads at the courts of Philippe Auguste, Richard the Lionheart and the King of Aragon. The "mad monk", as he called himself, carried off first prize at the Courts of Love Literary Tournament and won the Golden Hawk at a contest at Le Puy.

Winning barrels (16C) – During the Wars of Religion, **Captain Merle** was escorting a convoy of supplies for the Huguenots when Catholics ambushed him in a gorge. Merle ordered the men to cut the mules' traces and flee. After they had gone some distance, he stopped the stampede, having calculated that the Catholics would fall upon the casks of wine instead of pursuing his men. He proved to be right; after rallying his men, he counter-attacked, wiping out his drunken adversaries.

OLD TOWN

Turreted houses still grace the town centre, testifying to the city's former prosperity.

▶ For a tour of the old city, allow 20–30min. Leave from place de l'Hôtel-de-Ville. Turn left towards place de Monaco.

Note the elegant turreted house at No. 4 passage du Chevalier-des-Huttes.

▶ Turn left towards place de Monaco.

▶ **Population:** 2 003.
▶ **Michelin Map:** 330: D-5. 20km/12.4mi NE of Aurillac – Local map see Monts du Cantal.
▶ **Info:** Av. André-Mercier, 15800 Vic-sur-Cère. ℘04 71 47 50 68. www.carlades.fr.
▶ **Location:** Vic-sur-Cère lies along the Aurillac–Murat road.
▶ **Don't Miss:** The Château de Pesteils.
▶ **Timing:** Allow half a day.

Maison des Princes de Monaco

South of the church, off rue Coffinhal. This 15C house *(No. 4)* served as a residence on several occasions for the princes of Monaco, to whom Louis XIII had given the Carladez region–and thus Vic, its capital–in 1642. It remained in their possession until the Revolution.
The house has a mullioned window and a door surmounted by a badly damaged bas-relief depicting the Annunciation.

▶ Continue on rue Coffinhal.

Maison Dejou

At No. 5, there is a small *hôtel particulier* from the late 17C with a semicircular pediment.
Retrace your steps. On the left, note the tower adjoining the façade of the École St-Antoine on rue du Moine-de-Montaudon.

▶ Walk down to place de l'Église, pass behind the east end and follow the path to the waterfall.

Lou Cap Del Liou

Pretty old mill spanning the Iraliot.

▶ Walk up to the church.

DISCOVERING AURILLAC, CHÂTAIGNERAIE & MONTS DU CANTAL

Église St-Pierre

This partly Romanesque building has undergone many alterations. Note the graceful apse and the curious modillions on the south façade. Opposite the church, the former bailiwick is now private property. Walk up to the calvary along rue du Dr-Civiale. From the chapel there is a fine panoramic view of the town.

WALKS

Cascade du Trou de la Conche and Rocher de Maisonne

Behind the church, take the street leading to a footbridge over the Iraliot. On the other side of the torrent, walk up a very steep path.

At the top of the rise the road divides: *(left)* to Trou de la Conche cascade; *(right)* to the top of Maisonne rock, giving a fine view of Vic and the valley below.

Grotte des Anglais

Leave Vic on N 122 towards Murat and immediately turn onto the road to La Prade. Park on the platform.

A small knoll commands a nice view of the spa, with Curebourse plateau and wood in the background.

Go to Fournol village (vestiges of a Roman bridge down below). Bear left to rejoin and cross N 122.

Opposite, slightly to the right, a sign-posted trail leads to the **Grotte des Anglais**, a cave that gave shelter to bandits and highway robbers during the Hundred Years War (1337-1453).

EXCURSIONS

Thiézac

9km.5.6mi NE along N 122.

This is a sunny summer resort with a Gothic church (Église St-Martin) and a chapel (Chapelle Notre-Dame-de-Consolation) overlooking the village. It was after undertaking a pilgrimage here that Anne of Austria conceived, after 22 childless years of marriage, the future Louis XIV.

Cascade de Faillitoux

5km/3.1mi to the W. Leave Thiézac on the road to Vic and, soon after the graveyard, turn right onto D 59.

Around 3km/2.1mi further on, the road goes through Lasmolineries village, offering views of the Faillitoux waterfall flowing from its basalt ledge.

DRIVING TOUR

UPPER GOUL VALLEY AND CARLADÈS

80km/50mi. Allow one day.

Leave Vic to the SE on D 54, heading for Raulhac and Mur-de-Barrez.

Rocher des Pendus

Leave the car near Col de Curebourse and take the path on the right, opposite Auberge des Monts.

From this rock there is an extensive **panorama**★★ over the Cère valley, the Cantal mountain range, Carladès rock, the Châtaigneraie and the Aurillac basin.

Continue along D 54.

Église de Jou-sous-Monjou

Interesting Romanesque church with a fine belfry and a porch resting on a slender column.

Take D 59, then D 600 until you reach Raulhac.

On the way, note the Château de Cropières (*not open to the public*), a typical manor from the Cantal region.

Continue along D 600 towards Mur-de-Barrez.

Château de Messilhac

Occasional guided tours (45min) mid-Jun–Aug. €6. 04 71 49 57 86. www.messilhac.com.

VIC-SUR-CÈRE

Visiting the Rocher de Carlat with a VR headset

At the end of a track, this former fortress stands proudly in a delightful bucolic setting. The Renaissance façade, flanked by two square towers crowned by pointed roofs, is pierced with mullioned windows.

▶ On leaving Mur-de-Barrez, D 990 and D 459 (right) lead to Ronesque rock.

Rocher de Ronesque★★

This basalt rock forms a plateau dominating the entire countryside. It was formed in the same way as Carlat rock; first covered by volcano activity, then deeply gashed by large valleys. The picturesque hamlet at the foot of the rock is typical of the Cantal, where the houses often have roofs of stone slabs called *lauzes*.

Rocher de Carlat★★

🕐 Jun–early Jul and Sep Fri–Sun 2–6pm; Jul–Aug Mon–Fri 2–7pm, Sat–Sun 10am–7pm. €7; Children 6–16. €4. www.rocherdecarlat.fr.

The scenery here is typical of the Carlat area. The region was covered with basalt by lava flows from the volcanoes of Cantal; erosion fragmented the coating of rock, isolating a few flows which now stand, sheer-sided, at the top of steep hillsides. Today, it boasts delightful valleys and houses with steeply sloping hipped roofs of stone slabs surrounded by gardens and orchards.

The Rock once housed a massive fortress, deemed the most awe-inspiring in the South of France. A virtual reality tour of the now-defunct 15C and 16C fortress is now possible via VR headset or smartphone.

▶ Cross the breach and skirt, to the left, the north side of the rock.

Climb the Escalier de la Reine carved out of the rock to reach the northern edge of the plateau; there is a wonderful **view**★ of the mountains of Cantal. Climb Murgat rock, topped by a statue: the view stretches southwards beyond the village, to the Carlat region.

▶ Continue on D 990 to Vézac. D 208 on the right leads to Polminhac.

Château de Pesteils★

🕐 Apr–Jun, Sept, mid-Oct–early Nov 2–6pm (Jul–late Aug 10am–7pm). €8.50. 📞 04 71 47 40 03. www.chateau-pesteils-cantal.com.
🕐 *Costumed medieval visits are organised in summer.*

This beautiful medieval castle, built on a rocky promontory on the north bank of the Cère overlooking the town of Polminhac, was one of the strongholds designed to defend the valley. The imposing 13C square keep is crowned with a machicolated watch-path.

DISCOVERING AURILLAC, CHÂTAIGNERAIE & MONTS DU CANTAL

Murat ★

Murat lies in the pleasant Alagnon valley, in a scenic **setting**★★. Its grey houses with stone-slabbed roofs rise on picturesque terraces on the slopes of the basaltic Bonnevie hill. Two other steep peaks overlook the small town: Chastel rock to the north-west and Bredons rock to the south-east, topped by an interesting Romanesque church. Murat is an ideal centre from which to tour the volcanoes of Cantal and enjoy rambling in the surrounding state-owned forest. In August, a large influx of music lovers come to enjoy the International Festival of World Music and Dance.

> **Population:** 1 991.
> **Michelin Map:** 330: F-4. 25km/15.5mi NW of St-Flour – Local map see Monts du CANTAL.
> **Info:** pl de l'Hôtel de Ville, 15300 MURAT. ☎04 71 20 09 47. www.murat.fr.
> **Location:** Murat lies in the Alagnon valley, west of St-Flour, along the road to Aurillac.
> **Parking:** In the centre.
> **Don't Miss:** Stroll around the streets and stop for a coffee.
> **Timing:** Murat is not large; a couple of hours will suffice.

A BIT OF HISTORY

Nothing is impregnable to the French – The **Count of Anterroches**, who was born near Murat, is remembered for his reply to the proposal by the English, at Fontenoy, to fire first: "Gentlemen, we never fire first. Fire yourselves." This was not simply a gesture of courtesy but rather an application of the tactic by which troops would come under fire first and then march on the enemy while the latter were reloading their muskets. Anterroches is also credited with another famous saying: as he stood before Maastricht, someone declared that the town was impregnable. "Nothing," replied Anterroches, "is impregnable to the French."

THE TOWN

A brochure about this town of steep, narrow streets is available from the tourist office.

Église Notre-Dame-des-Oliviers

The church dates from the late Gothic period but has a modern west front.

Halle

This covered market is a fine example of 19C ironwork architecture.

Former Bailiff's Court

The building dates from the 16C and opens onto rue de l'Argenterie through a doorway decorated with moulding.

Maison Rodier

This elegant Renaissance-style building has some attractive bonding in trachyte (a type of volcanic rock) and a corbelled watch-tower.

Consul's Residence

Faubourg Notre-Dame.
The late-15C stone façade has two storeys with narrow windows topped by an ornament. Note the two carved angels above the door, part of which consists of linenfold panels.

Rocher de Bonnevie

The sides of this hill feature strange basalt columns which are remarkable for the uniformity and length of their prisms. A castle once stood on the hill but it was razed on the orders of Richelieu; it did, however, take six months and six hundredweight of gunpowder to complete the task. From here, there is a fine view over Murat, the Alagnon valley, the mountains of Cantal and the Chevade valley.

MURAT

Murat

Maison de la Faune
Jul–Aug 10am–noon, 2–6pm (Sun, 2–6pm); rest of the year Tues–Sat 3–6pm. €4.8 (child 6–15, €3). 04 71 20 00 52. www.murat.fr.
This former mansion has retained a late-15C turret. Inside, a large collection of beetles and butterflies, stuffed birds and animals are displayed in reconstructions of their natural environment.

EXCURSIONS

Église de Bredons★
SE along D 926. Contact the town hall for information. 04 71 20 02 80.
The small fortified 11C church is all that remains of the Benedictine priory. The doorway on the south side has billet moulding. Inside, note the monumental giltwood altarpiece completed in 1710 for the High Altar; the intricate detail and abundance of gold and polychrome make this a grandiose piece of decoration. The Resurrection is depicted in the centre. Other giltwood altar screens decorate the chapels.

Albepierre-Bredons★
5km/3mi SW on D 39.
This tiny village built on a volcanic hill overlooks the Alagnon valley. Underground houses were once built into the caves in the rock. From the top of the village, there is an interesting view of Murat below and of the Rocher de Bonnevie in the distance.

ADDRESSES

STAY

Chambre d'Hôte La Gaspardine – *Gaspard, 15300 La Chapelle d'Alagnon.* 04 71 20 01 91. www.cantal-hote.com. *4 rooms.* Isolated in a peaceful place, this former farm, just 2km/1mi from the town, opens onto a beautiful flowery terrace with a most agreeable view over the Alagnon valley. The rooms are decorated with good taste, and the dinner menus favour the specialities of the region.

EAT

Le Jarrousset – *3km/1.8mi E of Murat via N 122 dir. Clermont-Ferrand.* 04 71 20 10 69. www.restaurant-le-jarrousset.com. *Closed Sun eve and Tue (except Jul–Aug) and Mon, closed Jan.* This rural restaurant in a pavilion set back from the road has a contemporary-style dining room with a veranda giving onto the garden and a terrace in summer. Fine dining without the pretensions of haute cuisine; a peaceful place for a relaxing evening.

Salers★★

Salers is one of the prettiest little towns in Upper Auvergne and has a very distinctive character. It stands at an altitude of 951m and has retained from its military and judicial past a rare set of ramparts and old houses grouped together on a pinnacle, giving a magnificent view of the confluence of the River Aspre and River Maronne. Salers also lends its name to a tasty farmhouse cheese made from unpasteurised full-cream milk.

A BIT OF HISTORY

Arms and the gown (15C–16C) – The twofold character of the buildings in Salers can be explained by the town's history. Initially unwalled, it suffered cruelly at the hands of the English and the mercenaries or "free companions", who roamed the highways; as a result the ramparts were built and still stand today. In the 16C Salers became the seat of the bailiwick of the Upper Mountains of the Auvergne, and the established *bourgeois* families, from which the judges were selected, started building their impressive turreted houses.

WALKING TOUR

Eglise St-Mathieu★

A 12C porch still remains from the Romanesque church that pre-dated the present church, begun in the 15C. The bell-tower, which was struck by lightning, was rebuilt in the 19C.

▶ On leaving the church, pass a fountain on the left and follow rue du Beffroi uphill.

Go under the Tour de l'Horloge (clock-tower, also known as Belfry Gate), flanked by a round tower with machicolations. Just beyond the gate, on the right, is the house of Pierre Lizet with its Gothic window and Renaissance portal.

▶ **Population:** 357.
Michelin Map: 330: C-4. 20km/12.4mi SE of Mauriac – Local map see Monts du CANTAL.
Info: Pl. Tyssandier-d'Escous, 15140 Salers. ℘04 71 40 58 08. www.salers-tourisme.fr.
Location: Salers lies 20km/12.5mi SE of Mauriac, and 45km/28mi from Aurillac, via the D 680.
Parking: There is generous parking around the centre.
Don't Miss: A gentle stroll through the old streets is needed to fully appreciate the timeless beauty of the village.
Timing: Allow half a day, and enjoy a relaxing lunch.

Place Tyssandier-d'Escous

The old houses of dark lava stone with their clean, sober lines, corbelled round or polygonal turrets and pepper-pot or many-sided roofs look like a stage-set; the scene is completed by a fountain in the centre. On the main square, a monument has been raised to Tyssandier d'Escous, who improved the region's breed of cattle in the 19C and made it famous.

House known as the "Ancien Baillage"

This Renaissance building, the former Bailiff's Court, stands at the corner of rue du Beffroi. It is a vast residence of fine architectural design, flanked by two corner towers. It is not open to visits from the public.

Maison de Flojeac

Opposite the tourist office. The house has a turret with canted corners.

Maison de la Ronade

This building has a tower rising five storeys high. It has been converted into a tearoom.

SALERS

Salers

▶ At the entrance to rue du Couvent, on the right, a wooden door leads to a large courtyard.

Maison des Templiers – Musée de Salers

Rue des Templiers. ⓒ*Mon–Thu and Sun 10am–12.30pm, 2–5.30pm, Sat 2–5.30pm; open til 6.30pm in summer.* ⊚€5. ℘04 71 40 75 97. www.salers-tourisme.fr.

The 15C building houses an exhibition on the town's folklore and past: reconstruction of Auvergne interiors, cheese-making, chemist's shop dating from 1890, religious objects and garments.

▶ Turn left onto avenue de Barrouze.

Esplanade de Barrouze

The small, shaded park here offers an impressive view★ of the Maronne, Rat and Aspre valleys and also of the Puy Violent massif.

▶ Retrace your steps.

Maison Bertrandy

The house has a round tower and an attractive door.

▶ Return to Grande-Place, then take rue du Beffroi back to the church.

EXCURSIONS

Les Burons de Salers ★

4km/2.5mi from Salers on the road to Puy Mary.
ⓒ*Apr–Sept 10am–7pm.* ⊚€5. ℘04 71 40 70 71. www.buronsdesalers.fr.
Appropriately located in a restored *buron* (shepherd's hut), this "cheese house" retraces the history of the Salers breed of cattle and of the local cheese-making tradition; fine collection of tools. Another *buron* presents the history of the local liqueur made from the gentian plant. Reserve in advance to enjoy a typical truffade lunch.

La Maison de la Salers

7km/4.5mi from Salers via D22.
ⓒ*Feb–Jun and Sep–Nov 10am–noon and 2–6pm; Jul–Aug 9am–7pm daily; end-Dec–early Jan 10am–noon; 2–6pm.*⊚€7;⊚€4.5 for children. ℘047140 54 00. www.maisondelasalers.fr.
Located within a typical 17C Auvergnat barn, this interactive locale complete with short films allows visitors to learn all about Salers cattle, beef, and cheese.

Anglards-de-Salers

10km/6.2mi N on D 22.
The Auvergne-style church with its octagonal belfry is quite purist in its architectural style.

183

DISCOVERING AURILLAC, CHÂTAIGNERAIE & MONTS DU CANTAL

SALERS — Map

WHERE TO STAY
- Bastide du Cantal (La) .... ①
- Saluces (Hôtel) .... ②
- Voyageurs (Hôtel Les) .... ③

WHERE TO EAT
- Bailliage (Le) .... ①
- Diligence (La) .... ②
- Évasion (L') .... ③

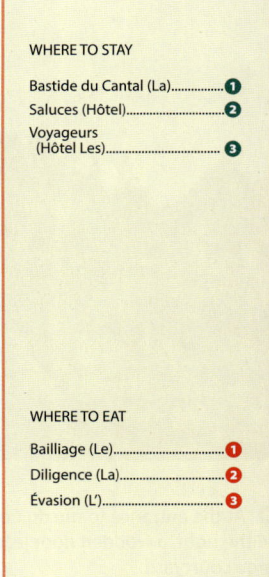

Below it stands the 15C **Château de la Trémolière** (May–Sept. €5. ℘04 71 40 05 72) which houses a collection of 16C Aubusson tapestries.

▶ You can extend your tour by pressing on to Mauriac (see MAURIAC).

Brasserie 360

13.3km/8.3mi W on D680 and D922. ℘04 71 68 98 63. www.brasserie360.fr. Open May–mid-Jun Fri-Sat 10.30am–7pm; mid-Jun–late Jun Mon-Sat 4pm–7.30pm; Jul–Aug 4pm–7.30pm daily; Sept. Mon-Sat 4pm–7.30pm.
This brewery located within the Parc Naturel Régional des Volcans d'Auvergne brews beers from the pure water of the wild Maronne river. Perched at 100 metres of altitude, it overlooks glacial valleys and beautiful volcanoes.

Pleaux

Pleaux enjoys a modest workaday atmosphere, a mutually supportive community and a smattering of sturdy bourgeois houses in the Renaissance style along the narrow streets that ripple from the Grand Place and the broad square where the market is held.

ADDRESSES

🛏 STAY

⊜ **Hôtel Les Voyageurs** – *15380 Le Falgoux. ℘04 71 69 51 59. hotel-restaurant-des-voyageurs-hotel.business.site/. Closed Nov.–mid-Dec. 14 rooms.* Auberge in the true Auvergnat tradition with an inglenook fireplace lined with benches in the bar. The rooms have been refurnished and are soberly rustic but well kept. Regional dishes in the restaurant.

⊜⊜ **La Bastide du Cantal** – *rte de Puy Mary – 1km/0.5mi NE via the D 680. ℘04 77 69 35 49. www.villagefani.com. 25 rooms.* Above the town in a peaceful park, a modern and functional place to sleep peacefully. The rooms have all been refurbished and some are equipped with balconies or terraces with views over the valley. The hotel also boasts a pool.

⊜⊜ **Hôtel Saluces** – *rue de la Martille 15140 Salers. ℘04 71 40 70 82. www.hotel-salers.fr. 8 rooms.* This charming hotel in a former 17C private mansion boats a calm,

RIOM-ÈS-MONTAGNES

lush courtyard – the perfect place for breakfast. Rooms have gorgeous exposed beams and hardwood floors. Not suitable for thos who cannot climb stairs.

⌘ EAT

La Diligence – R. du Beffroi. ☏04 71 40 75 39. www.ladiligencesalers.com. Closed mid Nov–Mar. Don't be fooled by the modern look of this establishment – the dishes served here are traditional local fare. If the *crêpes* won't satisfy your appetite, the *truffade*, *tripoux*, *pounti* or *potée auvergnate* will, especially when washed down with a native wine.

Le Bailliage – R. Notre-Dame. ☏04 71 40 71 95. www.salers-hotel-bailliage.com. Closed mid-Nov–Feb. An inviting dining room and lovely terrace on which to enjoy the mouthwatering cuisine of the Auvergne. The hotel element has large rooms overlooking the garden or the surrounding countryside. An agreeable retreat.

L'Evasion – 11 rue Notre-Dame. ☏04 71 40 74 56. Closed Thurs. In the heart of the picturesque village, this simple, modern table works with local products like Saint-Flour lentils and Corrèze apples for creative, unique dishes.

Riom-ès-Montagnes ★

Situated in the western part of the Parc Régional des Volcans, Riom-ès-Montagnes is a small town linking the Rhue valley to the Cantal mountain range and a thriving commercial centre with an important cheese industry. The production of an aperitif based on the gentian plant contributes to the prosperity of the town, which is the ideal starting point for excursions through the high pastures and Romanesque churches of gentian country.

> - **Population:** 2 798.
> - **Michelin Map:** 330: E-2
> - **Info:** 1 av. Fernand-Brun 15400 Riom-ès-Montagnes. ☏04 71 78 07 37. www.tourisme-gentiane.com.
> - **Location:** 24km/15mi from Bort-les-Orgues via the D 922.
> - **Don't Miss:** Visit the beautiful valley of the Cheylade.
> - **Kids:** Exploring the countryside.

SIGHTS

Église St-Georges ★
The only remaining parts of the original 11C are the chancel, the apse, the dome and the transept.

Espace Avèze
⏱ Mid-Jun–mid-Sept 10am–noon, 3–7pm; the rest of the year by appointment. ♿ ⌘ No charge. ☏04 71 78 03 04. www.aveze.com.
This company, founded in 1929, produces an aperitif based on the gentian plant picked in the surrounding mountains. An exhibition space offering a view of the bottling hall is devoted to the drink, the only one extracted by soaking the plant for nine months in a mixture of water and alcohol.

Gentiane Express
⏱ Departures Apr–mid-Jun and mid-Sep–mid-Oct Thurs. & Sun. at 3pm (mid-Jun– mid-Jul and Sept. Tues.-Sun., mid-Jul–Aug Mon–Fri 10am and 3pm; Sat.–Sun. 3pm). 2½h round trip. Booking essential; check website for details. ⌘€16 (child 4–12, €9). ☏04 73 39 72 21. www.gentiane-express.com.
This tourist train takes passengers across high pastures where the famous Salers cattle graze in summer. The itinerary links Bort-les-Orgues and Lugarde via

185

DISCOVERING AURILLAC, CHÂTAIGNERAIE & MONTS DU CANTAL

Castle ruins, Apchon

Riom-ès-Montagnes and the Barajol viaduct.

EXCURSIONS

St-Étienne-de-Choimeil
14km/8.7mi NW along D 3 then D 205. Turn right before the Romanesque church.

Botanical trail
3.5km/2.2mi round tour. Allow 1h.
This pleasant ramble through woodland offers the opportunity of discovering the local flora in its natural environment.

DRIVING TOUR

2 CHEYLADE VALLEYS AND GENTIANE COUNTRY★★
90km/56mi. About one day.
see map p158.

After crossing the dry Sapchat valley, and the Rhue de Cheylade valley, the road overlooks the wooded Véronne valley and runs along its hillside. Riom-ès-Montagnes appears in the midst of a fresh pastoral setting.

▶ Head S from Riom along D 3.

Soon a superb **panoramic view** unfolds to the left over the Dore mountain range and the upper plateaux of the Cézallier area. Beyond lie the ruins of the Château d'Apchon and the mountains of Cantal.

Apchon
This is a typical Cantal village its sturdy houses. A footpath leads off from rue de la Porte-du-Barre to a viewing table and the **castle ruins** *(30min on foot there and back; access to the ruins could be dangerous for children).*

▶ Leave Apchon S (D 249) then turn right onto D 63.

Collandres
The Romanesque church of this tiny village stands on the site of a former look-out post over the Véronne valley. The road, which goes past the church, runs across high pastures where cattle graze in summer. In the Cantal region, these pastures extend over an area of some 80 000ha.
Turn left at the first junction towards La Chatonnière. The road runs through woodland and pastureland dotted with burons (shepherds' huts) and farms. Besides cattle grazing in the fields, you are likely to see birds of prey and herons.

▶ Return to Collandres and leave the village S along D 263.

Cascade du Pont d'Aptier
This waterfall in its unspoilt setting is the ideal place for a picnic.

▶ Beyond the bridge, turn left onto D 249.

RIOM-ÈS-MONTAGNES

Chapelle de la Font-Sainte
This 19C place of pilgrimage can be seen in the middle of the fields.
The road *(D 49)* runs through St-Hippolyte and down to the Rhue de Cheylade. After crossing the river, the Puy Mary is visible to the right of a long ridge starting at the Puy de Peyre-Arse.

Cheylade
This resort above the Rhue is popular with anglers and is a good starting point for rambles.

▶ 2.5km/1.5mi S of Cheylade, turn right on D 262. Park near a bridge and walk a further 100m to the right.

Cascade du Sartre★
The waterfall is formed by the Rhue which flows down a drop of 30m. Continue along D 262 and, beyond another bridge, turn right on a path offering an attractive view of the **Cascade de la Roche**, a waterfall formed by a tributary of the Rhue which drops down over the rocks in a series of mini-cascades.

▶ Turn back and continue along D 62.

Le Claux
This small resort is ideal for a variety of outdoor activities: cross-country skiing and snowshoeing in winter (**Maison de Montagne** – ☎04 71 78 93 88), paragliding, climbing, riding and rambling in summer.
Beyond Le Claux, the view of the Puy Mary and the Cheylade valley with its forested floor becomes increasingly impressive. The road rises in a series of hairpin bends and continues through woods until it reaches the alpine pastures. It then crosses Col de Serres and arrives at the Impradine valley, hollowed into a bowl shape by ancient glaciers. During the final climb up to Pas de Peyrol, the road crosses the Eylac pass, clings to the sheer sides of the Puy Mary and provides a number of splendid **views★** over the Impradine and Rhue de Cheylade valleys, the Dore mountain range, and the Cézallier area.

Pas de Peyrol★★ –
See Monts du CANTAL.

▶ Go back 3km/1.9mi along D 62, then turn right onto D 23, heading for Dienne.

The road hugs the steep Impradine and Santoire valleys.

Puy Mary★★★ –
See Monts du CANTAL.

▶ Leave Puy Mary along D 680 then turn right onto D 12 towards Le Falgoux. Beyond Col d'Aulac, turn left as you enter the Marihou woods.

Site de Cotteughes et Preydefont
The remains of drystone huts abandoned during the Middle Ages testify to the area's long-standing cattle breeding tradition.

Trizac
This large village is renowned for its cattle markets.

▶ Turn right onto D 205.

Menet
As the road runs down towards the village, it affords views of its harmonious white buildings. The nearby lake offers relaxing activities (angling, pedalo, etc).

▶ Leave Menet E; D 36 runs through woodland back to Riom.

ADDRESSES

♀/ EAT

Le Garage – 2 route Mauriac. ☎04 71 78 60 79. le-garage-trizac.wixsite.com/le-garage-trizac. ⏰ mid-Jul–mid-Sep lunch daily, dinner by reservation; off-season Tues–Fri lunch; weekends by reservation.
Traditional Auvergnat fare is on the menu at this delightful gas station-turned-restaurant.

DISCOVERING AURILLAC, CHÂTAIGNERAIE & MONTS DU CANTAL

Mauriac★

Situated between the Dordogne and Puy Mary, this small town, an important agricultural trading centre, consists of black, lava stone houses on the edge of a vast basalt plateau.

> - **Population:** 3 977.
> - **Michelin Map:** 330: B-3 – 19km/11.8mi NW of Salers.
> - **Info:** 1 r. Chappe-d'Auteroche, 15200 Mauriac. ℘04 71 68 19 87. www.tourisme.paysdemauriac.fr.
> - **Location:** 20km/12mi NW from Salers, 50km/31mi north of Aurillac.
> - **Timing:** 2–3 hours to wander.

SIGHTS

Basilique Notre-Dame-des-Miracles★

This is the most important Romanesque building in Upper Auvergne, erected between the 12C and the 14C. The vast main doorway at the west front is the best piece of Romanesque carving in the area. Around place Georges-Pompidou are a few old houses including one with double Romanesque bays. Note the old houses with twinned Romanesque openings surrounding place Georges-Pompidou.

Monastère St-Pierre

Jul–Aug 10am–noon, 2.30–5.30pm; Sept. 2–6pm. Sun am and Tue in Sept. €3. ℘04 71 68 07 24.

This monastery was once a daughter-house of Église St-Pierre-le-Vif in Sens. It is possible to see a few Gallo-Roman remains, some of the foundations of the Carolingian church (early 9C), the 11C chapter house (columns made with local marble) and part of the cloisters (14C–15C).

> Follow rue du Collège.

Hôtel d'Orcet

Currently the Sous-Préfecture. This 16C–18C building incorporates the 12C tympanum that decorated the doorway into the monastery refectory.

> Continue along rue du Dr-E.-Chavialle; the first left leads to the museum.

EXCURSIONS

Puy St-Mary

Climb up to the chapel at the top of Puy St-Mary. From here there is a panoramic view of Mauriac, the mountains of Cantal and the plateaux bordering the Auvergne and the Limousin.

Château de la Vigne

Ally. ℘04 71 69 00 20. www.chateaudelavigne.fr.

This 15C castle is flanked by two round towers topped by pepper-pot roofs, and a square tower that served as a keep and to which, in the 18C, a second building was attached. Inside, there are 16C frescoes on the walls and ceiling of the Salle de Justice. It is also possible to **spend the night** in one of four beautiful rooms.

🚗 DRIVING TOUR

CHURCHES OF THE NORTHERN PLATEAUX
Round trip of 70km/44mi. Allow a day.

> Head NE from Mauriac on D 922 and turn right onto D 678.

Église du Vigean

In the small church is a **reliquary★** made of 13C Limousin enamelwork.

> Follow D 678. About 2km/1mi before reaching Moussages, take D 12.

188

MAURIAC

Monastère St-Pierre, Mauriac

Moussages
Overlooking a square decorated with an old fountain and surrounded by old houses is the church, whose Romanesque east end has carved modillions.

▶ Leave N on D 22 then turn right.

Château d'Auzers★
Apr–Jul 3–6.30pm; Jul–Aug daily 2–6.30pm; Sept.-Oct. Sun, Mon, Thurs, Fri 3–6.30pm. ℘04 71 78 62 59. www.auzers.com.
This 14C and 16C castle comprises a central building flanked by two high turrets crowned by pepper-pot roofs.

▶ 2km/1mi after leaving Auzers, turn right onto D 22, heading to Saignes.

Saignes
This small summer resort perched above the Sumène valley has a Romanesque church and several quaint 15C houses.

▶ Turn right towards Le Monteil then left onto D 36.

Chastel-Merlhac
Its circular shape makes this eroded lava flow look like a basalt fortress.

▶ Return to Saignes and turn NE onto D 236 towards Riom; turn right onto D 15 then right again onto D 3.

Antignac
The **Jardins ethnobotaniques** (*℘04 71 40 21 16*) grow plants of medieval origin found on archaeological sites.

▶ Leave Antignac on D 3 to Bort-les-Orgues; turn left on D 15, then D 315.

Ydes-Bourg
Insectes du Monde (*Jul–Aug 2–7pm; Sept–Jun by appointment only. €3. ℘04 71 40 59 81*) is mainly devoted to butterflies and moths.

▶ Rejoin D 922; right to Bassignac.

Bassignac
The **Jardin Délirant** (*10am–8pm; €4 (children, €2.50). ℘04 71 67 32 50*) is a garden growing more than 150 species of textile plants.

▶ Rejoin D 922 to return to Mauriac.

DISCOVERING AURILLAC, CHÂTAIGNERAIE & MONTS DU CANTAL

Saint-Cernin

This small town is a pleasant base from which to explore the western Cantal mountain range.
One of the most striking features of the surrounding countryside is the castle of Anjony. Strategically located on the tip of the Tournemire promontory, it dominates the lush landscape of the Doire valley with its four tall towers.

- **Population:** 1 155.
- **Michelin Map:** 330: c-4
- **Info:** Le Bourg, 15140 St-Martin-Valmeroux. 04 71 69 44 41.
- **Location:** 20km/13mi N of Aurillac via the D 922.
- **Kids:** Château d'Anjony.
- **Timing:** Allow half a day and enjoy a leisurely stroll and maybe a coffee.

ST-LOUIS CHURCH

The 12C **Église St-Louis**, dominated by its bell-tower, was altered in the 15C and boasts some fine **woodwork**★ (note in particular the misericords on the 14 choir stalls, from the chapter-house at St-Chamant), a handsome Louis XIV lectern near the pulpit and lovely **corbels** carved into the basalt of the church's east end.

🚗 DRIVING TOUR

GORGES DE LA MARONNE★
55km/34.2mi round tour. Allow 2hrs.

▶ Leave St-Cernin to the N towards D 922; head for Mauriac and turn onto the first road on the right.

Château du Cambon
🍃 *Jul–Aug 2.30–6.30pm; Jun and Sept by arrangement.* ⊛€6. 04 71 47 60 48.
This fine 18C castle, built of dark basalt stone, has been whitewashed. The owner takes visitors on a guided tour, from the chapel and the first-floor bedrooms to the ground-floor reception rooms.

▶ Rejoin D 922 towards Mauriac.

St-Chamant
The **church** contains eight choir stalls decorated with **painted panels**★. The **château** (🍃 *guided visits Jul–Aug 2.30–6.30pm.* ⊛€5 (park and interior). 04 71 69 26 85. http://saintchamant.free.fr) is 17C with a 15C square machicolated keep; inside are wonderful **tapestries**★, in very good condition, decorated with themes including spring, mythological events and the crusades. The castle chapel houses a lovely gilded wooden altarpiece (18C) depicting the Holy Family.

▶ Leave St-Chamant to the W on D 42. Rejoin D 922.

St-Martin-Valmeroux
A small glove-making centre with a Gothic church, an old fountain and the ruins of château de Crèvecœur.

▶ Leave St-Martin to the W on D 37.

The winding road to Loupiac dominates the Maronne valley, flanked by luxuriant slopes. Beyond Loupiac stands the ruins of Branzac castle.

Château de Branzac
This massive keep with corner towers representative of Cantal fortified architecture is now just a picturesque ruin on the end of a promontory.

▶ Return to D 37.

🚶 Opposite the last house in St-Christophe-les-Gorges, on the road to St-Martin-Cantalès, take the path *(45min on foot there and back)*, cross the railway tracks and go to the chapel Notre-Dame-du-Château.

SAINT-CERNIN

GORGES OF THE MARONNE

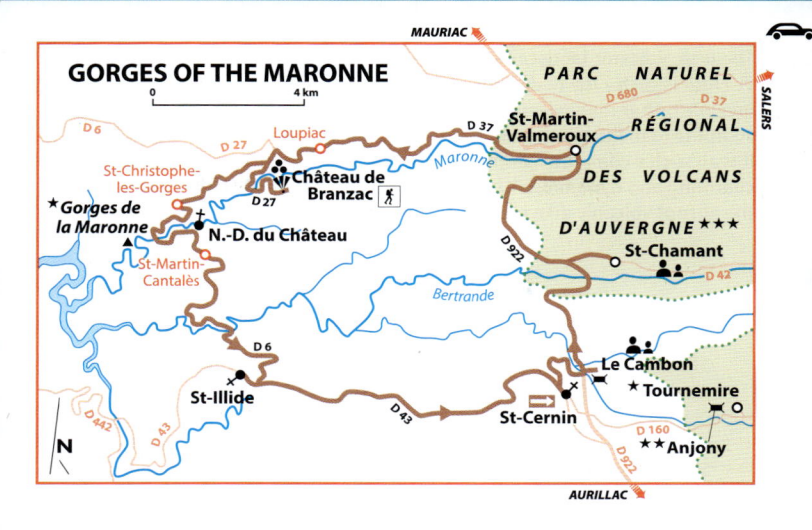

Notre-Dame-du-Château
The chapel is an attractive building roofed with *lauzes*, sitting in a lovely **setting**★ overlooking a double meander of the river.

▶ Leave St-Christophe-les-Gorges to the south on D 6.

Gorges de la Maronne★
The valley narrows and enters a canyon bordered by lush vegetation.

▶ Continue along D 6, entering the Gorges de la Bertrande.

Église de St-Illide
This Romanesque church (*closed to the public*) was enlarged in the 15C.

▶ Leave St-Illide E and follow D 43 back to St-Cernin.

EXCURSIONS

Tournemire★
6.5km/4mi to the E of Saint-Cernin via the D 160.
This lovely village in the heart of the Cantal mountains has been recognised as one of the most beautiful villages in France. The lava-stone houses are covered with slate roofs, and the small, Romanesque church is built of coloured volcanic tufa.

Château d'Anjony★★
Guided tours daily (except Tues.) Feb–Mar and Oct–Nov at 2.15, 3.15, and 4.45pm; Apr–Jun and Sept at 2.15, 3.30, 4.45, and 6pm; Jul–Aug daily at 10.45am and noon except Sun, 2 and 6.15pm. €9. ℘04 71 47 61 67; www.anjony.fr.

This castle of reddish basalt is one of the most remarkable in Auvergne. Strategically located on the tip of the Tournemire promontory, it dominates the lush landscape of the Doire valley with its four tall towers.

The castle was built in the 15C by Louis II of Anjony, companion of Dunois and Joan of Arc, near the towers of Tournemire, which his family had held in joint fief with the Tournemires since 1351. This dual ownership led to three centuries of bloody rivalry between the families: one of old feudal stock, the other having prospered through business and service to the royal family.

The main hall on the first floor boasts a coffered ceiling with three tiers of beams, and throughout the castle are fine furnishings and furniture: a vast fireplace, tapestries from Aubusson and Flanders, a tester bed and a reclining seat. The Knights' Hall on the second floor has **frescoes**★ of Michel of Anjony and his wife Germaine of Foix in late-16C dress and scenes illustrating the legend of the Nine Valiant Knights from a medieval poem.

ST-FLOUR SANFLORAIN AND MARGERIDE DU CANTAL

The lush, volcanic landscape of green hills and glacial valleys that surrounds St-Flour is such a joy to explore, a place where the metronome of life is set at *andante* rather than *allegro*, and the harmonies between man and the land combine to make a pastoral symphony worthy of the greatest composers. It is all such a complete contrast to St-Flour itself, a place at once both charming and dynamic, with its narrow streets climbing to the upper town on the abrupt volcanic dike of Planèze.

Highlights

1. Exploring the upper town of **St-Flour** and buying local produce at the Saturday market (p194)
2. Walking the path to the tiny **Sailhant waterfall** (p197)
3. Exploring the rugged **Gorges de la Truyère** (p198)
4. Admiring the **Garabit viaduct**, built by Gustave Eiffel before he created the Eiffel Tower (p199)
5. Stepping back in time at the **Château d'Alleuze** (p200)

Dark Rocks

The local rock around St-Flour, as elsewhere in Cantal, is the dark and sombre basalt. As a result, many of the buildings have a gloomy façade. But this belies the attractions of the place, not least of which is the Gothic cathedral, with its twin towers dominating the countryside. Of this elevated town, the saying goes: "None ever took you by force except the wind!"

What's in a Name?

Originally, the name of "Margeride" applied only to a lordship, in this case one whose castle was ruined in the 15C, and to a forest area. The original location is near Védrines Saint-Loup on the road from Saint-Flour Langeac. It gradually became the generic name for all of the surrounding mountains. The National Forest finally formalised the name in the 19C, and geographers later extended the name to the entire granite plateau in the 20C.

Flora

The vegetation across the region largely consists of pine and beech forests (in the damp areas), with man-made forests of spruce and extensive areas of broom heath and heather. There are also bogs in which you can still find relics of Ice Age plants (especially the rare dwarf birch and willow of Lapland).

Gorges de la Truyère at Laussac

© Christian Guy/hemis.fr

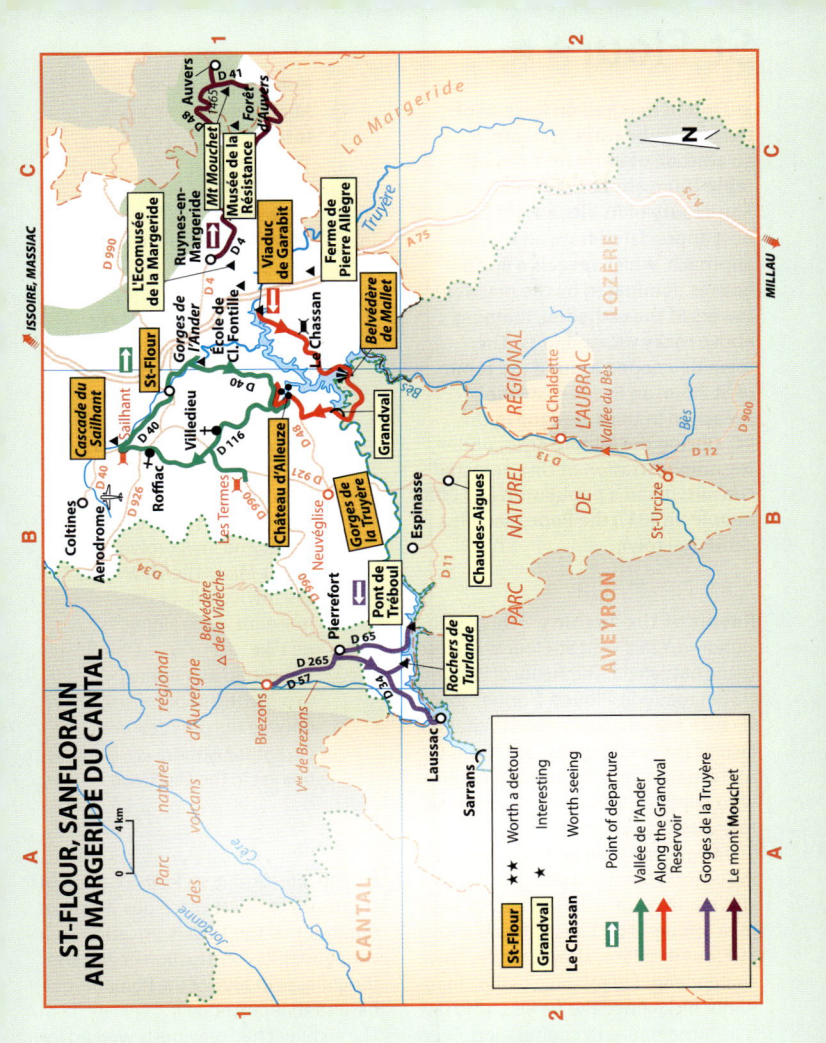

Sanflorain Lands

At the centre of Les Pays du Sanflorain sits the Planèze: a vast, virtually flat area of basalt plateaux. Until quite recently, the area hosted crops of rye, peas, lentils and other grains. With better sunshine and lower rainfall than the areas to the west, protected by the mountains, the Planèze was for many years regarded as the granary of the Upper Auvergne, over which St-Flour was the guardian. From this heart radiated different landscapes, each with its own strong identity and culture.

Feeling Sheepish

In the 16C, Margeride adopted the agro-pastoral system of farming, similar to that used in Planèze. This was based on extensive use of rangelands for livestock in combination with cereal cultivation around the village (mainly rye).

Sheep farming was of great importance, as it ensured the fertilisation and management of the land. The sheep were entrusted to a shepherd who brought the flock back into the village every night.

St-Flour ★★

St-Flour is perched on the end of the *planèze* bearing its name, at an altitude of 881m on a basaltic table 100m above the River Ander. The beauty of its **site★★** can be best appreciated from an eastern approach, which reveals a line of houses dominated by the massive towers of the cathedral, looming above rocky escarpments. The town developed around the tomb of St Flour, an Evangelist who preached in the Auvergne in the 4C. During the Middle Ages, under the administration of three elected consuls, it had a population of 7 000 people. In 1317, the Pope made it a cathedral town.

A BIT OF HISTORY

Revolt of the Tuchins – During the Hundred Years War, St-Flour was close to the battlefield. The Treaty of Brétigny (1360) made St-Flour a frontier town, "France's key to Guienne" (Aquitaine). Fear of the English grew, but it was the mercenaries, more than the English, who controlled the country from the fortresses of Saillant and Alleuze.

The town was often attacked, its outlying districts burnt and pillaged. The consuls made pacts with the enemy who, for a fee, agreed to leave the people of St-Flour in peace. However, the truce was endangered by some of the inhabitants, nicknamed the *Tuchins,* who saw it as tantamount to capitulation. Seen as patriots by the lower classes, they secretly banded together and waged implacable guerilla warfare on the occupant. After 1384, the *Tuchins* also attacked the rich and privileged orders and became outright robbers. Having become dangerous to local authorities, they were overcome by the troops of the Duc de Berry.

CATHEDRAL DISTRICT
Cathedral★
9am–6pm (Jul–Aug 8.30am–7pm). 04 71 60 22 50.

- **Population:** 6 630.
- **Michelin Map:** 330: G-4.
- **Info:** 17 bis, pl. d'Armes, 15100 St-Flour. 04 71 60 22 50. www.pays-saint-flour.com.
- **Location:** There are two towns: one modern and busy on the plain; the other, perched on a huge rocky upthrust overlooking the Ander and Lescure valleys. It is here, within the network of old streets and cranky buildings, that Saint-Flour's interest lies.
- **Parking:** There are ample parking areas in both the upper and lower town.
- **Don't Miss:** The view from the town walls, or the museum in the Hôtel de Ville.
- **Timing:** Half a day to explore the upper town; beware the *priorité à droite*. On Saturday there is a lively market in the Old Town.

Built in late-Gothic style, the cathedral stands on the vast place des Armes, a reminder of the town's vocation as a stronghold. Its construction begun after the collapse in 1396 of the Romanesque basilica that preceded it.

The architect had previously worked for the Duc de Berry, which explains why the construction is not in the usual style of the region. The right-hand tower is pierced with square mullioned windows, letting daylight into the two rooms once used as a bishop's residence.

Inside, the lines of the five aisles are strikingly sober. Under the organ loft, a 15C mural depicts **Purgatory and Hell**.

Old Streets

From place d'Armes, lined with arcades and old façades (particularly at the corner of rue de Belloy), walk to rue Sorel and the church of St-Vincent, a former

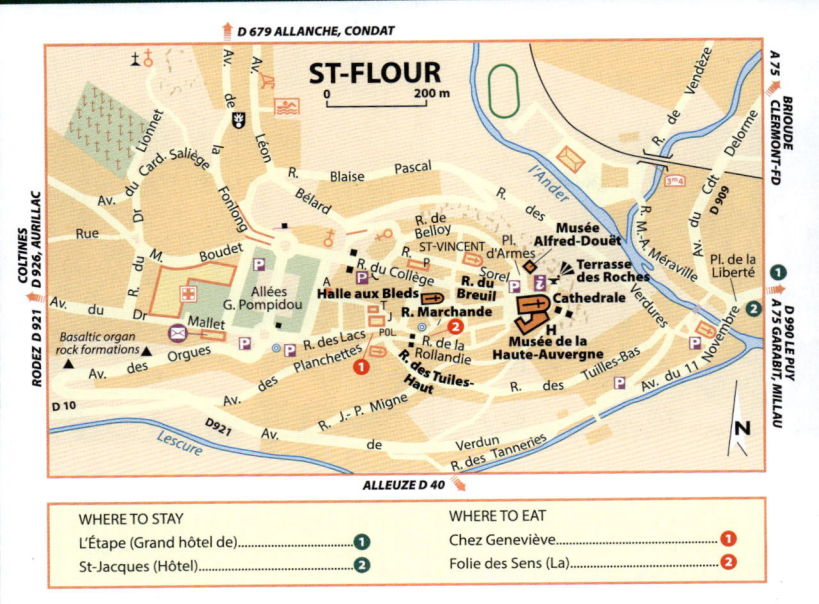

WHERE TO STAY		WHERE TO EAT	
L'Étape (Grand hôtel de)	1	Chez Geneviève	1
St-Jacques (Hôtel)	2	Folie des Sens (La)	2

Dominican convent that is occasionally open to the public for exhibits.

Follow rue des Jacobins on the left, then rue de la Collégiale, named after a disused 14C church: **Notre-Dame collegiate church** or **Halle aux Bleds**. This building was completey renovated in the 2000s and today features a series of contemporary windows. Open to the public during the Saturday weekly market from Nov.–March and in summer during exhibits.

Rue Marchande has a few interesting old houses, including No. 31, a 15C mansion that is now the governor's house and whose façade and courtyard can be seen. At No. 15, Hôtel Brisson has a 16C courtyard and original windows separated by columns with rope moulding. Other interesting streets include **rue du Breuil** (15C house at no. 8), and **rue des Tuiles-Haut** (old houses).

Ancienne Maison Consulaire

The façade of this former consul's residence dates from the 16C. The courtyard (enter through No. 17 bis), from which can be seen three houses successively bought by consuls in the 14C and 15C to serve as their consular establishment, has an old well, a 15C staircase turret and various painted inscriptions. It houses the Musée d'Art et d'Histoire Alfred-Douët (see Museums below).

Terrasse des Roches

Behind the east end of the cathedral.
From this square on the old ramparts there is a lovely view of the lower part of the town, the Ander valley and the Margeride mountains.

MUSEUMS

St-Flour prides itself on its rich cultural heritage and its many museums, which will enlighten you on local art and history.

Musée de la Haute-Auvergne

Place d'Armes. Nov–Mar Thu–Fri 2–5pm; Oct and Apr–Jun Wed–Sat 2–6pm; Jul–Sept daily 10.30am–6.30pm. 1 Jan, 1 May and 25 Dec. €4 (free 1st Sun of month) 04 71 60 22 32.

This museum is located in the former bishop's palace rebuilt in the 17C. Displays in the low 15C vaulted rooms explain how blue-veined Fourme cheese is made (including Cantal and

St-Flour

Salers varieties) and the different facets of pastoral life, particularly the shepherd's huts or *burons* where cheese is made. On the ground floor, in the former chapel, note a 12C polychrome wooden statue of St Peter from the church at Albepierre-Bredons, a 14C statue of St Flour, nine 16C carved wooden panels and a lovely set of Marian statues from the 12C to the 18C. The next room leads to the chapter-house, the only vestige of the Cluniac priory, where the treasure of the cathedral of St-Pierre and portraits of bishops are displayed.

The exhibits on the first floor concentrate on Auvergne folklore: popular music and its traditional instruments, hats and headdresses, a collection of regional carved-wood pieces, Cantal furniture (chests, cupboards, dressers, wooden bed panelling). The contents of the archaeological section mainly come from the digs at Mons and from Laurie, near Massiac. A beautiful bronze **brassard**★ consisting of six rings attached with a bar, and bracelets and swords, are the main items on display.

Musée d'Art et d'Histoire Alfred-Douët
⊙*Nov–Mar Thu–Fri 2–5pm; Oct and Apr–Jun Wed–Sat 2–6pm; Jul–Sept daily 10.30am–6.30pm.* ⊙*24 Dec–2 Jan.* ⊛€4 *(free 1st Sun of month, except Dec–Jan).* ☏*04 71 60 44 99. www.musee-douet.com.*

Beyond the entrance hall with its collection of ancient weapons is the library, which boasts Diderot's *Encyclopaedia*; the guard-room with its monumental fireplace and the Consul Room where fine tapestries hang, containing Renaissance furniture. The Louis XVI bedroom with painted wood panelling displays 18C furniture, and the gallery is exclusively decorated with 17C paintings and furniture. In addition, you will see fine Limousin enamels and glassware as well as a collection of pewter and copper.

EXCURSIONS
Roffiac
2km/1.2mi W along D 40.
An old restored mill, **Moulin du Blaud** (♿⊙*Jun–Aug Tue–Sat 1–6pm*), houses a trout information centre providing all you want to know about this freshwater fish, which you can catch *(no licence required; fishing tackle hiring facilities)* in the lake. The museum includes an observation laboratory, aquariums and a model of a dam. A nature-discovery trail runs round the lake.

Vallée de Brezons
36km/22mi S along D 65 and D 39.
One of the most beautiful glacial valleys in Europe thanks to its pronounced U shape, the Brezons valley is located at the base of the Plomb du Cantal. Here, about 50 sources unite and give visitors access to several waterfalls and

paths (detailed leaflet available at the Pierrefort Tourism Office.)
A massive lava cap overlooks the valley with an appearance like that of a lion's head. Climb to the top of the Col de la Griffoul, near the village of Arzalièz, and look to the right for a fantastic **view**★.

Coltines
13.5km/8.4mi NW. Leave St-Flour on the D 679 then take the D 40. Turn right onto D 14 for Coltines.

Musée de l'Agriculture★
Jul–Aug 9.30am–noon, 2–6.30pm; rest of the year 10am–noon daily except Sun, 2–5pm. 1 Jan, 25 Dec. €6 (children under 10, €3.50). 04 71 73 27 30.
Located in a 17C house, this interactive museum is devoted to agriculture in the Auvergne region from the turn of the 20C to the 1950s.

Aerodrome Saint-Flour Coltines
04 71 60 94 95. www.aerodrome-stflour-coltines.fr
Soar above the Auvergne peaks with ultralight aviation planes, hot air balloons and more. This aerodrome also offers the unique opportunity to fly alongside wild migratory birds.

Massiac
28km/17.3mi N of St-Flour on E 11.
This old village by the River Alagnon, is enlivened by a traditional weekly market (Tuesday mornings) and two picturesque annual fairs (Jun and Oct). The town's past is evidenced by the town hall, a fine 17C wooden house with a round stone tower belonging to the former ramparts.

Musée Municipal Élise-Rieuf
May–Jun and 1st 2 weeks of Sept, Sun and public holidays 2.30–6pm; Jul–Aug daily except Mon 2.30–6.30pm. 04 71 23 03 95.
www.musee-elise-rieuf.org.
The museum displays portraits of people from the Auvergne and China, Provençal and Scandinavian landscapes and Italian towns painted by Élise Rieuf, a native of Massiac (1897–1990).

DRIVING TOURS

VALLÉE DE L'ANDER
40km/25mi. Allow 4h.

▶ Leave St-Flour E onto D 990. After crossing the River Ander, turn right onto D 250.

Gorges de l'Ander
Continue along the edge of the river, which runs between both rocky and wooded slopes. The path ends in a very picturesque meander at the hamlet of Le Bout du Monde ("World's End").

▶ Turn around and at the crossroads take D 250 on the left, then left again onto a small road leading to Grizols. After the village, turn left onto D 40.

Site du Château d'Alleuze★★
see GORGES DE LA TRUYÈRE Driving Tour.

▶ Leave Alleuze to the N on D 116.

Villedieu
The church, half-Romanesque, half-Gothic, has an attractive door with a wrought-iron knocker. In the chancel, notice the beautiful High Altar, the staffs and finely carved lectern.

▶ Continue along D 116. At the intersection turn right onto D 921, then onto D 926, heading for Murat.

Église de Roffiac
The church is a little Romanesque building from the beginning of the 12C.

▶ Leave Roffiac to the N on D 104. Park in the hamlet of Le Sailhant.

Cascade du Sailhant★★
15min on foot there and back.
The path to Le Sailhant (or Le Babory) waterfall weaves among the houses bordering the beautiful volcanic rocks on

197

which the Château du Sailhant is built. The tiny cascade falls into a semicircle of tall cliffs; in the hollow lies a small lake. It is also possible to park at the entrance to the château and walk the short distance to the edge of the cliff, which offers a bird's-eye view of the cascade and its rocky surrounds.

Château du Sailhant★★

Apr–May Wed–Sun 2–6pm; Jun Wed–Sun 10am–noon, 2–6pm; Jul–Aug daily 10am–noon, 2–6pm; Sep Tues–Sun 10am–noon, 2–6pm. Guided visits every hour; every half-hour on summer weekday afternoons. €10 (€5 children 5–12). 04 71 60 98 00. www.sailhant.com.

This 1000-year-old fortress stands tall over a magnificent 30m-high rockspur. The fortress was modified over the course of the 19C and has been entirely restored and renovated by American architect Joseph Pell Lombardi beginning in 1997. Historic tours offer access to the great room, the lord's chambers, the library, and the chapel.

Leave Le Sailhant S along D 40. Further on, D 979 leads back to St-Flour.

ADDRESSES

STAY

Hôtel St-Jacques – *8 pl. de la Liberté. 04 71 60 09 20. www.hotelsaintjacques.com. Closed Nov–Jan. 28 rooms.* A former staging post on the way to Santiago de Compostela. Family rooms; city views.

Grand Hôtel de l'Étape – *18 av. de la République par D 909. 04 71 60 13 03. www.hotel-etape.com. 23 rooms. Restaurant.* 1970s building with large and practical rooms; ask for one with views of the mountains. The restaurant menu takes full advantage of home-grown produce.

EAT

Chez Geneviève – *25 r. des Lacs. 04 71 60 17 97. Closed Sun and Mon except Jul–Aug.* A friendly ambiance and hearty regional cuisine using fresh, local produce make this small restaurant very popular. Reservations are advised.

La Folie des Sens – *36 r. de la Rollandie. 04 71 60 42 21. www.folie-des-sens.fr. 71 60 17 97.Open Thurs.–Mon; closed Sun. evening in winter.* In the heart of the medieval city, this local team serves a seasonal haute cuisine menu devoid of pretension featuring local cheeses, blond Saint-Flour lentils, Aubrac beef, and more.

Gorges de la Truyère★★

The River Truyère has carved narrow, deep, sinuous gorges, often wooded and rugged-looking, through the granite plateaux of Upper Auvergne. These are among the most attractive natural sites in central France. Dams, built to serve the needs of hydroelectric power stations, have transformed them into one long lake without affecting their beauty, except when the waters are low. There is no road alongside the river, though many cross it, offering lovely views.

- **Michelin Map:** 330: H-5 to I-6 – 4km/2.5mi N of Chaudes-Aigues.
- **Info:** Tourist Office 15320 Ruynes en Margeride 04 71 23 43 32.
- **Location:** The gorges lie a short distance to the south of St-Flour.
- **Don't Miss:** The Viaduc de Garabit.
- **Timing:** A visit to the gorges can be combined with a tour of St-Flour (*see St-FLOUR*). Allow at least a day to visit both.

GORGES DE LA TRUYÈRE

🚗 DRIVING TOURS

1 ALONG THE GRANDVAL RESERVOIR★★
60km/37mi. About 2h.

▶ From the 165m-long Garabit bridge there is a view of the viaduct.

Viaduc de Garabit★★
The Garabit viaduct is an elegant, bold construction designed by an engineer named Léon Boyer and built (1882-84) by Gustave Eiffel. It has total length of 564m and stretches across the River Truyère at a height of 123m. Its 448m superstructure is supported by a bold metal arch.

Since the Grandval dam was built, the water below the viaduct has risen to the level of the supporting piles of the bridge, which still stands 95m above the maximum level of the dam's waters. It was the experience gained in Garabit that enabled Eiffel to design and build his famous 300m tower in Paris for the 1889 World Fair.

At night, the viaduct is lit up to show off its beautiful "metal lace." Lights stay on until 10pm in spring and autumn, 1am in summer, and until 9pm on weekend evenings in winter.

▶ At the southern end of the bridge turn right to Faverolles.

The route crosses the rocky Arcomie ravine and the Arling stream and continues to Faverolles, where the Cantal, Margeride and Aubrac mountains come successively into view.

Château du Chassan
🟢 *May–Oct by arrangement (except Jul–Aug daily 2–6.30pm).* €6.
☏ 04 71 23 43 91.
In a region where medieval fortresses abound, this château provides a more peaceful addition to the landscape. In the 18C Jean-François de Ponsonnaille demolished the feudal castle of Faverolles in order to build the present house, which has remained in the family ever since.

The main building, with its austere façade, is embellished by a carved balcony and flanked by two wings, one of which is still lived in; the other has been turned into an exhibition hall. The hallway has a stone staircase topped with a basket-handled arch. A 15C horse-blanket on the wall bears the Ponsonnaille family coat of arms: three bells or cowbells flanked by two lions and topped with the count's coronet. In the dining room, the oak dresser still occupies the place for which it was made; its well-proportioned design distracts from any inherent heaviness.

Belvédère de Mallet★★
Park after a sharp left-hand bend and walk to the promontory (🚶 10min there and back).

From here, there is a splendid view over Grandval reservoir. From D 13 turn right on D 40 through Fridefont, and down along a twisting route to the ridge of the dam itself.

Barrage de Grandval★
This multiple-arch concrete dam is supported by thick buttresses. The central arch houses a circular power station beneath a metal dome. It produces 144 million kWh per year. The lake formed upstream of the dam is 28km/17mi long.

▶ After a very sharp left-hand bend, the road drops into a wooded valley, offering splendid views of the ruins.

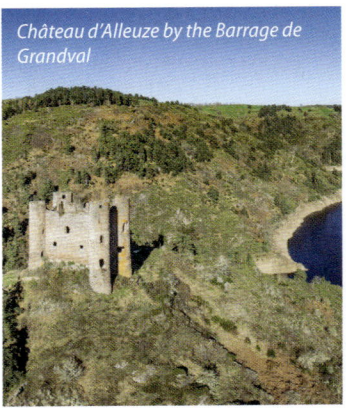

Château d'Alleuze by the Barrage de Grandval

© Francis Cormon/hemis.fr

Château d'Alleuze★★

The castle ruins may be reached by car along D 48. Park the car near the graveyard and follow the steep path for 5min.

The fortress was built in the 13C by the Constables of the Auvergne but belonged to the Bishops of Clermont when, during the Hundred Years War, **Bernard de Garlan** – an adventurer who sided with the English – took it by storm and set up camp. For seven years he terrorised the region, pillaging a wide area and holding it ransom.

The D 48 scenic road west of Barry skirts the narrow Alleuze valley, providing breathtaking **views★★** of the castle and its ruins, a vast keep flanked by four round towers standing on a spur of barren rock. An even better view of the site may be had from the village of **La Barge**. Park beside the war memorial and turn left towards the church.

In Alleuze, turn back and take D 48 towards Lavastrie, then D 921 left to Chaudes-Aigues.

2 THE PLANÈZE★

40km/25mi. About 2h.

At the foot of the Plomb du Cantal, the St-Flour planèze unfolds to the east and south-east, a vast plateau where fields of crops stretch as far as the eye can see, earning the region its reputation as the agricultural heart of Upper Auvergne.

Chaudes-Aigues

Chaudes-Aigues is ideally situated in the picturesque Remontalou valley, within the **Aubrac natural regional park**. Hot springs have made it not only a spa resort, but also a town where hot running water has been piped to houses since 1332.

Today, 32 of the springs are tapped (they are said to be the hottest in Europe). The springs were slow to find widespread popularity, largely because of the difficult access. However, they now seem to be on the verge of a massive boom, firstly due to the opening of the A 75 motorway and secondly thanks to the ongoing renovation work undertaken to develop the spa. Dominating the town on the south side is the Tour du Couffour, which still features its circular medieval keep and today is home to a gastronomic restaurant.

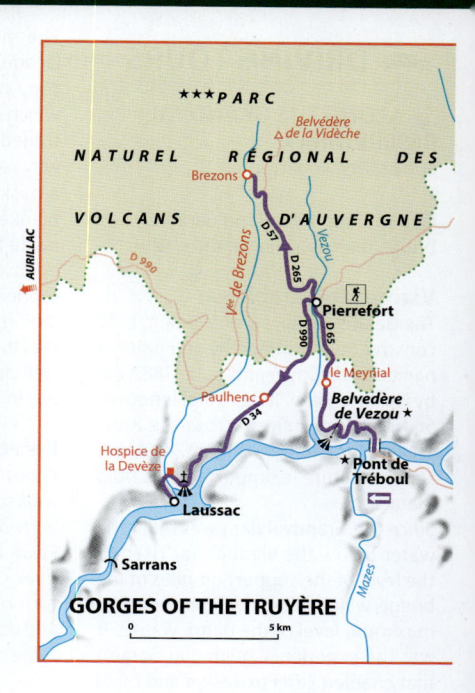

The route briefly follows the west bank of the Truyère valley then turns right onto the *planèze*, which offers views of St-Flour plateau, as well as the Cantal, Margeride and Aubrac mountain ranges.

Espinasse

This small village offers plunging views over the River Truyère.

From Auzolles on, the road clings to the steep sides of the **Lévandes valley**. A long, vertiginous descent follows, with breathtaking views of the wooded valley floor and southern slopes. After crossing the Lévandes, the road runs along the **Sarrans reservoir**, a particularly beautiful lake when water levels are high.

GORGES DE LA TRUYÈRE

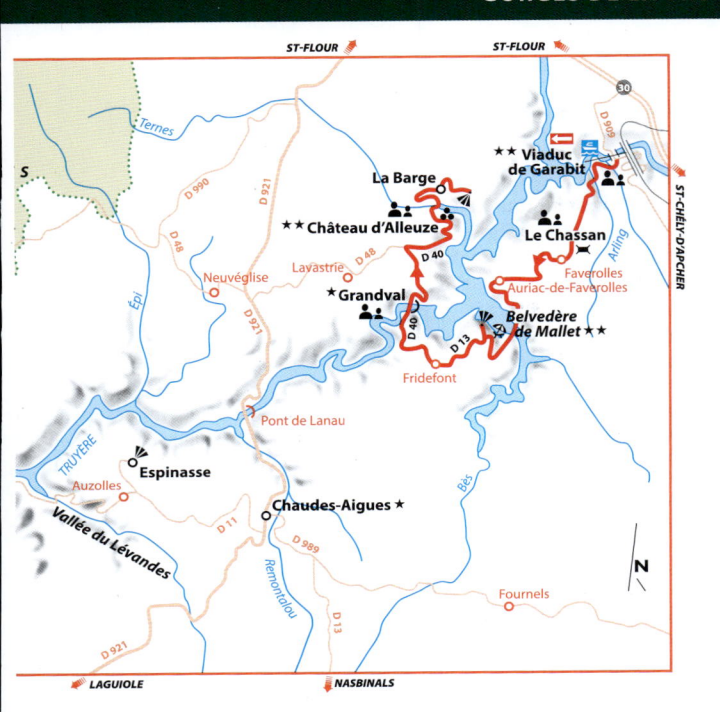

Pont de Tréboul★

This suspension bridge is a stunning piece of modern engineering. It replaced a Gothic bridge, built by the English in the 14C, which was submerged, together with the village of Tréboul, when the valley was flooded.

◐ Cross the bridge and turn left to Pierrefort. Park the car 600m after the overhead bridge, beyond a bend to the right.

Rocher de Turlande★

Take D 34 from Pierrefort and turn left after the church.

This magnificent site can be accessed after the charming village of **Pierrefort** (home to two fantastic butchershops near the main square). Park about 200 meters before the site, near a farm, and walk the path towards a sublime view overlooking the Truyère Valley and the shockingly blue Sarrans lake. The highest of these rocks was once home to a castle, destroyed in the 14C. Only the chapel remains; it is occasionally open to visits.

Laussac

The village is built on a promontory that the flooding of the valley has turned into a peninsula. *The northern part of the gorge is described in this guide, whereas the south-western section is described in the Languedoc-Roussillon-Tarn Gorges guide (see ENTRAYGUES-SUR-TRUYÈRE).*

ADDRESSES

♀ EAT

Restaurant Serge Vieira – *Le Couffour, 15110 Chaudes-Aigues.* ✆04 71 20 73 85. www.sergevieira.com. *Closed Tues.–Wed.* Located in a contemporary dining room juxtaposing the medieval fortress in which it is set, this restaurant offers panoramic views of the scenery and a devilishly creative menu marrying technical acuity, aesthetic ingenuity and sumptuous flavors.

Ruynes-en-Margeride

La Margeride is a granite range lying parallel to the volcanic mountains of Velay. It stretches from the River Allier in the east to the high volcanic plateaux of the Aubrac in the west. The highest section consists of extensive plateaux covered with vast pastures interspersed with forests of pines, fir and birch. Below the Montagne lie "Les Plaines", undulating stretches of land broken by numerous rock spurs.

- **Michelin Map:** 330: H-4.
- **Info:** Le Bourg, 15320 Ruynes-en-Margeride. 04 71 23 46 69.
- **Location:** 13km/8mi SE of St-Flour via the D 4.
- **Timing:** Allow a full day or more to drive around the plateau.

L'ECOMUSÉE DE LA MARGERIDE★

Since 1975, this open-air museum has specialised in a study of rural society in this region. It helps to preserve the natural and cultural heritage and gives visitors an insight into traditional lifestyles through the restoration of typical buildings, exhibitions, walks and regional discovery holidays.

The three sites here reveal different aspects of rural life in the Margeride region. The **Ruynes tower** at Ruynes-en-Margeride focuses on the aromatic and edible plants of yesteryear in the St Martin garden. At Loubaresse (17km/10.5mi to the south of Ruynes), **Pierre Allègre's farm★** portrays the life of a local family in the late 19C. At Signalauze (5km to the south of Ruynes), a reconstructed classroom from the **Clémence Fortille school** depicts school life in the first half of the 20C.

🚗 DRIVING TOUR

LE MONT MOUCHET
50km/31mi. Allow 3h.

Mont Mouchet (1 495m) is one of the peaks in the Margeride range. In May 1944, it became one of the main centres of the Resistance against Nazi Occupation in the Massif Central. On 2 June, 3 000 men from the French Maquis pushed enemy forces back beyond Paulhac. On 10 June, after occupying Ruynes-en-Margeride, where 27 civilians were massacred, a large German detachment pillaged and set fire to Clavières but were halted by the Resistance and had to withdraw to St-Flour. The following day the Germans again attacked Clavières, but the Maquis had time to organise its defences.

A national monument to the French Resistance was erected here and faces the Mont Mouchet Forestry Commission Centre, which had been used as the headquarters of the Auvergne Resistance. A **museum** (*May–Jun and Sept daily except Mon 10am–12.30pm, 2–6pm; Jul–Aug daily 10am–1pm, 2–6pm). €5. 04 71 74 11 91. www.gorgesallier.wixsite.com/musee-mont-mouchet*) contains documents from the war.

The road wends its way through **Auvers Forest**, known locally for its mushrooms and blueberries.

▶ Go back to D 113, turn left, then 2km/1mi further on, turn left again onto D 41.

Auvers

Near the church, a granite base supports a monumental bronze statue depicting "**La Bête du Gévaudan**", a wild animal that devoured cattle and terrorised local farmers in the area. It was eventually hunted down and shot near Auvers by Jean Chastel on 19 June, 1767.

▶ Continue along D 41, which skirts the east slope of the Mont Mouchet. After 5km/3mi, turn left onto D 412. D 4 will take you back to Ruynes.

VELAY AND BRIVADOS

When you think of Velay, three words should spring instantly to mind: *dentelle* (lace), *lentilles* (lentils) and *verveine* (a green liqueur flavoured with the herb verbena). But Velay is far more than this. The Brivadois to the north-west, while mainly located in the Haute-Loire, overflows into Puy-de-Dôme and Cantal. The area is largely composed of small plains *(limagnes)*. The Livradois and Mergeride, meanwhile, are known for their foothills. Largely given to agriculture in one form or another; this is a peaceful and relaxing countryside.

Verveine du Velay

The "formula" for Verveine liqueur was discovered in 1859 by a herbalist named Joseph Rumillet-Charretier and was initially marketed under his name. The plant, known as verbena in English, has long been attributed with magical properties. The Romans notably called it the "herb of Venus" because of its alleged aphrodisiac qualities.

Volcanic Plateaux

Many local villages throughout the region are built on or of volcanic stone, and a tour of this region therefore gives an excellent overview of the landscape. Take in St-Paul-de-Tartas, with its Romanesque church built of purplish volcanic rock, or the once-fortified village of Pradelles, where a house with Renaissance windows on the market square is home to a local museum. The Musée Vivant du Cheval de Trait (Draught-Horse Museum) is housed in a 19C inn and includes reconstructed workshops and a collection of carriages dating from the end of the 19C.

Highlights

1. A leisurely exploration of **Puy-en-Velay** (p205)
2. Taking a driving tour around **Vallée de la Borne** (p212)
3. Tasting **Puy lentils**, France's first AOP vegetable (p214)
4. Wandering the old streets of **Brioude** (p215)
5. Visiting Auvergne's largest Romanesque church **St Julian's Basilica** (p215)

"Caviar of the Poor"

Lentils were likely one of the first crops cultivated by humans and have been part of our diet since Neolithic times. They have the third-highest protein content of any plant-based food. Le Puy-en-Velay is renowned for its particular variety of green lentils, grown on the thin soils of the region. The so-called "caviar of the poor" has a distinctiive flavour and is commonly served with

Basilique St-Julien, Brioude

© Christian Guy/hemis.fr

VELAY AND BRIVADOS

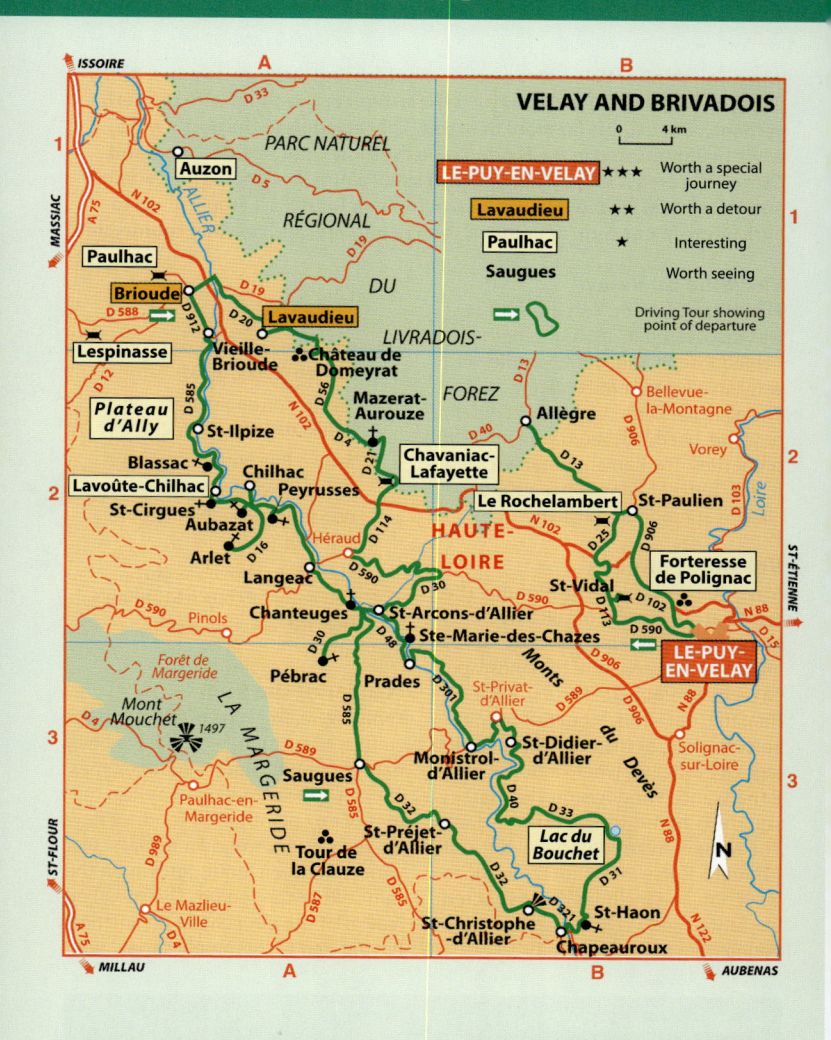

sausage in the Auvergne. In 1996, Puy lentils became the first vegetable to receive an AOC distinction.

La Bête du Gévaudan

La Bête du Gévaudan is said to have been a wolf-like animal that roamed the Auvergne in the 18C, killing about 100 people. Every effort to slay the beast failed, and the story ultimately achieved national notoriety. The King himself – Louis XV – took a personal interest, because of the unrest the killings caused in an area already burdened with religious and political tension. Many descriptions of the beast were put forward, ranging from the fantastic to the prosaic, but none has ever been confirmed. That said, unlike other popular stories of monsters, La Bête du Gévaudan is unique: whatever it was, it left behind 100 corpses as proof of its presence.

Le Puy-en-Velay with St-Michel-d'Aiguilhe, Rocher Corneille and Cathédrale Notre-Dame

Le Puy-en-Velay★★★

Out of a rich plain set in a depression rise the enormous volcanic peaks that make up Le Puy en Velay: the steepest, Saint-Michel rock (or Rocher d'Aiguilhe) is surmounted by a Romanesque chapel. The largest, Corneille rock (or Mont Anis) is crowned by a monumental statue of the Virgin Mary. This splendid vision is complemented by a visit to the cathedral of Notre-Dame du Puy, the a starting point of the Santiago de Compostela pilgrimage venerated for its Black Virgin.

On Saturday, market day, the town is a striking sight: place du Breuil and the old streets between the square and the market teem with crowds. In autumn, the Festival of the Bird King (Fête du Roi de l'Oiseau) is held in commemoration of an age-old local custom to discern the town's best archer. The festival is celebrated in a Renaissance atmosphere that pervades the upper end of the town.

A BIT OF HISTORY

City of the Virgin Mary – The site of Le Puy seems to have been an ancient place of pagan worship (remains of a 1C sanc-

- **Population:** 19 712.
- **Michelin Map:** 331: F-3.
- **Info:** 2 pl. du Clauzel, 43000, Le Puy-en-Velay. 04 71 09 38 41. www.lepuyenvelay-tourisme.fr
- **Location:** Le Puy-en-Velay is situated south-west of Lyon and St-Etienne, and is accessible from the A 75.
- **Parking:** There are plenty of car parks around the southern ring road, but precious few within the town itself.
- **Don't Miss:** St Michel-d'Aiguilhe.
- **Timing:** Head for the cathedral area first, and then wander the streets, or follow one of the Town Walks. Allow a full day to explore.

tuary are among the cathedral foundations), evangelised in the 3C. Apparitions of the Virgin Mary and miraculous cures near a dolmen capstone (since) known as the "Fever Stone") encouraged the first bishops to come and settle here,

DISCOVERING VELAY AND BRIVADOIS

The Puy Basin

The Puy basin owes its formation to the collapse of the Vellave plateau, an after-effect of the alpine folding during the Tertiary period. Sediment stripped from the hills partly filled the basin, which was then cut by the River Loire. At the end of the Tertiary Era a series of volcanic eruptions convulsed the region; the bed of the Loire was shifted east.

During the Quaternary Era, erosion began again, forming spurs from the most resistant of the volcanic reefs of various origins; these include basalt tables, the remains of lava flows (Polignac rock), volcanic chimneys (St-Michel rock, Espaly and Arbousset peaks) and parts of eruptive cones (Corneille and Ceyssac rocks, Denise volcano). As the lava flow cooled, combinations of prismatic columns were formed, such as those at Espaly. It is to these volcanic phenomena that the basin owes its highly original physiognomy.

---

probably at the end of the 5C. A basilica was erected, then a cathedral, around which a town soon developed.

In the Middle Ages, pilgrimages to Le Puy were popular: not only was it a point of departure for the pilgrimage to Santiago de Compostela in Spain, but, along with Chartres, Le Puy is the oldest site of Marian worship in France. Kings, princes and crowds of humble origin flocked here to invoke the mother of God.

In the 12C, the havoc wrought by a group of privateers known as **Les Cotereaux** posed a serious threat to the pilgrimages and all they contributed to the town in terms of prosperity and renown. The **Black Virgin** brought even greater fame to Le Puy. The present statue, dating from 1856, replaced the original, mutilated and burnt during the French Revolution.

City of lace – In Le Puy and the Velay, as well as in the region of Arlanc, handmade lace was long an important part of the local economy. The art probably originated in the 17C and soon began to develop to such an extent that a special organisation was established. Women in local villages worked at home for merchants in the neighbouring towns, and "collectors" who provided the lacemakers with thread and cartoons (patterns), served as intermediaries.

Originally reserved for the gentry, lace became so popular that, in 1640, the Toulouse Parliament outlawed its use as clothing. A Jesuit priest, moved by the distress of the lacemakers who suddenly found themselves out of work, managed to have the ban lifted. Saint-Régis invited his fellow missionaries to make Le Puy lace known throughout the world and later became the patron saint of lacemakers.

The lace trade retained its religious overtones for a long time: the art was passed on not only from mother to daughter but also by religious women known as "les Béates," who also taught catechism and cared for the sick.

WALKING TOURS

1 THE TREASURE TRAIL★★★

The cathedral dominates the upper part of the town, which is one large conservation area. Start from place des Tables with its graceful Chorister Fountain (15C) and walk up to the cathedral via the picturesque rue des Tables lined with stone steps bordered by several old houses.

Cathédrale Notre-Dame★★★

This marvellous Romanesque building, a departure point for the Camino de Santiago de Compostela and a UNESCO World Heritage Site, owes its unusual appearance to the influence of the East. Byzantine influence, a result of the crusades, can also be seen in the octagonal domes over the nave.

The original church corresponds to the present east end. When work was

LE PUY-EN-VELAY

CATHÉDRALE NOTRE-DAME

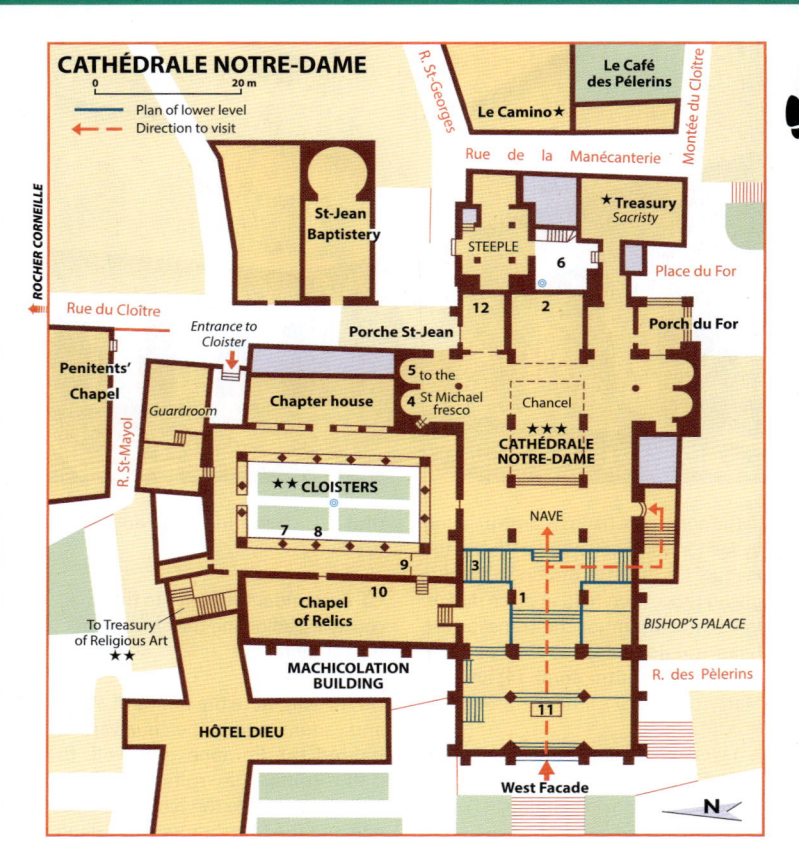

Plan of lower level
Direction to visit

begun to extend it in the 12C, shortage of space quickly became a problem. The last bays of the nave (built two by two, in two stages), together with the west porch, were built virtually above a sheer drop, with the tall arcades serving as open piling. At the end of the 12C, the For Porch and St-Jean Porch were added. Extensive restoration was carried out on the cathedral in the 19C.

Route Under the Cathedral

Steps lead to the main door under the four bays built in the 12C. At the level of the second bay, two 12C **panelled doors**★ close off two side chapels; their faint decoration in relief recounts the life of Christ. Go through the main door, framed by two red columns.
Straight ahead, the main staircase leads right into the cathedral, opposite the High Altar. This configuration led to the saying that: "One enters Notre-Dame du Puy through the navel and leaves through the ears."

▶ Take the central staircase or, if it is closed, the right-hand one, which leads to a door in the side aisle.

Interior

The most unusual feature of the church is the series of domes that cover the nave (the one over the transept crossing is modern). Note the pulpit (**1**) and the beautiful high altar (**2**), which supports the wooden statue replacing the original Black Virgin burnt during the Revolution. The Baroque organ, recently restored, is located at the west end of the nave. Bishop Jean de Bourbon's 15C fleur-de-lis tapestry hangs at the end of the chancel.

207

DISCOVERING VELAY AND BRIVADOIS

Cloisters, Cathédrale Notre-Dame

In the north aisle hangs a large painting by Jean Solvain known as the "Vow of the Plague" (1630) (**3**) illustrating a thanksgiving procession held in place du For. In the north arm of the transept are beautiful Romanesque frescoes: the Holy Women at the tomb (**4**) and the Martyrdom of St Catherine of Alexandria (**5**).
A gallery on the left contains a **fresco of St Michael**★ (late 11C-early 12C). It is the largest known painting in France depicting the Archangel Michael.
The famous stone known as the **"Pierre des fièvres"** (**12**) is in the chapel next to St-Jean Porch.

For Porch
This porch with highly elaborate capitals dates back to the late 12C. The smallest door is known as the "Papal Door" because of the inscription above it. From the small place du For, there is an attractive overall view of the site and a particularly good view of the belfry.

▶ Walk around the east end via rue de la Manécanterie.

St-Jean Porch
This porch preceded by a large flattened arcade was designed for sovereigns to pass through; it connects the cathedral to the 10C and 11C baptistery, whose entrance is flanked by two stone lions. The leather-covered doors have beautiful 12C strap hinges (wrought-iron brackets).

▶ Pass under the belfry to the small courtyard adjoining the east end of the cathedral.

On the way, note the tombs of abbots and canons, and in the courtyard (**6**), behind the Romanesque well, the Gallo-Roman bas-relief sculptures incorporated into the base of the east end and the frieze above: they depict hunting scenes.

Cloisters★★
The beautiful cloisters abut the north face of the cathedral. Each gallery is from a different period; the oldest, to the south, is Romanesque.
The **historiated** capitals in the west gallery include one (**7**) depicting a dispute over an abbot's crook, and another (**8**) showing a centaur.
A remarkable **Romanesque railing**★ (**9**) closes the west gallery. From the southwest corner of the cloisters, a Romanesque chimney can be seen rising above the altar boys' house.
Around the cloisters, above the arcades, is a delicately decorated **cornice** illustrating a medieval bestiary. The polychrome arch stones and the quoins with their black, white, red and ochre lozenges form a decor reminiscent of Islamic art.

LE PUY-EN-VELAY

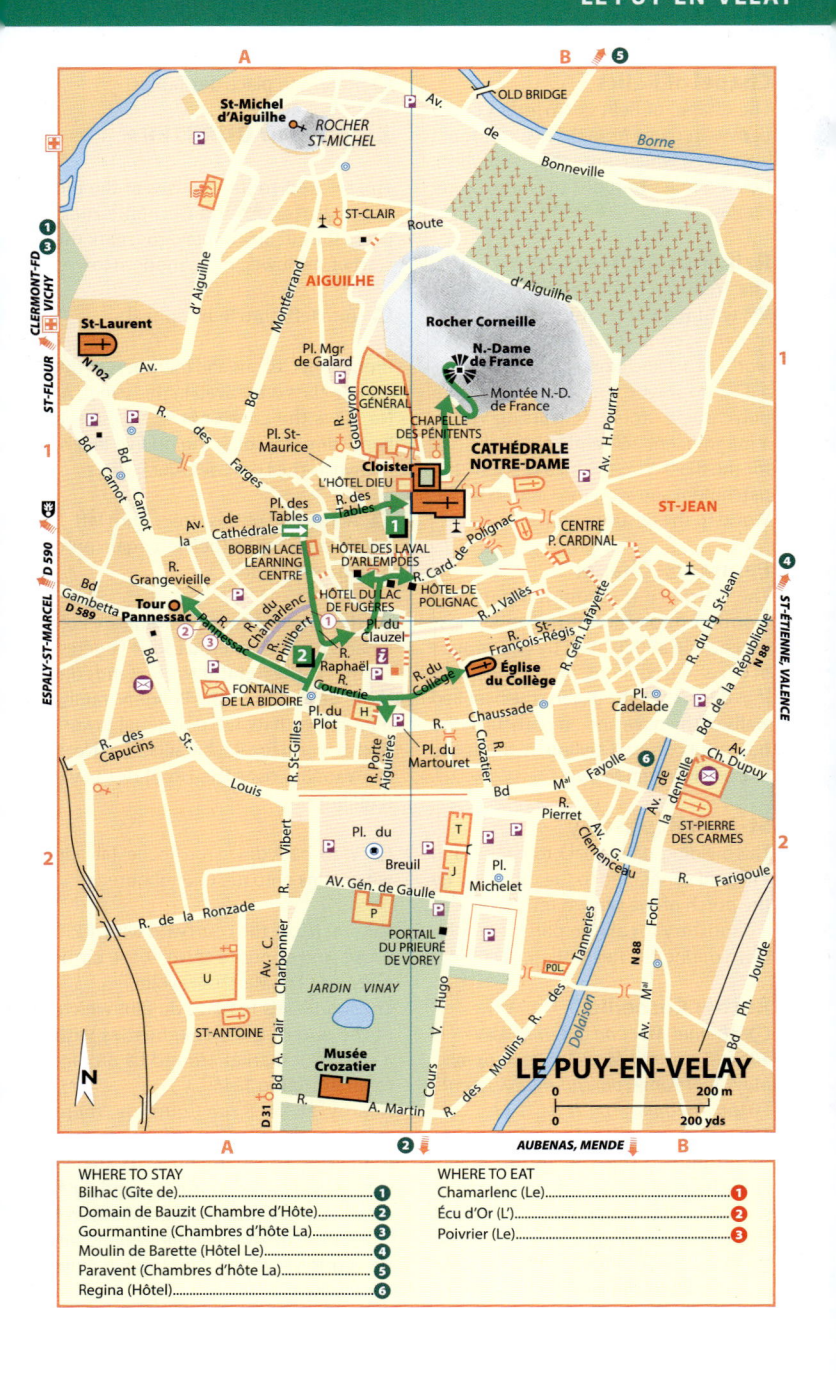

WHERE TO STAY	
Bilhac (Gîte de)	①
Domain de Bauzit (Chambre d'Hôte)	②
Gourmantine (Chambres d'hôte La)	③
Moulin de Barette (Hôtel Le)	④
Paravent (Chambres d'hôte La)	⑤
Regina (Hôtel)	⑥

WHERE TO EAT	
Chamarlenc (Le)	①
Écu d'Or (L')	②
Poivrier (Le)	③

209

DISCOVERING VELAY AND BRIVADOIS

Chapel of Relics
The Chapel of Relics or Winter Chapel derives its name from the beautiful gold altarpiece which, until the Revolution, housed relics brought to Notre-Dame du Puy.

Religious Art Treasury★★
The Treasury, displayed in the former Velay State Room above the Chapel of Relics, contains a large number of works of art, including an 11C silk cope, a 13C engraved enamel reliquary, a polychrome-stone 15C Nursing Virgin, a magnificent 16C embroidered cloak for the Black Virgin, and a piece of 15C parchment showing the Genesis of the World to the Resurrection.

Penitents' Chapel
The entrance is through a panelled wooden door carved in the Renaissance style and flanked by two groups of wreathed columns. Inside, the paintings decorating the gallery, the panelled walls of the nave and, in particular, the beautiful coffered ceiling, recount the Life of the Virgin Mary.

St-Jean Baptistery
This building, dating back to the 10C and 11C, and connected to the cathedral by the porch of the same name, served as a baptistery for all the parishes in the town during the Revolution.

Rocher Corneille
Feb–mid-Mar and Oct–mid-Nov 10am–5pm; mid-Mar–Apr 9am–6pm; May–Sept 9am–7pm (Jul–Aug 7.30pm). Mid Nov-Jan. ☏04 71 04 11 33.
This is the remainder of a cone, no doubt belonging to the volcano of which St-Michel rock is the chimney. The rock is surmounted by a monumental statue of Notre-Dame-de-France erected in 1860 by national subscription. This cast iron statue is 16m high and weighs 110t.
An outstanding 213 cannons, among the trophies from the capture of Sebastopol given to contractors by Napoleon III, were melted down to cast it.
It is possible to go up inside the statue to neck level.

▶ Return to place des Tables.

2 THE OLD QUARTER★

The tall, red-roofed houses of the old town cluster around Corneille rock, while the circular boulevards mark the start of the lower, more modern town.

▶ Turn left onto Rue Raphaël.

Prominent citizens and members of the middle class once lived in this street. At No. 38 is the Lace Centre; No. 56 is a handsome 16C building on five levels, known as the Logis des Alix Selliers.

▶ At the end of this street, turn left onto rue Saulnerie then left again onto rue Rochetaillade.

On the corner with rue Cardinal de Polignac is the 15C Hôtel du Lac de Fugères. Further to the right, at No. 8, stands the Hôtel de Polignac, the Polignac family mansion with its 15C polygonal tower. Back beyond rue Rochetaillade, at No. 3 rue Vaneau, rises the Hôtel des Laval d'Arlempdes.

▶ Walk back down rue Roche-Taillade which runs onto rue Chênebouterie.

Note, at No. 8, the courtyard with a 15C turret, and opposite at No. 9, the birthplace (16C) of Marshal Fayolle.
The road leads to place du Plot which, at the end of the week, bustles with a colourful market around La Bidoire fountain, dated 1246.
Nearby, at No. 8 rue Courrerie, there remains an interesting 16C façade next to the Hôtel de Marminhac. Its arched windows bear keystones carved with masks. Continue to place du Martouret – the site of many executions during the Revolution – where the Hôtel de Ville now stands.

▶ Return to place du Plot and follow rue Pannessac.

This part-pedestrianised street is bordered by elegant 16C and 17C Renais-

LE PUY-EN-VELAY

sance houses with overhanging fronts, sometimes flanked by a tower or watch-turret (Nos. 16, 18, 23).

To the right, some of the alleys – rue Philibert, rue du Chamarlenc – retain a medieval character.

The façade of No. 16 rue Chamarlenc, known as the Demeure des Cornards (the Cornards were companions whose prerogative it was to poke fun at the town's burghers) is adorned with two horned heads, one laughing, the other sticking out its tongue, surmounted by satirical inscriptions.

At No. 42 Rue Pannessac, the Logis des André, and at No. 46 the 17C Logis des Frères Michel are decorated on the ground floor with masks and carved quoins, and on the upper storeys with masks, garlands and scrolls. Both reveal the opulence of the wealthy merchant who lived in this district.

At the end of the street, the 14C **Pannessac Tower** retains a level of trefoiled machicolations. It is the last remaining trace of the original 18 fortified gateways, with twinned towers which allowed access through the town walls.

▶ Retrace your steps.

Église du Collège

At the beginning of the 17C, a Jesuit priest named Martellange built a building in the new Italian Baroque style for the order's newly founded college.

ADDITIONAL SIGHTS

St-Michel-d'Aiguilhe★★

Feb–mid Mar and Christmas period (except 25 Dec) 2–5pm; mid-Mar–Apr and Oct–mid-Nov 9.30am–5.30pm; May–early Jul and Sept 9am–6.30pm; Jul–Aug 9am–7pm. *1 Jan, 25 Dec.* €5. *04 71 09 50 03. www.rochersaintmichel.fr.*

St-Michel Chapel crowns St-Michel rock, a gigantic needle of lava which rises up in a single shaft to a height of 80m above ground level. Its slender belfry, in the form of a minaret, looks like a pointed finger of rock.

▶ Walk up montée de Gouteyron linking the Aiguilhe rock and the upper town. Alternatively, you can reach the foot of the rock by car and park nearby.

This chapel probably replaced a temple dedicated to Mercury. The building standing today, which dates from the 10C–12C, shows Eastern inspiration in its trefoil portal, its decoration of arabesques and its black, white, grey and red stone mosaics. Inside, the highly irregular ground plan follows the contours of the rock. The complexity of the vaulting testifies to the architects' ability to make the most of the site. The small columns, which form a sort of ambulatory around a short nave, are surmounted by carved capitals.

The vaulting above the small apse is decorated with 10C paintings. On the right, objets d'art found under the altar in 1955 are on display; note in particular a small 11C wooden reliquary Christ and a 13C Byzantine ivory cask.

A covered watch-path goes around the chapel, overlooking Vieux Pont, the old cusp bridge that spans the Borne.

Musée Crozatier

11am–6pm (except Tues). €6 (free for children under 18). *04 71 06 62 40. www.musee.patrimoine.lepuyenvelay.fr.*

An eight-year renovation project saw the addition of a modern building of glass and concrete to the preexisting 19C building erected at the bottom of the Henri Vinay garden. The museum visit is divided into four parts: the historic gallery presents local collections from prehistory through the Renaissance; the Velay gallery is dedicated to ancestral pilgrimages and lacemaking; the Beaux-Arts gallery is home to works including the 15C Vierge au manteau; the science and technology gallery shows off extensive paleontological and natural history collections.

The dome room boasts a contemporary creation by Franck Chalendard and a remarkable view over the upper city.

Église St-Laurent

The church of St-Laurent is a rare example of Gothic art in Velay; it dates from the 14C and was part of a Dominican convent.

🚗 DRIVING TOURS

VALLÉE DE LA BORNE
Round trip of 60km/37mi. Allow half a day.

▶ Leave Le Puy SW on D 590 to Espaly-St-Marcel.

Espaly-St-Marcel
Shortly before reaching the railway, turn right towards the car park.

Piton d'Espaly
This peak was formerly crowned with a castle which, after serving as a residence for the bishops of Le Puy (King Charles VII was given hospitality here during his frequent pilgrimages), was ruined during battles involving the Catholic League *(private)*.

Rocher St-Joseph
⊙Sanctuary: daily 10am–6pm. ℘04 71 09 16 71. www.josephbonespoir.org.
The upper terrace, built at the foot of the statue, offers a **view★** of Le Puy-en-Velay.

▶ Rejoin D 590 and continue towards Chaspuzac. Turn right onto D 113 then right again onto D 112.

Forteresse de St-Vidal
⊙Mar–mid-Apr Wed 2–5pm; mid-Apr–May Wed–Sun 2–5pm; Jun Tues 2–5pm, Wed–Sun 10am–noon, 2–5pm. Jul–Aug 10am–7pm daily; Sep Wed–Sun 10am–noon, 2–5pm. Guided tours daily when open; see site for times. ℘09 81 43 68 00. www.saintvidal.com.
The massive towers of this fortress dominate the village, which clusters below around a rise in the Borne valley. Once the fief of Baron Antoine de la Tour, governor of Velay in the 16C, the castle has retained from its feudal days the vaulted cellars and Gothic kitchen with its immense fireplaces. Gothic and Renaissance decorative elements from the alterations carried out in the 15C and 16C still remain, including the galleries with ribbed vaulting lining three sides of the inner courtyard, the beamed ceiling and carved stone doorway of the State Rooms, and the southern façade. Regular visits and shows, both day and night, allow visitors to explore French and regional history; see site for times and details.

▶ Return to D 113, turn right towards Chazelle then left onto N 102 and right again onto D 25. When the castle appears in the distance, turn left.

Château le Rochelambert
🍃Guided visits only (45mn); reservations required: May–Oct daily 2pm, 3pm, 4pm, 5pm; Nov–Apr daily 3pm, 4pm. ⊙1 Jan, 25 Dec. ⊛€7 (children, 5–12, €5). ℘07.66.83.19.01. www.chateau-de-la-rochelambert.com.
Built on the banks of the River Borne, this 13C–16C castle set in pastoral surroundings was the setting of one of George Sand's novels, *Jean de la Roche*.

▶ Continue along the minor road for 2km/1.2mi then turn left onto D 13.

Allègre
This village nestles around the ruins of a feudal castle built on the southern edge of the Boury volcano. Once through the Porte de Monsieur, you see the Chapelle de Notre-Dame de l'Oratoire standing in the centre of the square.

Tourbière du Mont Bar
🚶 *2h there and back. The climb is rather steep, but shaded by fir trees.*
This Stromboli-type volcano is the only one of its kind in France, for its crater is filled with a peat bog. A marked footpath leads to the bog and enables visitors to walk all the way around.

▶ Leave Allègre S along D 13.

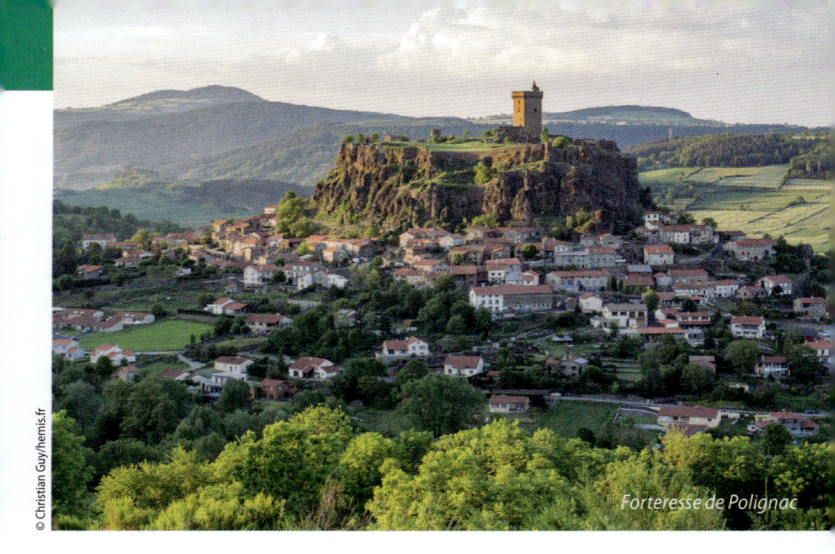

Forteresse de Polignac

St-Paulien
Once the capital of the Velay region, this village was a bishopric until the 6C. The church is a fine example of Romanesque style from Auvergne.

▶ Leave St-Paulien S along D 906 then follow D 102.

Polignac★
Rising on its basalt hillock, the fortress of Polignac still has imposing remains of its powerful martial past from both Antiquity and the Middle Ages. The view of the site, from D 102, is superb.

Church
This is a beautiful Romanesque building with a Gothic porch and a 12C Romanesque-Byzantine dome.

Forteresse de Polignac
Feb–Mar 1.30–5pm; Apr–Jun and Sept–Oct 10am–noon, 1.30–6pm; Jul–Aug 9.30am–7pm; 1st 2 wks in Nov 10am–noon, 1.30–5pm. €5. 04 71 04 06 04. www.forteressedepolignac.fr.
The building, which could house 800 soldiers as well as the family and servants, is perched on an enormous basalt platform, the remaining fragment of a lava flow; the platform sits on a softer strata of rock which has been protected from erosion as a consequence.

▶ Return to D 102 which leads back to Le Puy.

ADDRESSES

STAY

Dyke Hôtel – *37 bd du Mar.-Fayolle. 04 71 09 05 30. www.dykehotel.fr. Closed Christmas week, 1 Jan. 15 rooms.* The contemporary rooms are small but tidy.

Gîte de Bilhac – *Bilhac, 43000 Polignac. 04 71 09 72 41. www.gite-bilhac.com. 4 rooms.* This beautiful fully restored family farm has kept the rustic character of the hostel it once was. Accommodation is very simple, but well maintained.

Chambre d'Hôte Domaine de Bauzit – *43750 Vals-Près-le-Puy. 04 71 03 67 01. www.domainedebauzit.fr. 5 rooms.* Nestled in a vast area, this former monastery exudes serenity. The decor of the rooms pays tribute to four different countries in Asia, while the fifth and last, "Auvergne", is simpler but equally comfortable.

Chambre d'hôte La Gourmantine – *Chemin de Ridet, 43000 Polignac. 04 71 05 94 29. www.gourmantine.fr. 5 rooms.* Located at the foot of the castle, this fully restored 18C farmhouse enjoys a quiet corner of the village. Cosy rooms and home cooking.

Chambre d'Hôte La Paravent – *43700 Chaspinhac. 10km/6mi NE of Le Puy via D 103 dir. Retournac, then D 71. 04 71 03 54 75. www.la-paravent.com. 5 rooms. Restaurant.* The decor is authentic and the cosy bedrooms are very welcoming.

Hôtel-Restaurant Régina – *34 bd Maréchal Fayolle, 43000 Le*

DISCOVERING VELAY AND BRIVADOIS

Puy laces

Puy-en-Vélay. ℘04 71 09 14 71. www.hotelrestregina.com. 25 rooms. **Restaurant**. This comfortable hotel located in an early 20C building offers several different categories of simple rooms and suites and a restaurant serving tasty, market-driven fare.

EAT

Le Chamarlenc – *19 r. Raphaël.* ℘*04 71 02 17 72. Tue–Sat, lunch–dinner.* This small restaurant in the historic centre serves simple, rustic fare.

L'Écu d'Or – *59-61 r. Pannessac.* ℘*04 71 02 19 36. www.restaurantlecudor.com. Closed Wed and Sun evening (and Thurs in low season).* In the pedestrianised part of town, this picturesque, medieval-themed restaurant has an arched dining room decorated with murals. Regional cuisine.

Le Poivrier – *69 r. Pannessac.* ℘*04 71 02 41 30. www.lepoivrier.fr. Closed Sun–Mon.* Sleek restaurant; specialities include beef from Haute-Loire.

SHOPPING

Market – *Pl. du Plot. Sat morning.* On the public square with a water fountain, the country comes to pay its respects to the city in the form of baskets overflowing with the finest farm produce; berries and mushrooms in season.

Marché aux Puces (Flea Market) – *Pl. du Clauzel. Sat.* Bargain hunters, second-hand buffs and bric-a-brac enthusiasts should visit the Place du Clauzel.

Centre d'Enseignement de la Dentelle au Fuseau (lace-making centre) – *38/40 r. Raphaël.* ℘*04 71 02 01 68.* *www.ladentelledupuy.com. Closed public holidays.* We can thank St. François-Régis, patron saint of lace workers, for inspiring the creation of this establishment allowing us to discover lace in an original manner!

Distillerie de la Verveine du Velay-Pagès – *Z.I. de Blavozy, approx. 6km/3.6mi E of Le Puy via N 88, exit ZI de Blavozy, dir. St-Étienne, 43700 St-Germain-Laprade.* ℘*04 71 03 04 11. www.verveine.com. mid-Mar–Jun, Sep–Dec Tues–Sat 10am–12.30pm; 2–6.30pm; Jan–mid-Mar Wed–Thur 10am–12.30pm; 1.30–5pm; Jul–Aug Mon–Sat 10am–12.30pm; 2–6.30pm. €6.50.* The Pagès distillery takes visitors on a discovery tour of the production of Verveine du Velay liqueur.

Sabarot – *15 rue Courrerie 43000 Le Puy-en-Velay.* ℘*04 71 00 10 15. www.sabarot-shop.com.*
Oct - Jun Tues-Fri 10am-6.30pm, Sat 9am-7pm; Jul - Sept Mon-Sat 10am - 7pm; every day from July 14th–end Aug 10am-7pm (6pm on Sun). Founded in 1819, Sabarot was originally a flour mill. A century later, the company branched out into the sorting and packaging of Puy green lentils. In 1970, the company diversified into other pulses and grains, and in 1984, into the wild mushroom business.

ON THE TOWN

Le Michelet – *5 bis pl. Michelet.* ℘*04 71 09 02 74. Mon–Wed 7.30am–1am, Thu 7.30am–2am, Fri–Sat 9am–4am.* 1960s America and its symbols seem to attract the young people of Le Puy to this nightclub and bar.

Brioude ★★

Built on a terrace overlooking the plain, Brioude is a beautiful and active city in the Val d'Allier with a pronounced southern style and rich heritage. Vieille-Brioude *(4km/2.3mi)*, meanwhile, once the former center of the Brivadois thanks to its now-defunct winemaking industry, boasts a beautiful Romanesque church. Take time to stroll the streets of both and admire the beautifully restored façades of canonical houses. In the vicinity of Brioude, particularly along the banks of the Allier, many churches and castles wait to be discovered.

> - **Population:** 7 042.
> - **Michelin Map:** 331: C-2.
> - **Info:** Place Grégoire de Tours, 43100 Brioude. ☎04 71 74 97 49. www.ot-brioude.fr.
> - **Location:** Brioude is southeast from Clermont Ferrand, and accessible via the A 75.
> - **Parking:** Limited parking in the town centre.
> - **Don't Miss:** The town walk is especially agreeable.
> - **Timing:** A relaxing half-day would be sufficient, including lunch.

A BIT OF HISTORY

A saint, and a bandit from the Alps – Legend has it that a tribune of the Roman Legion named Julian, who was born in the Vienne region and converted to Christianity, sought refuge in Brioude and was martyred in the year 304. Pilgrims flocked to Brioude to pray at St Julian's tomb, particularly during the time of St Gregory of Tours (6C).

From the 9C onwards, the God-fearing town was subject to the authority of the canon-counts of St-Julien and remained so until the French Revolution, which put an end to their aristocratic tyranny. Folk tales in Brioude still make reference to Mandrin, the notorious smuggler from Dauphiné. On 26 August 1754 he entered the town with a band of armed men, sought out the manager of the warehouse where tobacco was stored and taxed (the Farmers General held a monopoly on the sale of tobacco) and made the unfortunate man purchase a large batch of contraband Nicotine grass at an excessively high price. Mandrin then withdrew, while the people of Brioude turned a blind eye; they were delighted at the trick played on a system they hated. The victim never recovered from the shock; he died eight days later.

BASILIQUE ST-JULIEN★

St Julian's Basilica is the largest Romanesque church in the area, a "vast stone-built shrine standing over a famous tomb" (Bernard Craplet). It is typical of the Romanesque style seen in the Auvergne, with its tiered east end and varying colours of masonry, though it differs in other respects – the portals are topped with smooth or carved coving or zigzag moulding instead of the traditional string-course of billet moulding. The ornamentation at the east end is also noticeably Burgundian in style.

Exterior

Building began on the church as it stands today with the main entrance (the narthex) in 1060 and was completed in 1180 (chancel and east end). Its nave was raised and given rib vaulting in 1259, but the west front and square bell-tower above it were rebuilt in the 19C, as was the octagonal bell-tower above the transept crossing.

The fine concentric layout of the **east end★★** makes this the most remarkable part of the building. It is one of the last examples of Romanesque architecture in the Auvergne.

The side **porches★** with their groin vaulting constitute the oldest part of the church. They have an unusual appearance, the result of their use as chapels during the 16C and the inclusion of a gallery over the top.

DISCOVERING VELAY AND BRIVADOIS

Interior

The nave is particularly striking for its size and the warm hues of the red sandstone walls and pillars. The pebble **pavement**★ dating from the 16C in the nave and from the pre-Romanesque era in the fifth bay in the centre was uncovered, together with the small crypt beneath the chancel, following restoration and excavation.

The church contains a large number of **capitals**★★ embellished with acanthus leaves, narrative scenes or themes common in Auvergne churches.

The basilica contains a number of **altarpieces** and old **statues** that are worthy of note. The walls and pillars in the first bays, the ambulatory and the north gallery above the narthex still contain traces of 12C and 13C **paintings**★, which are surprising for their diversity, modernism and spirited representations of human figures. Turn to the right on entering the basilica to see:

(1) (south aisle) 14C statue of Christ the Leper (Crucifix), carved in wood with canvas backing, brought here from the former leper hospital in La Bajesse, near Brioude.
(2) (south aisle) 14C statue of Virgin Mary in childbirth in wood.
(3) (south aisle) 14C statue of Madonna with Bird carved in lava stone.
(4) (5th bay, south pillar) capital of Christ surrounded by the Evangelists.
(5) (first pillars of transept) carved corbels of heads of royal figures.
(6) (chancel) carved altarpiece (17C) behind the High Altar.
(7) (chancel, north pillar) capital depicting the Holy Women.
(8) (north aisle) 14C gilt wooden statue of the Madonna with Bird.
(9) (Chapel of the Cross) altarpiece attributed to 17C sculptor Vaneau.
(10) (3rd bay, north pillar) two capitals of groups of soldiers around a wounded soldier or prisoner.
(11) (south pillar in narthex) capital of the Punishment of the Money-lender; painting of a woman in profile, with an enlarged eye.
(12) (St Michael's Chapel) – in the south gallery of the narthex *(access by a spiral staircase)* – 12C frescoes; capital depicting donkeys playing musical instruments.

🐾 TOWN WALK

Hôtel de Ville

City hall is built on the site of the former castle of the canon-counts of St-Julien. There is a fine view over the Brioude section of the Limagne plain and the Livradois range from the adjacent terrace.

Old Houses

In the district around the basilica is a network of narrow streets with old buildings and remarkable façades.

To the north, on the corner of rue Talairat: 17C mansion with turrets and carved door; rue du 4-Septembre: no. 29, Lace Centre *(see below)*; No. 25, 16C

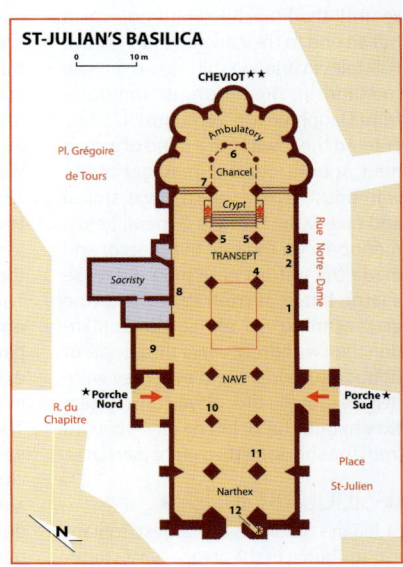

ST-JULIAN'S BASILICA

shop with arcades; No. 22, 15C building known as **Mandrin's House**; place St-Julien: 15C half-timbered house; south of the basilica: No. 21 rue de la Tour d'Auvergne, 18C mansion; place Eugène-Gilbert, Romanesque house with turret.

Hôtel de la Dentelle
May–Oct Mon–Sat 9.30am–6pm, Sun 2.30–6pm; Apr Mon–Sat 9am–noon, 2–6pm; Nov–Mar Mon–Fri 9am–noon, 2–5:30pm. €8. 04 71 74 80 02. www.hoteldeladentelle.com.
The centre, housed in the 15C former residence of the counts of Brioude, contains collections of lacework and lace-making equipment as well as a workshop where lace-makers can be seen at work.

Maison du Saumon et de la Rivière
Apr–Jun and Sept Mon–Fri 10am–noon, 2–6pm, Sat–Sun, 2–6pm; Jul–Aug Mon–Fri 10am–12.30pm, 2–7pm, Sat–Sun 2–6pm; Oct and early Nov Mon–Sun 2–6pm; winter vacation Mon–Fri 2–6pm. €6.50. 04 71 74 91 43. www.aquariummaisondusaumon.com.
The Atlantic salmon, which reaches the spawning grounds of the Upper Allier at the end of its 800km/500mi journey upstream, is part and parcel of Brioude's history. Before learning about the importance of salmon fishing in the Brioude area in bygone days, you can see over 30 local species of river wildlife. The main attraction is the "salmon river", a curved length of glass where migratory fish swim in simulated currents.

EXCURSIONS
Château de Paulhac★
5km/3mi NW of Brioude via the D 20. Closed for restoration following fire damage. 04 71 50 27 76.
This magnificent fortress was first mentioned in documents in the 10C. The three towers and dungeon were built in 1160, and the castle itself rebuilt in the 15C and 19C.

Château de Lespinasse★
11km/7mi SW of Brioude via the D 588. After 10km/6mi turn left towards Lubilhac, then immediately turn left. Guided tours mid Jul–Aug at 3pm, 4pm, 5pm. €7. 04 71 76 82 12. www,chateaudelespinasse. blogspot.com.
Erected on the site of an ancient Gallo-Roman town, this medieval castle is one of the oldest buildings in Brivadois. Its square tower was built in the 12C. In the 15C, the advantageous marriage of Louis, the son of the Lord of Lespinasse, to Jeanne, dauphine of Auvergne, allowed the construction of circular towers. From the castle you get a magnificent view of the mountains of the Livradois.

Plateau d'Ally★
22km/13.5mi SW of Brioude. Leave along the D 588, in the direction of Aurillac. After about 1km/0.5mi, turn left onto the D 12, then left again at the D 122, and then continue to Ally.
On the borders of Haute-Loire and Cantal, the small town of Ally lies on the edge of a plateau at around 1 000m. Until the last century, the people of Ally were mainly involved in farming along with craft production and mineral mining. This declined gradually, leading to a new emphasis on tourism. Today its mines, windfarms and mills (04 71 76 77 22) all welcome visitors.

DRIVING TOUR

HAUT-ALLIER AND SÉNOUIRE VALLEY★★
120km/75mi. Allow one day.

Leave Brioude to the E on N 102, heading for le Puy-en-Velay.

Vieille-Brioude
An impressive winepress dating from 1873 stands in place de la Croix, testifying to the town's important wine-growing past. A whole network of cellars and galleries was dug through the rocky spur on which Vieille-Brioude is perched.

DISCOVERING VELAY AND BRIVADOIS

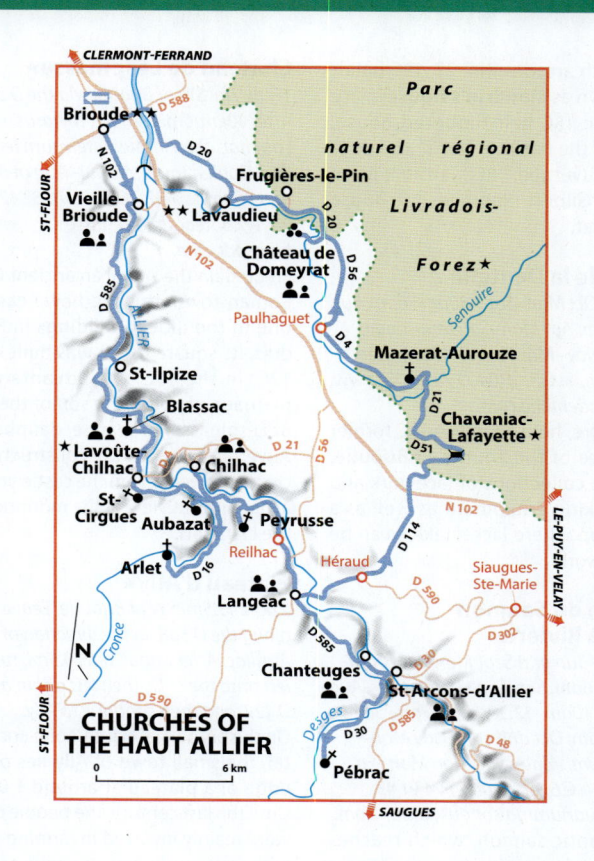

CHURCHES OF THE HAUT ALLIER

Musée-jardin de la Vigne
Easter–1 Nov 9am–7pm.
04 71 50 92 44.
www.museejardindelavigne.fr.
A Romanesque church stands in the middle of a garden where flowers grow next to herbs and medicinal plants. A vineyard festival takes place every October.

▶ In Vieille-Brioude, turn right onto D 585, which follows the upper valley of the Allier to Lavoûte-Chilhac.

St-Ilpize
This medieval town, clinging to a basalt rock and towering above the River Allier, is crowned by the ruins of a castle. The defensive walls enclose a 14C **chapel**.

▶ Rejoin D 585; turn right onto D 144.

Église de Blassac
The church is built on a flow of basalt. Its chancel contains a set of 14C frescoes.

▶ Rejoin D 585.

Lavoûte-Chilhac
This village stands on the banks of the Allier, which washes up against the walls of the houses. It has an elegant 11C bridge, restored in the 15C, as well as a Gothic **church** and 18C Benedictine abbey.

Maison des Oiseaux du Haut-Allier
Jul–Aug Sun–Thur, weekends rest of the year, reservations recommended.
04 71 77 43 52.
This information centre presents the bird population of the Gorges de l'Allier and organises nature walks.

BRIOUDE

▶ Rejoin D 585, which at this point hugs a meander in the Allier, giving a good view of the countryside.

Église de St-Cirgues
Inside, the two bays and the splays of the windows in the chancel are covered with interesting frescoes.

▶ Carry on along D585.

Église d'Aubazat
This village in a pleasant setting has a church with a Pietà and wooden statues representing an Entombment (15C).

▶ Rejoin D 585 for a further 500m, and at the crossroads turn right onto D 41, and then right again onto D 16.

Église d'Arlet
This hamlet at the bottom of the Cronce valley has a Romanesque church.

Chilhac
Small village built on a terrace of columnar basalt. Its **Musée Paléontologique** (Easter–Oct by appointment; Jul–Aug daily 2–6pm. €5 (child 6–18, €3). 04 71 77 47 71/47 26. www.museechilhac.com) presents artefacts uncovered on local excavation sites since 1960.

Église de Peyrusses
This church contains a Virgin Mary in Majesty and splendid – if somewhat faded – frescoes.

▶ Follow D 585 through Reilhac.

Langeac
This busy little town lies in a cultivated "corridor" at the downstream end of the Allier gorge. One or two old houses can still be seen along its streets.

▶ Leave Langeac S along D 585.

Église de Chanteuges
This attractive Romanesque church belonged to a local abbey that used to be the summer residence of the abbots of La Chaise-Dieu.

▶ Turn right under a bridge, onto D 30.

Pébrac
After running along the pretty little valley of the Desges between pine-covered slopes, the road brings you to this quiet hillside village with red-roofed houses and the ruins of an 11C **abbey**, which underwent extensive alteration in the 15C. Beautiful carved capitals have survived from the Romanesque era.

▶ Return to the intersection with D 585 and carry on along D 30, crossing to the opposite bank of the Allier.

St-Arcons-d'Allier
The **church** has a very classic Romanesque nave with basalt columns. Its arcades are roofed by sturdy relief arches. The **Musée du Fer Blanc** displays miscellaneous items made of tinplate: lamps, moulds etc.

▶ Cross the River Allier, drive through St-Arcons and take D 302 to Saugues. Turn left onto D 590, heading for Langeac. When you reach the locality called "Héraud", turn right.

Château de Chavaniac-Lafayette
Daily except Tues 10am–noon, 2–6pm. Guided visits Jul–Aug Tues–Fri 10am, 3pm. Off-season by reservation. €7 (€7 for children 8–16). 04 71 77 50 32. www.chateau-lafayette.com. The residence where Marie-Joseph-Gilbert, **Marquis de La Fayette**, was born on 6 September 1757 stands on one of the final outcrops of the Livradois area above the Allier valley.
A general biographical exhibition provides an introduction to the visit; next comes the kitchen where La Fayette's childhood is evoked, then the treasure room where personal objects and letters are displayed; this leads to the bedroom where he was born.

DISCOVERING VELAY AND BRIVADOIS

▶ Leave Chavaniac to the W on D 51; at the first crossroads, turn right onto D 21, then take D 4.

Mazerat-Aurouze
This village has a lovely church built of pink stone, with frescoes depicting the lives of monks and peasants.

▶ Go back to Brioude via the Sénouire Valley, by taking D 4 to Paulhaguet, then D 56.

Domeyrat
The castle (*Jul-Aug Sun–Fr 2.30pm, 4.30pm. 0471768295. €8, €6 children 6–17*) ruins dominating the Sénouire and its Romanesque bridge are a fine example of medieval military architecture. Dismantled in 1795, it still towers proudly above the River Sénouire spanned by the five arches of a Romanesque bridge.

▶ Continue along D 20, then D 203.

Lavaudieu★★
see LAVAUDIEU.

▶ Return to Brioude on D 20.

Lavaudieu★★

This hamlet, established on the banks of the Sénouire, is still home to the remains of an abbey founded in the 11C by St Robert, the first abbot of La Chaise-Dieu. The Benedictines continued to live here until the French Revolution.

SIGHTS
Abbey Church
The octagonal belfry has two storeys of semicircular bays. Inside, the nave is decorated with fine 14C **frescoes★** in the Italianate style: they represent scenes from the Passion and such calamities as the Black Death.

ADDRESSES

STAY
Ermitage St-Vincent – *Pl. de l'Église, 43100 Vieille-Brioude.* ℘06 80 67 17 45. www.ermitage-saintvincent.fr. *Closed Dec–Jan. 5 rooms.* Comfortable rooms and a garden bursting with flowers. A typical local meal is served every evening.

EAT
La Poste et Champanne – *1 boul. du Dr Devins 43100 Brioude.* ℘04 71 50 14 62. www.hotel-de-la-poste-brioude.fr. *Tue–Sun lunch; Tue, Wed, Sat dinner. Closed 2 weeks in Nov.* Generous, flavorful local cuisine. Part of a charming, recently renovated **hotel** (*16 rooms*) near the town centre.

SHOPPING
Cave Saint-Julien – *17 r. du Commerce.* ℘04 71 74 90 18. Wines from all corners of France line the shelves of this shop.

Gilles Guinet – *10 r. du Commerce.* ℘04 71 50 12 47. Vanilla *bavarois*, nougatine and caramelised pears *(le Manon)* vie for attention in this pastry shop.

- **Population:** 238.
- **Michelin Map:** 331: C-2.
- **Info:** Le Bourg, 43100 Lavaudieu. ℘04 71 76 46 00.
- **Location:** A peaceful setting midway between Clermont-Ferrand and Le Puy-en-Velay. 10km/6.2mi SE of Brioude.
- **Timing:** 2-3 hrs will suffice.

Cloisters★★
Guided visits by arrangement, call or check website for details. €6.
℘04 71 76 08 90.
www.abbayedelavaudieu.fr.
Little remains of the abbey buildings, but there are particularly fine restored

Octagonal belfry, Lavaudieu

cloisters that include charming single or double colonnettes, some of them twisted, some cylindrical or polygonal, with capitals decorated with carvings of foliage and animals.

The projecting upper storey is supported by oak posts. In the refectory is a 12C **mural** (restored) which covers the entire end wall.

Maison des Arts et Traditions Populaires

Same conditions and hours as the Cloisters. 04 71 76 08 90.

This Traditional Arts and Crafts Museum is housed in an old peasant baker's house dating from the late 19C. The oven, well, bread trough and counter are still visible. On the ground floor, the living room contains a collection of everyday domestic items. The byre houses tools from old crafts (clog-making, carpentry). Beside it is the *veillade*, the room where people gathered in the evening to chat, sing and tell stories. The cupboard contains an interesting collection of headdresses and nightcaps. On the first floor are three bedrooms. The so-called Lacemaker's Room contains superb samples of pillow, crochet and bobbin lace and several lengths of trimmings.

EXCURSIONS

Frugières-le-Pin

3.5km/2.2mi E on D 20.

A museum devoted to the French Resistance and the deportation of many of its members was set up here as a tribute to Joseph Lhomenède, who was mayor of the municipality and who died in Buchenwald in 1944.

Musée de la Résistance, de la Déportation et de la Seconde Guerre Mondiale

Jun–Oct 10am–noon, 2–7pm; Nov–May weekends only. €6. 04 71 76 42 15.

Located near the former station, the Second World War Museum contains numerous documents, posters, weapons and uniforms as well as moving photographs showing the sacrifices made by underground activists.

Vallée de la Sénouire

see BRIOUDE.

ADDRESSES

STAY
THE ABBEY INN

Auberge de l'Abbaye – 04 71 76 44 44. *www.auberge-de-labbaye-lavaudieu. com. Closed Sun evening except summer, and Mon.* A pleasant rustic atmosphere reigns in this village inn housed in an old stone residence. The tasty regional fare is served in a dining room with exposed beams and a hearth.

DISCOVERING VELAY AND BRIVADOIS

Saugues

This small town favoured by anglers is the site of a number of large markets. It is dominated by an ancient keep known as the "Englishmen's Tower". Between the Margeride and the Allier, which cuts an almost uniformly narrow valley forming magnificent gorges, lies Saugues country with its stone walls, mountain streams and harsh climate.

> **Population:** 1 933.
> **Michelin Map:** 330: D-4 – 44km/27mi SW of Le Puy-en-Velay.
> **Info:** Cours St-Gervais, 43170 Saugues. 04 71 77 71 38. www.gorges-allier.com.
> **Location:** 44km/27.5mi SW of Puy-en-Velay.
> **Timing:** Half a day. On Maundy Thursday, at nightfall, a long-standing traditional Procession of the Penitents is held.

SIGHTS

Musée Fantastique de la Bête du Gévaudan
Guided visits. Daily mid-Jun–mid Sept 2.30–6.30pm (Jul–Aug 10am–noon, 2.30–6.30pm); off-season Nov 10 3pm, Nov 20 1.30pm. €5.50 (children €3.50). 04 71 77 64 22. www.musee-bete-gevaudan.com.
This museum is dedicated to the notorious creature that slayed and devoured countless sheep, goats and shepherds in the 18C, locally known as "La Bête du Gévaudan".

Tour des Anglais
Daily Jul–Aug 10am–noon, 2.30–6.30pm. €2.5. 04 71 77 71 30.
The name of this tower dates back to the Hundred Years War. The Treaty of Brétigny (8 May 1360) put an end to the contracts of the "mercenaries" enlisted in the English army. They became **free companions**, dubbed "The Englishmen", living on pillage and robbery and soon took over the town. The royal troops did not succeed in ousting them, and it was only once they had been paid off in gold that they finally left.

Church
The church, surmounted by an octagonal bell-tower, houses a 12C Auvergne Virgin and a 15C Pietà as well as the shrine of St Bénilde.

Diorama sur St Bénilde
Jul–Aug 3–7pm. 04 71 77 82 53.
Thirteen set-pieces retrace the life of **Pierre Romançon** (1805-62), Brother Bénilde of the Christian Schools, the first state primary school teacher in Saugues, who was canonised in 1967. The exhibition is held in the actual school where he taught and was the principal.

EXCURSIONS

Tour de la Clauze
10km/6.2mi SW of Saugues on D 33.
This impressive-looking tower was originally built to keep watch over La Margeride. What remains of the formidable citadel is the *donjon*, once surrounded by fortified walls. The stronghold played a major role during the Wars of Religion but subsequently slipped into neglect.

DRIVING TOUR

FROM THE ALLIER GORGES TO THE DEVÈS
Round tour of 105km/65.2mi. Allow 4h.

> Leave Saugues to the N on D 585.

St-Arcons-d'Allier –
See BRIOUDE.

> Take D 48 which runs along the east bank of the Allier.

Chapelle Ste-Marie-des-Chazes
This isolated chapel on the east bank of the Allier stands on a peaceful spot

SAUGUES

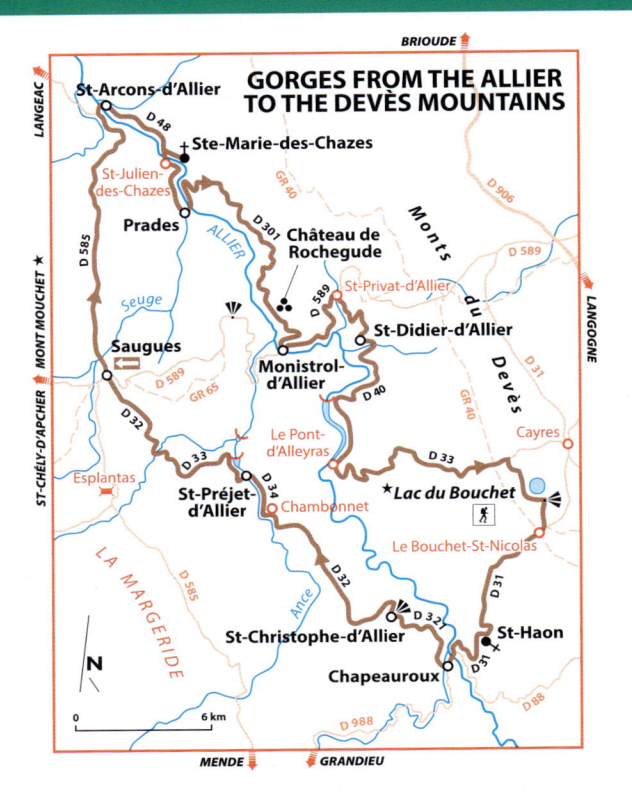

at the foot of a striking basalt rock. A monumental flight of 30 steps leads to a porch-belfry (rebuilt in the 19C) crowned by a conical lantern.

▶ Cross the Allier once more before going through St-Julien-des-Chazes and carrying on along D 48.

Prades
This small village is situated in a splendid **setting★** hemmed in by the valley sides. The sinuous D 301, half cut into the valley slopes, commands some beautiful views. After dropping downhill a little, it runs along the foot of the ruins of the **Château de Rochegude.**

Monistrol-d'Allier
This village lies in a very impressive **setting★** in the Allier valley.

▶ Leave Monistrol E on D 589, and turn right in St-Privat-d'Allier onto D 40.

St-Didier-d'Allier
This small village occupies a precarious site on a steep-sided rock.

▶ Take D 40 as far as Le Pont-d'Alleyras, then turn left onto D 33.

Lac du Bouchet★
A woodland footpath leads round the lake. Allow 45min.

🚶 This lake is 28m deep and at the bottom of an old crater, which explains its almost circular shape. The surrounding lake shore is covered with pine, spruce and fir trees planted between 1860 and 1900. No river or stream is known to feed the lake, nor any overflow channel, yet the clarity and freshness of the lake's waters show that they are being constantly renewed.

DISCOVERING VELAY AND BRIVADOIS

St-Haon
The village built on the edge of the plateau has a church with a remarkable late-12C apse.

▶ Follow D 31.

Chapeauroux
This hamlet is built on the confluence of the Allier and the Chapeauroux in an attractive valley crossed by a sweeping railway viaduct with 28 arches.

▶ On leaving Chapeauroux, turn right onto D 321.

St-Christophe-d'Allier
From the road leading up the steep slope to this village there is a broad view of the Allier gorge.

▶ Follow D 32 and just before it crosses the Ance, turn right onto D 34.

St-Préjet-d'Allier
This village on the eastern flank of the Margeride has two dams spanning the Ance: La Valette and Pouzas.

▶ Take D 33 alongside the graveyard. It leads back to Saugues.

ADDRESSES

STAY
Chambre d'Hôte des Gabales – *Rte du Puy-en-Velay. ℘04 71 77 86 92. www.lesgabales.com. Closed Dec–Jan except during Christmas school holidays. 5 rooms. Reservations required.* Skillful renovations have given this bourgeois house built in the 1930s new appeal.

RECREATION
Sportival Haut-Allier – *43300 Langeac. ℘06 80 35 20 82. www.sportival.fr. Open all year.* This centre offers many outdoor activites: climbing, canoeing, kayaking, adventure trails, walking, off-road biking and more. The site is magnificent, in the heart of the Allier gorge.

Le Monastier-sur-Gazeille

This large village in the Haute-Loire derives its name from the largest Benedictine monastery in the Velay area, founded in the late 7C. St Calmin, Count of Auvergne, founded the monastery and became its first abbot.

- **Population:** 1 806.
- **Michelin Map:** 331: G-4.
- **Info:** Mairie, 43150 Le Monastier-sur-Gazeille. ℘04 71 08 37 76.
- **Location:** The village is 17km/11mi south-east of Le Puy-en-Velay.
- **Timing:** Allow one hour to visit the church.

SIGHTS

Abbey Church
The Romanesque church built in the 11C underwent extensive alterations in the 15C. The abbey's treasures include a stone Pietà dating from the 15C and two lengths of Byzantine silk used to shroud the bodies of the founding saints.

Musée d'Art Populaire
May–Sept 2:30–7pm (closed Mon). ℘04 71 03 81 31. €5.
The local museum is housed in the vaulted chambers of the abbey castle. The collections illustrate the history of regional life (lace, traditional costumes), and the prehistoric period in the Upper Loire valley. One of the rooms deals solely with Robert Louis Stevenson.

LE MONASTIER-SUR-GAZEILLE

Stevenson's Travels

In front of the post office is a memorial commemorating the travels undertaken across the Cévennes, in the autumn of 1878, by the Scottish writer **Robert Louis Stevenson**, author of *Treasure Island*. As much to satisfy his wish to travel as to try and retrace the spirit that once fired the *Camisards,* or Protestant rebels, Stevenson, then aged 28, decided to cross the Cévennes on foot from Le Monastier to Alès, accompanied only by a somewhat capricious donkey. Sleeping outdoors or in any inns he happened to come across (with one menu for all, and all visitors sleeping in the one room), he took 12 days to reach Alès. His travel notebook is a mine of humorous and penetrating observations on the wonderful countryside he discovered and the people he met on his way.

His travels were full of comic incidents, which he recounts with glee. To carry the strange sleeping-bag that he had made, Stevenson acquired the donkey which he immediately christened Modestine. The conflict between the obstinacy of the Scottish novelist and the strong will of the donkey from the Velay lasted for the entire trip: "Modestine's pace is quite beyond description. It was something much slower than a stroll, when a stroll is much slower than a walk. She held back each hoof for an incredibly long time…"

DRIVING TOUR

LAUZE COUNTRY
125km/77.6mi. Allow 1 day.

Château de Vachères
(*Not open to the public*) A massive keep flanked by towers with pepper-pot roofs gives this 13C castle with its blocks of black basalt outlined in white mortar a typically Velay-style appearance.

Lac d'Issarlès★
Like a sapphire set in a deep crater, this pretty lake is breathtaking in spite of being used for hydroelectric purposes, which vary the levels of the water.

▶ Join the D 16 heading for Béage and follow directions for Ste-Eulalie.

Summit of Gerbier-de-Jonc

DISCOVERING VELAY AND BRIVADOIS

Ste-Eulalie
This village belongs to the municipality of Gerbier-de-Jonc and lies at the source of the River Loire. On the way to the Mont Gerbier-de-Jonc, another traditional broom-covered farmhouse, **Ferme Philip**, can be visited.

▶ Continue along D 122, heading towards Lachamp-Raphaël until you reach the intersection with D 378.

Ferme de Bourlatier★
May–Jun Wed–Fri 2.30–5.30pm, Sat–Sun 10.30am–6pm; Jul–Aug daily 10.30am–6pm; Sept Wed 2.30–5.30pm, Sat–Sun 2–6pm; Oct Wed, Sat–Sun 2.30–5.30pm. €4.50. 04 75 38 84 90. www.bourlatier.fr.
A fine example of regional rural architecture with its *lauze* roof tiling, this stately farmhouse has been extensively restored in local tradition. Its most salient feature is probably its superb framework, shaped like an inverted hull, able to support the 150-tonne roofwork!

▶ At the crossroads take D 378, for Les Estables and Gerbier-de-Jonc.

Gerbier-de-Jonc★★
The Gerbier-de-Jonc looks like a giant haystack or a huge heap of sheaves when seen from a distance.
The word "Gerbier" is a Latinisation of the Indo-European root *gar* meaning "rock". Similar names are found in other regions of France, in particular in the Pyrenees (Pic du Gar, Pic du Ger, Pic du Jer). The word *jonc* is derived from the Latin *jugum* meaning "mountain". Gerbier-de-Jonc therefore literally means "rocky mountain". The Gerbier de Jonc, which is part of the Mézenc range, consists of phonolithic rocks that have a tendency to flake, forming unstable scree slopes and clothing the mountainside in a scaly shell. At the foot of the south-western slope are several small streams; the sources of the Loire.

The Climb
From the top there is an impressive **panoramic view★★**. On the north-east side, the view extends over the dip formed by the Eysse, a tributary of the River Eyrieux. Mont Alambre, the Mézenc and the volcanic Sara close off the north horizon; Montfol obstructs the view to the west; the conical La Barre, recognisable by its tabular outline, lies in the foreground on the south side. A stretch of the Alps can be seen in clear weather.

▶ D 328 then D 36 to Les Estables.

Les Estables✻
This small mountain village lying in the foothills of the Mézenc massif is a popular winter resort offering a wide choice of pistes for both Alpine and cross-country skiing.

▶ Cross the village heading N and turn right for Mont Mézenc via the Peccata Cross.

Mont Mézenc★★★
The volcanic Mézenc range (the final "c" is not pronounced) forms a natural barrier that divides the rivers flowing to the Atlantic from those flowing to the Mediterranean. The Mézenc massif forms the centre of a volcanic trail that cuts across the axis of the Cévennes. It is flanked to the west by the granite mountains at La Margeride and to the east by the crystalline plateaux of the Upper Vivarais.
A vast tract of land called the **Zone Nordique du Mézenc** is popular in the winter months for the cross-country skiing it offers.

Access via the Boutières Cross
2.5km/almost 2mi from Les Estables via D 631 E. Park at the Boutières Cross (1 508m).
From the rock above the pass at the Boutières Cross, to the right, there is a superb **view★★** over Sara, Roche Borée and Les Boutières.

▶ Follow the footpath numbered GR7 (1h15 there and back) which climbs up to the left towards the summit.

LE MONASTIER-SUR-GAZEILLE

The Mézenc massif

Hillsides with contrasting appeal – On the Velay side of the Mézenc massif, the range looks like a vast, bare plateau. In the summer months it resembles a windswept steppe dotted with low farmhouses crowned with thatched or stone-slabbed roofs. The Vivarais side of the range is rugged terrain, suddenly sweeping down towards the Rhône. The streams have worn the ground down to the granite rocks underneath.

Splendid basalt flows – On the hillsides flanking the valleys, erosion has revealed extensive basalt lava flows that are particularly impressive in the upper reaches of the River Ardèche and its tributaries (the Volane, Bourges, Fontaulière and Lignon). These flows, which now take the form of prismatic columnar basalt, have created famous beauty spots such as the Ray-Pic waterfall, the Thueyts causeway, Pourcheyrolles rock, Jaujac and Antraigues.

Flora in the peaks – The upper Mézenc massif has flora which will delight botanists, including a variety of groundsel which, in all the Massif Central, can only be found at the summit of the Mézenc massif: the famous "Mézenc grass" with silvery leaves and beautiful bright-yellow flower-heads. The great mountain violet, Alpine anemone, all sorts of gentians, globe flowers, arnica, willow-herb and saxifrages are the commonest of the plants but it is when the narcissi flower in June that the mountain acquires its finest appearance. A traditional market of medicinal herbs, known as the "Violet Fair", is held in Ste-Eulalie every year.

Head for the south summit via the flat ground in between the two peaks.

Access via the Peccata Cross
3km/2mi NE from Les Estables. Park at the Peccata Cross then follow the path on the right (1hr on foot there and back).

This route climbs up through the woods then twists and turns amid the heather and juniper bushes.

Bear left towards the north summit (1 749m) topped by a cross.

Panoramic View★★★
From the summit there is a sweeping **panorama**. To the north are the Meygal and Forez mountains; to the west, the Puy basin, the Velay area and the mountains of the Auvergne; to the south lie Lake Issarlès and a string of volcanic cones; and to the east the Saliouse and Eysse gorges, both of which cut into the Boutières area towards the Upper Eyrieux, where deep ravines are interspersed with ridges and peaks.

Rejoin D 274 to the N.

Chaudeyrolles
Typical of the Mézenc, this village has a number of houses built from volcanic stone and roofed with *lauzes*. At the **Maison du Fin Gras du Mézenc**, there is an explanation of the methods of cattle rearing that produce the AOC beef of the region.

Moudeyres
The village still has several typical cottages, namely the **Ferme des Frères Perrel** (guided visits: mid-April–mid-July Sat–Sun 10am–noon, 2–6pm, Wed 2–6pm; mid-Jul–mid-Sept 10am–1pm, 2–6pm. €6. 06 27 59 14 52. www.ecomuseefermeperrel.com/). Apart from its basalt walls, its *lauze* tiles over the living quarters and its thatched roof crowning the outbuildings, it has kept its original furniture and farming tools.

Turn back and rejoin D 500. Turn right towards Le Monastier-sur-Gazeille.

Freycenet-la-Tour
The tower has long since disappeared but the village is still worth a visit for its Romanesque church and its typical houses roofed with *lauze* tiles.

THIERS AND THE LIVRADOIS-FOREZ

The Livradois and Forez look out over a land of grass and trees, a land of long-established traditions. In the east of the Massif Central, there is a marvellous, amorphous realm of wide, open spaces, a landscape that is hard to take in at first glance. Through the middle flows the River Dore, with its nourishing waters. On its right bank, the Monts du Forez, covered with pine, seem untouched since the dawn of time. On the left, the Livradois reigns, made up of a series of plateaux and granite outcrops, divided by hollows.

Highlights

1. Bird watching in the **Livradois-Forez national park** (p230)
2. Taking a walk around the old part of **Thiers** and treating yourself to a fine piece of **Thiers** cutlery (p231)
3. Tasting some local **Fourme d'Ambert** blue cheese (p239)
4. Visiting the paper-making mill **Richard de Bas** in Ambert (p239)
5. Admiring exquisite 16C tapestries at the abbey of **La Chaise-Dieu** (p243)

Crafty Museums

The residents of the areas around the park are proud of their history and the craftsmanship they have practised over the centuries, which is reflected in various local museums: cutlery-making (Thiers); lace-making (Arlanc); paper-making (Richard-de-Bas); cheese-making (Ambert); ceramics (Lezoux).

La Moule Perlière

Rediscovered in 1994, the cool and clear waters of the Livradois-Drill have yielded pearl-bearing mussels, although they are small and of little value. One can neither eat them nor gather them: the so-called "pearl mussel" has protected status in Europe, which prohibits any interference either with the mussels themselves or their environment.

Water, Water Everywhere

The importance of water cannot be underestimated, especially in Thiers. The combination of the Dore and the spirited Durolle enabled the town to become the capital of cutlery-making from the 16C.

In Ambert, meanwhile, water paved the way for a profitable paper-making industry; in the 16C, more than 300 paper mills operated in the area. A special reminder of those pioneering times remains at Richard de Bas Mill, which today houses an ecomuseum that brings the history of the industry back to life.

Cloisters, Église Abbatiale St-Robert, La Chaise-Dieu

Luxurious Peasant Dishes

As in many other regions, the authentic local fare of the Auvergne is cheap yet nourishing, often featuring a combination of potatoes, pork and vegetables. The Auvergne speciality "Potée" is a hotpot-type dish containing lard, ham hock, ribs, fresh local sausage, root vegetables, beans, cabbage and potatoes, and clearly adheres to the underlying principles of peasant cooking.

Saint-Pourçain *andouillette* (a type of sausage) and marbled, melt-in-your-mouth Mézenc beef served with green Puy lentils are just some of the choice dishes you'll find at the Auvergne table. This area is also home to one of the Auvergne's five AOP-protected cheeses. Fourme d'Ambert is one of the mildest of French blues, with a sweet, nutty aroma.

Parc Naturel Régional Livradois-Forez★

One of the largest protected areas in France, the Livradois-Forez National Park was set up in 1986 and covers an area of 297 000ha of woodlands and farmland. The park seeks to revitalise a declining rural environment and to present and promote local heritage, especially crafts and industry. A haven for nature lovers, the landscape and its flora and fauna have been shaped by altitude, numerous waterways and a varied terrain.

- **Michelin Map:** 326: H/J 8/11 and 330 I/L 1/3.
- **Info:** Maison du Parc 63880 Saint-Gervais-sous-Meymont. ✆04 73 95 57 57. www.parc-livradois-forez.org.
- **Location:** 65km/40mi SE of Clermont-Ferrand.
- **Don't Miss:** The music festivals of La Chaise-Dieu and Thiers.
- **Kids:** Explore the walking trails.
- **Timing:** You can spend a whole day here; visit in spring or autumn to see migrating birds.

VISIT

The Maison du Parc offers information about getting around, and can give details about the **Livradois (Agrivap) discovery trains** (*see p230*) that make exploring the vast area a bit easier. There are numerous waymarked paths crisscrossing the park, dedicated to walking and biking, as well as facilities for water sports and paragliding.

ADDRESSES

STAY

Auberge de Chabanettes – *Côtes de Chabanettes, 63590 Auzelles. 29km/18mi E of Issoire. ✆04 73 72 86 27. www.aubergedechabanettes.com. Closed Jan. 5 rooms.* This delightful family run boutique-hotel and spa in the heart of the Livradois-Forez National Park, offers a splendid and peaceful escape from city life. Restaurant with good wine list, parking, WiFi, Whisky bar, spa, sauna and riverside terrace. Perfect for a touch of escapism.

Parc naturel régional Livradois-Forez near Ambert in winter

© Christian Guy/hemis.fr

Thiers★★

The town located on a ravine through which the River Durolle flows has a magnificent view over the Limagne and the Dômes mountain range. This, and the town's historic district, make Thiers an attractive tourist destination. The waters of the Durolle helped make Thiers' fortune: paper and knives have been made here since the 15C, and although paper-making has nearly disappeared, cutlery-making continues to contribute to the town's renown. The town was first founded on the south bank of the Durolle, around the original church of Le Moutier.

- **Population:** 11 685.
- **Michelin Map:** 326: I-7
- **Info:** Hôtel du Pirou, 63300 Thiers. ℘04 73 80 65 65. www.vacances-livradois-forez.com
- **Location:** Thiers lies within the Parc Naturel Régional du Livradois-Forez, just 40km/25mi east of Clermont-Ferrand.
- **Parking:** Beside the Eglise St Genès, and at the northern end of town.
- **Don't Miss:** The view from the Terrasse du Rempart; Maison des Couteliers.
- **Timing:** Allow half a day to explore this lovely town.

WALKING TOURS

1 THE OLD CITY★

A number of 15C, 16C and 17C half-timbered houses have been restored in the centre of the old town (Vieux Thiers). These picturesque houses line narrow, winding streets known as *peddes*, many of them reserved for pedestrians.

▶ Start from place de la Mutualité and walk down rue Prosper-Marilhat leading onto rue Terrasse.

Terrasse du Rempart★

The terrace offers a beautiful **panorama**★ of the Limagne and the Dore and Dômes mountain ranges. The view of the sunset can be magnificent from here. The viewing table is made of enamelled lava stone.

▶ 50m further on, turn right onto rue du Bourg.

Rue du Bourg

At Nos. 10 and 14 note the 15C Volvic-stone doorways; No. 20 is a 16C house.

Thiers Cutlery Trade

The origin of Thiers' cutlery specialisation dates back to the Middle Ages: legend has it that Auvergne knights returned from the First Crusade (1096–99) bearing the secret of cutlery manufacture. The local metallurgical industry dates back to the 14C; by the 16C, the town's cutlery trade had developed sufficiently to start exporting products to Spain, the Netherlands and Lombardy.

Blades of all types were once sharpened on grinding wheels powered by the waters of the Durolle. Cutlery production has subsequently been modernised, and the traditional figure of the knife-grinder lying face down over his grinding-wheel with his dog on his legs to keep him warm is now but an image of the past. Technological and electrical developments have paved the way for enormous factories, but today, Thiers still boasts nearly 300 manufacturers or craftsmen.

DISCOVERING THIERS AND THE LIVRADOIS-FOREZ

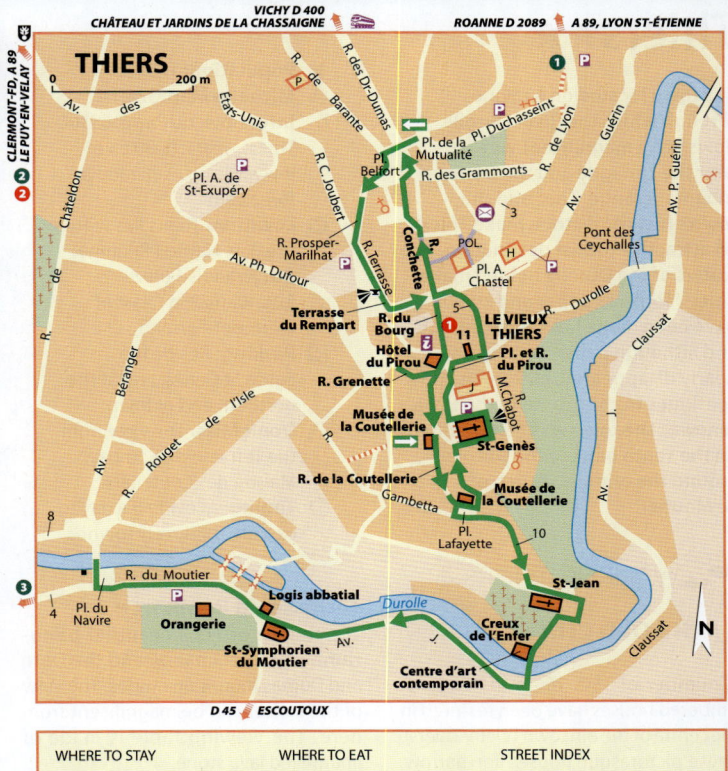

WHERE TO STAY	WHERE TO EAT	STREET INDEX
Aigle d'Or (Hôtel L')............ 1	à la Belle Excuse................ 1	Clermont (R. de)............... 4
Eliotel (Hôtel)................... 2	4 Chemins (L'Auberge des).... 2	Dumas (R. Alexandre)........ 5
Clos St-Eloi (Le)................ 3		Mitterand (R. F.)............... 3
		Voltaire (Av.)................... 8
		4 Septembre (R. du).......... 10

Place du Pirou

This square is dominated by the early-15C **Hôtel du Pirou★**. The house, with its pointed gables and timbered façade, is a handsome example of civil architecture of the Middle Ages.

Rue Grenette

No. 8 is a 16C and 17C house (Maison dite de Lauzun).

Rue de la Coutellerie

Note the unusual houses at Nos. 12 and 14, the latter with wooden corbels carved in a somewhat free and vigorous style. No. 21, the Maison de l'Homme des Bois (15C), is decorated with an enigmatic ape-like figure. This house and the ancient alderman's house at No. 58 contain the Cutlers' Centre and the Cutlery Museum.

Musée de la Coutellerie

23 and 58 rue de la Coutellerie.
Guided visits (1h30): Feb holidays–May, Oct and Christmas holidays daily except Mon 10am–noon, 2–6pm; Jun and Sept daily 10am–noon, 2–6pm; Jul–Aug daily 10am–12.30pm, 1.30–7pm. €7.5 (Jun–Sept; €5.9 otherwise). Jan, 1 May, 25 Dec. 04 73 80 58 86. www. ville-thiers.fr/Musee-de-la-Coutellerie.

At No. 21, five rooms are devoted to the history of the cutlery industry in Thiers: history and origins, crafts and techniques, working conditions, leisure, commercialisation and advertising etc.

Creux de l'Enfer, Centre d'Art Contemporain

At No. 58, craftsmen may be watched working on the different phases of knife manufacturing. Workshops on the ground floor specialise in the polishing, shaping, mounting and carving of top-quality knives in limited numbers. In the basement sound-and-light show evokes the deafening world of the forge (power-hammer, furnace etc).

▶ Follow rue Chabot on the left and take the first street on the left leading to the steps; turn left then first right onto impasse Jean-Brugière.

Église St-Genès

This Romanesque church has undergone many alterations. The west front and the bell-tower have been rebuilt, but the south transept retains the interesting decoration on its gable and graceful windows.

▶ Walk through the public gardens surrounding the east end of the church of St-Genès.

The north door, which leads onto place du Palais, is preceded by an 18C porch, the wall of which boasts an elegantly carved 14C recess.

▶ Turn right onto rue du Palais and leave place du Pirou to the right.

Rue du Pirou

At No. 11 stands the **Maison des Sept Péchés Capitaux**, named after the decorations evoking the Seven Deadly Sins on the seven beams supporting the first floor; at No. 9, note a corbelled construction.

Further along is the "Coin des Hasards", an intersection dominated by the tower of Maître Raymond (15C).

▶ Continue along rue Alexandre-Dumas and place Antonin-Chastel. Take a few steps to the left and follow rue Conchette.

Rue Conchette

In the courtyard at No. 4 there is a 16C staircase; at No. 10, an inner façade on pillars. At No. 18, in the courtyard with its turret, two 16C medallions.

▶ Return to place de la Mutualité.

② THE OLD MANUFACTURING VALLEY

This tour starts from the Maison des Couteliers. The return journey is by local bus (TUT).

▶ Walk down rue du Quatre-Septembre, heading towards the Creux de l'Enfer (signposted itinerary). You will reach place St-Jean and its church.

Église St-Jean

This 15C church occupies a picturesque site overlooking the Durolle.

▶ A path to the right as you leave the church runs around the church and leads to Creux de l'Enfer.

Creux de l'Enfer, Centre d'Art Contemporain
Daily except Mon 2–6pm. 1 May and 25 Dec; 2 weeks in Jan. ℘04 73 80 26 56. www.creuxdelenfer.net.
This contemporary arts centre is set up on the premises of a former factory facing the impressive Durolle waterfall. Exhibitions focus on unusual aspects of modern art that draw inspiration from the nearby landscape. The site is also used as an artists' workshop for experimental projects.

▶ Walk along avenue Joseph-Claussat.

Vallée de la Durolle
The route follows the Durolle. The river's many waterfalls once operated numerous cutlery operations. There were at least 140 falls over a distance of 3km/2mi. The most picturesque are those known as the **Creux de l'Enfer** ("Hell-Hole"), just before St-Jean bridge, and the **Creux du Salien**, just after Seychalles bridge (15C).

Église du Moutier
The church was part of the powerful Benedictine abbey founded in the 7C. At the corner of avenue Joseph-Claussat stands the fortified **Logis Abbatial du Moutier**, the last remains of the abbey.

Orangerie
. ℘04 73 80 53 53. www.ville-thiers.fr.
Located in Moutier park, the orangery now occasionally hosts events linked to sustainability and the environment. The large hothouse is landscaped: pool, walls of plants and exotic species contrast with a desert environment.

▶ Continue along rue du Moutier to place du Navire (note the Pont du Navire, listed as a historic monument) then travel back to the town centre by public transport (from the church of Moutier).

EXCURSIONS
Château et Jardins de la Chassaigne
Leave Thiers N towards Vichy. Beyond the tunnel, turn left onto D 94C, and follow signposts to the castle. Visitors enter through the gardens. Guided tours of the interior. Jun–mid-Sept daily except Tue 2.30–6pm. €6. ℘04 73 80 59 08.
The 15C manor, which had already suffered during the Revolution, was dismantled at the beginning of the 20C; its trees were also felled, with the exception of the lime tree in the main courtyard. Although the castle was still inhabited, its upkeep was neglected until new owners acquired it in 1986.

Lezoux
15km/9mi to the W of Thiers.
In the 2C, Lezoux was a major centre of the ceramics industry, fuelled by the clay quarried in the Limagne. Within a radius of 3km/2mi, the remains of more than 200 potters' kilns have been uncovered, and pottery made in Lezoux has been found as far afield as England and Prussia. The town, in which there is now a large oil-making plant, still has a 15C belfry topped by a tower. It stands adjacent to one of the old town gates.

Musée Départemental de la Céramique
39 rue de la République, 63190 Lezoux (15km/9.3mi from Thiers). Daily except Tue. Oct–Mar 10am–5pm (2–6pm weekends); Apr–Sep 10am–6pm (2–7pm weekends). 1 May, 1 Nov, 11 Nov, 25 Dec. €5. ℘04 73 73 42 42. www.musee-ceramique.puy-de-dome.fr.
This ceramic museum offers a fun, informative discovery of the region's rich past via finds from archaeological sites in and around Lezoux. The museum traces the history of potters from ancient times to the present, projecting visitors into the daily life of a Gallo-Roman family in this, the most important centre of ceramic production in the Roman Empire. Great for kids and adults alike.

Ravel
6km/3.7mi SE of Lezoux along D 223.
This village, set among the pasture and woodland of the Limagne, is easily identified by the château★ (*guided visits May–Aug Tue–Sun 10am–5pm; Sept–Apr Sat–Sun only 2–5pm, except public holidays. €7. ℘04 73 62 95 15; www.chateauderavel.com*) which overlooks its houses and its church. In 1294, the castle was given by Philip the Fair to his chancellor Pierre Flotte and passed by inheritance and marriage to the D'Estaing family, who had it renovated in the 17C. The most beautiful and best preserved part of its decoration dates from the 18C.

Church
The building has two 14C stained-glass windows in the nave and another (late 13C) in the sacristy.

ILOA "Les Rives de Thiers"
12km/7.5mi. At the large roundabout at the entrance to Thiers, head for Vichy. Take the fork at the toll-booth and at the next roundabout turn left.
This large leisure park offers facilities for a great many sports: rambling, cycling, riding, swimming, tennis and golf.

St-Rémy-sur-Durolle
9km/6mi N on N 89 and a small road on the left.
The scenic road winds through woodland before reaching St-Rémy. This cutlery-making centre is built on the southern flank of "Thiers mountain", an extension of the Bois Noirs massif.

▶ In St-Rémy, take a road uphill on the left to the wayside cross. Leave the car near the sports ground and walk to the top of the cliff (15min there and back).

From the wayside cross, the **panorama**★ includes the Forez mountains, the Margerides, the Plomb du Cantal and the Dômes mountain range. Northeast of St-Rémy, on the right of D 201, a large lake offers various watersports such as swimming, sailing and rowing.

DRIVING TOURS

1 LES MARGERIDES★
5km/9.5mi. Allow 3h.

A delightful drive across the plateaus and valleys of Les Margerides (*see RUYNES-EN-MARGERIDE*).

▶ Leave Thiers NE along N 89 towards Lyon.

From the look-out point by the turn-off to St-Rémy, there is an attractive view over to the right of the Durolle gorge, Thiers and the Limagne.

▶ In Château-Gaillard, take the first turning to the right.

Vallée des Rouets
Walking boots recommended.
Guided visits in the mill – €4.3, rest of the visit unguided. Jul–Aug noon–7pm; Jun noon–6pm; Sept 2–6pm. ℘04 73 80 58 86. www.ville-thiers.fr.
The various paths formerly used by craftsmen have been restored and are now clearly signposted, offering interesting views of both architectural features and natural sites. There used to be 27 cutlery workshops in the valley; the last one in operation was the Rouet Lyonnet (1816) which closed in 1976. One can still visit the last working mill in the valley.

▶ Beyond Château-Gaillard and Bellevue turn right on D 320.

The road crosses the river and winds through green and fertile countryside.

▶ On leaving Vernières there is a view of the Durolle valley and the village of St-Rémy on the mountainside; D 102 descends to Thiers and makes a right-hand bend near Borbes rock.

Rocher de Borbes
From the rock, there is an extensive **view**★ of the Limagne, the Dômes and

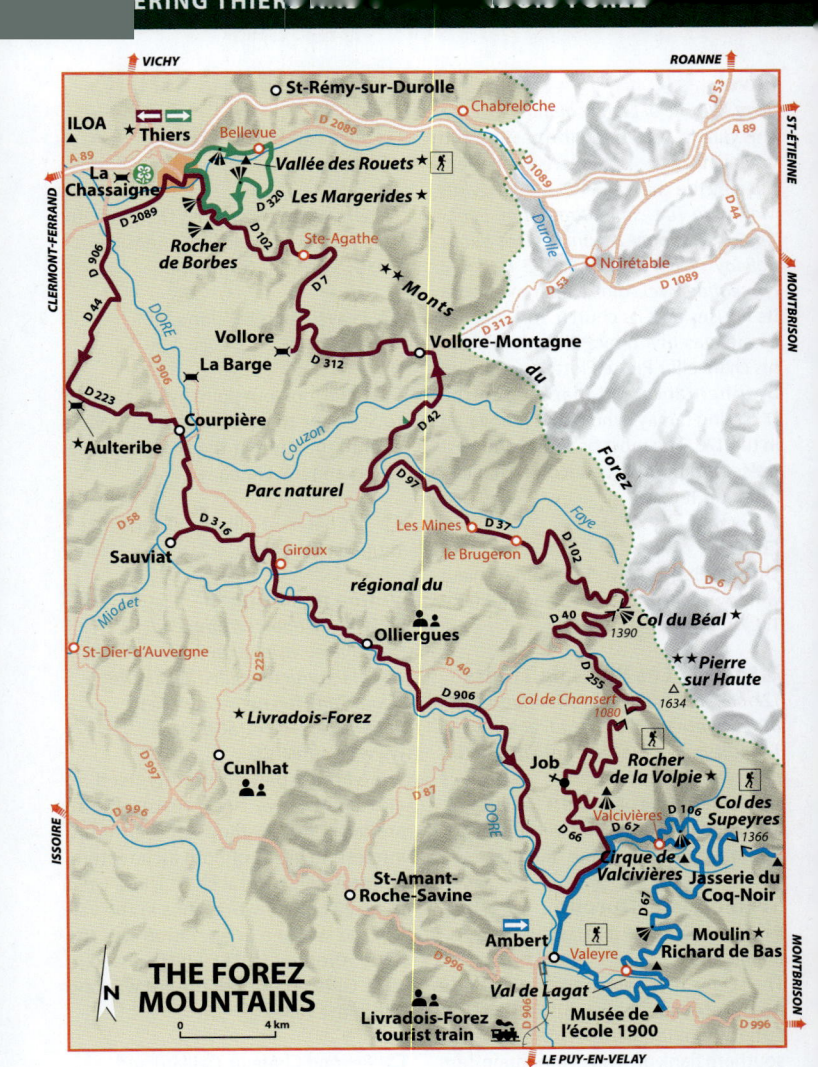

the Dore mountain ranges, the Livradois and, in clear weather, the Cantal mountains.

▶ Continue on D 102 to return to Thiers.

② LA DORE TO MONTS FOREZ★★
130km/81mi. Allow one day.

The Dore is a tributary on the right bank of the Allier, rising in the mountains of the Livradois area. It flows down in a south-easterly direction into deep, granite gorges then turns northwards to cross the Ambert plateau.

▶ Leave Thiers to the W and drive up to Pont-de-Dore to cross the river. Follow D 906, then D 44 on the right.

Château d'Aulteribe★
5km/3mi NW along D223.
Jan–mid-May and mid-Sept–Dec daily except Mon 10am–noon, 2–5.30pm; mid-May–mid-Sept daily 10am–noon, 2–6.30pm. 1 Jan, 1 May,

236

1 and 11 Nov, 25 Dec. ∞€6. ℘04 73 53 14 55. www.chateau-aulteribe.fr.
This castle was rebuilt in the 19C in the Romantic style, on the site of an austere medieval construction. The estate was bequeathed to the National Historic Monuments Trust in the 19C.

▶ Take D 223 then turn right onto D 906.

Courpière

The town lies at the entrance to a gorge formed by the River Dore. In addition to its picturesque houses, Courpière boasts a number of interesting castles in the vicinity and is the ideal starting point for excursions through Livradois country.

Church★

This Auvergne-style Romanesque building is topped by a Gothic bell-tower.

Château de la Barge

2km/1mi N on D 58 in the direction of Escoutoux. &.● *Guided visits Jul–Aug Mon–Fri 2pm, 3.30pm, 5pm; May and Sept–Oct by appointment.*
℘04 73 53 14 51.
This handsome residence is still circled by its moat. In the 16C the former citadel was converted into a Renaissance château. Two centuries later, it was graced with a terraced garden which its present owners are constantly refurbishing.

▶ Beyond Courpière, continue to Ambert on D 906; right onto D 316.

Sauviat

This village stands high above a meander of the River Dore as it flows through a narrow valley.

▶ Drive down on D 316 and rejoin D 906 on the right.

Olliergues

Situated on the north bank of the Dore, over which is a 15C bridge, Olliergues boasts terraces of houses rising up the hillside and features a castle that once belonged to Marshal Turenne's family.

▶ Continue towards Ambert and 3km/2mi before reaching Ambert, turn right onto D 66 and right again onto a road leading to Volpie rock.

Rocher de la Volpie★

🚶 From the rocky Volpie peak, the **view★** stretches over the Livradois mountains with the Ambert plain in the foreground. Those reluctant to tackle the climb can take a path to the right beyond the farm, which leads across the meadows to the foot of the rock *(20min there and back)*.

▶ Rejoin D 66 and turn right.

Église de Job

Superb 15C church topped by a large square belfry.

▶ D 255 to the right then D 40 leads to Col du Béal.

Col du Béal★

From this pass, there is a wide, panoramic view over the mountains of the Auvergne and the Lyonnais area.

▶ Leave Col du Béal on D 102.

The road crosses vast expanses of pasture and soon provides a superb view of the mountains of the Livradois area.

▶ In Brugeron, take D 37 towards Olliergues and, when you reach the hamlet of Les Mines, turn right onto D 97.

The road follows the Faye valley.

▶ Shortly after crossing the River Faye, turn right onto D 42.

Vollore-Montagne

This mountain village is an ideal centre for walkers. The forests, the landscapes of woodland and meadow, and local beauty spots make this part of the journey most enjoyable.

▶ Drive W on D 312.

Château de Vollore
8km/5mi E along D 7. Guided visits Jul–Aug daily by reservation. €15 (unaccompanied visits Jul–Aug €5). 04 73 53 71 06. www.chateauvollore.com.
This 17C building of pale granite stands on a spur, and is flanked to the south by a large 12C keep and to the north by a 14C tower. It has been in the same family for over two centuries. Stay at one of the château's **5 rooms** for a royal experience.

▶ N along D 7; 7km/4mi beyond Ste-Agathe, the road begins its descent to Thiers via the Margerides route.

3 LE VAL LAGAT *see AMBERT.*

ADDRESSES

STAY
Hôtel l'Aigle d'Or – *8 r. de Lyon, 63300 Thiers. 04 73 80 00 50. www.hotel-restaurant-aigle.fr. Restaurant open Mon–Sat evenings (Sun July–Aug). 18 rooms.* Founded in 1836; comfortable lounge and cosy, soundproofed rooms.

Le Clos St Eloi – *49 av. du Général-de-Gaulle. 04 73 53 80 80. 31 rooms. Restaurant.* Quiet rooms, spacious and colourful; a nice retreat between town and country.

Hotel Eliotel – *51, rte de Maringues, Pont de Dore, 63920 Peschadoires. 6km/4.8mi W of Thiers via N 89. 04 73 80 10 14. www.eliotel.fr. 17 rooms. Restaurant.* Only 3 minutes from the A89, this hotel offers comfy rooms and excellent cuisine, often combined as packages to encourage a little indulgence.

EAT
L'Auberge des 4 Chemins – *Rte de Clermont, Pont de Dore, 63920 Peschadoires. Closed Mon and Tue. 04 73 80 25 68. www.aubergedesquatrechemins.com.* Located at a crossroads, this unpretentious family-run inn welcomes gourmets to a small terrace in a courtyard or either of two dining rooms. Surrounded by flowers, you will find simple and traditional cuisine infused with strong flavours of the region.

La Belle Excuse – *6 rue du Bourg, 63300 Thiers. Tue–Sun (Mon in summer) 04 82 79 52 08. www.restaurant-la-belle-excuse.com.* A warm setting with beamed ceilings at the centre of town. The chef prepares simple and tasty traditional dishes from the region.

Ambert

The small, seemingly-isolated town of Ambert lies in the middle of a low, wide plain between the Livradois and Forez mountains. Ambert is a centre of diverse economic activity, including the manufacture of braiding and the production of the eponymous local blue cheese. It is also the ideal starting point for excursions across the surrounding high pastures.

SIGHTS
Église St-Jean★
Place St-Jean.
The church of St-Jean is a typical example of flamboyant Gothic architecture.

- ▶ **Population:** 7 206.
- **Michelin Map:** 326: J-9.
- **Info:** 4 pl. de l'Hôtel-de-Ville, 63600 Ambert. 04 73 82 61 90. www.vacances-livradois-forez.com.
- **Location:** At the heart of the Livradois-Forez, 77km/48mi from Clermont Ferrand and 79km/49mi from St-Étienne.
- **Timing:** Half a day to explore; market Thursday morning.

AMBERT

Moulin Richard de Bas

Hôtel de Ville
Boulevard Henri IV.
An unusual rotunda made famous by Jules Romains' *Copains* novel.

Passage Kim en Joong
Pl Charles de Gaulle
This space unites more than 100 works from South Korean artist Kim en Joong, known here for the beautiful windows he created for the Dominican chapel.

Mus'Energie
Apr–Nov Tue–Sat 2–6pm (Jul–Aug daily 10.30am–1pm, 2–6.30pm.) €7 (children 6-12 years €5). 04 73 82 60 42.
This museum installed in a former saw mill boasts a large collection of steam-powered machines from the early 20C.

Maison de la Fourme d'Ambert et des fromages d'Auvergne
Guided tours (45mn). Oct, late Dec, Feb, Apr Mon–Sat 10am–12.30pm; 2–6pm (May–mid-Jul until 6.30pm); mid-Jul–mid-Aug 10am–6.30pm. €6; €10 for visit+cheese workshop+tasting Tue–Fri at 2.15pm in summer. 04 73 82 49 23. www.maison-fourme-ambert.fr.
This museum devoted to cheese-making is housed in a 15C building. Guided tours describe the manufacture of Fourme d'Ambert, the delicious local blue cheese. Tastings and workshops are offered in summer.

EXCURSIONS

Livradois–Forez tourist train★
Leaves Ambert at 10.30am and 2.15pm; mainly operates in Jul–Aug and some out-of-season days; check website for details and reservations. €17 (children, €13). 04 73 82 43 88. www.agrivap.fr.
In the summer, a panoramic tourist train departs from Ambert to La Chaise-Dieu, through typical landscapes of the Livradois-Forez Regional Park.

Moulin Richard de Bas★
5km/3mi E of Ambert via D 996, and then the D 57. Guided tours (1h) daily all year 9.30am–12.30pm, 2–6pm (mid-Jul–Aug 9.30am–6.30pm). 1 Jan and 25 Dec. €8.30 (child 6–17, €5.60). 04 73 82 03 11. www.richarddebas.fr.
Old houses and paper mills are evidence of the industrial importance of the Lagat valley which, for several centuries, was one of the main paper-making centres in France. Today, Richard-de-Bas is the only remaining mill in production.

🚗 DRIVING TOURS

LE VAL LAGAT
60km/37mi. Allow one day.
See THIERS for tour map (route 3).

▶ Leave Ambert E along D 966, heading towards Montbrison.

👥 Musée de l'École 1900
In Saint-Martin-des-Olmes. ⏱Apr–Jun and Sept–Oct daily 2–7pm; Jul–Aug daily 10am–6pm. ⏱1 Jan, 25 Dec. €5.50 (child 6–12, €3.50). ☎04 73 72 66 80. www.ecole1900.fr.

The village school, dating from the 1880s and closed in 1989, houses this interesting school museum which recreates the atmosphere of a 20C classroom.

▶ Turn around and take the first road on the right.

👥 Moulin Richard-de-Bas★
(see Excursions).

▶ At Valeyre, turn right onto D 67.

🚶 A discovery trail, Le Chemin des Papetiers, starts from Valeyre and runs along a steep mule track.

Cirque de Valcivières
This attractive *cirque* shelters several hamlets on its stream-strewn slopes and among the fields.

▶ Turn right onto D 106, and up to the Col des Supeyres.

Col des Supeyres
Alt. 1 336m.

This pass on the eastern edge of the Livradois-Forez Nature Park is surrounded by a landscape of badly-drained mountain pastures. A farm, the **Ferme des Supeyres**, sells artisan fourme d'Ambert every day except Thurs and Sun (10am–12.30pm; 3–5.30pm).

Un colporteur et des Jasseries
🚶 From Col des Supeyres, walk through high pastures along a discovery trail, following in the footsteps of pedlars.

👥 Jasserie du Coq-Noir
⏱Noon–7pm: Jul–Aug daily; May–Jun and Sept Sat–Sun and public holidays. No charge. ☎04 73 95 31 33. www.coq-noir.fr.

This former summer farm offers valuable insight into mountain farming, roof thatching and cheese-making. Cultural events like concerts and hikes are offered in summer.

▶ Return to Col des Supeyres and Valcivières.

After Valcivières the route follows a rock-strewn ravine to emerge above the Ambert plain and then descends the lower slopes of the Forez mountains.

▶ D 66, then D 906 back to Ambert.

LIVRADOIS TO THE DORE★
100km/62mi round trip. Allow one day. (see region map).

▶ Leave Ambert W along D 996, for St-Amand-Roche-Savine. The Le Monestier/St-Amand road takes you past a small castle, the Domaine Nobles des Escures.

St-Amand-Roche-Savine
Every summer, this charming hamlet nestling amid the Livradois heights welcomes many visitors, especially during the lively rock festival.

▶ Drive N; 1km/0.5mi after St-Amand, turn right onto D 87, then D 65.

Cunlhat
Pretty trading community formerly specialised in wool-making, surrounded by lush wooded vegetation.

AMBERT

▶ Leave Cunlhat to the S and drive along D 105 to St-Eloy-la-Glacière; turn left after entering the village.

La Ferme des Bois Noirs

Unaltered since it was built in 1763, this farmhouse illustrates the life and work of a peasant family in the Livradois region, a poor mountainous area where men had to take on seasonal work to supplement the meagre income the family derived from farming.

▶ Drive back to St-Eloy and turn left onto D 105 to Fournols.

Fournols

This small summer resort boasts several fine old mansions and a priory.

▶ D 37 will lead to St-Germain-l'Herm.

St-Germain-l'Herm

Summer holiday resort offering a wide range of activities.

▶ Follow D 999 and turn right onto D 999A; drive through St-Bonnet-le-Chastel, and continue to Novacelles.

Novacelles

This small village is tucked away in a valley watered by the Dollore.

▶ Take D 105 to St-Sauveur-la-Sagne, then D 38 along the Dore gorges. Turn right onto D 907.

La Chaise-Dieu★★

See La CHAISE-DIEU.

▶ Drive N out of La Chaise-Dieu along D 906 then turn right onto D 202.

Dore-l'Église

The village, situated at the confluence of the Dore and Dorette, has a 12C church that underwent alterations in the 15C. To the left of the church is a Gallo-Roman memorial.

▶ Take D 906 N.

Arlanc

This small market town is hemmed in between Forez and the Livradois mountains. The **Musée de la Dentelle** (*☎04 73 95 00 03, open May–Jun, Sept weekends and holidays 2–6pm; Jul–Aug 10.30am–noon, 2–5pm; ∞€4*) is housed in the vaulted cellars of the town hall.

Jardin pour la Terre

Daily except Wed, May–Sept 2–6.30pm; ∞€6; Jul–Aug daily 2–8.30pm; ∞€6.50. ☎04 73 95 00 71. www.arlanc.com/Jardin.html.
This garden retraces the history of small trees and shrubberies from all five continents and their adjustment to European climatic conditions.

Marsac-en-Livradois

On the square to the south of the church stands the old White Penitents' Chapel, which houses a museum (open Jul–Aug) bursting with memorabilia relating to this brotherhood.

▶ Go back to Ambert on D 906.

ADDRESSES

🛏 STAY AND 🍴 EAT

Hôtel-Restaurant La Renaissance – *64 Route Nationale, 63220 Arlanc. 15km/9mi S of Ambert. ☎0473 72 96 10. 7 rooms.* A fine hotel-restaurant good location. Relaxing rooms, spacious and fully equipped.

Hôtel-Restaurant Les Copains – *42 bd Henri-IV. Closed Feb school holidays, Sun evening and Sat. ☎04 73 82 01 02. www.hotelrestaurantlescopains.com. 10 rooms.* . This restaurant is across from Ambert's unusual town hall. Run by the same family since 1935, the décor is no longer contemporary but the ambience is ever amiable. Ten comfortable rooms.

La Chaise-Dieu★★

Set amid lush green countryside with gently rolling hills, the vast buildings and ornate architectural style of the famous abbey of La Chaise-Dieu come as a magnificent surprise. The abbey derives its name from the Latin *Casa Dei*, meaning "the House of God".

A BIT OF HISTORY

Founding the abbey – In 1043 Robert de Turlande, a former canon from Brioude, withdrew with a few companions to this desolate plateau. He was soon joined by increasing numbers of followers and founded a monastery under the Benedictine Rule for which, in 1052, he obtained the Pope's protection. Its success continued to grow to the extent that, at Robert's death in 1067, the monastery had 300 monks and 49 priories. Increasing numbers of priories continued to be founded, and this made La Chaise-Dieu the third most important French monastic order in the mid-12C. The abbot was all-powerful. He was accountable to no-one but the Pope. In the 12C and 13C the abbots maintained the Order's independence and kept alive the spirit in which the abbey had been founded, thereby avoiding the excesses which weakened the great abbey at Cluny.

Papacy of Clement VI – The situation suddenly deteriorated in the early 14C, when the abbot's authority was undermined and several priories broke away from the mother-house. The election,

- **Population:** 652.
- **Michelin Map:** 331: E-2 40km/25mi NE of Le Puy-en-Velay.
- **Info:** Rue de la Gare, 43160 La Chaise-Dieu. ℘04 71 00 01 16. www.lepuyenvelay-tourisme.fr.
- **Location:** La Chaise-Dieu is all about its abbey, so the best way to orient yourself is to wander the maze of streets and see how it would have dominated the original community here.
- **Don't Miss:** The old houses in the narrow streets adjacent to the place de l'Église.
- **Timing:** Explore first, and then spend some time in the abbey, especially the cloisters; allow at least half a day.

Tapestries and the choir stalls in the chancel, Église Abbatiale St-Robert

however, in Avignon, of Pope Clement VI – one of the abbey's former novices and monks – brought a halt to this decline. The Pope had the church rebuilt as it is today between 1344 and 1352 to designs by an architect from Southern France named Hugues Morel. The Pope's nephew, Gregory XI, completed the building (last three bays in the nave and the abbey buildings).

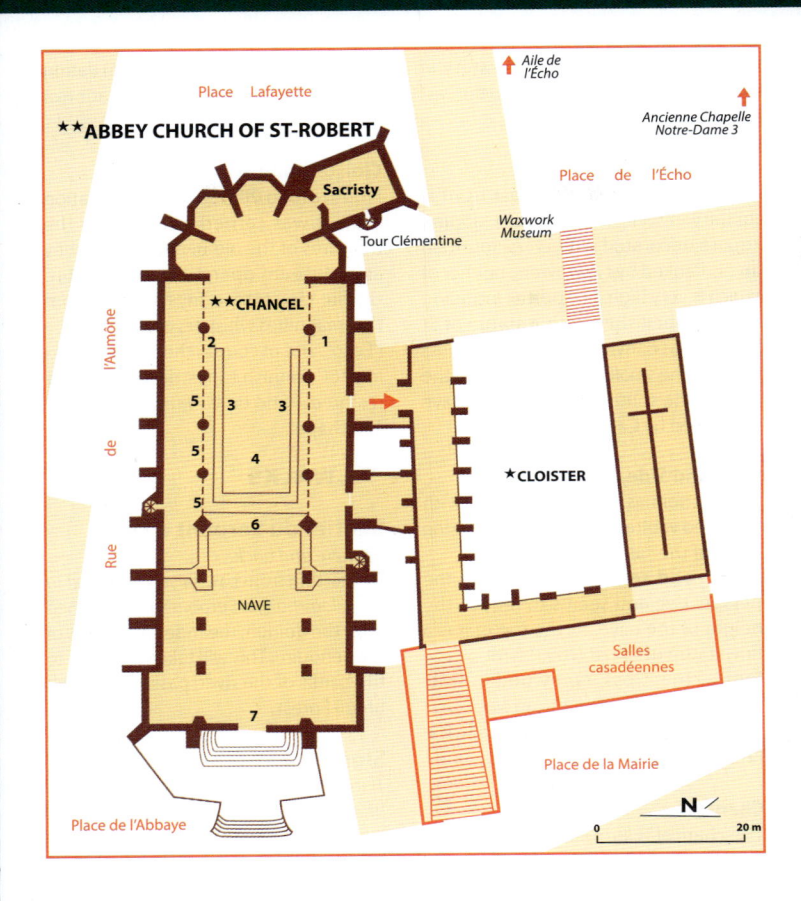

In the early years of the 16C, Jacques de St-Nectaire gave the abbey a dazzling set of tapestries.

Contemporary rebirth – After centuries of decline, the abbey finally attracted attention in the early years of the 20C. It was not completely restored, however, until after World War II.
In 1965 the pianist **Georges Cziffra** fell in love with the abbey and founded a festival of religious music in aid of the restoration project. The Festival de la Chaise-Dieu continues to make a name for itself as one of the main festivals of its kind in France.

ABBEY
Église Abbatiale St-Robert★★
Guided visits only: daily Jul–Aug at 11am, 2.30pm, 4pm, except during the festival in Aug. No charge; donations encouraged. €7 to visit tapestry room. ℘04 71 00 05 55. www.abbaye-chaise-dieu.com.

Solidly built of granite, the church gives an impression of grandeur and austerity which seems to reflect the personality of its founder, Clement VI. In 2019, after three years of restoration, the precious collection of 14 tapestries made between 1501 and 1518 was restored to the abbey. They depict the story of Christ, from the Annunciation to the Last Judgment.

West Front
The architecture of the west front is military in style. It overlooks a sloping square decorated with a 17C fountain and is flanked by two towers, neither of which is very high. The portal, including a pier embellished with a statue of St Robert, was damaged by the Huguenots in 1562. The small house concealing the base of the south tower is said to have been used by Cardinal de Rohan.

Nave and Side Aisles
The interior has a vast nave roofed with flattened vaulting and is flanked by side aisles of the same height.
A 15C **rood screen** (1) breaks up the perspective and seems to reduce the height of the nave. At the top of it is a fine statue of Christ (1603) with, at the foot of the Cross, two wooden statues representing the Virgin Mary and St John (15C). The superb **organ loft**★ (2) facing it dates from the 17C.

Chancel★★
The chancel is surrounded by 144 oak **choir stalls**★★ (3) dating from the 15C, decorated with particularly fine carvings depicting a wide range of subjects.
In the middle of the chancel is **Clement VI's tomb** (4). The Pope had it made during his own lifetime and carved by Pierre Roye, Jean David and Jean de Sanholis. The north aisle features the famous fresco of the **Dance of Death**★ (5) (2m high and 26m long): the three panels juxtapose the great and famous of this world and the dead; the dead are shown inviting the living to dance with them, a reminder of what lies before them.
The fresco depicts the powerful to the left, the wealthy in the middle and the craftsmen to the right. This theme was frequently depicted in the 15C, yet never before has it been treated with such realism and such a sense of movement. In the south aisle lies the mutilated **tomb** of Abbot Renaud de Montclar (6) dating from the 14C; it still has its decoration of carved cherubs.

Cloisters and Museum★★
From 2010 to 2022, a great restoration project was carried out, uniting the treasures of the old Benedictine abbey as a museum open to visits. The 14C Gothic cloisters, a mysterious room that magnifies whispers called "Salle de l'Echo", and of course, the 14 breathtaking 16C Flemish tapestries – now fully restored – and on view in the restored 17C chapel.

WALKS

Sentier du Serpent d'Or
2h there and back.
Starting from La Chaise-Dieu *(next to the village hall)*, is Serpent's Lane, named after the golden, meandering waters of the Sénouire. This will take you down to the banks of the river, passing through Breuil Forest.

Signal de St-Claude
1km/0.6mi E. Beyond the railway bridge, turn right onto the path that leads to the summit some 600m further on.
Fine view of Pierre sur Haute, the mountains in the Forez and Lyon areas, Mont Pilat, the Cévennes, the mountains of Cantal and the Dore mountain range.

ADDRESSES

STAY AND EAT

Chambre d'Hôte La Jacquerolle – *R. Marchédial. ℘04 43 07 60 54. www.lajacquerolle.com. 4 rooms.* Set in the lower part of the village, this handsome house built of local stone has a dining room furnished in period pieces.

Écho et Abbaye – *Pl. de l'Écho. ℘04 71 00 00 45. www.echo-et-abbaye.com. Closed mid-Nov–Mar and Wed except Jul–Aug. 10 rooms.* A tranquil inn behind the abbey with a creative restaurant.

VAL D'ALLIER AND ALAGNON

Allier is the most prosperous of all the departments in the Auvergne; it is also in parts the flattest. Small, vibrant market towns are nestled amid a countryside of meadows, forests, over 1 000 lakes (many with beaches and sporting activities) and rivers – not least of which are the eponymous Allier and the Alagnon. There are more than 500 châteaux in Allier, many open to the public. Not surprisingly, the economy tends to revolve around agriculture and tourism, with revenue from the latter increasing steadily each year.

Auvergne AOC
Perhaps not instantly thought of as a wine-producing region, the Auvergne nevertheless has its own AOC distinction, used by five distinct areas: Madargue, Châteaugay, Chanturgue, Corent and Boudes. The quality of the wine has improved greatly in recent years, thanks in no small part to the influx of natural winemakers within the region.

The Heady Scent of Garlic
Modern Billom plies a wide variety of economic activities, including sawmills, wood veneering, car body workshops and industrial ironware works. Cultivation of the regional speciality, garlic, is declining, but many companies continue to store and sort fresh garlic.

Highlights
1. The view from the top of the clock tower in **Issoire** (p248)
2. Passing a few quiet hours in the sleepy hillside village of **Mareugheol** (p251)
3. Remarkable stained-glass windows in the gothic **Sainte-Chapelle** in Vic-le-Comte (p252)
4. Exploring narrow streets in the medieval district of **Billom** (p254)
5. A long and leisurely drive through the **Alagnon Gorge** (p256)

Along the Alagnon
The Alagnon river, a tributary of the Allier, flows for 86km/53mi through the centre of France. It rises near the village of Laveissière, not far from the Plomb du Cantal. The river takes a generally northeasterly direction, passing through Cantal (Murat and Massiac), Haute-Loire (Lempdes-sur-Allagnon – note the double "ll" used in Haute-Loire) and the Puy-de-Dôme (Beaulieu). The river finally joins the Allier at Auzat-la-Combelle.

A Bird in the Hand
Embedded in the meanders of the Allier River, the Allier Nature Reserve is home to a great variety of birds, not least of which are the squacco heron, osprey, whiskered terns and small passerines en route to the Limagne during their annual migration.

Gorges de l'Alagnon near Léotoing

© Luc Olivier/Photononstop

VAL D'ALLIER AND ALAGNON

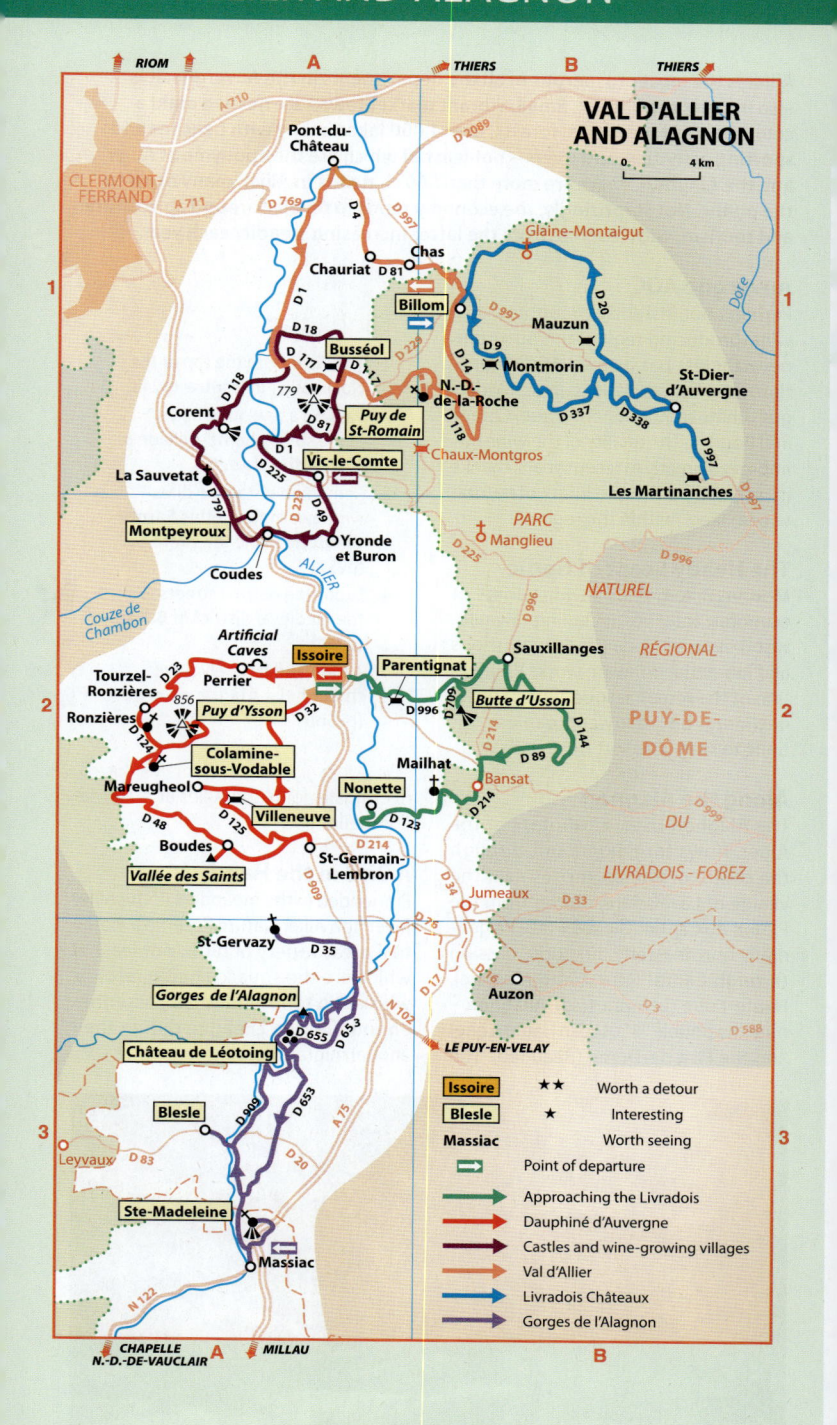

Issoire ★★

Issoire is located on the Couze river, near its junction with the Allier, on the fertile Limagne plain. The town is said to have been founded by the Arverni, a powerful Gallic tribe that inhabited the present-day region of Lyon and gave their name to this region – Auvergne. During the 17C religious wars of the Reformation, Issoire suffered greatly, and most of the old town was destroyed.

- **Population:** 14 662.
- **Michelin Map:** 326: G-9.
- **Info:** 9, place Saint Paul, 63500 Issoire. ℘04 73 89 15 90. www.issoire-tourisme.com.
- **Location:** Most shops, restaurants and bars cluster around the clock tower.
- **Parking:** Ample car parking in the centre of town.
- **Don't Miss:** The view from the top of the clock tower.

A BIT OF HISTORY

Reformed City – In 1540 a former Dominican monk arrived in Issoire from Germany and converted the Consuls to the Lutheran faith. He was burnt alive on the bailiff's orders, but his death led to numerous additional conversions. As a result, Issoire was washed in the blood of martyrs.

Architecturally, pride of place goes to the ornate 12C Abbatiale Saint-Austremoine, formerly the church of a Benedictine abbey, and one of the largest Romanesque churches in Auvergne. But there is an agreeable, provincial ambiance about the place that rewards even the shortest break. Today, surrounded by boulevards, the town is bright, refreshing, and a delight to explore, not least for its remarkable Renaissance **clock tower**, formerly the town belfry (see Tour de l'Horlage).

WALKING TOUR

The early-19C **granary** has been turned into an entertainment centre.
Follow rue Ponteil, which starts opposite and leads to the **Tour de l'Horloge** (clock tower see Sights).
On reaching place de la République (the former Grande Place), where a busy market takes place on Saturday mornings, note the 15C **Maison Charrier** with its Gothic doorway and the **fountain** adorning the centre of the square, designed in 1823 by the architect Ledru. Ahead and to the left is the **Maison aux Arcades**; turn left onto rue des Fours and admire the 15C–17C **Hôtel Bohier**, which houses a Renaissance staircase. Turn left at the end of the street to reach the **Centre Pomel** (see Sights). Opposite, on the corner of square Cassin, the Maison de la Bascule (weights and measures building) houses the **Musée de la Pierre Philosophale,** containing a collection of 1 000 minerals. Walk around the cathedral and back to place de la République. Turn right onto rue de la Berbizialie; on the corner, note the 15C **Maison du Chancelier Duprat** with its rectangular corbelled tower. Continue to place St-Avit; the 18C Maison Bartin on the left has fine wrought-iron balconies.

ABBATIALE ST-AUSTREMOINE★

St-Austremoine, once the church of a Benedictine abbey, was built in the 12C and dedicated to the first bishop of the Arverni people, martyred in the 3C. It is now the parish church, replacing the neighbouring Église St-Paul, destroyed shortly after the French Revolution.

Exterior

The **east end**★★ stands on a wide esplanade, a consummate example of Auvergnat Romanesque architecture. No other church boasts such harmonious proportions, such purity of line and such restraint in its decoration. Its powerful, well-balanced design consists of vari-

DISCOVERING VAL D'ALLIER AND ALAGNON

Exteiror decorations, Abbatiale St-Austremoine

ous different elements; note the mosaics and sculptures representing signs of the Zodiac.

Interior
The two-storey **nave** is striking for its magnificent proportions; the painted decoration was added in the mid-19C. At the southern entrance to the ambulatory is one of the finest and most complete views of the building. Walk around the chancel; it is particularly interesting for its superb narrative **capitals★**.

Crypt
This is one of the finest crypts in the Auvergne. The stocky columns supporting the vaulted roof give an impression of strength that is further emphasised by the total lack of decoration.

SIGHTS
Centre Pomel
This houses the **Centre d'Art Roman Georges-Duby** (&⊙Jul–Aug Tue–Sun 10am–12.30pm, 2–6pm; May–Jun and Sept–Oct Tue–Fri and Sun 2–6pm, Sat 10am–12.30pm, 2–6pm. ☏04 73 89 56 04. http://centre-artroman.issoire.fr), which displays the vestiges of the Monastère St-Austremoine.

Tour de l'Horloge
⊙Mar–Jun and Sep–Nov Tue–Sun 2–6pm (Sat 10am–12.30pm, 2–6pm); Jul–Aug Tue–Sun 10am–12.30pm, 2–6pm. ⊙Dec–Feb, 1 May. ∞€2. ☏04 73 89 07 70. tour-horloge.issoire.fr.
The chimes of the Renaissance belfry (15C) can still be heard throughout town. Temporary exhibitions are also organised. From the top of the tower, there is a fine view over the town, the Limagne landscape, the Monts-Dore and Livradois mountains.

EXCURSION
Auzon★
28km/17mi SE of Issoire.
Auzon's dramatic **setting★** on a sheer-sided rock spur is best appreciated when seen from D 5 coming from the Allier valley. This old fortified town still has many traces of its ramparts and castle and boasts a fine collegiate church.

🚗 DRIVING TOUR

APPROACHING THE LIVRADOIS
45km/28mi round trip. Allow 2h. (⬥see region map).

▶ Leave Issoire on D 996 to the SE.

ISSOIRE

Château de Parentignat★
Guided visits. Jun and Sept Sat–Sun 2–6pm; Jul–Aug daily 10.30am–12.30pm, 2–6pm. €10. ℘04 73 89 51 10. www.parentignat.com.

The château was built towards the end of Louis XIV's reign (early 18C) and has remained in the same family since. The main courtyard has formal grass parterres, contrasting with the English-style landscape gardens bordered by orange trees and roses. The ancestral treasures include furniture as well as paintings by Nicolas de Largillière, Mme Vigée-Lebrun, Rigaud and Van Loo. Regular guided visits (45 minutes) are offered with more or less regularity depending on the season.

▶ Continue along D 996 towards Sauxillanges. After 6km/3.7mi, take D 709 on the right.

Butte d'Usson
The basaltic rock of Usson was once the site of a formidable castle, of which nothing remains but the memory of Marguerite de Valois. "Usson is a town situated on a plain where there is a rock, and three towns one on top of the other in the shape of a Pope's mitre", says an ancient text. The castle was built by the Duc de Berry and was believed to be impregnable. On the door was written "Mind the traitor and the tooth!" meaning that only treason or famine could get the better of it.

View
From a viewing table off D 709 to the north of the town there is a beautiful view of the Limagne d'Issoire in the foreground and the Puys chain in the background.

Puy d'Usson
A gentle path leads to the summit on which a chapel has been built; it provides a good **panorama**★ of the region. During the climb, a beautiful set of basalt columns can be seen in an old quarry.

▶ Return to D 996.

Sauxillanges
The 11C church with 15C alterations contains a mural depicting the Deposition and a 15C statue of Our Lady of the Woods. The Prior's Chapel, now a heritage centre, **Maison du Patrimoine** (Jul–Sept 2.30–6.30pm; Tues 10–noon; off-season by appointment. ℘04 73 96 85 10. www.musee-sauxillanges.com), is part of the remains of a priory founded in 927 and attached to the Cluniac Order. The Gothic vaulting is decorated with interesting hanging keystones bearing the coats of arms of the various priors. Take the direct route (D 214) or go the long way to St-Étienne-d'Usson on D 144 towards Sarpoil.

▶ In Bansat, turn right onto D 24, then turn left in St-Martin-des-Plains, heading for Mailhat.

Église de Mailhat
The small Romanesque church has a square belfry with double openings and a five-sided apse.

▶ D 123 leads to Orsonnette, then to Nonette.

Nonette★
The village is built on a promontory overlooking the Allier. The half-Romanesque, half-Gothic **church**, once part of a priory, has a carved Romanesque doorway and, inside, a superb late-14C bust of Christ (north chapel). The ruins of the 14C **castle** *(45min on foot there and back via a steep path)* stand on a height offering a splendid **panorama**★.

DAUPHINÉ D'AUVERGNE★
60km/37mi. Allow half a day.

At the end of the 12C, the region of rugged countryside scored by Couzes flowing between hilly outcrops and basalt plateaux to the southwest of Issoire between the Cézallier and the Allier valleys formed the Dauphiné d'Auvergne. The lords of this royal fief set up glit-

DISCOVERING VAL D'ALLIER AND ALAGNON

tering courts in Champeix, Vodable and Mercœur successively.

▶ Leave Issoire to the W on D 996, towards Champeix.

Perrier
Overlooking the village of Perrier is a plateau bristling with bizarre rocks, evidence of violent eruptions thousands of years ago in the Dore mountain region. These unleashed gigantic flows of mud mixed with boulders, or **lahars**.

Artificial Caves
1h walk there and back. From the church in Perrier, take the footpath to the caves ("Chemin des Grottes").
These caves were hollowed out of the volcanic rock and used as troglodytic dwellings.

▶ From the caves, follow the route indicated as "vue panoramique".

From the plateau there is a remarkable **view**★ of the surrounding rocks, the feudal keep, the village and the Couze de Pavin.

▶ On leaving Perrier, take D 26 left (2km/1.2mi), then left onto D 23.

Tourzel-Ronzières
Small wine-growers' houses in this village bear witness to a viticultural past, specifically during the 18C and 19C, when Tourzel's main source of income was wine. One of these lava-walled houses is home to a small **museum** devoted to the pork butcher's trade.

▶ Follow D 23 for another 1km/0.6mi, then turn left onto D 124.

Ronzières
At the entrance to the village, a narrow track (*closed to traffic*) climbs up to a basalt plateau on which stands a pre-Romanesque church. In the graveyard, on the edge of the plateau, two viewing tables give information on the view of the surrounding countryside, which stretches over the Puy d'Ysson, the Couze de Pavin, the Perrier plateau and the Lembron plain.
Examples of the volcanic features so characteristic of the Dauphiné d'Auvergne region are easy to pick out.

▶ Take D 124 as far as Vodable and turn left onto D 32 to Solignat.

Puy d'Ysson★
This cone was formed by the chimney of a volcano; the plug of lava was laid bare by erosion.
From the summit, there is a **panorama** of the Dore mountain range, the extinct volcanoes of the Comté region, the Limagne around Issoire, the Livradois mountains and the Cézallier.

▶ Drive back down to Solignat and take D 32 back to Vodable.

Église de Colamine-sous-Vodable
The church stands surrounded by its graveyard, on the side of a combe. It boasts a Romanesque chancel and a group of wooden statues.

▶ Rejoin D 32 and travel for 4km/3mi towards Dauzat-sur-Vodable, then turn left onto D 48.

Boudes
Neatly sheltered by a range of hills to the north and by the Avoiron peak, this village boasts good soil, and local vines thus produce fine quality wine, including a particularly well-regarded white. The layout of the vineyards, on a single slope with good sun exposure, alongside the brightly coloured houses, form a striking sight. Note the fine dovecots.

▶ Leave Boudes to the S, crossing the Couzilloux, and take the track to the right running along the side of the graveyard.

Vallée des Saints★
2h walk return.
A waymarked path enables visitors to explore this area and admire its giant red and ochre pyramids. Their outland-

ISSOIRE

ish silhouettes have earned the valley its name.

▶ Return to Boudes and turn right at the church to rejoin D 48.

St-Germain- Lembron
This small, once-fortified village in the midst of an agricultural region still boasts some 18C houses with double-gabled roofs.

▶ Take D 48 towards Boudes once again, then turn off to the right after 1km/0.6mi onto D 125.

The road climbs towards Chalus, with beautiful views of the volcanic necks and tables rising above the Limagne.

Villeneuve
Narrow streets lined with old houses and wash-houses surround a 15C church.

Château de Villeneuve-Lembron★
Guided visits. Jan–mid-May and mid-Sept–Dec daily except Mon 10am–12.30pm, 2–5.30pm; mid-May–mid-Sept daily 10am–12.30pm, 2–6.30pm. 1 Jan, 1 May, 1 and 11 Nov, 25 Dec. €6. ℘04 73 96 41 64. www.chateau-villeneuve-lembron.fr.
This seigneurial castle was built for the Aureille family, one of whose members was the diplomat Rigault, who served under Louis XI, Charles VIII, Louis XII and François I and fought alongside Charles VIII in the Italian campaigns.

▶ Follow D 125; left onto D 720.

Mareugheol
Mareugheol is a typical example of a fortified village, built during the Middle Ages to protect the inhabitants from the marauding bands of robbers that plagued the region. Old stone houses stand along narrow streets within a rectangular fortified wall of which only a few stretches and a stump of corner tower remain.

▶ Take the D 719, then turn right onto the D 32, back towards Issoire.

ADDRESSES

STAY
Château de Grange Fort – *63500 Les Pradeaux. 7km/4.2mi SE of Issoire, take A 75, exit 13, dir. Parentignat and D 34, rte d'Auzat-sur-Allier. ℘04 73 71 02 43. www.lagrangefort.com. 3 rooms.* A 17C château with superb crenellated towers set in the bosom of a park surrounded by mountains. The rooms may feature a canopy bed, a sculpted door, a parquet floor or original mouldings. A campsite with chalets is also on-site.

EAT
Le Boudes La Vigne – *63340 Boudes. 15km/9mi S of Issoire via D 909 and D 48. ℘04 73 96 55 66. http://leboudeslavigne.franceserv.com.* Set in the heart of a quaint wine-making village, this hotel-restaurant, part of which is in the cellar, takes full advantage of local ingredients.

La Bergerie de Sarpoil – *63490 St-Jean en Val. 10km/6mi E of Issoire via D 999. ℘04 73 71 02 54. http://labergeriedesarpoil.com. Sun–Mon lunch; Thur–Sat dinner.* A coaching inn and sheepfold in the olden days, this restaurant, featuring old stone walls in the dining room boasts a high-class contemporary menu.

Origines – Le Broc – *r. du Clos de la Chaux 63500 Le Broc – Issoire. 5.4km/3.3mi S of Issoire via D 716. ℘04 73 71 71 71. http://restaurant-origines.fr. Wed–Sun; Wed–Sat dinner.*

This beautifully located restaurant perched above the Auvergne serves an audacious menu blending authenticity and modernity.

Table d'Arthur – *35 r. Saint-Antoine, 63500 Issoire. ℘04 73 54 95 06. http://tabledarthur.com. Tues–Sat lunch and dinner (Sun lunch).* Refined, delicate cuisine with fresh, local products. Reservations recommended.

DISCOVERING VAL D'ALLIER AND ALAGNON

Vic-le-Comte★

With its white stone houses and orchre-coloured roofs, Vic-le-Comte has a real southern feel to it. The region's sun-drenched valleys bear witness to its past: a series of volcanoes form a transitiion between the plain and the Livradois mountains. More than 50 peaks, once coovered in grapevines, are now shrouded in woodlands. Today, Vic-le-Comte boasts lovely timber-framed houses dating to the Middle Ages and 19C winemakers' homes. It is also home to a paper mill owned by the Bank of France, which makes the watermarked paper used for bank notes printed in Chamalières.

- **Population:** 5 037.
- **Michelin Map:** 326: G-9 – 16km/10mi N of Issoire.
- **Info:** Sauteyras, 63970 Lac d'Aydat 04 73 79 37 69. tourism.mondarverne.com.
- **Location:** Vic-le-Comte is 25km/15.5mi from Clermont Ferrand, and 16km/10mi from Issoire, via the A 75 autoroute.
- **Parking:** There are a number of car parks both in the centre and just outside.
- **Don't Miss:** The fortified village of La Sauvetat.
- **Timing:** Allow half a day for a leisurely walking tour.

WALKING TOUR

Le Trampoline
Pl. de l'Olme. 06 75 49 43 99. www.letrampoline.com.
This contemporary art centre hosts a great variety of temporary exhibits from artists both local and far-flung.

Sainte-Chapelle★
A beautiful Gothic building heralding the Renaissance. The richly coloured **stained-glass windows**★ depict scenes from the Old and New Testaments. The very fine stone **altarpiece**★ (1520) is the work of Florentine artists.

Old Houses
Rue Porte-Robin has several buildings with 15C and 16C façades. The old town gate, **Porte Robin**, is all that remains of the fortified curtain wall.
Continue straight ahead towards rue du Palais, at the entrance to which are two corbelled houses.

▶ Take the covered passage on the right, rue des Farges, then rue de Coulogne beyond; turn back.

DRIVING TOUR

CASTLES AND WINE-GROWING VILLAGES
45km/28mi. Allow half a day.

▶ Drive S out of town along D 49. In Yronde, take D 136.

Yronde
This is where Le Bouchet abbey once stood. Note the lovely small church.

Buron
The road runs round the village, overlooked by the ruins of a castle.

▶ Cross the River Allier; take D 229 left.

Coudes
This ancient village at the confluence of the Allier and Couze de Chambon once thrived on a major river traffic in wine.

▶ Continue along D 229, across the A 75 motorway, then turn right on D 797.

Montpeyroux

Montpeyroux★

This fortified hillside village overlooks the Allier to the east. A medieval gateway gives access to narrow twisting lanes leading to the three-storey 13C **keep**. Most of the old houses in the village have been restored and their cellars are a reminder of the wine-growing past of the village, which now welcomes a colony of artists and craftsmen.

▶ Continue along D 797. In Authezat, turn left on D 96.

La Sauvetat

This once-fortified village surrounded by fertile plains has retained a 13C keep. Its name is a reference to its past as a home to warrior-monks known as the Hospitaliers. The village has also retained the magnificent Porte Saint-Jean, a square tower, and a chapel that is hope to a gilded copper Vierge en Majesté.

Guided tours of the village are organized once a week in Jul–Aug.

▶ Leave La Sauvetat NE along D 630, cross the A 75 and rejoin D 96.

Corent

This village overlooking the River Allier clings to the north-eastern slopes of the Puy de Corent; it is known for its high-quality wine, one of the five vintages making up the Côtes d'Auvergne *appellation*. On the plateau, an **archaeological site** reveals one of three Arvenii oppida south of the basin of Clermont.

▶ Follow the D 118 to cross the River Allier. Turn left to join the D 1.

The road follows the east bank of the river, jotted with wine-growing villages such as Mirefleurs, La Roche-Noire and St-Georges-sur-Allier.

▶ On leaving St-Georges-sur-Allier, turn right on D 759.

Château de Busséol★

Guided visits. mid-Jun–mid-Sept daily 10am–noon, 2.30–6pm; mid-Sept– mid-Nov and Apr–mid Jun Sat–Sun and public holidays 2.30-6pm. €9.
04 73 69 00 84.
The main façade collapsed in 1963 but has since been rebuilt with Romanesque-style windows.

▶ Leave Busséol S and follow D 4 then continue on D 229. In Benaud hamlet, turn right on D 116 then take D 81. Park at Saint-Maurice.

Puy Saint-Romain

90min on foot there and back.
The setting of the puy is striking; the summit, an ancient place of worship, offers a **panormama**★ encompassing the *Comté Puys*, the Forez mountains, the Livradois mountains, the Dore and Dôme mountain ranges, Clermont-Ferrand and the Limagne.

▶ Go to Longues on D 758 and D 1, then follow the D 225 back to Vic-le-Comte.

Billom★

Billom is situated on the Limagne plain at the foot of the Livradois mountains. It flourished in the Middle Ages and had a university before Clermont-Ferrand. This university, transformed in the 16C, became the first Jesuit college and was well known in the Auvergne.

A BIT OF HISTORY

During the Reign of Terror, in the wake of the French Revolution, Couthon, a member of the Convention, issued a famous edict ordering the demolition of all belfries in the province on the basis that they were "contrary to equality"; this was how the church of St-Cerneuf lost its elegant little tower.

WALKING TOUR

MEDIEVAL DISTRICT

From the *Hôtel de Ville* follow quai de la Terraille to place du Creux-du-Marché, surrounded by old houses. Cross Pont du Marché-aux-Grains: three troughs and gutters hewn out of Volvic stone are visible on the parapet on the right – they were used to measure grain.

> **Population:** 4 882.
> **Michelin Map:** 326: H-8.
> **Info:** 13 r. Carnot, 63160 Billom. ℘04 73 68 39 85. www.billom.com.
> **Location:** Billom lies 27km/17mi SE of Clermont-Ferrand.
> **Parking:** Parking is limited in the centre of town.
> **Don't Miss:** A walk around the Medieval district.
> **Timing:** 2–3hrs would suffice, but stay for lunch.

Walking up rue de l'Étézon, note the 16C belfry on the right and the 16C Maison du Bailli at the top of the street.

▶ Turn left, and walk past the former trade tribunal to place des Écoles.

Maison du Chapitre

This 15C mansion, known as the chapterhouse, was part of the medieval university and was used as a prison during the Revolution.

Fontaine du Cibony, Place de la Halle, Billom

© Christian Guy/imageBROKER/age fotostock

BILLOM

Porte de l'Évêché
This gateway into the medieval town marked the first line of fortifications.

Église St-Cerneuf★
This Gothic church was erected over an old Romanesque church, of which a **crypt**★ remains.

▶ Turn right on leaving the church, and turn left onto rue Pertuybout.

Maison de l'Échevin
The entrance to this 16C alderman's house features an attractive staircase tower and a well with a wheel.

Rue des Boucheries
This narrow street paved with pointed stones is flanked by medieval houses, including the Maison du Doyen, which has a beautiful basket-handle arch over its window and a Renaissance staircase. The 15C Maison du Boucher has stone walls on one side, half-timbered walls on the other and two overhanging upper floors.

🚗 DRIVING TOURS

VAL D'ALLIER
50km/31mi. Allow 3h.

▶ Leave Billom along D 997 for Pont-du-Château and turn left onto D 81.

Chas
This old fortified village has kept its gateway and turret as well as its Romanesque church, fronted by a Renaissance porch and a pretty fountain.

Chauriat
Located north of the Comté, this small wine-growing village stands out thanks to its two churches. The deconsecrated Église Ste-Marie was built in Merovingian times. The Église St-Julien is characteristic of the Auvergnat Romanesque style.

▶ Drive to Pont-du-Château along D 4.

Pont-du-Château
This strategically important town was long fortified: it was the location of the only bridge spanning the Allier between Moulins and Brioude. During the 19C, Pont-du-Château boasted a busy port; this history is recalled in the **Musée Pierre-Mondanel** *(Jul–Aug 10am–noon, 2.15–6pm (closed Mon); rest of the year by appointment. ☎04 73 83 73 98)*, housed in the kitchens of an old château.

▶ Leave Pont-du-Château to the S and take D 1 heading towards Vic-le-Comte.

The road meanders along the banks of the River Allier, offering pretty views of the mountain ranges.

▶ Turn left onto D 117, which crosses Mirefleurs. Follow a steep slope towards the road to Busséol.

Château de Busséol
See VIC-LE-COMTE.

▶ Continue along D 117, then D 301 towards St-Julien-de-Coppel.

Drive up through Notre-Dame-des-Roches, a small chapel perched on a rock, for a view of Billom country.

▶ Continue on D 118 to see the ruins of Coppel Tower; just before La Beauté, turn left. D 14 will take you back to Billom through the lush Angaud valley.

LIVRADOIS CHÂTEAUX
45km/28mi. Allow 3h.

This route provides lovely views of the first Livradois summits and gives access to the main strongholds in the Pays de St-Dier.

Château de Montmorin
Jul–Aug, daily, 2–6pm. ≤€6. ☎04 73 68 30 94.

This former citadel used to consist of a keep flanked by round towers; it now lies

DISCOVERING VAL D'ALLIER AND ALAGNON

largely in ruins. Rooms in the main building have been turned into a museum.

▶ Take D 337, then D 338 towards St-Dier-d'Auvergne.

St-Dier-d'Auvergne
The 12C church here was fortified in the 15C; it has a buttressed west front with arcading.

▶ Drive 5km/3mi to the S on D 997.

Les Martinanches
Nestling at the bottom of a valley is a **castle** (*guided visits afternoons only mid-Jul–Aug, closed Sat. €6. ☎04 73 70 81 98; www.chateau-des-martinanches.com*), built originally in the 11C but altered in the 15C and the 19C. Inside there are beamed ceilings, fine porcelain and earthenware, and period furniture. The château also offers **8 hotel rooms**.

Château de Mauzun
The mighty fortress (*guided visits 3pm, 4.30pm, 6pm. May–mid-Jul and Sep Sun, mid-Jul–Aug daily except Mon. €7. ☎06 70 10 22 20. www.chateaude-mauzin.fr*) standing on a spur of basalt rock, once the property of the bishops of Clermont-Ferrand, offers a fine view of the Limagne plain. Although still in ruins, the castle retains its two defensive walls and 20 towers.

▶ Take D 20 to Neuville, then D 152 and D 229 back to Billom.

Massiac

The rocky headlands of St-Victor and St-Madeleine frame this ancient village, situated at the confluence of three rivers: the Alagnon, the Alagnonnette and the Arcueil.

SIGHTS
Église Saint-André
This church is notable for its 17C painting by Guy François, *L'Adoration des Bergers*.

Musée Municipal Élise-Rieuf
Jul–Aug daily except Mon 2.30–6.30pm; May–Jun and Sept Sun and public holidays 2.30–6pm. ☎04 71 23 01 17. www.musee-elise-rieuf.org.
This museum displays portraits of people from the Auvergne and China, Provençal and Scandinavian landscapes and Italian towns painted by Élise Rieuf, a native of Massiac (1897–1990).

- **Population:** 1 875.
- **Michelin Map:** 331 H-3
- **Info:** pl. de la Gare, 15500 Massiac. ☎04 71 23 07 76. www.pays-saint-flour.fr.
- **Location:** 28km/17.3mi N of St-Flour on E 11.
- **Timing:** There is a traditional weekly market (Tue am) and two annual fairs (Jun and Oct).

🚗 DRIVING TOUR

GORGES DE L'ALAGNON
70km/43.5mi round tour. Allow half a day.

The road alongside the lower reaches of the River Alagnon between Le Babory-de-Blesle and Lempdes-sur-Allagnon offers a most appealing drive.

MASSIAC

▶ Drive N out of Massiac towards Clermont-Ferrand; at the roundabout, take the small road that skirts the motorway slip road then passes under the motorway.

Site de la Chapelle Ste-Madeleine★

This small 11C chapel stands on top of a spur of basalt rock, at the south-eastern extremity of the Chalet plateau.
On the opposite bank of the river, another spur of basalt rock (735m), the Plateau de St-Victor, once occupied by prehistoric Man, later served as a lookout to keep watch over the Alagnon valley and the river crossing.

▶ Return to the roundabout and follow D 909 N. In Le Babory, turn left onto D 8 which crosses the Alagnon.

Blesle★

This ancient village on the west bank of the Voireuze was founded around a Benedictine abbey. **Église St-Pierre**★ (11C–12C) has some interesting furniture and statues in the treasury.
Other monuments of note include a great square **keep**, a 14C **bell-tower**, all that remains of the church of St-Martin (destroyed in the Revolution), 15C and 16C houses, and the turret and doorway (17C) of the old hospice.
Do not fail to visit the **Musée de la Coiffe** (May–Jun, Sept 3–6pm; Jul–Aug 10am–noon; 3–6pm. €4. 04 71 76 27 08), set up in a former 16C hospital and presenting over 400 typical headdresses from the Auvergne and Velay areas.

▶ Return to the right bank of the Alagnon by taking D 8 in the opposite direction and turn left onto D 909.

Further north, the ruins of Léotoing Castle can be seen on high ground to the right (see below). The valley becomes narrower and wilder.

▶ In Lempdes head N on D 909, in the direction of St-Germain-Lembron. After 3km/2mi take D 35 on the left, then D 141 on the right.

St-Gervazy

The **castle** was once a ruin but has been restored since the town acquired it in 2002. It is home to several medieval rooms, exhibition rooms featuring paintings and photographs, and a **Toy Horse Museum** (Jun–Sep Sat–Sun 3–6pm; Jul–Aug Wed, Sat, Sun 3–6pm. €3. 04-73-96-43-72.) The Romanesque **church** houses a replica of the 12C Virgin Enthroned.

▶ Return to Lempdes; follow D 653 S over a distance of 4km/2.5mi then turn right onto D 655.

Léotoing★

The chapel located at the entrance to the village houses a model of the site and several panels providing information on local history, architecture and traditions. The fine view encompasses the Alagnon gorge, the Cézallier, the Brioude plain, the Livradois, the Plateau de la Chaise-Dieu and the Monts du Velay.

Castle

The tour of the ruins is undertaken at the visitor's own risk; it is not advisable for children or anyone suffering from vertigo; good walking shoes are recommended.
Substantial remains of this 14C fortress overlooking the River Alagnon are still visible. To reach them, walk through the fortified gate. The Romanesque **church** contains traces of a fresco depicting the Deposition and carved capitals.

▶ At the foot of the hill, take D 909 on the left. On leaving Lanau, turn left onto D 19 which later meets up with D 653. Return to Massiac via Grenier-Montgon.

LIMAGNE PAYS DES COMBRAILLES, GORGES DE LA SIOULE

This largely low-lying area is pierced north to south by the spectacular gorges of the Sioule, a river that rises in the foothills of the Monts du Sancy, ultimately joining the Allier near St Pourçain sur Sioule. The Combrailles form a mosaic of tiny villages, châteaux, mills, churches and chapels around which a vast area of open space proves ideal for walking, mountain biking and horse riding. Elsewhere, an abundance of museums allow you to discover different aspects of life and culture in this beautiful region, not least its remarkable geology, history and prehistory.

Highlights

1 A day or so exploring the elegant town of **Riom** (p260)
2 Strolling the footpath around the green waters of **Lake Tazenat** (p264)
3 Taking a trip to the spa town of **Châtel-Guyon** (p266)
4 Relaxing in charming **Aigueperse** (p267)
5 The **Gorges de la Sioule** are unmissable, and a canoe trip is a special way to explore (p269)

The Limagnes

The Limagnes are low-lying, fertile, plains drained by the Dore and the Allier. Almost entirely arable, and the plains boast rich, nearly black soil: perfect for producing tobacco, wheat, vegetable and seed crops, and fruit.

To the east, the Varennes is a hilly area of marshes, woodland, cropland and lush pastures, where alluvium has been washed down from the mountains of the Forez.

Ancient Combraille

The origins of the ancient lordship of Combraille date from Celtic times, with the local Gallic tribe, the Cambovices. The original region was divided into three departments in 1790: Allier, Creuse and Puy-de-Dôme.

A Castle Out of its Time

The 1789 French Revolution is often painted as the end of the French monarchy, but this wasn't quite the case. While Louis XVI and Marie-Antoinette lost their heads and the first French Republic was founded, the royal family would continue to have profound influence in France through the middle of the 19C. In 1830, Louis-Philippe, Duke of Chartres, was placed on the throne; the château of Randan, which he had acquired with his sister in 1821, therefore became a royal estate – the very last to ever be built in France.

Limagne plain

© Christian Guy/hemis.fr

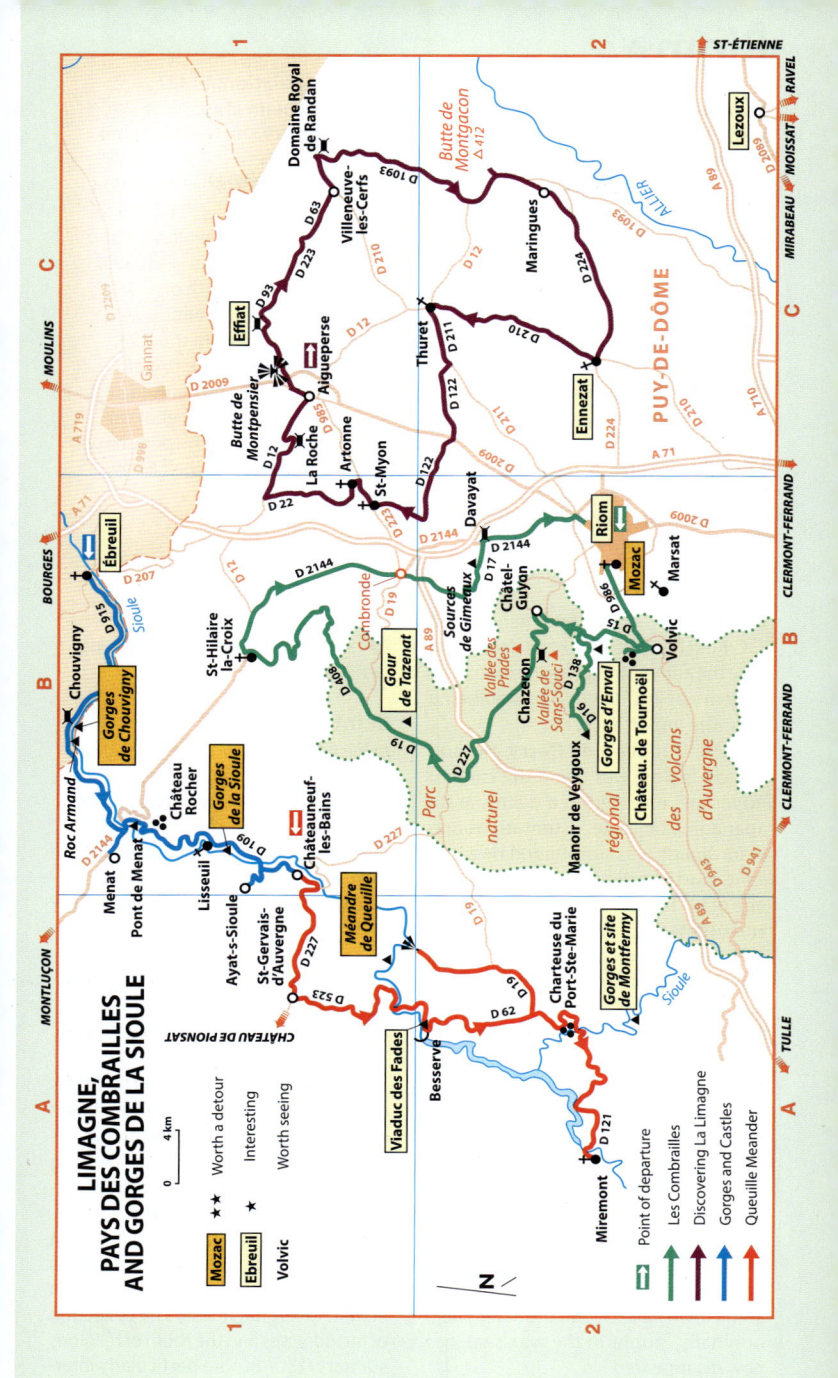

LIMAGNE, PAYS DES COMBRAILLES AND GORGES DE LA SIOULE

Riom★

The old town of Riom perched on a small hill on the western edge of the Limagne region still reflects the splendour of bygone days, with the ring of boulevards laid out on its now demolished walls. It is a city of considerable elegance, preserving a noble integrity thanks to its former position as the capital of the province of Auvergne. But it is also a festive, modern city, skilfully blending music, heritage, gastronomy and *savoir-faire*. A lively summer of events ends with a popular jazz festival. The city also boasts no fewer than 16 classified historical monuments, earning it the appellation *Ville d'Art et d'Histoire*.

- **Population:** 19 487.
- **Michelin Map:** 326: F-7 – 15km/9.5mi N of Clermont-Ferrand.
- **Info:** 27 Pl de la Fédération, 63204 Riom. ✆04 73 38 59 45. www.terravolcana.com.
- **Location:** Riom is situated 15km/9mi north of Clermont-Ferrand, accessible from the A 71.
- **Parking:** The centre of Riom is pedestrianised, but there are a number of car parks around the periphery.
- **Timing:** Allow half a day.

A BIT OF HISTORY

Capital city – At the beginning of the 13C, King Philippe Auguste's decision to base the administration of the monarchy in Riom was instrumental in establishing its future importance.

In 1360, Duc **Jean de Berry**, the son of Jean le Bon, was given the Land of Auvergne, elevated to a duchy, as an apanage. The Duke, ostentatious and extravagant, was surrounded by a brilliant court of artists. He chose Riom as one of his favourite places of residence and ordered extensive work to be carried out on the old castle, which he had converted by the architect Gui de Dammartin.

After the Duke's death, Riom and the Duchy of Auvergne passed to the Bourbon family. The town remained very much attached to the king and reputed for its wealth; indeed, when Joan of Arc needed powder and arrows for the siege of La Charité-sur-Loire, she appealed to the people of Riom. They pledged 60 gold écus but were slow to send them; in 1430, the townspeople received a letter of reminder which rhas been preserved at the town hall, though the Saint's hair, originally caught in the wax seal, has now disappeared.

WALKING TOUR

Start from place des Martyrs-de-la-Résistance.

Sainte-Chapelle★

In the Palais de Justice. Jul–Aug Wed–Fri 10am–noon, 3–5pm; Jun and Sept Wed–Fri 3.30–5pm; Tues 4.30 pm year-round. €1. ✆04 73 38 59 45.

The chapel (14C), all that remains of the Duke of Berry's castle, has some remarkable late-15C **stained-glass windows★** in the chancel.

Musée Régional d'Auvergne★

Mid-May–mid-Nov 2–5.30pm (Jul–Aug 2.30–6pm). 14 Jul, 1 and 11 Nov. ✆04 73 38 17 31.

This Regional Museum of Arts, Crafts and Traditions, laid out on three floors of a former 19C private mansion, houses a remarkable collection of farming implements, rural and craft tools, furniture, games, domestic items and costumes. Don't miss the reconstruction of a typical Auvergne home, which was disassembled and reassembled from an actual Auvergnat house. The collection of headdresses and the room of religious statuary (13C-18C) are particularly interesting.

RIOM

WHERE TO STAY
Château de Bourassol............ ❶
Maison de la Treille
 (Chambre d'hôte La)............ ❷
Pacifique (Hôtel Le)............... ❸

WHERE TO EAT
Flamboyant (Le)..................... ❶

Cour de l'hôtel
 Guymoneau..........................B
Hôtel Arnoux
 de Maison-Rouge................R
Hôtel de ville..........................H
Maison des Consuls................K
Tour de l'Horloge...................G

▶ Walk along rue de l'Hôtel-de-Ville.

Musée Mandet★

⊙ Tue–Sun: Sept–Jun 10am–noon, 2–5.30pm; Jul–Aug 10am–noon, 2.30–6pm. ⊙ 1 Jan, Easter Sun, 1 May, 14 Jul, 15 Aug, 1 and 11 Nov, 25 Dec. ∞€3, no charge on Wed, or for under 18. ℘ 04 73 38 18 53.

This museum is arranged into two private mansions: one, Hôtel Dufraisse (built 1740), houses the painting collections as well as a department dedicated to design and contemporary decorative arts from the 1950s to today. The other, Hôtel Desaix, houses the Richard Bequest.

On the first floor, rooms decorated with delicate woodwork present a series of paintings from the 17C Flemish and Dutch Schools and the 17C and 18C French Schools. The second floor is given over to 19C painting, particularly the works of Alphonse Cornet, an artist from Riom.

Hôtel de Ville

∞ Tours of the courtyard. ⊙ Mon–Fri 8am–5.30pm. ⊙ 1 Jan, 25 Dec. ℘ 04 73 33 79 00.

An enamelled stone plaque in the vestibule reproduces a letter from Joan of Arc to the people of Riom. The lovely 16C **courtyard**★ is enclosed by two buildings decorated with vaulted arcades; note the basket-handled arches and a staircase turret with a carved door. Beneath the arcades stand two bronze sculptures by Rodin, including *Gallia Victrix* (modelled on Camille Claudel) and a marble sculpture by Rivoire (the Kiss of Glory).

Maison des Consuls★

Fine 16C residence. The ground floor of the Consuls' House has five archways. The first-floor windows support an elegant frieze crowned by two busts of women and two busts of Roman emperors. The wooden house opposite dates from the 15C.

Carrefour des Taules★

Near this crossroads, which forms the intersection of the main streets of old Riom, stand some of the town's most interesting old houses. There are façades with carved windows at the corner of rue de l'Hôtel-de-Ville and rue de l'Horloge.

Rue de l'Horloge

The street is lined with old mansions boasting remarkable courtyards *(see below)* and beautiful windows such as those of no. 4 and above all no. 12. The town's belfry, with its gilt clock face, stands at the beginning of the street.

261

Tour de l'Horloge★
Tues–Sun 10am–noon; 2–5pm.
1 Jan, 1 Nov, 11 Nov, 25 Dec. €1 (free Wed). 04 73 38 99 94.
www.ville-riom.fr.
Surmounted by a 17C dome, this octagonal Renaissance tower rests on a square medieval base. It houses an exhibition retracing the history of the town.

Hôtel Arnoux-de-Maison-Rouge
7 rue de l'Horloge.
The corridor, lit with oval windows, leads to a delightful early-17C courtyard.

Cour de l'Hôtel Guymoneau★
12 rue de l'Horloge.
16C door. Go through the corridor into the attractive courtyard. The staircase is decorated with delicate carvings including an Annunciation. On the left, the gallery incorporates four statuettes representing, from left to right, Fortitude, Justice, Prudence and Temperance.

▶ Return to carrefour des Taules and turn right onto rue St-Amable.

Basilique St-Amable
Only the nave and part of the transept remain from the original 12C church. The early 13C chancel is a combination of Romanesque and Gothic (capitals with full-face figures and large crockets). The northern side chapels, with their fine ribbing on carved figure bases, date from the 15C; the southern side chapels and the west front are 18C. The sacristy features fine wood panelling (1687) around the chapter's chancel, and an interesting collection of silks.

▶ Follow rue du Commerce, turn right onto rue Hyppolyte-Gomot and walk to the intersection with rue Sirmon.

The numerous fountains that were erected in Riom in the 17C and 18C make strolling through the town very pleasant. One of the most famous is the 17C Adam and Eve Fountain, decorated with caryatids, by local sculptor Languille.

▶ Return to the crossroads and take rue du Commerce.

Rue du Commerce
The modern sculptures of lava stone contrast with older works of the same material. At No. 36, note the caryatids of the Hôtel Valette de Rochevert.

Église Notre-Dame-du-Marthuret★
This church, built in the Languedoc style, dates from the 14C and 15C. The west front was extensively damaged during the French Revolution. A copy of the Virgin with a Bird stands against the pier. On place J.-B.-Laurent, the fountain

Basilique St-Amable

12C capital, Eglise abbatiale Saint-Pierre-et-Saint-Caprais, Mozac
© Christian Guy/hemis.fr

recalls the Hero of the Battle of Marengo, General Desaix (1768–1800), who was born in Ayat-sur-Sioule.

DRIVING TOUR

LES COMBRAILLES
Round trip of 75km/46.6mi. Half a day.

The Combrailles is a crystalline plateau traversed north to south by the Sioule gorge which irrigates the area. The land is bordered to the west by the Combraille Limousine (Auzances region), to the east by the Riom plain and the Chaîne des Puys in the Bourbonnais bocage, and north and south by the Sancy (1 886m) and the upper valley of the Dordogne.

▶ Leave Riom W on D 986 towards Pontgibaud.

Mozac★★
This town lies at the gateway to Riom and is famous for the capitals and treasure in its church. An abbey was founded here by St Calmin in the 7C.

CHURCH★
The church was built in the 12C based on a design inspired by the great churches of the Auvergne. It underwent major reconstruction in the 15C following an earthquake. During the French Revolution, the cloisters and part of the abbey buildings were demolished.

Remains from the Romanesque period include a series of fine **capitals**★★ in the nave and north side aisle, which are renowned for their importance in the history of Romanesque sculpture. Two of these beautiful 12C capitals sit in the nave; they were originally part of the ambulatory, which no longer exists. On the approach to the chancel is a rich Romanesque bestiary, with griffins, men astride goats, dragons, a corded monkey (third pillar on the left), centaurs, birds of paradise, masks etc.

On the floor of the chancel is a third capital depicting four angels closing the mouths of four other characters; this is an illustration of a passage from St John's Book of Revelations. The chancel also contains 15C stalls. A 15C wood carving of the Madonna with a Bird stands near the baptistery.

TREASURY★★
The most priceless object is the enamel **reliquary of St Calmin**★★, said to date back to 1168. It is displayed in a glass case in the right arm of the transept.

▶ Rejoin D 986 and follow it towards Pontgibaud.

Volvic – *see VOLVIC.*

▶ N of Volvic, before the D 15-D 83 junction, turn left.

Château de Tournoël★★
See VOLVIC.

▶ Return to Volvic and take D 15 left alongside the graveyard. At the D 15 exit to Enval, leave the car just before the bridge spanning the Ambène.

Gorges d'Enval★
🚶 Having crossed the bridge, take a path uphill to the left along the shaded banks of the river. After a few minutes of occasionally strenuous walking, cross the ford over the mountain stream, which forms a waterfall that drops down into a picturesque gorge.

▶ Continue to Charbonnières-les-Varennes then turn left onto D 16 towards Paugnat.

Manoir de Veygoux
♿ ⏰ Apr–Jun and Sept–early Nov 10am–6pm daily except Sun–Mon; Jul–Aug daily 10am–7pm. €8.90 (child 5–15, €5.90). ☎04 73 33 83 00. www.veygoux.com.

The manor where General Desaix spent his childhood is partly concealed by a building added in recent years. Walk around the building to see the restored façade. Inside, there is a modern illustration of the life of this general who won fame during the Revolution and later in Bonaparte's army. Treasure hunts and other kid-friendly activities are regularly planned here.

▶ Return to Charbonnières-les-Varennes then drive to Châtel-Guyon.

Châtel-Guyon ✝
See CHÂTEL-GUYON.

ÉGLISE STE-ANNE
The church is decorated in a modern style. The stained-glass windows made of Baccarat crystal distil light onto **Byz-antine-style frescoes** painted by the Estonian artist Nicolas Greschny in 1956.

▶ Leave Châtel-Guyon on D 415 towards Manzat.

Château de Chazeron
⏰ Jul–Aug daily except Mon; Apr–May, Sept–Oct Wed, Sat, Sun. Guided visits 2pm, 5.30pm, 6.30pm; treasure hunt 3:30pm. €6 (tour); €8 (treasure hunt). ☎07 68 65 00 54. www.chateau-chazeron.com.

This medieval castle was altered in the 17C by the architect Mansart. A staircase was built on the site of the former east tower. Three of the outer walls were demolished and the moat filled in, then two wings were built, one of them containing the servants' kitchen (south wing).

Guided tours provide a lively insight into the history of the castle, while a daily treasure hunt provides a fun means of discovery.

▶ Follow D 415 to the junction with D 227. Turn right at Pont de la Ganne on D 19 towards Combronde.

Gour de Tazenat★
🚶 A footpath leads around the lake: leave from the refreshment stand in an anticlockwise direction. The first part of the footpath is flat but becomes steep in places along the second part. The green waters of Lake Tazenat lie in a volcanic crater. The lake marks the northern boundary of the Puys range.

▶ In Charbonnières-les-Vieilles, take D 408 NE to Montcel then turn left to St-Hilaire-la-Croix.

Église St-Hilaire-la-Croix
This attractive building stands on the shores of the "Red Lake", whose waters once mingled with the blood of martyrs, or so says local tradition. The lofty late-12C church shows strong Limousin influence (capitals decorated with palmettes and foliage motifs).

Gour de Tazenat

▶ Take D 1244 to Combronde, then S of the village take D 412.

Sources Pétrifiantes de Gimeaux

Not currently open to the public; call for updates. ✆04 73 63 57 59.
These natural thermal mineral springs are a geological phenomenon known locally as the "volcano". The industry of encrusting objects with lime dates back to the early 19C.

▶ Carry on along D 17 on the banks of the Danade.

Château de Davayat

Guided visits Jul–Sept daily except Sat 2.30–6pm. €5. ✆04 73 63 30 27.
A fine avenue of chestnut trees leads to this Louis XIII manor built by Blaise Roze, a wealthy merchant from Riom. The ambitious plans for the house and gardens were curtailed at Roze's death.

▶ Return to Riom via St-Bonnet along D 2144.

ADDRESSES

STAY

Chambre d'Hôte La Maison de la Treille – *25 r. de l'Église, 63200 Davayat.* ✆04 73 63 58 20. http://honnorat.la.treille.free.fr. *4 rooms.* Beautiful mansion dating from 1810 inspired by Italian neo-Classicism. The rooms are cosy and are located in an orange grove in the garden.

Hôtel Le Pacifique – *52 ave de Paris, 63200 RIOM.* t04 73 33 71 00. www.hotel-lepacifique-riom.com. *16 rooms.* This peaceful hotel on the outskirts of Riom boasts clean, colourful rooms.

Chambres d'hôtes Château de Bourassol – *57 allée Léon Blum, 63200 Ménétrol.* ✆04 43 97 35 85. www.chateau-bourrassol.fr. *5 rooms.* This 17C château effortlessly blends comfort and authenticity, with spacious rooms in a natural environment.

Clos des Noyers – *12 rue du Gén Desaix, 63460 Combronde.* ✆06 82 25 52 60. www.closdesnoyers.fr. *4 rooms.* Located in a beautiful 19C residence and surrounded by a calm lovely park.

EAT

Le Flamboyant – *21 bis r. de l'Horloge.* ✆04 73 63 07 97. www.restaurant-le-flamboyant.com. *Closed Wed, Sun lunch and Mon.* Located in a historical edifice of the old town that used to be a girls' school, this restaurant welcomes diners in three small rooms and serves regional and traditional cuisine.

La Croix de Fer – *16 rue de la Croix de Fer.* ✆04 73 86 09 96. www.lacroixdefer.fr. *Open Thurs–Sun lunch; Wed dinner. (Jul–Aug Wed–Sun dinner).* This restaurant serves up traditional local fare on an outdoor terrace with a panoramic view over Riom.

En Attendant Louise – *9, Grande Rue, 63200 Ménétrol.* ✆06 07 97 23 75. www,enattendantlouise.fr. *Tues–Sat, lunch only.* This traditional restaurant cooks up delightful local cuisine, specializing in truffade and pigs' feet.

Brasserie BHV 2.0 – *44 blvd Desaix, 63200 Riom.* ✆04 73 33 92 18. www.bhv-riom.fr. *Tues–Sat, lunch only.* Inventive, convivial cuisine abounds in this modern, cozy wine bar and restaurant.

Châtel-Guyon

Located on the edge of a regional park (Parc Naturel Régional des Volcans d'Auvergne), Châtel-Guyon is named for Count Guy II of Auvergne, whose castle once stood here.

> **Population:** 6 200
>
> **Info:** Office de Tourisme Terra Volcana, 1 avenue de l'Europe. ☏04 73 86 01 17. www.terravolcana.com.
>
> **Location:** 22km/13.6mi NNW of Clermont Ferrand.

A BIT OF HISTORY

Spa – The 12 springs of Châtel-Guyon provide water with the highest magnesium content in Europe to this spa resort, which enjoyed a massive boom in the 19C. The temperature of the natural spring water varies from 27.5°C to 38°C. The spa itself boasts Roman and Ramanesque architecture, and during the Belle Epoque period was much sought after by the maharajas of India and by French intellectuals like Guy de Maupassant and George Sand. The resort specialises in the treatment of digestive and gynaecological disorders. Today, life in the resort centres on the casino-theatre, the park at the foot of Mont Chalusset containing the Grands Thermes, and avenue Baraduc which is lined with cafés and souvenir gift shops.

SIGHTS

Aïga Resort

This state-of-the-art thermal resort seeks to renew the wellness world of Châtel-Guyon. Within the Art Deco style building lies a thermal spa boasting a focus on natural, local products with a design inspired by the rich red of the area's volcanic history. The "nutri-gastronomic" **restaurant** ensures guests have a revitalizing and renewing experience inside and out.

ADDRESSES

STAY

Hôtel-Restaurant Le Chante-Grelet – Bulle de Détente–*32 ave du Général Degaulle.* ☏*04 73 86 02 05. 26 rooms.* Just across the street from the new thermal resort, hotel boasts a spa with a sauna, hammam, covered, haeted pool, and jaccuzzi.

Hotel Spa Thermalia –*20 ave Baraduc.* ☏*04 73 86 00 11. www.hotel-spa-thermalia.com. 26 rooms.* Just a few steps from the thermal resort, this hotel boasts a covered heated pool, fitness center, and restaurant.

EAT

La Table Brayaude

12 rue de la République. ☏*04 73 86 00 27. latablebrayaude.com. Open Thur–Sun lunch and dinner.* ⊘ *Nov.* Market-driven restaurant boasting a menu of pizzas as well as more traditional local fare.

Grands Thermes

© David Frobert/Office de Tourisme Terra Volcana

Aigueperse

This charming town in the heart of the Limagne is surrounded by avenues that have replaced the former ramparts. The Hôtel de Ville (town hall) is housed in a 17C convent building; note the three Jack o' the clocks that chime the hours.

> **Population:** 2 700.
> **Michelin Map:** 326: G-6.
> **Info:** Office de Tourisme Terra Volcana, 27 rue de la Fédération, 63200 Riom. 04 73 38 59 45. www.terravolcana.com.
> **Location:** 34km/21mi NNE of Clermont Ferrand.

EXCURSIONS

Domaine Royal de Randan★
16km/10mi E of Aigueperse via D223. Daily except Tues, May–Jun, Sept 2–7pm; Jul–Aug 10am–7pm. 1hr guided tour of castle and chapel; 45mn guided tour of hunting museum. VISITS €5. 07 68 65 00 54. www.domaine-randan.fr.

Randan is the very last royal estate ever built in France, beginning in 1822. Owned by the family of the Dukes of Orléans, this monument was victim of a blaze in 1925, leaving it in ruins. Luckily, the most beautiful furniture pieces were saved and are on display, including 4 remarkable 19C pianos and a service of 60 unique pieces of cutlery sporting the marks of the royal Manufacture in Sèvres and of the Château of Randan itself.

The **chapel** and the kitchen wing are open for visits.

At the beginning of the 20C, Ferdinand of Orléans, Duke of Montpensier, created a hunting museum of 450 animals he had killed on his travels. Thanks to English taxidermist Rowland Ward, this collection has been displayed via dioramas.

DRIVING TOUR

DISCOVERING LA LIMAGNE
70km/43.5mi. Allow 3h.

This itinerary runs across the Limagne, a vast, fertile plain extending north of Clermont-Ferrand towards the Bourbonnais region.

> Leave Aigueperse via the N. D 2019, then D 2009 to the Butte de Montpensier, 4km/2.5mi further on.

Butte de Montpensier

A fortress once stood on this hilltop, and it was here that King Louis VIII, the father of St Louis, died in 1226, on his return from the Albigensian Crusade. The castle

Domaine Royal de Randan

Gate of Château d'Effiat

was razed to the ground on the orders of Richelieu in the 17C.

▶ Take the D 151.

Château d'Effiat★
6km/3.7mi NE of Aigueperse.
Guided tours daily Jul–Aug (except Mon) at 2.30pm, 4pm and 5.30pm. (interior only). €9. ℘04 73 63 66 76. www.chateau-effiat.com.
On the Vichy to Aigueperse road stands the Château d'Effiat, a fine Louis XIII building of considerable historic and architectural interest.

▶ Take D 93 and drive to Bas-et-Lezat, then take D 63.

Villeneuve-les-Cerfs
A picturesque **dovecote★** stands in a meadow at the entrance to the village.

▶ Continue along D 63 until you reach the intersection with D 1093 and turn right.

Maringues
This large village of Gallo-Roman origin, once a busy agricultural trading centre, stands along the recently canalised Morge. Until the mid-19C, wool and leather-working were the traditional local activities: around 1850 there were 60 tanneries operating along the river.

▶ Leave to the SW and take D 224, heading for Riom.

Ennezat
Ennezat, a large farming village on the Limagne plain, lies near marshes in a landscape of vast, geometrical fields separated by drainage ditches and rows of aspen trees and willows. It is also home to one of the oldest Romanesque **churches★** in Auvergne, with superb 15C frescoes.

▶ Leave Ennezat and follow the diverted route to Vichy on D 210.

Thuret
The 12C Romanesque church is home to beautiful sculptures and no fewer than 64 sculpted capitals as well as a black Virgin.

▶ Leave Thuret on D 211 and drive to Sardon. Enter Sardon on D 51, then, on leaving the town, turn left onto D 122 to the junction with D 985. Turn right onto D 985 to St-Myon.

St-Myon
There is a small Romanesque church here with a fine stone-slabbed roof.

▶ Continue along D 223 to the E.

Artonne
St Martin of Tours came here to pray at the tomb of St Vitaline.
🚶 A nature discovery trail "Coteau du Puy St-Jean" leads to a viewpoint overlooking the village.

▶ Take the D 985 back to Aigueperse.

ADDRESSES

🛏 STAY

Chambres d'hôtes Pinczon – *2 Grande Rue 63260 St-Agoulin. ℘04 73 33 00 49. 1 room.* This beautiful room is located within the medieval château of Saint Agoulin, restored in 1870, surrounded by a park of centuries-old trees.

Hôtel l'Atelier – *5 rue de l'Horloge 63720 Ennezat. ℘04 73 38 95 41. 12 rooms. www.hotel-latelier.fr* This peaceful, comfortable hotel is located in the heart of the Limagne plain.

Gorges de la Sioule ★★

The upper course of the River Sioule has a winding, undulating character as it flows down the Dômes mountain range, contrasting with the lower course, which is flat, with numerous islands in the Limagne basin. As erosion brought down the level of this basin, the Sioule, flowing at an increasing speed, cut into the granite plateau upstream, thereby hollowing out a gorge between the outlying areas of Ébreuil and Châteauneuf-les-Bains. An intricate network of footpaths and bridleways enable visitors to discover the attractions of the area, which is also ideal for fishing and canoeing.

- **Michelin Map:** 326: C-5 to E-7.
- **Info:** 63390 Châteauneuf-les-Bains, 04 73 85 80 94.
- **Location:** 30km/18.6mi NW of Riom. Access to the gorges is effected to the NW of Riom, by the D 2144 (direction Montluçon).
- **Don't Miss:** The gorges de Chouvigny, and the Méandre de Queuille.
- **Timing:** You will need a whole day to do the gorges justice.
- **Kids:** Visit the Château de Chouvigny.

DRIVING TOURS

1 GORGES AND CASTLES
40km/25mi. About 3h.

This delightful itinerary explores the gorges and leads to an important château.

Ébreuil
The small town lies on the banks of the Sioule, which, having crossed the famous gorge of the same name, flows through a wide, fertile valley. The **Église St-Léger★**, built in the 10C and 13C, was part of a Benedictine abbey whose buildings were replaced in the 18C by the present hospice (to the right of the west front) and by an abbot's palace (behind the east end) that is now a retirement home.

The belfry-porch, remarkable for the purity of its architectural design, was added to the 11C west front around 1125.

▶ Leave Ébreuil to the W on D 915.

The corniche road, 4km/2.5mi after Ébreuil, overlooks the Sioule. On the steeper, more rugged slope on the right, bare granite alternates with heather. Beyond Péraclos, the road descends to the river's edge.

Château de Chouvigny
Guided visits only (45mn): Jul–Aug daily except Mon 2–6pm; visits on the quarter-hour. €5 (cash only). 04 70 59 81 77. www.chouvigny.net.

This Bourbonnais-style fortress is built on a spur of rock in a delightful **setting★** in a valley, its impressive crenellated silhouette towering high above the gorge of the Sioule flowing below.

Gorges de Chouvigny★★
At the entrance to the gorge, the road cuts through a rocky headland, the left part of which, detached from the rest, is called **Roc Armand**. The summit can be reached by a staircase cut out of the rock.

Upstream, there is a beautiful view of the gorge – wooded slopes spiked with granite tips – whereas downstream, Chouvigny Castle can be seen. Beyond Armand rock, the gorge becomes very picturesque.

At the entrance to a tunnel, there is a **viewpoint** on the left, over a bend in the Sioule dominated by high cliffs. Upstream, the Sioule flows silently and smoothly down.

Gorges de Chouvigny

Below the viewpoint, however, it flows quickly and noisily through a mass of pebbles; it is gradually wearing down a shelf which interrupts the natural slope. The picturesque valley unfolds a succession of wild-looking gorges and green narrow stretches.

Menat

This small village was once home to a 6C Benedictine monastery. Today there remain the 12C abbey church, vestiges of the 15C cloisters, and buildings housing the town hall and the Museum of Palaeontology.

MUSÉE DE PALÉONTOLOGIE: "LE GÎTE À FOSSILES"

mid-May–Sept daily (except Tue) 10.30am–noon; 2–6.30pm. €5. 04 73 85 50 29.
The museum is chiefly devoted to the small geological basin of Menat, dating from the end of the Secondary Era. The exhibition "La Marche vers l'Homme" illustrates the evolution of life on earth from the first cell up to modern Man.

PONT-DE-MENAT

This is an ideal point of departure for canoeing and kayaking. Crossing the river, there is an attractive view *(right)* of the old humpback bridge.
Soon, on the edge of a cliff ahead, the romantic ruins of **Château-Rocher** (13C) loom into sight. Immediately below the ruins is an attractive view of a bend in the Sioule, a typical example of an incised meander: the concave bank *(this side)*, excavated by the direct attack of the current, is steep; the convex bank *(opposite)*, which receives the alluvial deposits, is low and cultivated.
The road then rises, providing greater views of the river; it reaches its culmination just before the intersection with D 99 from St-Rémy-de-Blot. Forming a ledge above a small, still-active mill, it offers a fine view of the entire valley.

Lisseuil

Here, the road reaches the bottom of the valley. The village church has a beautiful Romanesque Virgin (13C) in its restored chancel.

Ayat-sur-Sioule

An attractive road leads to this village, once the home of General Desaix (1768–1800), one of Napoleon's officers.

Châteauneuf-les-Bains

This thermal spa actually consists of several hamlets. Twenty-two springs are tapped here, providing cold water for bottling and hot water (ranging from 28–36ºC) for the baths treating rheumatism and nervous disorders. To taste the water, stop at **Source Lefort**.

GORGES DE LA SIOULE

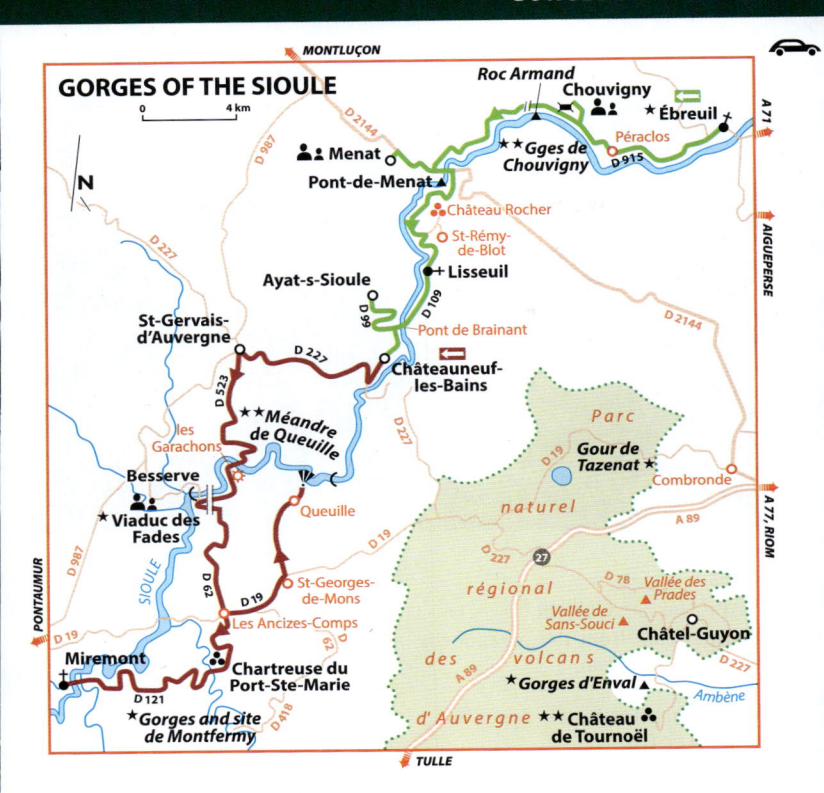

GORGES OF THE SIOULE

② QUEUILLE MEANDER
60km/38mi. About 3h30.

This remarkable geographical feature is well worth a visit; the time will come when it is no longer there.

Châteauneuf-les-Bains
See above.

▶ Take D 227 W.

St-Gervais-d'Auvergne
The village is built on a knoll. Its Gothic church still has some Romanesque features. Beautiful lime trees shade the terrace by the church. The **Tourist Office** *(Rue du Général Desaix, 63390 St-Gervais d'Auvergne; 04 73 85 80 94)* provides information on the area.

South of St-Gervais, the road winds through the middle of a wood, offering some lovely views of the Sioule before crossing the river. It then runs along the east bank, which follows numerous meanders and circumvents the seams of porphyry which lie in its path.

Viaduc des Fades★
This structure, built by the engineer Vidard at the beginning of the 20C, is one of Europe's highest rail viaducts.

BARRAGE DE BESSERVE
The dam, located upstream of the viaduct, is a gravity dam – its strength is provided by its sheer mass.

Méandre de Queuille★★
🚶 Walk behind the east end of the church and continue through the undergrowth to a viewpoint at the end of the promontory overlooking the Queuille meander, which was formed by the Sioule after it was widened by a dam. This side, the concave bank of the loop, is high and spiked with rocks; opposite, on the convex side, the river forms a tight circle around the Murat "peninsula", a long wooded headland.

271

Viaduc des Fades above the Sioule

BARRAGE DE QUEUILLE
Downstream from the meander is another gravity dam.

▶ Return to Les Ancizes-Comps and turn left on D 61.

The road provides a magnificent descent through the Sioule valley.

Chartreuse de Port-Ste-Marie
At the bottom of the valley, perched on a rock, are the ruins of a 13C Carthusian monastery.

Miremont
The 12C Romanesque church, with its massive square bell-tower, rises up on a peak dominating a loop in the river. Miremont is also home to a beautiful neo-Renaissance château built in the 19C, of which the gardens are open to the public.
The **Musée Retour sur le Passé** (May–Nov daily 9am–8pm) provides a reconstruction of everyday life in the Combrailles at the beginning of the 20C with costumes, old trades, and a school installed in traditional houses.

ADDRESSES

STAY
Castel Hôtel 1904 – *63390 St-Gervais-d'Auvergne.* ℘04 73 85 70 42. www.castel-hotel-1904.com. 15 rooms. Restaurant. This 17C manor became a hotel in 1904. The inviting interior is a reminder of centuries past with its period furniture, waxed parquets, grandfather clocks and statuettes.

RECREATION
Sioule Loisirs – *Pont de Menat, 63560 Menat.* ℘04 73 85 52 87. www.sioule-loisirs.com. Mid-April–mid-Sept from 9am. Reservations required. Canoe and kayak rentals for trips down the Sioule. All-day and half-day itineraries possible. Horse riding, mountain bikes, fishing, aerial sports.

CanOvergne – *Pont de Menat, 63560 Menat.* ℘04 73 52 35 48. https://canoe.gorgesdelasioule.com/en/. May–Sept. Reservations required. Restaurant. Canoe and kayak rentals for trips down the Sioule. All-day and half-day itineraries possible.

BOURBONNAIS

Bourbonnais is an ancient province, one that corresponds roughly with the present-day department of Allier with a little bit of Cher thrown in. Its capital was, and still is, Moulins. The region marks the northern edge of the Massif Central, and takes the form of gently rolling countryside covered with a delightful patchwork of fields edged by hedgerows, which tend to give the area a wooded appearance. The Besbre, the Cher and the Aumance are the principal valley through-routes.

Vichy Pastilles

At the end of the 19C, the Empress Eugénie discovered these little sweets, introducing them to her ladies-in-waiting. The result was immediate: in 1885 an imperial decree recognised the originality of the pastilles of Vichy. Used as an aid to digestion, the original pastilles were pure bicarbonate of soda. Later they were made using salts extracted from Vichy water. Today's are flavoured with mint, lemon and aniseed.

Cluny

Founded in 910, Burgundy's Abbey of Cluny gave way to the largest monastic ensemble in Western Europe. For 9 centuries, the Clunastic order developed a rich cultural heritage that still exists today. In the Bourbonnais, six sites are recognized as *sites clunisiens,* including the former necropolis of the Dukes of Burgundy and the Romanesque church of Notre-Dame de Châtel-Montagne, with its square tower.

Highlights

1. The artworks and stained-glass windows of the **Notre-Dame Cathedral** in Moulins (p276)
2. A guided walk in the **Tronçais Forest** (p289)
3. "Taking the waters" at one of the **Vichy** springs (p293)
4. An evening of music at the Vichy **Opera House** (p300)
5. The world's largest rolling ball clock in **Lavoine** (p307)

The Oldest Vineyards in France?

Tradition has it that grapevines first appeared on the hillsides of the Bouble and the Sioule valleys a little before the Christian era. The stony ground of this region is ideal for vine growing, which developed rapidly during Roman times, and later at the demand of the monasteries and local squires.

Bourbon-l'Archambault and its medieval fortress

© Philippe Blanchot/hemis.fr

BOURBONNAIS

BOURBONNAIS

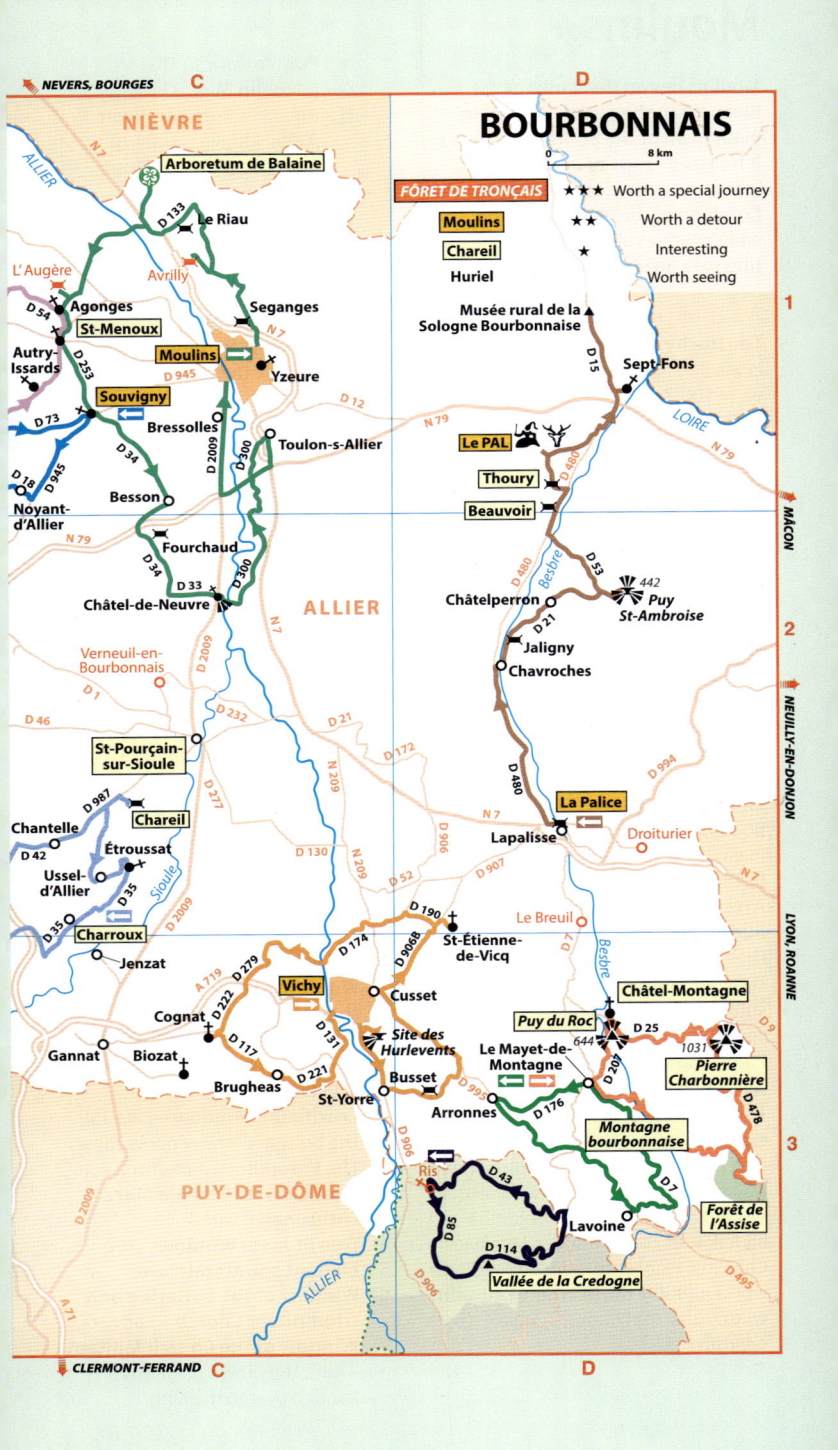

FÔRET DE TRONÇAIS ★★★ Worth a special journey
Moulins ★★ Worth a detour
Chareil ★ Interesting
Huriel   Worth seeing

0   8 km

NEVERS, BOURGES

NIÈVRE

Arboretum de Balaine
Le Riau
L'Augère
Avrilly
Agonges
Segranges
St-Menoux
Autry-Issards
Moulins
Souvigny
Yzeure
Bressolles
Toulon-s-Allier
Besson
Noyant-d'Allier
Fourchaud
Châtel-de-Neuvre

Musée rural de la Sologne Bourbonnaise
Sept-Fons
LOIRE
Le PAL
Thoury
Beauvoir
Châtelperron
Puy St-Ambroise 442
Jaligny
Chavroches

MÂCON

ALLIER

Verneuil-en-Bourbonnais

St-Pourçain-sur-Sioule

Chantelle
Chareil
Étroussat
Ussel-d'Allier
Charroux
Jenzat
Cognat
Gannat
Biozat
Brugheas

La Palice
Lapalisse
Droiturier

NEUILLY-EN-DONJON

Le Breuil
St-Étienne-de-Vicq
Vichy
Cusset
Puy du Roc
Châtel-Montagne
644
1031
Pierre Charbonnière
Site des Hurlevents
Le Mayet-de-Montagne
Busset
St-Yorre
Arronnes
Montagne bourbonnaise
Forêt de l'Assise

LYON, ROANNE

PUY-DE-DÔME

Ris
Lavoine
Vallée de la Credogne

CLERMONT-FERRAND

275

DISCOVERING BOURBONNAIS

Moulins ★

Moulins lies on the banks of the River Allier, the quietly charming main town of the Bourbonnais area. It boasts a range of economic and industrial activities linked to the rich farmland of the Moulins region. The wide avenues and streets of the old town are an ideal place for a stroll.

- **Population:** 20 103.
- **Michelin Map:** 326: H-3.
- **Info:** 11 r. François-Péron, 03000 Moulins. ℘04 70 44 14 14. www.moulins-tourisme.com.
- **Location:** Moulins lies roughly midway between Nevers and Clermont-Ferrand, and is accessible from the A 71.
- **Parking:** Park around the edge of the town centre rather than in it.
- **Don't Miss:** Take a tour around the lovely streets of the cathedral district.
- **Timing:** The heritage here merits a three-day visit.
- **Kids:** Visit the Val d'Allier nature reserve.

A BIT OF HISTORY

The Duchy of Bourbonnais – Bourbon lands first appeared in literature in the early 10C, but it took more than three centuries for the lords and counts of Bourbon to create a state capable of rivalling their neighbours, Berry and Burgundy. The Bourbons achieved their aim by taking advantage of their geographical location between the kingdom of France and the duchies of Auvergne and Aquitaine, placing their troops at the service of the crown. This alliance with royal authority, combined with a skilful policy of marriage (Béatrice de Bourbon married Robert, Count of Clermont, St Louis' sixth child, in 1265), facilitated the building of a vast State and led to eight Bourbons becoming King of France. In 1327 the Barony of Bourbon became a duchy and, in the following year, it was raised to the peerage by Philip VI.

Arts at the Court of Moulins – The duchy enjoyed its golden age during the 15C and, at the same time, the court in Moulins entered a period of splendour and brilliance, with artists summoned here by Charles I, Jean II, Pierre II and Anne of France: Pierre de Nesson recounted the misfortunes of Jean I; the Flemish musician Jean Ockeghem sang for Charles I before moving on to the king's chapel. Sculpture flourished under Jean II, firstly with Jacques Morel, then with Michel Colombe and his followers, Jean de Rouen and Jean de Chartres. Painters produced the finest works, notably the **Master of Moulins** who created the famous "Triptych" (&see opposite).

CATHÉDRALE NOTRE-DAME

Daily 9am–6pm; Easter–Nov 1 8am–7pm (Sun–Mon 9am–7pm; Sat 8am–6pm) During services. ℘04 70 20 57 77. www.moulins-tourisme.com.
Work began on a church in the 15C; it was made into a cathedral in the 19C. Notre-Dame is particularly interesting for its works of art and **stained-glass windows★★**, which depict famous figures from the Court of the Bourbons.

1) **St Catherine's or the Dukes' Window** – Late 15C. The window shows the Cardinal of Bourbon on the right and Pierre II and Anne of France on the left, worshipping St Catherine.
2) **Crucifixion Window** – Late 15C. The bottom of the window shows **The Entombment of Christ★** (16C).
3) **Window of the Virgin Mary Enthroned** – Late 15C.
4) **Tree of Jesse Window** – 16C.
5) **Elegant spiral staircase**.
6) **Window of the Suffering and Triumphant Church** – Early 16C.
7) **Window of the Church Militant** – 16C. The Crown of Thorns is handed over to the King.

MOULINS

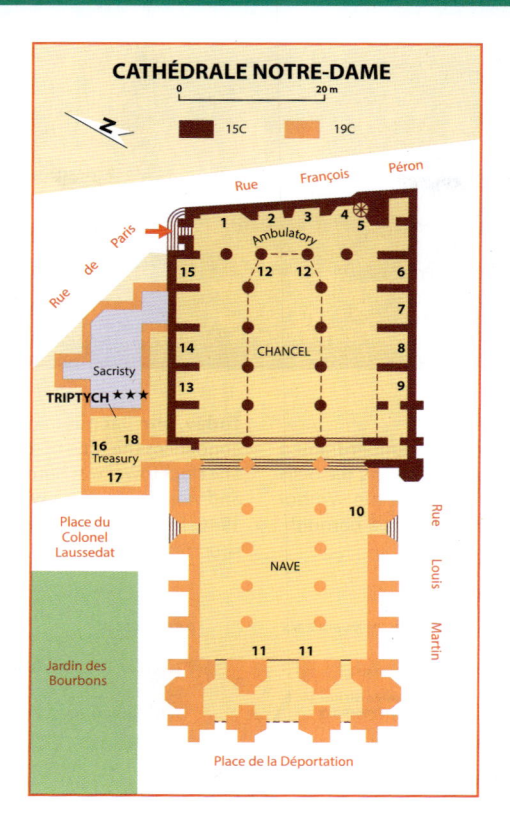

8) **Chapel of the Black Virgin** – The Black Virgin, a replica of the one in Le Puy-en-Velay, serves as a reminder that Moulins was one of the stopovers used by pilgrims on their way to Le Puy-en-Velay and Santiago de Compostela.
9) **Chapter Chapel** – The centre of the stained-glass window depicts the martyrdom of St Barbara.
10) **Classical Painting** – Two Carthusian monks.
11) **The Annunciation** – 18C painting on each side of the doorway.
12) **Window depicting the life of the Virgin Mary**.
13) **St Mary Magdalene Window** – 16C.
14) **Window of Christ on the Cross** – Late 15C.
15) **St Elizabeth of Hungary's Window** – Early 16C.

The Salle du trésor displays **Triptych by the Master of Moulins**★★★ (*see INTRODUCTION, Architecture*). This splendid painting on wood, probably completed in 1498, is considered to be one of the last masterpieces of Gothic painting in France.

The room also contains a 17C ivory crucifix reliquary **(16)** mounted on an ebony stand, the Aubery Triptych **(17)** and the Bethlehem Triptych **(18)** attributed to 16C Flemish painter Joos van Cleve.

WALKING TOUR

CATHEDRAL DISTRICT
See map p267.

▶ Leave the cathedral by the north door, walk around the east end of the church and go down rue Grenier, then rue des Orfèvres.

Église du Sacré-Cœur, the cathedral and the Régemorte Bridge over the Allier

Jacquemart★

The belfry, topped by a timber-framed roof and a campanile housing the bells and automata, was once the symbol of the town's privileges as a borough. Today, the Jacquemart family still announces the time of day for the city. The clock tower was burnt down in 1655 and was once again ravaged by fire in 1946. in 1947, it was rebuilt by public subscription.

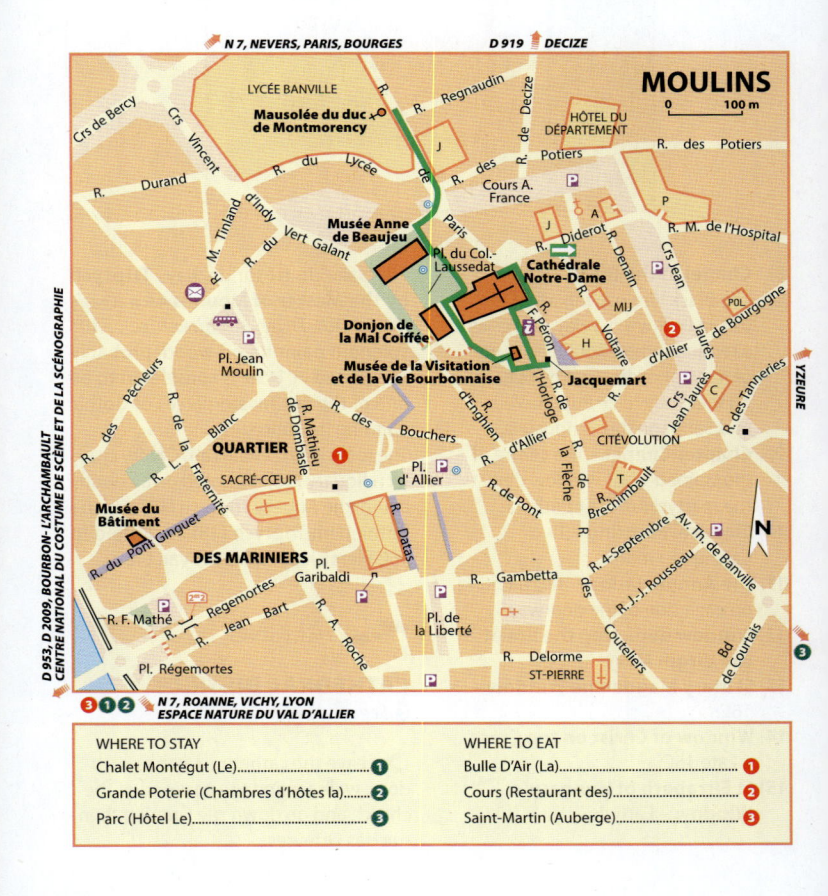

WHERE TO STAY		WHERE TO EAT	
Chalet Montégut (Le)	❶	Bulle D'Air (La)	❶
Grande Poterie (Chambres d'hôtes la)	❷	Cours (Restaurant des)	❷
Parc (Hôtel Le)	❸	Saint-Martin (Auberge)	❸

MOULINS

▶ Take rue de l'Ancien-Palais.

Donjon de la Mal Coiffée
All that remains of the old castle is a massive keep restored in the 15C and named "The Dishevelled" because of its roof. Used as a prison until 1986, its walls bear the inscriptions of past prisoners.

Pavillon dit d'Anne de Beaujeu
The so-called Anne de Beaujeu Pavillon is the only remaining part of the extension to the ducal palace commissioned by the princess around 1495.
This elegant construction is one of the earliest examples of Renaissance architecture in France and was used in later years by King Charles VIII.
A porch tower stands in front of the Italianate façade, which presents six arcades decorated with the initials of Peter and Anne of Beaujeu and the emblems of the Bourbons: the belt of hope, thistle and stag beetle.

Musée Anne de Beaujeu★★
Jan–Jun and Sep–Dec Tue–Sat 10am–noon, 2–6pm, Sun 2–6pm; Jul–Aug Mon–Sat 10am–12:30pm, 2–6.30pm. 1 Jan, 1 May, 25 Dec. €5. 04 70 20 48 47. www.musees.allier.fr.
This museum occupies the so-called Anne de Beaujeu Pavilion, the only remaining part of the extension to the ducal palace.

Mausolée du duc de Montmorency★
The mausoleum, completed in 1653, is the work of Parisian artists, the Anguier Brothers, and was commissioned by the wife of Henri II of Montmorency after she was widowed in 1632 and sent to the Convent of the Visitation in Moulins (now the high school). It was transported in pieces by road from Paris to Montargis and then by waterway.

QUARTIER DES MARINIERS
While visiting the historical heart of Moulins, explore the neighbourhood formerly occupied by the town's community of bargemen, starting from the Église du Sacré-Cœur.

Musée du Bâtiment
18 rue du Pont-Guinguet. May–Oct Fri–Sun 2–6pm. €3.50. 04 70 34 23 69. http://musee-batiment.planet-allier.com.
Tools, building materials and techniques but also fixtures and fittings of bygone days are displayed in this unusual and interesting museum housed in a fine 18C building.

ESPACE NATURE DU VAL D'ALLIER
8 boulevard de Nomazy. Individual self-guided tours and group tours all year. Public holidays. No charge. 07 77 82 88 30.
The **Val d'Allier Nature Reserve** extends along both banks of the River Allier, between Moulins and St-Pourçain-sur-Sioule. Information about guided nature rambles organised by the Ligue pour la Protection des Oiseaux (LPO) is available from the Espace Nature.

DRIVING TOURS

CHÂTEAUX IN THE BOURBONNAIS
100km/62mi. Allow one day.

This itinerary is a good way of getting to know the Bourbonnais.

▶ Leave Moulins to the NE heading towards N7, then turn right onto D 12.

Yzeure
The village of Yzeure is older than Moulins, and was the seat of the parish until the Hundred Years War.

Château de Seganges
Closed to the public.
Small château built at the same time as the Anne de Beaujeu Pavilion.

▶ Continue on D 29, turn right onto D 29.

DISCOVERING BOURBONNAIS

The road wends its way through Munet Forest, offering pretty glimpses of both coniferous and broad-leaved trees.

▶ Leaving the forest, take D 133 on the left. At the entrance to Auroüer, continue along D 133 on the left.

Château du Riau
Guided tours Jul and Sept daily (except Sat) 2–7pm. €7. ☎04 70 43 34 47. www.chateau-du-riau.com.
The Riau estate comprises several buildings dating from the 15C to the 18C, which lie in a lovely green setting on the border of the Allier and Nièvre regions. The most remarkable building is the **tithe barn**★, built in 1584, with its stables on the lower ground floor and grain storage on the three upper floors; the top floor, with its beautiful timber roof, provides an attractive view of the castle, moat, **fortified gatehouse** and dovecote. The gatehouse contains the chapel and the guard-room. In the square tower, a 15C staircase with a wooden balustrade leads to **bedrooms** decorated in Louis XV, Louis XVI and Empire styles. There is also a permanent exhibit of miniature furniture and dolls from the 19C.

▶ Continue along D 133 until you reach Villeneuve-sur-Allier. On leaving the village, turn right onto D 433.

Arboretum de Balaine★
Daily Mar–Nov 9am–noon, 2–7pm. €11. ☎04 70 43 30 07. www.arboretum-balaine.com.
This botanical garden founded in 1804 is landscaped in the English style and includes numerous species: various types of fir (Caucasian, Spanish, Douglas), giant sequoias, oaks, Cedar of Lebanon and locally grown varieties. The trees are pleasantly set amid beautiful shrubs of rhododendron, azalea, bamboo and dogwood.

▶ Return to Villeneuve-sur-Allier and take D 133 to Bourbon-l'Archambault on the right. After leaving Bagneux, D 133, then D 13 cut across the forest of Les Prieurés Bagnolet. Leave D 13 at the end of a straight section; right onto D 54.

St-Menoux★
see BOURBON-L'ARCHAMBAULT.

▶ Leave St-Menoux to the S on D 253.

Souvigny★★ – *see SOUVIGNY.*

▶ Leave Souvigny to the E on D 945, heading for Moulins. On leaving the village, turn right onto D 34, which crosses the railway line.

Besson
This village has an interesting Romanesque church with a single nave. Note the Château de Rochefort, whose ruins overlook the Guèze valley.

▶ Leave Besson to the SW on D 34. At the crossroads, turn left onto D 291, then take D 292 on the right.

Château de Fourchaud
Imposing castle featuring two massive towers with pepper-pot roofs and a sturdy-looking keep. Originally erected in the 14C, the stronghold was heavily restored during the following century.

▶ Continue along D 292. In Bresnay, take D 34 for 4km/2.5mi, then turn left onto D 33.

Châtel-de-Neuvre
Pretty village with a Romanesque church built on a promontory dominating the Allier valley. Enjoy the **view**★ extending over the nearby river and landscape.

▶ Leave Châtel-de-Neuvre to the E on D 32, crossing the Allier, then turn left onto D 300.

Toulon-sur-Allier
This hamlet used to be an important centre for the production of pottery in Gallo-Roman times.

▶ Leave Toulon-sur-Allier to the S on N 7, then take N 79 on the right.

MOULINS

After crossing the Allier, take N 2009 to Moulins on the right.

Bressolles
Small village situated north-east of the charming Prieurés Moladier forest.

SITES CLUNY
183km/113mi. Allow a half-day.
This tour allows you to discover five of the six remaining Cluny sites in the Bourbonnais region. (The last, St-Léger in Arronnes, is closed to the public.)

▶ Leave Moulins on D 945 to Souvigny.

Prieurale St-Pierre St-Paul
(see SOUVIGNY).

▶ Head south on D 2009 to Broût-Vernet.

Eglise Saint-Mazeran
This church still boasts two paintings given by Empress Eugénie.

▶ Head east on D 6 towards Seuillet.

Prieuré St-Germain-des-Fossés
This small rural priory is home to a church, convent buildings, and a dovecote. Frequent live shows and exhibits.

▶ Head SE on D 25 to Châtel-Montagne.

Eglise Notre-Dame de Châtel-Montagne
This superb example of Auvergnat Romanesque architecture is home to original capitals and traces of 12C and 13C wall paintings. Don't miss its **square** belltower. The Chemin des Dames offers a lovely **view** of the building.

▶ Head N on D 7 to Droiturier.

Eglise St-Nicolas Ste-Croix
With the exception of the cloister and belltower, this priory church remains mostly intact. Don't miss the two beautiful capitals.

▶ Return to Moulins via D 480.

ADDRESSES

STAY

Le Parc – *31 av. du Gén.-Leclerc. ☏04 70 44 12 25. www.hotel-moulins.com. 28 rooms. Restaurant.* A few steps from a verdant park and the train station. Modest bedrooms and two dining rooms, rustic and contemporary.

Chambre d'Hôte La Grande Poterie – *9 r. de la Grande-Poterie, 03000 Coulandon. ☏04 70 44 30 39. www.lagrandepoterie.com. 4 rooms. Open mid-Mar–Oct. Restaurant.* Ancient farm at the centre of a woodland park.

Le Chalet Montégut – *26 rte du Chalet, 03000 Coulandon. ☏04 70 46 00 66. www.hotel-lechalet.fr. 28 rooms. Restaurant.* In the centre of a park; quiet, delightful and provincial.

EAT

Auberge Saint-Martin – *Place du Bourg, 03000 Coulandon. ☏09 70 98 31 81. Closed Sun, Mon and Tue evenings.* Traditional dishes served in a rustic but homely dining room.

Restaurant des Cours – *36 cours Jean-Jaurès. ☏04 70 44 25 66. www.restaurant-des-cours-moulins.fr. Closed Wed.* This fetching bourgeois house in the heart of the city is embellished by a lacework of Virginia creeper.

Bulle d'Air – *22 place d'Allier. ☏04 70 34 24 61. Closed Mon–Tues.* This modern, creative restaurant takes advantage of fresh, organic products.

TAKING A BREAK
Le Grand Café – *49 pl. d'Allier. ☏04 70 44 00 05. Summer: daily 8am–1am; rest of the year: closed Sun eve, 1 Jan and 25 Dec.* Built in 1899, this café is classified as a historic monument. An imposing fresco honouring Gambrinus, the god of ale, surrounds customers.

DISCOVERING BOURBONNAIS

Bourbon-l'Archambault

The name of this little town serves as a reminder of the Celtic god, Borvo, protector of thermal springs. The spring water has been appreciated since Roman times; it emerges at a temperature of 55ºC and is recommended for the treatment of rheumatism, paralysis and functional rehabilitation. The town is overlooked by the ruins of its feudal castle.

- **Population:** 2 615.
- **Michelin Map:** 326: F-3.
- **Info:** 1 pl. de l'Hôtel de Ville, 03160 Bourbon-l'Arachambault. 04 70 67 09 79. www.ot-bourbon.com.
- **Location:** Bourbon lies north of Clermont Ferrand, accessible along the A 71.
- **Parking:** Gare Routière on Av Charles Louis Philippe or at the covered market.
- **Timing:** Allow half a day.

SPA RESORT
The thermal establishment, built in 1885, is situated in the middle of the park, along with the casino. The thermal establishment contains ceramics from the Parvilliers workshops, dating from 1885.

SIGHTS
Musée Augustin Bernard
Apr–Oct Thu–Fri 3–6pm (guided visit on Fri). €4. 06 47 79 68 10.
Founded in 1937, this museum is housed in the former pump rooms, also known as the "King's House", built by Gaston of Orléans in the town centre. The first floor includes a reconstruction of a local home, and regional headdresses and costumes are on display. Farm implements testify to the region's rural past.

Église St-Georges
This church was erected in the 12C and altered and enlarged in the 15C and again in the 19C. Walk down to the town centre along rue de la République and admire the view of the fortified old town and the ruins of its fortress.

Forteresse Médiévale
> *mid-Feb–Jun and Oct–mid-Nov 10am–noon, 2–6pm; Jul–Sep 10am–7pm. Mon.*
Guided visits mid-Feb–Nov (1h30). €8 (€6 unguided). 04 70 67 02 30. www.forteressebourbon.fr.
Louis II of Bourbon turned Bourbon castle into a princely residence, but the destruction wrought in the Revolution left nothing but three towers.

DRIVING TOUR

BOCAGE BOURBONNAIS
Round trip of 45km/28mi. Allow 2h.

Leave Bourbon-l'Archambault heading N on D 1 towards Nevers.

The Bocage Bourbonnais is a pleasantly undulating region, crisscrossed by hedges and dotted with forest groves which thrive in the heavy clay soil otherwise unsuited for farming.

Église de Franchesse
The church of Saint-Etienne was built in the 12C–13C, surmounted by a slender steeple characteristic of the region.

Take D 135 towards Ygrande.

Les Vignes
This hamlet is the home of the **Musée Émile-Guillaumin** (*May–Sept Thu, Sat, Sun and public holidays 3–6pm €2.5.* 04 70 66 37 90). This farmer-writer (1873-1951) chronicled the joys and griefs of the tenant farmers of the Bourbonnais area.

BOURBON-L'ARCHAMBAULT

▶ Drive SW from Les Vignes on D 953.

Église d'Ygrande
The 12C church boasts one of the most beautiful stone spires in the region, more than 25m in height.

▶ Leave Ygrande SE along D 192. In St-Aubin-le-Monial, turn left on D 492. At the crossroads, turn right onto D 18. Drive through Gipcy and turn right onto D 11. Continue to Meillers.

Église de Meillers
Dedicated to Saint Julien, this 12C Romanesque church is renowned for its beautiful tympanum and frieze of animals playing musical instruments. The church is crowned by an unusual belfry.

▶ Leave on D 18. After the crossroads with D 11, turn right onto D 58. Halfway along this road to St-Menoux is Autry-Issards.

Église d'Autry-Issards
The main entrance to the church is topped by a signed lintel.

▶ Drive NE out of Autry-Issards along D 58 which leads to St-Menoux.

Église de St-Menoux★
At the heart of a peaceful village lying between Bourbon-l'Archambault and Moulins stands one of the loveliest churches in the Bourbonnais.
The present church was erected during the second half of the 12C, on the site of a 10C sanctuary built in honour of Menulphus, a Breton bishop, who died in the village in the 7C.

▶ You can return directly to Bourbon l'Archambault on D 953 or choose to continue a little way along the D 58.

Église d'Agonges
Pretty church carved in pink sandstone. The friezes on the façade are decorated with animal motifs and the interior features figurative capitals.

Distinguished Visitors
The waters at Bourbon, brought back into fashion by Gaston of Orléans, Louis XIII's brother, attracted many famous figures of the 17C, including Madame de Montespan, Louis XIV's mistress who died here in disgrace in 1707, and Charles-Maurice de Talleyrand-Périgord (1754–1838), Prince of Bénévent and France's Minister of Foreign Affairs.

▶ Leave to the NW and drive on D 54 for 4km/2.5mi until Franchesse, where you turn left. The D 139 will take you back to Bourbon-L'Archambault.

ADDRESSES

⭑ STAY

Chambre d'hôte Le Chalet de la Neverdière – Les Ferrons, 03160 Ygrande. 10km/6mi SW of Bourbon-l'Archambault. ☏04 70 66 31 67. 4 rooms. Restaurant. A curious chalet dating from the early 20C, it has an ochre-edged façade and a roof in the clouds.

Grand Hôtel Montespan-Talleyrand – Pl. des Thermes. ☏04 70 67 00 24. www.hotel-montespan.com. Closed mid-Nov–Mar. 39 rooms. Restaurant. Mme de Montespan, Mme de Sévigné and Talleyrand are among the famous guests who have sojourned in these three houses attached to the spa.

Château Ygrande – Le Mont, 03160 Ygrande. ☏04.70.66.33.11. www.chateauygrande.fr. 16 rooms. This striking 19C establishment is home to stables, extensive grounds, and a lovely restaurant serving fresh produce grown on the estate.

DISCOVERING BOURBONNAIS

Souvigny★★

Souvigny, which lies among wooded hills in the middle of a rich farming area, retains the most beautiful sanctuary in the Bourbonnais region, a reminder of the town's past splendour. It is renowned for its 11C church wherein lie the tombs of many of the most influential dukes of Bourbon. The town has the status of "Grand Site of the Auvergne" and is keenly promoting its important architectural heritage.

> - **Population:** 1 961.
> - **Michelin Map:** 326: G-3 – 13km/8mi W of Moulins.
> - **Info:** Mairie de Souvigny, 03210 Souvigny. ☏04 70 43 60 38. www.ville-souvigny.com.
> - **Location:** Lying 13km/8mi west of Moulins along the D 945, Souvigny is equally accessible from Bourbon-l'Archambault.
> - **Don't Miss:** A visit to the museum.
> - **Timing:** To make the most of Souvigny and the surrounding area, allow a full day.

A BIT OF HISTORY

Resting place of the Dukes of Bourbon – In 916, Aymard, lieutenant of the Duke of Aquitaine, sold his land at Souvigny to the monks of Cluny; in doing so he bestowed an uncommon destiny upon the former Carolingian villa.

Two famous abbots from the powerful Burgundian abbey died in the monastery founded here: St Mayeul in 994 and St Odilon in 1049. The saintliness of the two men, soon united in the same tomb, drew numerous pilgrims to Souvigny, and the oldest of the Cluny priories, showered with gifts, developed dramatically. The lords of Bourbon, descendants of Aymard, created a state around Souvigny which was to become the Duchy of the Bourbonnais. In the 14C and 15C the monastery underwent further alterations, when Duke Louis II and Duke Charles I decided to make the sanctuary their necropolis.

ABBEY

Église Prieurale St-Pierre-et-St-Paul★★

The west front of the original Romanesque edifice, of which only the left door remains, was preceded in the 15C by an avant-corps with a portal and a wide Flamboyant opening.

Two Romanesque bell-towers, connected since the 15C by a gable with a rose window, dominate the priory. The three Romanesque bays in the centre of the façade belonged to the original building consecrated in 1064. The north side shows the church's different stages of construction: the towers, the second aisle and the ambulatory are 12C whereas the upper part of the nave and the transept are 15C.

Nave and aisles – The interior has surprisingly large dimensions: 87m by 28m. The double side aisles flanking the nave and the double transept are evidence of Cluniac influence. The inner aisles, built in the 11C, are very narrow with barrel vaulting, whereas the outer aisles, which came later, have groined or pointed vaulting.

Chapelle Vieille★

The old chapel has a beautiful stone screen in Flamboyant Gothic style.
- Tomb of **Louis II of Bourbon**, known as Louis the Good, and his wife, Anne of Auvergne. The two marble recumbent figures are still extremely realistic, despite the defacements.
- 15C **Entombment**.

Chapelle Neuve★★

The new chapel is larger than the old chapel and has a very fine enclosure.
- Tomb of Charles I and his wife, Agnes of Burgundy by Jacques Morel. The figures, clothed in flowing cloaks, rest on a black marble slab.
- A graceful Mary Magdalene from the late 15C.

SOUVIGNY

- The Virgin, Child and St John (16C).
- Small 15C Pietà.

Cloisters
Only one side of these 15C cloisters remains, with groined vaulting because of the arrangement of the pillars. French-style gardens have been laid out on the site of the priory buildings.

SIGHTS

Musée de Souvigny
⏱ *Apr–May and Oct–Nov daily except Tue 9am–noon, 2–6pm; Jun and Sept daily 9am–noon, 2–6pm; Jul–Aug daily 9am–noon, 1–6pm.* ⊘ *Sun mornings all year.* ≤4€ *(museum and garden)* ✆ *04 70 43 99 75. www.ville-souvigny.com/Musee.*

This museum houses local history collections as well as a glass-working exhibition. Next to the sarcophagi, recumbent figures and capitals stands a 12C **calendar**★★, the most striking piece in the collection. This 1.8m octagonal pillar, weighing 840kg/1 848lb (over 0.75t), is carved on two sides with scenes showing the labours of the months and the corresponding signs of the Zodiac; symbols of strange peoples and fabulous animals adorn the other faces.

Local history is recalled in the Souvigny glassworks founded in 1755: the master glassmakers' tools and examples of glassware (carafe stoppers, pharmacy bottles, champagne glasses) on show are reminiscent of this ancient craft.

🚗 DRIVING TOUR

COMBRAILLE BOURBONNAISE
65km/40.5mi. Allow 4h.

This lush bocage countryside with its pretty churches will charm visitors.

▶ Leave Souvigny to the SW on D 945, heading for Le Montet.

Noyant-d'Allier
The most striking feature of this former miners' town is its pagoda, surrounded by Buddha statues.

Tomb of Louis II of Bourbon and Anne of Auvergne, Église Prieurale St-Pierre-et-St-Paul

▶ Continue N on D 18.

Église de Meillers
See Bourbon-l'Archambault, Driving Tour.

▶ Leave Meillers to the S on D 18, then turn right onto D 106.

The Côtes-Matras command an enjoyable vista of the Allier plain.

▶ At Champs-Regneauds, take the D 945 right towards Le Montet.

Le Montet
The 12C Église St-Gervais-et-St-Protais was fortified in the 14C, but today only the nave and the side aisles have survived.

▶ Leave Le Montet to the W on D 22, heading towards Cosne-d'Allier. After 9km/5.6mi, turn right onto D 68.

Buxières-les-Mines
The very last open-air coal mine in the area can be found here.

Église St-Maurice
This church has a curious two-tier bell tower and a blind nave crowned by barrel vaulting.

▶ Return to Souvigny via D 289, then D 11, driving along the Gros-Bois and Messargesoak forests.

285

DISCOVERING BOURBONNAIS

Montluçon

The economic capital of the Bourbonnais area, facing the first outcrops of the Cobraille hills mainly huddles around the castle that once belonged to the dukes of Bourbon, but its industrial suburbs stretch over a long distance northwards, up the Cher valley.

- **Population:** 39 217.
- **Michelin Map:** 326: C-4.
- **Info:** 67 ter boulevard de Courtais, 03110 Montluçon. 04 70 05 11 44. www.valleecoeurdefrance.fr.
- **Location:** Montluçon lies north-west of Clermont-Ferrand and is easily accessed using the A 71 autoroute.
- **Parking:** There are several car parks in the centre of town.
- **Don't Miss:** the Château des Ducs de Bourbon.
- **Timing:** Montluçon is a bustling place; you may find it useful to allow a full day to explore.

A BIT OF HISTORY

Successful rebirth – The completion of the Berry Canal in 1841 linked the iron seams of Berry and the coalfields of Commentry. Because of this, Montluçon enjoyed rapid expansion throughout the Second Empire, as the steel industry began to develop. It became the centre of a major railway network, and its functions as a trading and administrative centre spilled over into the surrounding countryside. By the turn of the 20C, the iron and coal seams were exhausted.

Musical son – André Messager (1853-1929), the composer, first became known as a conductor in Covent Garden in London, then in the Opera House in Paris. He then quickly gained a reputation as a composer of operettas and ballets.

OLD TOWN★

Start from avenue Marx-Dormoy and head for the castle.

Rue Grande, Montluçon

Château des Ducs de Bourbon

The castle was built during the Hundred Years War (14C–15C) by Louis II de Bourbon and his successors, Jean I and Charles I. Banks of flowers climb the old walls, and the castle itself consists of a vast rectangular building flanked, on the town side, by a turret and a large rectangular tower with crenellations.

Turn right onto rue des Serruriers and continue along Grand-Rue.

This old street is lined with 15C houses (Nos. 42, 39 and 27). Continue to place Notre-Dame with its 18C buildings. Stroll through **passage du Doyenné**, which leads to place de la Comédie. On Saturday mornings, this part of town is filled with colour thanks to its flower market.

Musée des Musiques Populaires

Jun–Aug daily 10am–7pm; Sept–May Tues–Sun 10am–noon, 2–6pm. 1 Jan, 1 May, 25 Dec. €7.50 (child 7–12, €2; 13–18, €4). 04 70 02 19 62. www.mupop.fr.
This museum is home to over 700 instruments and a number of workshops making and repairing hurdy-gurdies, bagpipes, brasses, and strings.

MONTLUÇON

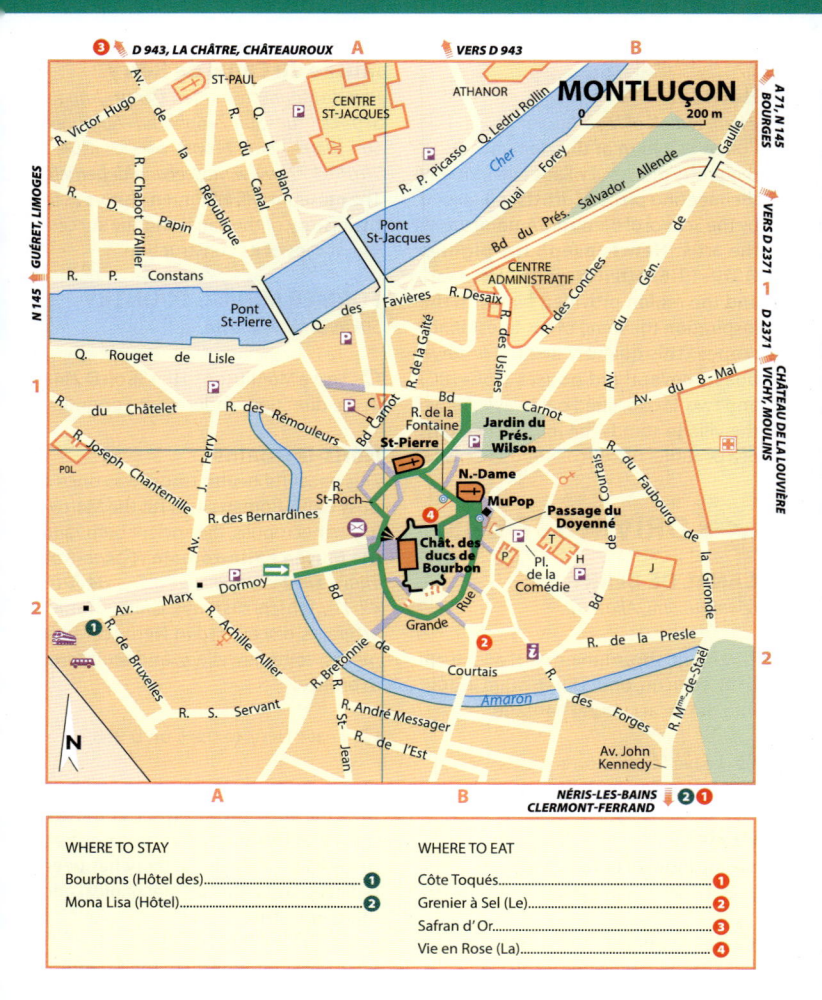

WHERE TO STAY	
Bourbons (Hôtel des)	❶
Mona Lisa (Hôtel)	❷

WHERE TO EAT	
Côte Toqués	❶
Grenier à Sel (Le)	❷
Safran d'Or	❸
Vie en Rose (La)	❹

Église Notre-Dame
The church was built but never completed on the orders of Louis II de Bourbon on the site of a Romanesque sanctuary.

▶ Turn left along rue du Petit Château.

Castle Esplanade
From here there is a **view**★ over the entire town, the industrial estates beyond and, in the distance, the first outcrops of the Massif Central, the peaceful Cher valley and the Berry region.

▶ Return to place Notre-Dame and turn left onto rue de la Fontaine.

On the right, rue Pierre-Petit leads to the **Président-Wilson Gardens**; rue des Cinq-Piliers on the left leads to the picturesque place St-Pierre.

Église St-Pierre
The church of St-Pierre, built in the 12C and 13C, is hidden by houses, some of which date from the 15C.

▶ Rue St-Roch and rue des Serruriers lead back to the foot of the castle opposite the statue of Marx Dormoy, former Mayor of Montluçon.

287

DISCOVERING BOURBONNAIS

EXCURSIONS

Hérisson
24km/14mi N of Montluçon.
Coiled in a loop of the Aumance river, this pretty medieval village was formerly the meeting place of artists influenced by the School of Barbizon. Among these, the artist **Henri-Joseph Harpignies** (1819–1916) often stayed in Hérisson, and the region provided him with the inspiration for some of his finest landscapes. This quaintly attractive town boasts several old houses (15C–18C) and two 15C fortified gateways. Above the village stands the impressive ruins of a beautiful russet-coloured 13C castle.

DRIVING TOURS

CANAL DE BERRY
65km/40.5mi. Allow 3h.

This round trip, running west and north of Montluçon, offers interesting insight into the local cultural heritage.

▶ Leave Montluçon to the NW on D 916, heading for Boussac.

Huriel
12C **Donjon de la Toque** (9am–11am (10am Tues), 2–3pm; Wed, Sat, Sun, €3).

▶ Leave Huriel to the N and take D 40 to La Chapelaude, then take D 943 on the left for 11km/6.8mi. At the locality called Goëlat, turn right.

Église de St-Désiré★
This remarkable Romanesque construction was once an 11C priory.

▶ Take D 479 N of St-Désiré.

Vallon-en-Sully
A charming village in local pink sandstone, set alongside the Berry canal.

▶ Return towards Montluçon on D 301, running along the River Cher and the Berry Canal. Stop at Magnette; from there cross the canal.

Musée du Canal de Berry
Port de Magnette, Audes. Apr–Jun, Sep–Oct Tue–Sun 2–6pm; Jul–Aug Tue–Sun 10am–noon, 2–6pm. €5. ☏04 70 06 63 72. www.museecanaldeberry.fr.
The museum will enlighten visitors as to the history of the canal and the successive stages of its construction.

FORMER MINING COUNTRY
50km/31mi. Allow 3h.

▶ Leave Montluçon to the SE on D 2144 in the direction of Clermont-Ferrand.

Néris-les-Bains
This peaceful health resort was once a busy Gallo-Roman city. Visit the Merovingian necropolis, the ancient baths and the **Musée gallo-romain** (Apr–Nov Thurs–Sat 2–5.30pm. €3.5. ☏04 70 03 42 11), which displays Gallo-Roman artefacts discovered in Néris: ceramic pieces, coins, jewellery, and sculptures in bronze.

▶ Leave Néris to the E on D 998.

Commentry
Until the end of World War I, Commentry was at the heart of an area devoted to mining. Today this activity has been replaced by chemical, mechanical and other industries.

▶ Leave Commentry to the SE and continue along D 998.

Église de Colombier
Crowned by an elegant 12C belfry, the church and its nearby priory, defended by a citadel, form a harmonious architectural ensemble.

▶ Leave Colombier N on D 200.

Malicorne
Jardin-Verger is a dazzling garden-orchard bursting with colour: the rose garden alone boasts several hundred varieties.

FORÊT DE TRONÇAIS

▶ Leave Malicorne to the N on D 69. Turn left onto D 438, which will take you back to Montluçon.

ADDRESSES

STAY

Hôtel Des Bourbons – *47 av. Marx-Dormoy. ℘04 70 05 28 93. www.hotel-des-bourbons.com. 44 rooms. Restaurant.* Opposite the station, a renovated 19C building with functional rooms and traditional menus served in a modern setting.

Hôtel Mona Lisa – *40 r. Boisrot-Desserviers, 03310 Néris-les-Bains. ℘04 70 08 79 80. http://hotel-monalisaneris.monalisa.fr. 57 rooms. Restaurant.* The Belle Époque façade of this hotel opposite the casino conceals well-equipped, air-conditioned rooms.

EAT

La Vie en Rose – *7 r. de la Fontaine. ℘04 70 03 88 79. www.resto-lavieenrose03.com. Closed Sun lunch.* Outside, a pretty pink façade; inside, orange-toned walls, old photos and advertising posters round out this restaurant's bistro-style decor. The menu offers Bourbon specialities featuring Charolais beef, served with soft jazz in the background.

Le Grenier à Sel – *Pl. des Toiles. ℘04 70 05 53 79. www.legrenierasel.com. Closed Sat lunch in winter, Mon lunch in Jul–Aug, Sun evening and Mon rest of year.* This attractive, ivy-covered manor in the old quarter of Montluçon is surrounded by a walled garden. The contemporary fare is flavoursome and the spacious, pleasantly furnished rooms are conducive to a good night's sleep.

Safran d'Or – *12 pl. des Toiles. ℘04 70 05 09 18. Closed Sun and Tue evenings, and Mon.* Small restaurant in bistro style, serving traditional cuisine.

Côté Toqués – *21 rue Hoche, Néris-les-Bains. ℘04 70 03 06 97. Open Tues–Sat lunch, Fri-Sat dinner.* Creative cuisine from the owners of nearby La Cave des Toqués wine shop featuring high-quality local ingredients.

Forêt de Tronçais★★

The Tronçais forest is located at the junction of the Berry and Bourbonnais regions; it has a total surface area of over 10 000ha. Its many pools and beauty spots make it a popular recreational area.

- **Michelin Map:** 326: D-3.
- **Info:** Pl. du Champ-de-Foire, 03350 CÉRILLY. ℘04 70 67 55 89. www.pays-de-troncais.com.
- **Location:** 30km/19mi N of Montluçon, accessed by the D 2144, via Meaulne. From Moulins it is best to go via Cérilly and along the D 953.
- **Kids:** Take a ride in an electric boat.
- **Timing:** At least half a day, more if possible.

EXCURSIONS

Ainay-le-Château

3km/1.9mi N of the forest on D 953. Formerly part of Berry and old Aquitaine, Ainay became a Bourbonnais stronghold in the late 12C. Although the castle has not survived, there remain vestiges of the ramparts (towers, sections of wall). The 12C Porte de l'Horloge in the main street was once used as a guard-room and prison.

The **Église St-Étienne** was built in the 16C on the site of a former Romanesque church. The west doorway, giving onto a small square overlooking the Sologne, is adorned with a fine Virgin with Child from the 17C.

DISCOVERING BOURBONNAIS

The Largest Oak Forest in Europe

Trials and tribulations – Once administered by the Dukes of Bourbon, the Tronçais Forest was confiscated in 1527 with the other lands owned by the High Constable. Poorly managed and neglected in the 16C and 17C, it slowly deteriorated. The devastation wrought by livestock, the improper use of certain parts of the forest by neighbouring parishes or lords, and the uncontrolled felling of trees meant that by 1670 nearly three-quarters of the forest was ruined.

To meet the country's requirements for ship timber, Colbert undertook to protect and replant the royal forest. The new plantations were not to be used until the trees were 200 years old. In 1788, the opening of the Tronçais Iron Foundry led to fresh destruction of the forest with two-thirds of its surface area reduced to coppice with standards in order to produce the charcoal needed for the manufacture of cast iron. In 1832, conservation measures were fortunately taken, and the forest was replanted on the basis of a cutting cycle of 160 years. This was extended to 180, then to 225 years in 1928.

Cultivating the forest – Tronçais forest is divided into series, which in turn are divided into blocks. Oak trees account for 70 percent of its plantations, with beech and Scotch fir the second most densely planted species.

The main aim of the forest remains the production of high-quality timber. The most sought-after trees are therefore of exceptional dimensions, their trunks sometimes more than 20m high and 1m in diameter at a man's standing height. To achieve this, the area around the most promising oaks must be surrounded by other trees during the oaks' growth period, then gradually cleared by successive felling. Logs with a diameter of 50cm and more are sliced in specialised industrial yards far from the forest. Some are exported to other EU countries (particularly Germany). The veneers produced supply the cabinet-making industries and are eventually sent abroad – to Sweden, the USA, and Belgium. Oaks that are 40–50cm in diameter provide wood for cooperage (split or made into staves to make barrels); Tronçais oak is particularly prized for the maturing of Cognac and claret. Oak trees of small diameter or lesser quality are converted into building timber or firewood.

🚗 DRIVING TOURS

1 EASTERN SOLOGNE REGION★★★

20km/12.5mi. About 2h. This itinerary takes a tour of the Pays de Tronçais.

Cérilly

This was the home of the Charles-Louis Philippe (1874-1909), author of semi-autobiographical novels. His birthplace (🕐 *May–Sep 3–6pm.* 📞 *04 70 67 52 00*), at No. 5 of the street bearing his name, is open to the public.

▶ Leave Cérilly to the N on D 111 which leads through the eastern part of the forest. Cross over Rond de Brot roundabout and D 978A, then take the first tarmacked road on the left, Ligne de Cros-Chaud.

Étang de Pirot★

Rond des Pêcheurs offers a lovely overall **view** of the vast Lake Pirot.

▶ Take Ligne des Pêcheurs, then turn right on D 978A.

Fontaine Viljot

On the right-hand side of the road (170m). Park on the left verge.
Oaks and conifers form a charming border to the crystal clear water of this spring. Legend has it that if a maiden wishes to marry, she must throw a pin

FORÊT DE TRONÇAIS

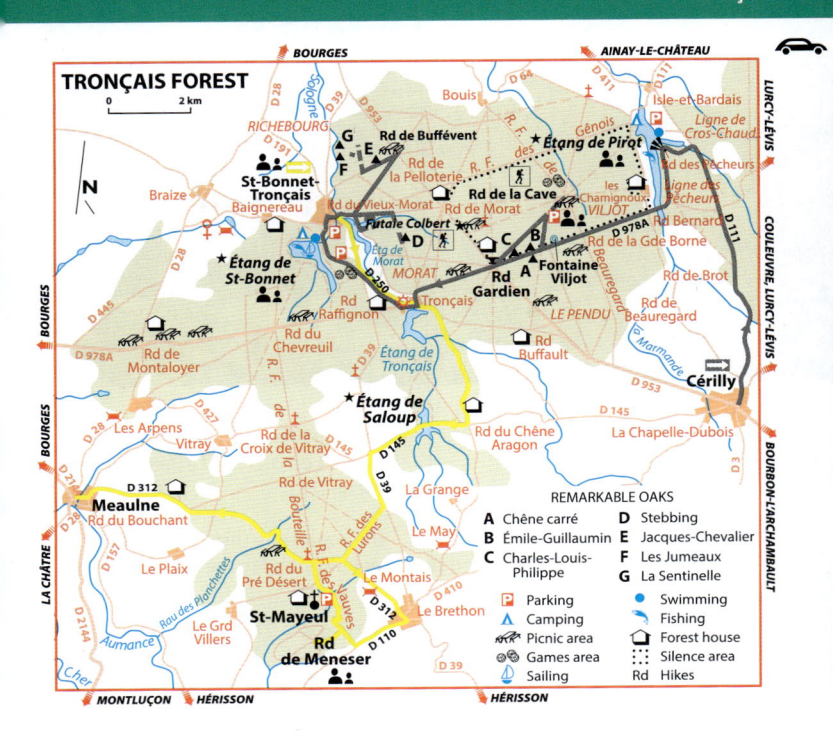

into the spring; if the pin pricks the bottom, the maiden has "pricked a heart." South of the Rond Viljot, walk to the **Square Oak** (*Chêne Carré*). This 300-year-old tree has a total height of 26m and a circumference of 5.96m.

Émile-Guillaumin and Charles-Louis-Philippe Oak Trees

These two trees close to the roadside to the north commemorate two novelists from the region.

At Rond Gardien, turn sharp right onto the Planchegross forest road (one-way) up to the car park.

Rond de la Cave
30min on foot there and back.

This large, sheltered picnic area lies at the very heart of the forest. Return to **Rond Gardien** (*viewing table*) and continue to Tronçais. The factory here was built on the edge of Lake Tronçais.

Take D 250 on the right.

Étang de St-Bonnet★

The lake, to the left of the road, sits in a very attractive setting. The bathing area and path around it are popular destinations for a walk.

Futaie Colbert★

30min on foot.

There is a marked trail from Rond du Vieux-Morat. Beautiful plantation of 300-year-old oaks in a cool, undulating setting (protected area).

Stebbing Oak

1.5km/0.9mi from Rond du Vieux-Morat.
Isolated in the middle of a plantation of young trees is a typical 300-year-old oak (37m high and 3.95m in circumference).

Rond de Buffévent

2km/1mi from Rond du Vieux-Morat.
Short walks along the forest road lead to magnificent 300-year-old oaks: **Jacques-Chevalier**, **Jumeaux** (the Twins) and **Sentinelle** (the Sentry).

Forêt de Tronçais at Rond Gardien in autumn

2 WESTERN SOLOGNE REGION★
30km/19mi. About 1h.

St-Bonnet-Tronçais
A pleasant place to stay on the edge of the forest. Guided tours of the surrounding area are organised by the **Centre Permanent d'Initiatives Pour l'Environnement** *(CPIE – Avenue Nicolas-Rambourg, Tronçais 03360 St-Bonnet-Tronçais;* ☏ *04 70 06 14 69).*

▶ From St-Bonnet-Tronçais take D 250 S. Beyond Tronçais factory turn right, at Rond du Chêne Aragon turn right on D 145.

Étang de Saloup★
The road bisects the lake.

▶ Turn left on D 39, then follow route Forestière des Lurons. From the car park, take the footpath (past a no-entry sign).

The path ends at **St-Mayeul Chapel** overlooking a ravine.

▶ From the car park turn right onto the narrow route Forestière des Vauves winding through the ravine and right to Rond de Meneser.

Rond de Meneser
Various paths provide pleasant walks *(minimum 30min on foot there and back).*

▶ Continue on the forest road; turn left on D 110; in Le Breton turn left on D 312.

The road runs through the forest to **Meaulne**, and to the Aumance valley.

ADDRESSES

🛏 STAY AND 🍴 EAT

Le Tronçais – *12 Avenue Nicolas Rambourg, 03360 Tronçais.* ☏ *04 70 06 11 95. Closed Sun evening, Mon and Tue off-season. 12 rooms. Restaurant.* Calm, spacious bedrooms. Bright dining room with bay windows opening out onto the countryside.

Au Coeur de Meaulne – *20 place de l'Eglise, 03360 Meaulne.* ☏ *04 70 02 21 11. www.aucoeurdemeaulne.com. 7 rooms. Restaurant.* Calm, spacious bedrooms with beautiful windows allowing you to see sunrise and sunset.

SIGHTSEEING
"Discovering the forest" – The forest offers walkers additional attractions besides the contemplation of its oak trees. Mushroom pickers will find boletus, hydnum, russula and chanterelles. There is also quite a large population of red deer, roe deer and wild boar. Great crested grebes can often be glimpsed on Pirot Lake.
In season, **guided tours** of the forest are organised *(for 1–2 months in summer, from the rond de Tronçais; contact for information* ☏ *04 70 46 82 00; for information on tourist activities, call* ☏ *04 70 67 55 89).*

Vichy

A world-famous spa resort and holiday town, Vichy attracts numerous visitors because of its high-quality shopping facilities and the wide range of entertainment it has to offer: casino-theatre, cabarets, festivals, concerts, exhibitions, lectures horse races, and more. The parks along the banks of the Allier add to the pleasure of staying here. The multi-purpose sports centre, situated north of the town, is one of the best designed sports complexes in Europe. The Sporting Club completes the complex with its 18-hole golf course, tennis courts and swimming pool. Lake Allier, created after the construction of a dam bridge on the river downstream from the town, is used for international competitions (rowing, regattas, water-skiing etc.

> - **Population:** 25 756.
> - **Michelin Map:** 326: H-6.
> - **Info:** 19 Rue du Parc, 03200 Vichy. 04 70 98 71 94. www.vichy-destinations.fr.
> - **Location:** NE of Clermont-Ferrand, set on the River Allier.
> - **Parking:** There is ample parking in the town centre.
> - **Don't Miss:** The Spa district
> - **Timing:** You can comfortably explore the town in half a day, but a longer period will give you time to experience its spa facilities.

THE SPA RESORT

The healing properties of Vichy water were appreciated by the Romans, who built a small spa town here – Vicus Calidus. After a long period of relative obscurity, Vichy's vocation as a spa was resurrected in the 17C, and since then, countless celebrities have come to spend a pleasant holiday here while tending to their health.

THE SPA DISTRICT★

The "spa resort" architecture of the late 19C and early 20C, the period when Vichy, the "Queen of Spa Towns", was at its most popular, is well worth a closer look. The buildings of the Vichy spa complex have been carefully restored and listed as protected for some years now, making up a rich and unique part of France's architectural heritage.

Parc des Sources★

This beautiful park planted with chestnut and plane trees was laid out on the orders of Napoleon I and links a number of springs. The spa district effectively grew up around it, and it has remained the centre of the town's spa industry and leisure facilities.

In the mornings, the district is permeated with the peculiar atmosphere of the spa, punctuated by the comings and goings of people taking the waters, gathering in clusters around the springs as they await their "glass of water". In the afternoons and on gala evenings, fashionable society comes to life, going for an evening stroll, having a drink on the terrace of the Grand Café or attending some glittering function.

Halle des Sources

Fed by the waters of Vichy's six thermal springs, the **Pump Room** is built of glass and metal, and its very transparency and the fluidity of its design bring to mind the element dispensed within.

Centre Thermal des Dômes

The luxury assembly rooms in a neo-Moorish style were designed by Charles Lecoeur, architect of the Grand Casino, and inaugurated in 1903. The central dome and corner cupolas are covered in gold enamelled roof tiles.

Grand Casino★

The Grand Casino, which opened in 1865, represents the influence of general good spirits on people's health. The

DISCOVERING BOURBONNAIS

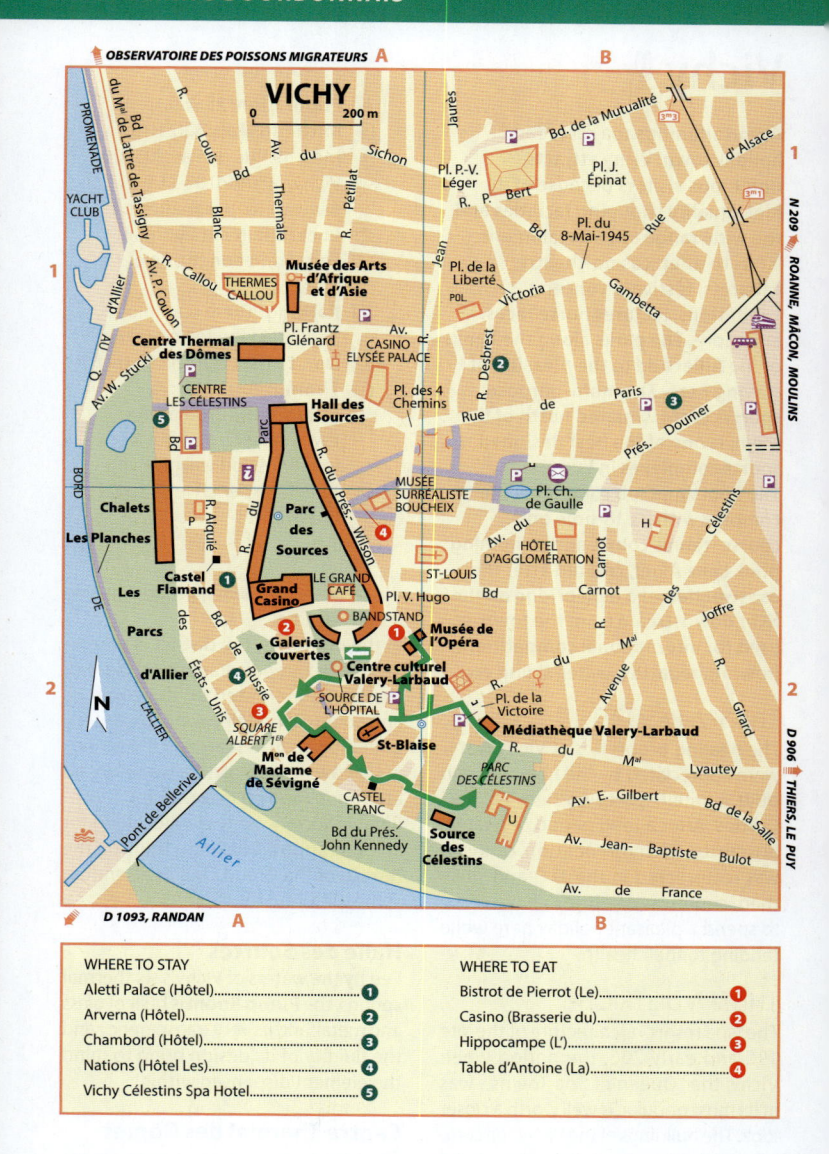

WHERE TO STAY	
Aletti Palace (Hôtel)	①
Arverna (Hôtel)	②
Chambord (Hôtel)	③
Nations (Hôtel Les)	④
Vichy Célestins Spa Hotel	⑤

WHERE TO EAT	
Bistrot de Pierrot (Le)	①
Casino (Brasserie du)	②
Hippocampe (L')	③
Table d'Antoine (La)	④

first of its kind in France, it housed various assembly rooms and gaming halls beneath a single roof. From 1900 to 1903, it was renovated and extended with the addition of an opera house under the direction of architect Charles Lecoeur. Inside, the superb Art Nouveau decor is the work of wrought-iron worker Émile Robert and master glass-artist François Chigot.

Covered Arcades

These beautifully delicate Art Nouveau creations in wrought iron were crafted by Émile Robert for the 1889 World Exhibition in Paris and transferred to Vichy in 1900.

The balustrade of the bandstand, also the work of Robert, forms a garland of musical motifs *(concerts in season)*.

VICHY

The Vichy Government

From early July 1940 until 20 August 1944, Vichy was the capital of the French State during Nazi German occupation of the north of France. Vichy, with a direct railway line to Paris (the "Thermal-Express"), relatively modern telephone links, and many hotels which could be requisitioned for government offices, was chosen in preference to cities such as Clermont-Ferrand, Marseille or Toulouse. It had the added advantage of being quite close to the line of demarcation between occupied and unoccupied France. Maréchal Pétain, hero of Verdun during World War I, was granted full executive powers by the French parliament.

The disproportionate centralisation of government power in this city was accompanied by a strictly monitored exercise of power and the laying aside of the fundamental principles of democracy. During the dark days of the Vichy regime, the city was subject to a permanent police presence, with the oppressive atmosphere further heightened by furtive and unexplained comings and goings, cowed public apathy and an overriding austerity totally at odds with the city's previous role as a health and leisure resort. On 20 August 1944, the representatives of the toppled regime who had remained in place were taken back to Germany by the Nazis as they retreated.

Hotels, Chalets and Villas

Despite the demolition of the prestigious Queen's Hotel, most of the grand hotels on which Vichy's reputation is based have survived. The Hôtel du Parc is among the most impressive neo-Baroque buildings in town. Walk along rue du Parc and turn onto rue Prunelle *(first on the right)* where the mansion at No. 8 is a pastiche of an English cottage. Take a glimpse along rue Alquié *(on the right)* which looks like an English street. The row of **chalets★** lining avenue des États-Unis (Nos. 101 to 109bis) was built from 1862 to house Napoleon III and his entourage, who used to come regularly to take the waters at Vichy. Turn onto rue de Belgique *(second on the left)* to admire the Venitian-style villa with St Mark's lions at No. 7 and the **Castel Flamand★** at Nos. 2–2bis. Retrace your steps and turn left onto rue Alquié leading to boulevard de Russie.

The Palais des Parcs (the old Ruhl) at No. 15 is another neo-Baroque hotel. It was after the fall of the Empire that architects unleashed the full power of their imagination to create truly eccentric buildings. There are some remarkable examples of florid design along boulevard de Russie (neo-Classical at Nos. 17, 19 and 21★, Art Deco at No. 29).

WALKING TOUR

OLD VICHY

▶ Start from the Source de l'Hôpital. Follow avenue A.-Briand to reach square Albert-1er (signposting).

Note the Ermitage du Pont-Neuf Hotel, which exemplifies Art Deco style. The **Maison de Madame de Sévigné**, constructed during the time of Louis XIII, has been extensively restored and converted into a hotel (Pavillon Sévigny). The Marquise of Sévigné would stay here when she came to spend the season at Vichy.

▶ Continue along rue de la Tour (on the right) then rue Verrier (on the right) and walk past the 16C Castel Franc, remodelled in the 19C when it became the town hall.

Source des Célestins

The water from this spring now flows as far as the Pump Room, but it is worth taking the short walk to have a look at the elegant Louis XV pavillion that houses the spring itself. The **Célestins Park** contains some magnificent evergreen trees, as well as traces of the old

295

convent after which the spring and the park are named.

▶ Head for rue du Mar.-Lyautey.

Médiathèque Valéry-Larbaud★
Guided tours by reservation.
04 70 58 42 50.
The local multimedia library presents an exhibit on the author **Valéry Larbaud**, who was born in Vichy in 1881. Around 14 000 books, 180 manuscripts, 8 800 letters and many other documents are displayed on antique furniture.

▶ From place de la Victoire, turn left onto rue d'Allier. Look to your right along rue Besse; no. 2 was the birthplace of the famous reporter Albert Londres (1884–1932).

Église St-Blaise
The old church, altered many times over, has a highly venerated Black Virgin, known as Our Lady of the Sick and Suffering; only the statue's head is original (12C).

▶ On leaving the church, follow rue Hubert-Colombier, lined with villas illustrating a variety of styles. Turn left onto rue du Mar.-Foch.

Musée Municipal de Vichy
Daily except Sun and Mon 2–6pm. 14–22 Aug and 24 Dec–1 Jan.
04 70 32 12 97. www.ville-vichy.fr/musees.
Set up in the **Centre Culturel Valéry-Larbaud**, this small museum is devoted to local archaeology, contemporary painting, and postage stamps, coins and medals from Vichy. There is a collection of modern painting and sculpture with works by Gustave Moreau and Picasso.

▶ The Opera Museum is opposite.

Musée de l'Opéra de Vichy
May–mid-Dec daily except Mon and public holidays 2–6pm. €5. 04 70 58 48 20. www.operavichy-musee.com.
This museum presents a rotation of the archives of the Grand Casino Theatre, faithfully kept until the 1960s: costumes, accessories, posters, stage documents, programmes of all the operas performed from 1901 onwards, and 10,000 photographs of artists, of famous people who visited the town.

ADDITIONAL SIGHTS
Musée des Arts d'Afrique et d'Asie
16 avenue Thermale (opposite Thermes Callou). May–Oct daily except Mon 2–6pm. €4. 04 70 97 76 40. www.musee-aaa.com.
The former Musée du Missionnaire contains exhibits collected by missionaries and private donations. A quarter of the collection is displayed in eight rooms, inside a 19C house.

Parcs d'Allier★
These beautiful landscape gardens created at the request of Emperor Napoleon III are built on land reclaimed from the river. They are graced with trees of various species, lakes with swans and ducks, rock gardens, rose gardens and flowerbeds, and are ideal for long, peaceful strolls. The Parc du Soleil provides all sorts of attractions for children.

EXCURSION
St-Pourçain-sur-Sioule★
29km/18mi NW of Vichy
This small market town, an important crossroads on the Sioule, is popular with anglers and walkers alike. It owes its name to St Pourçain, a former slave turned monk who defended the Auvergne from the ravages of Thierry, son of Clovis, king of the Franks.
From place Maréchal-Foch, with its attractive fountain dominated by the belfry of the monastery, **walk★** through the covered passageway to the restored cours des Bénédictins, which offers a beautiful view of the bell-tower and imposing roof of the **Church of Ste-Croix**. This vast former abbey church was built in several stages from the 11C to the 15C. Whimsical carvings decorate the 15 stalls' misericords.

The Vichy Springs

Vichy's mineral and thermal springs contain mainly bicarbonate of soda and carbonic acid. The main springs belong to the State and are operated by a contracting company founded in 1853. The waters here are used to treat conditions of the liver, gall-bladder and stomach, diabetes, migraines, nutritional and digestive disorders, and also rheumatological complaints.

Waters from the Grande Grille, Hôpital and, in particular, Célestins springs, are bottled and exported the world over.

Hot springs – These are the basis of the Vichy drinking cures. The **Grande Grille** is named after the grille that used to protect it from thirsty animals. The bubbling water (temperature 40°C) comes up from a depth of 1 000–1 200m. The **Chomel** (temperature 41°C) is named after the doctor who captured the spring in 1750 and managed the waters. A third hot spring, the **Hôpital** (temperature 33°C), rises in a rotunda-shaped pavilion behind the Casino.

Cold springs – Part of the regimen includes drinking the water. The **Parc** (temperature 24°C) gushes forth in the Parc des Sources. The **Lucas** (temperature 24°C) is named after the doctor and inspector who bought the spring at the beginning of the 19C on behalf of the State. The **Célestins** has a temperature of 21.5°C.

Thermal establishments – The Centre Thermal des Dômes can provide up to 2 500 people with thermal and related treatments each morning. The Callou pump room, like that of the Célestins, boasts the latest technical innovations.

Hall des Sources

DISCOVERING BOURBONNAIS

Fishing on the Sioule by the town centre, St-Pourçain-sur-Sioule

Musée de la Vigne et du Terroir★
Jun and Sept Sat–Sun 2–5pm;
Jul–Aug Tue 2.30–6pm, Wed–Sun 10am–12.30pm, 2.30–6pm).
€3. 04 70 45 62 07. www.museedelavigne.fr.
Great care has been taken in presenting the history of the region's main agricultural activity. A spiral staircase in the clock tower (15C) leads to rooms with attractive beams and stonework where a large number of items show the different aspects of vine-growing and wine-making.

DRIVING TOURS

AROUND VICHY
75km/46.6mi. Allow 2h30.

▶ Leave Vichy to the SE on D 906. Before entering Abrest, turn left onto D 126, heading for Cusset, then right onto D 270 to Vernet. At the entrance to the village, on the right, a narrow road leads to a platform.

Site des Hurlevents
The view extends over the Vichy basin, the Allier valley, the Limagne, the Monts Dôme and Bois Noirs.

▶ Rejoin D 906 and continue until you reach the entrance to St-Yorre.

St-Yorre
This small town famed for its numerous mineral springs has become a major centre for glass-making.

▶ Leave St-Yorre to the E on D 121.

Château de Busset
Erected on a granite promontory overlooking the Allier valley, this elegant castle has belonged to the same family for 14 generations. Although considerably remodelled since it was built in the 13C, the edifice has retained a drawbridge and four defensive towers including the fine Tour d'Orion. It is now a **hotel**, with 11 beautiful rooms and a restaurant. (Nov–May.)

▶ On leaving Busset, turn left onto D 121 running by the cemetery, then take D 995 on the left. D 995 crosses the River Sichon, offering pleasant views of the lower valley.

Cusset
This town on the outskirts of Vichy is surrounded by wide avenues lined with century-old trees. Place Victor-Hugo has

VICHY

AROUND VICHY

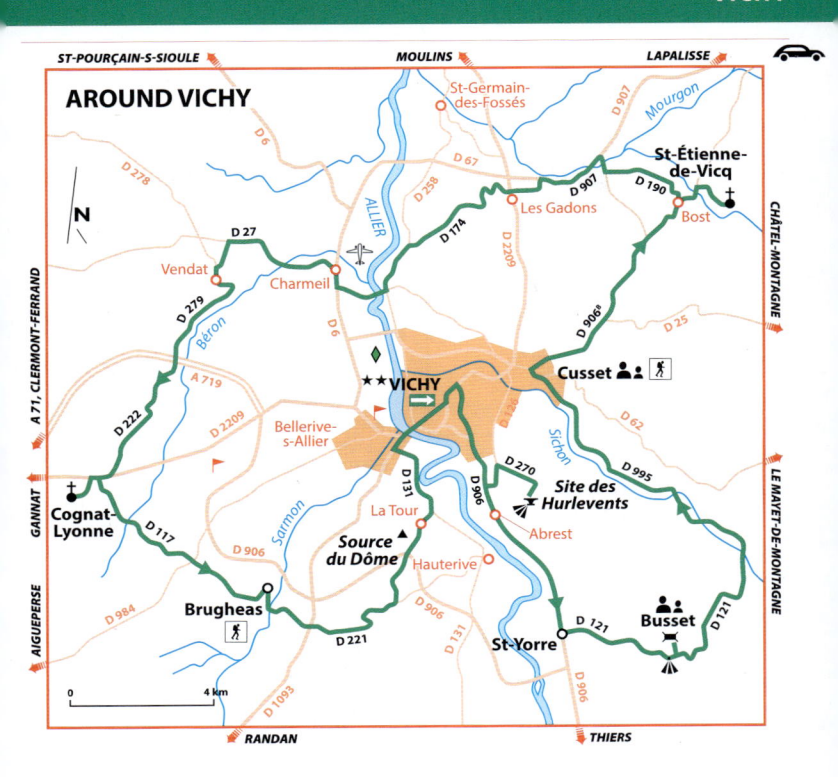

several gabled houses, notably the Taverne Louis XI.
The door and window of the Maison Barathon are embellished with fine late-16C sculptures. Set up in the only vestiges of the 15C curtain wall, the **Musée de la Tour Prisonnière** (*guided tours of the underground passages at 2pm, 3pm, 4pm, 5pm (Jul–Aug 6pm): May–Jun and Sept Sat–Sun; Jul–Aug daily. 04 70 96 29 17. €5)* presents an exhibition on local history through an extensive collection of documents, weapons, costumes, drawings, paintings and street plaques.

▶ Leave Cusset to the NE on D906B.

St-Étienne-de-Vicq

This hamlet has a Romanesque church with unusual architectural features.

▶ Take D 2209 towards D 6. Take D 67 to D 390, then take D 190.

Cognat

300m beyond the village, turn left onto a lane leading to the church.
This unusual 12C building stands on a knoll commanding a pretty **view** of the Limagne and Monts Dôme.

▶ Return to Cognat and turn right onto D 117.

The road cuts across Montpensier Forest (*see AIGUEPERSE*).

Brugheas

Lying on the banks of the Sarmon, this village is an ideal starting-point for country walks and bicycle rides.

▶ Leave Brugheas to the SE on D 221, heading for Hauterive. Before reaching the area known as "La Tour", turn left onto the narrow lane bordered by meadows and small ponds.

DISCOVERING BOURBONNAIS

Source du Dôme
This bubbling spring, the hottest in the Vichy basin, yields algae that are used in the preparation of mineral mud baths.

▶ The path runs through a small wood then across pastoral countryside. On reaching the surfaced road, turn left onto D 131 which leads back to Vichy via Bellerive bridge.

ADDRESSES

STAY
Arverna Hôtel – 12 r. Desbrest. ✆04 70 31 31 19. www.arverna-hotels-vichy.com. *23 rooms.* A family hotel in a shady street between the train station and the spas. Bedrooms are small but functional.

Hôtel Chambord – 82-84 r. de Paris. ✆04 70 30 16 30. www.hotel-chambord-vichy.com. *26 rooms.* Three generations of the same family welcome you to this hotel with sound-proofed rooms.

Les Nations – 13 bd Russie. ✆04 70 98 21 63. www.hotel-lesnations.com. *Open mid-Mar–mid-Nov. 62 rooms.* Enjoys a central location, functional rooms and traditional food. Restaurant.

Aletti Palace Hôtel – 3 pl. Joseph-Aletti. ✆04 70 30 20 20. www.hotel-aletti.fr. *129 rooms.* Belle Epoque architecture and ambience in this palatial former spa near the Parc d'Allier.

Vichy Célestins Spa Hotel – 111 bd des États-Unis. ✆04 70 30 82 00. www.vichy-spa-hotel.fr. *129 rooms.* A big, modern and very chic hotel on the banks of the Lac d'Allier. Bright, sizeable rooms. Restaurant.

EAT
Brasserie du Casino – 4 r. du Casino. ✆04 70 98 23 06. www.brasserie-du-casino.fr. *Closed Tue–Wed.* Experience an authentic brasserie from the 1930s! It's all here: the old-fashioned atmosphere, the ambient gaiety, and tables so close to one another that you can eavesdrop on your neighbour.

La Table d'Antoine – 8 r. Burnol. ✆04 70 98 99 71. www.latabledantoine.com. *Closed Thu evening in winter; Sun evening and Mon (except public holidays).* Inventive, savoury cuisine.

L'Hippocampe – 3 bd de Russie. ✆04 70 97 68 37. www.restaurant-hippocampe.com. *Closed Tue lunch, Sun evening and Mon.* A good place to enjoy seafood.

Bistrot de Pierrot – 22 rue de la Source de l'Hôpital. ✆04 43 03 69 49. *Tue–Wed 8am–5pm; Thurs–Sat 8am–5pm, 7pm–9pm.* Simple, tasty bistro with seasonal food and an open kitchen.

ON THE TOWN
Le Blue Note – Vichy Célestins Hôtel, 111 bd des États-Unis. ✆04 70 30 82 00. www.vichy-spa-hotel.fr. *9am–11pm.* An inviting piano-bar frequented by spa-goers and celebrities visiting Vichy. Live music from 7pm onwards Fri, Sat and Sun.

Le Samoa – 13 sq. de la Source-de-l'Hôpital. ✆04 70 59 94 46. *Opens at 8.30am. Closed Sun morning in winter.* Under the shady arcades lining the square, this Vichy institution is popular.

Casino de Vichy "Élysée Palace" – Passage de la Comédie. ✆04 70 97 93 37. *Mon–Fri 10am–3am, weekends until 4am.* Slot machines and traditional games (*boules*, blackjack, French and English roulette) vie for the favours of enthusiasts.

SHOWTIME
Palais des Congrès – Opéra de Vichy, 5 r. du Casino. ✆04 70 30 50 50. www.congres-vichy.fr. *Tickets: Tue–Sat 1.30–6.30pm; phone reservations: Tue–Fri 10am–12.30pm. Closed Sun–Mon except performance days.* A citadel of Vichy culture, this handsome Art Nouveau-style opera house has opted for an exacting programme alternating opera, theatre, dance and even pop music.

Lapalisse

Lapalisse lies on the banks of the River Besbre and is dominated by the outline of its castle. This is a good spot to use as a base for exploring the Besbre valley, renowned for its many châteaux.

- **Population:** 3 247.
- **Michelin Map:** 326: I-5 – 23km.14.3mi NE of Vichy.
- **Info:** 9 place Charles Bécaud, 03120 Lapalisse. 04 70 99 08 39. www.lapalisse-tourisme.com.
- **Location:** Lapalisse occupies a central position in France to the NE of the Auvergne and 90km/56mi from Clermont Ferrand.
- **Timing:** This is a complex area to explore, and to do so can take one or more days.

SIGHTS

Château de La Palice★★

Guided visits Apr–Oct daily (except Tues) 9am–noon, 2–6pm. €7. 04 70 99 37 58.

Little remains of the original medieval castle; the early Renaissance building standing today dates from 1527 and was designed by Florentines.

The drawing room once had walls covered with leather from Cordoba; it contains the Chabannes family portraits.

The **Golden Salon★★** is decorated with a magnificent gilded coffered ceiling and two tapestries of knights, representing Godefroi de Bouillon and Hector. The tapestries, of 15C Flemish manufacture, come from a series of hangings 3.80m high and 4m wide, with a 30cm border. The chapel was rebuilt in the mid-15C but was pillaged during the Revolution. In the outbuildings (fine timber ceilings) there is a collection of standards and flags gathered by a priest from Doyet.

EXCURSION

Neuilly-en-Donjon

27km/17mi NE along D 994 then right onto D 989.

This small village is mostly known for the delightful **porch★** of its Romanesque church, characterised by painstaking detail and remarkable craftsmanship.

Château de La Palisse

© Hervé Lenain/hemis.fr

Monsieur de La Palice

15C–16C – Jacques II de Chabannes, Lord of La Palice, Marshal of France, won renown for his valour during the campaign to capture the Milan region. He was killed at the Battle of Pavia in 1525. The French expression *une verité de La Palice* – meaning something that is so obviously true that it hardly bears pointing out – has its sources in a poem his officers wrote in his honour.

> M. de La Palice est mort,
> Mort devant Pavie.
>
> Un quart d'heure avant sa mort
> Il était encore en vie.

Although they meant to express that he had fought bravely up to the last instant, the words "A quarter hour before his death, he was still alive" have lost their meaning of courage in the face of battle and come to imply naïvety bordering on dim-wittedness.

DRIVING TOUR

BESBRE VALLEY★
60km/37mi. Allow 4h.

▶ Leave Lapalisse to the NW on D 480, along the left bank of the Besbre.

The Besbre valley contains a surprising variety and number of castles. Only a few are open to visitors, but they are all worth a close look. This quiet little river, which rises in the Bois Noirs (Black Woods) at the foot of the Puy de Montoncel, flows into the Loire south of Bourbon-Lancy.

Chavroches
As it climbs towards the castle, the road gives a glimpse of the 15C main building. The gate and outer walls are 12C-13C.

▶ Drive along the one-way street then turn right and follow D163 then D205.

Jaligny
This little town is well known in France for being the adopted home of poet, journalist and novelist **René Fallet**. There is an **exhibition** (⏲Tues, Fri 4–6pm, Wed 10am–noon, 3–6pm, Thurs 10am–noon, Sat 10am–noon, 2–4pm. 11am–noon. ✆04 70 35 68 79. ≤€5.) about him in a space dubbed **Les Pieds dans l'eau**.

Jaligny is also an agricultural centre famed for its fair. The **Château**★ (🔑 *not open to the public*), visible from afar, consists of two sturdy towers with Renaissance windows.

▶ Leave Jaligny heading NE along D 21.

Châtelperron
Small, secluded village dominated by the rounded turrets of its château (🔑 *not open to the public*).

Préhistorama
⏲*Apr–Sept daily except Tue 10am–noon, 2–6pm (Sun and public holidays 2–6pm); Oct–Mar Wed–Sun 2–5pm. ≤€4.* ⏲*Jan.* ✆*04 70 34 84 51. www.03web.fr/prehistorama.*
This museum is housed in the former railway station. It retraces the daily life of Neanderthal man.

▶ Continue to St-Léon then turn left.

Puy St-Ambroise
The **view**★ stretches over the entire Besbre Valley and, to the north and west, over the Sologne Bourbonnaise, a flat region studded with copses.

LAPALISSE

▶ Return to St-Léon; follow D 53 to Vaumas to rejoin the Besbre valley.

Château de Beauvoir★

Gardens: open all year 9am–7pm (Nov–Apr 10am–5pm). Sat–Sun from May–mid-Oct. ☎04 70 42 00 44. €2
This ancient 13C stronghold shows traces of the 15C renovations carried out by the La Fin family. It differs from the other castles in the region because of its layout: the buildings are set at right-angles to each other. The old watchtower is a typical example of Bourbonnais architecture.

▶ Continue along D 480, then turn left onto D 296.

Château de Thoury★

Gardens only: mid-Apr–mid-Oct 10am–noon, 2–6pm. ☎04 70 42 03 95.
This attractive 11C, 12C and 15C stronghold is surrounded by a park. High curtain walls link the two main buildings and the machicolated entrance gate, which has two turrets with pepper-pot roofs; it is reached via a drawbridge over a moat.

▶ On leaving the château, turn right.

Parc le Pal★

Open mid-Apr–Sept at variable hours and days; check website for current details. €30 (children under 10, €27). ☎04 70 42 68 10. www.lepal.com.
The amusement park is laid out around place de la Gaîté, a copy of a Parisian square in the middle of the countryside. A dozen or so different attractions include a monorail, rafting, a water train, a caterpillar, a rollercoaster etc.
The zoo is home to more than 500 species of animals – including elephants, giraffes, big cats, monkeys, deer, waterfowl, parrots and birds of prey – which roam at semi-liberty in an environment reproducing their natural habitat.

▶ From the park, turn left onto the road back up to D 480. Drive through Dompierre-sur-Besbre, then turn N onto D 55.

Abbaye de Sept-Fons

This abbey is housed in 18C buildings; the church was rebuilt in 1955.
An audio-visual presentation describes monastic life. The monks make excellent organic food, including a wide range of delicious jams.

▶ Take the D 15 as far as Beaulon.

Musée rural de la Sologne Bourbonnaise

Open by appointment. ☎06 48 18 78 99.
This museum contains one of the most comprehensive collections of rural life in Bourbonnais.

▶ Return to Lapalisse by the D 15, D 55, then D 480.

ADDRESSES

STAY

Maison des Collines Autour – *Le Pouthier, 03300 La Chapelle. ☎06 62 23 35 43. Closed 3 weeks at Christmas. 3 rooms.* This country inn in the hills was designed with sustainability and green living in mind.

EAT

Auberge de l'Olive – *Av. de la Gare, 03290 Dompierre-sur-Besbre. ☎04 70 34 51 87. www.auberge-olive.fr. Closed Sun evening (Dec-15 Apr) and Fri (except Jul-Aug).* This inn on a busy road is full of surprises. The light and airy veranda is a very inviting setting for a meal, as is the more rustic dining room with fine wooden beams and a lively blue theme.

DISCOVERING BOURBONNAIS

Charroux ★

Charroux is built on a hilltop and was one of the 19 castellanies of the Barony of Bourbon. The old houses, built of dressed stone and ornamented with carved mouldings, have been restored and make the village particularly attractive.

- **Population:** 390.
- **Michelin Map:** 326: F-5 – 15km/9.3mi N of Gannat.
- **Info:** Maison de Tourisme ℘04 70 56 87 71. www.charroux.com.
- **Location:** Charroux en Bourbonnais (to be precise) is just 10min from the exit of the A 71, midway between Montluçon (N) and Clermont Ferrand (S).
- **Timing:** Leave plenty of time for the driving tour.

WALKING TOUR

Église St-Jean-Baptiste
This fortified 12C building was once part of the town walls. The belfry rises above the transept crossing, but its pyramid-shaped spire has been truncated.

▶ Leave via the north aisle.

On the square, there is a **medieval house** with an overhanging upper storey. On the left stands the belfry, a square tower once used as a watchtower.

Rue de la Poulaillerie
An old stone well stands in the centre of this picturesque cobbled street.

Musée de Charroux
Apr–Jun Fri–Mon and public holidays 11am–1pm, 2–6pm; Jul–Aug daily 11am–1pm, 2–7pm. Sep–Dec open weekends. ≤€4. ℘04 70 58 39 93. www.musee-charroux.net.
This **Regional History Museum** is set up in a house decorated with carvings of animal heads, figures and nailhead moulding; objects and documents provide an insight into the history of the Charroux area.

Porte d'Orient
The East Gate was one of the bastions in the town wall. The defensive system is still visible today.

EXCURSIONS

Gannat
13km/8.5mi S on the D 42 and D2009.
This ancient town on the edge of the Limagne plain and the granite base below the mountains of the Auvergne is also on the threshold of the "Gateway to Occitania", the point of contact between two old forms of French language – *langue d'oc* and *langue d'oïl*. The area has archaeological importance, and digs have uncovered rhinoceros skeletons thought to be at least 23 million years old, together with the remains of crocodiles and fossilised birds.

Every summer the town is filled with the sounds of traditional folk dancers, musicians and singers for the colourful international 10-day **World Cultures Festival**.

Jenzat
6km/3.7mi SE on D 42.
The late-11C church here is decorated with 15C paintings in tempera known as "Frescoes by the Masters of Jenzat". The **Maison du Luthier** (*Jul–Aug Sat–Wed 2.30–6.30pm; Jun and Sept Sat–Sun 2.30–6.30pm. ≤€4. ℘06 80 80 35 27. www.maison-luthier-jenzat.fr*) contains a museum on the craft of making musical instruments, in particular hurdy-gurdies.

Église de Biozat
18km/11.1mi SE.
This Romanesque church is typical of the Limagne area with its barrel-vaulted nave. From here you can drive 4km/2.5mi to Effiat and join up with the Limagne discovery trail (*see AIGUEPERSE*).

Medieval half-timbered house, Charroux

DRIVING TOUR

BOURBON COUNTRYSIDE
60km/37mi. Allow 2h30.

▶ Leave Charroux W and follow D 35 for 2km/1mi, then turn right onto D 68. Cross the motorway and take D 183 left.

Veauce
Nestling in a large shaded park, the castle (9C–15C), is perched on top of a rocky outcrop overlooking the River Veauce.

▶ Leave Veauce N on D 118, then D 987. At Croix des Bois, take D 284 right.

Forêt des Colettes
This forest of beech, oak and pine is dominated by the Signal de la Bosse.

▶ At D 998/D 987, turn right, cross Coutansouze, take D 68 on the right.

Bellenaves
This village has a fine Romanesque church.

▶ Leave Bellenaves to the N on D 42.

Chantelle
On a steep promontory stands a Benedictine abbey, built on the ruins of a former castle and monastery.

▶ Take Grand-Rue (D 987) to rue Anne-de-Beaujeu, which leads to the Abbaye St-Vincent.

The church dates from the Romanesque era. Only the nave is open.

▶ Leave Chantelle to the E on D 987. After 6km/4mi, take D 115 on the right.

Château de Chareil-Cintrat ★
Mid-Jun–mid-Sept daily (except Mon) 10am–noon, 2–6pm. 1 Jan, 1 May, 1 and 11 Nov, 25 Dec. €3.50. 04 70 56 94 28. www.chareil-cintrat.fr.
This former stronghold, restored in the 16C, is owned by the State. Part of the exterior has recently been restored (the doorway, the terrace and the 19C well). The interior is notable for its two imposing Renaissance fireplaces and its 16C **mural paintings**★ in shades of brown, representing mythological themes (Mars, Venus, Cupid, legend of Adonis).

▶ Go back to D 987, heading for Chantelle, then take D 115 on the left and proceed to Ussel-d'Allier.

Ussel-d'Allier
A dirt track to the left of the D 223 leads to a raised viewing table offering a panorama of the Bourbon countryside.

▶ Return to D 223.

Église d'Étroussat
The church boasts 14 modern **stained-glass windows**★ attributed to Frédérique Duran.

▶ Leave Étroussat to the S on D 35 and drive back to Charroux.

Montagne Bourbonnaise

Comprising the Black Forest and the mountains of Madeleine, the Montagne Bourbonnaise is a place of gently sloping pastures backed by woodlands of beech, oak and spruce. It rarely exceeds 1 000m. The main activities here are walking and fishing in summer and skiing in winter.

- **Michelin Map:** 326 F/H 5/7.
- **Info:** R. Roger-Dégoulange, 03250 Le Mayet-de-Montagne. ℘04 70 59 38 40. www.tourisme-montagne-bourbonnaise.com.
- **Location:** 27km/17mi SE of Vichy by the D25.
- **Kids:** The Ecomusée at Lavoine.
- **Timing:** Allow a full day or more to explore fully.

Vallée de la Credogne★

From a high rock at the side of the road, the Credogne river forms the **Cascade du Creux-Saillant**. A tributary of the Dore, la **Credogne** runs along a pretty valley, through which the D 114 tracks it for much of the way.

🚗 DRIVING TOURS

1 LA VALLÉE DU SICHON
50 km/30mi. Allow 3h.
See map opposite.

Maison de l'Artisanat
Sept–mid-june Mon 10am–noon; Tues, Thurs–Sun 2.30–6.30pm; mid–June–Sept daily (except Wed) 10.30am–12.30pm, 2.30–6.30pm. ℘04 70 59 75 24.
On the other side of the church this house is an outlet for craftsmen and farmers; it also provides tourist information.

▶ Leave Le Mayet-de-Montagne on the rue de Vichy then the D 62 for 500m, then turn left onto the D 176 as far as Arronnes.

Arronnes
An ancient Cluniac site, the village was built around the only remaining priory church of the 11C St Leger. A waymarked trail explains the local history.

Maison de la Paysannerie
Jul–Sept Fri 2–6pm, Sat–Sun 10am–6pm. ℘04 70 41 80 81.
Two galleries are devoted to the life and times of farmers, bakers and blacksmiths. There is also a small farm shop.

▶ Take the D 995 heading SE in the direction of Ferrières-sur-Sichon.

Glozel
In the world of archaeology, Glozel was the subject of controversy during the 1920s. A young farmer supposedly discovered the so-called "Field of the Dead" here with some votive tablets, the significance of which still occupies the minds of scientists.
An interesting **museum** (*Call or check website for opening hours: ℘04 70 41 12 96; www.museedeglozel.com; €4*) contains many bones, ceramics, stones and engravings, some of which date to the Upper Paleolithic period.

▶ Follow the D 995 to Cheval-Rigond, and take the little lane on the left climbing to the château.

Château de Montgilbert
From the parking lot walk up to the remains of the château, but take care in doing so.
This imposing 13C fortress, flanked by four round towers and a square tower, is reinforced by an outer wall. **La Maison de la Vallée du Sichon** houses a small exhibition about the history of the castle.

MONTAGNE BOURBONNAISE

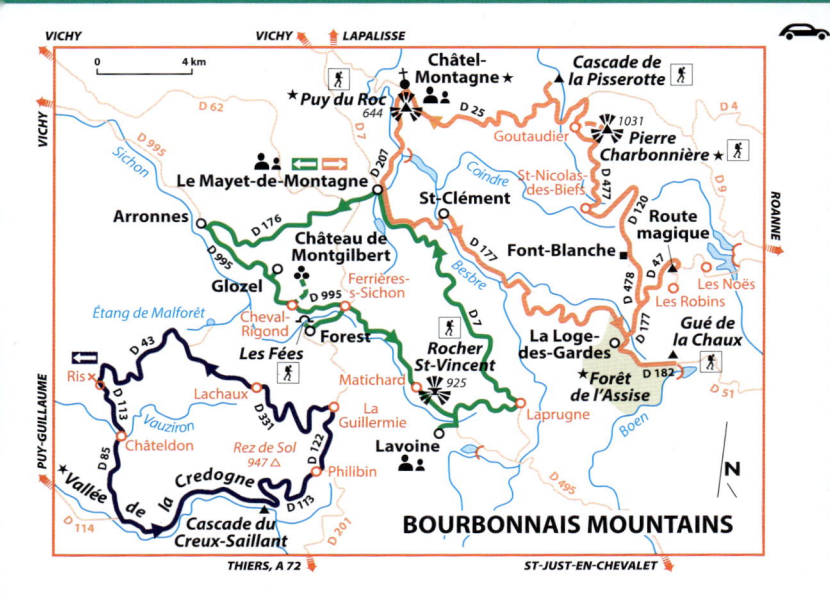

Return along the D 995 and head towards Ferrières-sur-Sichon where you turn right (D 122).

Grotte des Fées
9am–noon, 2–7pm (torches supplied at Maison de la Vallée du Sichon). 04 70 41 11 47.
A road and then a path lead down into the Sichon valley to this cave.

Return to Ferrières-sur-Sichon, head SE on the D 995. Keep an eye open for the Cascade du Sichon.

Rocher Saint-Vincent
30min there and back. The access road begins on the left, 1km/0.5mi after the hamlet of Matichard.
A path leads to the top of the rock from which there is an extended panorama. The rock stills bears traces of the 11C Pyramont castle.

Follow the D 995, and turn right on the D 422 towards Lavoine.

Lavoine
Don't miss the biggest **horloge à billes** (a rolling ball clock; 30sq m) in the world in the village square!

Écomusée du Bois et Scierie à Eau
May–Oct 2.30–6pm, closed Mon. €3. 04 70 59 35 69. www.ecomusee-bois-foret.com.
At the gateway to the Black Forest, this museum in a natural wooded environment details the flora and fauna of the area as well as the life and times of a forester.

Return along the D 995 and take the road to Laprugne. From this village the D 7 leads back to Mayet-de-Montagne.

2 LES MONTS DE LA MADELEINE★

The Monts de la Madeleine roughly parallel the peaks of the Bois Noirs.

Leave Le Mayet-de-Montagne heading SE and taking the D 7 for 2.5km/1.5mi, then turn left onto the D 120.

Saint-Clément
They still make wooden clogs in this small village on the Besbre. Following the reunification of Germany in 1990,

307

DISCOVERING BOURBONNAIS

Saint-Clément was the geographical centre of the member countries of the European Union.

▶ Leave Saint-Clément heading SE and take the D 177.

The route follows the heavily wooded valley of the Besbre and provides improving views as height is gained in the valley of Sapey on the left.

Forêt de l'Assise★
The route descends through the forest to reach the **Loge-des-Gardes** (a small winter sports station) and the **Maison Forestière de l'Assise**, at the centre of the massif forest.

▶ Follow the D 182.

Gué de la Chaux
🚶 *1h.*
On the plateau de la Verrerie, a flora and fauna trail has been created in the middle of a huge bog.

▶ Make a U-turn and take the D 177 on the right. At the crossroads at Grand-Borne, turn right on the D 47, for Les Noës. Just before les Forges, turn right towards les Robins.

La "Route magique"
About 50m before a junction, stop the car as it is descending and see what happens… With the car in neutral, the car rolls backwards, giving the impression of going up the slope. This strange optical illusion has no explanation, but draws the curious.

▶ Return to the intersection with the D 177, and turn right onto the D 478.

The route passes close to the small winter sports station of **Font-Blanche** and then provides lovely views of the Monts de la Madeleine, to the right.

▶ Follow the D 478 then, at the col de la Rivière, take the D 120 on the left. As you approach Saint-Nicolas-des-Biefs, take the D 477 on the right.

Pierre Charbonnière★
At Goutaudier, take a track climbing on the right; follow this for 500m.
🚶 *1h30 there and back.*
The trail climbs through the woods to an assembly of rocks, from where there is a superb view to the east of Roanne and the Monts de la Madeleine.

▶ Follow the D 477 to Trapière, and then turn left onto the D 25.

Cascade de la Pisserotte
🚶 *1h30 there and back.*
The Barbenan falls in two stages into a very beautiful setting.

▶ Continue on the D 25.

Puy du Roc★
Beyond the crossroads, immediately after a tower house, turn left and, 200m further on, turn left onto a trail that climbs to the top of the rock.
🚶 *45min there and back.* A path leads to the summit (644m), which provides a splendid **panorama**★ to the north of the Bourbonnais, to the west of the Monts Dôme and Monts Dore and to the south and east of the Bois Noirs and the Monts de la Madeleine.

▶ Follow the D 25.

Châtel-Montagne★
In the village you can visit eight workshops belonging to artists and craftsmen, along with the Heritage House, dedicated to the Romanesque.

Église Notre-Dame
The remains of a former Benedictine priory, this 12C church is a fine example of Romanesque architecture in the Bourbonnais.

▶ Leave Châtel-Montagne heading SW and take the D 207 which leads back to Le Mayet-de-Montagne.

LYON ★★★

Twenty centuries of history and a superb geographical situation at the confluence of the Saône and the Rhône give Lyon an appearance quite unlike any other and justify its inclusion on UNESCO's World Heritage List. Too often, it is bypassed by tourists in a hurry, when it is perfectly equipped to serve as a stopover for a few days, or a prime destination in itself.

Introducing Lyon

The rivers Rhône and Saône provide the magnificent sight of their very differing courses as they flow past the foot of the two famous hills, Fourvière and La Croix-Rousse, facing the low plain of Dauphiné. Flowing down from the north, the Saône skirts the small Mont-d'Or range and enters the Pierre-Scize gorge gouged out between Fourvière and La Croix-Rousse. The Rhône arrives from the Alps, a wide river that washes the lower slopes of La Croix-Rousse. During Roman times, the confluence lay at the foot of the hill. The alluvium built up by the Rhône gradually pushed the confluence further south, and the resulting peninsula became the main centre of the city. The Fourvière and La Croix-Rousse hills have numerous terraces from which to admire the town; the views from some of these are famous, including the Fourvière Basilica viewing table, place Rouville and rue des Fantasques in La Croix-Rousse. Further away but no less outstanding are the panoramic views from the Esplanade de Ste-Foy and Mont Thou.

Lyon's current prosperity serves as a reminder of the fact that the city's finest hours, during the Roman Empire and the Renaissance, were times when trade was of major importance and the city succeeded in taking full advantage of its outstanding geographical situation. It is, after all, on the road to Italy, between Central and Eastern France, and midway between Northern France and the southern provinces.

Lyon is not only an industrial city specialising in metalworking, chemistry and building trades, and famous for its silk and synthetic fabrics; it is also a university town and a world-famous

Highlights

1. Taking a river tour on a unique **bateau-mouche** (p314)
2. The views from the various *montées* on **Fourvière Hill** (p324)
3. The unusual architecture of the **Fourvière basilica** (p325)
4. The bustling streets of **La Presqu'île** and its squares (p328)
5. The outstanding collections at **Musée des Beaux-Arts** (p330)

Quai Général Sarrail along the Rhône and the passerelle du Collège

309

LYON ★★★

LYON'S MOST BEAUTIFUL AREAS AND MONUMENTS

MUSÉE DES BEAUX-ARTS	★★★	Worth a special journey
Rue St-Jean	★★	Worth a detour
Musée Gadagne	★	Interesting
Opéra		Worth seeing

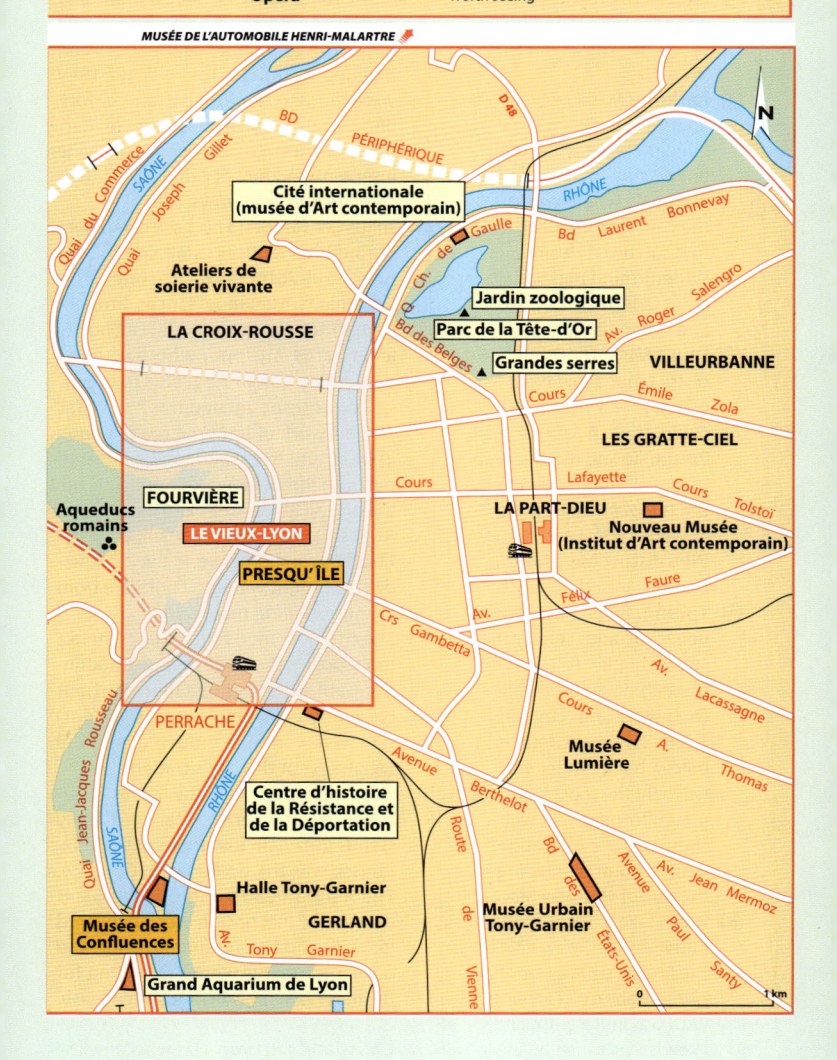

MUSÉE DE L'AUTOMOBILE HENRI-MALARTRE

- Cité internationale (musée d'Art contemporain)
- Ateliers de soierie vivante
- LA CROIX-ROUSSE
- Jardin zoologique
- Parc de la Tête-d'Or
- Grandes serres
- VILLEURBANNE
- LES GRATTE-CIEL
- Aqueducs romains
- FOURVIÈRE
- LE VIEUX-LYON
- PRESQU'ÎLE
- LA PART-DIEU
- Nouveau Musée (Institut d'Art contemporain)
- PERRACHE
- Musée Lumière
- Centre d'histoire de la Résistance et de la Déportation
- Halle Tony-Garnier
- GERLAND
- Musée Urbain Tony-Garnier
- Musée des Confluences
- Grand Aquarium de Lyon

LYON ★★★

▶ **Population:**
City: 513 275; Conurbation: 2 265 375.

Michelin Map: 327: H/I-5 – Local map see Monts du LYONNAIS.

Info: Pl. Bellecour, 69214 Lyon. ℘04 72 77 69 69. www.lyon-france.com.

Location: Lyon lies in a natural plain in the Rhône valley, 460km/287mi ESE from Paris.

Parking: Massive underground car park beneath place Bellecour, but be sure to make a note of exactly where you left the car – getting back to it can be confusing. Underground parking also at les Célestins, les Terreaux and la République.

Don't Miss: The Fourvière district, but allow most of a day for a worthwhile exploration. A tour of Presqu'île and its squares is time well spent; check out the *traboules* (alleyways) in Vieux Lyon. La Part-Dieu district has a fine pedestrianised precinct.

Timing: Begin from place Bellecour, and wander the streets aimlessly; this is no place to be methodical! Organised tours covering 1, 2 or 3 days are detailed below, but a longer stay will gain the most from this magnificent city, as will "free range" exploration; make a point of heading for the out-of-the-way places.

Kids: Take a boat trip in a bateau-mouche, or visit the Musée de l'Automobile Henri-Malartre. A session with Guignol is popular; likewise visit the Parc de la Tête d'Or.

centre in the field of medicine. It has a Court of Appeal and an Archbishopric (the Archbishop of Lyon bears the title "Primate of the Gauls"). The city is also famous for its cuisine: it is one of the best-known gastronomic centres – perhaps the capital of food – in France.

Twenty Centuries of History

Capital of the Gauls – According to a Celtic legend, two princes, Momoros and Atepomaros, stopped here one day at the confluence of the rivers and decided to build a town. While they were digging the foundations, a flock of crows flew down around them. Recognising the event as evidence of divine intervention, they decided to call their city **Lugdunum** (Crows' Hill).

Julius Caesar set up his base camp here during his relentless campaign to conquer Gaul. After his death, one of his lieutenants, Munatius Plancus, brought Roman settlers here (43 BCE). Shortly afterwards Agrippa, who had been ordered by Caesar Augustus to organise Gaul, chose Lugdunum as his capital. The network of imperial roads began in Lyon, and five major routes radiated out from the city towards Aquitaine, the Ocean, the Rhine, Arles and Italy. Caesar Augustus stayed in the town; Emperor Claudius was born here. In the 2C, aqueducts brought water to Fourvière from the surrounding mountains.

The city, governed by its council, held a monopoly in the trade of wine throughout Gaul. The mariners in its harbour were powerful ship-owners; its potters were veritable industrialists. The wealthiest of the city's traders lived in a separate district, on the Île des Canabae, around where St-Martin-d'Ainay stands today. On the slopes of La Croix-Rousse was the Gallic town, Condate. The Amphitheatre of the Three Gauls (the votive inscription was uncovered in 1958) and the Temple of Rome and Caesar Augustus were the setting for the noisy Assembly of Gauls once a year.

Christianity in Lyon – Lyon became the meeting-place for businessmen from all over the country. Soldiers, merchants and missionaries arrived from Asia Minor and began spreading the new gospel. Soon, a small Christian community developed in the town.

In AD 177, a people's revolt broke out and led to the famous martyrdom of St Pothin, St Blandine and their companions. Twenty years later when **Septimus Severus**, having defeated his competitor Albin (who enjoyed popular support from the locals), decided to set fire to the town, he found that there were still 18 000 Christians in Lyon. He had them massacred; among them St Irénée, St Pothin's successor.

A focus on faith has continued through the ages. On 8 December each year, the **Feast of the Immaculate Conception** is celebrated in Lyon with a great deal of pomp and enthusiasm. In the evening, thousands of multicoloured lanterns can be seen in the windows of the city. The origins of this **"Festival of Lights"** date from the occasion of the consecration of the gilded Madonna of Fourvière in 1852. Floods had delayed the work of sculptor Fabish, who was not able to deliver the statue by the deadline of 8 September. Accordingly, the ceremony was postponed until 8 December, the Feast of the Immaculate Conception.

On the day itself, heavy rainfall resulted in cancellation of the evening festival. However, contrary to all expectations, the rain stopped at precisely the time the festivities had been scheduled to start. All over the city, thousands of balconies were lit up by tiny lights placed there in a spontaneous gesture by Lyon residents. This religious custom has become a traditional festival during which the city councillors and store owners inaugurate their Christmas displays.

Lyon in the Middle Ages – After Charlemagne's reign, Lyon passed from one family to another through legacies and dowries. Finally, the city was placed under the authority of its archbishops. During this period, a large number of major building projects were completed. Churches and abbeys sprang up in Lyon and the surrounding area. The Pont du Change (Exchange Bridge) was built over the Saône; the Pont de la Guillotière, designed by the Pontiff Brothers, provided access to the other bank of the Rhône.

In the early 14C, Lyon was annexed to royal authority and obtained the right to elect 12 consuls. A municipal charter was proclaimed at Île Barbe in 1312. The consuls, all of them members of the rich *bourgeoisie*, raised taxes and ensured that there was law and order. The people of the working classes, who were quick to rebel and who had not hesitated in besieging the archbishop in his palace, discovered that the consuls were even more heavy-handed than the clergy had been.

A cultural centre – At the end of the 15C, fairs and the development of banking attracted traders from all over Europe. Social, intellectual and artistic life blossomed, stimulated by a visit from François I and his sister, Marguerite, who held the most dazzling court. Famous "booksellers" took the fame of Lyon's printers far and wide. There were 100 printers' workshops in the town in 1515, and more than 400 by 1548.

Painters, sculptors and potters, all of them steeped in Italian culture, paved the way for the French Renaissance. Lyon boasted brilliant poets and storytellers such as **François Rabelais** (1494–1553). He was a doctor at the local hospital and, for the fairs in 1532 and 1534, published his works *Gargantua* and *Pantagruel*. It was, though, a woman, **Louise Labé**, who embodied the spirit of the day, not only for her grace and beauty but also for her skill in poetry. At the age of 20, Louise had developed comprehensive linguistic (Greek, Latin, Spanish and Italian) and musical talents.

After a stint at the siege of Perpignan (not for the faint-hearted!), she eventually married a gentleman-rope-maker (*cordier* in French) from Lyon and opened a salon for poets, artists and men of learning, just as Madame de Sévigné was to do a century later.

LYON★★★

GETTING AROUND

Maps – In addition to the maps included in this guide, Michelin town plans 30 and 31 and Michelin map 110 (the surroundings of Lyon) will be useful.

Access – By road via motorways A 6, A 7, A 42 and A 43. The city also boasts a regular 2hr link with Paris by TGV. Perrache and La Part-Dieu stations are close to the town centre by métro. There are flights to and from most major cities via Lyon-St-Exupéry airport, linked to the town centre by a shuttle service.

Parking – There are several underground car parks strategically placed for easy access to the town centre. Some of these are architectural gems, the most spectacular being the Parc Célestins by Buren, whose columns adorn the Jardins du Palais-Royal in central Paris.

Public transport – The underground train/subway (métro) is the most convenient mode of public transport, and is especially well adapted to the needs of tourists. The best-value ticket to buy is the 1-day **ticket-liberté**, for unlimited travel on the Lyon urban transport network (métro, bus, funicular railway, trolley-bus). Details from TCL (Transports en Commun Lyonnais) kiosks or call ☎04 26 10 12 12, www.tcl.fr.

Cultural Pass – You can buy a 1–4-day Lyon City Card *(www.lyoncitycard.com)* which will gain you admission to museums, sights and transport, as well as reductions at theatres, on shopping, etc. Adult prices range between 1 day (€25), 2 days (€35), 3 days (€45), 4 days (€55). *(discount for online purchase).*

TOURING THE CITY

Planning your visit – If you have only **one day** to spend in Lyon, then you must devote the morning to Old Lyon (on foot), to the Fourvière terrace and the Roman theatres (use the funicular), but you will not have time to visit the museums; the afternoon should be spent touring the Presqu'île with its Fabric Museum and, either visiting the Fine Arts Museum or an enjoyable walk around the Gros Caillou, on the slopes of the Croix-Rousse.

Two days will enable you to get better acquainted with Fourvière and the various museums and to stroll along the River Saône on the first day. The second day should be devoted to touring the Presqu'île on foot and to visiting its museums (fabrics, printing and hospice museums); you should even have time to take a stroll in the Croix-Rousse district.

Organised tours – Lyon, which is listed as a "Town of Art and history", offers discovery tours conducted by guide-lecturers approved by the Ministry of Culture and Communication. Information at the tourist office or on www.vpah.culture.fr. The Lyon tourist office offers tours of the city on foot, or by bus, boat, taxi or even helicopter *(discount for online bookings).* **Lecture tours** are available around Old Lyon, Croix-Rousse and the Tony Garnier district.

Bateaux-mouches river trips – *☎04 78 42 96 81. www.lesbateauxlyonnais.com. From quai des Célestins.* These unique long-boats enable visitors to discover a different side of Lyon. Several different routes are possible, allowing you to see a great variety of Lyon's major sites.

"La Belle Cordière", as she was known, penned some pleasing verse herself, as well as encouraging others.

Scientific advances – Literature and the arts reigned in the Lyon of the 16C. Science became all the rage in the 18C, with the **Jussieu brothers** (famous botanists) and Bourgelat, who founded the first veterinary school in Europe in Lyon in 1762. In 1783 **Jouffroy** tested steam navigation on the Saône with his "Pyroscaphe", the first really viable steamboat; however, it brought him nothing but the ironic nickname of "Jouffroy the Pump". In 1784, **Joseph Montgolfier** and **Pilâtre de Rozier** succeeded, at Les Brotteaux, in rising into the air on board a hot-air balloon. This was one of the first flights. A few years later, **André-Marie Ampère**, the great physicist, and **Joseph-Marie Jacquard**, who invented a weaving loom, showed their own form of inventive genius.

"Lyon is no more" – During the French Revolution, the residents of Lyon resisted the Convention. Retribution was harsh: on 12 October 1793 the Committee of Public Safety declared that "Lyon waged war on liberty. Lyon is no more." Houses were destroyed, countless local people died, and Lyon was renamed a "Free Commune".

Lyon's "Mr Punch" – Guignol, the popular wooden puppet who is well-known throughout France, his dutiful wife Madelon, and his usual sparring partner, Gnafron, whose fine bass voice has coarsened somewhat through excessive consumption of Beaujolais, all embody the popular spirit of the local people in a way that provokes laughter without giving offence. **Laurent Mourguet** (1769–1844), who created Guignol, was a local weaver. The few neighbours for whom he first performed his comedy shows were enthusiastic. Soon, as his success grew, so did his audience: he staged performances all over Lyon, in the Petit Tivoli, and in the main avenue in Les Brotteaux where, on Sundays, three rows of chairs were set out. After Mourguet's death his 16 children, all of whom had been trained by him, perpetuated his art form. Nowadays, comedies based on current affairs are played out on the stage of the Guignol de Lyon theatre.

LYON ★★★

Threads of History

Silk, the fibre from cocoons produced by the caterpillars of the Bombyx moth, otherwise known as silkworms, was first discovered in China and was brought to France by Louis XI in 1466. The French silk industry did not really begin to evolve until the 16C; at this time Lyon was chosen as the central silk depot, and cultivation of the mulberry bushes on which silkworms feed was begun on a large scale. The industry's expansion continued under Louis XIV, with notable innovators such as Philippe de Lassalle playing a major role in its development. It was brought to an abrupt end by the outbreak of the French Revolution but gained new importance under Napoleon's Empire, finally reaching its apogee in c. 1850, shortly after which a devastating silkworm plague broke out, decimating French silkworm breeding centres. This was a blow from which the French silk industry never fully recovered. It subsequently had to contend with strong foreign competition, the discovery of artificial fibres and mass industrialisation. Nonetheless, Lyon silk production has remained a standard of quality for the fashion world and among French luxury materials.

Sericulture, or the production of silk, involves raising silkworms in special silkworm farms (in French, *magnaneries*) from the egg to the cocoon stage. The silkworm chrysalids are suffocated in steam so that the cocoon can be unravelled as a single long filament of silk. The raw silk obtained at this stage is not strong enough to be woven and so undergoes a preparatory process – reeling, in which the silk fibres from several cocoons are wound together to form a single strand. Bobbins of this thread are arranged on a special frame, then unreeled in batches onto a warp frame. Next the warp is stretched on a draw loom to form parallel threads, across which the weft threads are drawn by a shuttle. To allow the shuttle to pass along with the weft, various mechanical systems for lifting the appropriate warp threads were developed, one of the most famous of which was Jacquard's (using punched cards). Various types of plain weave are possible using silk, to produce taffeta, silk serge and satin, for example. The manufacture of fancier, figured fabrics (with decorative motifs in coloured threads) requires a more complex system, however, using cords known – funnily enough – as simples. As for woven pile fabrics such as velvet, it is necessary to have a second set of warp threads which form the pile. Such fancy fabrics can be smooth (damask, lampas) or textured (brocade, brocatelle).

Silk can also be processed after it has been woven, for example in silkscreen-printing, or the manufacture of figured or watered silks.

The silk industry – It was silk that, in the 16C, made Lyon a major industrial city; until then most of the silk fabrics in France had been imported from Italy. Two main figures dominate the history of this new industry. In 1536, **Étienne Turquet**, a man from Piedmont, offered to bring silk and velvet weavers from Genoa and set up a factory in Lyon. François I, who was anxious to stem the flow of money out of the country as a result of purchases of foreign silks, accepted his offer. In 1804 **Joseph-Marie Jacquard** invented a loom which, by using a system of punched cards, enabled a single worker to do the work of six. The Croix-Rousse district was filled with house-workshops – the upper storeys contained the looms on which the workers wove the silk provided by the manufacturer.

In 1875, a revolution occurred in the silk industry; the introduction of mechanical looms and the change in fashion away from figured fabrics and brocades quickly reduced the silk-workers to abject poverty. Only a few looms continued to exist in Lyon, capable of

Vieux Lyon by Montée du Gourguillon

producing special fabrics at exorbitant prices. Ordinary silks were made by workers in rural areas where labour was less expensive.

Today natural silk imported from Italy or Japan now represents only a minute proportion of the quantities of fabric processed here. It is subject to extremely meticulous care and attention in the silk-workers' centre (Maison des Canuts, *see below*). The so-called "silk-style" weaving, though, using all sorts of fibres (glass, carbon, borum and aramide) remains one of Lyon's specialities.

The traditional know-how of the silk weavers has found direct applications in the production of highly sophisticated parts for the aeronautics, space and electronics industries.

Lyon Fair – In the Middle Ages, Lyon was "one of the keys to the kingdom", situated as it was on the frontiers of Savoy, Dauphiné, Italy and Germany on one side, and Beaujolais, Burgundy, Languedoc, Forez and the Auvergne on the other. In 1419, the heir to the French throne, the future Charles VII, having realised the value of this geographical situation in commercial terms, ordered two fairs to be held here every year; he made Lyon one of the largest warehouses in the world. Traders and merchants flocked here from every direction.

From 1463 onwards, thanks to Louis XI, the fairs were held four times a year. Re-established in 1916 after a long break, the **Lyon International Fair** maintains the city's tradition as a major centre of international business.

A European crossroads – Lyon lies at the centre of a motorway network that links the city to northern and southern Europe in the north–south direction and to the Massif Central, Switzerland and Italy in the east–west direction, via St-Étienne, Clermont-Ferrand, Geneva, Annecy, Chambéry and Grenoble.

Since 1981, in addition to the many fast rail links with the rest of France, Lyon has enjoyed even more rapid communications due to the high-speed train (TGV) service. There is a busy international airport, **Lyon-St-Exupéry**, to the east of the town and the Édouard-Herriot harbour to the south of the Gerland district is full of heavy barges waiting to sail up to Auxonne on the Saône.

Lyon puts on a new face – There has been much development in Lyon since the "daring" tower blocks of the 1930s. In order to ensure its success in the future, Lyon is developing a number of science and technology parks, which bring together scientific research, higher education and industry. The **Cité Internationale** is the site of an International Conference Centre, the head offices of Interpol, a hotel complex and a Museum of Contemporary Art. To the east, around the university campus, there are major technical research offices and, further out of town, the St-Exupéry TGV station, designed by Spanish architect Calatrava to resemble a bird taking flight, which provides a TGV link to the local airport.

DISCOVERING LYON

Vieux Lyon★★★

Lyon's old town, between Fourvière Hill and the Saône, includes the **St-Jean district** in the centre, the **St-Paul district** to the north and the **St-Georges district** to the south. This was once the town centre and the seat of all the corporations, in particular those representing silk-workers. Traders, bankers, clerks and royal dignitaries lived here in magnificent townhouses. Almost 300 of these mansions still stand, forming quite an exceptional example of Renaissance housing.

> **Location:** Sandwiched between the Saône and Fourvière Hill.
>
> **Kids:** The Musée des Automates; the astronomical clock in the cathedral; one of the performances by Le Guignol (even if you don't understand it).
>
> **Don't Miss:** The beautiful buildings of rue St-Jean and the neighbourhood; Galerie de Phillibert Delorme.

OLD TOWN

One of the main features of the old town is the numerous passages or alleyways known as **traboules** (from the Latin *trans ambulare* meaning "walking through") especially between rue St-Jean, rue des Trois-Maries and quai Romain-Rolland, rue St-Georges and quai Fulchiron. Since there was not enough space to build an extensive network of streets, these passageways, all perpendicular to the Saône, were built to link the buildings together; they are quite fascinating. The houses reflect their period of construction (15C–17C) and there are several architectural styles.

The **Late Gothic houses** are distinguishable by the elegant decoration on the Flamboyant façades. The windows are often set asymmetrically into the walls. Most of the old houses, among them the most beautiful of all the mansions, are built in the **Renaissance style**. The basic structure remains unchanged, but the buildings are bigger and include new decorative features of Italian inspiration. The staircase turrets are beautiful; each courtyard has galleries, one above the other, each with surbased arches.

The **French Renaissance houses** are fewer in number. There is a noticeable return to Antiquity with the inclusion of architectural orders. The famous architect **Philibert Delorme** (1515–70), a native of Lyon, launched the new fashion with the gallery on squinches at No. 8 rue Juiverie. The main staircase, which was often rectangular, was set in the centre of the façade.

The **late-16C and pre-Classical houses** are distinguished by severe architectural lines. The decoration on the façade appears above the ground floor and includes triangular pediments with a central arch stone in relief, and rusticated bonding. The galleries overlooking the courtyard show Florentine influence with rounded arches supported by round columns.

WALKING TOURS

1 ST-JEAN AND ST-PAUL DISTRICTS

Place St-Jean
In the centre is a fountain with four basins topped by a small pavilion. To the east of the square is the cathedral of St-Jean and the choir school.

Manécanterie
To the right of the west front on place St-Jean is the 12C choir school. The front of the building, which lost 0.80m of its overall height when the ground level was raised, is decorated with a blind storey topped by red-brick encrustations, colonnettes and niches containing statues of human figures.

VIEUX LYON

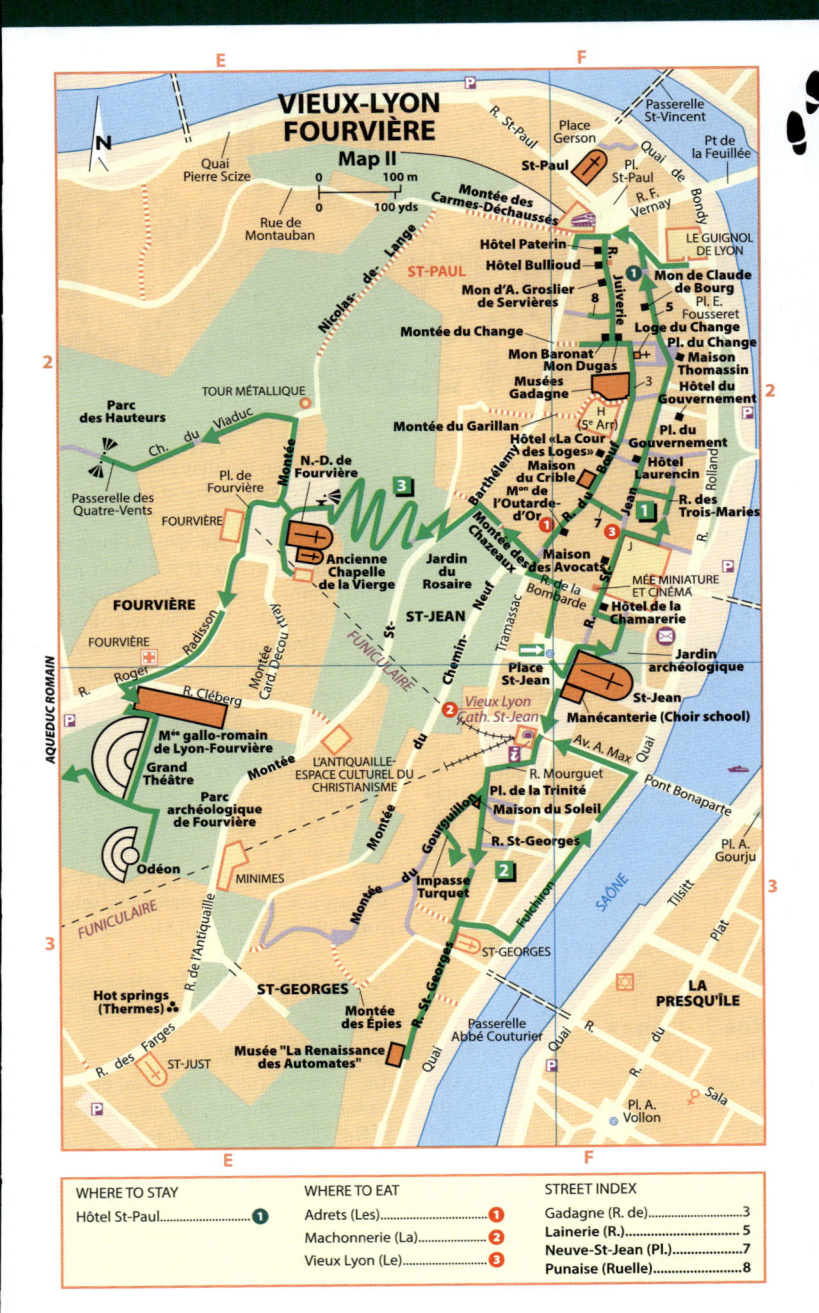

WHERE TO STAY	WHERE TO EAT	STREET INDEX
Hôtel St-Paul............①	Adrets (Les)............①	Gadagne (R. de)............3
	Machonnerie (La)............②	Lainerie (R.)............5
	Vieux Lyon (Le)............③	Neuve-St-Jean (Pl.)............7
		Punaise (Ruelle)............8

Primatiale St-Jean★

Dating originally from the 12C, St-Jean Cathedral is a Gothic building erected to complete a Romanesque apse. On the exterior the most notable features are the four towers, two on the west front and two over the arms of the transept. They are only slightly higher than the nave. In 1245 and 1274 the cathedral was the setting for the two Councils of Lyon.

319

Place St-Jean, Basilique Notre-Dame on the Fourvière Hill in the background

In the following century it was chosen for the consecration of Pope John XXII. In 1600, Henri IV married Marie de' Medici here.

▷ Skirt the cathedral to the right on rue St-Étienne and go to the archaeological gardens.

Jardin Archéologique

In this archaeological park visitors can see the remains of several buildings that have occupied the former site of the church of St-Étienne to the north of the present cathedral, since the 4C. They include Gallo-Roman baths, a palaeo-Christian baptistery and an arch from the 15C church of Ste-Croix.

▷ The narrow rue Ste-Croix leads to rue St-Jean.

Rue St-Jean★★

This was the main street in the old town of Lyon and, as such, royal corteges and religious processions passed along it. **No. 7** has a Flamboyant Gothic façade. The old **Hôtel de la Chamarerie** at **No. 37** was built in the 16C for the cleric responsible for overseeing the cathedral cloisters, who was known as the chamarier.

The arcading in the galleries of the **Maison des Avocats★** (Barristers' House) is supported on massive columns, and the outbuildings have pink roughcast. Seen from rue de la Bombarde, the house presents a fine example of 16C architecture in the Italian style. **No. 58** has an unusual feature in the shape of a well with a tripartite roof so that it is accessible from the courtyard, the staircase and the workshop. At **No. 54**, the **longest traboule** in old Lyon crosses five courtyards before reaching **No. 27 rue du Bœuf**. Walk past the Palais de Justice to **No. 52**: the house of printer Guillaume Leroy (late 15C) has a spiral staircase in a round tower. The bays are supported on arches. **No. 50** is a fine example of a renovated courtyard enhanced by galleries and a spiral staircase.

The same features can be admired at **No. 42**, which has retained its corbelled passageway resting on sculpted consoles. At **No. 36**, a house dating from the late 15C, there is a polygonal tower containing a spiral staircase.

▷ Take rue du Palais-de-Justice and turn left onto rue des Trois-Maries.

Rue des Trois-Maries

The "Street of the Three Marys" derives its name from the niche on the pediment of **No. 7** containing a statue of the Virgin Mary flanked by two Holy Women. On the same side of the street, numerous traboules lead off downhill to the Saône. At **No. 3** a handsome example of French Renaissance has a staircase surmounted by a tower in the centre of its façade; this feature is repeated in the house at **No. 5 place du Gouvernement**. The façade of **No. 4** is adorned with a regular arrangement of fluted pilasters and, in the courtyard, a tower in which the spiral staircase is clearly visible.

VIEUX LYON

▶ Retrace your steps to No. 6, and cross the traboule leading across two restored courtyards to No. 27 rue St-Jean.

The façade at **No. 27** has mullioned windows framed by fluted pilasters. **No. 28** conceals a magnificent **courtyard**★★ with an imposing tower with a spiral staircase inside it. The **Hôtel Laurencin** at **No. 24** has a crenellated octagonal tower containing a spiral staircase.

▶ Cross place de la Baleine and go to place du Gouvernement.

Place du Gouvernement

The façade of **No. 5**, its doorways topped by wrought-iron imposts and a stone balcony, dates from the early 17C. **Hôtel du Gouvernement** (16C) stands at **No. 2**. The upper courtyard lies at the end of a long roofed passageway. All that remains of the well to the right is the shell-shaped top (note the *traboule* at No. 10 quai Romain-Rolland).

▶ Rejoin rue St-Jean and walk on until you reach place du Change.

Place du Change

This square, originally called place de la Draperie, was frequented by moneylenders in the 15C and 16C. The **Loge du Change** was designed mainly by Soufflot, the architect who altered the original design between 1747 and 1750. On the upper storey are engaged columns topped by Ionic capitals and carved entablatures. Opposite is the **Maison Thomassin** which has a 15C façade built in the 14C style. On the second floor the mullioned ogee bays rising to trefoiled arches are set into Gothic arches decorated with coats of arms.

▶ Continue along rue Lainerie.

Rue Lainerie

Note the vaulted corridor of **No. 18**. The **Maison de Claude de Bourg** at **No. 14** has a 15C flower-decked façade which is typical of Lyon, with ornate accolades.

▶ To the right is rue Louis-Garrand and the Guignol puppet theatre.

Rue Lainerie opens onto place St-Paul, where you can glimpse the train station and, further back, the **church**.

▶ Turn left onto rue Juiverie.

Rue Juiverie★

The Jews were expelled from this street in the late 14C and the Italian bankers who replaced them had luxurious mansions built. The **Hôtel Paterin**, also known as "Henri IV's House", at **No. 4** is an outstanding example of Renaissance architecture. The **staircase** in the courtyard, with its three tiers of arches, one above the other, supported on massive columns, is particularly impressive.

At **No. 8**, the second courtyard in the **Hôtel Bulliod** contains the famous **gallery**★★ designed by **Philibert Delorme**, a gem of French Renaissance architecture in Lyon. Delorme built it in 1536 on his return from Rome. The Renaissance façade on the **Maison Antoine Groslier de Servières** (**No. 10**) has five arches on the ground floor topped by triangular or broken pediments of black marble. In the courtyard is a round tower with mullioned windows containing a spiral staircase. The corbels on the balcony on the first floor are carved with human figures. The house at **No. 21** has ogee windows with rounded frontons. There is

Gallery, Hôtel Bulliou, no. 8 rue Juiverie

© M&G Therin-Weise/age fotostock

321

DISCOVERING LYON

Le Guignol de Lyon – Compagnie des Zonzons

Guignol, the satirical puppet, is characterised by his black cap under which he has a short plait he calls his *sarsifis*. His naïvety and waggish banter make him a perfect example of the "urchins" of Lyon. His wife, Madelon, with whom he has frequent arguments, is a model wife, if somewhat prone to grumbling. His inseparable friend is Gnafron whose most notable features are his tall stature and his ruddy nose, an indication of his marked liking for Beaujolais. If anybody asks him what he does for a living, he answers, "Educated people call us cobblers or botchers; the uneducated call us gowks" *("gnafres")*. Shows at the Guignol theatre are now a blend of tradition and modern innovation, influenced by contemporary authors and even films.

a Gallo-Roman cellar in its basement. Between **Nos. 16** and **18** rises the picturesque, steep **ruelle Punaise**, which leads onto montée St-Barthélémy. In the Middle Ages it served as an open sewer. The mansion at **No. 20** was built by a wealthy 15C gentleman, E Grolier. The façade is decorated with mullioned windows flanked by colonnettes. At **No. 22** is the **Maison Baronat**, which has a corbelled corner turret overlooking montée du Change. At **No. 23**, at the corner of rue de la Loge, is the **Maison Dugas** whose long façade is decorated with bosses and lions' heads.

▶ Turn left onto rue de la Loge, then right into rue de Gadagne.

Musée Gadagne★

This mansion stretches from No. 10 to No. 14 rue de Gadagne and is the largest Renaissance building in the old town. In 1545, it was purchased by the **Gadagne Brothers**, bankers of Italian origin who had amassed a colossal fortune. Indeed, the expression "as rich as Gadagne" became a local figure of speech.

Musée Historique de Lyon★
In the Local History Museum the rooms on the ground floor have been laid out with **religious sculpture★**, including bas-relief sculptures from old churches or abbeys in Lyon, in particular from Ainay, St-Pierre and Île Barbe (Annunciation bas-relief, a mantelpiece known as "Charlemagne's Crown").

Musée International de la Marionnette★
The exhibits of this museum include not only Guignol and a number of glove puppets, but also an outstanding collection of string and rod puppets and shadow figures from France, England, Belgium, Holland, Venice, Turkey, Russia and the Far East.

▶ Walk across place du Petit-Collège and along rue du Bœuf.

Rue du Bœuf

This street owes its name to the statue of a bull at the corner of place Neuve-St-Jean.
The street contains some lovely examples of Renaissance architecture, some now occupied by luxury hotels. At **No. 6**, "La Cour des Loges" Hotel occupies a fine set of four restored houses. It is possible, with discretion or perhaps stopping for refreshment, to have a look at the beautiful courtyard with its U-shaped galleries on three floors.
No. 14 leads into a pretty courtyard with a polygonal tower and galleries supported on arches surmounted by a frieze of Greek motifs.
The **Maison du Crible★** at **No. 16** dates from the 17C. It has an ornate doorway with bosses and ringed columns topped by a pediment decorated with a small carving of the Adoration of the Magi said to have been the work of Giambologna. An alleyway leads to an inner courtyard in which the elegant round tower, with

staggered openings, owes its name, **Tour Rose** (Pink Tower), to the colour of its famous roughcast. *Do not go up to the terraced gardens.*

Place Neuve-St-Jean
This old street was transformed into a square under the Consulat. At **No. 4** is a vast building set slightly back from the others which features a superb staircase over arches corresponding to galleries with surbased arches.

▶ Return to rue du Bœuf.

The **Maison de l'Outarde d'Or** (House of the Golden Bustard) stands out at **No. 19** because of its carved stone sign. The courtyard is particularly interesting for its two turrets. One of them is round; the other, corbelled, is a rectangle built on an upturned pyramid.

Another building of interest can be seen at **No. 27** (the longest *traboule* in Lyon, leading to **No. 54** rue St-Jean) with an elegant 16C spiral staircase preceding three courtyards.

No. 36 opens onto a pretty courtyard decorated with restored galleries. It is interesting to compare these with those of **No. 38**, which are largely sealed up by additional structures. Most of the galleries were closed off when the district's fortunes sank to make more space and to retain heat.

▶ No. 31 opens onto rue de la Bombarde (on the right). Almost opposite, take rue des Antonins, which leads back to place St-Jean.

From St-Jean métro station it is possible to take the funicular railway up to the top of Fourvière hill and come back down the same way after visiting the Basilica, Gallo-Roman Museum and Roman theatres.

2 ST-GEORGES DISTRICT

▶ Walk from place St-Jean to place de la Trinité (follow rue Mourguet).

Place de la Trinité
The **Maison du Soleil**, which became famous after inspiring the backcloth for the Guignol puppet theatre, lends an old-fashioned touch to the square.

Montée du Gourguillon
Set on the hillside in the Fourvière district, this was the usual route taken by carriages heading for the Auvergne in the Middle Ages. It is difficult to imagine the heavy loads coming up such a steep slope. It was also the direct route between the cloisters of St-Jean belonging to the Canon-Counts, and St-Just, the fortified town of the Canon-Barons. At **No. 2** stands a Renaissance house. Slightly further up the hill is the **Impasse Turquet**, a picturesque passageway with old timber galleries.

Rue St-Georges
The ground floor of **No. 3** has basket-handled arches and the springer of the door is decorated with two rampant wrought-iron lions. At **No. 3 bis** the springer is decorated with a phoenix rising from the flames. At **No. 6**, the 16C house has a fine interior courtyard (art gallery). The spiral staircase is set in a round tower with sloping windows.

▶ Continue to no. 100 if you want to visit the Automata Museum.

♿♙ Musée des Automates
100 rue St-Georges.
♿*Daily 2–6pm.* *1 May, 3rd Mon in Sept, 25 Dec.* €7 (child 3–17, €5).
04 72 77 75 28.
www.museeautomates.com.
Seven rooms house 250 automata in perfect working order, displayed according to cultural, traditional and regional themes.

▶ Turn right at Église St-Georges and return via quai Fulchiron.

3 THE MONTÉES
see FOURVIÈRE HILL

Fourvière Hill★

The Fourvière district of Lyon stands on a hill of the same name; the term **Fourvière** is said to come from the Latin *forum vetus*, relating to the forum situated in the heart of the Roman colony established in 43 BCE; its theatre, odeon and aqueducts have survived to this day. The forum, which stood on the site now occupied by the esplanade in front of the basilica, is said to have collapsed in 840. In the 3C, people moved from the side of the hill and the stones were reused to rebuild the town at the bottom of the slope. In the Middle Ages the hill was largely given over to farming (in particular vineyards). In the 17C, numerous religious orders set up monasteries and convents here, which inspired the historian, Michelet, to make his famous comment about Fourvière, "the hill that prays" opposite La Croix-Rousse "the hill that works". Nowadays Fourvière, with its basilica, Roman monuments and museum is, with the old town below, one of the most popular tourist venues in Lyon.

- **Location:** Situated to the W of the Saône, dominating Vieux-Lyon.
- **Kids:** The tree-climbing adventure (Go Ape in the UK).
- **Don't Miss:** The spectacular view from the Fourvière Basilica.

WALKING TOUR

3 THE MONTÉES
see p307 for map.

The *montées*, or rises, consist of winding flights of steps or steeply sloping streets that climb the Fourvière hill, providing superb views down over the old town. Each of them has its own charm.

Montée des Chazeaux
With its 228 very steep steps, it leads onto montée St-Barthélémy.

Jardin du Rosaire★
Daily, 6.30am–9.30pm.
The **great rose gardens** are laid out between the lake and quai Achille-

---

Les Montées

Winding staircases or steep streets, "Les Montées" scale Fourvière Hill, offering dramatic views over the old town.
Montée des Carmes-Déchaussés – This derives its name (Rise of the Barefoot Carmelites) from the monastery founded in the early 17C which now houses the Regional Archives; it has 238 steps.
Montée du Change – This links rue de la Loge to montée St-Barthélémy. On the way down, there are interesting views of the spires on the church of St-Nizier which rises from the buildings on the banks of the Saône.
Montée du Garillan★ – This is a remarkable series of zigzag flights of steps (224 steps).
Montée du Chemin-Neuf and Montée St-Barthélémy – From these steps there is an extensive view over the rooftops of the old town and St-Jean Cathedral.
Montée du Gourguillon – See St-Georges district, p311.
Montée des Épies – This rise climbs up above the St-Georges district, high above the church dedicated to St George, a neo-Gothic building designed by Bossan, the architect also responsible for Fourvière Basilica.

FOURVIÈRE HILL

Lignon, and boast 70 000 plants representing 350 varieties which are a stunning sight between June and October. The road, which climbs in zigzags (30min) is used each day by students attending a nearby school, by employees keen to find parking spaces close to Vieux Lyon and by pilgrims: note the numbered brass roses marking the route. The zigzags criss-cross woodland areas of maple, yew and boxwood. Owned by the church but managed by the city council, the garden is adorned with small flowery interludes. With its stunning vistas over the city and its welcome shade, the place is a popular location for picnics.

For a 360-degree **panoramic view**★★ climb to the foot of the basilica's observatory; from there the hillsides of the Lyonnais area, Mont Pilat and Mont-d'Or are visible and, in good weather, the Alps and Mont Blanc to the west and the Puy de Dôme to the east.

Lyon viewed from Basilique Notre-Dame

Basilique Notre-Dame★

The history of the religious buildings erected in honour of the Virgin Mary on the site of the Roman forum spans 800 years. The massive basilica standing today at the top of Fourvière hill is an integral part of the Lyon landscape. The basilica is a famous place of pilgrimage built to designs by an architect named Bossan after the Franco-Prussian War (1870) in fulfilment of a vow taken by Monsignor de Genouilhac, the Archbishop of Lyon, who undertook to build a church if the enemy did not approach the city.

Crenellated walls with machicolations, flanked by octagonal towers, form an odd blend of Byzantine and medieval features. The abundance of decoration inside (nave and crypt) is no less unusual.

Ancienne Chapelle de la Vierge

To the right of the basilica stands the real pilgrimage chapel dating from the 18C: the former Lady Chapel containing a statue of the Virgin Mary (16C).

Musée de Fourvière

This museum, housed in the chapel and buildings once belonging to the Jesuit Order, contains a collection of polychrome wooden statues (12C–19C), various projects designed for the basilica in the 19C, and votive offerings.

▶ Take the montée Nicolas-de-Lange to the right of the basilica.

Montée Nicolas-de-Lange

The 560 steps here mean that there a total of 798 steps lead to place St-Paul from the metal tower (Tour Métallique) on Fourvière.

Parc des Hauteurs

Follow a path to the left, just before the Tour Métallique.

This ambitious project was set up to enhance visitors' appreciation of Fourvière hill by laying out panoramic walks. The most original construction is that of the "Chemin du Viaduc", a footbridge that gives a breathtaking **view**★ down onto Lyon and La Croix-Rousse.

Musée de Gallo-Romains de Lyon-Fourvière

Musée de Gallo-Romains de Lyon-Fourvière★★
♿⏰*Tue–Fri 11am–6pm, Sat–Sun 10am–6pm (Roman theater 15 Apr–15 Sept 7am–9pm; 16 Sept–14 Apr 7am–7pm).* 🚫*1 Jan, 1 May, 1 Nov, 25 Dec.* 💶*€6, free 1st Sun of the month.* 📞*04 72 38 49 30.*
lugdunum.grandlyon.com.
This museum stands on the hill at Fourvière, at the heart of the district that was once the plateau of the ancient town of Lugdunum. The museum displays thematic exhibitions of its mainly Gallo-Roman collections.
An adjacent archaeological site, opened in 1933, brought to light ancient and medieval public buildings in the district: Gallo-Roman baths in rue des Farges, remains of early basilica in rue des Macchabées and quai Fulchiron.

Théâtres Romains
The group of buildings uncovered near rue de l'Antiquaille includes a theatre built during the reign of Caesar Augustus (1C BCE) and extended during the reign of Hadrian (2C) and an odeum.

Grand Théâtre
This is the oldest theatre in France. It is similar in size to those in Arles and Orange (108m in diameter) but smaller than the one in Vienne. The number of tiers of seats was later increased by building on top of the promenades.

The outer circular wall of the theatre shows substructures in which archaeologists have noted the particular attention paid by the builders to exits via underground corridors and to ground drainage through a system of pipes and sewers. The stage curtain machinery, housed in the orchestra pit, is some of the best preserved of its kind in the world.

▶ Climb the staircase leading to the top of the tiers of seats.

From here, the full size of the theatre can be appreciated. It is possible to walk round the upper section by following the Roman road of large granite slabs.

▶ Walk down the Roman road to the odeum.

Area Overlooking the Theatre
Beyond the paved road behind the theatre, recent excavations have revealed the existence of an impressive residence and not, as was thought at one time, a temple dedicated to Cybele. From the late 1C BCE there stood on this huge rectangular esplanade a vast and magnificent house, bordered on one side by shops sheltered by a portico.

FOURVIÈRE HILL

Life at the Crossroads

As the "Gateway to the south of France", Lyon combines the better qualities of the north of France in a more Mediterranean context, embodied not least by the red pantile roofs. Lyon enjoys not only the reputation of being a major, hard-working city, but also of having an outstanding standard of living in which good food plays a leading role. Life in Lyon is characterised above all by its lack of stress or complication. The Lyonnais are creatures of habit, and some of their favourite pastimes can be appreciated by visitors to the city as well, such as watching (perhaps even playing!) the odd game of boules, especially during the boules tournament at Whitsun; taking a quiet stroll along the banks of the Saône or Rhône or a gentle wander around the sloping streets of La Croix-Rousse, or indulging in a little shopping spree on the peninsula or in the Part-Dieu district. Then there is the pleasure of drinking in the sumptuous Renaissance architecture in the old town, or the peacefulness of the Tête d'Or park early in the morning, not forgetting the rose garden which is an absolute must in June. Locals enjoy lengthy conversations over a bottle of Beaujolais in one of the city's cafés, the somewhat noisier delights of local festivals, convivial lunches in a crowded Lyon *bouchon*, surrounded by the delicious rich smell of Lyonnais cuisine; and finally, for those who are young at heart, a Sunday afternoon spent watching the antics of the Guignol puppets.

Aqueducs Romains
On either side of the start of rue Roger-Radisson (once the road west to Aquitaine) are the interesting remains of one of the four aqueducts that provided the town's water supply.

SAINT-JUST QUARTER★

The long shopping street, rue de Trion, runs along the site of an ancient necropolis that flanked three Roman roads, hence its name.

▶ Turn right into rue St-Alexandre.

The square of the same name has a few low houses, one with a turret staircase.

▶ Take the charming rue des Macchabées, climbing between garden walls until you reach the church of St-Irénée.

The church and calvary of St-Irénée were rebuilt in the 19C, but the church occupies the site of an ancient 5C basilica, which houses the relics of St-Irénée, on of the founders of the Christian community in Lyon.

▶ Continue along the rue des Macchabées, then take the montée de Choulans.

Mausolées de Choulans
In the centre of place Wernert are three mausoleums that serve as reminders of the Gallo-Roman burial ground situated outside the town walls. The one in the centre, the oldest of the three (1C BCE), bears an inscription on one of the sides indicating that the monument was built by emancipated slaves once belonging to Calvius Turpion.

Rue des Macchabées
The street owes its name to the former cloister of the Maccabees. This important property was destroyed by Protestants in 1562, but a mural on the wall of no. 17 (as well as marks on the ground of the archaeological garden a little further to the right, revives the memory.

▶ Continue as far as rue de Trion and turn right towards rue des Farges.

Thermes Romains
Go under the porch of the residence that faces church of St-Just to discover the foundations of some of the municipal baths built around year 50; the visible part is the south side of the building.

▶ Retrace your steps to the funicular, by which you can return to the cathedral.

Place des Terreaux with the fountain by Bartholdi

La Presqu'île and its Squares★★

Lyon's main city centre districts lie around place Bellecour. "La Presqu'île" – the Peninsula – has long been the setting of the Lyon trading centre, and until the 19C, commerce centred on rue Mercière. Two main pedestrian precincts run across it linking place des Terreaux to Perrache railway station. They are rue de la République to the north and rue Victor-Hugo to the south. La Presqu'île is the modern face of Lyon, and it was an important counterpoint to Vieux-Lyon during the Middle Ages and the Renaissance. Many picturesque streets still exist from this time. The Rue de la République in particular is bustling with department stores, shops, cinemas and bistros, and the street is lined with buildings typical of 19C Lyon. Their façades incorporate tall windows and lintels decorated with cut sheet-metal signs. The districts to the south of place Bellecour skirt the former Île des Canabae district, the site of Ainay Abbey.

> **Location:** A walking tour of La Presqu'île, sandwiched between the Rhône and the Saône, is the best way to get a feel for the city; this is where you'll find most of the shops and restaurants. The area is well served by the metro (A), and at the centre is the huge place Bellecour.
>
> **Don't Miss:** The Musée des Beaux-Arts; the painted walls of the City of the Creation.

WALKING TOURS

1 PLACE DES TERREAUX TO SAINT-NIZIER

Place des Terreaux
This square is the hub of city life. It derives its name from the filling-in of a former bed of the Rhône by soil or leaf mould. The confluence of the rivers was situated nearby in Roman times. The famous monumental **lead fountain**★ was made by the sculptor Bartholdi. Its four quivering horses symbolise the rivers running towards the ocean. The south side of the square is bordered by the 17C façade of the Palais St-Pierre. In

LYON
LA PRESQU'ÎLE
map III

WHERE TO STAY

Artistes (Hôtel des).................. ①
Célestins (Hôtel)...................... ②
Élysée (Hôtel).......................... ③
Résidence (Hôtel La)................ ④
St-Vincent (Hôtel).................... ⑤

WHERE TO EAT

Brunet...................................... ①
Caro de Lyon........................... ②
Étage (L')................................. ③
Fédérations (Café des)............. ④
Jura (Le).................................. ⑤
Mercière (Le)........................... ⑥
Poêlon d'Or (Le)...................... ⑦
203 (Café le)............................ ⑧

1994, D Buren was entrusted with the restoration of the square. He added an area of granite paving slabs in a harmonious pattern with 14 pillars and 69 water jets. The whole installation is illuminated to great effect at night.

Hôtel de Ville
This remarkable city hall, part Louis XIII in style, was designed by Simon Maupin. It consists of a large rectangle of buildings flanked by pavilions. Inside is the main courtyard, an unusual construction on two levels separated by a semicircular porch. The original façade of the Hôtel de Ville facing place des Terreaux was destroyed by fire in 1674. Jules Hardouin-Mansart and Robert de Cotte were commissioned to refurbish the building, and they radically transformed the façade. The side pavilions and belfry were topped by a dome. In the centre, a large rounded tympanum supported by telamones is adorned with an equestrian statue of Henry IV.

Palais St-Pierre★
Pl. des Terreaux.
This 17C and 18C building was formerly the abbey of the Ladies of St Peter, one of the oldest Benedictine abbeys in Lyon, whose nuns were recruited among the highest ranks of French aristocracy. Inside, the buildings have retained part of their original Italianate decor, particularly in the refectory and main staircase. The building fell into disuse during the Revolution and was turned into a museum in the 19C. In 1884 the artist Puvis de Chavannes painted the "Sacred Wood" in the staircase at the entrance to the Fine Arts Gallery.

Ancienne Église St-Pierre
Next to No. 23 rue Paul-Chenavard.
Note the narrow 12C façade of the former church of St-Pierre and the austere Romanesque doorway flanking superb 18C wooden doors.

Musée des Beaux-Arts★★★
20 pl. des Terreaux. Daily except Tue and public holidays 10am–6pm (Fri 10.30am–6pm). Museum €8; Exhibitions €9; Combined ticket €12. 04 72 10 17 40. www.mba-lyon.fr. At the heart of the museum, Les Terrasses Saint-Pierre café-restaurant offers light meals.
From place des Terreaux, enter the gardens in the former cloisters, where the galleries are surmounted by terraces. Tall loggias crown the corner pavilions on the south side. The statues here include The Shadow by Rodin and Carpeaux at Work by Bourdelle. The Musée des Beaux-Arts ranks among the finest museums in France. Its splendid collections, carefully displayed, have been further enriched by the donation of 35

Courtyard, Musée des Beaux-Arts

LA PRESQU'ÎLE AND ITS SQUARES

Exploring the Traboules

The *traboules* are private property and some are therefore kept closed by their owners. However, many of the most interesting are open to visitors under the terms of an agreement drawn up between the city of Lyon, the owners and the urban community. They can be accessed by pressing the entry button, usually to be found above the intercom or entry-code number pads by each main street door. Other *traboules*, not usually open to the public, can be visited as part of a guided tour organised by the Lyon tourist office. Before beginning a visit, it is advisable to ask at the tourist office for the list of passages that are open to visitors. The best time to explore many of the interior courtyards described in this section is in the morning.

---

famous Impressionist and modern paintings of Jacqueline Delubac's private collection. The Fine Arts Gallery presents an exceptional overview of art through the centuries, throughout the world. Its collections are organised into five separate departments: painting, sculpture, antiquities, objets d'art and medals.

Paintings
The rooms contain a selection of works from the great periods in European painting.

Sculpture
There are works from the Romanesque to the Gothic and Renaissance periods. Among the 17C to early-20C works, the most outstanding are busts by Coysevox and Lemoyne, and marble and bronze statues by Etex, Pradier, Bourdelle, Maillol and Rodin.

Antiquities
This department consists of three sections organised by theme. The **Egyptian** section contains the most extensive collections covering art from all the Ancient Egyptian periods.
In the **Near and Middle East section**, note the "priest's head" from Assyria, heads of statues from Cyprus and lead sarcophagi from Roman Syria (3C–6C). The final section covers art from **Ancient Greece and Rome**, and includes an exceptional Korah (statue of a young girl) from the Acropolis illustrating the degree of skill attained by the sculptors of Ancient Greece.

Objets d'Art
This section of the museum comprises a huge variety of exhibits from all ages and all continents.

Quai St-Vincent
From the quay there are views over the meander in the Saône overlooked by a row of buildings with Art Nouveau façades (caryatids, floral patterns).
Upriver is a vast architectural complex, known as Les Subsistances, consisting of an early-17C cloister, later turned into an army supply-storage space and extended by the addition of a large square building with two mills in the centre. The restored complex is now occupied by artists (*visits: information available at the mill*).

▶ Turn back along the quai St-Vincent.

Quai de la Pêcherie
Secondhand booksellers occupy the quai at weekends. The fresco of the city library opposite is dedicated to writers of the region (Rabelais, Stendhal, Clavel, Saint-Exupéry, Chevallier…).

▶ Follow the rue de la Platière as far as place Meissonier.

Quartier de Saint-Nizier
The central fountain (19C) is dedicated to Pleney, a benefactor of the city.

▶ Take rue Paul-Chenavart on the right to return to the place St-Nizier.

DISCOVERING LYON

Église St-Nizier
Tradition has it that the present church of St-Nizier, much of which dates from the 15C, was built on the site of Lyon's very first church. On the outside, the nave is supported by double flying buttresses, which can be seen clearly from rue de la Fromagerie. The spires on the bell-towers of the church of St-Nizier are one of the outstanding features of Lyon's urban landscape.

▶ The rue de la Fromagerie leads to rue Édouard-Herriot.

The ancient street of the Empress, displaying the influence of Haussmann, contains many banks and luxury shops. At the corner of rue de la Poulaillerie, the **clock** is driven by Guignol and his friends.

▶ Take the rue de la Poulaillerie. Go into No. 13 to admire the magnificent Renaissance courtyard, which houses the Printing Museum.

Musée de l'Imprimerie★★
13 rue de la Poulaillerie.
Daily except Mon and Tue 10.30am–6pm. 1 Jan, 1 May, 1 Nov, 25 Dec. €6 (€8 during temporary exhibits). 04 78 37 65 98. www.imprimerie.lyon.fr.
The splendid late-15C Hôtel de la Couronne, once the property of a rich merchant, houses this printing museum. The collections retrace the glorious history of printing, from the invention of the printing press in the 15C.

Rue de la République
Many banks line the street leading to the **Stock Exchange★**. Renovated in 1994, the gardens around the Exchange have attractive displays of magnolia, rhododendron and azalea contained by box hedgerows. The façade of the **Palais du Commerce**, contemporary with the rue de la République, is decorated with allegories of trade, peace and abundance. The faces of the many buildings are typical of 19C Lyon, with high windows and decorative lintels, decorated with cut sheet-metal signs. The pedestrian precinct, Les Cordeliers, is very commercial and popular; this "street of the king" is bustling with department stores, shops, cinemas and brasseries.

▶ Turn right into the rue de l'Arbre-Sec, then turn into the rues du Garet and Pizay.

Rues de Bouchons
The Lyonnais version of a bistro is known as a *bouchon*, and in the evening, the lively streets close to Lyon Opera House come alive with the chatter of diners. Tables spill out onto the street, and the aroma of Lyon's finest food lingers in the air. The rue Pizay opens out onto the place de la Comédie where street dancers perform to hip-hop and rap. On the left stands the Opéra de Lyon, also known as the Grand Theatre.

Opéra de Lyon
See ADDRESSES for ticket information.
On the south side of the square, opposite the Hôtel de Ville, stands the Lyon opera house, the result of a successful modernisation scheme.
The façade of the old building has been preserved and the eight muses of the pediment appear to hold up the immense and splendid glass semi-cylindrical roof, the design of the architect **Jean Nouvel**. With a capacity of 1 300 seats, The Opéra includes an orchestra (60 musicians), a ballet (30 dancers), a choir (26 singers), a troupe and a solid expertise. With Ivan Fischer holding the baton, l'Opéra National de Lyon is an international-class company.
A 200-seat amphitheatre is the stage for a more varied programme, including classical, jazz and world music. The building takes on a particularly impressive appearance during the evening illuminations, which floodlight it in predominantly red tones, throwing its architectural contours into sharp relief.

LA PRESQU'ÎLE AND ITS SQUARES

Place Louis-Pradel
The square is decorated with a fountain and sculptures by Ipoustéguy. It is an aesthetic combination of old and modern forms.

2 LES CORDELIERS TO BELLECOUR

Église St-Bonaventure
St Bonaventura Church, cherished by the people of Lyon, has retained its original Franciscan layout. The bareness and simplicity of the architecture are a reminder of the Franciscans' respect for all forms of poverty.

Rue Grenette
This street was bustling with commerce at the time of the Renaissance, although you will no longer find any traces of that period; even the granary has disappeared. At the corner of rue Edouard Herriot stop to admire the symbolic mirrors and staffs in the secular café of the traders.

Rue Mercière★
Today pedestrianised, the rue Mercière was formerly one of the most important arteries of Lyon; the name itself, originally "Mercatoria", means "merchants". Today the street stands as a monument to those past times, and you will see many arches, and the remnants of old shops. Nos. 48, 50 and 52 in particular have beautiful Renaissance façades of red sandstone. No. 56 was where the first book in French was printed. This large mansion conceals a courtyard with galleries in the Italian style.

Place des Jacobins
The main feature of the square is the majestic Dominicans' fountain, erected in 1886 in memory of four local artists: Philibert Delorme, Hippolyte Flandrin, Guillaume Coustou and Gérard Audran.

Quartier des Célestins
The charming place des Célestins, which faces the 19C Italian theatre, is planted with magnolia. Beneath it, you will find the most amazing architectural achievement, of which a periscope in the middle of the square gives a general view.
To access the **underground Célestin-car park★**, take the elevator on the right. A spiral ramp loops around a central well, and the architectural lines are accentuated by alternating black and white paintings. At the bottom, a tilted circular mirror reflects the arches viewed through the periscope above. Titled "Sens dessus dessous" (Above and Below), the car park was designed by Daniel Buren and Michel Targe.

▶ Take the rue des Archers, then to the left the rue Émile-Zola. The high arcades of this little street host luxury shops.

Place Bellecour
This famous Lyon square, overlooked by the distinctive outline of Fourvière Basilica on its hill to the west, is one of the largest in France. The huge symmetrical Louis XVI façades lining the west and east sides of the square date from 1800.

The equestrian statue of Louis XIV is known to the locals as the "Bronze Horse". The pedestal is decorated with two bronzes by the Coustou brothers (17C–18C) representing the Rhône and the Saône, each facing in the direction of its respective river. On either side of the pedestal is the inscription: "Masterpiece by Lemot, Sculptor from Lyon." An earlier equestrian statue of the great King by Desjardins (1691) was erected on this spot in 1713. The symbol of royalty was overturned, smashed and melted down during the French Revolution. The present statue (1828) was itself threatened in 1848: it was about to be pulled down when the Commissary Extraordinary of the Republic saved it by suggesting that, if the pompous inscription in honour of Ludovicus Magnus were replaced by an homage to the talent of Lemot, this would constitute just as much of an attack on royalty.

To the south-east of the square, the bell-tower of the 17C former almshouse, the **Hôpital de la Charité**, stands on its own in front of the main post office.

Musée des Tissus

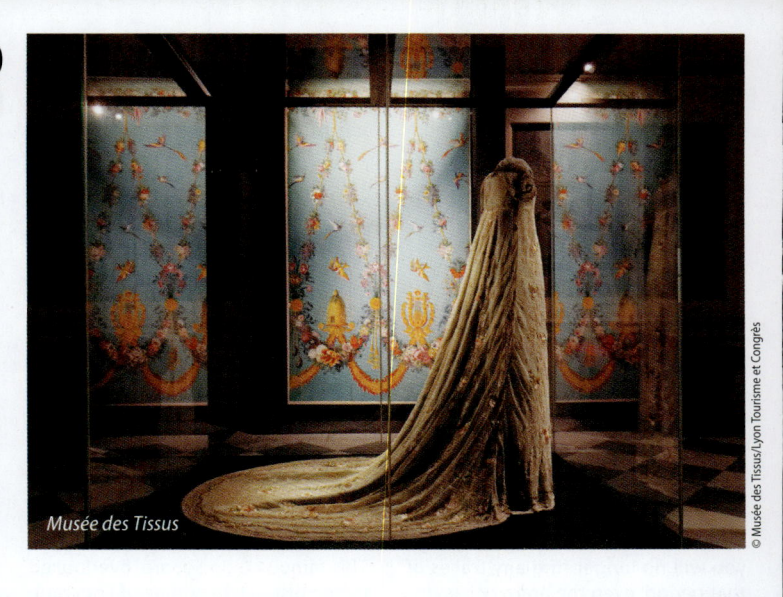

To the north-east of the square, the Banque Nationale de Paris stands on the site of the cinema where the first films by the cinematographer **Lumière** were shown.

3 FROM BELLECOUR TO CARNOT

Place Bellecour
See Place Bellecour p321.

Basilique St-Martin-d'Ainay
This church consecrated by Pope Pascal II in 1107 has undergone major alterations. The porch-belfry is topped by a pyramid roof, surrounded by unusual corner acroteria which give it its characteristic outline. Note the animal frieze beneath the cornice between the second and third levels, and the decoration of inlaid bricks.

Musée des Tissus★★★
34 rue de la Charité. Daily except Mon 10am–6pm. Public holidays, Easter. €12 (combined ticket with Musée des Arts Décoratifs).
04 78 38 42 00. www.mtmad.fr.
The Textile Museum, founded by the Lyon Chamber of Commerce over a century ago and housed in the Hôtel de Villeroy (1730), former residence of the governor of the province, is the pride of the Lyon people, and a veritable "repository" of decorative fabrics. The prestigious collections come from the most influential Western and Eastern countries as regards fabric design and production.

Musée des Arts Décoratifs★★
34 rue de la Charité. Same as Musée des Tissus. €12 (combined ticket).
This museum is mainly devoted to 18C furnishings. The collection includes pieces of furniture, objets d'art, musical instruments, tapestries, porcelain and faience. Among the sections devoted to Medieval and Renaissance art, the gallery containing over 200 examples of Italian majolica is of special interest.

Musée des Confluences
86 Quai Perrache. Tue–Wed and Fri 11am–7pm; Thu 11am–10pm; Sat–Sun and public holidays 10am–7pm.
1 Jan, 1 May, 25 Dec. €9. 04 28 38 12 12. www.museedesconfluences.fr.
Open in December 2014, the Musée des Confluences, at the very end of Presqu'île, is Lyon's most ambitious museum, seeking to tell the story of the world. This is an all-embracing museum that should not be missed.

La Croix-Rousse

La Croix-Rousse (literally "The Russet Cross") owes its name to a coloured stone cross which stood at one of the district's crossroads in the days before the French Revolution. The district still has all the character and flavour of a small village community and today remains the last bastion of true Lyon traditionalism. The most fiercely proud inhabitants of La Croix-Rousse are deeply attached to the "Plateau" and look down from a distance on the hustle and bustle below. They might even spend months on end without going down the hill.

> - **Location:** The Croix-Rousse hill dominates Presqu'île to the north. Park, for safety, in one of the car parks in Presqu'île not on the hill, as cars are sometimes vandalised.
> - **Don't Miss:** The view from the rue Justin-Godart; the silk workshops; the gardens of the Grande-Côte.

A BIT OF HISTORY

The invention of new looms by **Joseph-Marie Jacquard** (1752–1834) led the "canuts" or silk-workers to abandon the low cottages in the St-Jean district and move to larger austere buildings with wide windows that let in the light. The *traboules* in La Croix-Rousse were used to move bolts of silk about the district without any risk of damage from inclement weather. In 1831, and again in 1834, they were the scene of bloody uprisings when the silk-workers waved black flags symbolising poverty and bearing the famous motto: "Life through work or death through conflict."

WALKING TOURS

1 HISTORIC TEXTILE WORKERS DISTRICT
Round tour starting at place des Terreaux.

Go to No. 6 (near the fountain), which communicates with rue Ste-Catherine. Turn right and walk down rue Romarin until you reach rue St-Polycarpe. Keep walking towards the church.

The **"Condition Publique des Soies"** at No. 7 has a porch in which the upper arch is decorated with a majestic lion's head and mulberry leaves. It was on these premises during the 19C that the hygrometric packing of silk cloth was monitored since, due to the fact that silk can absorb up to 15 percent of its weight in water, checks had to be made to ensure that the weight of the fabric actually complied with the official norms.

Walk up rue de l'Abbé-Rozier.

From No. 19 rue Leynaud (opposite No. 14), the passage Thiaffait (derelict) leads up a double flight of steps to rue Burdeau. Opposite No. 36 montée du Per-

> ### Ateliers de Soierie Vivante★
>
> This association was founded in 1993 to protect and promote the heritage of the Croix-Rousse silk working industry. It organises a number of tours of authentic family-run silk workshops, leaving from the Atelier Municipal de Passementerie, the municipal furniture trimmings workshop. Other workshops included in the tour are hand-loom weaving, machine-loom weaving, velvet weaving, making silk-wrapped thread and trimmings (gimping) and hand painting on silk. (21 rue Richan; guided tours (30min) 2pm and 4pm Tue–Sat. P7. t04 78 27 17 13. www.soierie-vivante.asso.fr).

DISCOVERING LYON

LYON
LA CROIX-ROUSSE
Map IV

WHERE TO EAT

Bouchon des Filles (Le).................. 1
Maison Villemanzy........................ 2

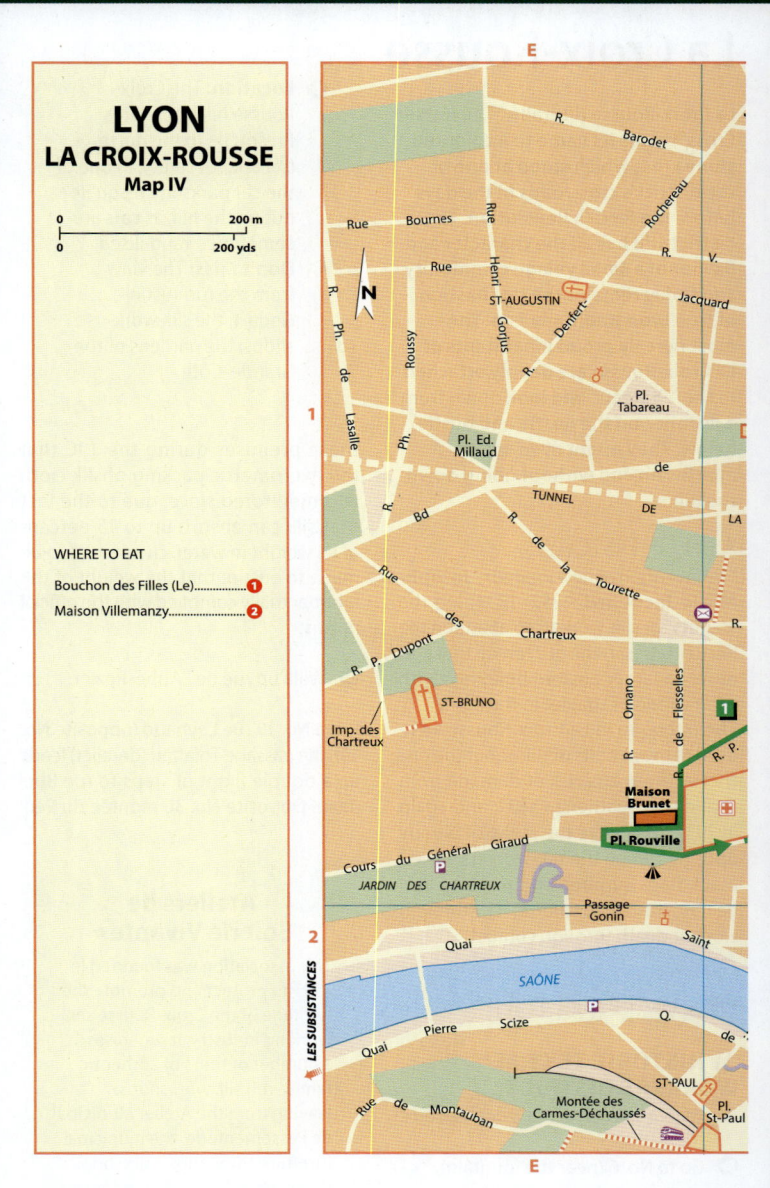

ron climbs up to **place Chardonnet**, on which stands the monument erected in memory of Count Hilaire de Chardonnet (1839–1924), the inventor of artificial silk.

▶ Turn right onto rue des Tables-Claudiennes (steps).

Rue des Tables-Claudiennes (street of the Claudian Tablets) owes its name to the inscriptions on bronze discovered by the draper Gribaud in his vineyard.

▶ Take No. 29 opposite, which communicates with cour des Voraces

LA CROIX-ROUSSE

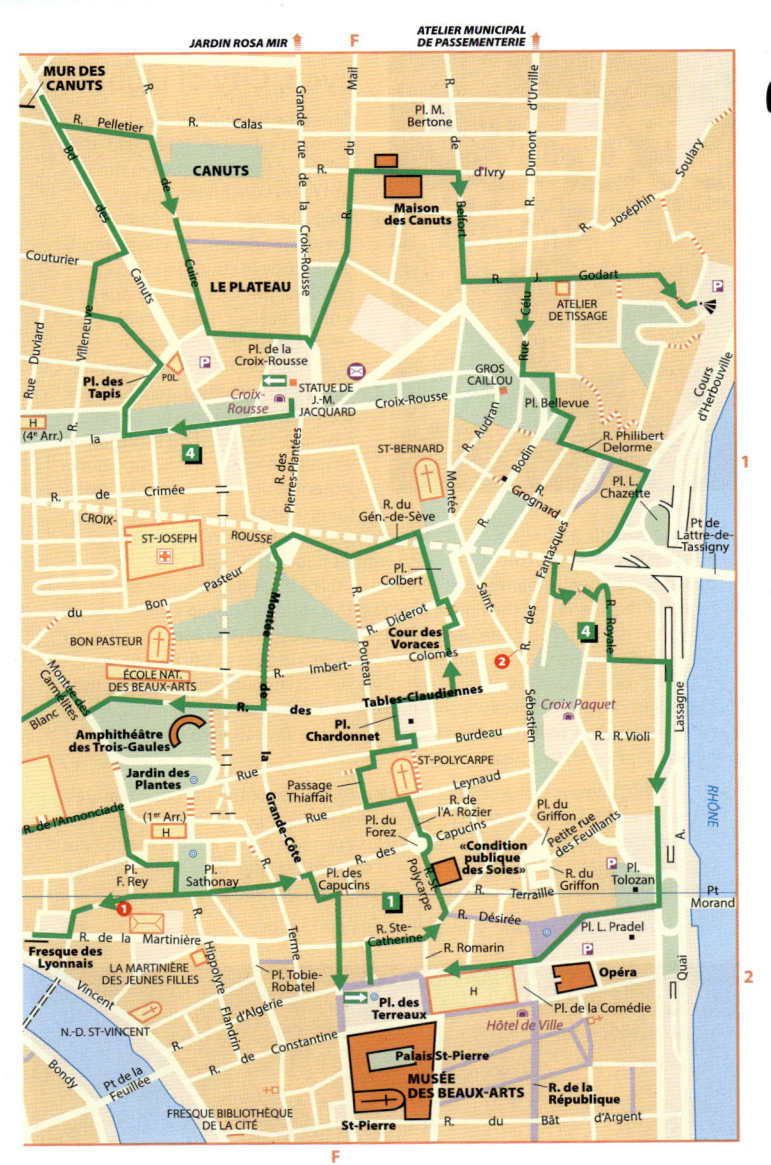

(steps and lane on the right, then turn left level with a street lamp).

Cour des Voraces with its imposing flight of steps is an impressive sight. In the 19C it was the meeting place of a silk workers' guild known as the *Voraces* or *Dévorants* ("The Ravenous").

Grande-Côte★

The Grande-Côte "montée" is well named; fortunately, you go down it. To compensate for the destruction of many old houses in its upper part, the Grande-Côte has benefited from much redevelopment.

337

DISCOVERING LYON

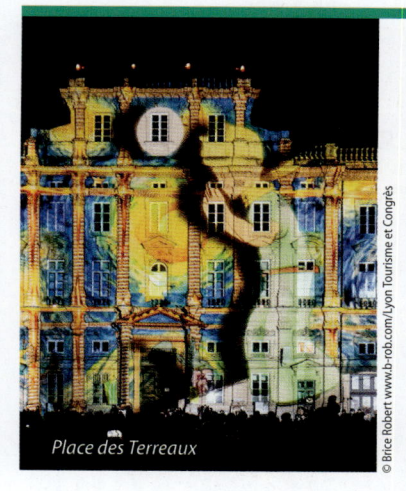

Lyon, City of Light

Given the tradition of the famous Festival of Lights held here on 8 December, when the city twinkles with the light of thousands of candles, Lyon was already predisposed to investing generously in street-lighting. It has done just that in the shape of a project called "Plan Lumière", which places the emphasis on public safety and the highlighting of the city's architectural heritage. Over 100 monuments and locations have been selected for inclusion in a comprehensive and homogenous system of illumination, which gives them a whole new dimension.

Place des Terreaux

Fourvière Basilica stands out like a lighthouse on the top of its hill; the opera house takes on a futuristic appearance with its huge glass superstructure glowing red; squares such as place des Terreaux or place de la Bourse and the banks of the Saône and the Rhône are lit up by subtle lighting in a variety of colours in warm or cold tones depending on the location. The Part-Dieu district with the distinctive Crédit Lyonnais tower soaring up from it, the Port St-Jean, the Hôtel-Dieu and many more of the city's famous monuments feature in this huge light show which weaves an atmosphere of fairy-tale and magic. Along with the various events put on in the evenings, this invitation to explore "Lyon by night" proves irresistible.

Such is the drama and the skill of the artists that many of the sites that feature in the Fêtes des Lumières need to be revisited to fully appreciate the magic of it all. Over the course of the four days, visitors are free to stroll around the "City of Light", appreciating a life-size art show at the cutting edge of technology. It is a breathtaking experience, and rightly praised and renowned.

A guide to the "Plan Lumière" is available from the tourist office. www.lyon.fr.

The Saône, Presqu'île and Part-Dieu viewed from Basilique Notre-Dame on Fourvière Hill

LA CROIX-ROUSSE

The agreeable garden, planted in 2000, is oriented to best view the neighbourhoods of St-Paul, St-John and Fourvière.

▶ Go down as far as the rue des Tables-Claudiennes.

Amphithéâtre des Trois Gaules
According to the dedication discovered at the bottom of a well in 1958, this venerable spot was built in 19 BC by Rufus as a meeting place for delegates from the 60 Gallic tribes.

Jardin des Plantes
The garden remains virtually in name only. The Orangery developed in the late 18C was transplanted to the Tete d'Or in 1856.

▶ In the montée des Carmélites, take the rue Pierre-Blanc on the left, then the rue de Flesselles.

Place Rouville
From the square there is a fine **view**★ over Lyon. Jutting out from above the seemingly endless sea of red rooftops on the peninsula is the belfry of the Hôtel de Ville and the Part-Dieu district overlooked by the tower of the Crédit Lyonnais bank on the left. On the north side of the square, **Maison Brunet** is a typical silk-worker's dwelling.

Place Sathonay
On the north side of the square are the monumental steps of montée de l'Amphithéâtre, flanked by two lion-shaped fountains.
At the beginning of the street, on the right, there is a fine painted wall known as the **Fresque des Lyonnais**★.

▶ Turn into the rue Terme on the left, then take the rue des Capucins. At the place des Capucins, steps and the rue Ste-Marie lead to the place des Terreaux.

2 LE PLATEAU★

▶ Begin on place de la Croix-Rousse, where there is a statue of Jacquard.

Place des Tapis
The square, shaded by a double line of plane trees, combines cinemas, terraces for a relaxing coffee, and daily market. A popular place with the Croix-Roussiens.

▶ Follow the rue Jacquard and the rue Villeneuve, to rejoin the boulevard des Canuts.

Quartier des Canuts★
At the junction of boulevard des Canuts, rue Denfert-Rochereau and rue Pelletier stands a tall **wall**★ adorned with a trompe-l'œil mural covering an area of 1 200sqm. Painted in December 1987 and updated in 1997, it serves as a picturesque reminder of life in one of the districts in La Croix-Rousse.
Note, in the windows, the puppet-theatre characters of Guignol, his wife Madelon and the Bailiff.

▶ Take the rue Pelletier, then the rue de Cuire et the little rue piétonne Victor-Fort.

A little market can be found each morning in place de la Croix-Rousse.

▶ Go down the narrow rue du Mail, a shopping street, then the rue d'Ivry on the right. The uniformity of the façades, enlivened by alternating shades of tan and pink, is typical of the silk-workers area.

Maison des Canuts
10 r. d'Ivry. Guided tours (50min) at 11am and 3:30pm: Mon–Sat 10am–6.30pm. 6–8 Jan and public holidays. €2 (€7.5 for tours). 04 78 28 62 04. www.maisondescanuts.com.
At No. 10 and No. 12, craftsmen and women from the home-workers cooperative perpetuate the traditions of the Lyon silk-workers and promote the high-quality fabrics they produce.

Left Bank

The Left Bank of the Rhône has allowed the original 18C town to expand. From the Parc de la Tête d'Or to the very modern Gerland, passing buildings of glass and brick of the International City, the extension has brought together the most diverse areas and offers an ideal ecological lifestyle, combining water and green spaces.

> **Location:** This area is north-east of Lyon's old town, on the left bank of the Rhône.
>
> **Kids:** The open spaces and animals of the Parc de la Tête d'Or; the Gerland park.
>
> **Don't Miss:** The architecture of the Musée d'Art Contemporain, and of the Cité Internationale.

THE BANKS OF THE RHÔNE

Cité Internationale

This vast complex, comprising an imposing Conference Centre (Palais des Congrès), cinemas (14 screens), hotels and a Museum of Contemporary Art, was installed between the Tête d'Or Park and the Rhône.

Musée d'Art Contemporain★

Cité Internationale: 81 Quai Charles-de-Gaulle.
Tue–Fri 11am–6pm; Sat and Sun 11am–7pm. €16. 1 Jan, 25 Dec. 04 72 69 17 17. www.mac-lyon.com.
This cultural museum is built around the atrium of the old market hall. Its modern structure allows for great flexibility of display and for works of art to be exhibited to their best advantage.

Parc de la Tête d'Or★

The name of the English-style gardens surrounding the Conference Centre derives from local folklore, which claims that a golden head of Christ is buried here. The entrance is marked by huge wrought-iron gates. The park is an ideal place to go walking and cycling and there is also a narrow-gauge railway.

Serres★ and Jardin Botanique

Alpine garden Mar–Oct–9–11.30am; Main garden Oct–Mar 9am–5pm; Apr–Sept 9am–6pm; Greenhouses Oct–Mar 9am–4.30pm; Apr–Sept 9am–5.30pm (5pm Sun). 04 72 69 47 78. www.jardin-botanique-lyon.com

The botanical gardens are laid out to the south-east end of the park and consist of acres of outdoor plants, great glasshouses containing tropical vegetation including numerous palm trees, and an Alpine garden.

Jardin Zoologique

Nov–Mar 9am–5pm; Apr and Oct 9am–6pm; May–Sep 9am–6.30pm. 04 72 69 47 78. www.zoo.lyon.fr.
The **Zoological Gardens**, located north of the botanical gardens, are among the oldest in Europe (1858). They have 1 100 animals including numerous wild animals from outside Europe. West of the zoo lies the deer park.
Between the two, on place de Guignol, children's activities (merry-go-round, games) and Guignol shows are organised by the **Véritable Guignol du Vieux Lyon** team (*06 12 42 48 71. http://theatre-guignol-lyon.fr*).

Quaysides along the Rhône

Quai Augagneur, by the Hôtel-Dieu, is lined with imposing bourgeois houses built in the late 19C. This wonderful esplanade beneath the plane trees is enhanced by the lively atmosphere of an open-air market *(except Mondays)*, and is particularly attractive in misty weather, when the river is turbulent and fast-flowing. The district of Les Brotteaux, with its geometrically laid-out streets, stretches to the east; it lies on the site of sandbanks *(brotteaux)* once deposited by the Rhône, hence its name.

From Wilson bridge the **view**★ extends to the heights of La Croix-Rousse on the other bank, where the tall houses of the former silk-workers rise one above the other.

Centre d'Histoire de la Résistance et de la Déportation★

14 av. Berthelot. Wed–Sun 10am–6pm. *Public holidays except 8 May.* €8. 04 78 72 23 11.
The museum is set up in part of buildings that from 1882 to the early 1970s were the Military Medical School and, from 1942 to 1944, housed the headquarters of the Gestapo in this region.

Halle Tony-Garnier

20 place des Docteurs. Guided visits by appointment. No charge for admission during events. 04 72 76 85 85. www.halle-tony-garnier.com.
The town planner, Tony Garnier created this massive symbol of construction in iron. It has been neglected for many years, but since its restoration in 2000, the hall hosts concerts, shows, exhibitions and other events.

Gerland District

This district sits opposite the confluence of the Rhône and the Saône and has a covered meat market at its centre. The area is one large "Science and Technology Park" and incorporates a high-level technical college, the Institut Pasteur, the Institut Mérieux and a sports centre. The International School is a glass construction overlooking the Parc Gerland.

THE PART-DIEU DISTRICT

This vast complex spread out over what was once Army land is built around a pedestrian precinct and consists of a large number of buildings and towers, including government offices, a shopping centre, the radio studios and the impressive library.
The **Crédit Lyonnais Tower** has now become the second most famous landmark in the city after the Fourvière Towers. Its brick-red colour blends in well with the rooftops of the old urban districts.

Musée des Moulages

87 cours Gambetta. Wed and Sat, 2pm and 6pm . 04 87 24 80 63.
This fascinating museum is devoted to the history of sculpture from Ancient Greece to the 19C.

Musée Lumière

25 rue du Premier-Film, Lyon-Monplaisir. Daily except Mon 10am–6.30pm. *1 Jan, 1 May, 25 Dec.* €7. 04 78 78 18 89. www.institut-lumiere.org.
Antoine Lumière, the father of Auguste and Louis, inventors of cinema, had this residence built between 1889 and 1901. The interior houses the **Institut Lumière** and hosts events based on still and moving pictures.

Musée Urbain Tony-Garnier

4 rue des Serpollières. Tues–Sun 2–6pm; guided visits of apartments and museum available; check website for times. €10 (€3 apartments). Public holidays. 04 78 75 16 75. www.museeurbaintonygarnier.com.
This group of buildings was built in the 1930s by the urban architect **Tony Garnier**. Since 1991, many of the blind walls of these large buildings have been decorated with murals painted by a group of artists calling themselves **"The City of Creation"**.

Halles de Lyon Paul Bocuse

102 Cours Lafayette. Mon–Sat 7am–7pm (10:30pm for restaurants); Sun 7am–1pm (4:30pm for restaurants).
Named for Lyon's most famous chef, this covered market is home to nearly food vendors from cheesemongers to butchers to winesellers. Most are closed on Mondays except for seafood vendors.

DISCOVERING LYON

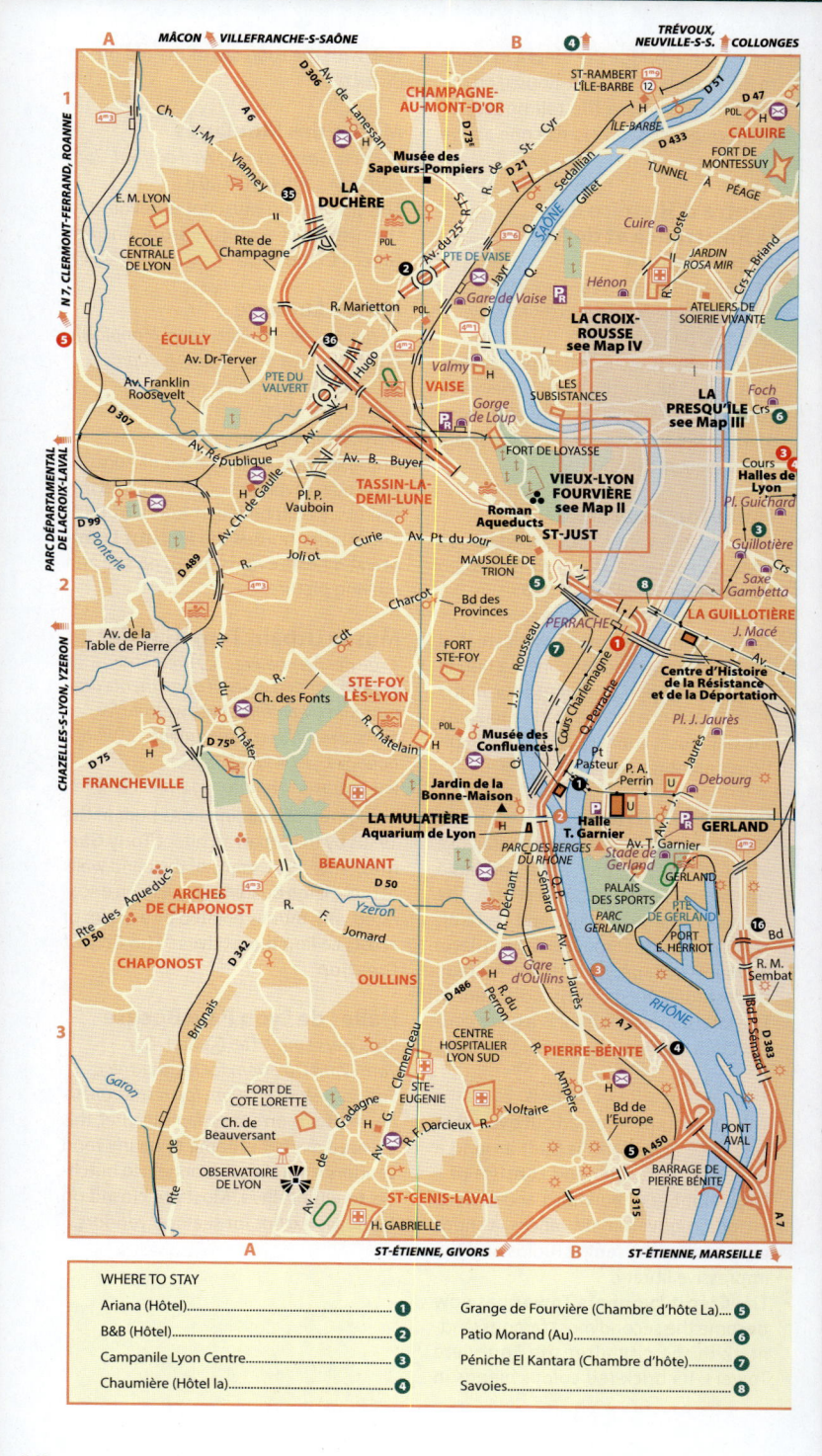

WHERE TO STAY

Ariana (Hôtel) 1	Grange de Fourvière (Chambre d'hôte La) 5
B&B (Hôtel) 2	Patio Morand (Au) 6
Campanile Lyon Centre 3	Péniche El Kantara (Chambre d'hôte) 7
Chaumière (Hôtel la) 4	Savoies 8

342

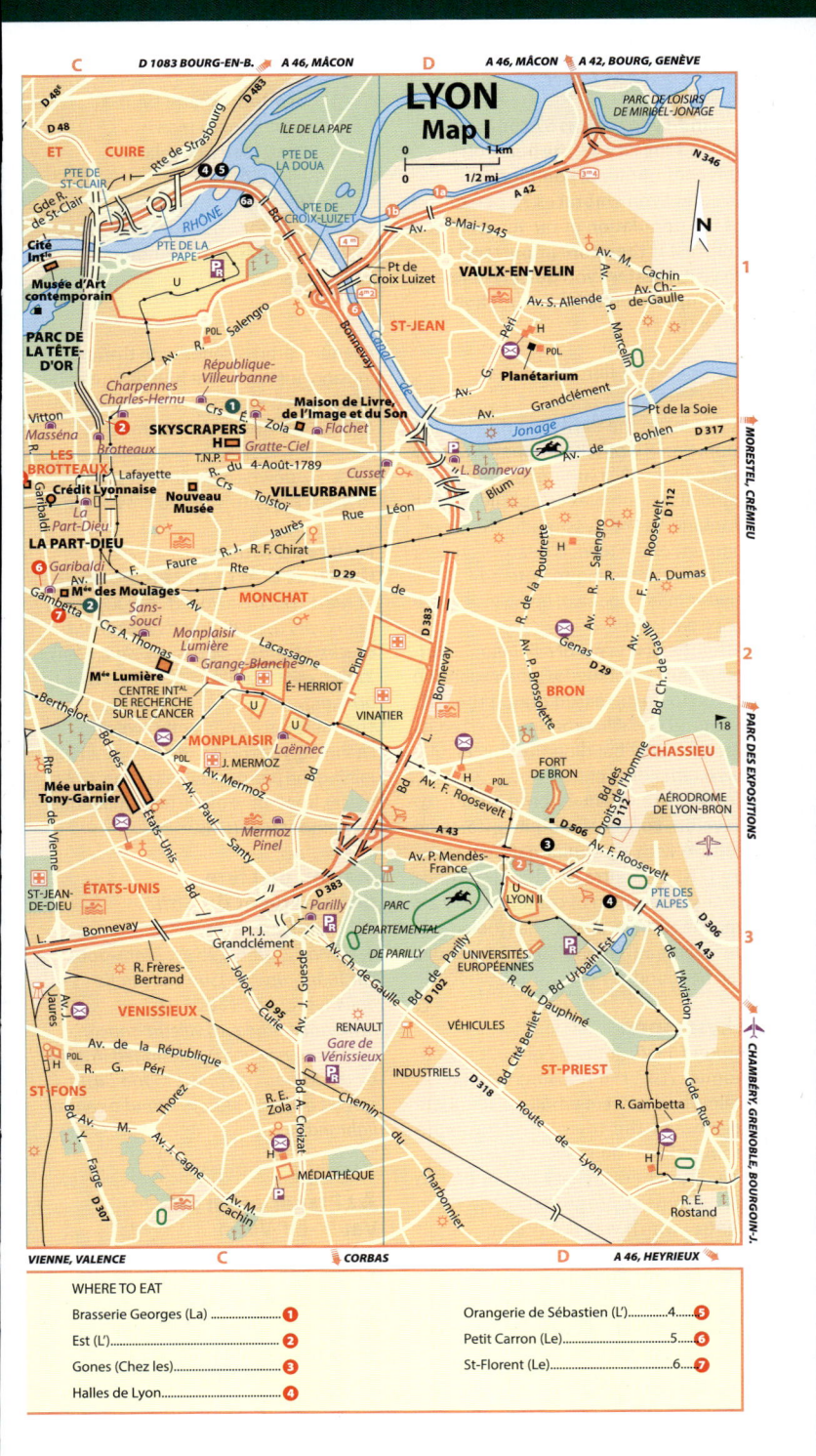

OUTSKIRTS

LYON Map I

WHERE TO EAT

Brasserie Georges (La) .... ①	Orangerie de Sébastien (L') .... ④
Est (L') .... ②	Petit Carron (Le) .... ⑤
Gones (Chez les) .... ③	St-Florent (Le) .... ⑥
Halles de Lyon .... ④	

343

Outskirts

"Grand-Lyon" unites 57 communes around the city. At the heart of this community of communes, Greater Lyon embraces 75 percent of the population of the Rhône. The contrast is therefore important, and to visit Greater Lyon quickly gives the impression of having escaped from the city.

> **Location:** Greater Lyon extends more than 20km/13mi from place Bellecour.
> **Kids:** Planetarium Vaulx-en-Velin; the aquarium of Lyon.
> **Don't Miss:** The automobile museum.

VILLEURBANNE AND THE EAST

Adjacent to the Part-Dieu district, the municipality of Villeurbanne owes its name to the Villa Urbana, an important agricultural complex established by the Romans on the Cusset hill. The development of the town is relatively recent and it is interesting to note how it has always made a point of being independent from Lyon.

After the first wave of silk manufacturers at the end of the 19C, the expansion of the town increased during the 20C. In the 1930s, Villeurbanne asserted its specificity by building the spectacular skyscraper district.

Today, the town is continuing to develop, concentrating its efforts on culture with a popular national theatre (TNP), an ultra-modern reference library, a museum of contemporary art and the antique-dealers' hall (boulevard de Stalingrad) where 150 antique shops can be found.

Skyscrapers

Around 1930, at the height of the economic crisis, the housing facilities in Villeurbanne were wholly inadequate in view of the town's fast-growing population. The mayor, Lazare Goujon, launched his city into a daring development programme: the town centre, which was the first project to be completed, was soon nicknamed **"Skyscraper City"** as its unique architectural style was more reminiscent of North-American buildings than of French suburbia.

Avenue Barbusse ends with the imposing and austere **town hall** designed by R Giroud: a belfry towers over the façade decorated with fluted columns.

> Walk down cours de la République towards cours Tolstoï and cross over.

Nouveau Musée (Institut d'Art Contemporain)

11 rue du Docteur-Dolard. Opening hours vary according to daylight hours; check web site for details. 1 Jan, 1 May, 25 Dec. €6. 04 78 03 47 00. www.i-art-c.org.

This museum is constantly evolving and changing, with new and visiting exhibits joining the permanent collection, rich in pieces from some of the most influential contemporary artists.

Maison du Livre, de l'Image et du Son

247 cours Émile-Zola. Mon 2–7pm, Tue–Fri 11am–7pm, Sat 10am–6pm. Sun and public holidays. 04 78 68 04 04. http://mediatheques.villeurbanne.fr.

This reference library, designed in 1988 by the famous architect Mario Botta, is spread over five storeys round a central light shaft.

VAULX-EN-VELIN

Planétarium de Vaulx-en-Velin

11km/7mi E of Villeurbanne. Wed 1:30–5pm, Sat–Sun 10:30am–5pm (check website for seasonal changes). late-Aug and Sept. €10 (children under 12, €8). 04 78 79 50 13. www.planetariumvv.com.

OUTSKIRTS

As a prelude, a scientific display reveals the secrets of the heavens. The 15m hemispherical screen surrounds you, and captivates young and old alike.

MIRIBEL

Carillon
13km/8mi to the NE of Villeurbanne.
Open only during concerts.
04 78 55 61 16.
Built between 1939 and 1947, this belltower is 30m high and overlooks a spectacular amusement park and the Miribel canal.

LA MULATIÈRE

Jardin de la Bonne Maison★
99 chemin de Fontanières.
Exit the A 7 for La Mulatière, then follow the directions for Oullins-Centre. At the 2nd crossroads, turn right for Ste-Foy-lès-Lyon, then at the 1st set of traffic lights, turn right.
Mar–Oct mornings; check website for seasonal hours. €8. 04 78 37 38 37.
www.labonnemaison.org.
Located in the residential part of Mulatière and surrounded by walls, this garden offers an exceptional display of shrubs, perennials and bulbs. There are also more than 750 varieties of rose.

Grand Aquarium de Lyon★
7 rue S.-Déchant (large car park).
Wed–Sun 11am–7pm (school holidays, daily). 1 Jan, 25 Dec. €15 (child 5–10, €11). 04 72 66 65 66.
www.aquariumlyon.fr.
This rather unobtrusive building on the banks of the Saône offers a journey to the different rivers and oceans of the world: impressive fish reign supreme in rivers of temperate climates; nearby, sharks swim round a wreck inside a huge pool on two levels; a myriad of small brightly coloured fish of all shapes feel quite at home in tropical waters.

WEST OF LYON

LA DUCHÈRE

Musée des Sapeurs-Pompiers
358 av. de Champagne. 10km/6mi NW along the A 6 (direction Paris), then the D 342. Wed–Fri 2–6pm; 1st weekend of each month 2–6pm.
€6. 04 72 17 54 54.
www.museepompiers.com.
This museum presents an impressive collection of equipment from the 18C to present times including hand, steam and motorised pumps. A memorial hall housing helmets, flags and portraits is dedicated to firefighters and recall two sad episodes in particular: St John (1930) and Feyzin (1966). There is a display of vehicles and rolling stock in the basement, but what is on view is only a small part of the total collection.

MARCY-L'ÉTOILE

Domaine de Lacroix-Laval
Rte de Sain-Bel. Leave Lyon heading NW (towards Mâcon), then follow the D 7 in the direction of Charbonnières.
Situated to the west of metropolitan Lyon, the Domaine de Lacroix-Laval (*daylight hours. 04 78 87 87 00*) serves as a welcome "green lung" for the city. Among the amenities in its 15ha/37 acre site is an interesting orienteering trail. At the edge of the park stands an elegant 16C **castle** where temporary exhibits are presented.
While wandering around the garden, do not miss the **vegetable garden**, where over 600 varieties of plant span four themes: Lyon horticulture; herbs and spices; a wild garden; and fruit and vegetable crops.

Charbonnières-les-Bains
10km/6mi (towards Mâcon), then D 307.
Set in woodland formerly worked by the charcoal burners, the Vale of Charbonnières is a traditional holiday resort popular with the people of Lyon. The ferruginous spring here was officially discovered by a priest in 1778. Pump rooms and a casino were soon opened. In 1900, people flocked to the

spa, which quickly gained a reputation for excellence.

SOUTH OF LYON
Givors
20km/12.5mi S by the A 7, then the A 47.
The ruins of the castle of St-Gerald (accessed through Les Étoiles) overlook the city hall, two churches and the Rhône.

Ternay
18km/11.3mi S along the D 307 (direction Vienne by the N 7).
The 12C church perched on the edge of a hill overlooking the Rhône is an interesting legacy of the Romanesque school along the Rhône. Formerly dedicated to St-Mayol, the church belonged to a Cluniac priory. Inside, the most endearing aspect is the main apse, with its vaulted arches and pilasters. The remains of the cloister are to the south of the church.

DRIVING TOUR

BANKS OF THE SAÔNE★
38km/24mi round tour. Allow 3h.

From its source at Vioménil in the Vosges, the River Saône flows southwestward into Haute-Saône *département* near Corre, where it meets the Canal de l'Est. It then continues through Gray to Pontailler-sur-Saône and crosses Côte d'Or department to enter Saône-et-Loire, where it is joined by the Doubs River, its major tributary. The river then passes Chalon-sur-Saône, Tournus, Mâcon and Villefranche before eventually joining the Rhône in Lyon. The river banks are a favourite weekend destination with Lyon residents, who come to stroll along the towpath, or to indulge in a light lunch of fried fish washed down with a bottle of Beaujolais in one of the many riverside restaurants.

▶ Leave Lyon to the N, in the direction of Trévoux. The pleasant D 433 follows the east bank of the river, bordered by vegetation, as far La Rochetaillée.

Musée de l'Automobile Henri-Malartre★★
Daily except Mon (other than public holidays) 10:30am–6pm; weekends only in Jan; afternoons only 3rd Fri of month. 1 Jan, 25 Dec. €6 (free for visitors under 26). ℘04 78 22 18 80. www.musee-malartre.com.
This restored 15C castle, and its terraced grounds overlooking the Saône, contain remarkable collections of motorcars (1890–1986), cycles (1818–1960), motorcycles (1904–64) and public transport vehicles (1886–1935), all in full working order. Of the 150 cars on show, 50 date from before 1914, and 18 were built in Lyon, a reminder of the fact that there were once over 100 manufacturers in the region. Some of the exhibits are unique, such as the Rochet-Schneider (1895), the Gobron-Brillié (1898), the Luc Court (1901) and the Thieulin (1908). The collection of cycles ranges from the hobby horse to Anquetil's bicycle, not forgetting the amazing "Penny Farthings". Over 50 motorcycles are on show, including a Herdtlé-Bruneau (1904), the Koehler-Escoffier (1935) ridden by Georges Monneret, sidecars and a Zundapp (1937) used by the German Army in Africa and Russia.

▶ Drive on to D 433 and turn right.

Neuville-sur-Saône
The town lies in a picturesque setting on a bend of the Saône. The church, topped by twin bell-towers dating from the 17C, contains a set of wood panelling by Perrache, a sculptor from Lyon (18C).

Trévoux
See VILLEFRANCHE-SUR-SAÔNE.

▶ Take D 933 and turn left onto D 504 towards Villefranche.

Villefranche-sur-Saône
See VILLEFRANCHE-SUR-SAÔNE.

▶ Return to Lyon on the A 6 (30min).

ADDRESSES

STAY

VIEUX-LYON

Hôtel St-Paul – *6 r. Lainerie. ℘04 78 28 13 29. www.hotelsaintpaul.eu/. 21 rooms.* This small, recently renovated hotel boasts a Renaissance style.

FOURVIÈRE

Chambre d'Hôte la Grange de Fourvière – *89 quai Pierre Scize. ℘04 72 33 74 45. www.grangedefourviere.fr. 2 rooms.* This charming B&B in the centre of Old Lyon was once a barn and stable.

PRESQU'ÎLE

Chambre d'Hôte Péniche "El Kantara" – *Quai Rambaud. ℘04 78 42 02 75. 2 rooms.* What could be more romantic or unusual than this magnificently restored barge moored on the river?

Hôtel St-Vincent – *9 r. Pareille. ℘04 78 27 22 56. 32 rooms.* Located in a narrow street close to the Saône, this hotel is very comfortable, with large rooms.

Élysée Hôtel – *92 r. du Prés.-Edouard-Herriot. ℘04 78 42 03 15. https://hotel-elysee-lyon.fr. 29 rooms.* A small family-run hotel where you can enjoy the vitality of the Presqu'île at affordable prices.

Campanile Lyon Centre - Berges Du Rhone – *4 r. du Mortier. ℘04 78 60 03 09. www.campanile.com. 126 rooms.* Just a five minute walk from place Bellecour, this modern hotel boasts functional rooms with air conditioning.

Hôtel La Résidence – *18 r. Victor-Hugo. ℘04 78 42 63 28. www.hotel-la-residence.com. 65 rooms.* Managed by the same family since 1954, this hotel borders a pedestrian street quite near the place Bellecour.

Hotel des Savoies – *80 r. de la Charité. ℘04 78 37 66 94. www.hotel-des-savoies.fr. 44 rooms.* This hotel boasts a façade decorated with the Savoie coat of arms. Inside, rooms are clean and simple, with pastel carpets. The convenient garage and reasonable prices make this a popular address.

Hotel Célestins – *4 r. des Archers. ℘04 72 56 08 98. www.hotelcelestins.com. 25 rooms.* Charming hotel in the heart of the city between place Bellecour and place des Jacobins. Perfect for exploring the city on foot.

Hotel des Artistes – *8 r. G-André. ℘04 78 42 04 88. www.hotel-des-artistes.fr. 45 rooms.* Giving onto the adorable place des Célestins and the theatre, this hotel has lovely rooms and a theatrical ambiance.

RIVE GAUCHE

Hôtel B&B – *93 cours Gambetta. ℘08 92 70 75 34. www.hotel-bb.com. 114 rooms.* A chain hotel in a central location near the railway station with spacious, comfortable rooms with king-size beds.

Au Patio Morand – *99 r. de Créqui. ℘04 78 52 62 62. www.hotel-morand.fr. 31 rooms.* This hotel has elegant rooms with a large bed and plasma TV screen. it also has a patio where you can breakfast.

THE OUTSKIRTS OF LYON

Hôtel la Chaumière – *11 av. du Gén-de-Gaulle, 69410 Champagne-au-Mont-d'Or. ℘04 78 35 10 60.* This contemporary building has bright, very well maintained rooms. A delightful alternative to chains.

Hôtel Ariana – *163 cours Émile-Zola, 69100 Villeurbanne. ℘04 78 85 32 33. www.ariana-hotel.fr. 102 rooms.* This is a practical address for those who wish to stay amid the 1930s high-rises of Villeurbanne. The hotel is modern, with air-conditioned, soundproofed rooms and a sober interior.

EAT

VIEUX-LYON

Le Vieux Lyon – *44 r. St-Jean. ℘04 78 42 48 89.* Local epicureans are all familiar with this tavern, in operation since 1947, where good humour and hospitality reign. Home-made Lyonnais cooking.

Les Adrets – *30 r. du Boeuf. ℘04 78 38 24 30. les-adrets.com. Closed Sat and Sun.* Exposed beams and tiled floor. Traditional dishes.

PRESQU'ÎLE

Le Café 203 – *9 r. du Garet. ℘04 78 28 66 65. www.moncafe203.com.* Customers come here for the fresh fare, slate menu and bistro setting.

La Brasserie Georges – *30 cours de Verdun. ℘04 72 56 54 54. www.brasseriegeorges.com.* Open since 1836, this brasserie near the Perrache train station is still a favourite Lyon haunt.

Le Jura – *25 r. Tupin.* ✆*04 78 42 20 57. www.bouchonlejura.fr. Closed Sun–Mon. Reservations requested.* Not far from the Rue de la République, this eatery with its 1920s decor and aproned matron overseeing the stoves is as genuine as they come.

Brunet – *23 r. Claudia.* ✆*04 78 37 44 31. Closed Tue. Reservations recommended.* An authentic Lyon *bouchon* (tavern), Brunet has elbow-to-elbow tables, Guignol-marked tableware and tasty dishes enhanced by an enticing selection of wines by the carafe.

Café des Fédérations – *8 r. Major-Martin.* ✆*04 78 28 26 00. http://restaurant-cafedesfederations-lyon.com. Closed Sun eve.* Unrivalled guardian of Lyonnais culinary traditions, served in a perfect setting and relaxing atmosphere.

Le Mercière – *56 r. Mercière.* ✆*04 78 37 67 35. www.restaurant-le-merciere.com. Reservations recommended.* Located in a passageway giving onto one of the most sought-after restaurant streets in town, this old house serves traditional fare in a classic Lyonnais setting.

Le Caro de Lyon – *25 r. du Bât-d'Argent.* ✆*04 78 39 58 58. www.lecarodelyon.fr. Closed Sun.* This restaurant behind the Opera House, designed to resemble a library, welcomes diners into an intimate atmosphere comprised of Murano chandeliers and antique knick-knacks.

L'Étage – *4 pl. des Terreaux.* ✆*04 78 28 19 59. www.letage-restaurant.com. Closed Sun and Mon.* The locals never tire of climbing the stairs leading to the humble silk workshop on the second floor. Charming setting and seductive, creative menus.

Le Bouchon des Filles – *20 Rue Sergent Blandan Ancienne Voie du Rhin. Lunch Fri–Sun, dinner daily.* ✆*04 78 30 40 44. www.lebouchondesfilles.fr.* This contemporary look at a classic bouchon offers delicious fare in a cozy dining room.

Le Poêlon d'or – *29 rue des Remparts d'Ainay.* ✆*04 78 37 65 60. www.lepoelon-dor-restaurant.fr. Closed Sat–Sun.* A classic bouchon with delicious Lyonnais fare.

LA CROIX-ROUSSE

Maison Villemanzy – *25 montée St-Sébastien.* ✆*04 72 98 21 21. www.maison-villemanzy.com. Closed Sun, and Mon lunch.* Perched on the slopes of Croix-Rousse, this restaurant offers a superb terrace view over the city. Family recipes and inventive cuisine.

RIVE GAUCHE

Le Petit Carron – *48 av. Félix-Faure.* ✆*04 78 60 00 57. www.lepetitcarron-restaurant.com. Closed 3 wks in Aug, Sat lunch and Sun. Reservations recommended.* The little puppet who inhabits the window of this tavern beckons you into a muted dining room featuring a slate *menu du jour*, composed based on market availability with a modern flair.

Chez les Gones – *102 cours Lafayette.* ✆*04 78 60 91 61. www.chezlesgones.fr. Tues–Sun (Closed Sun in summer), lunch only.* This tavern set in the bosom of the marketplace boasts typical Lyon dishes.

L'Est – *14 pl. J-Ferry.* ✆*04 37 24 25 26. www.brasseries-bocuse.com.* The décor is that of a big, old-fashioned brasserie where electric trains circumnavigate the dining room.

THE OUTSKIRTS OF LYON

La Terrasse St-Clair – *2 Grande Rue St-Clair, 69300 Caluire-et-Cuire.* ✆*04 72 27 37 37. www.terrasse-saint-clair.com. Closed Sat and Sun.* This tavern-like restaurant has a terrace sheltered by plane trees where you can dine on traditional cuisine.

Daniel et Denise Créqui – *156 rue de Créqui.* ✆*04 78 60 66 53. www.danieletdenise.fr. Closed Sat and Sun.* The combination of checked tablecloths, copper pans and photographs leaves you with the impression that you have gone back in time at this traditional *bouchon*.

SHOPPING

Markets *(Marchés)* – The Marché de la Création, quai Romain-Rolland and the Marché de l'Artisanat, quai Fulchiron are held on Sunday mornings. These are no run-of-the-mill craft markets, as the workmanship is outstanding. Used-book sellers line the quai de la Pêcherie every afternoon.

For food, head for the quai Saint-Antoine, where food markets with producers from all over the region set up stalls and sell their produce *(Tue–Sun, 7am–12.30pm)*.

ADDRESSES

There is also a Farmers' Market twice a week in the place Carnot *(Wed, 4–7pm; Sun, 5am–1.30pm)*, in front of the Gare Perrache.

ON THE TOWN

Rue Ste-Catherine – A very lively street featuring many establishments open until the early hours of the morning. **The Shamrock** is the most Celtic pub in town. Rum fans convene at **La Taverne du Perroquet Bourré** (The Tavern of the Plastered Parrot), while **L'Abreuvoir** is highly recommended for those who fancy good French music.

THEATRE AND ENTERTAINMENT

Le Guignol de Lyon – *04 78 28 92 57. www.guignol-lyon.com. Wed and Sat: 3pm and 4.30pm, Sun 3pm; daily during school holidays.* The Théâtre Bazar stages children's performances that marry burlesque and fantasy. The shows for adults, inspired by aspects and events of life in Lyon, are more malicious.

Auditorium-Orchestre national de Lyon – *149 r. Garibaldi. 04 78 95 95 95. www.auditoriumlyon.com. Tickets: Mon–Fri 11am–6pm, concert Saturdays 2–6pm. Closed most of Aug.* The Auditorium Maurice Ravel regularly hosts l'Orchestre National de Lyon.

Maison de la Danse – *8 av. Jean-Mermoz. 04 72 78 18 10. www.maisondeladanse.com. Tickets: Mon–Fri 11.45am–6.45pm.*

Marché de la Création

Closed mid-Jul–mid-Aug. From flamenco and tap dancing to ballet and the traditional dances of East and West, welcome to this, the citadel of the art.

Opéra National de Lyon – *1 pl. de la Comédie. 04 69 85 54 54. www.opera-lyon.com. Tickets: Mon–Sat 11am–7pm. Closed late Jul–end Aug.*

Halle Tony-Garnier – *20 pl. Antonin-Perrin. 04 72 76 85 85. www.halle-tony-garnier.com. Visits following schedule; phone ahead.* Since its restoration in 2000, this huge metallic structure presents a remarkable diversity of events from the Moscow State Circus to Lionel Richie.

Le Guignol de Lyon

BRESSE AND THE DOMBES

The area known as Bresse is endowed with many examples of fine architecture, not least Romanesque churches and Bressane farmhouses with clay walls, exposed beams and what are known as "Saracen" chimneys. The Dombes, to the south-west, is a major fish-farming area, with more than 1 000 lakes dotted across the countryside. Aquaculture in the region dates to at least the 12C, and today, more than 1 000 tonnes of fish are caught annually, most of which are bound for the markets of Germany.

Highlights

1 Tasting the local delicacy, **Volaille de Bresse** (see below)
2 Marvelling at the flamboyant **Royal Monstery** in Brou (p352)
3 The **Parc des Oiseaux** bird sanctuary, south of Villars-les-Dombes (p359)
4 Touring the lakes of the **Dombes** plateau (p360)
5 Medieval architecture in **Pérouges** (p362)

Volaille de Bresse

Local Bresse chickens are treated like fine wine: these blue-footed, red-crested chickens' right to roam and forage for real food is protected by law. The story of this famous chicken begins in 1591, when the bird was first mentioned in the town registers of Bourg-en-Bresse. Henry IV, having stopped here following an accident with his carriage, tasted it and demanded its inclusion on his courtly menu.

Described by the French as "the fourth gastronomic wonder of the world", Bresse chicken is dense and flavorful thanks to strict rules dictating that chickens must each have 10 square meters in which to run free, fed a lean diet of local cereals and skimmed milk that they supplement by foraging for local bugs and insects. The chickens finish growing in wooden coops in a dim, calm, well-ventilated structure; the resulting chickens are high in protein and low in fat.

Birdlife

With so much open space it is not surprising that the Dombes is known for its birdlife. The area includes ponds, marshes, wet meadows, deciduous forests, moorlands and arable fields and is home to 20 000 or more waterbirds. As a result, the area is hugely popular with birdwatchers and features such diverse species as black-winged stilt, squacco heron, marsh harrier, whisk-

Marshland, La Dombes

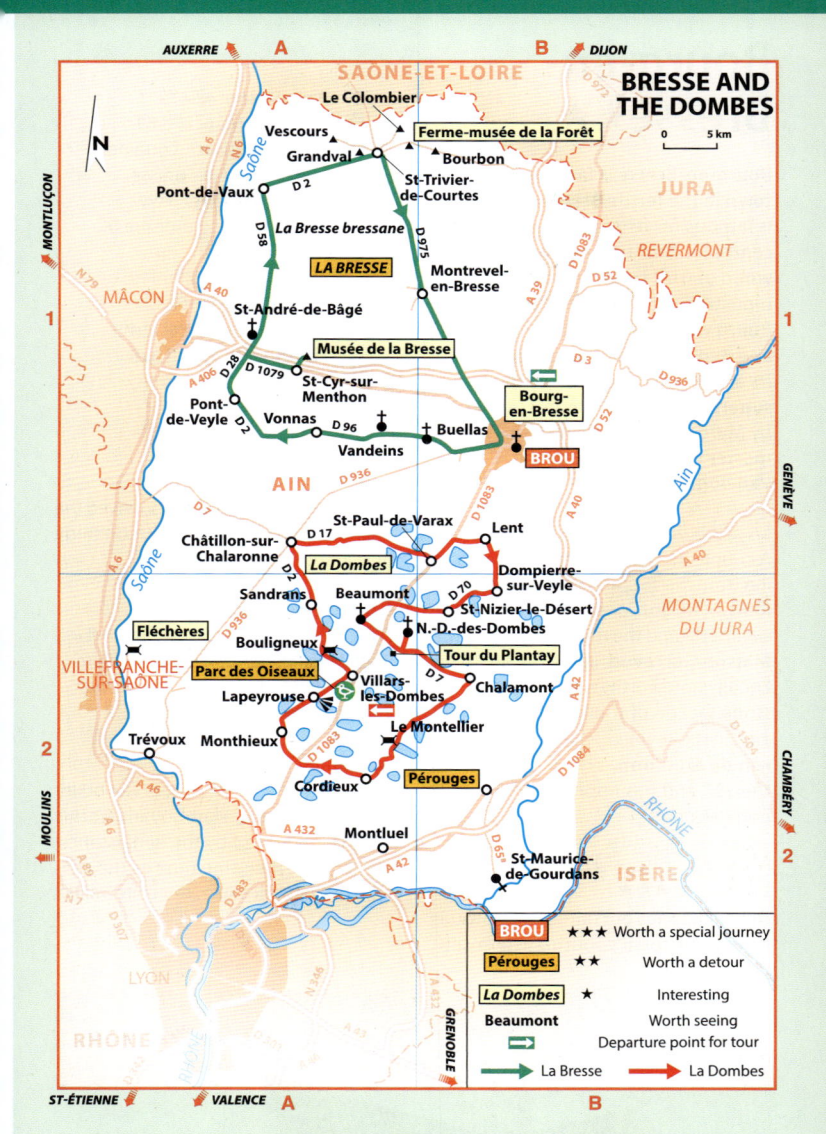

ered tern, red-crested pochard and purple heron. There are, however, conservation issues, not in the least because 90 percent of the area is used for hunting, with 70 percent given to farming.

Fermes Bressanes

The typical local farm in Bresse is characterized by a style unchanged since the Middle Ages uniting brick and wood. Low and long with distinctive roofs of channelled tiles and chimneys and a main entrance oriented towards the east, the oldest also use wattle and daub as part of their construction.

Today, some of these farms are protected as sites of local heritage, and many are open to visits.

Bourg-en-Bresse ★★

Bourg-en-Bresse, a large market town in the fertile Bresse region, is famous for its poultry and as a centre for furniture made from the wood of fruit trees. This and other industrial activities have endowed Bourg with the image of a lively and dynamic city. Bourg owes its architectural renown to the superb monastery commissioned by Marguerite of Austria to a master Flemish stonemason, Van Boghem.

- **Population:** 42 439.
- **Michelin Map:** 328 E3.
- **Info:** 6 av. Alsace-Lorraine, 01005 Bourg-en-Bresse. ℘04 74 22 49 40 www.bourgenbressetourisme.fr.
- **Location:** Bourg-en-Bresse is 62km/39mi NE of Lyon, via the D 1083.
- **Kids:** Visit a typical farm
- **Timing:** Allow half a day to explore at a leisurely pace.

OLD HOUSES

A couple of half-timbered houses, dating from the 15C, are worth visiting: the **Maison Hugon**, on the corner of the rue Gambetta and the rue V-Basch, and the **Maison Gorrevod**, in the rue du Palais. Equally noteworthy is the beautiful 17C stone façade of the **Hotel de Bohan**, and, in rue Teynière, the **Hotel de Marron de Meillonnas**, which dates from the 18C and has impressive wrought-iron balconies.

MONASTÈRE ROYAL DE BROU ★★★

Once a hamlet outside Bourg, Brou is now in the town's south-eastern suburbs. Happily, the buildings survived the Wars of Religion and Revolution fairly unscathed.

Church ★★

Daily: Jan–Mar and Oct–Dec 9am–noon, 2–5pm; Apr–Jun 9am–12.30pm, 2–6pm; Jul–Sept 9am–6pm. 1 Jan, 1 May, 1 and 11 Nov, 25 Dec. €9. ℘04 74 22 83 83.
www.monastere-de-brou.fr.
The church is deconsecrated. The building, in which the Flamboyant Gothic style is influenced by the Renaissance, was built at the same time as the château of Chenonceau in the Loire valley.

Monastère Royal de Brou

© Franck Guiziou/hemis.fr

Exterior

The tympanum above the fine **Renaissance doorway**★ shows Philibert the Handsome and Margaret of Austria and their patron saints at the feet of Christ Bound. On the pier is St Nicolas of Tolentino, to whom the church is dedicated (his feast falls on the day of Philibert's death). Surmounting the ornamental doorway arch is a statue of St Andrew; St Peter and St Paul flank the doorway on the arch shafts.

The decorative sculpture includes a variety of Flamboyant Gothic floral motifs (leaves and fruit), some showing a decidedly Renaissance influence (laurel, vine and acanthus), intermingled with symbolic motifs such as palms interlaced with marguerites. Other motifs include the initials of Philibert and Margaret linked by love-knots intermingled with crossed batons, the arms of Burgundy. The simpler façade of the north transept has a pinnacled gable. The five-storey belfry is on the south side of the apse.

The roof was modified significantly in 1759, so during restoration from 1996 to 1998 it was returned to its original design; Mansard frameworks were replaced by more steeply sloping forms. Flat roof tiles laid in a diamond pattern have been glazed in typical colours of the Burgundian style, evoking Margaret's status as Princess of Burgundy.

Interior

Nave – The pillars, formed by numerous little columns, thrust upwards in an un-broken line to the vaulting and open out into a network of ribs meeting at the carved keystones. A finely sculpted balustrade runs below the windows of the nave. The overall impression is one of elegance, magnificence and good taste. In the second bay of the nave (right) is a 16C black marble font bearing Margaret's motto.

The south transept is lit through a beautiful stained-glass window showing Susanna being accused by the Elders (above) and exonerated by Daniel (below).

To the right of the rood screen is the Montécuto Chapel which contains models explaining the construction of the church.

Rood screen★★ – The richly decorated screen, which separates the nave and transepts from the chancel, is composed of three basket-handled arches supporting seven religious statues. It once provided a passage for Margaret to access what were meant to be her private apartments; now accessible to the public, it provides an astounding view of the church from above.

Chancel – Margaret spared no expense to make this, the most important part of the church, as resplendent as possible. Taken as a whole, the sculpted decoration might border on the excessive, but the longer and closer one examines the ornamentation, the greater its charm, since the smallest detail is treated with quite extraordinary craftsmanship.

Choir stalls★★ – The 74 stalls, which line the first two bays of the choir, were carved from oak in just two years (1530–32). The master carpenter, Pierre Berchod, known as Terrasson, had to mobilise all the local wood craftsmen. They are carved in the same manner as the sculptures on the tombs, and the designs appear to be those of the same artist, **Jean de Bruxelles**. The stalls on the north side feature scenes from the New Testament and satirical characters, those on the south side show characters and scenes from the Old Testament.

The tombs★★★ – Many artists collaborated in the decoration of these three monuments, the high point of Flemish sculpture in the region. The designs were sketched by Jean de Bruxelles, who furnished the sculptors with life-size drawings. The ornamentation and the statuary, much admired by visitors, are attributed for the most part to a Flemish workshop which was set up in Brou, in collaboration with French, German and Italian sculptors. The statues of the three princely personages are the work of Conrad Meyt, born in Germany but trained in Flanders. The effigies of the prince and princess are carved in Carrara marble. Philibert and the two Margarets are represented, each lying on the tomb on a slab of black marble,

DISCOVERING BRESSE AND THE DOMBES

Choir stalls, Monastère Royal de Brou

their heads on embroidered cushions. A dog, emblem of fidelity, lies at the feet of the two princesses, and a lion, symbol of strength, at the feet of the prince. The tomb of Margaret of Bourbon occupies a recessed niche in the south wall of the choir.

The two other tombs differ in that they have two recumbent effigies: the first depicted alive and the second dead in a shroud. That of Philibert, the most sober in conception but also the most moving, is in the centre. The tomb of Margaret of Austria, with its huge canopy of chiselled stone, is north of the chancel. On the sole of her foot can be seen the wound which supposedly caused the princess' death by blood poisoning. Princess Margaret's motto is inscribed on the canopy: **Fortune in-fortune fort une** (Fate was very hard on one woman).
Stained-glass windows★★ – The windows in the centre of the apse show Christ appearing to Mary Magdalene (upper part) and visiting Mary (lower part), scenes taken from engravings by Albrecht Dürer. On the left and right, Philibert and Margaret kneel before their patron saints. The coats of arms of their families are above them: Savoy and Bourbon for the duke, and Imperial and Burgundian for the duchess.

Chapels and Oratories – The **chapel of Margaret**★★★ opens to the north of the choir. An altar screen and a stained-glass window, both fine works of art, deserve to be admired.

The **altar screen**★★★ depicts the Seven Joys of the Virgin Mary. This white marble masterpiece of delicate workmanship is exceptionally well preserved. A scene of the Seven Joys is set in each of the niches, designed for the purpose: on the left, below, is the Annunciation; on the right, the Visitation; above, the Nativity and the Adoration of the Magi; higher still are the Assumption, framed by Christ appearing to his mother, and Pentecost. The retable is crowned by three statues: the Virgin and Child flanked by Ste Mary Magdalene and Ste Margaret. On either side of the retable note St Philip and St Andrew.

The **stained-glass window**★★★ is inspired by an Albrecht Dürer engraving of the Assumption. The glass workers have added Philibert and Margaret kneeling near their patron saints.

The oratories of Margaret were arranged for her personal use. They are next to the Chapelle de Madame and are one above the other, linked by a staircase. These two chambers were effectively little drawing rooms. An oblique window, below a highly original arch, allowed the princess to follow the religious services. The nearby chapel has a remarkable **stained-glass window**★★ and a triptych ordered by Cardinal de Granvelle.

BOURG-EN-BRESSE

Museum and Cloisters★★
The museum is housed in the monastic buildings, which are arranged around two-storey cloisters, unique in France. From the roodscreen passage, visitors first access what were conceived as Margaret's apartments; she died before she was able to live here. These galleries, once used as offices, been converted into a museum to her life, with videos, maps, and interactive exhibits.
Following the apartments, one reaches a great room containing the museum's Renaissance art collections. Finally, one reaches the space dedicated to the artisan savoir-faire that contributed to the restoration of the monument. Of note are the 16C stained glass windows, which visitors can observe up close. All three sets of cloisters are now open to the public.

🚗 DRIVING TOUR

LA BRESSE★★
104km/65mi. Allow a whole day.

Bresse, which lies to the south of Burgundy, is a captivating land renowned for its traditions and gastronomy. This is bocage country, with many waterways running across the area. The landscape is easily recognisable by its meadows populated by white chickens, corn dryers and timber-framed farmhouses, some with distinctive chimney pots.

▶ Leave Bourg-en-Bresse to the west, taking the direction for Villefranche-sur-Saône. At Corgenon, turn right on D 45 and follow this as far as Buellas.

Buellas
The **church** has a beautiful Romanesque choir.

▶ Continue on D 45 to Vandeins.

Vandeins
The **church** is adorned with a carved doorway dating from the 12C, and the tympanum is clearly Romanesque work.

▶ Continue on the D 96 which leads to Vonnas.

Vonnas
This small, peaceful, flower-decked town is a popular gastronomic stop on the border between Bresse and the Dombes. By all accounts, for the best chicken dish you are ever likely to taste, try "Poularde de Bresse aux gousses d'ail et foie gras" (Bresse chicken with garlic and foie gras).

▶ Return to D 96 and follow it in the direction of Biziat. Once there, join the D 2.

Pont-de-Veyle
Watered by the River Veyle and surrounded by drainage channels, the town has grown since the 13C, and served as a haven for Protestants until the Edict of Nantes (1685). There are some interesting architectural details, not least the doorway of the **clock tower** (16C), the **Maison de Savoie** (15C, 66 Grande Rue) and the Jesuit-style **church** (1752).

▶ Leave Pont-de-Veyle heading north along D 28. 3km/2mi further on, turn right onto D 1079 in the direction of Bourg-en-Bresse.

Saint-Cyr-sur-Menthon
The town includes several outstanding examples of rural architecture. North of the D 1079, you can still see one of the largest poypes (feudal mounds) in the area – 46m in diameter, and 9.5m high.

▶ After St-Cyr-sur-Menthon, you can join the A 40 in the direction of Mâcon, turning off at the aire de répos.

👥 Musée de la Bresse
🕐 *Mar–mid-Nov daily except Tue 10am–6pm.* ≤€7. ☎03 85 36 31 22. www.patrimoines.ain.fr.
This is a beautiful example of Bresse architecture, built during the summer of 2005 in a semi-subterranean, contemporary building. Undulating glass panels reflect the environment, where you can discover Bresse through collec-

DISCOVERING BRESSE AND THE DOMBES

tions of costumes and jewellery, including exquisite Bresse enamels.
Following the plan of a farm courtyard, unusual in Bresse, the main area of the buildings is entered via a large porch, or "Passou". The house is remarkable for its Saracen chimney; it was built in 1490 and later restored using traditional techniques. From an inventory of 1784 found on the site, it is possible to reconstruct the organisation and equipment of the farm at that time. Behind the house, the garden has been recreated with remarkable attention to detail. Other buildings portray the building of a farm, livestock and poultry from Bresse.

◉ Go back to St-Cyr-sur-Menthon, take the D 1079 to the junction with the D 28. Turn right towards Bâgé-le-Châtel.

Saint-André-de-Bâgé

The Romanesque church, isolated in the cemetery on the left before the village, was built in the 11C by the monks of Tournus. An elegant octagonal spire, topped by a stone steeple, dominates the apse and two chapels.

◉ On reaching Bâgé-le-Châtel, continue northwards on D 58 to Pont-de-Vaux.

Pont-de-Vaux

This small town is dedicated to the memory of General Joubert, commander of the Italian army, and companion of Napoleon Bonaparte, who died in 1799 and was buried in the church of Pont-de-Vaux. Once a frontier town of Savoie, Pont-de-Vaux has developed in a meander of the Reyssouze, a tributary of the Saône. The river below the town has been channelled and allows navigation of the Saône as far as Pont-de-Vaux, with its half-timbered houses and 16C/17C façades. Each December, the town hosts one of the four annual *Glorieuses de Bresse* poultry competitions.

Musée Chintreuil
Apr–Nov daily except Tue 2–6pm.
€4. 03 85 51 45 65.
www.musee-chintreuil.com.
The museum displays interesting paintings by Jules Migonney (Vieille Mauresque) and Antoine Chintreuil (pupil of Corot).

Église Notre-Dame
The church dates from the 15C; its façade in the Jesuit style is decorated with Baroque shells. Because of space constraints, the church was built long and narrow and ends with a Gothic choir illuminated by large windows. In addi-

Ferme-musée de la Forêt

BOURG-EN-BRESSE

tion to the woodwork, which came from the monastery at Montmerle following the Revolution, the church is decorated with 11 large paintings by a student of Boucher, Nicolas Brenet (18C).

▶ Leave to the NE on the D 2 in the direction of St-Trivier-de-Courtes.

Saint-Trivier-de-Courtes

A former strategic possession of the Lords of Bâgé, the town is famous for its many Bresse farms with Saracen chimneys, notably:
Ferme de Grandval – 1.5km/1mi to the west by the D 2.
Ferme de Vescours – 5km/3mi to the west; turn right at the entrance to the village.
Ferme du Colombier à Vernoux – 3km/2mi to the north-east.
Ferme de Bourbon à Saint-Nizier-le-Bouchoux – 6km/3.5mi to the east.

Ferme-musée de la Forêt★
3km/2mi to the east. Apr–Jun and Oct Sat–Sun; Jun–Sept daily (except Mon) 10.30am–12.30pm, 2.30–6pm. €3 (children under 12, no charge). 04 74 30 71 89.
This beautiful 16C–17C farm has been restored and converted into a typical farm of Bresse. Note the latticed wooden balconies and the Saracen chimney. The building has a traditional interior with a fireplace 4m from the side of the room supported by a beam. In an adjacent building you will find a collection of antique farm equipment.

▶ Back in St-Trivier, take the D 975 to the south in the direction of Bourg-en-Bresse.

Montrevel-en-Bresse

A former stronghold of the Montrevel family, the town is also the "home" of St Peter Chanel (1803-1841), a missionary martyred on the island of Futuna and who became the patron saint of Oceania. The village of Cuets, next to the town, commemorates the saint (Musée Océanie).

The **farmhouse** has retained its beautiful 17C Sougey mitre square and Saracen chimney dating to 1461.
Set in the gravel pits of the Reyssouze valley, the **Montrevel Leisure Centre** is an important tourist attraction.

▶ Continue along the D 975 to arrive back at Bourg-en-Bresse.

ADDRESSES

EAT

La Coq'Hote – *15 rue Paul-Pioda, 01000 Bourg-en-Bresse. www.lacoqhote.fr/. 04 74 47 10 66 Closed Sun–Mon.* Local specialties are on the menu, including Bresse chicken prepared *en cocotte*.

Ô Beurre Noisette – *16 rue de la République, 01000 Bourg-en-Bresse. 04 74 21 26 45. Closed Sun–Mon.* A former butchershop has been converted into an authentic bistro serving local, seasonal fare. Beautiful terrace in summer.

Auberge Bressane – *166 Bd de Brou, 01000 Bourg-en-Bresse. www.aubergebressane.fr. 04 74 22 22 68. Closed Tues.* This ultra-traditional spot has an unsurprising focus on Bresse chicken, serving it spit-roasted or in a *vin jaune* and cream sauce.

RECREATION

Loisirs Plaine Tonique – *599, route d'Etrez, 01340 Malafretaz. www.laplainetonique.com.* This water park boasts beaches, waterslides, several pools, and facilities for volleyball, tennis, and more. Access to the beach and water park is free for those staying at the campsite.

Arbres et Sens Aventures
15km/9.3mi from Bourg-en-Bresse via autoroute A 40, exit 6 then N 83 towards Lons le Saunier. www.arbres-et-sens-aventures.fr. end-March–Oct Wed, Sat–Sun 2–7pm, Jul–Aug daily 10am–7pm.
The longest zipline in the Rhône-Alpes awaits at this adventure park.

DISCOVERING BRESSE AND THE DOMBES

La Dombes★

The Dombes plateau owes its charm and rather unusual appearance to the presence of more than 1 000 lakes dotted across its entire area. Here and there are low hills, formed by moraines, which were transformed in the Middle Ages into veritable fortresses of earth surrounded by moats. Rural housing in the Dombes region is built mainly of cob (pisé) whereas the castles and outer walls are built of rough red bricks known as carrons (terracotta).

The region's history, too, is somewhat out of the ordinary. Dombes was raised to the rank of a principality by François I following the confiscation of the property belonging to the Constable of Bourbon in 1523. A sovereign Parliament sat in Trévoux and remained until the mid-18C.

- **Michelin Map:** 328: C-4 to D-5.
- **Info:** 3, Place de l'Hôtel de Ville 01330 Villars les Dombes. ✆04 74 98 06 29. www.villars-les-dombes.com.
- **Location:** The Dombes plateau is situated between Lyon and Bourg-en-Bresse and is bordered by the River Ain and the River Saône.
- **Don't Miss:** A grand tour of the lakes.
- **Timing:** Allow a full day or two to explore the region.

A BIT OF GEOGRAPHY

The impermeable soil encouraged local people very early on in their history to turn their fields into lakes enclosed by mud dikes. The **Grand Étang de Birieux**, one of the most extensive of the lakes (now subdivided) dates from the 14C. In the 16C, Dombes boasted almost 2 000 lakes, many filled with stagnant water, which led to an unhealthy climate. Most of the lakes are intermittent, one being emptied to fill another: they are filled and stocked with fish for a period of six or seven years; then drained and for one year turned over to agriculture.

SIGHTS

Château de Fléchères★★

6km/3.5mi NE of Villefranche-sur-Saône via the D 933, in the commune of Fareins.

The early-17C château stands in a shaded 30ha park offering pleasant strolls. Built by a wealthy protestant from Lyon, the edifice included a temple (Protestant church) on the third floor of the central building. The huge hall beneath the church was used for gatherings of the local Protestant community.

The owner's living quarters were confined to the wings, which were lower than the central building. The interior is decorated with superb Italian frescoes (1632) believed to be the work of Pietro Ricchi.

Châtillon-sur-Chalaronne

To the N of the Dombes, along the valley of the Chalaronne; 25km/15.5mi SW of Bourg-en-Bresse.

This pretty town in the shadow of its 11C castle on the border between the Bresse and Dombes areas spreads along the Chalaronne valley. Coming into Châtillon from the south-west on the road from Villefranche (D 936), there is a fine **view** over the town's red rooftops, dominated by the impressive bell-tower of the former almshouse. The half-timbered houses with cob or brick walls built in the style typical of the Dombes area are brightened up in summer with bunches of flowers arranged in wicker baskets called *nids-de-poule* (hens' nests).

Highlights include the **ramparts** of the Vieux Château (the remnants of one of the largest strongholds in Bresse) and the **Maison St-Vincent**, where St Vincent de Paul was lodged by a Protestant,

LA DOMBES

A Bird's Paradise

The **Parc des Oiseaux**★ bird sanctuary *(1km/0.6mi south of Villars-les-Dombes on N 83. Daily late Mar–mid-Nov. From €20 (child 3–12, €15). 04 74 98 05 54. www.parcdesoiseaux.com)*, close to the Dombes Nature Reserve, lies along one of the main migration routes in Europe. Over 2 000 birds from five continents live in the park.

At the entrance, the "Birds' House" provides a warm, humid atmosphere for a wonderful selection of brightly coloured exotic birds. Enjoy a walk round the park along the footpaths running round the lakes, which are the breeding ground for large birds such as common and night heron as well as rarer species in giant aviaries. Besides the spectacular Vallée des Rapaces, the Volière du Pantanal and the Cité des Perroquets are also fascinating. The park is engaged in several conservation programmes aimed at endangered species. These are explained to children through various activities in the Maison des Enfants.

M Beynier, for five months while he was the incumbent of Châtillon. A municipal **museum** along the path leading up to the castle is devoted to rural life and ancient crafts, while the old **hospital**, commissioned by the Count of Châtelard in the 18C, now houses a regional arts centre.

Trévoux

Between Lyon and Villefranche-sur-Saône, its nearest neighbours.

This town is built on different levels along the steep bank of the Saône, its colourful façades and flower-filled gardens all facing southwards. Trévoux stands at the intersection of three Roman roads; it was once the capital of the Principality of Dombes, the seat of a sovereign Parliament, and was independent until 1762. After the Duke of Maine decreed that the town's magistrates and members of Parliament must also be residents here, a number of mansions were built in the 18C, along the alleyways of the old districts.

In the 17C and 18C the town was one of the most brilliant intellectual centres in France. Its printing house, founded in 1603, was famous. In 1704, the Jesuits published the first edition of the famous Trévoux Dictionary; under their supervision, the Trévoux Journal fought a relentless campaign against Voltaire and the "Encyclopædic" philosophers for 30 years.

Old Town Tour

▶ Park in boulevard des Combattants. Walk to place de la Terrasse, which over-looks the Saône. The Palais du Parlement is on the other side of rue du Palais.

Palais du Parlement de Dombes

Guided visits 3pm from tourist office: Apr–Sept Sat–Sun and public holidays. Oct–Apr, 1 Jan and 25 Dec. €4 (under 18, free). 04 74 00 36 32. www.patrimoines.ain.fr

This Parliament House was built at the end of the 17C; the Dombes Parliament sat from 1697 to 1771. The hall leads into the courtroom with its beautiful

Château de Fléchères

DISCOVERING BRESSE AND THE DOMBES

beamed ceiling with painted decorations.

Rue du Gouvernement
On either side of the street, just below the church, the Trévoux Dictionary and Journal were written and printed. The Jesuits who lived on the right, in the tall, spacious Maison des Pères, had only to cross the street to take their manuscripts to the printers opposite.
Further down are a number of old houses: the house of the Governor of Dombes, that of the Grande Mademoiselle and the Mint, their austere façades concealing terraces overlooking the Saône.

▶ Take Rue des Halles to the hospital.

Hôpital
Guided tours: same details as Parlement de Dombes.
The hospital was founded in 1686 by La Grande Mademoiselle; it still has the original wood-panelled pharmacy and a beautiful collection of pottery from Gien and Nevers.

▶ Return to rue des Halles and turn left onto rue du Port. Turn right onto rue de l'Herberie.

This street was once reserved for Jews. The intersection of rue de l'Herberie and Grande-Rue forms a triangle dominated by the square-shaped Arsenal Tower of 1405, later converted into a belfry.

▶ Walk up montée de l'Orme to the castle.

Château Féodal
Guided tours: same details as Parlement de Dombes.
Remains of the medieval castle (14C); from the top of the octagonal tower there is a view of the Saône.

▶ Walk down montée des Tours, then return along rue du Palais back to boulevard des Combattants.

🚗 DRIVING TOUR

TOUR OF THE LAKES★
Round trip of 99km/61mi from Villars-les-Dombes. Allow one day.

The region is well-known for its numerous lakes and the opportunities for fishing and bird watching.

Villars-les-Dombes
The unofficial capital of La Dombes, pleasant Villars is located on the right bank of the Chalaronne.

▶ Leave Villars on D 2 heading W.

Bouligneux
In a setting typical of this area stands a 14C brick-built castle that looks rather more like a fortress.

Sandrans
This village is known for its medieval fortress on which a large house was built in the 19C. Today a hillock remains, surrounded by a moat and crowned with a round tower.

Châtillon-sur-Chalaronne
See below.

▶ Leave Châtillon E on D 17 towards St-Paul-de-Varax.

St-Paul-de-Varax
The Romanesque church dates back to the 12C.

▶ Drive N along D 1083 then turn right onto D 64A.

Lent
The village still boasts fine 16C monuments: the church belfry (restored in the 18C) and some timber houses.

Dompierre-sur-Veyle
This village grouped around a Romanesque church is near the largest lake in the area (100ha/247 acres): **Le Grand Marais**.

LA DOMBES

▶ The D 70 road heading west to St-Nizier passes to the right of various stretches of water which are extensions of Le Grand Marais.

St-Nizier-le-Désert
This pleasant village offers facilities for fishing and gentle rambles.

▶ Follow D 90 which crosses D 1083 and leads to Marlieux. Drive through the village and join D 7. Just after a bend, take a small road towards Beaumont.

Beaumont
The **Chapelle Notre-Dame de Beaumont** stands on the lovely village square. This chapel was once a popular centre of pilgrimage, but subsequently fell into a state of disrepair. Restoration work has revealed 15C **frescoes★** which have been well preserved.

▶ Turn back along the small road on which you arrived to the first intersection. The road branching off to the right goes through the hamlet of Villardières, crosses D 1083 and leads to Le Plantay.

Le Plantay
The village is surrounded by the waters of the Grand Châtel. The **tower★** here (*not open to the public*), of large red bricks and decorated with white stone around the machicolations, is a symbol for the region.

Abbaye Notre-Dame-des-Dombes
Monks from this abbey, founded by Cistercians in the 19C, helped to drain the area and cultivated those sections of land which are fertile.

Chalamont
This is the highest point in La Dombes. Rue des Halles is lined with a few old houses (15C but restored) with overhanging storeys and a wash-house.

▶ Take D 61 to Joyeux, where there is an attractive 19C house.

▶ The castle at Le Montellier comes into view on the right.

Le Montellier
The brick castle (*not open to the public*), the most impressive in La Dombes, is flanked at one end by a keep rising on its earth mound.

Cordieux
A handsome red-brick manor house stands here.

▶ Rejoin D 4 and turn left (W) to St-André-de-Corcy; take D 82 to Monthieux.

Monthieux
Breuil manor house (16C), just north of the village, has an interesting Saracen well.

▶ Head towards Ambérieux-en-Dombes and turn right onto D 6.

Lapeyrouse
From the war memorial there is a delightful view of the Alps and, in the foreground, the Grand Glareins lakes and the 15C Château de Glareins (*not open to the public*).

▶ Take D 904 back to Villars.

ADDRESSES

STAY

Hostellerie des Bichonnières & Spa – *545 Route du 3 Septembre 1944, Rte d'Ars, 01330 Ambérieux-en-Dombes. 11km/6.6mi W of Villars-les-Dombes via D 904. ℘04 74 00 82 07. www.lesbichonnieres.com.* This recently renovated inn and spa boasts comfortable rooms and a beautiful outdoor garden.

361

Pérouges ★★

Pérouges is perched on a hilltop and surrounded by ramparts; it remains a model of medieval architecture, with narrow winding streets and ancient houses, making it very popular with visitors. Pérouges has such an authentic historical flavour that it is often used as the setting for period films by French directors.

> - **Population:** 1 238.
> - **Michelin Map:** 328: E-5.
> - **Info:** Route de la Cité, 01800 PÉROUGES. ℘04 74 46 70 84. www.perouges.org.
> - **Location:** Pérouge lies 34km/21mi NE of Lyon, and 38km/23.5mi from Bourg-en-Bresse.
> - **Don't miss:** The place de la Halle.
> - **Parking:** There is limited parking, but you will find a car park near the church.
> - **Timing:** Allow 2hrs to explore the town.

A BIT OF HISTORY

During the Middle Ages and up to the French annexation (1601), the town was disputed many times by the sovereigns of Dauphiné and Savoy. In the rich and active town centre, hundreds of craftsmen wove fabric from hemp grown in the surrounding fields.

In the 19C, the town's prosperity waned: Pérouges was too far from the railway line, and local craftsmen could no longer compete with industry.

In 1909–10, the town nearly disappeared altogether: many of the owners turned to mass destruction, and entire blocks of old houses were pulled down. Fortunately, a historical society from Lyon and a few artists from Pérouges stepped in, helped by the School of Arts. The most interesting houses were bought, restored, and classified as historical monuments.

Most of the houses in Pérouges mark the transition between the Gothic and Renaissance styles. The houses of the gentry and richer townsfolk have large dimensions and luxurious interiors. Those of the merchants were more modest, with semicircular openings to light the workshop or serve as counters to display their goods. The streets have barely changed since the Middle Ages. Narrow and winding, they had double-sloping paving with a drainage channel in the middle.

Pérouges viewed from the watchtower of Musée du Vieux-Pérouges

© Franck Guiziou/hemis.fr

PÉROUGES

PÉROUGES

WHERE TO STAY

M. et Mme Debeney-Truchon (Chambre d'hôte)............ ①

Petit Casset........................ ②

WHERE TO EAT

Coq (Auberge du).............. ①

Mollard (Auberge de Campagne du)................. ②

Vieux Pérouges (Ostellerie du)................... ③

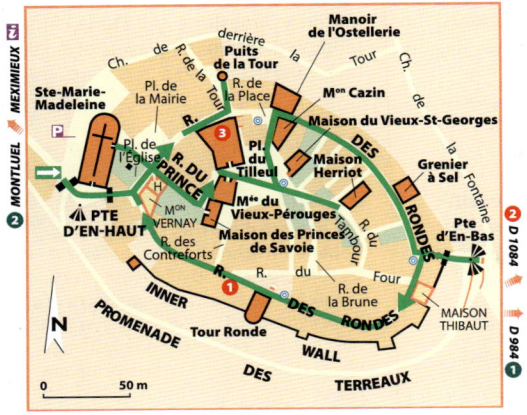

WALKING TOUR

OLD TOWN

Porte d'En-Haut★
This gateway, the main entrance to Pérouges, was also the most exposed. Its defence was reinforced by the fortress-church and a barbican.

Rue du Prince★
Butchers, basket-makers, drapers, the armourer and the apothecary held shop here. At one end stands the **Maison des Princes de Savoie**, which presently houses a museum.

Place de la Halle★★
This market square is one of the prettiest in France. It derives its name from the covered markets or **Halles**, which stood here and were razed in 1839.

Place du Tilleul★★★
Ostellerie
This inn has a sign bearing the town's coat of arms. The half-timbered east façade is 13C whereas the south front is Renaissance.
Musée du Vieux-Pérouges
(Apr–Oct Wed–Sun 10am–noon, 2–6pm. €4. 04 74 61 00 88).
This museum is housed partly in the Maison des Princes de Savoie and in the Maison Heer which opens onto place de la Halle.

Maison du Vieux-St-Georges
A shell-shaped niche on the façade houses an unusual wooden 15C statue of St George, patron saint of Pérouges, mounted on a horse.

▶ Take the narrow street which goes downhill from the corner of the square.

Maison Herriot
This sumptuous-looking house boasts semicircular and mullioned windows.

▶ Return to the square and take rue de la Place, to the N.

Maison Cazin
This lovely house has projecting upper floors and half-timbering.

▶ Turn right onto rue des Rondes.

Rue des Rondes★
This street still has most of its ancient paving and central drainage channel. The old houses on either side are protected by wide eaves.

Porte d'En-Bas
The Lower Gateway is older than the Upper Gateway. On the outside is an inscription referring to a siege in 1468, which can be translated as: "Pérouges of the Pérougians! Impregnable town! Those rascally Dauphinois wanted to take it but they could not.

DISCOVERING BRESSE AND THE DOMBES

So they went off with the doors, the hinges and the locks instead. May the devil take them!"

▶ Rue des Rondes leads round to place de l'Église.

Église Ste-Marie-Madeleine
This 15C church looks like a fortress, with its north-western wall incorporating crenellations, arrow slits and very high, narrow openings.

▶ Rejoin rue des Rondes which leads to rue de la Tour.

Puits de la Tour
For a long time, this well supplied water to the entire town. The tower built by the Romans was destroyed in 1749. A lantern in the upper part of the tower was used to send light signals to similar towers forming a relay right to Lyon.

The Two Curtain Walls
The path uphill from the Upper Gateway leads to **Promenade des Terreaux★** in the moat of the outer curtain wall of which only vestiges remains. The **Round Tower**, against which the house of the Sergeant of Justice is built, was formerly used as a prison.

EXCURSIONS
Montluel
Leave Pérouges on N 84 towards Lyon.
Montluel has retained several interesting buildings worth admiring. Take a stroll through the flower-decked town starting from the collegiate church of Notre-Dame-du-Marais (16C–17C) past the chapel of the former Visitation Convent then the 12C St-Stephen's porch; note the carved wood decoration of the apothecary's shop (guided visits May–Oct Wed and Sat 3–6pm; Nov–Apr Sat 3–6pm; public holidays; ℘04 78 06 06 23).

St-Maurice-de-Gourdans
12km/6.6mi S on D 65B.
This village lies on the edge of a plateau dominating the confluence of the River Ain and the River Rhône. The 12C church has been restored to reveal its original masonry: limestone and stone chippings with alternating layers of small bricks and flat pebbles.

ADDRESSES

STAY
Chambre d'Hôte M. et Mme Debeney-Truchon – *01150 Chazey-sur-Ain. ℘04 74 61 95 87. 5 rooms.* The simplicity and welcoming atmosphere of this village farm is seductive. If you have the time, the owner will show you how he makes his bread. Amateur *pétanque* players welcome.

Le Petit Casset – *96 imp. du Petit-Casset, 01120 La Boisse – 9km/5.5mi SW of Montluel. ℘04 78 06 21 33. www.lepetitcasset.fr. 18 rooms.* Quiet, renovated hotel in a residential area. The atmosphere is friendly and the rooms, all individually decorated, overlook the garden. Swimming pool.

EAT
Auberge du Coq – *R. des Rondes. ℘04 74 61 05 47. Open Wed–Sun lunch, Fri–Sat dinner.* In a cobbled street, this restaurant evokes the essence of yesteryear.

Auberge de Campagne du Mollard – *Le Mollard, 01320 Châtillon-la-Palud. 13.6km/8mi NE of Pérouges via D 984 and D 904, dir. Chalamont, and road on left. ℘04 74 35 66 09. www.aubergedumollard.com. Reservations required.* This farm and inn settled amid the fields invites guests to stay over in its rooms furnished with attractive sculpted wood pieces and serves traditional local fare.

Hostellerie du Vieux Pérouges – *pl du Tilleul, 01800 Pérouges. ℘04 74 61 00 88. www.hostelleriedeperouges.com.* The fame of this magnificent manor in the heart of the village has spread beyond national borders ever since Bill Clinton dined here in 1997. This is a beautiful place with a uniquely Bressan décor. Regional and traditional dishes.

BEAUJOLAIS AND THE MONTS DU LYONNAIS

Forever associated with the wines the region produces, Beaujolais' gently undulating landscapes are characterized by numerous mountain plateaux crisscrossed by narrow sinuous **valleys**. By contrast, the attractive Monts du Lyonnais south-west of Lyon have a gentle, pastoral countenance patterned by chestnut groves and oakwoods. Land in the low-lying valleys is used for market gardening, vineyards and orchards, although many pastures extend into the higher ground.

The Father of Physiology

Born in the village of St-Julien, Claude Bernard (1813–78) moved to Paris in 1834. His study of liver glycogen made him the "creator" of physiology – a branch of biology that deals with the functions and activities of life. His research has served as a foundation for modern medicine.

Grapes of Beaujolais

In 1935, the Gamay grape was forbidden in Burgundy. Beaujolais, to the south, decided to make the most of it and grew the grape in abundance. Today, the region is planted with around 98 percent Gamay, with Pinot Noir and Chardonnay taking up the remaining 2 percent. Covering no less than 22 250ha, Beaujolais is larger than the three Burgundy regions combined. The region is divided into two by the Nizerand river: to the north is Haut-Beaujolais, which has light soil, ideal for the Beaujolais-Villages wines and all ten crus. To the south are the Bas-Beaujolais, which produces around half of the total volume of wines at 10 percent alcohol, with a small amount of Beaujolais-Supérieur, which is a little stronger. Beaujolais Nouveau, the region's primeur wine, is released every year on the third Thursday of November.

UNESCO Soil

In Beaujolais, there are 500 million years under your feet. An amazing patchwork of colors and textures can be found, and in 2018, the region was designated a UNESCO Global Geopark site, highlighting the outstanding geological heritage of the region.

Highlights

1. Taking an amble around the old houses of **Villefranche** (p367)
2. Lining the streets to cheer the **Fête des Conscrits** in Villefranche (p368)
3. Touring the **Beaujolais vineyards** (p371)
4. Leisurely exploring the glorious **Monts du Lyonnais** (p377)
5. Seeing birds of prey in flight at **Courzieu Animal Park** (p378)

Village and vineyards of Chénas

BEAUJOLAIS AND THE MONTS DU LYONNAIS

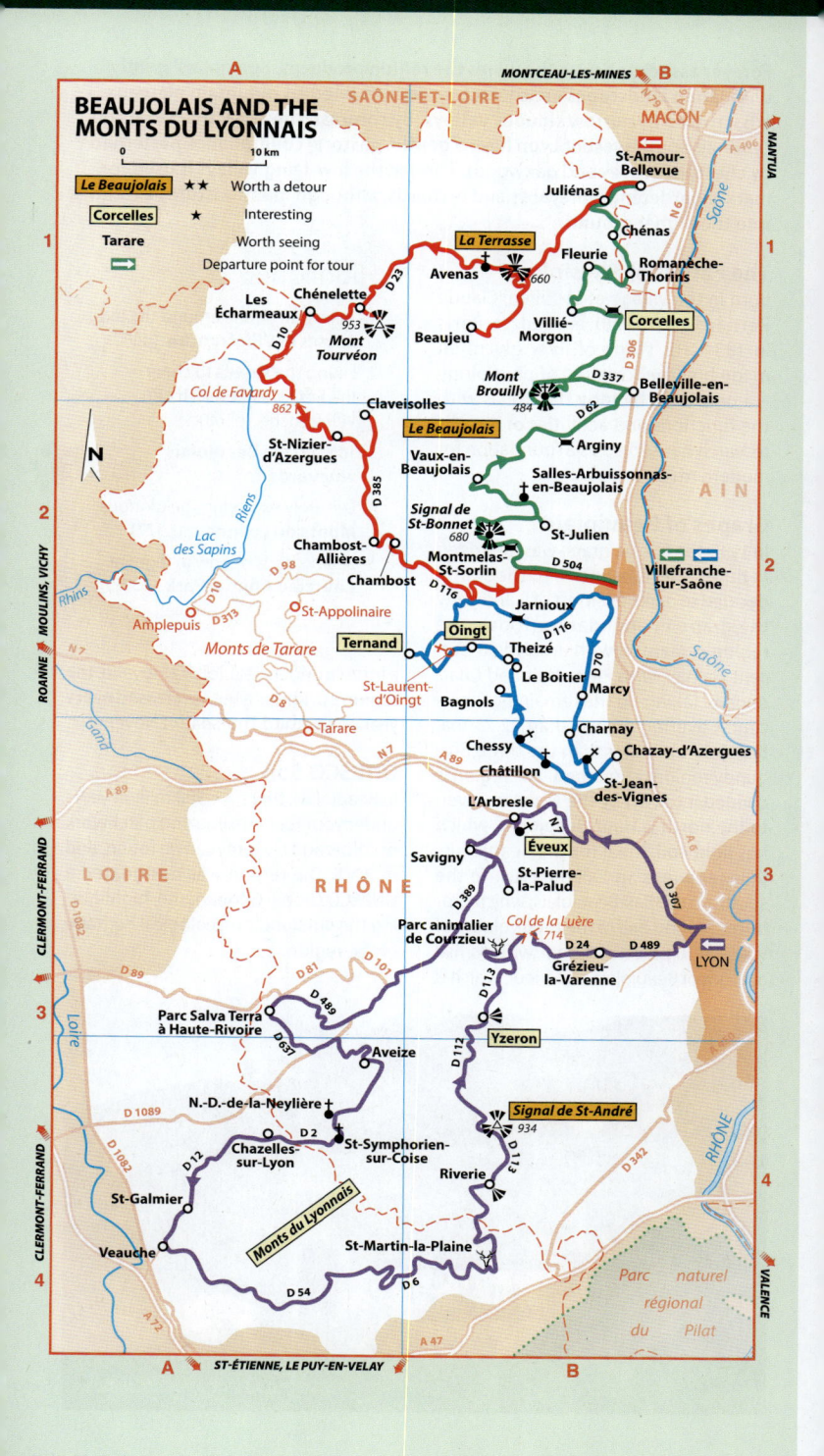

0 — 10 km

- *Le Beaujolais* ★★ Worth a detour
- **Corcelles** ★ Interesting
- Tarare — Worth seeing
- → Departure point for tour

MONTCEAU-LES-MINES · MÂCON · NANTUA · SAÔNE-ET-LOIRE

St-Amour-Bellevue · Juliénas · Chénas · Fleurie · Romanèche-Thorins · Villié-Morgon · **Corcelles** · Belleville-en-Beaujolais

La Terrasse · Avenas · 660 · Beaujeu · Les Écharmeaux · Chénelette · 953 · Mont Tourvéon · Col de Favardy · 862 · St-Nizier-d'Azergues · Claveisolles · Mont Brouilly · 484 · Arginy

Le Beaujolais · Vaux-en-Beaujolais · Salles-Arbuissonnas-en-Beaujolais · St-Julien · AIN

Lac des Sapins · Chambost-Allières · Chambost · Signal de St-Bonnet · 680 · Montmelas-St-Sorlin · Villefranche-sur-Saône

Ampuis · St-Appolinaire · Monts de Tarare · **Ternand** · **Oingt** · Theizé · Jarnioux · Le Boitier · Marcy

ROANNE, MOULINS, VICHY · Tarare · St-Laurent-d'Oingt · Bagnols · Chessy · Châtillon · Charnay · Chazay-d'Azergues · St-Jean-des-Vignes

L'Arbresle · **Éveux** · Savigny · St-Pierre-la-Palud · LYON

CLERMONT-FERRAND · LOIRE · RHÔNE · Parc animalier de Courzieu · Col de la Luère · 714 · Grézieu-la-Varenne

Parc Salva Terra à Haute-Rivoire · Aveize · **Yzeron** · *Signal de St-André* · 934

N.-D.-de-la-Neylière · St-Symphorien-sur-Coise · Chazelles-sur-Lyon · Riverie · VALENCE

St-Galmier · *Monts du Lyonnais* · Veauche · St-Martin-la-Plaine · Parc naturel régional du Pilat

ST-ÉTIENNE, LE PUY-EN-VELAY

366

Villefranche-sur-Saône

This busy industrial city is the capital of the Beaujolais region. It was founded in 1140 by the Lords of Beaujeu, to match the Anse fortress belonging to the Archbishops of Lyon. The settlement sprang up quickly, and in 1260, Guichard IV de Beaujeu granted the town a charter, which earned it the name of *Ville Franche*, meaning free town. In addition to its historical role as a wine trading centre, Villefranche now earns its living from the manufacture of sports and work wear (Joannès Sabot founded an overalls factory here in 1887), shirts and hosiery. The metallurgy, mechanical and food-processing industries are also represented here.

- **Population:** 37 266.
- **Michelin Map:** 327: H-4.
- **Info:** 96 r. de la Sous-Préfecture, 69400 Villefranche-sur-Saône. ⌀04 74 07 27 40. www.destination-beaujolais.fr.
- **Location:** The A 6 and D 306 link the town to Lyon, 34km/21mi to the south. The numbering of houses in Villefranche is based on a metric system, calculating the distance of each house from the beginning of the street. Street numbers run from rue Nationale east and west, and south from the north of town.
- **Parking:** There are numerous spacious car parks in the centre of town.
- **Don't Miss:** The lovely old houses along the rue Nationale.
- **Timing:** Normally allow 2 hours, but you can so easily be side-tracked.

SIGHTS

Old Houses

Guided tours (2h): check website for details. ⌀04 74 07 27 40. www.villefranche-beaujolais.fr.

Most of the town's oldest houses built between the 15C and 18C can be found along **rue Nationale**. They have relatively narrow façades, because of a 1260 tax imposed on their width, to make up for the exemption from taxes and the other privileges which had been granted to the town in its charter. The tourist office offers an urban route around the most important Renaissance courtyards, mansion façades, and more.

Odd-numbered side of the road

Note Nos. 375 (vaulted passageway), 401 (16C openwork spiral staircase in the courtyard) and, at No. 17 rue Grenette, the turret staircase with skylights. In the courtyard of No. 507, the well is surmounted by a shell-shaped canopy in the courtyard.

At No. 523, the **Hôtel de Mignot de Bussy** is a lovely Renaissance building with a spiral staircase, mullion windows and shell-shaped niche containing an elegant statue. Behind the splendid 1760 façade of No. 561, a vaulted passageway with sculpted supports leads to a 16C courtyard surrounded by pink-walled buildings. The **Maison Eymin** at No. 761 has an 18C façade with four levels of arches in the courtyard, hammer-wrought coats of arms (damaged) and an elegant turret housing a spiral staircase. No. 793, once the residence of the Roland de la Platière family, is indicated by a medallion and a commemorative plaque and features a monumental staircase with a wrought-iron bannister.

Even-numbered side of the road

From No. 400, there is a good view of the tower and stone balustrade of the Italian Renaissance house opposite. A 15C half-timbered house stands on the

DISCOVERING BEAUJOLAIS AND THE MONTS DU LYONNAIS

VILLEFRANCHE-SUR-SAÔNE

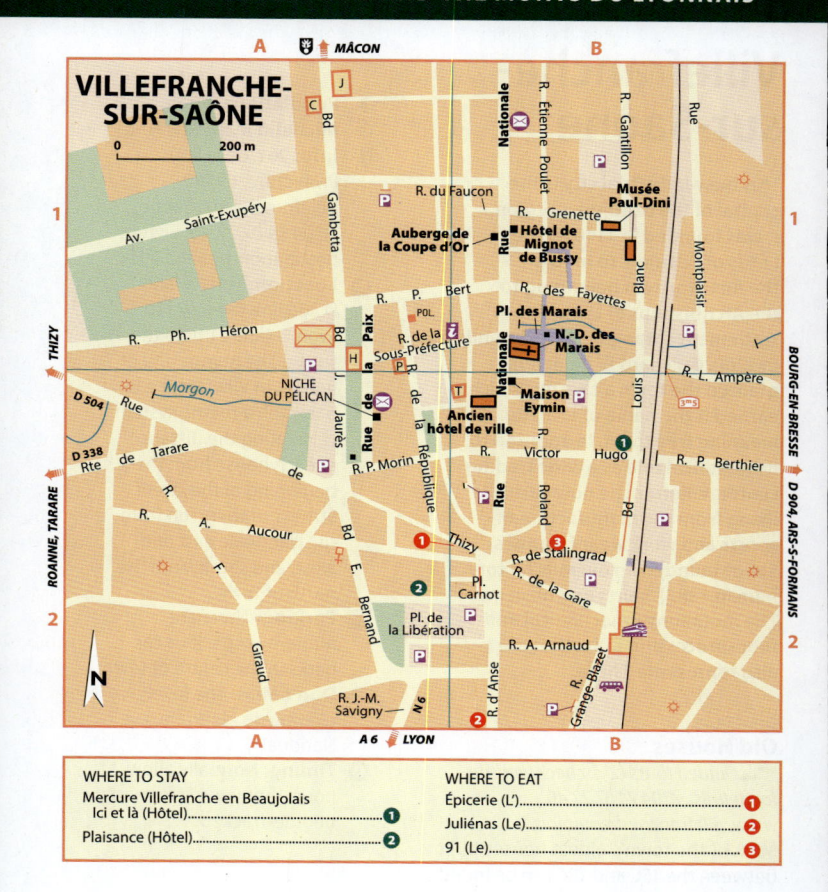

WHERE TO STAY	
Mercure Villefranche en Beaujolais Ici et là (Hôtel)	①
Plaisance (Hôtel)	②

WHERE TO EAT	
Épicerie (L')	①
Juliénas (Le)	②
91 (Le)	③

corner of rue du Faucon and rue Nationale (No. 476).

At No. 486, at the back of the alley on the right, a Renaissance bas-relief depicts two cherubs with chubby cheeks holding coats of arms with the date 1537.

The **Auberge de la Coupe d'Or** at No. 528 was the oldest inn in Villefranche (late 14C) before it was transformed in the 17C. On the corner of rue Paul-Bert, the façade on the right (No. 596) with crocket gables dates from the late 15C, and that on the left with moulded mullioned windows and medallions is Renaissance. Note the Gothic corner

La Vague de l'Amitié

Every year, on the last Sunday in January, to mark the end of military service, local conscripts celebrate the **Fête des Conscrits**. Those eligible to take part are men between the ages of 20 and 80. Dress code for the occasion is a black suit and top hat, decorated with a coloured ribbon (a different colour for each decade: 20s, 30s etc).

At 11am the participants form a procession, link arms and, clutching colourful bouquets of mimosa and carnations, make their way along rue Nationale close on each others' heels, in what is known as the Friendship Wave (*La Vague de l'Amitié*).

niche at No. 706. A passage at No. 810 leads to a restored courtyard.

The **town hall** at No. 816 was completed in 1660. The façade is built of golden Jarnioux stone and has a solid oak door decorated with cast-iron nails. The house at No. 834 was built in the late 15C and has a charming courtyard with a staircase turret.

Musée Paul-Dini

2 pl. Faubert. Wed 1.30–6pm; Thu–Fri 10am–12.30pm, 1.30–6pm; Sat–Sun 2.30–6pm. Mon-Tue, 9 May, 10 May, bank holidays. €6. 04 74 68 33 70. www.musee-paul-dini.com.

The former granary was converted in a museum by Paul Dini, director of Dauphiné Libéré; the museum houses a collection of regional paintings from 1875 to the present.

Rue de la Paix

The façade of the building to the south of the post office features a "pelican niche", a Gothic sculpture decorated with finials and pinnacles. Next to it, set slightly further back, is a pretty Renaissance well.

Place des Marais

This pretty square to the north-east of the church contains a fountain and is enclosed by modern houses with arcades, painted in shades of pink and ochre. At the intersection with rue Nationale, a ceramic plaque depicts Pierre II de Bourbon and Anne de Beaujeu in the same pose as that on the famous triptych by the Master of Moulins.

Notre-Dame-des-Marais

In the 13C, a chapel was built in honour of a statue of the Virgin Mary found in a nearby marsh *(marais)*; all that now remains of it is the small Romanesque tower above the chancel.

Aerial view of Villefranche-sur-Saône

ADDRESSES

STAY

CI & LA – *384 boulevard Louis Blanc. 04 37 55 09 09. www.hotelicietla.com. 78 rooms.* This modern hotel boasts lovely, comfortable rooms and a restaurant with seasonal food built around local products.

Hôtel Plaisance – *96 av. de la Libération. 04 74 65 33 52. www.hotel-plaisance.com. 68 rooms.* An impeccably managed hotel across from l'Esplanade de la Libération. The rooms, each with its own style, are clean and nicely furnished. Modern lounge bar to partake of Beaujolais.

EAT

Le 91 – Bar à vin – *91 rue Stalingrad. 04 74 03 14 10. Mon 11:30am–2pm, Tues–Fri 11:30am–11pm, Sat 10am–2pm and 5pm–midnight.* This convivial wine bar boasts a nice selection of wines (many local and organic) and a short-and-sweet selection of simple food.

Le Juliénas – *236 r. Anse. 04 74 09 16 55. www.restaurant-lejulienas.com. Closed Mon evening, Sat lunch and Sun.* In this bistro-style restaurant, Carine and Fabrice offer outstanding local wines and tasty seasonal dishes with a hint of the south, prepared and served with passion and conviviality in a charming dining room. There are four menus on offer plus the dish of the day and a children's menu. Colourful and imaginative cooking.

L'Epicerie – *55 rue Thizy. 04 74 62 04 04. www.restaurant-lepicerie-villefranche.fr. Lunch and dinner Mon–Fri, dinner Sat, closed Sun.* This traditional bouchon boasts a blackboard menu of delicious local fare including offal and charcuterie.

Village and vineyards of Theizé in autumn

Beaujolais ★★

According to an old French saying, Lyon is fed by three rivers: the Rhône, the Saône and… the Beaujolais. It is true that Beaujolais is renowned both within and beyond French borders largely as a wine-growing region, but although this industry makes a substantial contribution to local economy, it is by no means the region's only source of income.

- **Michelin Map:** 327: F-2/4/4, G-2/3/4, H-2/3/4.
- **Location:** The Beaujolais region lies north-west of Lyon and west of the Saône.
- **Don't Miss:** The 15C fortess: Château de Corcelles.
- **Timing:** Use Villefranche-sur-Saône as a base and allow two days to explore.

A BIT OF HISTORY

Beaujolais owes its name to the aristocratic Beaujeu family, at the height of their power from the 9C to the 11C. In 1400, Édouard de **Beaujeu** gave his estate to the House of Bourbon-Montpensier. The Beaujolais passed briefly into the hands of the Crown under François I, who confiscated it, among other territories, from the Connétable de Bourbon as punishment for his negative attitude towards the monarch. By 1560, the Bourbon-Montpensiers had been reinstated as landlords.

Anne-Marie-Louise d'Orléans, Duchesse de Montpensier, who was known as **"La Grande Mademoiselle"** (renowned for her love affairs and active support of the Roman Catholic Fronde movement), bequeathed the Beaujolais to the House of Orléans, who remained its owners until the Revolution.

A BIT OF GEOGRAPHY

The Beaujolais is a mountain range stretching between the Loire and Rhône valleys, on the line where the Atlantic and Mediterranean watersheds meet. Best described as hilly, rather than mountainous, the region's distinguishing features are numerous mountain plateaux crisscrossed by narrow sinuous valleys. To the east, the land drops sharply to the Saône, whereas to the west it slopes gently away. The cliffs formed by the subsidence of the Saône river bed are home to the vineyards of the "Côte Beaujolaise", whereas the rest of the region forms "La Montagne".

La Montagne – a region of picturesque hills, valleys and landscapes as varied as they are appealing. The upper slopes of the mountains are carpeted with broom and pines; lower down, there are stands of oak separated by wide clearings.

BEAUJOLAIS WINE

Beaujolais vineyards and the wine they produce have secured the region's reputation far beyond the borders of France. Unlike most other red wines, Beaujolais is best drunk young, served slightly chilled.

Vines have been cultivated here since Roman times. Today, the vineyards stretch from Mâcon in the north to the Azergues valley in the south. A single grape variety – Gamay – is used to produce the light and fruity red wines, whose characters are determined by the soil in which the grapes were grown. Beaujolais vineyards are divided into two areas of production:

Coteaux de Beaujolais – North of Villefranche, the soil is granitic and perfect for the Gamay vine. This is the region of **Beaujolais-Villages**: Moulin-à-Vent, Fleurie, Morgon, Chiroubles, Juliénas, Chénas, Côte de Brouilly, Brouilly, St-Amour and Régnié.

Pays des Pierres Dorées – Between Villefranche and the Azergues valley, the soil is composed more of sedimentary rocks, which alter the flavour of the wine. The wines here are "Beaujolais" and "Beaujolais Supérieur".

🚗 DRIVING TOURS

On the map opposite, the wine-producing area is shown in green – Names of grands crus are underlined in red.

1 BEAUJOLAIS VINEYARDS★
Villefranche-sur-Saône to St-Amour-Bellevue. 98km/61mi. Allow 5h.

The road winds its way through the vineyards, at first climbing the granite escarpments, then dropping down towards the Saône valley.

▶ Leave Villefranche on D 504, take D 19 on the right, then D 44 on the left.

Montmelas-St-Sorlin
Drive round to the north of the feudal castle, which was restored in the 19C by Dupasquier, a student of Viollet-le-Duc.

▶ Carry on from Montmelas as far as Col de St-Bonnet. From the pass, a track leads off to the right to the St-Bonnet beacon.

Signal de St-Bonnet
From the east end of the chapel, there is a view of Montmelas in the foreground, set against the hills and vineyards of the Beaujolais, and beyond them the Saône valley.

▶ From the pass, take D 20 on the right.

St-Julien
This pretty little wine-growing village is the birthplace of the doctor Claude Bernard (1813–78). The **Musée Claude-Bernard** (Apr–Oct Wed–Sun 10am–12.30pm, 2–6pm. 1 May, 1 Nov, 11 Nov. €5. 04 74 67 51 44) recalls his work in the field of physiology, in particular on the absorption of fats and sugars by the liver.

▶ Take D 19 as far as Salles.

Salles-Arbuissonnas-en-Beaujolais
In the 10C, the monks of Cluny founded a **priory**, now a museum (Mar–Nov Wed–Sun 10am–12.30pm, 2–6pm. 1 May, 1 Nov, 11 Nov. €4.5. 04 74 07 31 94). It was taken over by nuns of the Benedictine Order in the 14C, who ran it until they were replaced by "aristocratic" canonesses in the 18C.

▶ From Salles, take D 35, then eventually the D 49E to the right.

Vaux-en-Beaujolais
This wine-growing village and the ribaldry of its wine-tippling inhabitants inspired **Gabriel Chevallier** (1895–1969) to write his satirical novel *Clochemerle*. Today, the town is home to a small **museum** devoted to the man and the novel.

▶ Carry on along D 49E through Le Perréon, then the D 133, and then D 62 towards Charentay.

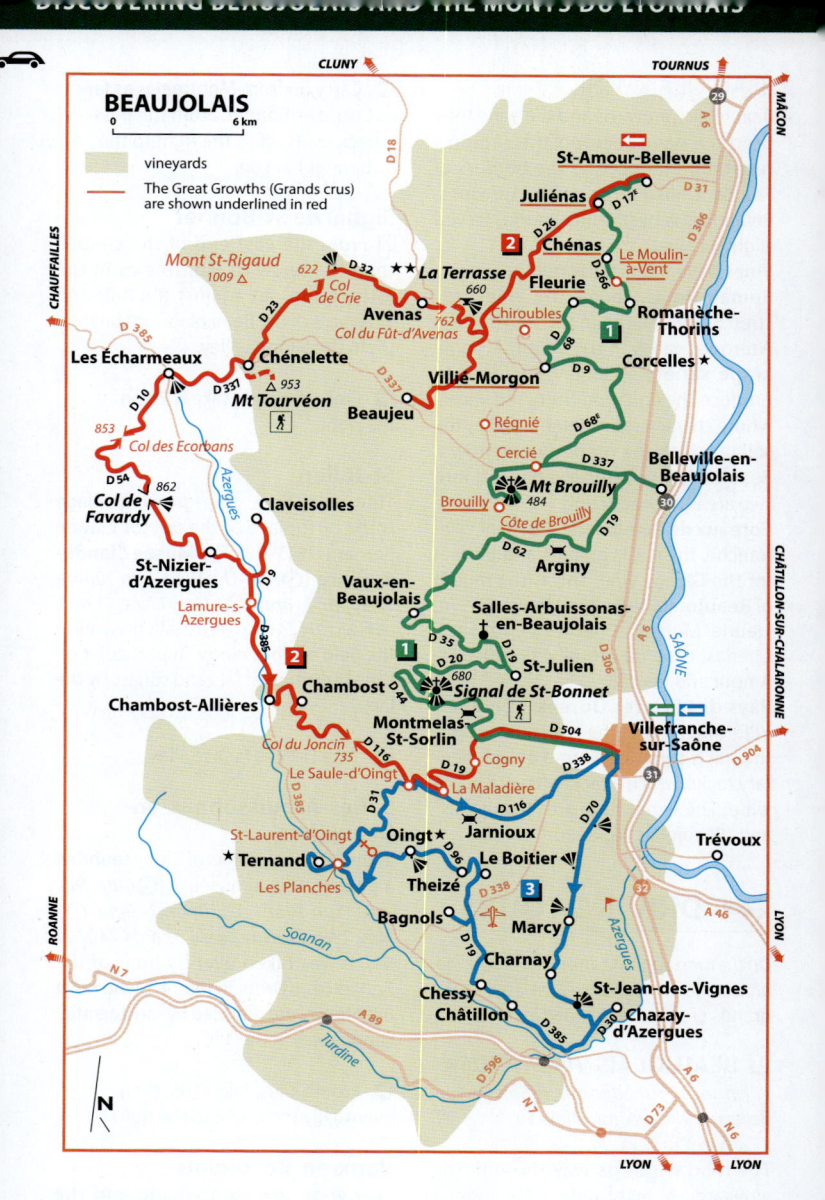

The unusual shape of the Château d'Arginy comes into sight 1km/0.6mi east of Charentay.

Château d'Arginy
All that remains of the castle is the great red-brick tower known as the Tour d'Alchimie: some say it was used by the Knights Templar to hide their treasure.

▶ Follow D 68, turn left onto D 19, then right onto D 37 to Belleville.

Belleville-en-Beaujolais
This old fortified town at the crossroads of communications routes is now a centre of wine-production and industry (manufacture of agricultural machinery). The **Hôtel-Dieu** (guided tours Wed–Fri 10am and 4pm, Sat–Sun 5pm (Jul–Aug,

BEAUJOLAIS

10am, 4pm, 5pm); ⏱Jan–mid-Apr, public holidays. ≤€5. ☏0474664467), built in the 18C to replace the old hospital, was in use for the care of the sick until 1991.

▶ Beyond Cercié (carry on along D37), the road skirts Mont Brouilly.

▶ Those wishing to climb Mont Brouilly should take D 43, turn left onto D 43E, then 100m further on take the road signposted "La Côte de Brouilly" to the left.

Mont Brouilly

Côte de Brouilly, a fruity wine with a fragrant bouquet, comes from the grapes harvested on the sunny slopes of Mont Brouilly. From the esplanade, there is a marvellous **view**★ of the vineyards, the Beaujolais hills, the Saône valley and the Dombes region.

▶ Return to Cercié. On leaving the village turn left onto D 68E towards the old village of Corcelles, then continue onto D 9 to the left.

Château de Corcelles★

♿⏱Mon–Sat: Apr–Oct 10am–6.30pm; Nov–Mar 10am–12.30pm, 1.30–5.30pm. ⏱Sun, 1 Jan, 15 Aug, 1 and 11 Nov, 25 Dec. . ≤€5. ☏04 74 66 00 24. www.chateaudecorcelles.fr.
This fortress was built in the 15C to protect the border between Burgundy and Beaujolais. Above the entrance to the keep is the family coat of arms of Madeleine de Ragny. The inner courtyard is surrounded by Renaissance arcades and contains a fountain with an ornate piece of 15C wrought-iron work on top.

▶ Rejoin D 9 to the right.

The road goes through vineyards of famous *grands crus* of the Beaujolais.

Villié-Morgon

Unusually for Beaujolais wines, the wine produced in Villié-Morgon matures well. It has a particularly fruity taste because of the broken-up schist soil in which the vines are cultivated.

▶ Leave Villié-Morgon N on D 68.

Fleurie

Fleurie wines are best drunk young.

▶ In Fleurie take D 32 E; left on D 186.

Romanèche-Thorins

The famous Moulin-à-Vent wine is produced here and in the neighbouring village of Chénas. There is a wine museum located in the railway station – **Le Hameau Dubœuf**★ (⏱daily 10am–6pm; ⏱25 Dec. ≤€20. ☏03 85 35 22 22; www.hameauduvin.com) displaying, among other things, one of the largest grape presses in France. The **Musée du Compagnonnage Guillon** (⏱Jan–May and Oct–mid-Dec 2–6pm; Jun–Sept 10am–6pm. ⏱1 May, mid-Dec–1 Jan. ≤€4. ☏03 85 35 22 02. http://musee-compagnonnage.cg71.fr) displays exhibits from the days of itinerant craftsmen; there are particularly fine examples of their work.

▶ At the Maison-Blanche crossroads on N 6, take D 466B, leading to St-Romain-des-Îles.

Parc Zoologique et d'Attractions Touroparc★

♿⏱Daily: Jul–Aug 9.30am–7pm; Sept–Oct 10am–6pm; Nov–Mar 10am–5.30pm. . ≤€20.50–23.50 (child 3–12, €16.90–19.90). ☏03 85 35 51 53. www.touroparc.com.
In a delightfully verdant setting dotted with ochre buildings, this zoo and breeding centre presents birds and animals from the five continents. Some attractions are closed in winter; check website for details.

▶ Rejoin D 266, which goes through the hamlet of Le Moulin-à-Vent, to D 68.

Chénas

Home to robust, top-quality Moulin-à-Vent and the lighter Chénas.

Juliénas

The strong wines from this locality can still be tasted in the **Cellier de** la Vieille Église (&⊙*Mar–May and Sept–Dec 10:30am–12:30pm, 3–6pm (May–Sept until 7pm.* ⊙*Tue from Oct–Apr.* ✆*04 74 04 42 98*), tasting cellars in an old converted church.

▶ Drive on to St-Amour-Bellevue.

St-Amour-Bellevue
This village at the northerly tip of the Beaujolais produces full-bodied dark-red wines and high-quality white wines.

2 MOUNTAIN TOUR★
St-Amour-Bellevue to Villefranche sur-Saône. 134km/83mi. Allow 6h.

This pretty drive continues from **St-Amour-Bellevue**, through vine-clad hills to dark pine forests, then drops to the Azergues valley.

▶ From Juliénas, take D 26 uphill, going through two passes.

Beaujeu
The capital of the Beaujolais lies amid vine-covered hillsides.

La maison du terroir Beaujolais
&⊙*Mar–Dec Mon–Sat 10am–12.30pm, 2–6pm, Sun and public holidays 10am–12.30pm, 3–6pm (7pm in Jul–Aug).* ⊙*Jan–Feb.* ≈€7. ✆*04 74 69 20 56. www.lamaisonduterroirbeaujolais.com.* This wine centre is devoted to the development of the Beaujolais area. The space is home to frequent art exhibits. Bike rentals are possible for those wishing to explore the area.

▶ Follow D 26 and D 18 to La Terrasse.

La Terrasse★★
The view from a bend in D 18 after Col du Fût d'Avenas covers the Saône valley, Bresse plateaux, Jura peaks and the Alps.

Avenas
The Roman road from Lyon to Autun once passed through this village.

▶ Take D 18E, then D 32.

Shortly before the pass (Col de Crie), there is a beautiful view north down the Grosne Orientale valley. As the road carries on downhill, it passes Mont St-Rigaud, the highest peak in the region.

Chénelette
This small village lies in a charming wooded setting. The **Tourvéon** towers above it. This summit was once the site of the great fortress of Ganelon, who betrayed Charlemagne's army, bringing about its defeat and the death of Roland at Roncevaux.

Les Écharmeaux
This summer resort is set against a backdrop of pine forests and meadows. From Les Écharmeaux, follow D 10 towards Ranchal. It crosses the Aillets pass and, after a stretch through forest, the Écorbans pass. Between Ranchal and St-Nizier-d'Azergues, D 54 affords **views★** of the Azergues valley.

St-Nizier-d'Azergues
This small town occupies a pleasant site above the Azergues valley. The pretty road carries on to Grandris.

▶ After Grandris, turn left onto D 504 as far as La Folletière, then left again on D 485 along the upper valley of the Azergues and through Lamure-sur-Azergues. In Le Gravier, turn right onto D 9.

Claveisolles
This little village is known for its conifers; in the 19C, the Comte du Sablon introduced Douglas firs from America.

▶ Drive back to D 485 and turn left to Chambost-Allières.

Chambost-Allières
This is an amalgamation of two very different villages: Allières in the valley, a busy place with lots of passing traffic; and Chambost, a rural hamlet above the valley.
The road from Chambost-Allières to Cogny via Le Saule-d'Oingt makes a **pretty drive★★**. It climbs to the Joncin

pass and then runs along the ridge, offering a **view★** of the Alps.

▶ In Le Saule-d'Oingt, turn left onto D 31, then left again onto D 19.

As the road drops down, the view stretches over the Saône valley, the Bresse region and the Jura foothills.

▶ D 504 leads back to Villefranche.

3 LE PAYS DES PIERRES DORÉES★★
Round tour from Villefranche-sur-Saône. 59km/37mi. Allow 4h.

This region, "the land of the golden stones," owes its name to the beautiful, ochre-coloured limestone used to build the farmsteads, castles and villages.

▶ From Villefranche, take the D 70 S.

Marcy
Outside this market town stands a **telegraph tower** (*Apr–Oct Sun 2.30–6pm. ☎0474670221 (town hall). €2*) built by Claude Chappe in 1799. The original semaphore mechanism was used to transmit messages until 1850.

Charnay
This small fortified town at the top of a hill still has the remains of its original citadel.

▶ Take a narrow road heading S from Charnay to St-Jean-des-Vignes.

St-Jean-des-Vignes
There is a good view of the countryside around Lyon from the small church perched on a hillside.

Espace Pierres Folles
Tue, Thu and Fri 10am –12.30pm, 2–5pm; Wed 2–5pm; Sat–Sun 2–6pm. Nov–Feb. €6. ☎0478436920. www.espace-pierres-folles.com.
This museum reflects the presence of a number of important geological sites in this area. It also boasts a botanical garden.

▶ Rejoin D 30 to reach Chazay-d'Azergues.

Chazay-d'Azergues
All that remains of the fortified town overlooking the Azergues is the belfry, a few 15C and 16C houses and a town gateway.

▶ Take D 30 as far as Lozanne, then D 385 to Châtillon.

Châtillon
A fortress built in the 12C and 13C to protect the mouth of the Azergues valley towers masterfully over this village. The **Chapelle St-Barthélemy**, originally part of the fortress itself, was extended in the 15C by Geoffroy de Balzac.

▶ Carry on along D 385.

Chessy
Near Chessy, a rich seam of copper belonging to Jacques Cœur was once mined. The ore obtained was known as **chessylite** and was a variety of azurite with a beautiful blue glint to it, highly prized by collectors.

▶ Take D 19 to Bagnols.

Bagnols
In this village is a 15C castle converted into a five-star hotel. There are pretty 15C–16C houses on the village square.

▶ Return to the D 19.

Le Boitier
As you leave this hamlet, the road takes you past Clos de la Platière, which belonged to the Rolands, who became famous during the Revolution. **Mme Roland de la Platière** stands out from her contemporaries as a cultured, well-educated woman. However, she made no secret of her antipathy towards Danton and Robespierre and paid for this in 1793 by being sent to the guillotine.

Theizé
This village, characteristic of the Pierres Dorées area, has two churches and two

castles. The main attraction is the **Site de Rochebonne** in the upper part of the village, which includes the former chapel and the château.

Oingt★

All that remains of the once mighty fortress here is the Porte de Nizy, the gateway at the entrance to the village, recognized as one of France's most beautiful. Narrow streets lined with gold-colored houses lead to the church, an old castle chapel dating from the 14C. From the top of the **tower** (*Apr–Oct Sat–Sun and public holidays 3–7pm (Jul–Aug daily 3–7pm). in rainy and windy conditions. 04 74 71 21 24. www.oingt.com*) there is a view of the Lyonnais and Beaujolais hills and the Azergues valley. The town is also known for having a large number of artisans including potters, painters, and leatherworkers.

▶ Carry on along D 96.

In St-Laurent-d'Oingt, note the church with a porch.

▶ Turn right at the junction with D 485.

Ternand★

The town retains some early fortifications, such as the keep and the watchpath, which have a good view over the Tarare hills and the Azergues valley.

▶ Turn back through Les Planches and follow the D 31.

The pass **road★★** over **Col du Sauled'Oingt** is very picturesque.

▶ At La Maladière turn right.

Jarnioux

The **castle** (*guided visits May–July and mid-Aug–Oct Sat 10am, 11am, 2pm, 3pm, 4pm; Sun 2pm, 3pm, 4pm; Jul–mid-Aug Mon–Sat 10am, 11am, 2pm, 3pm, 4pm; Sun 2pm, 3pm, 4pm. €5. 04 74 03 80 85*), built between the 15C and 17C, has six towers and includes a particularly charming Renaissance section.

▶ D 116 and D 38 back to Villefranche.

ADDRESSES

STAY

La Ferme Berger – *Le bourg, 69430 Les Ardillats. 04 74 04 80 20. Closed Jan. 4 rooms and 1 gîte. Restaurant (reservations required)*. A great stopover offering delicious meals and an attractive wine cellar dedicated to Beaujolais.

Chambre d'Hôte Domaine de La Grosse Pierre – *69115 Chiroubles. 04 74 69 12 17. www.chiroubles-passot.com. Closed Dec–Jan. 5 rooms.* The perfect address for getting away from it all in the heart of the Beaujolais region.

EAT

Le Coq à Juliénas – *Pl. du Marché, 69840 Juliénas. 04 74 03 67 51. www.lecoqajulienas.com. Closed all day Wed and Thu.* The cock is the king of wine country – or at least of this stylish establishment.

SHOPPING

In Beaujolais, many wine producers offer tours of their cellars, enabling visitors to discover different vintages.

La Maison des Beaujolais – *441 av. de l'Europe, 69220 St-Jean-d'Ardières. 04 74 66 16 46. www.lamaisondesbeaujolais.com. Restaurant*. The sign tells the name of the game: this establishment is dedicated to Beaujolais wines.

Le Comptoir des Beaujolais – *Pl. de l'Hôtel-de-Ville, 69430 Beaujeu. 04 74 04 81 18. May–Nov 10.30am–1pm, 2–7.30pm. Closed 3 wks in Jan.* The handsome bust of Bacchus points the way to this cellar on the lower floor of the Marius-Audin museum.

Moulin à Huile – *29 r. des Écharmeaux, 69430 Beaujeu. 04 74 69 28 06. www.huilerie-beaujolaise.fr. Tue–Sat 9.15am–1pm, 2–7pm. Closed 1st 2 wks of Jan, and public holidays.* The big old millstone of this 19C oil mill still crushes nuts and seeds to make the most flavourful virgin oils imaginable. Visits and tastings.

Monts du Lyonnais ★

This attractive, mountainous region lying to the south-west of Lyon has a pastoral appearance, with chestnut groves and oakwoods. Land in low-lying valleys is given over to market gardening, vineyards and orchards, whereas pastures extend over the higher ground. Traditional rural housing is still very prominent and adds to the charm of the region.

- **Michelin Map:** 327 F6, G5-6.
- **Info:** www.monts-du-lyonnais.fr.
- **Location:** Between St-Étienne and Lyon, above the Parc Naturel Régional du Pilat.
- **Kids:** Birds of prey at the Courzieu Animal Park.
- **Timing:** At least two days.

🚗 DRIVING TOUR

LYON ROUND TRIP
203km/126mi. Allow two days.

▶ Leave Lyon, heading west along the A 6. At the exit for Tassin-la-Demi-Lune, take the N 7 to L'Arbresle.

L'Arbresle
At the confluence of the Brévenne and the Turdine, this industrial city, which spcialised in silk products, is dominated by the remains of the castle of the Abbots of Savigny and by the pinnacles crowning the bell-tower (19C) of the church. L'Arbresle is the hometown of Barthélemy Thimonnier, inventor of the sewing machine.

▶ Take the D 19 to the SE of L'Arbresle.

Couvent de la Tourette ★
The convent of Sainte-Marie de la Tourette was built during the second half of the 1950s and is one of the most significant buildings of the work of Le Corbusier. *Guided visits: Sun 2pm, 2:45pm. Check website for details of guided visits in the off-season.* 🚫 24–31 Dec. €8. ☎0472 19 10 90. www.couventdelatourette.fr.

▶ Return to the D 389 and turn left.

Savigny
This town was built around a Benedictine abbey founded in the 8C. In the centre of the town, a little museum contains a number of sculptures dating from the 12C and 14C, from the abbey.

▶ Leave Savigny by the D 7, continue along this road to cross the D 389.

Musée de la Mine de Saint-Pierre-la-Palud
1 r. du Musée. ⏰ *Mar–Nov Sat-Sun and public holidays 2–6pm; Jul–Aug additional visits Tue and Thu at 3pm.* €6. ☎04 74 70 39 66.
The old mining site of this museum prospered from 1840 to 1972.

▶ Rejoin the D 389 towards St-Étienne. At Ste-Foy-l'Argentière, turn right onto the D 489, then take the D 81 to the left.

Parc Salva Terra à Haute-Rivoire
⏰ *Opening times are linked to school holidays: call or check website for details.* 🚫 *Nov–Jan.* €15.50 (children €6–€12.50). ☎04 74 26 35 92/06 10 65 09 33. www.salva-terra.com.
A journey through the 13C with a walled city and a chance to try your hand at fencing or throwing a javelin.

▶ Take the D 637 which leads to the D 389 and turn left onto it; turn right at the D 633 and follow the road to Aveize (where it becomes the D 4).

Aveize
At the entrance to the town, from the D 4, **view★** of Ste-Foy-l'Argentière in the valley of the Brévenne.

Head for St-Symphorien-sur-Coise on the D 4, then turn right at the D 662.

Notre-Dame-de-la-Neylière

In addition to the **chapel,** it is possible to visit the **Musées d'Océanie et de Jean-Claude Colin**, home of the Marist Fathers.

Saint-Symphorien-sur-Coise

A Gothic **church** dominates this ancient fortified town. Further on, **Chazelles-sur-Lyon** in the foothills of the Lyonnais area owes its fame to the production of high-quality felt hats, commemorated in the **Musée du Chapeau** (*04 77 94 23 29. www.museeduchapeau.com*).
The village of **St-Galmier** may not be well known, but its product is, although it was only in the early 19C that its naturally sparkling water was marketed, thanks to the enterprising spirit of **Augustin Saturnin Badoit**.

Veauche

Veauche's claim to fame is the manufacture of bottles needed for the water from St-Galmier. The church was originally a small priory dating from 970.

Head in the direction of St-Martin-la-Plaine.

Parc Zoologique de St-Martin-la-Plaine

Apr–Oct 9am–6pm; Nov–Mar 10am–4pm. 25 Dec. €16 (child 3–9, €12). 04 77 75 22 93. www.espace-zoologique.com.
This park specialises in breeding endangered species.

From St Martin, the route heads for the medieval market town of **Riverie** before continuing to St-André-la-Côte, 800m to the north-west of which is a path leading to **Signal de St-André**★★ (*45min there and back on foot*). Continue to the relaxing, stone-built village of **Yzeron**★, famed for raising goats and beautiful landscapes.

Follow the tortuous road to the **Parc Animalier de Courzieu** (*Apr–Nov, 10am–6pm (see website for details of activity times). €15, child 4–12, €11. 04 74 70 96 10. www.parc-de-courzieu.fr*) where outdoor displays of birds of prey in flight will particularly delight children.

Follow the D 24.

Grézieu-la-Varenne

This history of this town is closely linked to the activities of its laundry. It was here in the 17C that the clothes from religious communities were washed.

Return to Lyon via the D 489.

ADDRESSES

STAY

Logis Hostellerie du Forez – *6 r. Didier-Guetton, 42330 St-Galmier. 10km/6mi SW of Chazelles-sur-Lyon via the D 12. 04 77 54 00 23. 24 rooms.* This family-run hotel is close to the source of Badoit water.

Chez Jacotte et Elia – *Le Plat, 42330 St-Galmier. 3km/2mi from the centre on the D 12, towards Chazelles. 04 77 54 08 27. http://jacotte.elia.free.fr. 4 rooms.* Set in the countryside, this farm has been restored with style and taste.

EAT

Les 3 Archers de la Table Ronde – *Pl. du Marché, 69440 Riverie. 09 81 62 82 87. www.les3archers.fr. Closed Mon–Tue, closed for lunch Thurs.* The auberge was created in 1975. Local products and a relaxed service.

ROANNAIS AND LE FOREZ

The Roannais is a splendid region boasting a sweeping countryside of lakes, forests and mountains, with the river Loire lazily meandering through it. At the hub of several more well-known regions, the Roannais is within easy access of major cities (notably Lyon and St-Étienne), as well as towns and villages. The Forez is an ancient province of France, one that roughly equates with the central part of the Loire department. The inhabitants of the region are called Foréziens, and the dialect and language are unique, with subtle influences from the Auvergne. The celebrated Monts du Forez are a chain of mountains separating the valley of the Dore from the plain of Forez.

Roanne Excellence

Roanne is one of the most renowned centres in France for the production of industrial textiles, including rayon and other new fibres. Historically, the town was located at a strategic point at the head of the navigable Loire, but its status declined with the collapse of long-distance trade. From the 18C onwards, however, the rejuvenated navigation of the Loire contributed to the export of local products, especially the Beaujolais wine which, up until that point, had been transported overland, but also textiles and ceramics. In the 17C and 18C, almost half the population of Roanne was dependent in some way on water-borne transportation of goods, including carriers, carpenters, merchants, coopers, boatmen, journeymen, oarsmen and river labourers.

Highlights

1 The old medieval town of **Villerest** (p384)
2 The mountain village of **St-Germain-Laval** (p386)
3 The granite mountains of the **Forez** area (p390)
4 Winter sports at **Chalmazel** (p391)
5 The fascinating Ecomuseum of **Usson-en-Forez** (p398)

Say Cheese!

The delicious Fourme de Montbrison is a local cow's-milk blue cheese boasting a protected AOC status. One of the mildest blue cheeses, Fourme de Montbrison has a dry rind and a creamy yet firm texture. Unlike the similar Fourme d'Ambert, Fourme de Montbrison is salted before being placed in molds and has a smoother, more even texture.

Village and vineyards of Ambierle
© Bernard Jaubert/imageBROKER/age fotostock

ROANNAIS AND LE FOREZ

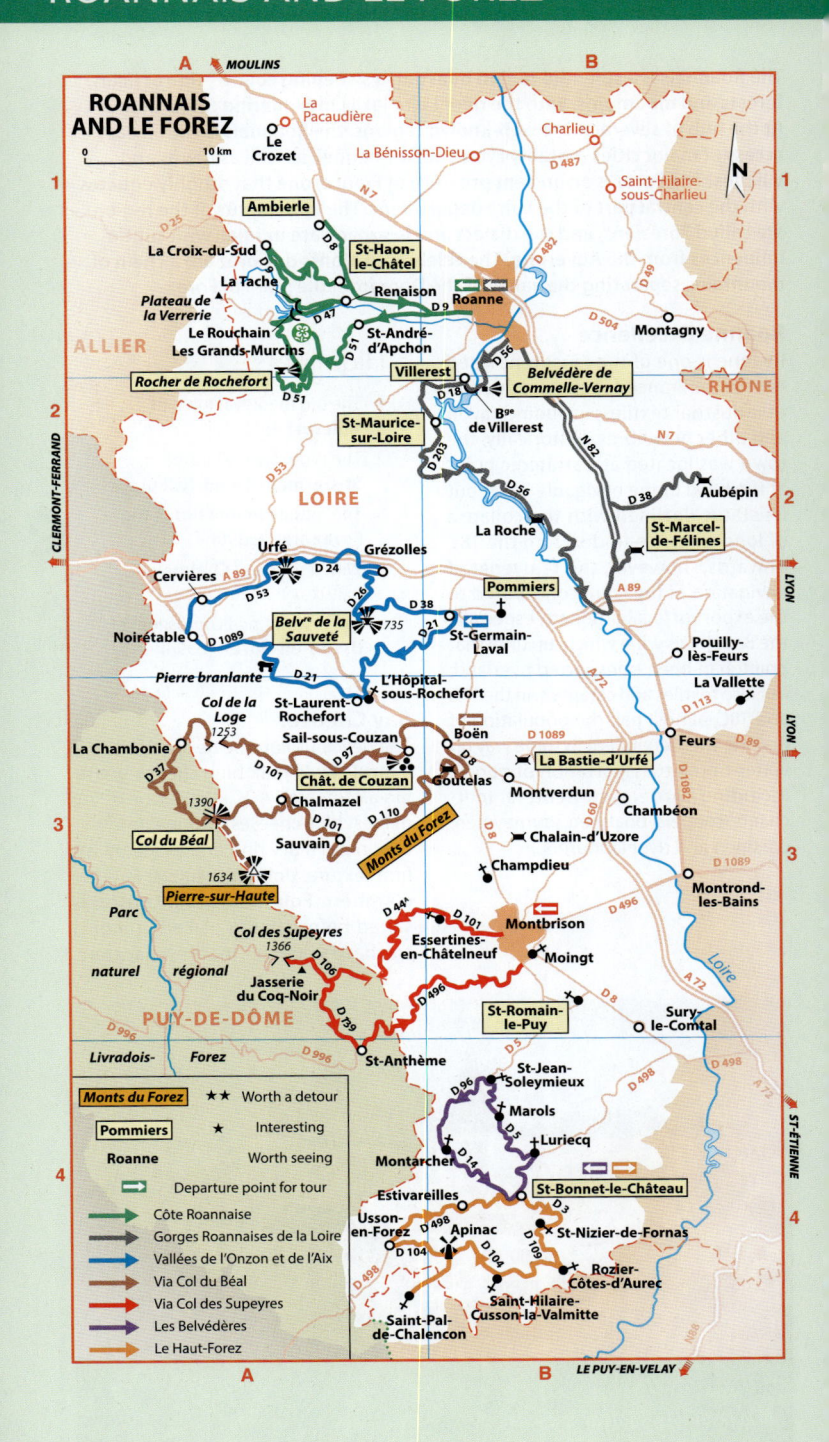

Roanne

Rodumna, as the town was called in ancient times, dates to more than a century before the start of the Christian Era. Later, in the 11C, the lords of Roanne built a fortress. The Seigneury of Roanne belonged in turn to the counts of Forez, Jacques Cœur, the dukes of Bourbon and the dukes of Roanne. The inauguration of the Roanne–Digoin canal in 1838 brought intense activity to the port of Roanne, thereby determining the town's industrial vocation.

ROANNE TODAY

Roanne is one of the best-known French textile centres for clothing, hosiery and knitted goods and towels. Its other economic activities are highly diversified and include food processing, metallurgy, armoured tanks, tools, boilermaking, tanning, dyes, paper mills and plastics. A Michelin tyre production unit has been operating in the north-east of the town since 1974.

Local gastronomy has a well-deserved reputation for excellence, and the town boasts several fine restaurants.

SIGHTS

Musée des Beaux-Arts et d'Archéologie Joseph-Déchelette

Daily except Tue 10am–noon, 2–6pm (Sat–Sun 2–6pm). €4.7. 04 77 23 68 77. This eclectic museum, housed in an early-18C mansion, was founded by the archaeologist **Joseph Déchelette** (1862–1914), a native of the town. He gathered the rich **collections,** which include many Gallo-Roman artefacts found over the course of excavations in the region. The museum is also known for its fine collections of faience, including items of 16C and 17C Italian **majolica**.

Place de-Lattre-de-Tassigny

The site of the old castle (part of its keep still stands) is flanked by the church of St-Étienne, with its 15C stained-glass window.

- **Population:** 36 749.
- **Michelin Map:** 327: D-3.
- **Info:** 8 place Maréchal de Lattre de Tassigny, 42300 Roanne. 04 77 71 51 77. www.leroannais.com.
- **Location:** Roanne lies 85km/52mi north-west of Lyon, accessible by the A 72.
- **Parking:** There are a number of car parks in the centre.
- **Don't Miss:** You will be delighted by a visit to the Musée des Beaux-Arts.
- **Timing:** Allow a full day to explore.
- **Kids:** Visit to the Parc des Canaux.

Muséo'Parc du Marinier

In Briennon. early Jul–Aug daily except Mon 2.15–6pm; Sep Sat–Sun. €4 (child 3–12, €2). 04 77 60 12 42. This park, located along the canal between Roanne and Digoin, has a lot to offer children, including a real barge turned into a museum and a hands-on system of miniature locks and barges.

Chapelle St-Nicolas-du-Port

The small chapel can be seen near the wharfs of the port. The date on the pediment – 1630 – marks the year the bargemen made a vow to erect a chapel to their patron saint if they were spared the death throes of the plague.

EXCURSIONS

Montagny

14km/8.7mi E along D 504.

On leaving Montagny, follow the signpost indicating "La Roseraie".

Roseraie Dorieux

Jul–mid-Sept, with free access to the rose garden; rest of the year, enquire for opening hours. 04 77 66 11 46. www.dorieux.fr.

DISCOVERING ROANNAIS AND LE FOREZ

> ### A Popular Marina
>
> The Port of Roanne, of substantial importance in 1945, declined rapidly from 1970 onwards, coming to a halt in 1992. This has since been by an increase in pleasure boating with the opening of locks on Sundays during the summer months. **Barge trips** *(several options offered from or to Roanne aboard the barge L'Infatigable; groups take priority; Marins d'Eau Douce, Port de plaisance de Briennon; 04 77 69 92 92)* are also organised on the canal.

This colourful and fragrant rose garden and nursery is freely accessible from July to September.

Plateau de la Verrerie

Leave Roanne W along D 9 to Renaison then follow D 47 to La Grand'Borne and turn right onto D 478 which leads to La Tourbière. To get back, follow D 39 from Col de la Rivière then D 9 to Roanne or D 4 if you fancy a detour via Briennon.

The solitary road climbs through the forest before reaching the Plateau de la Verrerie, which offers a pleasant ramble and a view of the Roanne plain.

Le Crozet

25km/15.5km NW on N 7.
Leave the car at the entrance to Le Crozet. The flower-decked houses of this small medieval town are spread out along the foothills of the Madeleine mountains. You enter the old main square by the Grand-Porte, flanked by two round towers that are truncated and partly concealed by houses.

Maison du Connétable

Fine front with wooden panels. The adjoining house with walled-in arcades used to be a cobbler's workshop (15C).

Maison Dauphin

A former meat market; a restored late-15C house with Renaissance windows.

Maison Papon★

Enter the courtyard to appreciate the Renaissance façade of enamelled ceramics and with mullioned windows.

Tour de Guet

The 12C keep near the 19C church has lost its machicolated crown.

Museum of Popular Arts and Traditions

Jun–Sept Wed–Sun 10.30am–noon, 3–7pm. €3. 04 77 63 00 87. www.museelecrozet.fr.
A peasant's interior has been carefully reconstructed in this 15C residence, alongside an old-fashioned smithy and a clog-maker's workshop.

🚗 DRIVING TOURS

CÔTE ROANNAISE★

Roanne to Ambierle. 100km/62mi. Allow half a day.

A line of vineyard-covered slopes running north–south, known as the "Côte", dominates the Roanne basin to the west. Contrasting with the harshness of the Madeleine mountains, the Côte is gentle and colourful, with rectangular houses, often roughcast with green shutters and red-tiled double pitched roofs. Its reddish soil is home to vineyards that produce reputed AOC red wines, as well as rosés and whites.

▶ Leave Roanne on the D 9 W and turn left onto D 51 to St-André-d'Apchon.

St-André-d'Apchon

At the centre of the town, in a secluded setting, stands a 16C château built for the Marshal of St-André.

▶ From the War Memorial, walk up the street with the Lion d'Or Hotel on the corner, then along the covered passageway 30m on the right, next to a butcher's shop.

ROANNE

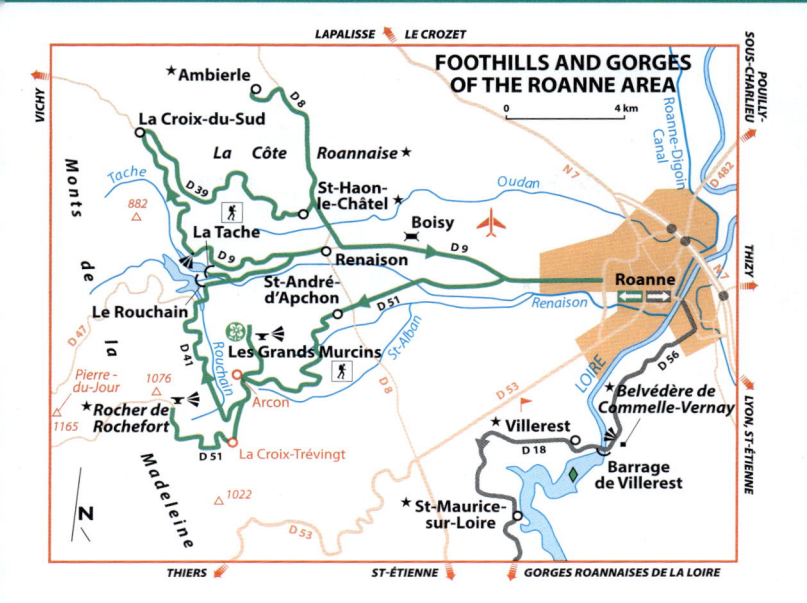

The Flamboyant Gothic church is decorated with 16C stained-glass windows.

▶ Continue along D 51 to Arcon.

The road twisting uphill above St-André offers vistas of the Roanne plain.

▶ Leave Arcon to the N, to Les Grands-Murcins and its arboretum.

Les Grands-Murcins
The arboretum, created in 1936–37 at the heart of a national forest, is particularly rich in coniferous trees, including Himalayan weeping pines.

▶ Return to Arcon and head S to La Croix-Trévingt. Turn right onto D 51 towards St-Priest.

Rocher de Rochefort★
The Rochefort Rock is equipped with a viewing table affording **views** of the Roanne plain, the Beaujolais and Lyonnais hills.

▶ Return to La Croix-Trévingt. Turn left onto D 51 and left again onto D 41 along the Rouchain valley to the dam.

Barrage du Rouchain
Duplicating the Tache dam to supply Roanne with drinking water, this dam (1977), made of rockfill, is equipped with a spillway on the River Rouchain, and occupies three valleys.

Barrage de la Tache
This dam was built between 1888 and 1892. It is a gravity dam: the sheer mass of it resists the pressure of the water.

Renaison
This is the economic heart of the Côte Roannaise. Its neo-Gothic church houses a Romantic organ by John Abbey.

▶ Turn back then follow D 9 to La Croix-du-Sud.

On the way, a **look-out rock★** on the left offers an attractive view of the Tache reservoir. The road up to the pass looks over the Madeleine mountain range.

La Croix-du-Sud
This pass is a major intersection on the rise separating the Madeleine mountain range from the Côte and the valley of the Teyssonne from that of the Tache.

St-Maurice-sur-Loire by the Loire, the Villerest dam in the background

St-Haon-le-Châtel★
The **fortified village★** has preserved its medieval appearance and some of its ramparts. The restored **church** (12C–17C) is a modest building, with typical furniture from the Forez region.

▶ Take D 8 N to Ambierle.

Ambierle★
This pretty town, exposed to the morning sun, is set amid vineyards that yield a pleasant rosé wine. There is an old Cluniac priory in the upper part of the village.
The **Musée Alice-Taverne** (⊙*Feb–Nov 10am–noon, 2–6pm.* ≤≤€5. ℘04 77 65 60 99; www.museealicetaverne.fr) focuses on traditional home life in the region including games, costumes and local superstitions. It also boasts recreations of various typical interiors (workshop, inn etc).

▶ Take D 8 and D 9 back to Roanne.

On the left is an attractive view of the large round tower of the **Château de Boisy** (⊶*not open to the public*). This castle (14C–16C) belonged successively to the Couzan family, Jacques Cœur and the Gouffier family, and occupies an important position in the history of Roanne.

GORGES ROANNAISES DE LA LOIRE★
Round trip of 139km/87mi.
Allow half a day.

▶ Leave Roanne to the S along avenue de la Libération. Turn right by the station onto D 43 and then right again onto D 56 to Commelle-Vernay viewpoint (signposted).

Construction of the Villerest dam upstream of Roanne created a new "Loire Lake", 33km/20.5mi long, which attracts sailing enthusiasts in the summer.

Belvédère de Commelle-Vernay★
The **view** encompasses Roanne and its outskirts and the Vernay bridge to the north, the town and dam of Villerest and the modern installations of the Villerest paper mills to the west.
A small **tourist train** ♿ (⊙*reservations recommended: Jul–Aug, daily at 3pm, 4.30pm and 6pm; May–Jun and Sept Wed–Sun at 3pm and 4.30pm.* ♿. ≤≤€6 (child 3–12, €3.50). ℘04 77 68 58 12) offers a 7km/4.3mi ride along the shores of Lake Villerest.

Barrage de Villerest
Designed to combat low water levels and floods on the Loire, this solid concrete arch gravity dam has a crown length of 469m. Its curved shape reinforces its stability. The variable-level reservoir is 30km/19mi long and has an average width of 250m.

▶ Cross over the dam to Villerest.

Villerest
The old **medieval town★** is a pleasant place to visit, with many houses boasting corbelled construction or timber-framed walls and the remains of ramparts. The 13C **Porte de Bise** is the starting point for a tour on foot; points

ROANNE

of particular interest are highlighted on information boards.
During the summer, crafts are sold from the traditional street stalls.

Musée de l'Heure et du Feu
*Jun and 1st 2 wks of Sept Sat–Sun and public holidays 2–6pm; Jul–Aug daily except Tue 2–6pm. €3.
04 77 69 66 66.
www.museedelheureetdufeuvillerest.fr.*
This unusual museum is divided into two parts; the **section on Fire**★ traces the history of the domestic fire since Antiquity and across different countries, while the section on time boasts a clock collection.

▶ Leave to the W and head for St-Maurice-sur-Loire.

St-Maurice-sur-Loire★
This town occupies a **site**★ overlooking the river. The old houses cling to a spur crowned by the ruins of a medieval castle.

▶ Drive towards Bully, down the hill towards the Loire and over the bridge at Presle. Turn right onto D 56 and along the east bank of the river.

La-Roche
Château de la Roche
*Guided visits. Mid-Apr–Jun and 1–mid-Sept daily except Mon 2–6pm; Jul–Aug daily 10am–noon, 2–7pm; mid-Sept–late Oct Sat–Sun 2–6pm. €5.50.
04 77 64 97 68.
www.lechateaudelaroche.fr.*
This medieval castle presents the history of the Gorges de la Loire area in a refined 17C decor and also offers an **escape game** *(Apr–Nov Fri–Sun)*.

▶ Shortly after the Chessieux viaduct the road meets N 82 near Balbigny; turn left towards Neulise. After 6km/4mi turn right onto D 5.

St-Marcel-de-Félines
This peaceful village facing the Forez mountains boasts a 12C fortified house altered in the 16C into a **château** (*guided visits only: Easter–Oct Sun–Mon and public holidays, 2.30pm, 3.30pm, 4.30pm. 04 77 63 54 98. www.chateaudesaintmarceldefelines.fr*). A bridge over the old moat leads to an inner courtyard of Italian inspiration. Inside, the decoration of the reception rooms is unified by the 17C wall and ceiling **paintings**★.

▶ Rejoin N 82 and continue to Neulise; turn right onto D 38. At Croizet turn right, cross the River Gand and take the path to the right.

Château de l'Aubépin
Daily except Tue and Thurs 10am–12.30pm, 2–5.30pm.
This lovely old château (16C–18C), flanked by corner pavilions is topped with a watch-turret set back from an avant-corps decorated with masks.

▶ Return to Roanne on N 82.

ADDRESSES

STAY
Grand Hôtel – *18 cours de la République (opposite the train station). 04 77 71 48 82. www.grand-hotel-roanne.fr. 31 rooms.* This well-maintained hotel dates from the early 20C.

EAT
Le Central – *58 cours de la République (opposite the train station). 04 77 67 72 72. www.troisgros.fr. Closed Sun–Mon. Reservations requested.* In the sober but elegant setting of a 1920s hotel, this bistro-grocery belongs to the famous Troisgros family. Simple, light cuisine in seasonal menus.

Troisgros – *728 Route de Villerest, 42155 Ouches. 04 77 71 66 97. www.troisgros.com. Closed Jan; Mon and Tue. Reservations essential.* With three Michelin stars, this is a veritable institution that sets the standard for French gastronomy. The Troisgros family receives its guests in a setting where modernism, quality, luxury and sobriety intermingle in perfect elegance.

St-Germain-Laval

This pretty mountain village is home to the River Aix which, along with the surrounding hills, form a delightful natural setting. Depending on the season, the vegetation transforms from deep green to golden brown.

- **Population:** 1 685.
- **Michelin Map:** 327: D-5.
- **Info:** 28 r. R.-Lugnier, 42260 St-Germain-Laval. 04 77 65 52 96.
- **Location:** The quickest approach is on the A 72, which passes 5km/3mi away. The town is 33km/20mi S of Roanne
- **Timing:** Allow 1–2 hours.

SIGHTS

The 18C **Église de la Madeleine**, crowned by a saucer dome, is used to host temporary art exhibitions in summer. The **parish church** at the far end of the village houses a stone statue of Moses (1065), on the right as you enter, and a small polychrome wooden Pietà in an alcove above the font.

The **municipal museum**, installed in a former private mansion (now the town hall) displays tapestries (including two splendid d' Aubusson tapestries) and furniture from France and abroad.

Place de la Mairie is lined with old houses, one of which has wooden panels: it is the birthplace of the explorer **Greysolon du Luth**.

EXCURSIONS

Chapelle Notre-Dame-de-Laval
1.3km/1mi via the D 38, W of St-Germain.

The Gothic chapel appears like a vision of grace at the edge of the Aix, which is spanned by a fine medieval bridge. The shrine attracted many pilgrims during the Middle Ages to the 17C, and was visited by Louis XI, returning from le Puy.

Pommiers★
3km/2mi to the E of St-Germain via D 21.

At the edge of Forez and Roanne, sits this enchanting hilltop village. The site was occupied from Roman times to the early Christian era but mainly developed in the 9C around a Benedictine monastery attached to Nantua. In the 14C, as surrounding villages were becoming increasingly concerned about security, Pommiers was surrounded by strong defensive walls.

Church – The church is today a Benedictine parish. This 11C–12C building's austerity is immediately striking, its vault pierced in places with small holes. The technique was used to improve the acoustics of the space. The north apse has retained an interesting series of wall paintings from the 16C.

In the 16C, the prior built a façade before the main building where he held his court sessions. In the 17C–18C, the priory was completely rebuilt with a a majestic cloister overlooking the Romanesque church.

DRIVING TOURS

VALLÉE DE L'ONZON AND VALLÉE DE L'AIX
90km/56mi. Allow 5h.

▶ Leave St-Germain to the S on D 1. In Boën (see Monts du FOREZ), take D 21 on the right to L'Hôpital-sous-Rochefort.

L'Hôpital-sous-Rochefort
This village was fortified in the 15C and has retained two of its doorways. The 12C church has a narrow nave housing a superb **Virgin with Child**★★ in polychrome wood dating from the late 15C. This life-size statue is a paragon of vivacity and grace.

ST-GERMAIN-LAVAL

Pommiers Priory

▶ Leave L'Hôpital-sous-Rochefort to the W on D 21, heading for St-Didier-sous-Rochefort. This road gives onto the lane leading to Rochefort (an old hilltop village). Rejoin D 21 and follow directions for St-Didier-sous-Rochefort.

St-Laurent-Rochefort
Note the fine 15C cross next to the church.

▶ Take D 21 to St-Didier-sur-Rochefort.

Between St-Didier-sous-Rochefort and St-Julien-la-Vêtre, a huge megalith, **La Pierre Branlante**, stands on the edge of the road (D 73).

▶ N 89 leads to Noirétable.

Noirétable
This pleasant mountain resort has retained its traditional economic activities (timber, cutlery). The 15C Flamboyant Gothic church has a remarkable porch, which used to be larger and served as a covered market. All the 17C statues carved out of black Volvic stone were brought here from the Hermitage monastery during the Revolution.

▶ Exit Noirétable W and take the D 24 N towards Cervières.

Cervières
Park the car on the esplanade at the entrance to the village.
The squat **Gothic church** has diagonal ribs resting on sculpted brackets depicting masks. Note the fine Renaissance house opposite the church. Walk through the vaulted passageway beneath the house and skirt the former fortifications on the left to a new granite arch; a steep street leads back to the church. The market ground beyond the town hall commands a lovely view of the surrounding countryside.

La Maison des Grenadières
Opposite the church. Apr–Oct Wed–Sun 2–6.30pm. €5 (€4 12–18, under 12s: no charge).
04 77 24 98 71. www.grenadieres.com.
Housed in a picturesque Renaissance residence, this museum is devoted to gold-thread embroidery and the skilful workers who decorate civil and military ceremonial clothes.

▶ Continue to les Salles on the D 24, then towards Champoly on D 53. Leaving Champoly (E), take the narrow signposted road leading to the site of Château d'Urfé.

Château d'Urfé
45min on foot there and back.

387

DISCOVERING ROANNAIS AND LE FOREZ

This 12C–15C stronghold *(Apr–Sept 10am–7pm, Oct–Nov and mid-Mar–Apr 10am–1pm, 2–5pm, Dec–mid-Mar Sat–Sun 10am–1pm, 2–5pm, |P4.3)* was once home to the Urfé family, before they moved to Bastie-d'Urfé (*see Château de la BASTIE-d'URFÉ*). The **viewing table** installed at the top of the keep affords a superb vista of the Monts du Lyonnais and the foothills of the Monts d'Auvergne.

▶ Drive back towards Champoly to take the D 24. After St-Marcel-d'Urfé, turn right onto the D 1.

Grézolles
Village dominated by the slate bell-tower of its 16C chapel.

▶ Go to St-Martin-la-Sauveté and, S of the village, turn left onto D 20, a path leading to the belvedere.

Belvédère de la Sauveté★
15min on foot there and back.
The path takes you to the foot of the watertower and a statue of the Virgin Mary, offering a sweeping **panorama** of the area.

▶ Return to St-Martin and take D 38 (on the right) to St-Germain-Laval.

Feurs

Owing to its strategic location in the Loire valley, this town was a thriving commercial centre back in the days of the Gauls. Trade remains an important activity today, as illustrated by the lively street markets. In fact, the name of the town is believed to be derived from the Latin word *forum*, symbolising a privileged place for communication and exchange.

> ▶ **Population:** 8 134.
> **Michelin Map:** 327 E-5.
> **Info:** Place Drivet, 42110 Feurs. ℘04 77 26 05 27. www.forez-est.com.
> **Location:** Between Roanne (41km/25.5mi to the N) and St-Étienne (50km/31mi to the S). At the centre of a plain, on the right bank of the Loire
> **Timing:** Allow 2 hours.

SIGHTS

Musée de Feurs
3 rue Victor-de-Laprade. Tue–Fri, 2–6pm; and one Sun of each month, 2–6pm (check website). 1 Jan, 1 May, 25 Dec and public holidays. €3.30. ℘04 77 26 24 48. www.feurs.org.
This recently renovated museum is devoted to Gaulish and Gallo-Roman archaeology as well as popular arts and crafts. The park is a delightful setting for the reconstructed villa displaying marble and stone exhibits, along with a pretty mosaic discovered in Feurs.

Église Notre-Dame
Flamboyant Gothic church with three naves. The ornate bell-tower with a 15C clock was remodelled in the 19C. Part of the 12C chancel is still standing. On the right, there is a Virgin with Child by J-M Bonnassieux. The wainscoting and stalls (18C) were taken from the priory in Pommiers.

EXCURSIONS

Plaine du Forez
Stray from the main roads and explore the more remote parts of the charming Forez basin: The volcanic spurs dotted around the landscape are often the sites of religious sanctuaries, namely St-Romain-le-Puy and Montverdun. Below, in the plain, *bocage* meadows alternate with ponds and old farmhouses.

Château de la Bastie-d'Urfé

Pouilly-lès-Feurs
7km/4.3mi N of Feurs on N 82 and D 58.
The unusual Romanesque church in this former fortified village was once attached to a Cluniac priory. West of Pouilly, a small Renaissance pavilion has kept its sculpted pediment and an upstairs loggia.

La Valette
7km/4.3mi NE of Feurs on D 113. 2km/1.2mi E of Salvizinet. After the bridge spanning the Charpassonne, turn right onto the tarmacked lane that starts by the inn.
This modest country church is nestled on a slope of the Charpassonne valley. The small Romanesque building boasts a single nave and a raised chancel. The somewhat crude furniture is unique to the Forez region.

Chambéon
Not far from St-Étienne airport and the River Loire, the **Écopole du Forez** *(6km/3.7mi S of Feurs via N 89 and D 107; signposted from Chambéon and Magneux-Haute-Rive; guided tours 1.30–6pm (7pm in Jul–Aug); Nov–Mar Wed and Sat–Sun; Apr–Oct daily. 1 Jan and 24–25 and 31 Dec. €3. 04 77 27 86 40; www.ecopoleduforez.fr)* is a preserved park that has become an important centre for studying migratory birds and aquatic fauna. Nature trails totalling 12km/7.5mi run along the banks of the Loire, enlightening visitors to the area's natural resources and riverside vegetation.

Château de la Bastie-d'Urfé★
19km N on D 8 and N 89. Guided tours. Apr–Sept 10am–7pm; Oct–Nov and mid-Mar–end-Mar 10am–1pm, 2–5pm; Dec–mid-Mar Sat–Sun 10am–1pm, 2–5pm. 1 Jan and 24, 25, 31 Dec. €4.3. 04 77 97 54 68.
In the 15C, the rough Lords of Urfé built a manor on the banks of the River Lignon. The family quickly rose to power, and during the Italian Wars, Claude d'Urfé spent several years in Rome as an ambassador. Upon his return to France, he converted Bastie Manor into a Renaissance château. **Honoré d'Urfé** (1567–1625), grandson of the ambassador and author of the first French novel, *L'Astrée*, grew up in these refined surroundings. The original manor (14C–15C) was enlarged in the 16C by Claude d'Urfé, who brought artists from Italy to help with the decoration.

Montverdun
18km/11.3mi W via the N 89 and D 42.
The Montverdun "Peak" is a geological curiosity rising between the Lignon valley and the Mont d'Uzore. It is a volcanic eminence that was historically topped by a fortified priory, below which the village developed. The church dates from the 12–15C, its severity is enhanced by the use of black basalt in its construction.

DISCOVERING ROANNAIS AND LE FOREZ

Monts du Forez★★

The granite mountains that are part of the **Parc Naturel Régional Livradois-Forez** form a range some 45km/28mi long. Along the edge are parallel offshoots separating the picturesque valleys, some of which run down to the Dore, others of which head for the Loire. The eastern slopes stand high above the Forez plain; the slopes to the west, the only part of the range in the Auvergne, drop sharply down to the Dore basin and include some magnificent views.

- **Michelin Map:** 327: B-5/6, C-5/6, D-5/6.
- **Location:** The Monts du Forez are part of the Parc Naturel Régional Livradois-Forez, so a good place to start is at the Maison du Parc in St-Gervais-sous-Meymont.
- **Parking:** At the Maison du Parc.
- **Don't miss:** The panorama from the col du Bréal and from the balcon du Forez.
- **Timing:** Allow at least a day-and-a-half to explore the region fully.

A BIT OF GEOGRAPHY

On the heights – Up to altitudes of 1 000m, the mountains are covered with fields (rye, potatoes) and meadows. The abundant supply of pure water rushing down the slopes is used to irrigate meadows, where it is cool even in the height of the summer. The water also serves to turn the waterwheels of mills, sawmills, and the last papermill in the Lagat valley; it also supplies the cutlery works in Thiers (*see p223*). At altitudes above 1 300m lie the summer pastures, called "Hautes-Chaumes."

DRIVING TOURS

1 VIA COL DE BÉAL★
84km/52mi. Allow one day.

Boën
Boën (pronounced "Bowen"), situated high above the left bank of the Lignon, specialises in metal-working and mechanical engineering. Boën was the birthplace of Father Terray (1715–78), Controller-General of Finances at the end of Louis XV's reign.
The unpopular measures he was forced to take in order to re-establish a balanced budget following the excessive spending of the royal court brought him the nickname "Emptier of Purses".

Musée des Vignerons du Forez★
Mar–Nov daily except Mon 2–6pm. Dec–Feb and 1 May. €4.50.
04 77 24 08 12.
www.chateaumuseeboen.fr.
The elegant 18C Château Chabert houses an authentic wine-making museum boasting reconstructions of traditional interiors and in technical presentations of wine-growing. A wine tasting is possible following the guided tour.

▶ Leave Boën on the D 1089. 2.5km/1.5mi on from Boën, turn left onto D 6 to Sail-sous-Couzan.

Sail-sous-Couzan
This peaceful village was the venue for the 1998 World Cup final between France and Brazil, won by the host country.

▶ Turn right off D 6 onto a very steep tarmacked road leading to the castle ruins.

Château de Couzan★
Park at the foot of the ruins; 15min on foot there and back. The ruins of this 11C fortress stand on a rocky promontory squeezed between the narrow valleys of the Lignon and Chagon. What

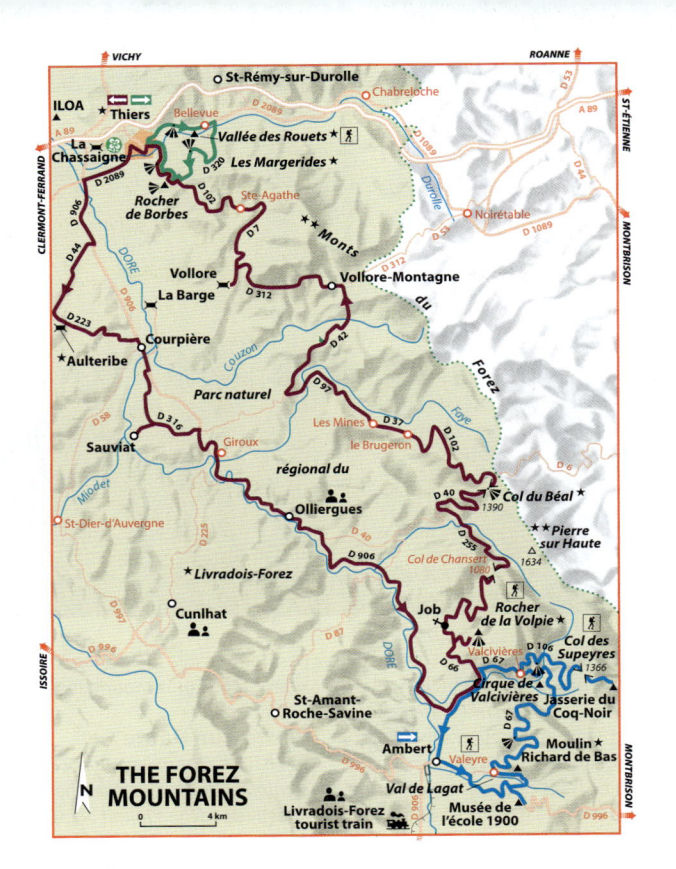

remains of the curtain walls and towers still suggests the strength of the Lords of Couzan, the oldest barons of the Forez. There is a good view of the castle walls from a rocky promontory behind the fort, and **panoramic views**★ over the countryside from the fortress (Jul–Aug 2.30–6pm. guided tours 3pm, 4pm, 5pm.)

▶ Return to Sail-sous-Couzan and turn left onto D 97 towards St-Just-en-Bas.

Summer Pastures

The Monts du Forez feature a wide range of scenery, much of it covered by dark pine forests. Once above the tree line, the mountain summits, often shrouded in mist or clouds, are vast bleak stretches of moorland – the Hautes-Chaumes. This somewhat eerie landscape can look more like a moonscape in certain lights. The vast bare wastes are broken only by granite rocks, deep peat bogs or clumps of broom. Nevertheless, man – or rather, woman – has attempted to scratch a living from this unwelcoming environment. A matriarchal society evolved in the mountain farmsteads *(jasseries)* during the summer months; while the menfolk were down in the valley dealing with the harvesting, the women and children would look after the livestock in the summer pastures, where they would also make the famous local Fourme cheese and gather medicinal plants.

This harsh way of life gradually died out, and there are now no more working *jasseries*. However, some of them have been converted into open-air museums which inform visitors about the daily work and traditions of these "Amazons of the Mountains".

DISCOVERING ROANNAIS AND LE FOREZ

Summits of the Monts du Forez and Pierre-sur-Haute, the Limagne hills in the foreground

The road runs along the crest of the hill above the upper Lignon valley, overshadowed by Pierre sur Haute before reaching Jeansagnière. Continue on to the pass, **Col de la Loge**, where a curtain of pine trees opens onto a clearing carpeted with grass. Before La Chamba, the forest gives way to more pastoral scenery and the route, skirting a succession of corries filled with fine pastures. This provides several outstanding views of the Dore basin and the Livradois area.

▶ Continue 2km/1.2mi beyond La Chamba and turn left towards Le Brugeron.

La Chambonie
A village nestling in a pastoral corrie.

▶ Immediately beyond a sawmill turn right onto D 37.

After a long climb up through the forest, there is a view over the Dômes mountain range. Beyond another stretch of road through the forest lie alpine pastures dotted with farmsteads *(jasseries)*.

Col du Béal★
From this pass there is a wide **panoramic view** over the mountains of the Auvergne and the Lyonnais area. The pass forms a threshold between the two sides of the Forez mountains.

Pierre-sur-Haute★★
2h30 on foot there and back; recommended in clear weather. Climb directly up to the summit across the alpine pastures and along the crest of the mountain, or take the chair-lift (mid-Dec–Mar. 04 77 24 85 09. www.loire-chalmazel.fr).

Pierre-sur-Haute, the highest peak in the Forez range (1 634m), is a dome-shaped granite mountain topped by military radar installations. The windswept moorland that carpets its slopes is gashed here and there by huge rockfalls. Small farmsteads dot the hillsides. From the summit to the right of the military installations, the **panorama** stretches right across the Forez, the mountains in the Lyonnais area and Beaujolais, the Limagne, the Dômes and Dore mountain ranges, Cantal and the mountains in Velay and Vivarais.

▶ About 7km/4mi from Col du Béal, a road cuts off to the right; it leads to the ski slopes and the Pierre-sur-Haute cable-car.

Chalmazel✷
This mountain village, which clings to the hillside in the Lignon ravine, is a

MONTS DU FOREZ

bustling place during the winter sports season. It is dominated by the old 13C **Château des Talaru-Marcilly**, a huge bastion flanked by corner towers, which still boasts its parapet walkway. The chapel is decorated with 16C frescoes.

▶ Take D 101 to Sauvain.

Sauvain
The most notable feature of this village is the **Musée de la Fourme et des Traditions** (*Jul–Aug, daily 10am–12.30pm, 2.30–6.30pm; May–Jun and Sept–Oct Sun and public holidays 2.30–6.30pm. €5. 04 77 76 30 04. www.museedelafourme.com*), an old 17C farmhouse that belonged to the inventor **Louis Lépine**, who founded a famous competition for the most innovative device or technique. The museum explores the history of local fourme cheese and the agricultural traditions surrounding it.

▶ Continue on D 101 in the direction of Montbrison. Soon after crossing the Lignon at Pont-de-Pierre, turn left onto D 110, for Col de la Pelletière. Drive to Trelins via La Bruyère and Prélion (D 20) and take D 20A on the right.

Château de Goutelas
The château stands on a terrace high above the Forez plain; it is a late-16C residence which has been restored and is now used to host courses and seminars. The courtyard is open to visitors and it is possible to walk round the exterior.

▶ Turn back and take D 8 back to Boën.

2 VIA COL DES SUPEYRES★
70km/44mi. Allow half a day.

Montbrison – *see MONTBRISON.*

▶ Leave Montbrison to the W along D 101 which climbs up the bare, rocky Vizery ravine. A short detour leads to the village of Essertines.

Essertines-en-Châtelneuf
From the village, with its small Gothic church boasting Flamboyant Gothic decoration, there is a view over the Forez plain from which emerges the rocky pinnacle of St-Romain-le-Puy.

▶ Regain D 101 and continue up the valley before turning left on D 44A. In Roche turn left onto D 44 and continue via D 113 to Col de Baracuchet.

From the road there are several glimpses of the Forez plain. The road continues to climb through valleys filled with farms and fields and dominated by wooded peaks. Near the pass, the trees become gnarled and twisted, until eventually they give way to a vast clearing from which there is a view of the Ance valley *(left)* and, opposite the road, the crest of the Forez mountains. The road climbs to Col des Supeyres through alpine pastures, carpeted with heather and dotted with farmsteads.

Col des Supeyres
See AMBERT, Le Val Legat.
The route down from the pass towards St-Anthème passes the group of farmsteads known as **Les Jasseries du Grand Genévrier**, one of which is open to the public.

Jasserie du Coq Noir
See AMBERT, Le Val Legat.

▶ As the road runs down to St-Anthème there are views of the volcanic cones in the Velay area – Meygal, Lizieux, Mézenc and Gerbier-de-Jonc.

St-Anthème
The red-roofed village nestles in the depths of the Ance valley.

▶ Follow D 496 from St-Anthème to return to Montbrison.

393

DISCOVERING ROANNAIS AND LE FOREZ

ADDRESSES

🍴 EAT

⊜ **Auberge du Mazet** – *42990 St-Georges-en-Couzan. ℘04 77 24 80 95. Closed Wed evening,Thurs.* A convivial atmosphere reigns in the vast dining room, ham, pork, and cheese are frequently on the menu.

⊜ **Auberge des Granges** – *Les Granges, 42920 Chalmazel (5km/3mi SW of Chalmazel dir. Le Col du Béal). ℘04 77 24 80 62. Closed Nov. Reservations recommended evenings.* This long chalet is a very convenient place to take it easy and re-energise after a hard day's skiing. The generous meals give healthy farm produce pride of place.

⊜⊜ **Gaudon** – *63880 Le Brugeron (6km/3.6mi S of La Chambonie via D 101 and D 37). ℘04 73 72 60 46. Closed Sun evening, Mon evening and Tue from mid-Sept–May.* In the bosom of the Monts du Forez, at the entrance of the village of Brugeron, this traditional house built in 1929 is a handy stopover.

Montbrison

The town is built around a volcanic mound and dominated by the 18C dome of the old Convent of the Visitation (today the law courts), and by the imposing belfry of its Gothic church, Notre-Dame-d'Espérance, which was founded in 1226 (restored 1970). The town was fortified following the attacks by the English army at the start of the Hundred Years War. During the Religious Wars, Montbrison was captured and pillaged by the Protestant forces in 1562, with the town's garrison thrown from the ramparts.

TOWN CENTRE

Opposite the church stands **La Diana** (*Wed and Sat 9am–noon, 2–5pm; Tue and Fri 2–5pm. ℘04 77 96 01 10. www.ladiana.com*), built in 1296 on the occasion of the marriage of the Count of Forez, Jean I, later served as a meeting place for priests; in Latin *Decanatus*, hence Diana.

The **Musée d'Allard** (*daily except Tue 2–6pm. 1 Jan and 25 Dec; €4. ℘04 77 96 39 15*) contains a fine collection of minerals and stuffed birds. The town also features several splendid **hôtels particuliers**, notably on rue St-Pierre and rue Puy-de-la-Bâtie.

> ▸ **Population:** 16 339.
> **Michelin Map:** 327: D-6.
> **Info:** 1 Place Eugène Beaune, 42600 Montbrison. ℘04 77 96 08 69. www.loireforez.com.
> **Location:** 44km/27mi NW of St-Étienne, via the A 72.
> **Timing:** Allow half a day.

Old Houses

The town features several splendid **hôtels particuliers**, notably on rue St-Pierre (*Nos. 1, 7, 10, 11, 13 and 17*) and rue Puy-de-la-Bâtie (*Nos. 5, 9, 11, 14, 18, 19 and 20*).

EXCURSIONS

Moingt

3km/1.8mi. Leave Montbrison S on D 8. This former Roman city has retained its medieval appearance and narrow winding streets.

Église de Champdieu

4.5km/2.8mi N on D 8.
Champdieu lies on the edge of the Forez plain and hills. It has a remarkable Romanesque **church** which was built for a Benedictine priory. In the 14C the church and priory buildings were heavily fortified. The most surprising feature of this church is the extent of its system of defence. High arcading forms machicolations on the south side and the south

Église de Champdieu

arm of the transept. A similar system runs along the walls of the priory, built in a quadrangle, with the church forming the south side. The church has two bell-towers; the more outstanding is the one over the transept, which dates from the Romanesque period. The second bell-tower, by the west front, dates from the 15C. Note, to the left of the west front's portal, the capital depicting a mermaid with two tails.

St-Romain-le-Puy

7km/4.3mi S of Montbrison.
The church of the former priory of St-Romain-le-Puy, which, at the end of the 10C, belonged to the abbey of St-Martin-d'Ainay in Lyon, rises on a volcanic peak emerging from the Forez plain. It dominates a St-Gobain glass-works at the foot of the peak. Water is bottled from a mineral spring north-east of the village near D 8.

Église du Prieuré★

Jun–Sept daily 2–7pm (6pm Sept); Apr–May and Oct Sat–Sun and public Holidays 2–6pm. 04 77 76 92 10.
From the plateau in front of the church, the panorama encompasses a vast circle of mountains: those of Forez to the west, the Monts d'Uzore to the north, and the Tarare and Lyonnais from the north-east to the south-east.

Chalain-d'Uzore

7km/4.3mi N, off the D 8.
The 14C–16C **château** (*guided visits Jul–Aug on Thurs at 4.30pm; €6. 04 77 97 13 12*) is notable for its former courtroom, converted into a village hall during the Renaissance (imposing fire-place) and for its gallery with sculpted doors.

Montrond-les-Bains

14km/8.7mi NE on D 496.
This spa resort, recommended specifically for obesity and diabetes, has retained its **château** (*Jul–Aug daily except Tue 2.30–7pm; Apr–May Sat–Sun and public holidays 2.30–7pm; Jun and Sept Wed, Fri–Sun and public holidays 2.30–7pm. Oct–Mar. €4. 04 77 94 64 74. www.montrond-les-bains.com*), whose ruins stand proudly on top of a hill near the Loire River. Although the castle was damaged by fire in the 18C, the outer walls have survived. Beyond the vast porch, decorated with fluted pilasters and capitals, stand the remains of the 14C and 15C building where the lord of the castle lived with his family.

DISCOVERING ROANNAIS AND LE FOREZ

Sury-le-Comtal
13km/8mi SE on D 8.
This small town's 17C **château** features lavish **ornamentation**★ consisting of sculpted ceilings and intricate wainscoting. There are also several fine fireplaces with carved panels.

St-Bonnet-le-Château★

St Bonnet is a village of considerable character, with its Gothic church and medieval streets climbing towards the collegiate church. It is also a small but active industrial centre, especially renowned for its *boules*.

OLD TOWN
On the road to the church stand two **Renaissance houses**★★ at the entrance to the streets opening onto place du Cdt-Marey. Further along are particularly noteworthy houses dating from the 15C–16C.
The **Chemin des Murailles**★ follows the outline the old fortifications to reach the 14C **porte de la Châtelaine**, the name given to Notre-Dame-du-Bon-Secours. At the time of the outbreak of the plague in the 18C, the Castel-Bonisontins was symbolically entrusted with the protection of the town by means of an oratory lodged in the gateway itself, which today lacks the original statue.

▶ Almost at the end of the road, cross the garden to the college.

From the terrace to the north of the Collegiale church, the **view**★ extends across the Forez plain, from which rises the prominent hill of St-Romain-le-Puy. The Gothic **collégiale**, dating from the beginning of the 15C, has two steeples.

ADDRESSES

STAY

Marytel – *95 rte de Lyon, 42600 Savigneux (1.5km/1mi E of Montbrison via D 496). ☎04 77 58 72 00. www.hotel-marytel.com. 33 rooms.* This modern edifice by the side of the road is protected from noise by efficient double-glazed windows. The basic, functional rooms are neat and tidy. A lovely tea salon also offers pre-dinner snacks and cocktails.

▶ **Population:** 1 637.
● **Michelin Map:** 327 D-7.
Info: 7 pl. de la République, 42380 St-Bonnet-le-Château. ☎04 77 50 52 48. www.pays-st-bonnet-le-chateau.fr.
▶ **Location:** 30km/19mi W of St-Étienne and 32km/20mi S of Montbrison.
Kids: The Ecomuseum of Forez.
● **Timing:** Allow half a day to explore the Old Town, and another to tackle the Driving Tour.

The **crypt** situated at the heart of the building is covered with 15C murals, depicting scenes from the New Testament.
The **Chapelle de la Charité** dates from the 17C and is especially interesting for its decoration and furniture.

🚗 DRIVING TOUR

LES BELVÉDÈRES
35km/22mi. Allow 1h30.

▶ Leave St-Bonnet on the D 498, to the N.

Luriecq
The simple Gothic **church** boasts a Renaissance porch.

ST-BONNET-LE-CHÂTEAU

Collégiale, St-Bonnet-le-Château

▶ Do a U-turn and take the D 5 to the right.

Marols

The church was fortified in the 14C. Of the two towers, the slimmer is a true defensive structure.

▶ Follow the D 5.

Saint-Jean-Soleymieux

The **church** is interesting for its 12C crypt. The village is located near an ancient thoroughfare, *Via Agrippa,* that linked the future Lyon with Bordeaux.

▶ Follow the D 96, then the D 44.

Montarcher

From the terrace of the little **church** (12C–15C) there is a fine **view★** over Mont Pilat, the Mézenc, the Yssingeaux region and the mountains of Margeride. The water of Montarcher was first marketed in 1999.

▶ The D 14 and the D 498 lead to back to St-Bonnet.

LE HAUT-FOREZ

50km/31mi. Allow about 2h.

▶ Leave St-Bonnet on the D 3 to the SE, and take the D 109 to the right.

Saint-Nizier-de-Fornas

The lovely **church** retains significant Romanesque elements. The rectangular tower, adorned with pinnacles and large gargoyles, gives the southern side a distinctive silhouette. Inside, there is a beautiful set of carved keystones.

▶ Continue on the D 109.

Rozier-Côtes-d'Aurec

The **church**, built in the 11C and 12C, is that of a Cluniac priory; the two-storey bell-tower has been rebuilt in its original form. The tympanum features a sculpted group representing the Adoration of the Magi and, in the long faces that are portrayed, shows a particular Spanish influence. Inside, the nave is supported with arches. Of note is the apse, decorated with a beautiful arch with fluted pilasters, characteristic of the Romanesque churches of the region.

▶ Turn round and take the D 104, to the left, then again turn left onto the D 42.

Saint-Hilaire-Cusson-la-Valmitte

This partially **Romanesque church** was rebuilt in the 15C and 19C. Note the small ambulatory behind the arches of the original apse. Two statues in polychrome wood date from the 15C.

DISCOVERING ROANNAIS AND LE FOREZ

▶ Turn around, and immediately turn left onto the road that lead to the D 104, which you take to the left.

Apinac
The church, dating from the 19C, is noted for its colourful stained glass windows.

Moulin de Vignal
Guided visits (1h): Jul–Aug Tue–Sun, 2.30–6.30pm; late-Apr–Jun and Sept–Oct, Sun and public holidays, 2.30-6.30pm. €5.. ☏04 77 50 80 23. www.moulindevignal.fr.
Saved by a local association, this set of **18C mill buildings**, which includes four mills, has been carefully restored. Today, they produce freshly ground flour as well as canola oil.

▶ Come back towards Apinac and turn left to take, the D 443 to the right. Continue on the D 24.

Saint-Pal-de-Chalencon
A fortified town of which several ancient gateways remain.

▶ The D 241 and D 91 lead to Usson.

Usson-en-Forez
The town, once fortified, is dominated by the 16C spire of its steeple. The nave of the church dates from the 15C.

Écomusée du Forez★
Quartier St-Joseph. Daily 2–6pm. 1 Jan, 25 Dec. €4 (child 8–16, €1.50). ☏04 77 50 61 40. www.ecomusee-usson-en-forez.fr.
Created in 1993 from a private donation, the museum makes good use of former convent buildings, restoring and reviving the lifestyles, customs and crafts of the region. From combs to the washing machine to lace clothing, family life in a village house is carefully replicated. The barn still houses typical tools, and upstairs, the focus is turned on the disappearing trades of clog-makers, carpenters, wheelwrights and lace-makers. In the adjoining building, you can listen to stories passed down during the long winter evenings and discover a collection of gleaming carriages. A pretty cottage garden, recreated from plans of Usson, completes the tour.

At the southerly exit from the town, 300m to the left of the D 498, the Romanesque apse of the **Chapelle de Notre-Dame-de-Chambriac** houses an ancient statue of the Virgin Mary.

▶ Take the D 498 towards Estivareilles.

Estivareilles
In August 1944, the regional *maquis* (the French Resistance force) hindered the withdrawal of German troops. As a result, the area saw fierce fighting during the liberation of Forez. The **Museum of 20C History** *(r. du Couvent. 2–6pm: mid-Apr–Oct; rest of year daily except Sat and Mon. Sat and Mon, mid Nov-Mar, 1 Jan, 25 Dec. ☏04 77 50 29 20)* describes the various stages of the campaign, and the upheavals of this turbulent century.

▶ The D 498 leads to St-Bonnet.

ADDRESSES

STAY

Hotel-Restaurant le Béfranc – *7 rte d'Augel, 42380 St-Bonnet-le-Château. ☏04 77 50 54 54. www.hotel-lebefranc.com. Closed 1wk in Oct, Feb, Sun evening and Mon except July-Aug. 17 rooms.* Clean and comfortable; choice of traditional dishes in the restaurant.

Chambre d'Hôte la Campagnarde – *Rte d'Estivareilles, 42380 St-Nizier-de-Fornas. ☏04 77 50 71 19. 3 rooms.* No frills, but a good atmosphere in this vast farm.

EAT

La Calèche – *2 pl. du Cdt-Marey, 42380 St-Bonnet-le-Château. ☏04 77 50 15 58. www.restaurantlacaleche.fr. Closed Mon evening of Oct–Mar; Tue, Sun evening, Tue evening, and Wed.* The restaurant is furnished in the style of the 17C and has three brightly coloured dining rooms.

ST-ÉTIENNE AND LE PILAT

The influence of adjacent departments is particularly evident throughout this region. To the west lies the Loire and the Haute-Loire, closely linked with their rivers; to the north-east lies Isère, and to the south-east is the Ardèche. There is no doubting the importance of St Étienne and its many services and facilities to the region, but within the greater area lie many parochial cultures and loyalties. Consuming a huge swathe of land is the Parc Naturel Régional du Pilat, which alone embraces no fewer than 50 towns and villages, all the while preserving a beautiful countryside of beech and fir forests, pastureland, orchards and vineyards.

More About Le Pilat

Spread across a rural area of more than 700sq km/270sq mi, Pilat Regional Park is especially rich and diverse in its natural and cultural heritage. Located in proximity to major urban centres and boasting a combined population of 50 000, it is a popular weekend getaway. Le Pilat's mountains, rising to 1 432m – higher than Ben Nevis, Britain's highest peak – lie where continental and oceanic influences collide. The result is an amazing and wide-ranging wealth of natural resources, and this is reflected in internal sub-divisions unique identities and cultures linger on: Pilat du Gier, Piemont-Rhodanien, the valley of Déôme, les Crêts and Haut Pilat. The convergence of so many influences has made this a particularly rich area in culture as well as natural bounty.

Highlights

1. Wandering the Old Town of **St Étienne** (p402)
2. 20C art in the **Museum of Modern Art** in St Étienne (p402)
3. Gateway to the gorges of the Loire, **Monistrol-sur-Loire** (p409)
4. Nature trails through the **Pilat Regional Park** (p410)
5. The spectacular panorama from **Crêt de l'Œillon** (p412)

Regional Parks

Regional parks are different from national parks in their concept and purpose. They are inhabited areas selected for development of the local economy through specific activities (the creation of cooperatives, promotion of crafts), the preservation of the natural and cultural heritage (museums, architecture) and the appreciation of the distinctive character of the region.

Château de Rochebaron, Monistrol-sur-Loire

ST-ÉTIENNE AND LE PILAT

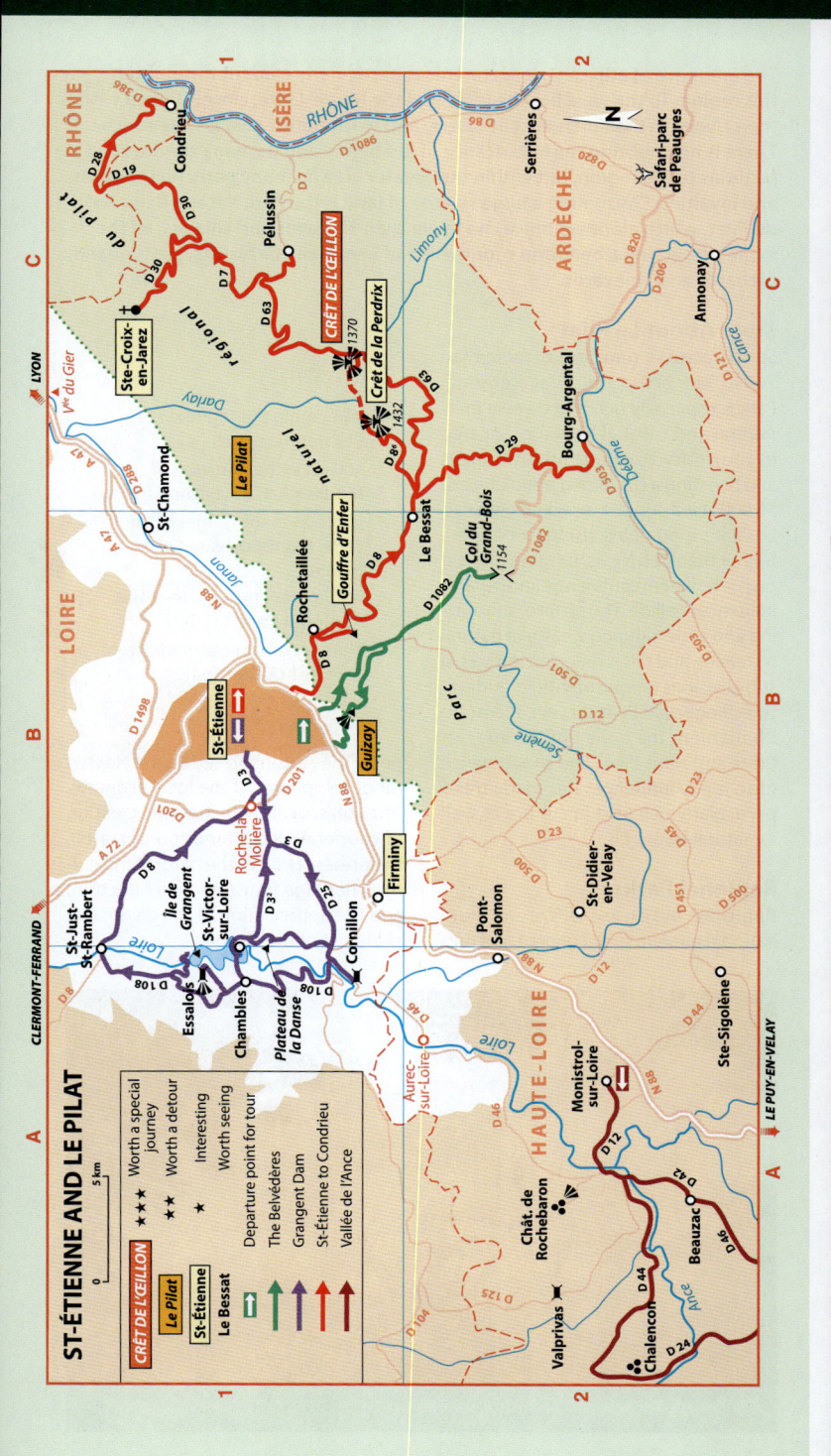

St-Étienne ★

St-Étienne lies in the Furan depression, close to the Massif du Pilat, Grangent lake and the Forez plain. The town is located at the centre of a coal basin, which supplied over 500 million tonnes of coal until the mines were closed in the 1980s. Since then, St-Étienne has adopted a new image: the façades of its buildings have been cleaned, and its gardens and parks have been renovated. The busiest area lies along a north–south axis: place Jean-Jaurès to place de l'Hôtel-de-Ville. The 15C and 16C main church of St-Étienne, locally known as the "Grand'Église", remains dear to the hearts of locals. The hometown of the composer Jules Émile Frédéric Massenet (1842–1912), has an intellectual and artistic presence that extends over the whole of Forez.

- **Population:** 174 985.
- **Michelin Map:** 327: F-7 – Local map see Le PILAT.
- **Info:** 16 av. de la Libération. 42000 St-Étienne. ℘04 77 49 39 00. www.saint-etienne-hors-cadre.fr.
- **Location:** Close to the Massif du Pilat, south-west of Lyon.
- **Parking:** The centre of St Etienne is a difficult place to drive and park, but there are parking areas at stages along the tram line.
- **Don't Miss:** The Museum of Modern Art and the Old Town.
- **Timing:** You will need at least a whole day, maybe more.
- **Kids:** Go star-gazing at the Planetarium.

A BIT OF HISTORY

In the 12C, St-Étienne was a village on the banks of the Furan, bypassed by major communication routes. Local coal, and the enterprising spirit of the inhabitants, brought about an extraordinary development; the population shot up from 3 700 in 1515 to 45 000 in 1826, then 146 000 in 1901, while the industrial estate spread west, east and north.

Armeville – In 1296, the people of St-Étienne started working the coal quarries: first for their personal needs, and then to feed the forges that produced knives. Soon after, St-Étienne pivoted to begin producing cutting and thrusting weapons, crossbows and, finally, firearms.
In 1570 the Arms Manufacturers' Lodge consisted of 40 trades, and mass production was already being practised. In 1746 the Royal Arms Factory was founded. During the Revolution, this activity would to earn the town the name of Armeville.

GETTING AROUND

TRAMWAY
The tramway is the best way to get around town. You can buy a one-day pass for unlimited travel throughout St-Étienne. *(www.reseau-stas.fr.)* An app available via the tourism website offers walking tour ideas and more.

From St-Étienne to Andrézieux – In May 1827, the first French railway, built to plans by Beaunier, was inaugurated: it ran between St-Étienne and Andrézieux over a distance of 21km/13mi and was used to transport coal. The wagons were pulled by horses. This ancestor of modern means of transport, perfected in 1829 thanks to the tube boiler developed by Marc Seguin, led to a revolution in transport and a boom in industry.

The town that made everything – The region of St-Étienne was already specialised in quality steels, tools, hunting guns, bicycles and automobile parts. To the ribbon industry, imported from

Italy, was added shirred fabric at the end of the 19C.

Industrial redeployment – The mines saw coal production decrease between 1960 and 1980. A gradual closing was planned, allowing the metallurgical and textile industries time to restructure themselves; they now operate in conjunction with diversified activities such as precision mechanics, electronics, food processing, plastics and cardboard manufacturing.

WALKING TOUR

OLD TOWN★

Start out from place du Peuple, a former medieval market square. On the corner of rue Mercière, a 16C tower rises above an arcade; a timber-framed house stands opposite.

Cross the avenue used by the trams to reach rue Denis-Escoffier, which marks the entrance to the old Outre-Furan district. At the junction of rue des Martyrs-de-Vingré is an unusual mid-18C house adorned with a statue as well as eaves with four rows of tiles and large, visible beams, typical of the urban architecture in Forez. On the left at no. 3 rue Georges-Dupré, a massive façade includes imposing lintels in one piece.

Turn back and follow rue des Martyrs-de-Vingré; numbers 19 and 30 are examples of 18C houses incorporating weaving lofts or workshops.

▶ After reaching place Neuve, turn right onto rue Nautin, which leads to rue Michelet.

Rue Michelet

This artery, pierced along the north-south axis parallel to rue Gambetta, contains some examples of innovative architecture from the 1930s (Nos. 34, 36, 42 and in particular No. 44, an imposing building in reinforced concrete).

▶ Continue along rue Nautin and rejoin rue Gambetta.

Place Boivin

This marks the site of the former 15C north rampart. Walk down rue Émile-Loubet; there is a fine façade adorned with five caryatids at no. 12, the 16C **Maison de "Marcellin-Allard"**.

Return to the square, one corner of which is occupied by the Grand'Église. To the right of the church, at the beginning of rue de la Ville, note the two handsome façades (15C and 16C): No 5, known as the **Maison François I** is decorated with five Renaissance medallions.

Grand' Église

The church of St-Étienne is the town's only example of Gothic architecture; its parish is the oldest in the city.

Place du Peuple

ST-ÉTIENNE

Musée d'Art et d'Industrie

▶ On leaving the church, turn right and rejoin rue Ste-Catherine, leading down to rue du Général-Foy. Turn left towards place Jean-Jaurès.

Place de l'Hôtel-de-Ville, the main town square, and place Jean-Jaurès form the hub of city life in St-Étienne.

Place Jean-Jaurès

In summer, this square is a delight, with its pretty bandstand and plane trees offering shade.

▶ Rue Gérentet leads to place Dorian, then rue Alsace-Lorraine will take you back to place du Peuple.

ADDITIONAL SIGHTS
Musée d'Art Moderne★★

4.5km/3mi from the city centre. Leave St-Étienne N via rue Bergson towards La Terrasse and follow signs to the Musée d'Art Moderne.

Daily except Tue 10am–6pm.
1 Jan, 1 May, 14 Jul, 15 Aug, 1 Nov, 25 Dec. €6.5 (guided visits €7.5); no charge 1st Sun of month. ℘04 77 79 52 52. www.mam-st-etienne.fr.

This vast art gallery located in the town of St-Priest-en-Jarez was designed by the architect D Guichard; it is devoted to 20C art, of which it provides an interesting retrospective owing to its policy of continual acquisition.

The sober, functional building looks like an industrial structure from the outside. Its walls, covered with black ceramic panels, are a reminder of the important local role of coal.

Musée d'Art et d'Industrie★★

Daily except Mon 10am–6pm.
1 Jan, 1 May, 14 Jul, 15 Aug, 1 Nov and 25 Dec. €6 (guided visits €7). ℘04 77 49 73 00. www.musee-art-industrie.saint-etienne.fr.

This Art and Industry Museum located in the former Palais des Arts is a real repository of local and regional know-how relating to tool-making and the evolution of equipment and machinery from the 16C up to the present day.

Puits Couriot, Musée de la Mine★

Daily except Mon 10am–6pm.
1 Jan, 1 May, 14 Jul, 15 Aug, 1 Nov, 25 Dec. €6.5 (guided visits €7.5).
℘04 77 43 83 23. www.musee-mine.saint-etienne.fr.

The visit begins in the **Salle des Pendus★**, a vast locker room where, as space was limited, miners' clothes were hung from the ceiling to dry. The adjoining shower is evidence of the collective life they led. Visitors are taken to the lower galleries in the cages used by miners for accessing the mines, bringing up coal and sometimes the injured.

DISCOVERING ST-ÉTIENNE AND LE PILAT

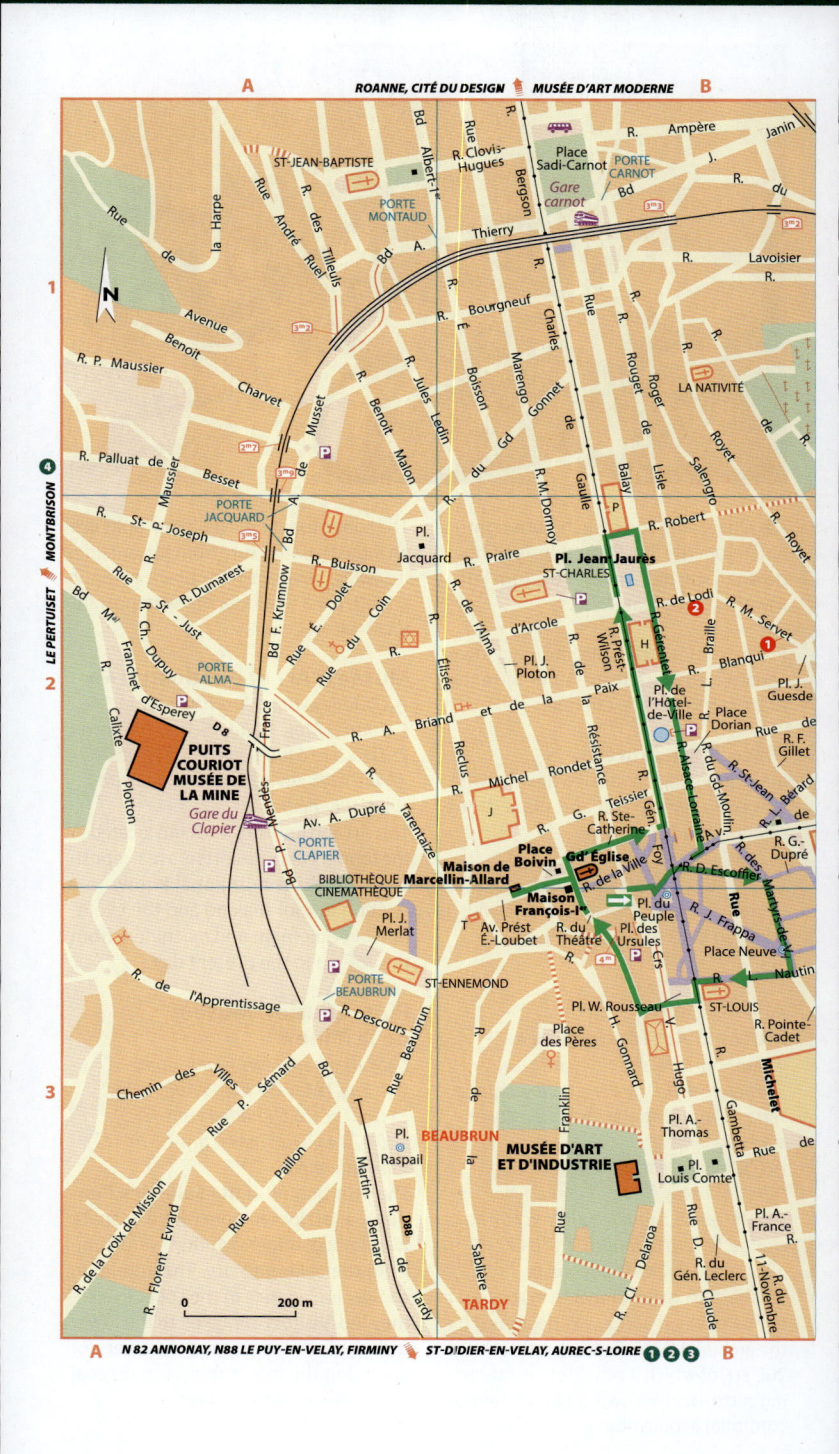

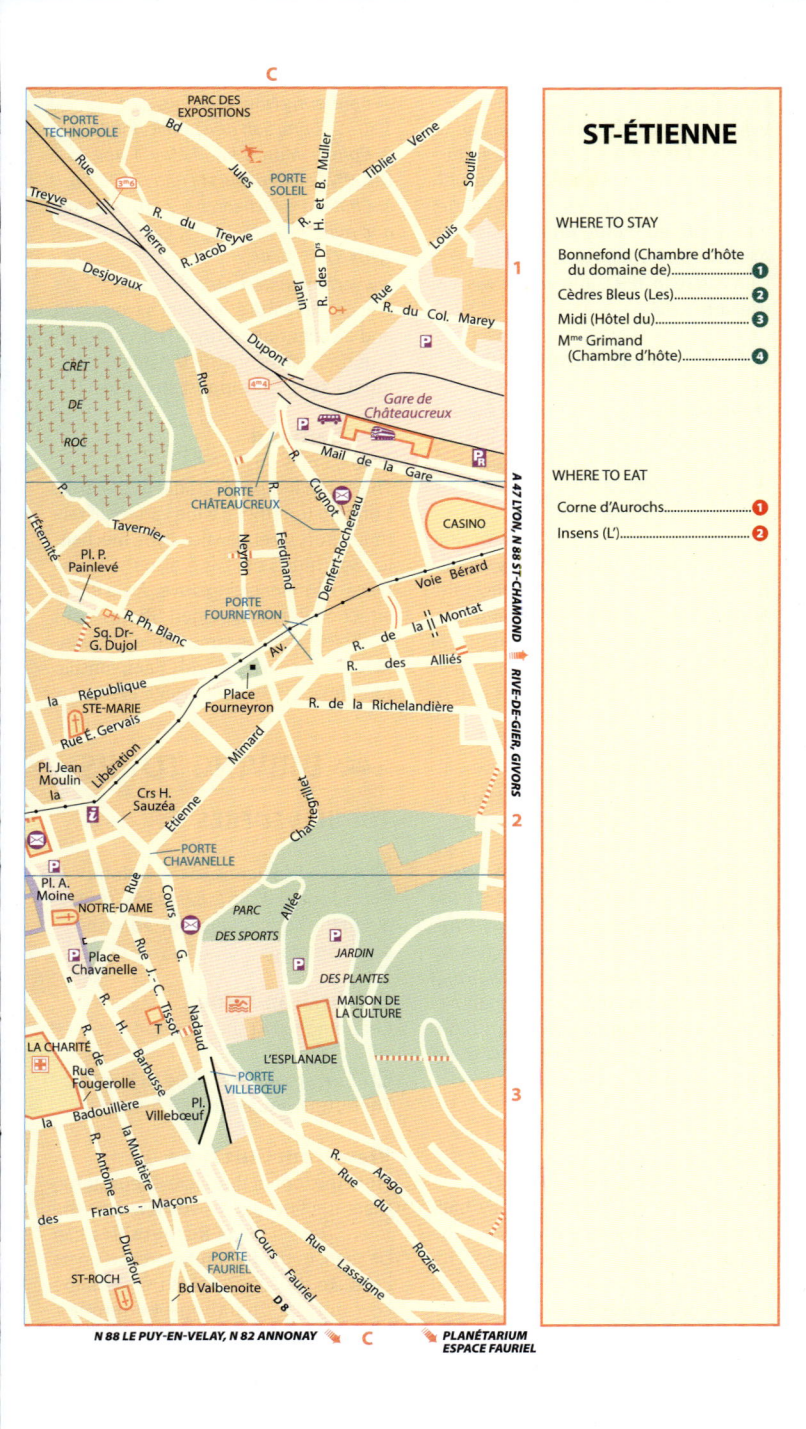

ST-ÉTIENNE

WHERE TO STAY

Bonnefond (Chambre d'hôte du domaine de)..................①
Cèdres Bleus (Les).......................②
Midi (Hôtel du)..............................③
Mme Grimand (Chambre d'hôte).....................④

WHERE TO EAT

Corne d'Aurochs...........................①
Insens (L').......................................②

DISCOVERING ST-ÉTIENNE AND LE PILAT

Site of the old Manufacture des Armes et Cycles de St-Étienne
Cours Fauriel.
Laid out under the Second Empire to be one of the showcases of the industrial expansion in St-Étienne along with Avenue de la Libération, cours Fauriel was occupied by the buildings of the Arms Factory, which were built by Léon Lamaizière in 1893, and which were in use until 1985.

♿ L'Astronef, Planetarium★
Espace Fauriel, 28 rue P.-et-D.-Ponchardier. ♿ *Call or check website for times of shows and visits.* *Sept, 1 Jan, 1 May, 25 Dec.* €10.30 (under 25, €8.20). 04 77 33 43 01. www.planetarium-st-etienne.fr.
Crowned by a hemispherical dome, this planetarium is fitted with highly sophisticated equipment, which enhances the appeal of its shows about the universe. Most impressive is the astronomical simulator, able to calculate and project the movements of the planets and of some 3 000 stars.

Atelier Weiss★
1 Rue Eugène Weiss. *Mon–Sat 9am–7pm. No tours from mid-Jul–mid-Aug.* 04 77 21 61 09. www.weiss.fr.
Local chocolate producer Etienne Weiss opened this factory and workshop to the public in 2016. The *passerelle* allows visitors to glimpse the chocolate-making process from above, with a walkway that traverses the factory floor from above. Chocolate-making workshops are regularly on offer; see website for timing and pricing details.

EXCURSIONS
Firminy
11km/6.8mi. Leave S on the D 88.
Firminy lies in the Ondaine valley, halfway between the mountains and the St-Étienne plain. The town is known for its urban appearance thanks to famed architect **Le Corbusier** boasting a housing complex, arts centre, stadium and St-Peter's Church (unfinished). It is the second **"Le Corbusier site"**★ in the world after Chandigarh in India.

♿ Écomusée des Bruneaux
Apr–early Oct daily except Mon 2–6pm; early Nov–Mar Tues–Sat 1.30–5.30pm, Sun and public holidays 2–6pm. *Mon, 1 Jan, 1 May, 1 Nov, 25 Dec.* *guided tours of mines 3:30pm.* *Château €4 (children €2.50); château and mine: €6 (child 6–15, €4.50).* 04 77 89 38 46. www.chateaudesbruneaux.fr.
The castle features a nailer's workshop and a collection of toys. The outbuildings house a reconstructed mine showing the types of support structures.

St- Chamond
7km/4.3mi W on the N 88.
This is the industrial cradle of the area, bringing together a wide variety of factories (iron, steel, plastics, dyes, mechanics, synthetics etc.). It is also the birthplace of former racing driver Alain Prost, affectionately nicknamed "Professor of the Track", who became famous by winning the Formula 1 World Championship four times (1985, 1986, 1989, 1993).

🚗 DRIVING TOURS

THE BELVEDERES

▶ Leave St-Étienne to the S along Cours Fauriel (D 8). N 82 makes its way along the Furet ravine, dotted with schist outcrops.

Col du Grand-Bois
Charming forest site.

▶ Turn around and drive to Planfoy. There, turn left and rejoin Guizay.

View from Guizay★★
From the foot of the Sacré-Cœur statue there is a fine, extensive view over the town. The village of **Rochetaillée** can be seen, to the far right, perched on its crest. To the left unfolds the Ondaine corridor: Le Chambon-Feugerolles, Firminy and the hills of Forez.

▶ The D 88 takes you back to St-Étienne.

ST-ÉTIENNE

GRANGENT DAM★★
80km/50mi. Allow 4h.

▶ Leave St-Étienne SW on the D 3 then continue on the D 25.

Along the road, the Pertuiset bridge marks the transition between the city and the wild landscapes of the Loire.

Château de Cornillon
At St-Paul-en-Cornillon.
The castle, perched on a spur overlooking the Loire, was once the seat of the most important baronies of Forez.

▶ Continue on D 108 for 10km/6mi.

The road runs along an escarpment offering **views**★★ over the meanders of the Loire.

Chambles
This site is one of the most beautiful gorges of the Loire. Next to the squat church, the tower of the old castle stands on the edge of a cliff overlooking the meandering Grangent, characteristic of the defensive system of castles dating from the Middle Ages.

▶ 2km/1mi after Chambles, take the road on the right towards the Château d'Essalois.

Château d'Essalois
The silhouette of the castle stands above the gorge; from this beautiful sentinel there extends a fine **view**★★ of the lake and the island of Grangent.
Close to the castle is a Celtic *oppidum* – a form of settlement – reflecting the strategic importance of the location. On the other side, the plateau of the Danse (prehistoric site) and St-Victor-sur-Loire provide alternative points of view over the gorge. The history of these places is the stuff of legend, shrouding them, even today, in an air of mystery.

▶ Return to Chambles by the same route, then take the D 108 and the D 3².

Île de Grangent with the remains of the 12C castle

Île de Grangent
This man-made lake has isolated a rocky spine bearing the remains of the 12C Château de Grangent.

▶ Take the D 108 heading north.

St-Just-St-Rambert
Located at the mouth of the gorges of the Loire, on the southern plains of Forez, St-Rambert is a former Gallo-Roman town, clinging to the side of a hill. St-Just is the modern part of the town, extending along the right bank.

Musée des Civilisations
Pl. Madeleine-Rousseau. Wed–Sun 2–6pm. 1 Jan, 1 May and 24–25 and 31 Dec. €4. 04 77 52 03 11. www.stjust-strambert.fr.
Local history is represented here, as well as collections from other countries. In particular: a collection of African art and Oceania, bronzes from Benin and an Egyptian mask.

▶ Take the D 8 towards St-Étienne, then turn onto the D 3 towards Roche-la-Molière where you rejoin the D 3² which leads to St-Victor-sur-Loire.

Plateau de la Danse
Leave the car in the car park and follow the path signposted "Point de Vue" that disappears into the woods.

407

This region, steeped in local history and legends, has a rocky belvedere commanding a lovely **view★** of Grangent dam and island, St-Victor promontory, Essalois Château, and the medieval tower in Chambles.

▶ Return to the car and drive to St-Victor.

St-Victor-sur-Loire

This pretty village adorned with roses overlooks the artificial lake formed by the Loire upstream of Grangent. The **sailing base** is a popular meeting-place in summer, and there are facilities for many other sports and leisure activities. The open-air theatre and the **castle** (www.chateau-saint-victor.com), sporting its 11C towers, are perched on top of the hill.

ADDRESSES

STAY

Chambre d'Hôte du Domaine de Bonnefond – 42660 St-Romain-les-Atheux. ☎06 71 10 57 04. www.chambres-hotes-equitation-pilat.fr. 3 rooms. This former farmhouse is situated in beautiful countryside. The rooms are tastefully decorated. Heated indoor pool.

Chambre d'Hôte Mme Grimand – Pracoin – 42230 St-Victor-sur-Loire. ☎04 77 90 37 95. www.chambre-hotes-loire.com. 3 rooms. Close to the gorges of the Loire and of the medieval village of St-Victor, this house has three harmonious and comfortable rooms.

Hôtel du Midi – 19 bd. Pasteur. ☎04 77 57 32 55. www.hotelmidi.fr. 33 rooms. Two buildings linked by a cosy lounge with an original fireplace. The rooms are a bit small, but practical and soundproofed.

Les Cèdres Bleus – Rte de Bas-en-Basset, 43110 Aurec-sur-Loire. ☎04 77 35 48 48. www.lescedresbleus.com. Closed Jan. 15 rooms. Restaurant (closed Fri and Sun evening, Mon and Tue lunches). Between the gorges of the Loire and the Grangent lake, in a park, are three wooden chalets.

EAT

Insens – 10, rue de Lodi. ☎04 77 32 34 34. www.insens-restaurant.fr. Open Tue–Sat. Following the modern "bistronomic" trend, this restaurant serves contemporary, inventive cuisine that won't break the bank.

Corne d'Aurochs – 18 r. Michel-Servet. ☎04 77 32 27 27. Closed all day Sat–Sun. Just a short walk from the hôtel de ville, this bistro serves Lyonnais tavern cuisine.

THEATRE AND ENTERTAINMENT

Comédie de St-Étienne, Centre Dramatique National – 7 av. du Prés.-Émile-Loubet. ☎04 77 25 14 14. www.lacomedie.fr. Tickets: Mon–Fri 1–7pm. Closed Aug, Christmas and public holidays. This centre was founded in 1947 in order to initiate and promote drama outside of the capital. Today it orchestrates a permanent troupe of actors, a stage set workshop and a costumes atelier, as well as four different performance halls.

Opéra Théâtre de St-Étienne – Allée Shakespeare, Jardin des Plantes, BP 237. ☎04 77 47 83 47. www.opera.saint-etienne.fr. Tickets: Mon–Fri 2–7pm. Closed mid-Jul–Aug. The focal point of cultural animation in St-Etienne offering theatre, ballet and operetta.

Le Triomphe – 4 sq. Violette. ☎07 83 97 63 60. www.comedietriomphe.fr. Tue–Sun 2–8pm. Closed Jul–Aug. This café-theatre in a converted cinema cultivates in its shows the spirit, the culture, the accents and the language of the region.

Nouvel Espace Culturel – 9 r. Claudius-Cottier, 42270 St-Priest-en-Jarez. ☎04 77 74 41 81. Tickets: Mon–Fri 10am–4.30pm. Closed Aug and weekends. The Nouvel Espace Culturel was created in 1991 in a suburb close to Saint-Étienne. Many professional and amateur theatre troupes from all over France appear here performing new works or repertory pieces.

Monistrol-sur-Loire

The town has a surprisingly Mediterranean feel about it, both in its appearance and its climate. Fortunately, the development of the city has spared this ancient town with its medieval streets.

THE OLD QUARTER
Château des Evêques
Check website for exhibition and opening dates. 04 71 61 63 66. www.monistrol-lesamisduchateau.org.
An avenue of lime trees leads to the large round towers of the old Bishop's Palace (14C–18C), which now houses the tourist office and hosts temporary exhibitions.

▸ Follow path round château on right.

From the church, take rue du Commerce, then the first street on the right. Take a stroll along the network of narrow alleyways, and travel back in time from the Middle Ages to the 17C (Classical façades of the Couvent des Ursulines and Couvent des Capucins).

EXCURSIONS
St-Didier-en-Velay
11km/7mi to the E via the D 12.
A small town in the heart of the Semène valley with an old quarter, Romanesque church and 19C corn exchange.

Pont-Salomon
9km/5½mi N via the N 88.
Nestled in the heart of the Semène valley, this factory-village began in the 19C. The **Musée de la Faulx**★ is located in one of the original buildings, where time seems to stand still (*visits can be arranged through the tourist office* 04 77 35 42 65, *or direct with the museum.* €4. 04 77 35 87 07. www.musee-delafaulx.fr).

Ste-Sigolène
9km/5.5mi SE via the D 44.
Four hundred years of weaving, 50 years of manufacturing plastics and a major

- **Population:** 9 266.
- **Michelin Map:** 331: H-2.
- **Info:** 14 Faubourg Carnot, 43120 Monistrol-sur-Loire. 04 71 66 03 14. www.tourisme-marches duvelayrochebaron.fr.
- **Location:** 45km/28mi north-east of Le Puy-en-Velay, and 30km/19mi south-west of St-Étienne.
- **Parking:** Limited parking in the town centre.
- **Timing:** Relax over a coffee and spend a few hours here.

industrial conversion is proof, if it were needed, of the determination and flexibility of the town's people.
The **Musée de la Fabrique** (*Jul–Aug and 1st Sun of month 3 –6pm.* €4. 04 71 75 01 55), run by a team of former weavers, tells this story.

Château de Valprivas
In Valprivas, 16km/10mi W. *Call for details.* 04 71 66 73 52. www.chateaudevalprivas.com.
In the court of honour, the round tower features an unusual spiral staircase entirely sculpted in oak, as well as a porch framed by caryatids and crowned by a coat of arms.

🚗 DRIVING TOUR

VALLÉE DE L'ANCE
46km/29mi. Allow half a day.

▸ Leave Monistrol on D 12, heading for Bas-en-Basset.

Château de Rochebaron
in Bas-en-Basset (7km/4mi W): 330m above place des Marronniers, take the path running to the left of the rampart.

DISCOVERING ST-ÉTIENNE AND LE PILAT

🚶 The ruins of this medieval castle (11C–13C), perched on a spur overlooking the Loire, are preceded by three rows of protective walls. The road follows the charming Ance valley and, after crossing Vert, develops into a **corniche★**. There are lovely views of the Loire basin, the Andrable valley and the Monts du Velay.

▶ In Tiranges, turn left onto D 24.

As you are descending towards the River Ance, the Tour de Chalencon looms into sight, perched on its promontory.

▶ Continue along D 24 until you reach the junction with D 9. Drive up D 9, then take D 29 on the right. Drive through St-André-de-Chalencon and take the road running along the cemetery. After 2km/1mi, park the car and continue on foot (15min there and back).

Château de Chalencon –
See Gorges de la LOIRE.

▶ Rejoin D 46 towards Beauzac.

Beauzac
The small 12C–17C **church** here has a Flamboyant portal and an elegant three-storey belfry; a Romanesque crypt lies under the apse. A few houses in the village, built within the old ramparts pierced by two gates, have unusual wooden galleries under the roof which rest on huge corbels.

▶ Return to Monistrol via Pont de Lignon on D 461 and then N 88.

Le Pilat★★

The influence of the Mediterranean to the east and the Atlantic to the west makes this massif something of a watershed, particularly at Chaubouret Pass; it also acts as a watertower for the St-Étienne region. The coolness of its fir plantations, swift streams and high pastures contrasts with the industrial aspect of the Ondaine, Janon and Gier valleys. Formation of the massif goes back to the Hercynian fold: it was then a high mountain with its folds lying in a south-west–north-east direction. During the Secondary Era, erosion reduced it to a plateau, sloping down towards the present-day Rhône valley; the plateau was covered with water, leaving several layers of sediment. During the Tertiary Era, the water withdrew. The Alpine fold then caused subsidence of the Rhône valley and tilting of the massif. Le Pilat, having been "rejuvenated", rose to an altitude of 1 500m while the rivers – the Gier in the north and the Limony in the south – slid to the foot of the faults. During the Quaternary Era, erosion took its toll once again.

- **Michelin Map:** 327: F-7 to G-8.
- **Info:** Maison du Tourisme du Pilat, Moulin de Virieu 42410 Pélussin. ℘04 74 87 52 00. www.pilat-tourisme.fr.
- **Location:** The Massif du Pilat lies to the east of St-Étienne, between the Loire basin and the Rhône valley.
- **Don't Miss:** The panorama of the valley from the Crêt de l'Œillon.
- **Timing:** Allow a whole day to explore; more if you can.

A BIT OF GEOGRAPHY
Grassy heights – Crêt de la Perdrix at 1 432m and Crêt de l'Œillon at 1 370m

LE PILAT

Rhône valley viewed from St-Sabin Chapel, Parc naturel régional du Pilat

bristle with strange piles of granite blocks called **chirats**, resulting from complete erosion of the summits. Many rivers rise near the summits and flow rapidly down towards the Gier, the Rhône or the Loire along steep-sided valleys. The Gier itself, close to its source, crosses a *chirat* at the **Saut du Gier** falls.

PARC NATUREL RÉGIONAL DU PILAT

Created in 1974, the park contains about 50 towns and villages in the Rhône and Loire *départements*. The countryside is diverse: forests of beech and fir at high altitude, pastureland on the plateaux, orchards and vineyards along the banks of the Rhône. Committed to preserving nature and the environment, Pilat Park promotes rural, craft, tourist and cultural activities.

Maison du Parc – Moulin de Virieu à Pélussin

Reservation centre and tourist office, Moulin de Virieu, 42410 Pélussin. 04 74 87 52 00. www.parc-naturel-pilat.fr. The park's main information centre also organises exhibitions, special activities and walks. To facilitate an introduction to flora and fauna within the regional park, there are 500km/310mi of marked footpaths (brown and white stripes), including sections of GR7 and GR42 (Grande Randonnée long-distance footpaths, marked with red and white stripes), three nature trails and eight special themed trails, each identified by a number.

The **Jean-Jacques Rousseau trail**, from Condrieu to La Jasserie, is a reminder of the philosopher's time at Mont Pilat in 1769; the **flora trail** takes the rambler from the almost Mediterranean vegetation of the Malleval region to the sub-alpine formation of Perdrix ridge, from prickly pear to mountain tobacco. The **ornithological trail**, between St-Pierre-de-Bœuf and St-Sabin Chapel features up to 90 registered species of birds (particularly from mid-May–mid-June). To promote traditional activities and revive near-forgotten crafts, the park has opened the **Maison de la Béate et de l'Allier à Marlhes** (*Jul–Sept Sun and public holidays, 2–6.30pm. 04 77 51 24 70*) in Marlhes, the **Maison de la Passementerie** (*early May–early Oct, Sun 2.30–6.30pm. 04 77 39 93 38. www.maison-passementerie.info*) in Jonzieux and the **Maison des Tresses et Lacets** (*Guided visits: Mar–Nov Wed–Sun 2.30pm and 4pm. €5. 04 77 20 91 06; www.tressesetlacets.com*) in La Terrasse-sur-Dorlay.

Tourist and sporting facilities include the St-Pierre-de-Bœuf Leisure Park which has an artificial river for canoeing and kayaking; the canoe base at

DISCOVERING ST-ÉTIENNE AND LE PILAT

Terrasse-sur-Dorlay; downhill skiing resorts at La Jasserie and Graix, and cross-country ski clubs at Le Bessat, Burdignes, St-Régis-du-Coin and St-Genest-Malifaux. Other sites are suitable for climbing, hang-gliding, cycling and orienteering.

Mountain-biking facilities are being developed, with numerous waymarked tracks categorised by degree of difficulty.

Festivals: Apple Day in November in Pélussin, the Farm Produce Fair in Bourg-Argental in June, the Wine Fair in Chavanay (second weekend in December) and the Cheese and Wine Fair in Condrieu in May provide an introduction to local produce.

Bourg-Argental

This small, busy town at the foot of the Pilat massif has specialised in local craft and industrial activities.

The church, rebuilt in the Romanesque style in the 19C, presents a sculpted doorway (12C).

🚗 DRIVING TOUR

ST-ÉTIENNE TO CONDRIEU
89km/56mi. About 6hrs, not including St-Étienne.

▶ Leave St-Étienne on D 8 SE.

Rochetaillée
This small village is perched on a narrow rocky channel between two ravines, below the ruins of a feudal castle.

Gouffre d'Enfer★★
🚶 *1h on foot there and back.*
To the right of the inn, Auberge de la Cascade, a path follows the bed of the old torrent to the foot of the dam.
The site is impressive: the heavily gouged walls of rock come together to form a dark, narrow gully, dramatically named "Chasm of Hell".
The dam was built in 1866 to supply water to St-Étienne; steps to the top.

▶ To get back to the car, turn left and follow the path on the right running past the Maison des Ponts et Chaussées.

Beyond Rochetaillée, there are attractive views (right) over the dams of Gouffre d'Enfer and Pas-du-Riot.

Le Bessat
Small summer and winter resort.

▶ Beyond Le Bessat, take D 63 towards La Croix-de-Chaubouret.

Crêt de la Perdrix★
Just after La Croix-de-Chaubouret turn left onto D 8A towards La Jasserie.
The road winds past spruce, mountain pastures and heathland.

▶ After about 5km/3mi, at the top of the climb, park near the path leading to Perdrix ridge (15min on foot there and back) which is crowned with a chirat (granite rock).

The panorama from the viewing table takes in the peaks of Mézenc, Lizieux, Meygal and Gerbier-de-Jonc.

▶ Rejoin D 8 and follow D 63 to Crêt de l'Œillon.

The road meanders alternately through fir trees and moorland covered in broom.

Crêt de l'Œillon★★★
15min on foot there and back.
At the Croix de l'Œillon pass, take the road on the left leading to the turn-off to the private road ending at the television relay station.
🅿 *Park in the car park. At the top, walk to the left around the fence; the viewing table is on the eastern end of the promontory, at the foot of a monumental cross.*
🚶 The panorama is one of the most spectacular in the Rhône valley. In the foreground, beyond the rocks of the Pic des Trois Dents (Three Teeth Peak), there is a view of the Rhône valley.

412

LE PILAT

▶ Continue to Pélussin.

Pélussin
Park on place Abbé-Vincent in front of the hospital. Walk down rue Dr-Soubeyran and take rue de la Halle on the left.
The old covered market provides a view of the Rhône plain and the town of Pélussin. Go through a fortified gatehouse and turn left. Note the ancient chapel and castle.

▶ Turn back the way you came and take D 7 right to Pavezin Pass. Continue to Ste-Croix-en-Jarez.

Ste-Croix-en-Jarez
The Carthusian monastery of Ste-Croix (Holy Cross) was founded in 1280 by Béatrix Roussillon. During the Revolution, the monks were forced to leave; the monastery was then split up, the cloisters demolished in 1840 and, in 1888, Ste-Croix became a municipality.

▶ Return to Pavezin Pass, turn left onto D 30 which, as it begins its descent, offers a beautiful view of the Rhône Valley. Continue to the D 28 for Condrieu.

Just before arriving, in a bend with a Calvary overlooking the town, there is a **panoramic view★** of the Condrieu basin and the bend in the Rhône below.

Condrieu
One of the largest markets in the region is held here, specialising in fruit and early vegetables.
The town is also famed for its excellent white wine, made from the viognier grape. The Maison de la Gabelle has an attractive 16C façade. The port is a pleasant place for a stroll, with its slightly Mediterranean feel.

Château de Virieu, Pélussin

ADDRESSES

STAY AND EAT

Chambre d'Hôte Le Moulin du Bost – *42131 La Valla-en-Gier (13km/8mi N of Le Bessat). ℘04 77 20 06 62. Closed Nov–Easter. 2 rooms. Restaurant.* An impassioned trekker and member of the *"relais randonneurs"* (lodgings for walkers), the owner of this house located in the Parc Naturel Régional du Pilat can recommend rambles adapted to your taste. Simple rooms and generous fare.

Chambre d'hôte La Rivoire – *42220 St-Julien-Molin-Molette (5km/3mi E of Bourg-Argental via N 82). ℘04 77 39 65 44. www.larivoire.net. Reservations required in winter. 5 rooms. Restaurant.* What a charming house, with its round tower and generous vegetable garden! It dominates the Vallée de la Déôme – an ideal vantage point with a splendid view that can be admired from all the bedrooms and the terrace.

Auberge du Vernolon – *42220 Colombier-sous-Pilat (8km/4.8mi E of Le Bessat). ℘04 77 51 50 07. www.aubergeduvernolon.fr. Reservations required. 4 rooms.* The *patronne's* able cuisine is delectable – to be enjoyed under the magnificent wood-framed ceiling in the barn or on the terrace with a panoramic view.

413

THE ARDÈCHE

THE UPPER VIVARAIS AND LE VELAY

(Map showing the region with the following locations and features:)

Towns and villages:
- Monistrol-sur-Loire
- St-Didier-en-Velay
- Beauzac
- Ste-Sigolène
- Roche-en-Régnier
- Retournac
- Chamalières-sur-Loire
- Montfaucon-en-Velay
- Montregard
- Mortesagne
- Suc d'Eyme
- Glavenas
- Barrage de Lavalette
- Yssingeaux
- Tence
- Lavoûte-Polignac
- Lavoûte-sur-Loire
- Chaspinhac
- Le Chambon-sur-Lignon
- St-Voy
- St-Pierre-Eynac
- St-Julien-Chapteuil
- Bigorre
- Maziaux
- Moudeyres
- Freycenet-la-Tour
- St-Front
- Chaudeyrolles
- Fay-sur-Lignon
- St-Clément
- Le Monastier-sur-Gazeille
- Croix de Peccata
- Les Estables
- Croix de Boutières
- Vachères
- Arlempdes
- Ferme du Bourlatier
- Mézilhac
- Ste-Eulalie
- St-Cirgues-en-Montagne

Features:
- Suc de Jalore 1076
- 1137
- Suc de Glavenas 1048
- Suc de Chauven 848
- Gd Testavoyre 1436
- Forêt du Meygal
- Pic du Lizieux 1388
- Lac de St-Front
- Viaduc de Recoumène
- MT MÉZENC 1753
- Gerbier de Jonc 1551
- Lac d'Issarlès
- Cascade du Ray-Pic
- PARC NATUREL
- HAUTE-LOIRE
- LE PUY-EN-VELAY

Directional indicators:
- ST-ÉTIENNE
- BRIOUDE
- MENDE
- AUBENAS

0 — 4 km

415

THE ARDÈCHE

THE LOWER VIVARAIS

0 — 5 km

AVEN D'ORGNAC	★★★	Worth a special journey
Thines	★★	Worth a detour
Viviers	★	Interesting
Vals-les-Bains		Worth seeing
→		Departure point for tour

Legend:
- → Le Coiron
- → Vallées de la Volane et de la Bourges
- → Col de l'Escrinet
- → Massif du Tanargue
- → Montagne and Haute Vallée de l'Ardèche
- → Défilés de l'Ardèche
- → Villages du Vivarais Cévenol
- → Corniche du Vivarais Cévenol
- → Route panoramique
- → Plateau d'Orgnac
- → Plateau des Gras

Places shown: Cascade du Ray-Pic, St-Cirgues-en-Montagne, Mazan-l'Abbaye, Forêt de Mazan, Burzet, Éperon de Pourcheyrolles, Montpezat-sous-Bauzon, Col de la Chavade, Chât. de Montlaur, Mayres, Thueyts, Chât. de Chadenac, Neyrac-les-Bains, Col de la Cr⁺ de Bauzon, Jaujac, Trappe de N.-D.-des-Neiges, Col de Meyrand, La Bastide-Puylaurent, St-Laurent-les-Bains, Valgorge, Montselgues, St-Jean-de-Pourcharesse, Thines, St-Pierre-le-Déchausselat, Payzac, Pied-de-Borne, Gravières, Chambonas, Les Salelles, Les Vans

Regions: LOZÈRE, GARD, Parc national des Cévennes, Monts d'Ardèche, Gges de la Borne, Gges de la Beaume

416

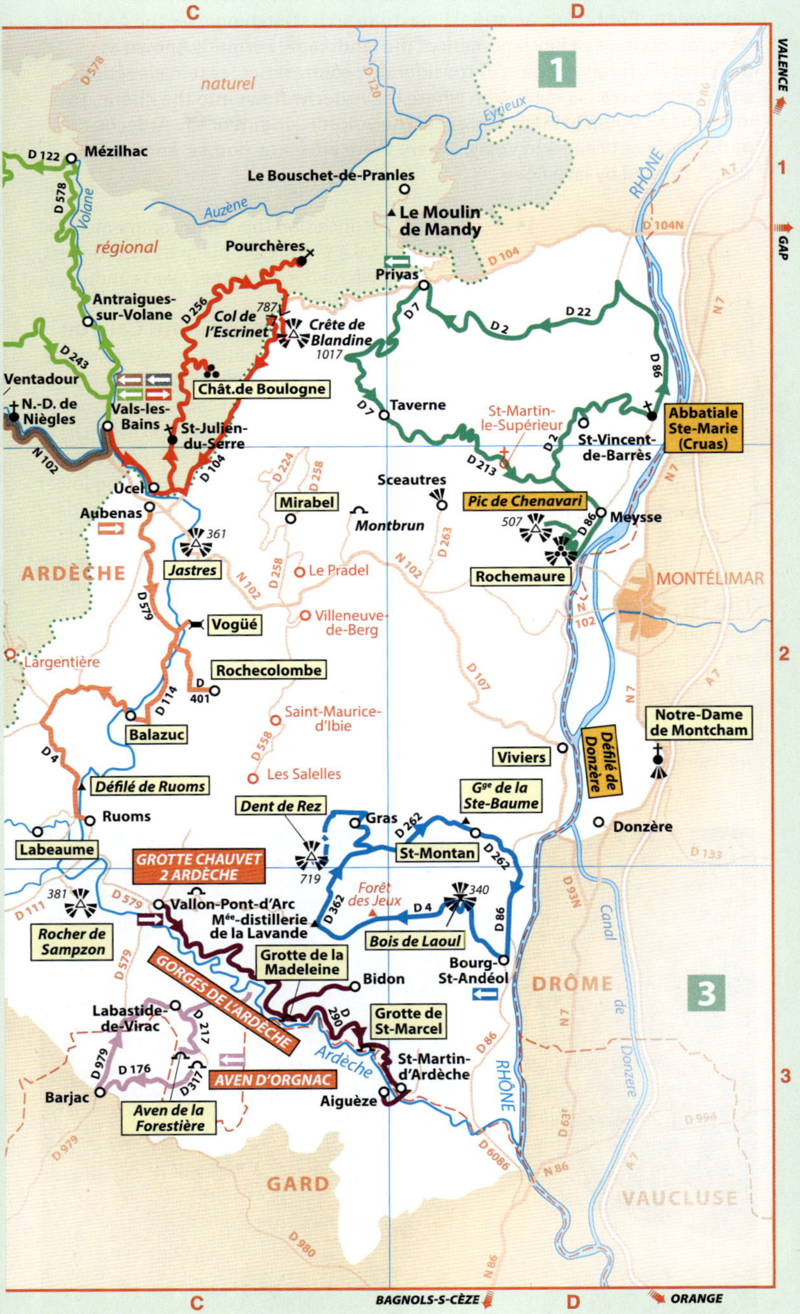
C
D
1
2
3
naturel
régional
VALENCE
GAP
BAGNOLS-S-CÈZE
ORANGE
Mézilhac
Le Bouschet-de-Pranles
Le Moulin de Mandy
Pourchères
Privas
Antraigues-sur-Volane
Col de l'Escrinet
787
Crête de Blandine
1017
Châtde Boulogne
Ventadour
N.-D. de Nièglès
Vals-les-Bains
St-Julien-du-Serre
Taverne
St-Martin-le-Supérieur
St-Vincent-de-Barrès
Abbatiale Ste-Marie (Cruas)
Ucel
Aubenas
Mirabel
Sceautres
Montbrun
Pic de Chenavari
507
Meysse
Rochemaure
361
Jastres
ARDÈCHE
Le Pradel
Villeneuve-de-Berg
MONTÉLIMAR
Vogüé
Largentière
Rochecolombe
Balazuc
Saint-Maurice-d'Ibie
Les Salelles
Viviers
Défilé de Donzère
Notre-Dame de Montcham
Défilé de Ruoms
Ruoms
Dent de Rez
Gras
Gge de la Ste-Baume
Donzère
Labeaume
St-Montan
GROTTE CHAUVET 2 ARDÈCHE
719
Forêt des Jeux
340
381
Vallon-Pont-d'Arc
Mée-distillerie de la Lavande
Rocher de Sampzon
Bois de Laoul
Grotte de la Madeleine
Bourg-St-Andéol
GORGES DE L'ARDÈCHE
Bidon
DRÔME
Labastide-de-Virac
Grotte de St-Marcel
St-Martin-d'Ardèche
Barjac
AVEN D'ORGNAC
Aiguèze
Aven de la Forestière
GARD
VAUCLUSE
Canal de Donzère
RHÔNE
Ardèche
Eyrieux
Auzène
Volane
D 122
D 578
D 120
D 86
A 7
D 104N
D 104
N 7
D 22
D 2
D 7
D 256
D 243
N 102
D 104
D 224
D 258
D 213
D 263
D 579
D 114
D 401
D 558
D 107
D 4
D 262
D 362
D 111
D 290
D 217
D 176
D 979
D 317
D 133
D 93N
D 6086
N 86
D 63E
D 994
D 980

THE ARDÈCHE

The Ardèche is known for its wild forests, trails, and rapids, with the emblematic Pont d'Arc, a natural limestone arch stretching over the Ardèche Gorges, serving as a key landmark of the landscape. Formerly known as the Vivarais, this is a region of considerable contrast not least in elevation, which ranges from a mere 40m where the Ardèche flows into the Rhône, to more than 1 700m in Mont Mézency. The volcanic origins of the Ardèche are particularly noticeable in Velay, where there are many domes, known as "sucs", formed by lava flows.

Highlights

1 Driving the **Corniche du Rhône** (p422)
3 A summer's day canoeing the **Ardèche Gorge** (p441)
2 Admiring the **Pont d'Arc** (p442)
4 The cave system of the **Aven d'Orgnac** (p447)
5 Exploring the **Défilé de Donzière canyon** (p453)

The First Hot-Air Balloon
On 4 June 1783, the **Montgolfier brothers**, natives of Annonay, launched a balloon made of fabric and paper, held together by some 1 800 buttons. The balloon remained in the air for 30min and landed more than 2km/1mi from its launch site. This feat is commemorated by a plaque on place des Cordeliers, where the experiment was conducted.

The European Grand Canyon
Ardèche is a nature-lover's paradise, cut through by incredible stone gorges that form a thirty-kilometre long canyon running from Saint-Martin-d'Ardèche to Vallon-Pont-d'Arc: the most recognizable landmark in the area. The lower part of the gorge forms the boudary between the Ardèche and the Gard. The gorges are a beautiful natural site to explore, ideal for boating, swimming, and sightseeing.

Beefing it Up
Rising to 1 753m, Mont Mézenc lies between the Ardèche and Haute-Loire, and is famous for its AOC beef, fed on the best hay in the mountain pastures.

Pont-d'Arc

© Gil Giuglio/hemis.fr

Annonay

Annonay is located in a deep cleft of the Vivarais plateau, at the confluence of the River Deûme and River Cance. In the Middle Ages, the exceptional quality of the water here encouraged the establishment of a leather and wool industry, which then flourished. One of the first towns to uphold the principles of the Reformation, Annonay suffered greatly during the Wars of Religion. However, in the 17C, following the establishment of the Johannot and Montgolfier families' paperworks, Annonay began to prosper again.

- **Population:** 16 720.
- **Michelin Map:** 331: K-2.
- **Info:** Pl. des Cordeliers, 07100 Annonay. 04 75 33 24 51. www.ardechegrandair.com.
- **Location:** Almost directly south of Lyon.
- **Don't Miss:** The Old Town.
- **Timing:** At least half a day.

WALKING TOUR

OLD TOWN
The old quarter on the hills overlooking the two rivers is currently undergoing a major restoration project.

▶ Begin from place de la Libération.

On this square stands a statue of the Montgolfier brothers, erected in 1883.

▶ Turn right onto rue Franki-Kramer.

Rue Franki-Kramer
Annonay's old high street, like the nearby place Grenette and place Mayol, is flanked by picturesque 16C–18C houses.

▶ Take rue de Trachin on the right, which opens out to the chapel.

Chapelle de Trachin
This Gothic chapel is all that remains of a priory founded in 1320 by Guy Trachin, a wealthy resident of Annonay.

Place de la Liberté
This square located in the centre of the old town becomes a bustling hub of trade on market days *(Wednesdays and Saturdays)*. The square is graced by a statue of Marc Seguin.

▶ From the bottom of place de la Liberté, turn onto Montée du Château.

Fortified Gates
Montée du Château forms a steep incline up to the old machicolated gate; a second gate also survives, at the end of rue de Bourgville.

▶ Rue Montgolfier leads to the bridge.

Pont Montgolfier
Upstream, the view is of the humpback Valgelas bridge (14C) and the convent of Ste-Marie (16C). Downstream, the Deûme flows into the Défilé des Fouines, a dark, narrow rocky gorge.

▶ Walk to Valgelas bridge and follow Voûtes Soubise, a vaulted passageway, to the steps of rue Barville. Turn right onto rue de Deûme and continue to avenue de l'Europe.

Avenue de l'Europe partly covers the Deûme. From the intersection with rue de la Valette, there is a view west over the Tour des Martyrs (12C–13C), the last remnant of the old ramparts.

Place des Cordeliers
The square owes its name to the former convent built on the site, where today there is a theatre. To the right, a plaque commemorates the first public enterprise of the Montgolfier brothers.

▶ Retrace your steps and then take the steps to Rue Grangeat. Turn left at rue Chalayer, then right.

DISCOVERING THE UPPER VIVARAIS AND LE VELAY

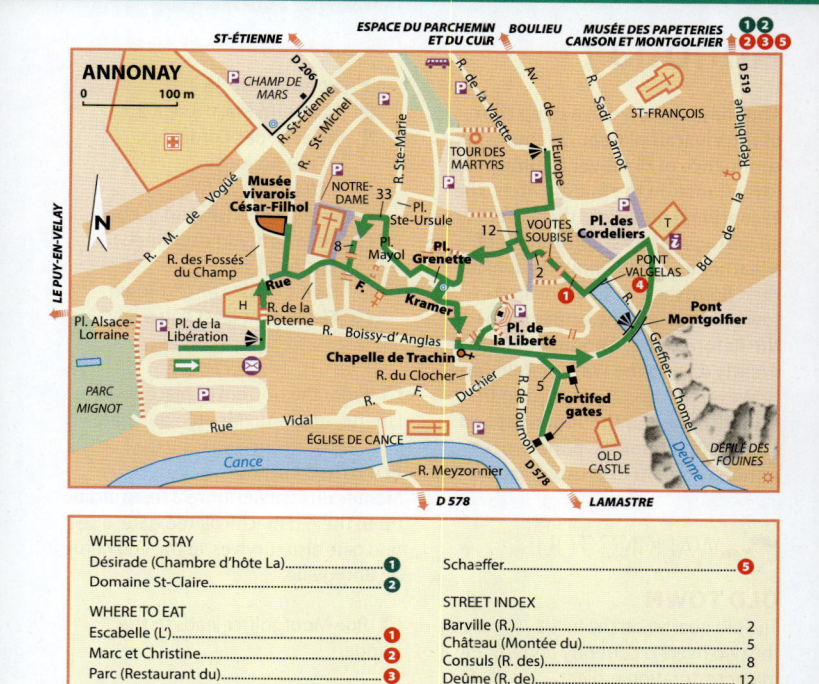

WHERE TO STAY	
Désirade (Chambre d'hôte La)	①
Domaine St-Claire	②
WHERE TO EAT	
Escabelle (L'è's)	①
Marc et Christine	②
Parc (Restaurant du)	③
Radicelles	④
Schaeffer	⑤
STREET INDEX	
Barville (R.)	2
Château (Montée du)	5
Consuls (R. des)	8
Deûme (R. de)	12
Réforme (R. de la)	33

Place Grenette
Built in 1585, this square retains the pillars and arcades of the ancient granary. At Nos. 1 and 3, notice the 16C doors.

▶ Turn right on rue Franki-Kramer, walk past the cathedral and turn right into rue Jean-Baptiste Bechetoille.

ADDITIONAL SIGHT
Musée des Papeteries Canson et Montgolfier
2.5km/1.5mi NE. Vidalon. Jul–Aug daily 2.15–6pm; rest of the year Wed and Sun 2.30–6pm. 24 Dec–1 Jan, Easter Sun. €5.50. 04 75 69 89 20. www.musee-papeteries-canson-montgolfier.fr.
This museum, in the house where the Montgolfier brothers were born, retraces the history of the local paperworks.

EXCURSIONS
Boulieu-lès-Annonay
5km/3mi to the N on avenue de l'Europe. Former fortified village with square ramparts flanking the main street.

Barrage du Ternay
10km/6mi via the D 206 to the N, then D 820 and D 306.
Constructed in 1867 to provide a water supply to Annonay; today it offers a lovely water space bordered by cedar.

Bourg-Argental
See Le PILAT.

🚗 DRIVING TOURS

NORTH OF ANNONAY
39km/24mi. Allow half a day.

▶ Leave Annonay to the NW, along the boulevard de la République. Follow the D 121, then the D 519 and finally the D 820 in the direction of Serrières for a further 6km/3.5mi as far as a roundabout, where you take the first exit. About 300m further on, turn left.

ANNONAY

👥 Safari-parc de Peaugres★
Check website, or call, for variable dates throughout the year. €24 (child 3–12, €21). ☎04 75 33 00 32. www.safari-peaugres.com.
Located at the foot of the Pilat massif, this nature reserve is home to 400 mammals, 300 birds and around 60 reptiles. There is an area exclusively for cars following the "safari" experience and a main zoo that can be explored on foot.

Serrières
This ancient city will remain forever associated with the epic tales of its boatmen on the Rhône. Ever since, annual nautical games have animated the banks of the river.

Réserve Naturelle de la Platière
Access to the island is impossible during floods, and dangerous in strong winds.
Come here early in the day, armed with a pair of binoculars, to observe the waterfowl. More difficult to spot are beavers, which tend to be active at night.

▶ Go back over the Pont de Sablons and then head S on the D 86.

Champagne
In spite of its location on the right bank of the Rhône, Champagne was a fifedom of the powerful counts of Albon, whose castle rises on the opposite bank. The **Musée des Mariniers** (*Jun–Sep 10am–noon and 2:30–6pm, closed Tues, ☎04 75 34 00 46 €4*), located within the Champagne church, details the history of traditional barge crossing and features some lovely 18C frescoes.

▶ Drive 2.5km/1.5mi further on the D 86 and turn right towards St-Désirat.

Musée de l'Alambic★
Mon–Fri 8am–noon, 2–6pm, Sat 10am–noon, 2–6.30pm, Sun and public holidays 2–6.30pm (Jul–Aug Mon–Fri 8am–noon, 2–6pm, Sat–Sun and public holidays 10am–noon, 2–6.30pm.
1 Jan and 25 Dec. ☎04 75 34 23 11. www.jeangauthier.com.
This museum within the Gauthier distillery, recalls the life of distillers and shows some interesting films.

▶ Follow the D 82 for Annonay. At St-Etienne-de-Valoux, turn left towards Thorrenc.

Château de Thorrenc
Recently restored, this 11C castle lies deep in the ravine of the Thorrençon.

▶ Beyond Ozas, you can return to Annonay by the D 370.

AY AND CANCE VALLEYS
Round tour of 48km/29mi. Allow 2h.

▶ Leave Annonay by rue de Tournon to the S heading for Lamastre.

Quintenas-le-Peyron
The village is dominated by the 14C belfry of its Romanesque church.

▶ In Quintenas, on the right, facing the church, follow directions for St-Romain-d'Ay.

The narrow road meanders through the countryside, affording pretty views of the Haut-Vivarais.

▶ Leave the church of St-Romain on your left and drive to D 6; turn left. After 90m, on the right, a steep road leads to Notre-Dame-d'Ay.

Notre-Dame-d'Ay
This modest sanctuary perched on top of a rocky outcrop is a popular place of pilgrimage.

ADDRESSES

🛏 STAY

Chambre d'Hôte La Désirade – *07340 St-Désirat. ☎04 75 34 21 88. www.hotel-desirade.fr. 8 rooms.* Amid grapevines and trees, this renovated 19C house has pleasant rooms giving onto either a courtyard or park and vineyard.

DISCOVERING THE UPPER VIVARAIS AND LE VELAY

Chambre d'Hôte La Palisse – *804 Rte de Cheval, 07340 Peaugres. 04 75 67 08 37. www.lapalisse-peaugres.com. 3 rooms.* You can almost imagine you are in an African safari park.

Domaine de Saint-Clair Golf & Spa, – *Route du Golf, 07430 Saint-Clair. 04 75 67 01 00. www.domainestclair.fr. 54 rooms.* This luxurious hotel boasts an 18-hole golf course, comfortable rooms and a creative, refined restaurant.

EAT

L'Escabelle – *1 av. de l'Europe. 04 75 67 64 09. Closed Wed and Sun.* Traditional cuisine served in a medieval setting below a vaulted ceiling.

Restaurant du Parc – *40 quai Jules-Roche, 07340 Serrières. 04 75 34 00 08. Closed Sun and Thu evenings, and Mon.* Delivering regional specialities like *ravio!a* and Ardèche sausages.

Schaeffer – *07340 Serrières. 04 75 34 00 07. www.hotel-schaeffer.com. Closed Sat lunch, Sun evening and Mon.* Cosy restaurant with rooms extended over the Rhône river; classic cuisine.

Radicelles – *21 rue Montgolfier. 0954 78 12 41. Lunch Tues–Sat, dinner (tasting menu only) Thurs–Sat. https://www.radicelles.fr.* Creative, modern restaurant using almost exclusively seasonal, local products.

Tournon-sur-Rhône★

This busy town on the Rhône overlooks Tain-l'Hermitage on the opposite bank, famed for its fine wines. Tournon is a lively shopping town, and the shaded quayside and castle ruins on the hillside give the town a characteristic Rhodanien atmosphere.

TOWN

Tournon-sur-Rhône boasts a 15C–16C **château** containing a museum about bargemen on the Rhône set in a charming **terraced garden★**.

The **Lycée Gabriel-Fauré** has an attractive Renaissance doorway, and a collection of busts and tapestries.

EXCURSIONS

Cité du Chocolat Valrhona
12 ave du Président Roosevelt, 26600 Tain l'Hermitage. Mon–Sat 9am–7pm, Sun 10am–6:30pm. €7.
Just across the river in lovely Tain l'Hermitage, known for its Crozes Hermitage wines, Valrhona welcomes lovers of all things chocolate for an interactive (and delicious) experience. Richly informative… and delicious!

- **Population:** 11 171.
- **Michelin Map:** 331: L-3.
- **Info:** 2 Place Saint-Julien, 07300 Tournon-sur-Rhône. 04 75 08 10 23. www.hermitage-tournonais-tourisme.com.
- **Location:** Not far from Romans-sur-Isère (20km/12.5 mi to the E) and Valence, to the S.
- **Parking:** There are car parks on the left bank of the Rhône, and around the Place de la République.
- **Timing:** Allow half a day, at least. Arrive in time for lunch.

🚗 DRIVING TOURS

CORNICHE DU RHÔNE★★★
43km/26.5mi. Allow 2h.

▶ Leave Tournon-sur-Rhône to the S via rue du Dr-Cadet and rue Greffieux towards St-Romain-de-Lerps.

From Tournon to Valence the **panoramic road★★★** along the hillside offers magnificent views.

Tournon-sur-Rhône, the Rhône and the vineyards of Tain-l'Hermitage

▶ In Plats turn left by the War Memorial onto GR 42.

St-Romain-de-Lerps★★★
This is one of the most impressive views along the Rhône: to the east, above the Valence plain, rises the Vercors bar, dominated by the Moucherolle needle and the dome of the Grand Veymont.

▶ Take the D 287 towards the S. At St-Péray, take the road in front of the Château de Beauregard. Park at the end of the road.

Crussol★★
On the hillside above the plain lie the famous castle ruins. The white stone of Crussol was often used elsewhere because of its fine grain. The **site★★** is one of the finest in the Rhône valley
🚶 *You reach the ruins of the castle by a path (1h there and back).*

GORGES DU DOUX VIA THE CORNICHE ROAD★
50km/31mi. Allow 2h.

▶ Leave Tournon-sur-Rhône on the road to Lamastre.

The road runs along the pretty orchards of the Doux basin. The **corniche road★** dominates the Doux gorges.

Boucieu-le-Roi
This village was once the seat of a royal bailiwick in the upper Vivarais area.

▶ Return to Tournon-sur-Rhône via Colombier-le-Vieux and D 534, running on the opposite side of the gorges, through wild vegetation.

DÉFILÉ DE ST-VALLIER★
60km/37.5mi. Allow 2h.

▶ Leave Tournon-sur-Rhône to the N on D 86.

Vion
The church, partly Romanesque, has a transept crossing with capitals.

▶ In Vion, take the narrow road that leads to D 532. At Croix de Fraysse, head for St-Jeure-d'Ay, then turn right onto D 6. About 7km/4.3mi further on, take D 506 on the right, leading to Ozon.

The steep descent to Ozon offers **views★★** over **St-Vallier Gorges★** and the orchards and vineyards along the river.

▶ Cross the Rhône between Sarras and St-Vallier, then follow the N 7. As you leave St-Vallier, take the D 51 to the left in the direction of St-Uze.

Maison de la Céramique de St-Uze
🕐 *Mar–Dec Wed 2–6pm (school holidays Wed–Sun 2–6pm).* ⌨ €4.
📞 *04 75 03 98 01. www.territoire-ceramique.com.*

DISCOVERING THE UPPER VIVARAIS AND LE VELAY

At the beginning of the 19C, the discovery of kaolin clay in the region gave rise to a number of ceramic enterprises and brought the town great renown.

▶ As you leave St-Uze, turn right towards St-Barthélemy-de-Vals. Go through the town and rejoin the D 500 towards Ponsas. After 1.5km/1mi, take a left into the forest.

Les Roches qui dansent

This section of the valley is evocative of the Rhône in medieval times: ruins of feudal strongholds and old defensive towers line the escarpments.

▶ Turn left towards Crozes-Hermitage. Go through the town and then follow signs for the Pierre-Aiguille.

Pierre-Aiguille Belvedere★

The far-reaching views from here encompass Tain-l'Hermitage and its vineyard; the town of Tournon across the river and the foothills of Vercors with the Alps in the background.

Vallée de l'Eyrieux★

The River Eyrieux rises to the north of St-Agrève then tumbles down from the high plateaux of the Vivarais area to flow into the Rhône after a distance of 70km/44mi. The upper valley has a mountainous appearance, with steep slopes covered with chestnut and spruce; this is the area known as Les Boutières. Downstream from Le Cheylard, the torrent flows into gorges, then less rugged basins and rocky narrows alternate down to the final plain and the Rhône valley.

A BIT OF GEOGRAPHY

The Eyrieux flows swiftly. Because of the sloping ground on its upper course, autumn storms suddenly swell the main river and its tributaries.

ADDRESSES

STAY

Hôtel de la Villeon – 2 Rue Davity, 07300. ℘04 75 06 97 50. www.hoteldelavilleon.com. 16 rooms. This beautifully restored mansion in the centre of Tournon is now a luxurious hotel boasting a bar, wine tasting cellar, and terrace with spectacular views over the town.

EAT

Le Chaudron – 6 rue du port, 01600 Trévoux. ℘04 74 00 43 52. Closed Mon; Tues and Sun eve. www.lechaudronrestaurant.fr. Simple, tasty food; house specialty of frogs' legs.

Le Carré d'Aléthius – 4 rue Paul Bertois, 07800 Charmes-sur-Rhône. ℘04 75 78 30 52. www.lecarredalethius.com. 16 rooms. Inventive, delicious food within a charming, 9-room hotel.

Michelin Map: 331: J-4 to K-4/5.

Info: 8 rue Paul Montrochet, 69002 Lyon ℘04 72 59 21 59. http://en.auvergnerhonealpes-tourisme.com.

Timing: Allow a day for each of the Driving Tours.

Old, isolated hamlets cling to the hillsides marked into strips by the low walls surrounding terraced fields. Larger villages and small towns grew up in the small inner basins in the valley, or at the mouth of tributaries.

Some of these have industrial activity, but the dominant character of the valley derives from farming peaches. In the spring, the peach trees turn this rugged valley into a carpet of pink-petalled blossom.

VALLÉE DE L'EYRIEUX

CORNICHE DE L'EYRIEUX

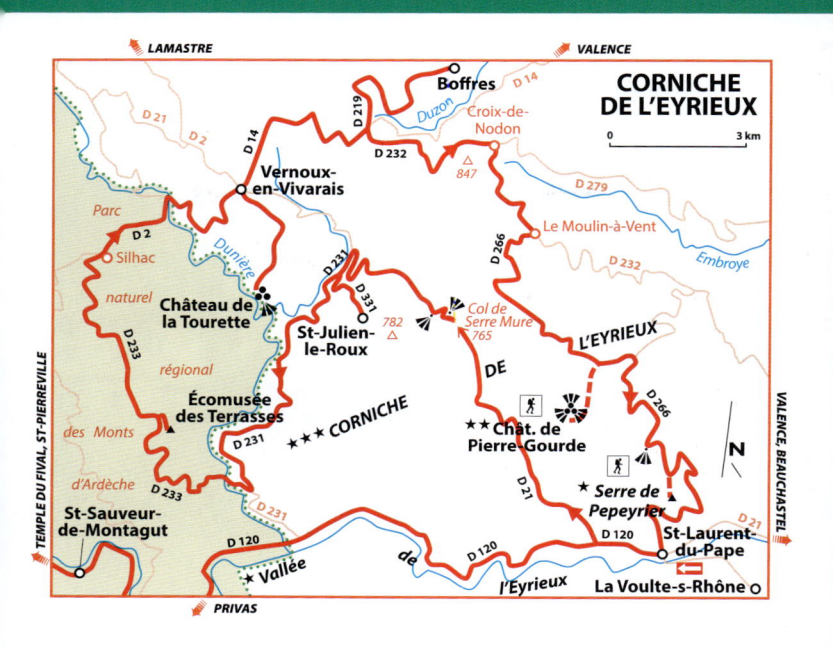

🚗 DRIVING TOURS

LA VOULTE-SUR-RHÔNE ROUND TOUR★
55km/34mi. Allow 3h.

La Voulte-sur-Rhône
Small town with an industrial past on the right bank of the Rhone, a place of narrow streets lined with old houses.

Beauchastel
Listed village at the foot of its castle ruins. A stroll through narrow alleys and streets takes you to the Maison du Patrimoine and the terrace, offering a pretty view of St-Laurent-du-Pape and the nearby valley.

▶ Rejoin D 21 and head towards St-Laurent-du-Pape.

St-Laurent-du-Pape
Attractive town at the valley entrance, enhanced by its bridge over the Eyrieux.

▶ Keep driving along the valley in the direction of Cheylard.

St-Sauveur-de-Montagut
Dominated by the ruins of Montagut Château *(access by D 244 and a forest lane)*, the village stands at the confluence of the Eyrieux and Gluyère.
The roads runs along the Gluyère valley, hugging the riverbanks almost up to St-Pierreville.

Temple du Fival
🕐 *Open Jul–Aug, Tue, Thu and Fri, 3–7pm.* ☎ *04 75 65 46 84.*
This ancient temple has been converted into a **museum** dedicated to the history of the Huguenots.

▶ Continue along the D 8, which runs for 11km/7mi to St-Pierreville.

St-Pierreville
The **Maison du Châtaignier** (🕐*Jul–Aug Thurs–Mon 10am–12:30pm and 2:30–6pm, Sun 10am–1pm. Sept–Oct and Apr–Jun Fri and Sat 10am–noon and 2–5pm.* 🕐*Nov–Mar.* ⚏€8. ☎ *04 75 66 64 33. www.maisonduchataignier. fr*) presents an exhibition on chestnut production and offers tastings.

DISCOVERING THE UPPER VIVARAIS AND LE VELAY

Village of Beauchastel

▶ Follow the D 102 towards St-Saveur-de-Montagut and then the D 120 back to Voult-sur-Rhône.

CORNICHE DE L'EYRIEUX★★★
Round tour from St-Laurent-du-Pape. 90km/56mi. Allow 3hr30.

▶ Leave St-Laurent-du-Pape on D 120, then right onto D 21 for Vernoux.

As it winds up to Serre Mure pass, this road offers views of the Vivarois ridges, the upper basin of the Eyrieux and the Boutières region, as well as a view of the western slopes of the Pierre-Gourde peak.

▶ Turn left onto D 231, then D 331.

St-Julien-le-Roux
From the church, mountains can be seen along the **horizon★**, above the ruins of Château de la Tourette.

▶ Go back to the D 231, and take the D 233 towards Silhac. Park at the entrance to Charayre.

Écomusée des Terrasses
⏱ *Open by appointment only.* ✆ 04 75 65 24 70. €4.5.
Several houses boast ancient cultivation terraces, perfectly maintained and evidence of determined hard work; restoration continues at a gradual pace.

▶ Take the D 233. At Silhac, take the D 2 to the right.

Vernoux-en-Vivarais
Vernoux stands on the Vivarais plateau, between the Eyrieux and the River Doux, in the centre of a large hollow.

Château de la Tourette
The ruins of this stronghold, which once marked the gateway to the States of Languedoc, lie in an unspoilt **setting★** and are among the most evocative in the Vivarais.

▶ Drive to Boffres situated 8.5km/5mi NE on D 14 and D 219.

Boffres
The village of Boffres is built on a projection in a semicircle at the foot of its simple church and the remains of a fortified castle. Just outside the village, a bronze

VALLÉE DE L'EYRIEUX

bust has been erected to the memory of **Vincent d'Indy**, the French composer and teacher (1851–1931), born in Paris, but descended from a family in the region. It was at **Château des Faugs**, west of Boffres, that d'Indy came to seek inspiration. He composed his third melody without words from a shepherd's song heard near Les Estables, and his opera *Fervaal* one misty morning on the peaks of Mont Mézenc.

▶ Drive to the D 14, turn left onto D 232.

The road runs along the hillside, offering views of Vernoux-en-Vivarais in the centre of the basin. Beyond Croix-de-Nodon, there are generous glimpses of the Rhône valley and clear views of the deep wooded Embroye valley.

▶ At Le Moulin-à-Vent turn right onto D 266.

After a long wooded section, the road runs along a spectacular stretch of ledge, opposite Pierre-Gourde peak, in front of the mountain ridges enclosing the Eyrieux valley.

▶ A track, off D 286 to the right, leads to the Château de Pierre-Gourde. Park at a pass, in sight of the ruins.

Panorama from the Château de Pierre-Gourde★★

This medieval castle, now in ruins, occupies a magnificent **site**★. At the foot of the peak on which the keep was built lie the ruins of the main building, parts of the curtain wall and the feudal village.

▶ Walk left around the ruins to reach a rocky terrace.

The **panorama** encompasses the Rhône and Trois-Becs, between the Vercors bar, the Baronnies and Mont Ventoux. Opposite, the backbone of Croix de Bauzon overlooks the Haut-Eyrieux gap.
During the descent, two panoramic bends offer views first of the Eyrieux valley, with its clearly delineated ridges, endlessly repeated, and then of the Rhône valley, on the left.

▶ About 5km/3mi from Pierre-Gourde, a sign on the right indicates the Serre de Pepeyrier ridge.

View from Serre de Pepeyrier★

There is a beautiful **view** from the ridge of the mouth of the Eyrieux valley with its vast peach orchards, the town of Beauchastel and the Rhône plain; in the background, Mont Ventoux.

▶ Rejoin the D 266 to return to St-Laurent-du-Pape.

Château de Pierre-Gourde

DISCOVERING THE UPPER VIVARAIS AND LE VELAY

St-Agrève

St-Agrève lies on the slopes of Mont Chiniac. There are few historic remains, because the town suffered repeatedly during the Wars of Religion.

- **Population:** 2 579.
- **Michelin Map:** 331 I-3.
- **Info:** 35 Grande-Rue, 07320 St-Agrève. 04 75 30 15 06. www.ville-saintagreve.fr.
- **Location:** Midway between Puy-en-Velay and Valence.
- **Timing:** Allow half a day.

SIGHTS
Mont Chiniac★★
A road leads to the summit, crowned with fir trees. The view encompasses the Massif du Mézenc, the Massif du Meygal and the Monts de Lalouvesc.

Devesset
The nearby **Lac de Devesset** is a leisure centre providing facilities for many water sports (swimming, sailing etc).

EXCURSIONS
Lamastre
The ancient upper town is dominated by the Château de Peychelard, while the lower town, Savel, has developed along the banks of the Doux.

Désaignes★
The existence of this former Gallo-Roman settlement is evidenced by a great many ruins, including a Roman road. It was to become the most densely populated city in the Vivarais.
Of its past glory there remain large sections of the ramparts, a 14C **castle** (*Apr–Jun and Sep–Oct Sat–Sun and public holidays 2–6pm; Jul–Aug daily 3–7pm. €4.50. 04 75 06 66 21*) housing the **Musée de la Vie Rurale**, and numerous Gothic houses.

🚗 DRIVING TOUR

LES BOUTIÈRES★★
80km/50mi round trip leaving from St-Agrève. Allow 4h.

▶ Leave St-Agrève to the S on D 120, heading towards Le Cheylard.

During the drive down, you will enjoy pretty views of the Mézenc, then the road enters the Eyrieux defile.

▶ Take D 120 south. At the exit to St-Julien-Boutières, turn right on D 101.

Fay-sur-Lignon
This mountain-village (pronounced *fa-yee*) offers cross-country skiing facilities in winter. There is a good **view★** of the surrounding mountains from the graveyard next to the church.

▶ Take D 262 S and turn left to St-Clément.

St-Clément
Once past the town, there are attractive **views★★** of the Gerbier de Jonc, Suc de Sara and Mont Mézenc mountains, in line with the valley of the River Saliouse.

▶ Beyond Lachapelle-sous-Chanéac keep following the D 278.

▶ In Armanas turn left and then right onto D 478 to Le Bourget and Rochebonne.

This is a winding and attractive route with lovely views over the basin of the upper Eyrieux and of the confluence of the River Eysse and River Eyrieux.

Ruins of Rochebonne★
Park by the side of the road.
🚶 The magnificent **site★★** is the setting for the fissured, granitic ruins of the medieval castle, overlooked to the west by Mont Mézenc. Walk down to the ruins (*30min there and back*).

▶ Continue along D 478 towards Beauvert and down to D 21 which leads back to St-Agrève.

# Yssingeaux

This is one of the largest communes in France, standing at the heart of a landscape of volcanic and wooded hills; a perfect base for walking.

🚗 DRIVING TOUR

MASSIF DU MEYGAL AND PAYS DES SUCS★
98km/61mi. Allow 3h30.

▶ Leave Yssingeaux to the S on D 7, then after 3km/2mi turn right onto D 42.

Forêt du Meygal
This forest, mainly conifers, was planted between 1865 and 1880.

▶ After the Araules crossroads, turn right onto D 18, towards Queyrières, then left onto the first forest lane, signposted in red and blue. At the next intersection, take the left-hand lane running along the east slope of the Grand Testavoyre.

Grand Testavoyre★★
🚶 A path through ferns and bilberry bushes leads to the summit from which there are splendid **panoramic views** over the volcanic landscape.

▶ Continue through the forest.

The west road goes past the **Maison des Copains,** which became famous after it was mentioned in a novel by the French writer **Jules Romains**.

▶ The left-hand forest lane leads to D 15. Turn left, then right onto the D 26, and again right onto the D 263.

Saint-Front
This village built on a large mound offers an excellent view towards the Mézenc.

▶ Take the D 39 to the west, then before Machabert, turn right towards Maziaux.

- ▶ **Population:** 7 568.
- ⊙ **Michelin Map:** 331 G-3.
- 🛈 **Info:** 16 Place Foch. ☎04 71 59 10 76.
- ◉ **Location:** 28km/17.5mi NE of Puy-en-Velay.
- ⏱ **Timing:** Allow 2 hours to up to half a day.

Maziaux et Bigorre★
These hamlets have a number of buildings specific to the Mézenc, with slate or thatched roofs and small windows.

▶ Turn right onto the D 39, then the D 49 which you follow to St-Julien-Chapteuil.

St-Julien-Chapteuil
The village occupies an unusual **site★** in the middle of a leafy basin watered by the Sumène, bristling with volcanic peaks. The **Musée Jules-Romains** is devoted to the life and literary achievements of the author **Jules Romains** (1885–1972).

▶ Leave St-Julien to the N and take D 26 towards St-Pierre-Eynac.

St-Pierre-Eynac
Pretty country **church** with a Romanesque doorway underneath a Renaissance porch. During the drive to Aupinhac, note the **view** of Le Puy and the basin to the left: you can see the Corneille rock and St-Michel-d'Aiguilhe.

▶ Continue towards St-Étienne village on D 26 after crossing N 88. Take D 71 N towards Malrevers. After Rosières, turn right onto D 7. Take the first road on the right after the cemetery on the road to Mortesagne.

The route is dominated by the Suc d'Eyme. During the drive down towards **Glavenas,** enjoy the **view★** of the curious landscape.

▶ Return to Yssingeaux on D 431 and N 88.

Privas

Privas occupies an unusual **site★** in the Ouvèze basin, at the foot of Mont Toulon; a good example of relief inversion, the lava flow on which it stands was once at the bottom of the valley and is now in relief since the ancient unprotected calcareous heights have been eroded. Business in the town concentrates on small industry (milling, sprung bed bases) and the manufacture of *marrons glacés* (candied sweet chestnuts), of which it is the capital.

- **Population:** 8 700.
- **Michelin Map:** 331: J-5.
- **Info:** 3 Pl. du Gén.-de-Gaulle, 07000 Privas. 04 75 20 81 81.
- **Location:** 30km/19mi from Aubenas (to the SW) and Montélimar (SE).
- **Timing:** Allow half a day to get a feel for the place.

SIGHTS
Montoulon
1h there and back – park near the museum and walk up boulevard du Montoulon.

A signpost marks the path to the right that goes to the hilltop, where there is a monumental **calvary** (three crosses) and a good **view★** over the town, the Ouvèze Valley, the Rhône and the Alps.

Pont Louis-XIII
South of the town centre. The bridge spanning the River Ouvèze has preserved its coping of rough-stone corbels and offers a good view of Privas.

EXCURSIONS
Le Bouschet de Pranles
15km/9.3mi N along D 2 and D 344.
A small **Protestant Museum** (May–Jun Sat–Sun and public holidays 2–6pm; Jul–Aug Mon–Sat 10am–6pm, Sun 2–6pm; Sept daily 2–6pm; Mon. €5. 04 75 64 22 74; www.museevivaraisprotestant.org) has been set up in the birthplace of Pierre Durand, one of the Desert Fathers in the 18C, and his sister Marie Durand. This 18C Huguenot heroine was locked up in the tower of Constance d'Aigues-Mortes for 38 years (1730–68).
Pranles has become the Mecca of Protestantism in the Vivarais region; a Protestant gathering is held here on Whit Monday every year.
Take the time to visit the **Moulin de Mandy** (Jul–Aug Sun, Tues, Thurs, Fri 2:30–6:30pm, Wed 10:30am–6:30pm), a working mill where you can see bread being baked every day at 11:30am.

Mirabel★
Mirabel is a stronghold that once commanded the main road from the Rhône to the Cévennes and played a strategic role during the Wars of Religion.

Grottes de Montbrun
45min there and back.
To discover these mysterious caves, descend by a difficult path down the left flank of a ravine.

Sceautres
This miniscule village, nestled on a grassy terrace at the bottom of the valley, seems crammed against the black basalt rock that dominates it.

DRIVING TOUR

PLATEAU DU COIRON★★
74km/46mi from Privas.
Allow half a day.

Head S from Privas along D 7, following signs to Villeneuve-de-Berg.

The deeply-eroded volcanic bar that forms the Coiron plateau marks, to the north, the limit of the Lower Vivarais area. Its black basalt rocks cut across the line of hills from the Escrinet pass to the River Rhône, creating the starkly contrasting Rochemaure dikes.
The upper part of the Coiron plateau takes the form of a vast, bare *planèze*

with an average altitude of 800m rising from the banks of the Rhône in a north-westerly direction.
The road crosses the Ouvèze basin, then enters the sun-baked Bayonne gorge. As the road climbs the hillside, there is a succession of superb views of Privas and the surrounding area. Suddenly, though, where the basalt has covered the base of the mountain, the scenery becomes darker and gloomier.

▶ At the junction with the road to Freyssenet, turn left towards Taverne.

The countryside stretches away as undulating moorland dotted with juniper bushes, box and broom, a landscape bereft of human habitation were it not for the hamlet of **Taverne**.

▶ In Taverne, take D 213.

Between the Col de Fontenelle and Les Molières, a broad gap in the hills provides a view of the Rhône in the distance. In the foreground are basalt columns down which runs a thin stream of water. On one of the hillsides to the right, erosion has worn the rock down to the underlying limestone layer. The road then runs steeply down to Les Molières along the side of the ravine where the various strata in the rock are clearly visible.

▶ Beyond St-Martin-le-Supérieur turn right along the Lower Lavézon valley. The river bed is covered with large, rounded, black and white boulders.

Meysse

15min on foot there and back.
The old village can be discerned behind its façade of more modern housing. Around the old Romanesque church is a network of narrow streets and vaulted passages.

▶ Follow D 2 up the Lower Lavézon Valley; turn right towards St-Vincent-de-Barrès.

The road runs through the vast **Barrès** basin with its fertile farmland. It then follows a tributary valley of the River Rhône, which separates the limestone uplands of Cruas to the east from the volcanic Coiron plateau to the west.

St-Vincent-de-Barrès

This is a lovely village perched on a basalt neck jutting out from above the Barrès plain. It is dwarfed by the basalt towers of its old fortress. From the esplanade in front of the church, there is a view over the Barrès area.

▶ Take the D 322 which winds to the east for 8.5km/5.2mi.

Cruas

Cruas pays a heavy price for its industrial development, but its unique heritage should not be overlooked. The town is dominated by an imposing tower and chapel.
In 804, Benedictine monks founded an abbey at Cruas, although the oldest part of the extant church dates from the 11C. To protect themselves from invasion and floods, the monks established themselves on a rocky ledge and later integrated this into the town's defensive structure, earning it the name 'The Castle of the Monks'. In the 16C-17C, the abbey was attacked by the Huguenots.

Former abbey church★

Guided visits possible: ask at the tourist office. €3–5 depending on season.
This beautiful Romanesque building is dominated by a powerful lantern tower. The interior is sombre, with a vaulted ceiling. The earthen flooring was damaged from the 15C to the 18C by flooding.
There is an 11C **crypt**★ under the choir, with many examples of Romanesque bestiary sculpture.

Dungeon-chapel

Take rue Jean-Jaurès, and after about 200m, turn left onto an ascending lane. Leave the car on an esplanade and walk from there to the ruins (*visit organised by tourist office*).
Note the group of medieval houses lower down.

ADDRESSES

STAY

Hôtel Chaumette – Av. Vanel. ℘04 75 64 30 66. www.hotelchaumette.fr. *36 rooms. restaurant*. Beyond the door of this hotel, discover the inviting interior featuring Provençal and African colours and decorative touches. Pleasant dining room with contemporary furniture and a wood parquet.

Chambre d'Hôte Château de Fontblachère – 07210 St-Lager-Bressac (15km/9mi SE of Privas). ℘06 11 18 23 83. www.chateau-fontblachere.com. *7 rooms. Restaurant*. This gorgeous home promises a peaceful stopover in an elegant setting.

EAT

Le Corentin – *2 pl. de la République.* ℘04 75 64 75 75. *Closed Wed evening and Sun.* On a small and shady square, this crêperie also serves well-prepared bistro fare and a regional menu, "Taste the Ardèche", perfect for discovering the flavours of the area.

La Boria – *3 cours du Palais.* ℘04 75 64 48 48. www.laboria.com. *Closed Sun evening and Mon.* This creative local bistro offers a great variety of seasonal fare in tasting menus big and small. The nine-course tasting menu (evenings and weekends only) is a delicious endeavor not for the faint of heart.

Vals-les-Bains

This spa resort lies in a surprising setting at the bottom of the deeply-encased Volane valley. The town has developed along the valley, resulting in a narrow urban corridor about 2km/1.3mi long but on average only 300m wide.

- **Population:** 3 522.
- **Michelin Map:** 331: I-6 Local map see Massif du TANARGUE.
- **Info:** 7 r. Jean-Jaurès, 07600 Vals-les-Bains. ℘04 75 89 14 97. www.aubenas-vals.com.
- **Location:** Just 5.5km/3.5mi N of Aubenas.
- **Timing:** Allow at least half a day to explore.

Intermittent Spring

East bank. This spring (discovered in 1865) gushes forth from the middle of the park at the southern end of town. It rises to a height of 8m every six hours *(11.30am and 5.30pm in summer, 10.30am and 4.30pm in winter).*

Rocher des Combes

2km/1.2mi E via a road alongside the hospital – 15min on foot there and back. This is one of many excursions starting from Vals.

From the viewing table there is a good view over the surrounding mountains.

DRIVING TOURS

VALLÉE DE LA VOLANE AND VALLÉE DE LA BOURGES★★
Round trip of 69km/43mi. Allow 4h.

Leave Vals on D 578 N to Mézilhac.

The Volane valley is lined with terraced hamlets, dotted with boulders and darkened by ancient basalt flows. The site of Antraigues, perched on its rocky promontory, marks the end of the lava flows.

Antraigues-sur-Volane

This delightful hill village is clustered around a shaded square lined with attractive terraces and popular among enthusiastic *boules* players in high season.

Mézilhac

The village stands on the sill between the Eyrieux and Ardèche valleys. From a basalt peak crowned by a cross, there is a splendid **view**★ north-west to the Gerbier-de-Jonc peak and the Mézenc range, north-east to the Boutières cirque and south down the Volane valley.

▶ Take D 122 along the crest to Lachamp-Raphaël then take D 215 down to Burzet.

Cascade du Ray-Pic★★
45min on foot there and back.
A path leads to the foot of these impressive falls, where the river gushes between two overhanging walls of basalt in an austere landscape at the bottom of a ravine.

Burzet
This village is renowned for its annual procession, commemorating Christ's Passion, up to a calvary overlooking the village and the River Bourges flowing beside it.

▶ Return to Vals via St-Pierre-de-Colombier, Juvinas and D 243. Or drive to Montpezat along D 26, then follow D 536 and join up with the tour described under AUBENAS.

COL DE L'ESCRINET★
85km/53mi. Allow 3h.

▶ Leave Vals S on D 578B.

Ucel
Ancient village built in a circle on a hilltop overlooking the River Ardèche.

▶ In St-Privat, turn left onto D 256, running along the Luol and Boulogne valleys.

It is a pleasure to drive through the pretty landscape of orchards and vineyards, alternating with pine and chestnut groves.

St-Julien-du-Serre
The village has an interesting 12C Romanesque **church** with an unusual silhouette, its apse supported by hefty flying buttresses.

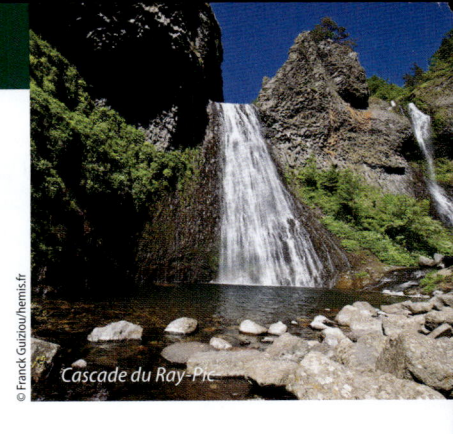

Cascade du Ray-Pic

▶ Drive through St-Michel-de-Boulogne to the ruins of the Château de Boulogne.

Château de Boulogne★
This was originally a fortress, built by the Poitiers family on a spur between two ravines. The castle was transformed over the centuries into a sumptuous residence which escaped the ravages of the Revolution, but was partly demolished in 1820.
The magnificent **gateway**★★, which René de Hautefort had built in the late 16C, incorporates twisted columns drawing on Renaissance tradition.

▶ Turn round and take D 256 on the right. Drive through Gourdon, then turn right onto D 122, skirting Roc de Gourdon. After 2km/1.2mi, turn left onto a narrow lane that leads to Pourchères.

Pourchères
The 12C church built on the nearby slopes features a single nave and a semicircular apse.

▶ Turn round and take D 122 on the left, then N 104, heading for Col de l'Escrinet.

Col de l'Escrinet
This pretty pass provides access to both the south of the Ardèche and the Plateau du Coiron. It offers a fine **panorama** encompassing the Plateau du Coiron, Privas valley, Tanargue massif and Mont Lozère.

DISCOVERING THE LOWER VIVARAIS

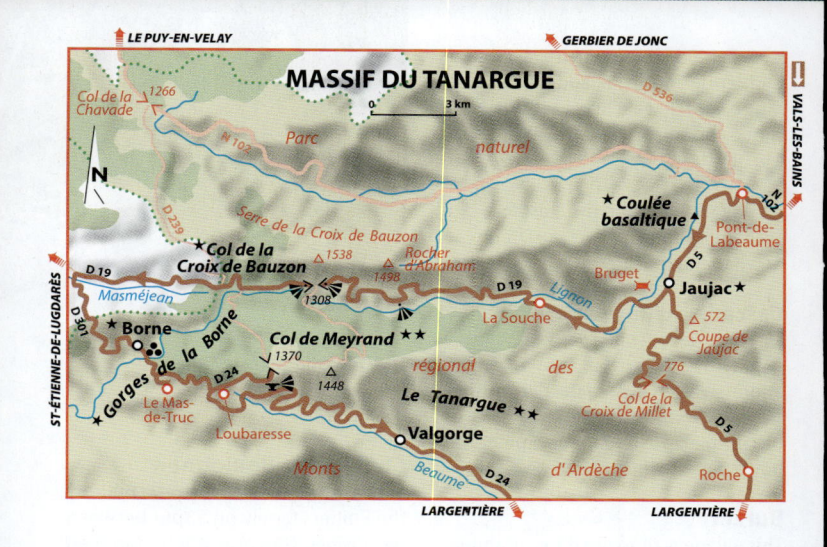

◐ Before driving down towards Aubenas, turn left onto D 224, heading for Freyssenet.

Crête de Blandine
Park the car on the flat area and head for the television transmitter. This crest is the highest summit of the plateau. The **view**★ extends over Privas to the east and Mirabel and Aubenas to the south.

◐ Return to Col de l'Escrinet, then drive back to Vals via St-Privat and Ucel.

THE MASSIF DU TANARGUE
80km/50mi round tour. Allow 3h.

The route passes the basalt flows of the Lignon valley; 2km/1.2mi beyond Pont-de-Labeaume, at a signpost, park and walk up to the edge of the volcanic platform on which the road runs; here and there the **basalt flow**★ takes on a striking appearance of perfectly vertical tube-like sections, some of a blue-grey colour.

Jaujac
This village has attractive 15C and 16C houses, especially in the Chastelas district on the west bank, and the ruins of its old fortified castle. To the south-east rises the "Jaujac dish", an ancient volcano from which the flows of the Lignon emerged, and where mineral springs emanate.

Col de la Croix de Bauzon★
From this pass the view extends over the valleys of the Borne and the Masméjean to the mountains of the Margeride; to the east, the Lignon basin continues into the Aubenas depression.
A small ski resort has been created at the foot of the Tanargue slopes, between La Souche and St-Étienne-de-Ludgarès.

◐ Follow D 19 towards St-Étienne-de-Lugdarès and turn left on D 301 (narrow road).

Gorges de la Borne★
Beyond a stretch of route across broom-covered moorland, the descent to Borne offers plunging views over the gorge. To the west is the profile of Le Goulet mountain. **Borne**★ itself is a village in a secluded site, on a ledge above the deeply embanked torrent.

◐ Continue to Col de Meyrand, via Loubaresse. As far as the village the road is narrow and sometimes impassable due to rockfalls.

VALS-LES-BAINS

Col de Meyrand★★
From this pass a splendid ledge is suddenly revealed. An extensive panorama is visible, from left to right, over the summit of the Tanargue, the Valgorge valley, the Ardèche depression overlooked by the Dent de Rez, the Valgorge ridge opposite and, to the right, the back of Mont Lozère.

▶ Turn back.

Beyond Loubaresse there are views along the channel down to Valgorge, then of stretches shaded by chestnut trees. The road drops downhill, twisting along the upper valley of the Beaume.

Valgorge
This small village is situated within a lush setting of vineyards and orchards.

▶ Continue on D 24 until you reach Roche and take D 5 on the left.

The road follows the Ligne valley up to Col de la Croix-de-Millet.

▶ D 5 leads back to Jaujac and Pont-de-Labeaume. There, take N 102 on the right, heading for Vals.

MONTAGNE AND HAUTE VALLÉE DE L'ARDÈCHE★
Approx 82km/51mi. Allow half a day.

▶ Leave Vals-les-Bains heading S, and then take the N 102 on the right and follow the valley as far as Pont-de-Labeaume. The take the D 536 on the right – in the direction of Montpezat-sous-Bauzon.

Éperon de Pourcheyrolles★
800m before Montpezat turn right, and then 600m after the path to the power plant take a short paved road. Leave the car at the end of the road and walk from there (⚐ 15min there and back).
About 100m below the last pylon there is a great view of the outcrop on which rest the ruins of the feudal castle of Pourcheyrolles.

▶ After the bridge over the Fontaulière, take the narrow lane to Chaudouards which branches on the right.

Église Notre-Dame-de-Prévenchère
The interior of this 12C–13C church is characterised by four short naves featuring Romanesque or Gothic vaulting. Driving back towards Montpezat, you encounter the **town** with its narrow main street flanked by old granite houses built in the mountain style: curved façades, with low porches resting on round arches.

Montpezat-sous-Bauzon
The old town of Montpezat has given its name to a major hydroelectric project, commissioned in 1954. It is the first example in France of a group of reservoirs straddling the watershed, and several dams serve to collect water from the upper Loire and its tributaries.

▶ Take D 536 for Suc de Bauzon until you reach D 110. Turn left to go to St-Cirgues-en-Montagne.

Saint-Cirgues-en-Montagne
The church is Romanesque and typical of those found in the mountains with its squat appearance and bell-tower.

▶ Take D 239 S heading towards Mazan-l'Abbaye.

Mazan-l'Abbaye★
In a clearing of Mazan forest, this 12C abbey was the first Cistercian sanctuary built in the province of Languedoc. The town also boasts a work form the Partage des Eaux art installation project *(www.lepartagedeseaux.fr)* entitled Un Cercle et Mille Fragments.

Forêt de Mazan★
Small waterfalls, moss-covered rocks and wild blueberries and raspberries provide a charming backdrop to a walk through the lush undergrowth.

435

DISCOVERING THE LOWER VIVARAIS

▶ Continue along D 239, which leads to Col de la Chavade and the start of the Ardèche valley.

Col de la Chavade

This pass marks the watershed between the Atlantic Ocean and the Mediterranean. N 102 between Le Puy and Viviers follows the traditional route from the Velay area to the Rhône valley. Just over a mile beyond the pass, the road crosses the Ardèche. This hilly drive offers beautiful views down the valley.

Mayres

This hamlet is situated in a wooded gorge. From a footbridge on the river, about 1km/0.6mi above the hamlet, there is a lovely view of the upper valley.

Thueyts★

This small town surrounded by orchards lies on a basalt flow, the remains of an ancient volcanic eruption.

A **waymarked footpath**★ (*1h30 return; follow the red arrows*) leads along the edge of the lava flow. Just upstream from the Pont du Diable, the Ardèche flows through a narrow gorge, making an interesting **scene**★ against the dark backdrop of the basalt cliffs. Steps lead up to the top of the basalt cliffs, affording pretty views of the valley.

Neyrac-les-Bains

This small spa town backs onto the slopes of the Soulhiol volcano. In the Middle Ages its bicarbonated hot springs were thought to cure leprosy.

▶ At the exit of Pont-de-Labeaume turn left following signs to Notre-Dame de Nièglès; the road drops into a valley before reaching a plateau. Park the car down on the right.

Notre-Dame de Nièglès

The church stands on a hill overlooking the river. Little remains of the original 10C building. The road back to Pont-de-Labeaume commands pleasant views of the medieval fortress of Ventadour.

Château de Ventadour

Guided visits: Jul–Sept Mon–Fri 9am–noon, 2–7pm, Sat–Sun 3–7pm. €5. ☏04 75 38 00 92 (Jul–Oct), or ☏03 23 55 50 67 (Nov–Jun).

Partly demolished and abandoned, this imposing medieval fortress would have eventually disappeared without the valiant efforts of Pierre Pottier and his wife who, since 1969, have undertaken to restore it.

▶ N 102 and then D 104 lead back to Aubenas.

ADDRESSES

☞ STAY

Grand Hôtel de Lyon – *11, Avenue Paul Ribeyre.* ☏04 75 37 43 70. www.grandhoteldelyon.com. *Apr–Oct. 34 rooms. Restaurant.* This hotel is centrally located, and has rooms that are spacious and well kept.

Château Clément – *Chemin de la Châtaigneraie.* ☏04 75 88 33 53. www.auchateauclement.com. *5 rooms.* This magnificent hotel boasts the luxury of a château and the comfort of an inn.

⏚ EAT

Le Tanargue – *Au Village, 07110 Valgorge.* ☏04 75 88 98 98. www.hotel-le-tanargue.com. *Closed Sun evening and Mon except Apr–Sept and school holidays. 22 rooms.* Inviting inn set in the Vivarois mountains; the restaurant serves a good selection of dishes every day.

Le Vivarais – *5 avenue Claude Expilly.* ☏04 75 94 65 85. www.hotel-helvie.com. *Closed Mon, closed Sat lunch and Sun dinner Sept–Jun.* This haute cuisine restaurant's chef adores creating tailor-made wine and food pairings.

ON THE TOWN

Casino – *Av. Claude-Expilly.* ☏04 75 88 77 77. www.casinodevals.fr. Located in a scenic, rather old-fashioned park also housing a theatre and a cinema, this casino is comprised of slot machines, a bar, and two restaurants.

SHOPPING

Brasserie Bourganel – *7 av. Claude-Expilly.* ℘*04 75 94 03 16. www.bieres-bourganel.com.* Set on the banks of the Volane, this brewery organises informative visits followed by tastings.

SPORTS AND LEISURE

Parc naturel regional des Monts d'Ardèche. ℘*04 75 94 35 20. www.destination-parc-monts-ardeche.fr.* Founded on the initiative of local chestnut growers, this nature park comprises 132 municipalities committed to the protection of the natural and cultural heritage of the Monts d'Ardèche.

Aubenas

Aubenas stands in an impressive **setting★** perched on a spur of rock overlooking the Ardèche. The roads hugging the Coiron cliffs to the east reveal a wonderful **view** of the valley below. Aubenas is known for its candied chestnuts and jam.

- **Population:** 12 563.
- **Michelin Map:** 331: I-6.
- **Info:** place de l'Airette, 07200. ℘04 75 89 02 03. www.aubenas-vals.com.
- **Location:** Aubenas is 40km/25mi W of Montélimar.
- **Parking:** There are numerous car parks in the centre of town.
- **Timing:** Allow half a day for a relaxed stroll around town.

A BIT OF HISTORY

Following a bitter winter in 1669–70, which killed all the local olive trees, rumours of new taxes fuelled deep-seated dissatisfaction: On 30 April 1670, a farm inspector was stoned in Aubenas; the ringleader of the attackers was thrown into prison, but the rioters, led by a country squire from La Chapelle-sous-Aubenas, **Antoine du Roure**, effected his release the very next day. While the governor of Languedoc played for time by holding negotiations, Roure's men captured Aubenas.

Towards the end of July, the rebels fought the royal army at Lavilledieu. The peasants were massacred, and Roure was subsequently executed in Montpellier. Aubenas and La Chapelle were condemned to pay heavy fines as a reflection of royal wrath.

SIGHTS

Château
Closed for renovations. www.aubenas-vals.com.
The oldest parts of this fine building date from the 12C. The castle was enlarged by a succession of families.

Château d'Aubenas

© Franck Guiziou/hemis.fr

Dôme St-Benoît
Guided tours Jul–Aug at 5pm. ℘*04 75 87 81 11.*
This hexagonal building is the former Benedictine chapel of Aubenas (17C–18C).

Old Houses

The 16C "House of Gargoyles" stands opposite the château; its tall polygonal turret is decorated with magnificent gargoyles. There is a charming 16C staircase-turret in the courtyard of the "Maison de Castrevieille" on place Parmentier; handsome town houses line rue Jourdan.

EXCURSION

Jastres Panorama★

7.5km/4.5mi SE via N 102. 4km/2.5mi beyond the bridge spanning the Ardèche, turn left on the access road to an industrial estate. After 200m, turn right onto a tarred road. After 1km/0.5mi turn left on a rocky uphill road. Park at the top.

The edge of the plateau was the site of a prehistoric settlement. Where the road ends, the view embraces the entire Lower Ardèche, the Aubenas valley and the Coiron range to the north-east.

DRIVING TOUR

DÉFILÉS DE L'ARDÈCHE★

44km/27mi. Allow 2h.

Take D 104 from Aubenas to St-Étienne-de-Fontbellon, then turn left onto D 579.

The light-filled Ardèche valley forms a wide dip stretching to the basin of the Lower Chassezac in the west. The river flows through fertile basins. Here the road runs close to the river, between orchards and vineyards.

Vogüé

The village of ancient, arch-spanned streets dominated by a castle is built against a cliff overlooking the Ardèche. The vast 16C **château** (*Apr–Jun and mid-Sept–early Nov Wed–Mon 10.30am–1pm, 2–6pm; early Jul–mid-Sept daily 10am–7pm. 1st wk in Jul. €5.5. 04 75 37 01 95. www.chateaudevogue.net*), which still belongs to the Vogüé family, replaced the original medieval fortress and now houses exhibitions on the Vivarais region.

Head back S to D 1, then D 401 on the left to Rochecolombe.

Rochecolombe★

The medieval village of Rochecolombe occupies a secluded **site★** overlooking a stream rising from a limestone corrie. There are in fact two villages of Rochecolombe: the upper one is the first, with houses clustered around a church.

From the square in the upper village, turn left onto a road down to a bridge across the stream. Park a little further along, just before a bend, and follow the footpath down to the water's edge.

On the right stands the **medieval village**, at the foot of the ruins of a square tower and the bell-tower of a Romanesque chapel. At the bottom of the corrie, enclosed by limestone cliffs are two **Vauclusian springs.**

Return towards Vogüé on D 401, turn left on D 114 after crossing the Ardèche.

In Lanas, the road crosses the river by a narrow bridge, offering a view of the Auzon confluence with the Ardèche.

In St-Maurice-d'Ardèche turn right onto D 579, then right onto D 294 just after the station in Balazuc.

Balazuc★

This once-fortified village is perched above a secluded gorge. Cross the bridge to the opposite bank for a good view of the charming village.

During the summer season, leave the car in the car park.

Like many villages in the Lower Vivarais area, Balazuc was founded by a Saracen colony in the 8C and 9C. It now makes a pleasant place for a stroll, particularly in the old streets up to the castle. It is also home to a **natural history museum** (🕒 Apr–Nov, 10am–12:30pm, 2–5:30pm. €7.7. www.museum-ardeche.fr) conveying the geological history of this region. 🚶 For a pleasant walk downstream along the banks of the Ardèche, take the dirt track to the left of the bridge at the foot of the village. Here the river flows through a narrow passage between walls of rock.

▶ Take D 104 to Uzer; on reaching Bellevue, follow D 4 to Ruoms.

The entrance to the Ligne gorge is marked by a narrow rocky passage.

A beautiful **view** unfolds upstream of the Ardèche at the confluence of the two rivers. The Ligne gorge is followed by the **Défilé de Ruoms**★, alongside which the road passes through picturesque tunnels in the rock.

▶ Take the bridge on the left to Ruoms.

Ruoms

The walled centre of this town lies within a quadrilateral of ramparts flanked by seven round towers.

▶ Return to Aubenas on the D 4, D 294, D 114 and D 579.

Les Vans

In the heart of the Lower Vivarais, in the middle of a fertile basin watered by the River Chassezac and dominated to the west by the jagged spire of the Barre ridge lies the town of Les Vans (pronounce the "s" of Vans). The setting, for those arriving from the Cévennes, is a magnificent Mediterranean scene, with an austere landscape of schist ridges to the north giving way to the dazzling white limestone of the south.

EXCURSIONS

Rocher de Sampzon
7km/4.2mi S of Ruoms.
🚶 *Leave the car below the church and go to the summit on the tarmac road, then on the path level with the platform.* From the top, the **panorama**★★ encompasses the Vallon basin, the Orgnac plateau and the River Ardèche.

Labeaume
3.5km/2mi W of Ruoms. on the D 245.
At the edge of a gorge with arcaded streets and galleried houses.
🚶 The walk along the left bank of the river to the **Gorges de la Beaume**★, is most pleasant, offering pretty views of the shimmering waters and the sculpted limestone cliffs.

- ▶ **Population:** 2 776.
- **Michelin Map:** 331: G-7.
- **Info:** Pl. Ollier, 07140 Les Vans. ✆04 75 37 24 48. www.cevennes-ardeche.com.
- ▶ **Location:** 38km/24mi SW of Aubenas.
- **Kids:** Go bathing at Mazet-Plage, or discover the rural life in Gravières.
- 🕒 **Timing:** You should allow a full day to appreciate the town and its surroundings.

🚗 DRIVING TOURS

VILLAGES DU VIVARAIS CÉVENOL★
34km/21mi round trip. Allow 2h30.

▶ Leave Les Vans on D 10 N, turn right on D 250.

Chambonas
This is a village with a part-Romanesque church (12C–17C) boasting towers covered in glazed tiles, and formal gardens said to have been laid out by Le Nôtre.

▶ Follow D 250.

DISCOVERING THE LOWER VIVARAIS

The road runs alongside the Chassezac, crosses the Sûre and climbs a sandstone slope between vineyards and stands of evergreens.

Payzac
There is a charming rural church (12C–15C) here.

▶ Take D 207 towards St-Jean-de-Pourcharesse.

The sandstone landscape modulates from grey to red tones. After the village of Brès the surrounding rock becomes schist and the road winds through chestnut groves.

St-Jean-de-Pourcharesse
A typical local church, built of schist with a roof covered in stone slabs *(lauzes)* stands in this village.

▶ Take the road to Lauriol village.

From here, the road passes more chestnut groves in a landscape slashed by ravines, to the edges of which cling tiny hamlets. Note the interesting stone-slabbed roofs.

St-Pierre-le-Déchausselat
This village is built on terraces. From the vineyards of the farm below the church there is an attractive view over the surrounding countryside.

▶ Return to Les Vans via Chambonas.

CORNICHE DU VIVARAIS CÉVENOL★
113km/70mi. Allow 5h.

▶ Leave Les Vans on D 901 towards Villefort and take D 113 right.

Gravières
The **church** (12C–15C) here has a sturdy belfry. Inside, in the wall of the chancel, there is a 14C Tree of Jesse of carved stone *(for visits call ☎04 75 37 31 07)*.
👥 A round tour (6km/3.5mi) starting from **La Virade du Batistou** runs right around the village inviting children to discover the rural life of the early 20C.

▶ Continue along D 113 and, beyond the bridge on the River Chassezac, turn right on D 413.

Les Salelles
This village overlooks a meander in the Chassezac. The **church of St-Sauveur** is a Gothic edifice built of warm red sandstone. The fortified belfry, destroyed by lightning, was rebuilt in the early 20C.

▶ Follow the valley along D 113.

Usine de Pied-de-Borne
At the confluence of the Altier, the Chassezac and the Borne, the hydroelectric plant is powered by the Villefort and the Roujanel, producing more than half of the total energy output for the valley.

▶ Having crossed the Borne, turn right on the D 151 towards La Bastide-Puylaurent.

La Bastide-Puylaurent
The village was founded in the 19C during the construction of the Paris–Nîmes railway line; it is a pleasant, cool resort in the upper Allier valley.

▶ Leave La Bastide going E on the D 906, and turn left onto the D 4.

Trappe de Notre-Dame-des-Neiges
This Cistercian abbey was founded in 1850; it is isolated among woodlands of conifer and beech, and sheltered from the winds that sweep the Vivarais mountains.
On the descent to St-Laurent-les-Bains, a bend on the left offers a **view★★** at the entrance to the Borne valley.

Saint-Laurent-les-Bains
Confined in a narrow valley, this small spa resort treats different forms of rheumatism. From the main street, where there is a hot fountain (53°C/127°F), there is a nice view of an old tower on the ridge above.

Village of Thines

▶ Continue on the D 4.

The road descends to cross the Borne and then climbs again passing through a beautiful pine forest that gives way to a more desolate landscape.

▶ Turn right towards Montselgues.

Montselgues
This tiny village in the middle of a vast plateau dotted with wild narcissi and broom in June, has a sturdy church with a lovely Romanesque doorway. The village is a cross-country skiing centre.

▶ Come back to the D 4, then take the D 513 on the right.

Thines★★
This small village sits on a spectacular **site★★** perched above the Thines torrent and its ravine. It boasts old houses clinging to the rock, narrow alleyways and a fine Romanesque **church**. The **east end★** is particularly attractive, with a cornice adorned with fanciful motifs below which is a blind arcade resting on carved consoles and engaged columns. The alternating colour of the stonework – pink sandstone, grey granite and white limestone – adds to the charm of the building.

▶ Go back as far as the crossroads with the D 4 and there turn right.

Shortly before Peyre, there is a good **view★** to the right of Thines down below.

▶ Return to Le Vans via Pont de Chambonas.

ADDRESSES

STAY

Camping La Source – *Chemin de la rouvière, 07460 Berrias-et-Casteljau (12km/7.2mi SE of Les Vans via D 901 and D 202). ☎04 75 39 39 13. Open Apr-Sept. Reservation recommended. 81 sites. Food service.* This fairly new campground has been well planned: the clearly defined sites are already protected from the sun. The bar, pizzeria and grocery, located in the same building, provide on-site sustenance. Enticing pool.

Le Carmel – *Montée du Carmel. ☎04 75 94 99 60. www.le-carmel.com. 26 rooms. Restaurant*. Dominating the medieval town, this former Carmelite convent has delightfull rooms, decorated with the fabrics and colours of Provence. Pretty garden, sunny breakfast room, shaded terrace and, at the table, dishes of the day.

La Santoline – *07430 Beaulieu. 13km/8mi SE of Les Vans via D 901, D 202 and D 252. ☎04 75 39 01 91. www.la santoline.com. closed mid Sept-mid Apr. 8 rooms.* Isolated in the middle of the garrigue, this 16C edifice will delight

DISCOVERING THE LOWER VIVARAIS

those who yearn for peace and quiet. Colourful elegance prevails in the rooms, none of which is alike. Supper, for residents only, is served in a pretty, arched dining room. There is a pool and a garden for your pleasure.

Camping La Source – *275 route de Chassagnes.* ℘04 75 37 34 35 www.domaine-des-chenes.fr. This four-star campground boasts a spa, restaurant, and on-site pool. There are also regular activities to occupy children.

EAT

Chez Vincent et Michèle – Pizzeria le "C4" – *07460 Berrias-et-Castlejau (10km/6mi E of Les Vans. Take D 901, D 252 and follow signs to VVF).* ℘04 75 39 35 33. *Closed mid-Sept–Apr. Reservation recommended.* Savour Le Lagon's fine cuisine by the waterfall pool Summertime, amid the rocky gorges or tuck into a pizza on the terrace next door.

Le Likoké – *7 Route de Païolive. Closed Sun–Mon in off-season; Sat–Sun in Jul–Aug. Closed Tues in Oct.* ℘04 75 88 09 74. www.likoke.fr. This beautiful, creative restaurant clearly evokes the passion and adventurous spirit of Chef Piet Huysentruyt.

Gorges de l'Ardèche★★★

The Ardèche gorge, overlooked by an audaciously engineered road, ranks among the most impressive sites of natural beauty in the south of France. A large part of the gorge is now a nature reserve. In 1993, this exceptional stretch of landscape was listed as a major national site (Grand Site d'Intérêt National).

A BIT OF HISTORY

Spates and droughts – In the upper valley, the Ardèche cuts a steep downhill course, but it is in the lower valley that the more interesting formations are to be seen. Here, the river has carved a passage through the limestone of the plateau, already undermined by subterranean streams. The Ardèche's tributaries accentuate its sporadic yet typically Mediterranean flow. During the autumn spates, when the river's volume can increase dramatically, there is a tremendous convergence of flood waters at Vallon-Pont-d'Arc.
The strength of these erratic floodwaters is such that the river pushes the flow of the Rhône eastwards and deposits alluvial debris in its river bed. In 1890, the

- **Michelin Maps:** 331: I-7 to J-8.
- **Location:** It is difficult to get a complete overview of the gorges, but the view from the panoramic road is as good as any.
- **Don't Miss:** The Pont d'Arc.
- **Timing:** You should allow a whole day to do a complete circuit.
- **Kids:** If the water is calm, take a canoe trip on the river.

force of the Ardèche spate was so strong that it cut right across the course of the Rhône and broke through the Lauzon dike on the opposite bank.

🚗 DRIVING TOURS

ROUTE PANORAMIQUE
38km/24mi starting from Vallon-Pont-d'Arc. Allow half a day.

The D 290 overlooks the gorge from the clifftops at the edge of the Gras plateau, giving views from the many look-out points *(belvédères)* along the way.

GORGES DE L'ARDÈCHE

Vallon-Pont-d'Arc
This town is the departure point for boat trips down the gorge. Southeast of the town, on the slope of a hill, stand the ruins of Vieux Vallon castle, a reminder of the old medieval village here.

La Grotte Chauvet 2 Ardèche★★★
(Opening variable depending on season, check website for details. www.grottechauvet2ardeche.com. Reservations recommended in high season.)

At the end of 1994, a set of cave paintings was discovered on the site of the Combe-d'Arc in the Ardèche gorge. Part of a vast network of underground galleries, the cave (Grotte Chauvet) features numerous prehistoric red and black paintings of some 400 animals, including horse, mammoth, bear, woolly rhinoceros, cat and auroch; figures of a hyena and an owl are also portrayed, which is exceptionally rare. Initial studies of the art date them to about 30 000 years ago. The number, quality and originality of the paintings place the cave on a par with the Cosquer cave east of Marseille and the Lascaux cave in the Dordogne, in terms of the importance of its contribution to the study of prehistory worldwide.

The Grotte Chauvet 2 Ardèche allows viewers to explore a reproduction of the paintings, as well as partake in interactive exhibits of local wildlife for the era. Children can create their own cave paintings.

▶ Head S for Pont-d'Arc on D 290.

The road skirts the ruins of Vieux Vallon castle and after crossing the Ibie, comes to the Ardèche. On the left is the Grotte des Tunnels, a cave through which an underground torrent once ran.

Pont-d'Arc★★★
At one time, the river skirted this promontory, and the arch would have been just a gully through which underground waters drained. General erosion and the river wore away the land around the arch, and then the river itself, during some particularly large spate, abandoned its old meander to slip through the passage. Beyond Pont-d'Arc the landscape becomes more impressive. The river follows a series of gentle curves, interspersed with rapids, at the bottom of a deserted gorge. After Chames the road veers round to the left at the bottom of Tiourre valley which forms an impressive, rocky **cirque**★ before reaching the edge of the plateau.

PRACTICAL INFO
A FRAGILE ENVIRONMENT
The Ardèche Nature Reserve is a conservation area, so every effort should be made to protect its ecosystem. In particular, visitors must not light a fire, leave behind rubbish, pick plants or stray from the signposted footpaths. Picnicking is possible all along the way. Camping or bivouacking is prohibited outside authorised camp sites (*see Where to Stay, p437*).

Belvédère du Serre de Tourre★★
Poised almost vertically above the Ardèche, this viewpoint offers a superb **view** of the meander known as the **Pas du Mousse**, with the ruins of the 16C Château d'Ebbo clearly visible on the rocky promontory.

Belvédère de Gaud★★
There is a fine view of the upstream sweep of the Gaud meander and the turrets of its small 19C castle.

Belvédères d'Autridge★
To reach the two viewpoints, take the panoramic curve. The needle of rock known as Aiguille de Morsanne soars up from the Ardèche like a ship's prow.

Belvédères de Gournier★★
These viewpoints are well situated, high above the Ardèche. Below, the Gournier

DISCOVERING THE LOWER VIVARAIS

farm lies in ruins in a meadow beside the river.

▶ Continue to the Marzal chasm along the road across the Gras plateau (D 590).

Aven Marzal★

Interior temperature 14°C; 743 steps. The chasm is a natural well, and leads to caves rich in stalagmites, stalactites and other limestone formations.
You can also visit the **Musée du Monde Souterrain** (♿⏱*Apr–early Nov 10.30am–5.30pm (Jul–Aug 9.30am–7pm).* ✆*04 75 04 12 45. www.aven-marzal.com*), a museum devoted to the history of speleology in France. The **Zoo Préhistorique** (♿⏱*mid-Feb–early Mar 2–4.30pm; Apr–early Nov 10.30am–5.30pm (Jul–Aug 9.30am–6.30pm).* ☞€9. ✆*04 75 55 14 82*) is laid out along a shaded route displaying life-size reproductions of extinct animals that lived from the Primary to the Quaternary Era.

▶ D 201 leads to Bidon.

Bidon

This is a tiny village of traditional houses built with drystone walls, where life has gone on peacably for centuries.

▶ Return to the La Madeleine junction.

This is the **Haute Corniche★★★**, the most outstanding section of the drive, offering views of the gorge from a series of viewpoints in quick succession.

Belvédère de la Madeleine★

From here there is an imposing view of the Madeleine "fortress", a rocky outcrop blocking the view of the rest of the gorge downstream. These are the highest cliffs of the entire gorge.

🚶 From the parking area, a stony footpath leads through dense vegetation to the Belvédère de la Cathédrale.

👥 Grotte de la Madeleine★

🕐*Daily: Apr–Jun and Sept 10am–6pm; Jul–Aug 10am–7pm; Oct–Nov 10am–5pm.* ☞€11 (child 6–15, €6.5). ✆*04 75 04 22 20. www.grottemadeleine.com.*
This cave was carved by an underground river which once drained part of the Gras plateau.
Enter through the Grotte Obscure, then follow a tunnel hewn out of the rock (⚠️*steep stairway*) which leads to the

444

GORGES DE L'ARDÈCHE

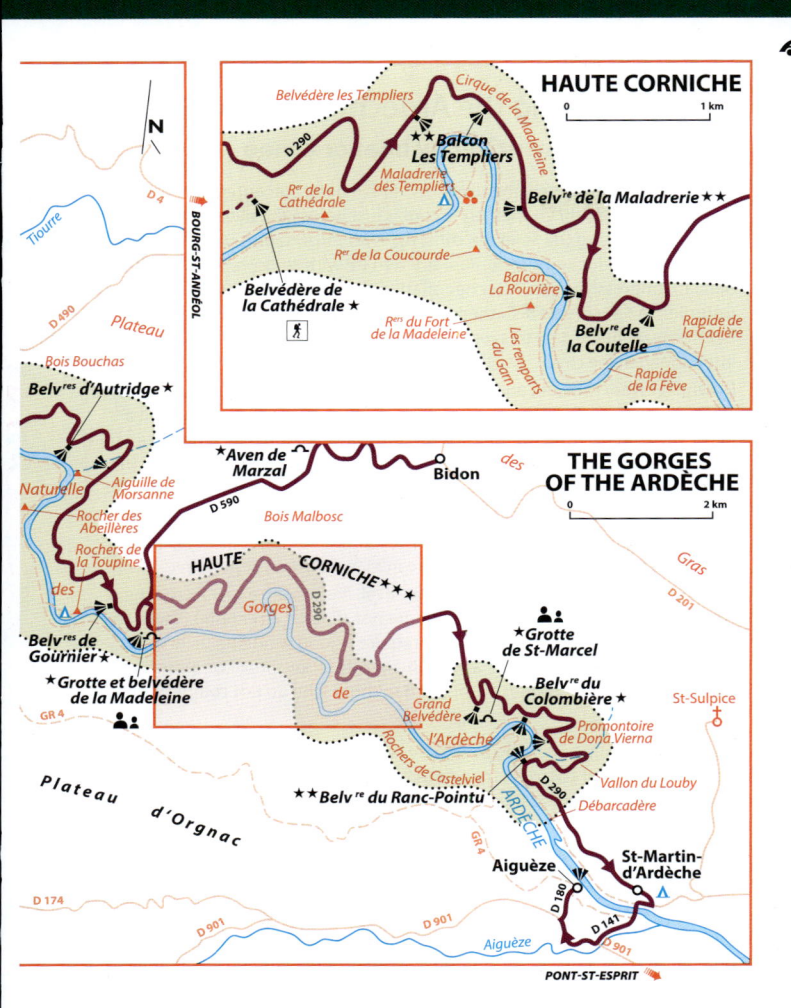

Salle du Chaos, a vast chamber divided into two by columns coming down from the cave roof.

Belvédère de la Cathédrale★★

This look-out gives an unparalleled view of one of the most fascinating natural sights along the gorge: an immense jagged rock known as the "Cathedral" rising above the river.

Balcon des Templiers

From the "Templars' Balcony" there are striking views of a tight loop in the river, cut deep into the magnificent surrounding rock walls.

Belvédère de la Maladrerie

From here there is a good view of the "Cathedral" rock upstream.

Belvédère de la Coutelle

This viewpoint overlooks the Ardèche. To the right is the end of the Garn ramparts; to the left, along the axis of the gorge, are the Castelviel rocks.

Grotte de St-Marcel★

Guided tours: Apr–Jun and Sept 10am–6.30pm; Jul–Aug 10am–7.30pm; Oct-early Nov 10am–5.30pm. €10.50 (child 6–15, €7). 04 75 04 38 07. www.grotte-ardeche.com.

445

Following the Ardèche Gorge★★★
Downriver by boat or canoe

After a long, calm stretch, the river flows into a bend and enters the gorge. The impressive Rapide du Charlemagne comes just before the natural arch of Pont-d'Arc. After passing the Saleyron cliffs, the river forms rapids before reaching the Gaud meander and cirque. Rapids alternate with smooth-flowing stretches beneath impressive cliffs. After negotiating the boulders of the Toupine de Gournier, the Rocher de la Cathédrale looms into sight in the distance. Just before you actually pass this rock, the river takes you past a natural opening into La Madeleine cave.

Downriver from the Coucourde rock (Provençal for "crane") and the Castelvieil cliff, the opening of St-Marcel cave appears on the left and, as you round a bend, the Dona Vierna promontory and the Belvédère du Ranc-Pointu can be seen. The cliffs melt away as the valley finally widens out, overlooked by the tower of Aiguèze on the edge of the rocky outcrop to the right.

The whole trip covers a distance of 30km/18.6mi; however, it is possible to shorten this by starting from Chames. The river can be explored by canoe year-round, although the best times are in May, June and September.

Depending on the season and the water level, it is wise to allow six to nine hours to complete the trip (departures are not allowed after 6pm). There are a few difficult passages (rapids) which require a good canoeing technique; in addition, it is essential to be able to swim. Life jackets must be worn by participants and heavy fines are applied to those who do not comply with regulations.

Canoe hire – Some 50 hiring companies offer unaccompanied and guided trips lasting one or two days for an average price of €40 (one day) or €55 (two days without accommodation) per person (children under 7 years of age are not allowed on these trips). A list of hiring companies is available from tourist offices. For unaccompanied trips, it is necessary to book an overnight stop from central booking offices located in the above-mentioned tourist offices.

Overnight stops – Overnight stops along the gorge are allowed in two places only: Aire Naturelle de Gaud and Aire Naturelle de Gournier. Longer stays are possible at two campsites: the naturist campground Camping des Templiers (℘04 75 04 28 58; www.camping-templiers-ardeche.com) and Camping des Grottes de St-Marcel (℘04 75 04 14 65).

Following the gorge on foot

Two-day walking tour (21km/13mi) with an overnight stop at the Gournier bivouac (booking essential), or a one-day walk for strong walkers. A chance to spot the rare Bonelli's eagle that reigns supreme over the gorge.

A topoguide (French), *Les Gorges de l'Ardèche et leurs plateaux* (No. 2, Gilbert de Cochet) is published by the Syndicat Intercommunal des Gorges de l'Ardèche et de leur Région Naturelle (SIGARN ℘04 75 98 77 31).

Also available, and in part passing through the Ardèche, is *The Grand Traverse of the Massif Central* (in English) by Alan Castle (Cicerone Press, 2010: ISBN 978-1-85284-571-1. www.cicerone.co.uk), a guidebook to mountainbiking, cycling or walking the 700km GTMC, Grande Traversée du Massif Central, in southern France, from Clermont-Ferrand in the Auvergne to Montpellier and Sête on the Mediterranean. The long-distance route is described in stages for walkers, and mountain bikers, with on road alternatives for road cyclists.

Ardèche Gorges at St-Martin-d'Ardèche

A tunnel dug through the rock leads into chambers and passageways lined with stalagmites and stalactites. Winemakers age their wines here and offer tastings paired with cave exploration *(www.speleo-oenologie.com/)*.

Belvédère du Colombier★

From here, there is a view over a meander enclosed by walls of rock. The road follows a loop along a dry valley, skirts the Dona Vierna promontory and makes a long detour along the Louby valley.

Belvédère du Ranc-Pointu★★

This viewpoint at the mouth of the Louby valley overlooks the last meander of the Ardèche. From here the landscape changes dramatically on the way down to St-Martin: the bare defile gives way to a cultivated valley which opens out as it gets nearer the Rhône. On the opposite bank, the village of **Aiguèze** can be seen clinging to a rocky crest.

St-Martin-d'Ardèche

This is the first settlement since Vallon and a haunt of anglers, walkers and canoeists.

▶ Cross the river via the narrow suspension bridge then turn left onto D 901 and right again onto D 180.

Aiguèze

This medieval village crowns the last clifftops along the gorge. The 14C fort has a watch-path which offers **views**★ of the mouth of the gorge, with Mont Ventoux in the distance and the suspension bridge linking Aiguèze to St-Martin-d'Ardèche in the foreground.

ADDRESSES

STAY

Hôtel-Restaurant Le Clos des Bruyères – Rte des Gorges, 07150 Vallon-Pont-d'Arc. ℘04 75 37 18 85. www.closdesbruyeres.fr. *Closed Oct–Mar. 32 rooms.* Take a break in this regional-style house whose arcades open onto the summer pool. Rooms with a balcony or on the ground floor. Seafood served in the restaurant with a terrace.

Camping Le Provençal – *1.5km/1mi SE of Vallon-Pont-d'Arc.* ℘04 75 88 00 48. www.camping-le-provencal.fr. *Open mid Apr–mid Sept. Reservations recommended. 200 sites. Food service.* Beyond its pretty, flowery entrance, this elongated terrain stretches to the banks of the Ardèche. An agreeable place to stay, with a children's playground, attractive pool and tennis court.

EAT

Auberge La Farigoule – Bidon. ℘0475 04 02 60. A typical country inn located between vines and lavender fields boasting traditional local fare. Come in winter to take part in a truffle-focused menu.

Aven d'Orgnac ★★★

Until 19 August 1935, the people of Orgnac-l'Aven had paid little attention to the swallowhole known to them as "Le Bertras". It wasn't until Robert de Joly (1887–1968), President of the Speleology Society of France, explored it that they became of its wealth. An engineer with the College of Electricity in Paris, he was a daring explorer of this area of the Cévennes, playing a vital role in the development of equipment and techniques used in underground explorations. The huge chambers in the swallowhole were formed by the action of underground water from infiltrations in the cracked limestone rocks. The first concretions, some of which were 10m in diameter, were broken by an earthquake at the end of the Tertiary Era. These truncated or overturned columns then became the base for more recent stalagmites.

- **Michelin Map:** 331: I-8 – Local map see Gorges de l'Ardèche.
- **Info:** 1pl. de l'Ancienne-Gare, 07150 Vallon-Pont d'Arc. ℘04 75 88 0401. www.vallon-pont-darc.com.
- **Location:** Located 15km/10mi from Vallon-Pont d'Arc, the Aven d'Orgnac is at the southernmost edge of the Ardèche. The location is well signposted, 25km/16mi west of the Rhône valley.
- **Timing:** You will need at least half a day for the cave and area.

UNDERGROUND MAZE

Temperature below earth 11°C. 700 steps, and return to the surface by lift.
Guided tours: Mar 10.30am, 11.30am 2.15pm, 3.30pm, 4.45pm; Apr–Jun every 30min from 10am–noon, 2–5.30pm; Jul–Aug all day; Oct–mid-Nov every 40min; Christmas holidays and Feb 2.15pm, 3.45pm, 4.45pm. €14.5 (child 6–14, €9.5). ℘04 75 38 65 10.
www.orgnac.com.

This fabulous cave system, discovered in 1935, is now a major tourist attraction and. The development of the caves was a difficult task, and today the paths are at the bottom of the cave system up to 120m below the surface.

The system is entered through a long tunnel leading down to the entrance hall. The various tours descend by walking from chamber to chamber, which collectively cover 5km/3mi and over 30 000sq m. In June 2004, the cave system was listed as a Grand Site de France.

Anyone contemplating touring the caves needs to be relatively fit and agile. The **Upper Chamber** (Salle Supérieure) is amazing for its sheer size (height: 17–40m; length: 250m; width: 125m) and the views in and around it. The dim light from the natural mouth of the swallowhole gives it a bluish tinge that appears somewhat unreal. It contains a number of magnificent stalagmites, in an incredible variety of shapes. The largest (in the centre) have the appearance of pinecones. For the most part, the height of the gallery roof has prevented stalagmites from joining up with the stalactites overhead to form columns; instead they have thickened at their base until some reach quite impressive dimensions. Other, more slender, stalagmites look like piles of plates, as a result of the slow oozing of water through the high, thin roof.

Beneath the lower sections of cave roof are slim **candle-like formations**, with straight or tapering sides. In the niche of a huge formation of draperies and stalagmites like organ pipes is an urn containing the heart of Robert de Joly. In the **Rockfall Chamber** (Salle du

Cave of Aven d'Orgnac

Chaos), filled with concretions from the Upper Chamber, there are magnificent "drapes" of various colours – white, red and brown – hanging from a crack in the cave roof.

The **Red Chamber** (Salle Rouge) has a fantastic decor centred around colossal pillars of calcite. It owes its name to the layer of clay, the residue of the dissolving calcite, which covers floor, walls and concretions alike.

The climax of the tour is the **Grand Theatre** viewpoint overlooking a huge chamber which, at first, is in total darkness; however, music gradually fills the cave and, combined with light effects underlining details round the rock walls, creates a spellbinding atmosphere.

La Randonnée Souterraine

Cave enthusiasts may like to take part in this one-hour underground ramble, available to groups of restricted size only, through the red chambers, a magnificent part of the cavern that has been left as it was when discovered, apart from the electric lighting. This walk is an ideal compromise between standard guided tours of caves and full-blown potholing "in the raw", and is not unduly problematic or physically taxing, although you will need to be reasonably agile.

Cité de la Prehistoire

The rooms, laid out around a patio, contain the finds from archaeological digs in Ardèche and the north of Gard. They date from the Lower Palaeolithic to the Iron Age (from 350 000 to 600 years BCE). Reconstructions, including an Acheulian hut from Orgnac 3, a flint workshop and a cave decorated with a Lion's Head provide an insight into the everyday life of prehistoric man.

🚗 DRIVING TOUR

PLATEAU D'ORGNAC

45km/28mi itinerary starting from Aven d'Orgnac; local map see Gorges de l'ARDÈCHE.

Barjac

The narrow streets of the upper town, lined with fine 18C houses surround the castle now a cultural centre (cinema and multimedia library).

From the esplanade overlooking the valley, there is a fine view of the Cévennes mountains.

Twice a year (Easter weekend and around 15 August), Barjac holds an antique fair which attracts enthusiasts and specialists from all over the region.

▶ Follow D 979 N. In Vagnas, turn right onto D 355.

Labastide-de-Virac

This fortified village on the boundary between the Languedoc and Vivarais regions is an ideal departure point for outings to the Aveyron gorge or the Orgnac plateau.

Just north of the village stands a 15C castle, the **Château des Roure** (*Jul–Aug daily 10am–7pm; Easter–Jun and Sept daily except Wed 1–6pm, mid-Oct–early Nov 1–5pm. €9.80). ☎04 75 38 61 13. www.chateaudesroure.com*), which guarded the passage through the gorge at the Pont-d'Arc.

The two round towers were pulled down in 1629 during the Wars of Religion. Since 1825, the castle has belonged to the family of sculptor James Pradier (1795–1825) whose forebears were tenant farmers to the Counts of Roure; he carved the statues representing Lille and Strasbourg on place de la Concorde in Paris.

449

The tour takes in the Florentine courtyard, a spiral staircase and the great hall with its fine chimney-piece.

The castle watch-path overlooks the Ardèche and Gras plateaux, and in fine weather Mont Lozère and Mont Mézenc can be seen to the north.

The tour ends with an exhibition of handmade silk goods. A working silkworm farm illustrates traditional methods of silkworm breeding.

▶ Beyond Labastide, turn left off D 217.

The road runs through **Les Crottes**, a ruined village *(partly restored)* destroyed during World War II. A stele commemorates the inhabitants who were shot by the Nazis on 3 March 1944.
Continue to the **Belvédère du Méandre de Gaud**. This promontory commands an excellent **view★★** of the Ardèche and the Gaud cirque.

▶ Drive back to D 217 and turn left. A minor road on the right leads to Aven de la Forestière.

Aven de la Forestière★

Guided visits: Apr–Sept daily 12.30–5pm (Jul–Aug 10am–7pm). €10. ℘04 75 38 63 08.

This cavern, first explored by A Sonzogni in 1966, was opened to tourists in 1968. It is not far below ground and is easily accessible. The cleverly lit chambers contain a wealth of fine concretions in interesting shapes and subtle colours. A small underground zoo is home to a variety of fish, shellfish, frogs, toads and insects.

ADDRESSES

☞STAY

⊜⊜ **Couvent de Vagnas** – *270 rue du Couvent, 07150 Vagnas. ℘04 87 22 00 30. www.couventvagnas.com. 3 rooms. Restaurant open Thurs–Sun eve.* This former 19C convent is ideally situated near the Pont d'Arc. Renovated in 2018, this hotel is located on a 2 hectare park and boasts an interior courtyard with 100-year-old trees and comfortable rooms with exposed stone walls.

⊜ **Prehistoric Lodge** – *Combe d'arc, 07150 Vallon Pont-d'Arc. ℘04 75 87 24 42. www.prehistoric-lodge.com. 8 lodges and 4 rooms.* This lodging option affords the choice between four cosy rooms and eight natural lodges.

♀/EAT

⊜ **Hotel-Restaurant les Stalagmites** – *07150 Orgnac-l'Aven. ℘04 75 38 60 67. www.lesstalagmites.com. Closed mid Nov–Feb.* A simple, very inexpensive family boarding-house with a warm welcome, located right in the village. In summer, the generous, traditional cuisine is served on the tree-shaded terrace.

⊜ **La Carabasse** – *Pleoux, 07460 Beaulieu. ℘06 17 89 73 58. www.restaurant-carabasse.fr. Open Fri–Sat night.* Fresh food made from local, organic products.

Bourg-St-Andéol

A bas-relief of the god Mithras, aged by time, is all that remains of the cult that flourished here before the evangelisation of St Andéol.

SIGHTS

The Romanesque **Église Saint-Andéol** dates from the 11C–12C, and impresses with the simplicity of its interior design. The **Palais des Évêques**, the former palace of the bishops of Viviers, has "Sleep-

- ▶ **Population:** 7 462.
- **Michelin Map:** 331: J-7.
- **Info:** Pl du Champ-de-Mars. ℘04 75 54 54 20. www.rhone-gorges-ardeche.com.
- ▶ **Location:** 28km/17.5mi S of Montélimar, via the D 86.
- **Timing:** Allow half a day.

BOURG-SAINT-ANDÉOL

ing Beauty" appeal with its monumental façade, huge chimneys and magnificent apartments.

At the entrance to the valley, between the sources of the **Tourne,** a bas-relief of Gallo-Roman origin has been carved into the limestone rock; it represents the god Mithras, and in spite of its dull appearance you can still distinguish the god in the process of killing a bull.

DRIVING TOUR

PLATEAU DES GRAS★

51km/32mi. Allow about 3h.

The plateau des Gras, dominated by the Dent de Rez, lies between the Rhône to the east, the gorges of the Ardèche to the south, and the valleys of Ruoms and Balazuc to the west. Almond orchards, patches of lavender, gnarled mulberry trees and hedges border the roads.

▶ Leave Bourg-St-Andéol on the D 4, in the direction of St-Remèze.

Belvédère du Bois de Laoul★

A splendid view of the Rhône valley, the Pierrelatte plain and the hills of Mont Ventoux and Tricastin.

▶ Continue climbing and pass the foot of the relay tower. About 1km/0.5mi further on, a small road branches off, opposite the Auberge de la Belle Aurore, and leads to a chapel.

Musée-distillerie de la Lavande

Saint-Remèze. Guided visits: Apr–Sept daily 10am–7pm. €6.90. 04 75 04 37 26. www.museedelalavandeardeche.com.
This distillery is set in a farmhouse on the plateau de Gras, surrounded by fields of lavender, and linked to a small museum.

▶ Retrace your steps and turn left onto the D 362. At the crossroads at Mas-du-Gras, turn left on the D 262.

Gras

A small hamlet of old houses. The vault of the church is decorated with curious medallions in bright colours.

Dent de Rez★

The curious profile of this rock, separated from the summit of Barres mountain by the col d'Eyrole, dominates the plateau.

▶ Return to Mas-du-Gras, and turn left onto the D 262.

Larnas

This village boasts a lovely Romanesque church surrounded by lavender fields.

Gorge de la Sainte-Baume★

After Larnas, the road plunges into a rocky gorge, where the heat of summer has earned it the name, **Val Chaud**.

Saint-Montan★

The ruins of the feudal castle that dominates the village is named after the hermit, Montanus. The village, with its arrangements of old houses, narrow streets, stairways and archways is especially engaging and pleasing.

▶ Return to Bourg-St-Andéol by the D 262 and the D 86.

ADDRESSES

EAT

⊜⊜**La Cigale et la Fourchette** – *15 Lot Ste-Agnès, 07220 Larnas. 09 70 35 96 97. www.lacigaleetlafourchette.fr. Closed Sun eve, Wed.* This country-style bistro is known for local cuisine and an organic wine list.

⊜⊜**La Table du Vigneron** – *Notre Dame de Cousignac, 07700 Bourg-Saint-Andéol. 04 75 54 61 41. www.domainedecousignac.fr. Open May, Jun, Sept, Oct Tues–Sat lunch, Fri–Sat dinner. Jul–Aug dinner nightly.* With 5 charming rooms and an organic vineyard, this estate's organic restaurant serving country fare is the definition of idyllic.

Viviers ★

This episcopal town created in the 5C gave its name to the province of Vivarais. Its location, boxed in between Jouannade hill and the rocky peak on which the upper town is built, meant that it remained almost untouched by the Industrial Revolution. Only the quarries, originally opened in about 1750 by the Pavin brothers in the hamlet of Lafarge north of the town to produce cement, are witness to the conversion of a small Ardèche business into a firm of international rank. The contrast between the cliffs on either side of the river, the isolated peaks in the middle of the gap and the stately flowing river upstream of Châteauneuf power plant form a picturesque sight.

- **Population:** 3 905.
- **Michelin Map:** 331: K-7.
- **Info:** 2 Avenue Mendès France, 07220 Viviers. 04 75 54 54 20. www.rhone-gorges-ardeche.com.
- **Location:** Viviers is easily reached from the A 7 and N 7; Montélimar is 17km/11mi to the N, Bourg-St-Andéol, 14km/9mi to the S.
- **Parking:** Limited centre parking; park near the Hôtel de Ville (see local map).
- **Don't Miss:** Take a tour of the Old Town.
- **Timing:** Allow 1–2 hours.

A BIT OF HISTORY

After Alba-la-Romaine, the Roman capital of the Helvia people, fell into ruins, Bishop Ausonne went to live in Vivarium, at the confluence of the Escoutay and the Rhône where the city had its port. In the 5C the upper town was fortified. Numerous donations and skilful politics gradually turned the Vivier bishops into overlords of an immense domain east of the Rhône – the Vivarais. They fiercely defended its independence against the Counts of Toulouse, sharing ownership with them of the Largentière mines and minting their own coins.

At the end of the 13C, the French monarchy wanted to expand its territory into the Rhône valley. The Bishop of Viviers finally recognised the suzerainty of the King of France in 1308; a large part of the Vivarais became "Crown" land, whereas the west bank of the Rhône remained "Empire" land, under the distant control of the Holy Roman Emperor.

Inside a second set of ramparts, a medieval city began to develop. All that remains of the defence towers and the main doors is a clock tower, the **Tour de l'Horloge**, extensively refurbished in the 19C. In 1498 Claude de Tournon, became Bishop of Viviers; he had the Romanesque cathedral destroyed and a Flamboyant Gothic chancel built.

Noël Albert, a nouveau-riche entrepreneur who had made his fortune in the salt trade and tax collection, had the Renaissance façade of the Maison des Chevaliers built. After becoming head of the Protestants, he captured the ecclesiastical city.

WALKING TOUR

OLD TOWN ★

The ecclesiastical town is distinct from the lower town. They communicated via the Porte de la Gâche to the west and Porte de l'Abri to the south. The houses in the lower town, in a tight cluster, are roofed with Roman tiles. They generally consist of two upper storeys and a ground floor housing a high cellar or a shop. Most of them have kept their medieval appearance despite many alterations over the centuries. The houses in the ecclesiastical town hide their gardens and courtyards behind bare walls with semicircular openings, sometimes surmounted by a coat of arms.

Park on place de la Roubine. Follow rue J.-B.-Serre and Grande-Rue as far as place de la République.

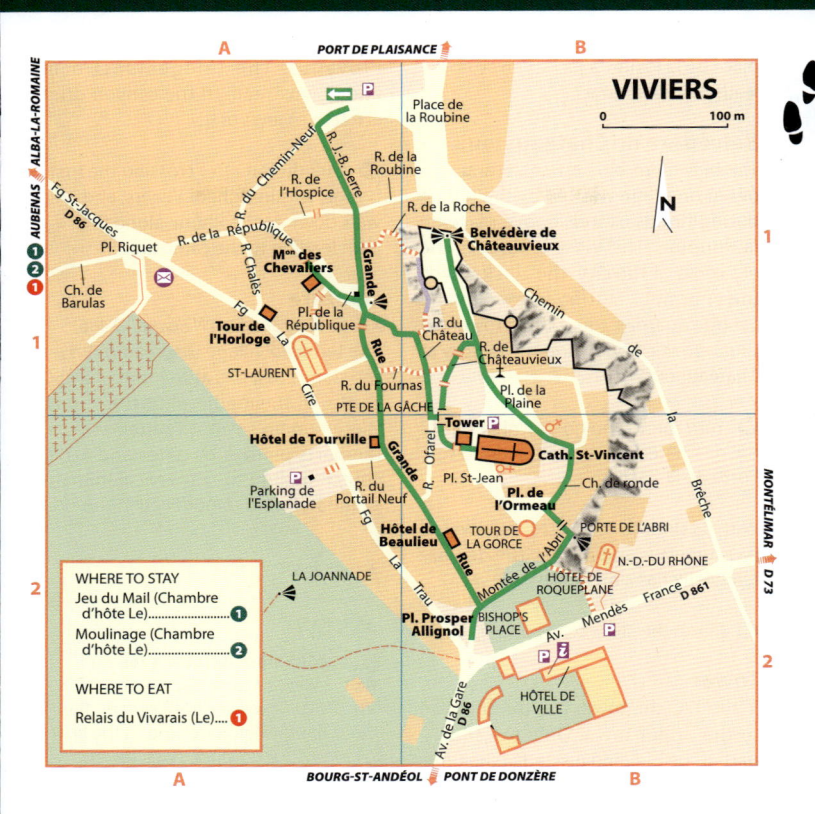

From the eastern corner of the square there is a view of the ruins of Château-vieux Tower.

Maison des Chevaliers

The "Knights' House", also called the House of Noël Albert, was built in 1546. The ornate window-frames on the first floor consist of columns and fluted pilasters with Ionic capitals; rams' heads and garlands of leaves have been carved on the lintels, between the modillions.

Grande-Rue

This street is lined with meticulously dressed façades, some with ornate portals surmounted by wrought-iron balconies such as **Hôtel de Tourville** and **Hôtel de Beaulieu** (18C). Grande-Rue leads to a series of little cross-streets, narrow, stepped and spanned by arches.

Place Prosper-Allignol

The square is flanked by two buildings erected between 1732 and 1738 by Franque. Their Classical symmetry and neat stonework makes them beautiful examples of 18C Viviers architecture.

◐ Walk up the steep montée de l'Abri, which passes under Porte de l'Abri and leads to place de l'Ormeau.

The street offers a fine view over the chapel of Notre-Dame du Rhône, rebuilt by Franque, and the mouth of the Donzère gorge.

Place de l'Ormeau

The square, lined with old canons' houses (17C) owes its name to a centuries-old elm tree *(ormeau)* which perished in 1976.

◐ Take the parapet walk (Chemin de Ronde) around the cathedral; from

DISCOVERING THE LOWER VIVARAIS

place de la Plaine, a passageway north leads to a vast terrace.

Belvédère de Châteauvieux

This belvedere, built on a natural acropolis at one time washed by the Rhône during floods, stands above place de la Roubine. The **view** embraces the old roofs of the city, the clock tower, the enormous cutting formed by the Lafarge quarries, the cooling towers of Cruas power station and the factory at Châteauneuf.

▶ Turn round and go downhill via rue de Châteauvieux (on the right) to Porte de la Gâche.

With its smooth cobblestones, covered passageways and arches, rue de Châteauvieux has a medieval air.

▶ Climb the steps to the tower.

Tower

In the 12C, this tower was the entrance to the upper town. Only the square part of the building existed at the time, with a Romanesque chapel dedicated to St Michael on the first floor.

Cathédrale St-Vincent

The only remains of the 12C Romanesque building are the porch, the west front and the lower part of the nave walls. The chancel is remarkable for its Flamboyant **ribbed vaulting**★.

EXCURSIONS

Chapelle Notre-Dame-de-Montcham Viewpoint★

The belvedere to the right of the chapel commands a lovely panorama of Mont Ventoux.

Défilé de Donzère★★

14km/9mi S on D 73 and D 144 to Donzère and then D 486 to the river.
This is a very picturesque canyon through which the Rhône flows. The vertical wall of the west bank contrasts with the isolated peaks lining the east bank. This point is traditionally considered to be the gateway into Provence. The bridges upstream and downstream of the canyon offer attractive views of it.

▶ Park the car after crossing the first bridge, within sight of Viviers, and walk down to the Rhône along the path leading to the campsite.

Donzère

About 5km/3mi S on N 86 and D 486.
The terraced village is spread out over the slopes of a hill, at the foot of a 15C castle. Of the medieval fortifications, there remain several vaulted streets, ramparts pierced by gates and a 12C church built in the Provençal Romanesque style and remodelled in the 19C.

ADDRESSES

STAY

Chambre d'Hôte Le Jeu du Mail – Alba-la-Romaine. ☎04 75 52 41 59. http://lejeudumail.free.fr. 4 rooms. In the 1970s, the owners were among the first to receive guests in the Ardèche and have continued to do so ever since, with evident pleasure. On the edge of town; swimming pool and garden.

Chambre d'Hôte Le Moulinage – Chemin des Carmes, 07220 St-Thomé. ☎04 75 52 62 11. www.le-moulinage.com. 2 rooms and a suite. This old silk mill, in a wild, natural setting has comfortable rooms and a delightful suite. *Table d'hôte* dinner with regional specialities and fresh, local produce of the season. You can swim all year; in winter in the original swimming pool on the mezzanine and in summer in the natural pools of the Carme.

EAT

Hotel-Restaurant le Relais du Vivarais – 31 Faubourg des Sautelles. ☎04 75 52 60 41. www.relaisduvivarais.fr. Closed Sun evenings, Mon lunch. 6 rooms. A warm welcome is assured in this family hotel-restaurant located in the lower town. Rustic dining room and pleasant summer terrace arranged under the willows. The kitchen specialises in local produce.

Château d'Alba-la-Romaine near Viviers
© Hervé Lenain/hemis.fr

DRÔME PROVENÇALE AND THE PRÉALPES DRÔMOISES

With a clear affinity to the landscapes to the south, the borders of La Drôme Provençale are a bit hazy and are not officially defined. The area lies between Dauphiné and Provence, and as such forms a gateway between North and South. Everything about La Drôme evokes the sights, sounds and smells of the South, and although it is not part of Provence in an administrative sense, it certainly has all the hallmarks of a Provençal department. The landscape vibrates with luxurious lavender fields and olive groves, while gentle hills lead to "perched" villages, and then to mountains and forests, epitomising the many varied landscapes of this remarkable region.

Highlights

2. Nougat from **Montélimar** (p458)
1. Exploring the medieval towns around **Montélimar** (p459)
3. The elegant **Grignan castle** and its remarkable collection of funiture (p461)
4. The **crocodile farm** near Grignan (p462)
5. Driving around the hills of the **Drôme** (p465)

The Perfect Cliché

Café terraces clustered beneath the ubiquitous plane trees, pastis, olives, wine… and *pétanque*; all the clichéd icons of the villages of the Drôme. The climate is Mediterranean, the sky an endless cerulean blue, the light exceptional; lavender fields, vines and orchards stretch as far as you can see. Hectic weekly markets (see *www.jours-de-marche.fr*) are loud with farmer-speak and vibrant with the colours of Provence. It isn't Provence… and yet it is.

A Little of What You Fancy

The wines of the Drôme have an excellent reputation, produced under the AOC Côtes du Rhône, in the case of wines from Hermitage and Crozes-Hermitage, and Côtes du Rhône Villages for wine from Rochegude, Vinsobres, Rousset and Saint Pantaléon. You will also find excellent black olives, truffles, goat's cheese (*picodon* and *foujou*) and, of course, nougat from Montélimar.

Pétanque… Or is it Boules?

Throughout the region, every town or village will have an area set aside for games of *pétanque*, a form of *boules* where the aim is to throw metal balls as close as possible to a small wooden ball *(cochonnet)* or jack.

The current form of the game is enjoyed by around 17 million people in France, and there are even 3 000 players registered in England!

For the record: in pétanque your feet must not move, and must remain within the throwing circle; in boules, it is permissible to take a stride before throwing.

Allées Provençales, Montélimar

© Camille Moirenc/hemis.fr

DRÔME PROVENÇALE AND THE PRÉALPES DRÔMOISES

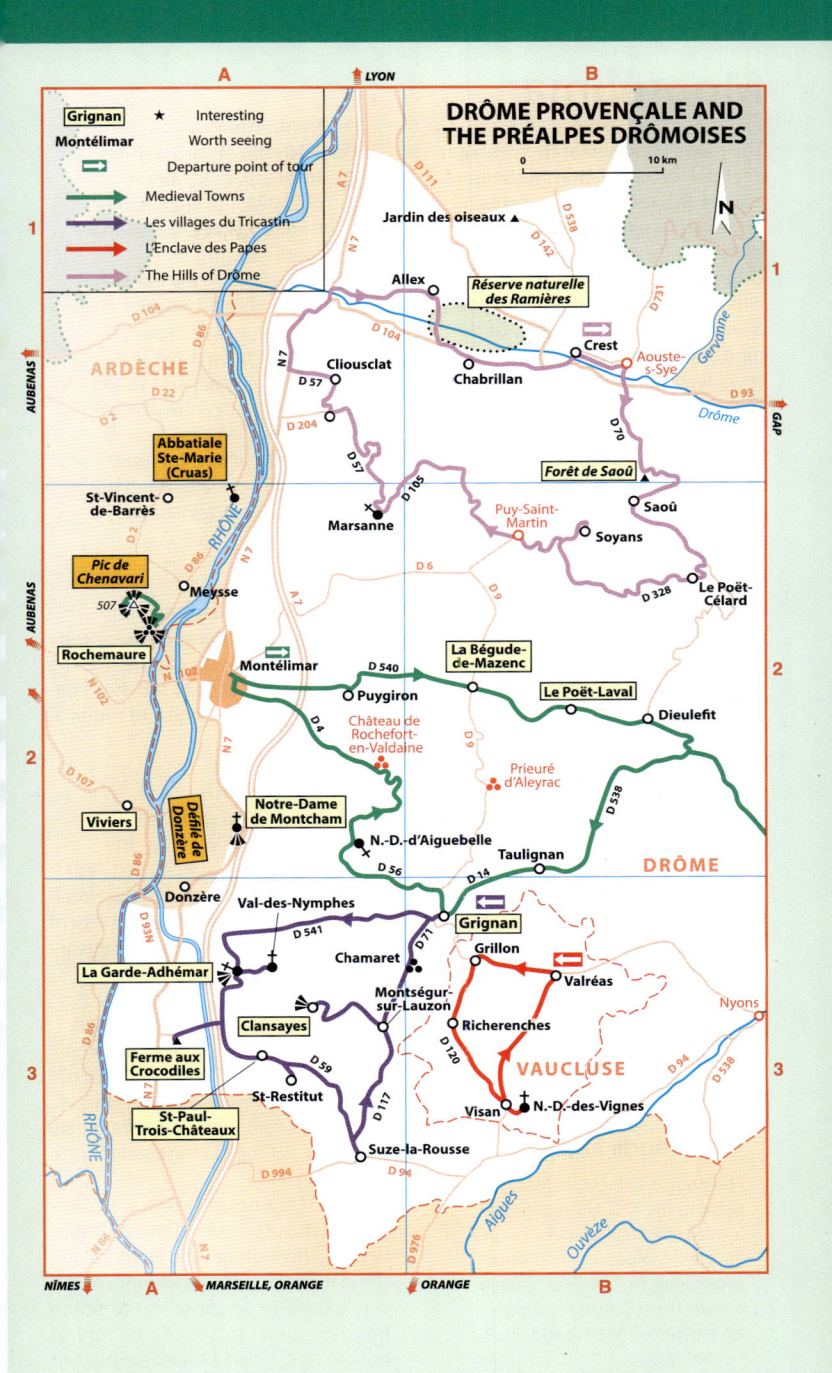

DISCOVERING DRÔME PROVENÇALE AND THE PRÉALPES DRÔMOISES

Montélimar

The name Montélimar derives from a feudal fortress, "Mont-Adhémar," built in the 12C by the powerful Adhémar family. The last member of the family was the Comte de Grignan who lived in the 17C and was the son-in-law of Madame de Sévigné, the lady of letters. Of the nine gates that were once part of the town walls, only the Porte St-Martin to the north of the town still stands. The diversion of the Rhône towards Montélimar feeds the Châteauneuf power plant.

- **Population:** 39 924.
- **Michelin Map:** 332: B-6.
- **Info:** Espace St Martin, 26200 Montélimar. ☏04 75 01 00 20. www.montelimar-tourisme.com.
- **Location:** On the banks of the Rhône, between Valence and Orange.
- **Parking:** There are numerous car parks in and around the centre of town.
- **Timing:** Take it easy and spend a whole day here.
- **Kids:** The Château and the Musée de la Miniature.

SIGHTS

Old Town
In the centre, around the 15C **Collégiale Ste-Croix**, most of the streets have overhanging eaves. **Place du Marché**, lined with arcades surmounted by façades and wrought-iron balconies, has a southern feel about it. On place Émile-Loubet is **Diane de Poitiers' house** with its fine façade.

Château des Adhémar
⏱10am–12.30pm, 2–6pm (Jul–Aug 10am–6pm). ⏱1 Jan, 11 Nov, 25 Dec, and Tue from Nov–Mar. €6 (under 18, free). ☏04 75 00 62 30. chateaux-ladrome.fr.
The original fortress (12C) to the east of the town was extended in the 14C by order of the Pope. Only the *seigneur's* lodgings (main apartments) and the watch-path are open to the public.

Almonds and Honey

The nougat industry in Montélimar dates to the 17C. Almond trees arrived in France from Asia in the 16C, and the popularity of almond-growing across the Gras plateau quickly grew. The ready supply of honey from Provence and the Alps, helped motivate the growth of the industry even further.

Allées Provençales★
The shaded pavements of these wide half-pedestrianised avenues are the hub of the town's activity and their boutiques offer a wide choice of regional products.

Musée de la Ville
⏱Jul–Aug daily except Mon 11am–6pm; rest of year Wed–Sun 2–6pm ⏱Jan. €3. ☏04 75 53 79 24.
Housed inside the chapel of the Hôtel-Dieu (19C), the museum of the city of Montélimar proposes various temporary exhibits.

Fabrique Arnaud-Soubeyran
Avenue du Gournier - Zone commerciale Sud, BP 148, 26204 Montélimar Cedex. t 04 75 51 01 35. www.nougatsoubeyran.com. ⏱Mon–Sat 9am–7pm, Sun 8am–noon, 2–6:30pm. €3, including tasting sample (free for under 16).
Since 1837, the Arnaud Soubeyran company has been producing world-famous nougat. This museum and factory along the Nationale 7, where vendors of the candy used to go car-to-car to sell to holiday-goers, traces the history of nougat and allows visitors to discover its production through windows onto the factory floor.

Château de Rochemaure

🚗 DRIVING TOURS

OVERLOOKING THE RHÔNE
Tour begins 12km/7.5mi NW. Allow 2h.

▶ Leave Montélimar on the D 11.

Château de Rochemaure★
Near Rochemaure church (follow signs). Guided tours Jul–Aug at 10am and 4pm; unguided visit 11am–1pm, 5–7pm. Rest of year. €3. ✆04 75 49 59 20.
The ruins of Rochemaure castle stand on an impressive **site**★★ on the southern edge of the Coiron plateau. The castle (12C–14C) was besieged by the Huguenots in the 16C and 17C and abandoned in the 18C.

▶ Turn left as you reach the plateau and park below the castle walls. A road veering to the left leads to the ruins.

The 12C square keep is surmounted by a pentagonal tower which enabled the archers to vary their angle of fire.

The Old Village
On your way back, take rue du Faubourg in front of the town hall (mairie), *then take rue de la Violle.* The streets are lined with medieval houses.

Pic de Chenavari★★
4.5km/2.8mi N of Rochemaure castle.
🚶 *At the foot of the Chapelle St-Laurent, take the road on the right, heading for Les Videaux. Turn left onto Chemin des Freydières and keep on climbing. Ignore the right-hand lane to a farmhouse and take the dirt track to the plateau. From here you can easily reach the summit (45min on foot there and back).*
From the top there is a **view** of Rochemaure castle, the Rhône, Vercors Barronies and the Lower Ardèche.

MEDIEVAL TOWNS★
87km/54mi. Allow approx 4h.

▶ Leave Montélimar on the D 540, then after passing beneath the autoroute, turn right towards Puygiron.

Notice along the Valdaine plain the small, rural homes built of limestone, a blank wall and curtain of cypress trees protecting them from the blasts of the Mistral.

Puygiron
Dominated by its ancient chateau (13C–16C), the village is worth visiting not least for its **view**★ of les Trois-Becs, Marsanne and the plateau du Coiron.

▶ Go back to the D 540 and turn right.

DISCOVERING DRÔME PROVENÇALE AND THE PRÉALPES DRÔMOISES

La Bégude-de-Mazenc★

At the crossroads in the centre of this modern town, turn left onto the D 9, then take the small paved road leading to the entrance of the old "perched" village; leave you car there.
You enter a wonderful maze of lanes by a fortified gate leaning against the church, which is partially Romanesque. A path climbs steeply to the top of a hill crowned by a beautiful pine forest.

▶ The D 540 climbs in the direction of Dieulefit, and the valley of the Jabron.

Le Poët-Laval★

This perched village, well restored and maintained, occupies a steep **site**★ and holds considerable medieval interest, not least a *commanderie de Malte*, a 12C dungeon, the remains of ramparts and of 15C houses.
Of the old church, only the tower and the Romanesque apse remain. The old temple, built in the 17C inside the house of a 15C knight at the centre of the village, houses historical documents on the region and a little museum dedicated to Protestantism in the area and the Dauphiné Reformation (*Apr–Jun and Sept–Oct 3–6.30pm (Jul–Aug 10am–noon, 3–6.30pm). Mon morning and Sun morning. €3.5. 04 75 46 46 33. www.museeduprotestantismedauphinois.com*).

▶ Return to the D 540.

Dieulefit

Beautifully situated at a point where the Jabron valley opens out, this small town with a strong Protestant tradition today survives on tourism and on visits by *"curistes"*, who visit the health centre. It is also renowned for its pottery; the Jabron valley is dotted with pottery workshops. In the centre of the town, a large house organises annual exhibitions of contemporary ceramics.
The D 538 descends through the Lez valley, dominated by the feudal remnants of Béconne and of Blacon (14C).

▶ Turn right onto the D 14, towards Taulignan.

Taulignan

On the boundary of Dauphiné and Provence, this ancient village has retained its medieval walls, circular and almost continuous, with 11 towers (nine round and two square) connected by curtain walls. To the north-east the Anguille gate is the only fortified gate to have survived. Wandering at random through the lanes you will discover ancient façades and houses with mullioned windows.

Atelier-musée de la Soie★

Apr–Sept daily except Sun and Tue 10am–12.30pm, 2–6pm.; end-Nov–Dec 2–5pm. 25 Dec, Jan–mid-Feb. €5.50. 04 75 53 12 96. www.musee-soie.com.
The museum houses an educational display about the plant and machinery needed to produce silk, and the manufacturing processes that prevailed in the region during the 19C.

Grignan★ (*See GRIGNAN.*)

▶ Leave to the N on the D 4, then turn left onto the D 56. After Réauville, turn right towards Notre-Dame-d'Aiguebelle.

Notre-Dame-d'Aiguebelle

The abbey was founded in 1137 at the instigation of St Bernard, Abbot of Clairvaux. Today the lives of the monks are governed by strict rules and they devote themselves to prayer, manual work and intellectual pursuits.

▶ Rejoin the D 4 heading N along the D 550 passing Montjoyer.

On the way you will notice the imposing ruins of the Château de Rochefort-en-Valdaine, dominating the wooded valley of the Citelles.

GRIGNAN

ADDRESSES

🛏 STAY

Hotel Beausoleil – *14bis, Boulevard du Pêcher.* ☎04 75 01 19 80. www.beausoleil-montelimar.com. *16 rooms.* This hotel features clean, colorful rooms.

Hôtel les Hospitaliers – *26160 Poët-Laval.* ☎04 75 46 22 32. www.hotel-les-hospitaliers.com. *Closed 10 Nov–14 Mar. 20 rooms. Restaurant.* Enjoying a select location in the village, this hotel occupies a cluster of stone houses with superb views of the valley and mountains.

🍴 EAT

Le Grillon – *40 r. Cuiraterie.* ☎04 75 01 79 02. *Closed Sun evening and Mon.* Located on a little street in the old town, this restaurant has an inconspicuous façade that leads to a big dining room.

ON THE TOWN

Café Cantante – *18 r. Roger-Poyol.* ☎04 75 00 01 30. *Mon–Sat 6pm–2am.* This unusually alluring, original night-spot is in a class of its own.

SHOPPING

Nougat Chabert and Guillot – *9 r. Charles-Chabert.* ☎04 75 92 20 20. www.nougat-chabert-guillot.com. *Closed public holidays.* For nougat aficionados, pros and amateurs alike, this establishment founded in 1913 makes a delicious Montélimar nougat.

Au Rucher de Provence – *35 blvd Desmarais.* ☎04 75 52 01 59. http://lartisan-nougatier.fr. *Shop: daily 8am–7.30pm.* The Bonnieu family makes high-quality nougat under two brand names: Stoupany, the oldest (since 1787), and Le Rucher de Provence, launched in 1938.

Escobar Patissier-Confiseur-Chocolatier-Glacier – *2 pl. Léopold-Blanc.* ☎04 75 01 25 53. www.nougats-escobar.com. There are 3 shops in Montélimar: Route de Marseille; Chemin de Gery, and Rue Pierre Julien. *Closed Sun and public holidays Jun–Aug.* This chef belongs to the elite set of genuine Montélimar artisans.

Grignan★

This hillside town became a fortified village in the 12C, developing around the base of its castle. The original town was protected behind 13C walls. Everywhere, changes in the population can be traced through the ornamental façades of the buildings, which date from the 15C to the 18C. Around the town, the countryside expands to embrace no fewer than 14 villages within the title "Pays de Grignan".

> ▶ **Population:** 1 587.
> ⊙ **Michelin Map:** 332: C-7.
> 🛈 **Info:** Pl. du Jeu-de-Ballon, 26230 Grignan. ☎04 75 46 56 75. www.tourisme-paysdegrignan.com.
> ⊙ **Location:** S of Montélimar, via the D 941 (Valréas).
> 👥 **Kids:** The Crocodile farm at Pierrelatte.
> ⏱ **Timing:** Allow 1–2 hours.

CHÂTEAU★★

⏱ *Daily 10am–12.30pm, 2–6pm (Jul–Aug 10am–6pm).* ⊘*Tue from Nov–Mar, 1 Jan, 11 Nov and 25 Dec.* ≈€8. ☎04 75 91 83 55.

The castle was built in the 16C by Louis Adhemar, governor of Provence, and extended between 1668 and 1690 by the son of Madame de Sévigné, who then lived here. It was largely destroyed during the Revolution, but was restored and regained its style and elegance in the 20C under the new owner and later by the Conseil Général de la Drôme. Walking around the exterior you discover the great Renaissance façade, then the Cour du Puits with its pool opening

461

DISCOVERING DRÔME PROVENÇALE AND THE PRÉALPES DRÔMOISES

out onto a terrace framed to the left by a Gothic gallery, and then the main building itself.

From the terrace there is a vast **panorama**★★ along the crest of the Montagne de la Lance to Mont Ventoux and the beautiful Dentelles de Montmirail, Comtadine plain and les Alpilles, the woodlands of Grignan and the mountains of Vivarais.

Inside the château there is a chance to see the grand staircase (17C), and visit the apartments of Madame de Sévigné and the Count of Grignan, the King's Hall and the oratory before descending by a Gothic staircase to the Great Gallery. There is a remarkable collection of furniture, including two magnificent cabinets, and Aubusson tapestries depicting scenes from mythology.

🚗 DRIVING TOUR

LES VILLAGES DU TRICASTIN
47km/29mi. Allow 3h.

▶ Leave Grignan west by the D 541, then take the D 472.

Chapelle du Val-des-Nymphes
In a valley kept cool by many waterfalls and which, as its name suggests, was once a place of pagan worship, stand the ruins of a 12C chapel. For a long while a ruin, this Romanesque chapel was restored from 1991, and an elegant timber ceiling now covers the nave.

La Garde-Adhémar
This old village is made visible from some distance away by its church, perched on a rise. It is an ideal spot for a stroll, with its picturesque limestone houses, its vaulted alleyways and its narrow, winding streets with their arches. In the Middle Ages this village was a major fortress belonging to the Adhémar family. In the 16C, a Renaissance château was built for **Antoine Escalin**, Baron de la Garde, who started life as a mere shepherd then became a soldier; he ended his career as one of François I's ambassadors and as General in charge of the French galleys. Old town walls can be seen on the north side; to the south of the village is a fortified gate and a few ruins, not far from the huge cross erected on a Roman base.

The Romanesque church is remarkable for its two apses and the attractive outline of its two-storey octagonal belfry topped by a stocky pyramid.

👤 La Ferme aux Crocodiles★
Pierrelatte. ♿🕐Daily: Nov–Feb 10am–4pm; Mar–Jun and Sept–Oct 10am–5pm; Jul–Aug 9.30am–6pm. €17 (child 3–12, €11). ☎04 75 96 09 37. www.lafermeauxcrocodiles.com.

This crocodile farm is stocked with a great many species from countries all over the world (Cuba, America, Egypt), installed in large basins. Further on, visitors can discover a vast hothouse containing tropical vegetation and superb exotic birds. From the many footbridges, visitors can watch some 300 crocodiles from the Nile region basking in the sun or swimming in dark waters.

▶ Go back along the D 59 and follow it SE after having re-crossed the autoroute.

St-Paul-Trois-Châteaux★
The old town is surrounded by the remains of ramparts, but has never had the three castles that its name – St-Paul-Three-Castles – would suggest. It was appointed capital of the region during Roman times, under the name "Augusta Tricastinorum".

During the second half of the 4C, the first part of its Roman name was replaced by the name Paul, commemorating one of the town's first bishops. The name of the old capital of "Tricastini" may possibly have been Frenchified by a clerk in the 16C to "Trois Châteaux", though there is no evidence for this theory. The town was a bishopric until the Revolution.

Modern St-Paul sits at the heart of the main truffle region of France. A wander through the walled city will allow you to discover its quiet beauty and historic significance.

GRIGNAN

Cathedral★
This imposing building, begun in the 11C and completed in the 12C, is a remarkable example of Provençal Romanesque architecture.
Most striking is the exceptional height of the transept walls and the powerful aspect of the nave.

Maison de la Truffe et du Tricastin
Open: Hours are variable according to the season; call for more information. €4. ℘04 75 96 61 29. www.maisondelatruffe.com.
The Truffle Centre, located inside the tourist centre, houses an exhibition with posters, showcases and a video projection on the cultivation and marketing of what is known as the "black diamond" of the Tricastin region, and an ingredient in many tasty local dishes.

St-Restitut
The village **church★** in Provençal Romanesque style has fine **carved decoration★**.

Suze-la-Rousse
The principal Tricastin village during the Middle Ages, Suze developed along the left bank of the Lez. The town is enclosed within walls, and includes many fine Renaissance houses, a Romanesque church and a massive old city hall with a beautiful 15C–16C façade.
An imposing **castle** (*daily Sept–Jun 10am–12.30pm, 2–6pm; Jul–Aug 10am–6pm; Tue from Nov–Mar, 1 Jan, 11 Nov and 25 Dec.* €6. ℘04 75 04 81 44) dominates a hill above the Garenne, embracing a park of 23ha. The main building (14C) is a beautiful example of medieval military architecture, and the interior was remodelled during the Renaissance as is reflected in the façades of the courtyard and the double staircase, which gives access to the first floor, where temporary exhibitions are arranged.
The Blue Room, decorated with stucco on the theme of the Four Seasons, and the octagonal room, which occupies a corner tower, are worthy of a visit, offering views of Mont Ventoux, the Lance mountains and the Dauphine alps.
In the other wing the guard room precedes the Salle des Armes, which boasts a magnificent ceiling.

▶ Take the D 117 to the N.

Montségur-sur-Lauzon
In front of the Mairie take the road to the left, then turn right and take a lane climbing to the summit of a hill on which the old village is built. A series of zigzag paths take you round the village and enable you to discover the ancient Romanesque chapel.

▶ Take the D 71 W, then the D 481.

Clansayes★
From here there is an extensive **view★★** over the Tricastin area and its peaks carved by erosion.

Chamaret
A beautiful belfry on a rock dominates the surrounding countryside, the view extending across the Tricastin area.

▶ Return to Grignan by the D 71.

ADDRESSES

STAY AND EAT

Tricastin – R. Caprais-Favier. 26700 Pierrelatte. ℘04 75 04 05 82. www.hoteldutricastin.com. 13 rooms. A simple hotel in a calm street near the city centre.

Gîte du Val des Nymphes – Val des Nymphes, 26700 La Garde-Adhémar. ℘04 75 04 44 54. 3 rooms. Restaurant. Located on the hills of the Tricastin, in the midst of peach trees, this traditional house is absolutely delightful.

Le Bistro – Hotel le Clair de la Plume, 2 pl. du Mail. ℘04 75 91 81 30. www.clairplume.com. Traditional bistro cuisine in this appealing hotel-restaurant (which also includes the acclaimed Michelin-starred Le Clair de la Plume restaurant). A good range of Rhône valley wines.

DISCOVERING DRÔME PROVENÇALE AND THE PRÉALPES DRÔMOISES

Valréas

Besides its geographical oddity – a chunk of the Vaucluse enclosed by the Drôme – Valréas is a particularly agreeable old city founded originally on the manufacture of cardboard boxes, but now given to producing wine and truffles.

- **Population:** 9 798.
- **Michelin Map:** 332: C-7.
- **Info:** Av. Maréchal-Leclerc, 84600 Valréas. ℘04 90 35 04 71. www.ot-valreas.fr.
- **Location:** 10km/6.2mi to the E of Grignan.
- **Timing:** 2 hours to visit the town.

SIGHTS
Musée du Cartonnage and de l'Imprimerie
Apr–Oct daily except Tue and Wed 10:30am–1pm. €5. ℘04 90 35 58 75. This museum is dedicated to the production of boxes and packaging.

DRIVING TOUR

L'ENCLAVE DES PAPES
22km/13.7mi. Allow 2h.

▶ Leave Valréas on the D941, in the direction of Grillon (5km/13mi).

Grillon
Surrounded by vineyards, this peaceful village has two faces: lower down is the place de la Bourgade with its neo-Gothic clock tower, and the upper village, wherein lies its medieval heart.

▶ Leave Grillon to the S and follow the D20 for 4km/2.5mi.

Richerenches
Founded in the 12C, this **commanderie de Templiers** was built to a rectangular plan, and has retained its walls flanked by four round corner towers.

▶ Leave Richerenches heading SE, and follow the D 120.

Visan
This large village has many winding alleyways around its medieval castle. Located at the top of a hill, its caves serve each year to house 10 000 magnums of red wine.
Just outside the village (in the *direction of Vaison-la-Romaine*), a modern housing estate shelters the **chapelle Notre-Dame-des-Vignes**, which houses a 13C statue of the Virgin Mary.

▶ Return to Valréas by the D 976.

Crest

The town of Crest (pronounced Crè), situated at the spot where the River Drôme flows into the Valence plain, is particularly proud of its castle keep. The town has grown up around it, with a dual role as market town and a community specialising in food processing. Among the many local gastronomic specialities are *défarde*, a stew made with lamb's feet and tripe, and *picodons*, small goat's cheeses.

- **Population:** 8 669.
- **Michelin Map:** 332: D-5.
- **Info:** Pl. du Général de Gaulle, 26400 Crest. ℘04 75 25 11 38. www.valleedeladrome-tourisme.com.
- **Location:** 28km/17.5mi SE of Valence.
- **Kids:** The bird sanctuary at Upie.
- **Timing:** Allow 1–2 hours to tour the keep.

CREST

SIGHTS

Keep★
184 steps to the upper terrace.
Jul–Aug daily 9am–7pm, Apr–Jun and Sept 10am–7pm, Oct and Nov school holidays 10am–6pm, Christmas holidays 2–6pm. 1 Jan and 25 Dec. €7.50. 04 75 25 32 53. www.tourdecrest.fr.

The keep in Crest is all that remains of a fortress that was dismantled in 1633 on the orders of Louis XIII. The keep was erected over Roman foundations on a spur of rock, in various stages between the 11C and the 15C. The north wall, the tallest of the four, reaches a height of almost 52m; the base of the tower lies at an altitude of 263m.

From the upper terrace there is a view over the rooftops of Crest and beyond, in a superb **panoramic view★** to the north-east over Glandasse Mountain and the outcrops of the Vercors, and to the south over the Roche-Courbe range with the Trois-Becs, and Roche Colombe further in the distance. To the west the horizon is broken up by the long narrow ridge of the Vivarais area rising to the Gerbier-de-Jonc and Mézenc.

Old Houses
Along the main thoroughfare and the neighbouring streets are some of the vast mansions built for the wealthy bourgeoisie in Crest in the 16C and 17C.

Jardin aux Oiseaux
In Upie, 11km/6.7mi N. Leave Crest on D 538 towards Chabeuil, then take D 142.
Jul–Aug 10am–7pm; Mar–Jun and Sept–early Nov 10am–6pm; Feb 1–5.30pm. Jan. €11.60–14.80 (child 10–13, €10–12.80; 3–9 years, €8.40–10.80). 04 75 84 45 90. www.jardin-aux-oiseaux.com.

This superb Bird Sanctuary is home to over 200 different European and exotic species: hummingbirds, crested grebes, flamingoes, pelicans, ostriches, parrots etc.

DRIVING TOUR

THE HILLS OF DRÔME★
83km/52mi. Allow 3h.

▶ Leave Crest E on the D 93.

The **Forêt de Saoû** is planted with beech, oak and pine. **Saoû** itself is a village known for its *picodon* goat's cheese.

▶ At Saoû, turn left onto D 538, then the D 328 on the right.

Le Poët-Célard – A town hall, a temple and a castle sum up this tiny village.

▶ Continue on the D 328, then the D 310 towards Pont-de-Barret. Cross the village and take the D 128.

The village of **Soyans** is dominated by the imposing ruins of its castle, burned during the French Revolution.

▶ Follow the D 57 to Mirmande.

The pretty houses of **Mirmande** spread out over a hill. Around 1930, painter André Lhote settled here, and many contemporary artists followed.

▶ Follow the D 57 to Cliousclat.

Charming **Cliousclat** is known for its artisanal pottery.

▶ Return to the N 7; head N to Livron-sur-Drôme, then to Allex by the D 93A.

Allex is built on a limestone hill and dominated by a tower, all that remains of an 11C castle.

Réserve Naturelle des Ramières★ is a protected area extending for 10km/6mi along the Drôme.

▶ Cross the Drôme by the D 125.

Chabrillan is known among "perched" villages for its gardens and its castle.

▶ Go back to Crest on the D 104.

465

VALENTINOIS AND THE LOWER DAUPHINÉ

Le Valentinois is the small alluvial plain extending along the left bank of the Rhône, formed by the lower valleys of the two rivers flowing into it, the Isère to the north and the Drôme to the south. The region takes its name from the city of Valence, built on a terrace overlooking the Rhône. In 1349, the Dauphiné was attached to the kingdom of France but retained a certain autonomy until 1457. Following the French Revolution, the region was divided into three departments: the Drôme, Hautes-Alpes and Isère.

Highlights

1. Strolling around **Parc Jouvet** in the city of Valence (p471)
2. The Old Town of **Romans-sur-Isère** (p473)
3. The unusual **Palais Idéal** in Hauterives (p475)
4. The emerald waters of **Lake Paladru** (p480)
5. The on-site museum at **St-Romain-en-Gal** (p487)

Hector Berlioz

Berlioz, the son of a wealthy local doctor, was born in La Côte-St-André in 1803. At the age of 17, he went to Paris to study medicine. He attended lectures but was also a frequent visitor to the opera and the library of the Royal Music Academy, where he later began learning composition. In 1830 he wrote his *Symphonie Fantastique* and won the Grand Prix de Rome.

Thereafter he worked as a music critic in order to earn a living, while at the same time continuing to compose works that brought him success and failure in turn. He seldom returned to La Côte-St-André. Having failed to win the fame he deserved during his lifetime, Berlioz died in Paris in 1869, but his genius earned him posthumous acclaim.

Pilate's Resting Place?

Not far from Vienne, La Pyramide, affectionately known as "L'Aiguille" (the Needle), is a fine white stone pyramid that rests on a small square plinth made from four columns and four arcatures. In the 4C, it adorned the central forecourt of the vast Vienne amphitheatre. A masterpiece of stone-cutting, it is held together without the use of cement. During the Middle Ages, it was thought to be the tomb of Pontius Pilate; according to legend, after leaving Jerusalem for Vienne, the Roman procurator, struck with remorse, threw himself into the Rhône. The Pilat mountain range is said to be named after this event (there is a similar legend attached to Mount Pilate near Lucerne in Switzerland).

Parc Jouvet, Valence

© Eric Bascol/iStock

466

VALENTINOIS AND THE LOWER DAUPHINÉ

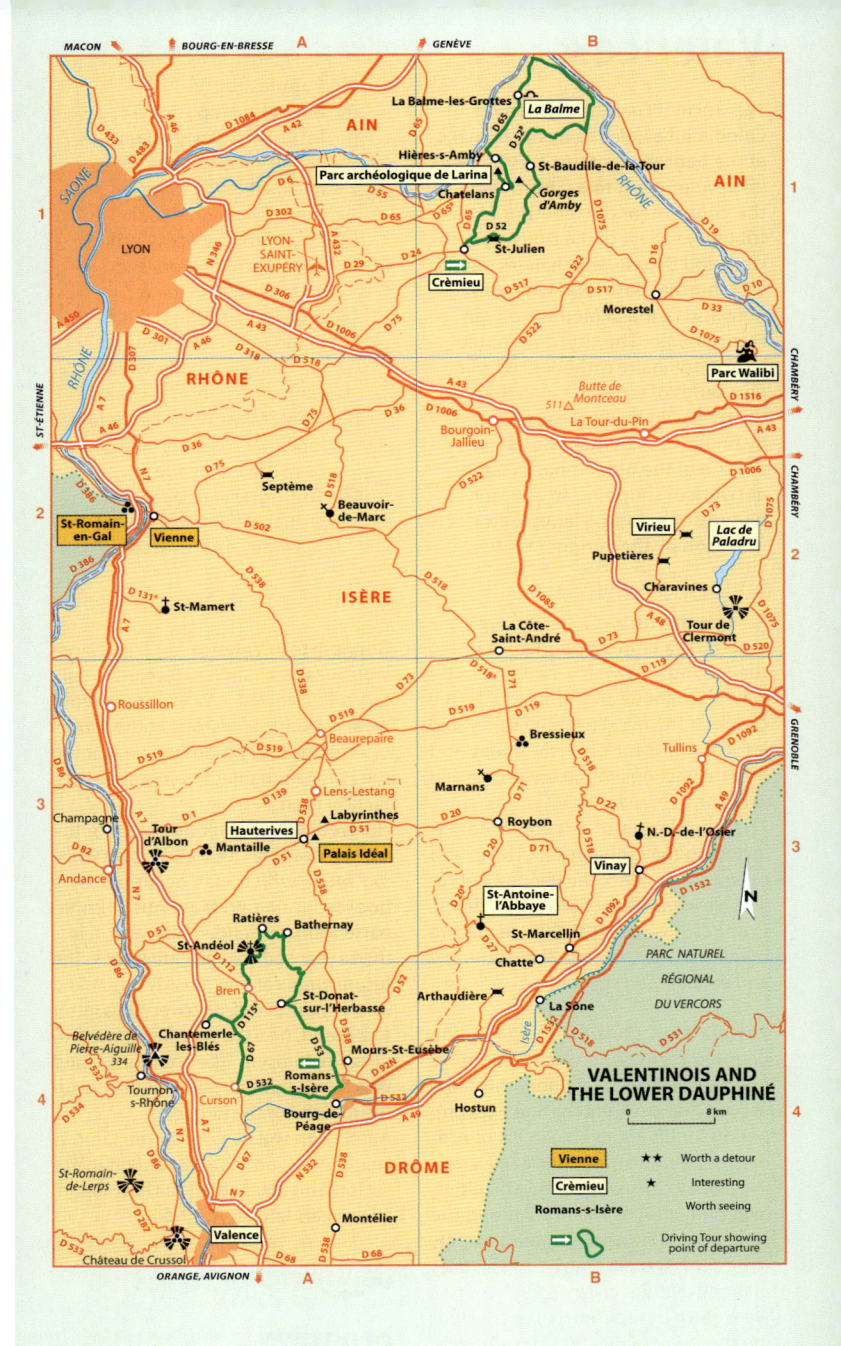

467

Valence ★

This ancient Gaulish city, named Colonia Julia Valentia by the Romans at the beginning of the 2C BCE, owes its development to its location on the Rhône, near the meeting of the tributary valleys of the Doux, Eyrieux, Isère and Drôme, which mark out a vast internal basin and where the flora and fauna of Mediterranean France begin. The city, dominated by St-Apollinaire cathedral, is built on a series of terraces going down to the river. Old Valence, surrounded by boulevards built in the 19C on the site of the old ramparts, has a network of shopping streets and picturesque sloping lanes, animated in season by the Summer Festivals.

- **Population:** 64 322.
- **Michelin Map:** 332: C-4.
- **Info:** 11 boulevard Bancel, 26000 Valence ☏ 04 75 44 90 40. www.valence-romans-tourisme.com.
- **Location:** Valence is 103km/64mi south of Lyon, and accessible from the A 7.
- **Parking:** Parking is difficult in the centre, but there are ample car parks within walking distance.
- **Don't Miss:** Try to be there for either sunset or sunrise from the Esplanade.
- **Timing:** Half a day is probably enough, but you can easily be distracted.

A BIT OF HISTORY

A regional hub – The city, which is served by a large network includuing the A 7 motorway, N 7 national highway, River Rhône and airport is the true centre of the middle Rhône valley and a focal point for entertainment and other attractions within the Drôme and Ardèche *départements*.

The population of Greater Valence, including the outlying suburbs spread out on either side of the Rhône – Bourg-lès-Valence, St-Péray, Portes-lès-Valence, Granges – is over 100 000, including numerous students enrolled at the law and engineering schools.

Rabelaisian studies – In 1452, the dauphin Louis, who was to begin his reign a few years later under the name of Louis XI and who, at the time, was preparing for his kingly role in his princedom of Dauphiné, founded a university in Valence consisting of five faculties, including an Arts Faculty. Among the students was **François Rabelais**. He was to recall his student days here in his tales of the adventures of Pantagruel. Courses were given by reputed masters, including the lawyer Cujas. Besides studying under this strict academic taskmaster, Rabelais is said to have had a love affair with his daughter.

Bonaparte in Valence – In 1785, Napoleon Bonaparte, then a 16-year-old military cadet, arrived in Valence to improve his knowledge of warfare at the School of Artillery. Every morning, he went to the Polygon to direct his bombardiers' tactical exercises.

He lived almost directly opposite the Maison des Têtes (*see Old Town Walking Tour*), which was occupied by a bookseller named Marc Aurel. Bonaparte soon befriended him, and in less than a year had read his entire stock. The future emperor had already embarked on a voyage of self-discovery. In a letter to a friend, he used a striking image to describe himself: "the southern blood which runs through my veins flows with the rapidity of the Rhône…"

Aurel's son was to publish the famous *Souper de Beaucaire*, in which Bonaparte set forth his ideas about the Revolution, a few years later in Avignon.

WALKING TOUR

OLD TOWN

Leave from Peynet kiosk.

VALENCE

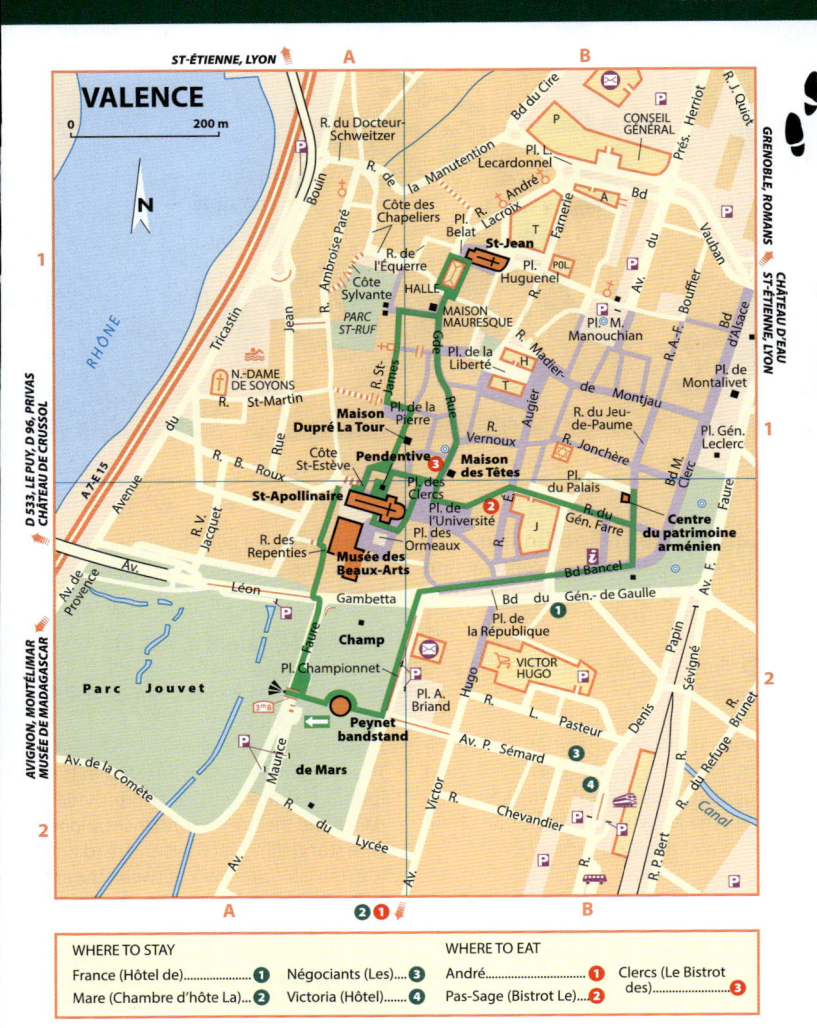

WHERE TO STAY		WHERE TO EAT	
France (Hôtel de)............ ①	Négociants (Les).... ③	André................ ①	Clercs (Le Bistrot
Mare (Chambre d'hôte La)... ②	Victoria (Hôtel)........ ④	Pas-Sage (Bistrot Le).... ②	des)....................... ③

Kiosque Peynet
This structure, built in 1880, owes its name to the artist **Raymond Peynet** (1908–99) who once drew a sketch of a pair of lovers seated beside it.

Champ-de-Mars
This vast esplanade, built on a hillside opposite the Rhône, overlooks Jouvet park. From the belvedere, there is a beautiful **view**★ of the Crussol mountains. The sunsets visible from here are famous; they throw the mountain range into relief. However, it is at sunrise that the view of Crussol is the most striking.

▶ Take the staircase below the belvedere and cross avenue Gambetta. The narrow rue des Repenties and côte St-Estève lead round the cathedral and onto place du Pendentif.

Pendentif
This small monument was built in 1548, in the Antique style. The structure is completely open with a semicircular arch on each side, and has lovely proportions. It draws its name from the shape of its vault, reminiscent of the pendentives of a dome.

469

Detail on the façade of Maison des Têtes

Cathédrale St-Apollinaire
This vast Romanesque construction was largely rebuilt during the 17C in the primitive style.

▶ Enter the cathedral through the north door.

Under the porch, on the left, notice the lintel from the original portal; its carved compartments represent the Annunciation, the Nativity, the Adoration of the Magi and the Magi before Herod.

Interior★
The influence of Auvergne Romanesque architecture is evident; the nave, with its barrel vaulting and transverse arches, is lit by the aisle windows.
An arcade separates the chancel from the ambulatory. Note the depth of the transept arms, unusual in Rhône buildings. Behind the chancel stalls is a cenotaph-bust of Pope Pius VI, who died in Valence in 1799.

▶ Leave through the south door.

Under the porch *(left)*, on the carved tympanum of the original portal, is Christ Giving Benediction, and on the lintel Christ Multiplying the Loaves.

▶ Walk around the east end.

Note the elegant billet-moulding above the arcades of the apse and the transept arms.

Musée de Valence, Art et Archéologie
Wed–Sun 10am–noon, 2–6pm. €6. 04 75 79 20 80. www.museedevalence.fr.
The Fine Arts Museum, located in the former bishop's palace, also provides dance and theatre performances, along with storytelling, lectures and readings to establish closer links between the art and arcaeology collections.

▶ Take rue du Lieutenant-Bonaparte, then rue Pérollerie to reach the Maison Dupré-Latour.

Maison Dupré-Latour
The interior courtyard of No. 7 has a Renaissance staircase turret with a door surrounded by a remarkable carved frame.

▶ From place de la Pierre, take rue St-James on the left, then follow rue Sabaterie and rue Malizard.

On the left stands the former St-Ruf temple. As you reach the public gardens, you will get a view of Crussol in the distance.

▶ Head for place St-Jean via côte des Chapeliers.

VALENCE

Église St-Jean
This church was rebuilt in the 19C. The porch features some interesting original Romanesque capitals.

▶ Walk along Grande-Rue.

Maison des Têtes★
The "House of Heads" at No. 57 is recognisable by the abundance and originality of the sculptures on its façade. Note two standing figures (Eve is on the left) and, under the roof, the four enormous haut-relief heads symbolising the winds, after which this Renaissance house (1532) was named.

▶ Grand-Rue, then rue Saunière, lead back to place du Champ-de-Mars.

Centre du Patrimoine Arménien★
14 r. Louis-Gallet.
Tue–Fri, Sat–Sun 2–6pm. €4.
04 75 80 13 00. www.le-cpa.com.
The Armenian Centre, located in a former law school, tells a poignant story of genocide and exile.
Take the rue du Jeu-de-Paume into the boulevard Bancel. Admire the beautiful façades by Haussmann along the Champ-de-Mars.

Parc Jouvet
This verdant setting in the heart of the city owes its existence to the generosity of a great vintner, Jouvet Theodor (1837–1905). You will find more than 700 species of trees here. Children will love the deer and the aviary.

EXCURSIONS

Châteaux d'eau de Philolaos
Take the autoroute towards Valence, leaving it at junction 32. Then head for Fontbarlette, Valence-le-Haut and parc Jean-Perdrix.
These water towers are the work of a sculptor, Philolaos, who frequently collaborates with architects and is responsible for works in Lyon, Évry, Créteil and La Défense.

Montélier
15km/9mi E via the D 68, then the D 538.
Montélier specializes in decorative trees and shrubs, with nearly 300 varieties. Take time to walk through the historical centre of the village, dominated by its 19C church. On some of the street corners, you will see works by contemporary artists, notably Christian Maas and Philippe Jamet-Fournie.

ADDRESSES

STAY
Hôtel Les Négociants – *27 av. Pierre-Sémard. 04 75 44 01 86. www.hotelvalence.com. 36 rooms.* A friendly, air-conditioned hotel close to the station.

Chambre d'Hôte La Mare – *Rte de Montmeyran, 26800 Étoile-sur-Rhône. 04 75 59 33 79. http://la.mare.free.fr. 2 rooms.* This family farm is the ideal place to become acquainted with the local *savoir-vivre* and the charm of the Drômois.

Hôtel de France – *16 blvd du Gén.-de-Gaulle. 04 75 43 00 87. www.hotel-valence.com. 46 rooms.* A modern, elegant hotel in tune with the times.

Hôtel Victoria – *37 rue Denis Papin. 04 28 99 01 60. www.hotel-victoria-valence.fr.* A charming hotel filled with elegance in the heart of Valence.

EAT
Le Bistrot des Clercs – *48 Grande Rue. 04 75 55 55 15. www.michel-chabran.com.* Bistro in the Parisian style, serving hearty food.

Le Pas-Sage – *4 rue de l'Université. 04 75 55 78 90. www.lebistrotdupassage.fr. Open Tues–Sat.* Fresh, contemporary Mediterranean fare.

André – *285 ave Victor Hugo. 04 75 44 15 32. www.anne-sophie-pic.com.* Michelin-starred chef Anne-Sophie Pic's bistro is a nod to her family heritage.

ON THE TOWN
Café Victor-Hugo – *30 av. Victor-Hugo. 04 75 40 18 11. www.restaurant-victor-hugo.fr. Open 6.30am–11pm.* Valence's chic literary café – chic but vivacious! Lunchtime, it is a noisy brasserie.

Café Bancel – *7 blvd Bancel.* ℘*04 75 78 35 98. Closed Sun.* A busy local hotspot in the heart of the city.

RECREATION

Marina – *Chemin de l'Épervière.* ℘*04 75 81 18 93. Apr–Oct daily 9am–noon, 2–8pm; Nov–Mar Mon–Sat 8am–noon, 2–6pm. Closed public holidays.* The Port de l'Épervière is the Rhône river's number one harbour. Several clubs organise sports activities here, including windsurfing, water skiing, para-skiing. There is also a bowling lane, a tennis facility, a pool, a campground, a hotel and several restaurants. The *centre aqualudique* boasts a water slide, pools, and a restaurant, L'Escale de Fonfon.

La Viarhôna – (en.viarhona.com) Cycling fans will love biking along a portion of this ambitious 815km cycling route joining Lake Geneva and the Mediterranean Sea, all the while following the picturesque Rhône river.

Romans-sur-Isère

The town is built on a hillside opposite Bourg-de-Péage, whose name is a reminder of the toll once collected by the Chapter of St Barnard to cross the bridge linking the two towns. Romans, a flourishing trade centre in the Middle Ages, was once the capital of footwear. Lovers of good food will appreciate the local *pogne* (a type of *brioche* flavoured with orange blossom), *saint-genis* (praline *pogne*) and goat's cheese, *Tomme*, which is also used to make the local dish, *ravioles*).

- **Population:** 34 095.
- **Michelin Map:** 332: D-3.
- **Info:** 34 place Jean Jaurès, 26100 Romans-sur-Isère. ℘04 75 02 28 72. www.valence-romans-tourisme.com.
- **Location:** 17km/10mi E of Tournon, 13km/8mi NE of Valence.
- **Parking:** There are central parking areas.
- **Don't Miss:** It's all about shoes; visit the shoe museum and *cité*.
- **Timing:** Allow at least half a day.
- **Kids:** Goblins and trolls at Le Monde Merveilleux des Lutins.

A BIT OF HISTORY

Dauphiné joins France – From the 11C on, the counts of Albon, natives of Vienne, gradually took over the region from the Rhône valley to the Alps that eventually formed Dauphiné. The origin of the name "Dauphin", given to members of the dynasty which then reigned over Dauphiné, remains uncertain. The last of the Vienne *dauphins*, Humbert II, lived mostly at Beauvoir Castle, opposite St-Marcellin. After the death of his son, which left him without an heir, he sold Dauphiné to the French crown. It was in St-Barnard Collegiate Church that the treaty unifying the Dauphiné region (formerly part of the Holy Roman Empire) to France, was solemnly signed on 30 March 1349. This province was to become the attribute of the oldest sons of the kings of France, who subsequently bore the title of Dauphin.

WALKING TOUR

OLD TOWN

▶ Start from place du Pont.

A maze of picturesque streets surrounds St-Barnard Collegiate Church and, half way down the hill from the church, place de la Presle and place Jacquemart.

ROMANS-SUR-ISÈRE

Collégiale St-Barnard
Quai U.-Chevalier. ✆ *04 75 72 25 87.*
In the 9C, St Barnard, Archbishop of Vienne, founded a monastery here. It was destroyed in the 12C and replaced by a Romanesque church of which the western porch, the northern portal and lower parts of the nave still remain. Towards the middle of the 13C, the chancel and transept were rebuilt in Gothic style. Largely destroyed by the Protestants in the 16C, the church was completely restored in the 18C.

▶ Take rue Pêcherie, opposite the west end of the church.

Escalier Josaphat
These **steps** go down from rue Pêcherie towards the houses with wooden balconies on place de la Presle. The stairway is part of the "Great Journey" or Way of the Cross, which attracts a large crowd of people on Good Friday.

▶ Rue du Fuseau runs straight onto rue de l'Armillerie.

At No. 15 rue du Mouton, off to the right, the Gothic windows on the first floor are now mullioned; above, the outline of a sheep's head carved in a projecting stone can just be made out.

▶ Continue towards place Fontaine-Couverte.

Place Fontaine-Couverte
This square in the heart of the old town is decorated with a modern fountain representing a flautist.

Côte Jacquemart
The hill is lined with 13C and 14C houses.

Le Jacquemart
This is an old square tower from the outer curtain wall of Romans, converted into a belfry in the 15C and given a Jack-o'-the-clock, which since 1830 has proudly sported the costume of a 1792 volunteer.

▶ Facing towards the river, turn left to côte des Cordeliers; walk down to rue Fontaine-des-Cordeliers and rue St-Nicolas.

Hôtel Thomé
This fine townhouse presents a Renaissance façade with beautiful mullioned windows on the upper floors.

▶ Continue towards the river via rue Sabaton and turn right onto rue des Clercs.

Rue des Clercs
The street is very picturesque with rounded cobblestones. Notice, opposite the town's archives, the portal decorated with fine chiselling.

Rue des Trois-Carreaux
This is an extension of rue des Clercs. At its intersection with place aux Herbes there is a monumental door, surmounted by an unusual corbelled construction with machicolations.

Place Maurice-Faure
Beside St-Barnard, to the right of the St-Jean door on the north side of the church, is a beautiful house with a corner tower.

SIGHTS

Musée International de la Chaussure★
Jan–Apr and Oct–Dec Tue–Sat 10am–5pm; May–Jun and Sept Tue–Sat 10am–6pm; Jul–Aug Mon–Sat 10am–6pm; Sun and public holidays all year 2.30–6pm. 1 Jan, 1 May, 1 Nov, 25 Dec, and 15 days following Christmas holidays. €6. ✆ *04 75 05 51 81. www.museedelachaussure.fr.*
The Shoe Museum is located to the east of town and reached through the gateway in rue Bistour, across terraced gardens in front of the building, which is adorned with an elegant colonnade. The museum aims to present the technical, ethnographic and aesthetic aspects of footwear. Numerous documents and other material trace the evolution of the craft.

WHERE TO STAY		WHERE TO EAT
Karene (Hôtel).........❶ Orée du Parc (Hôtel L')........❷		Mandrin............❶

In the old nuns' cells, the collections of footwear are displayed in chronological and thematic order from Antiquity to 1900. Some of them are extremely comprehensive, such as that of Paris designer Victor Guillen.

These sumptuous, amusing and enigmatic shoes reveal the ingenuity of their creators and evoke the customs of their country of origin and fashion throughout the ages: Roman sandals, cracowes whose length varied with social rank, patterns inlaid with tortoiseshell and pearl from Mauritania, Indian moccasins from North America, shoes from Ardèche used to open chestnuts and ankle boots from the Belle Epoque.

The 18C and 19C paintings on the theme of shoes and shoe-making add another angle of interest to the museum visit.

Cité de la Chaussure

Mon–Sat 10am–7pm. www.citedelachaussure.fr. 04 75 48 41 58. guided visits €6 (check site for times; reservation recommended).

This former supermarket has been converted into a space dedicated to shoe-making, with 5 workshops open to the public as well as a shop selling locally-made shoes.

EXCURSIONS
Bourg-de-Péage

1.8km/1mi S along the D 2092.

Located by the old bridge, Bourg-de-Péage gets its name from the toll that used to be charged here. The local specialty, **Pogne**, can be tried at Pascalis bakery (*www.pascalis.com*), which also offers information about its origins.

Mours-St-Eusèbe

4km/2.5mi N. Leave Romans on D 538 then turn right onto D 608.

The village church has kept only its bell-tower, at the west end, and the south wall of the nave from the 11C. It houses an interesting **Musée Diocésain d'Art Sacré**★ (*Sun mid-Jul–mid-Sept 2.30–6.30pm. €4. 04 75 02 36 16. museeartsacre.free.fr*) with rich sacred art (15C–20C) arranged according to a new theme each year.

Hostun

Leave Romans E towards St-Nazaire-en-Royans. Shortly beyond L'Écancière, turn right onto D 125C to Hostun.

An old farm (at Les Guerbys) has been turned into **Le Monde Merveilleux des Lutins** (the Wonderful World of Elves – *Jul–Aug 10am–6.30pm; Apr–May, Dec weekends 2–6pm; Jun* *daily except Mon 2–6pm, Sat–Sun 10am–6:30pm; Sept Sun 2–6pm.* 1 Jan, 25 Dec. €9 (children €7). 04 75 48 89 79. www.mondedeslutins.com), a fantasy realm where children can meet trolls, gnomes, sprites, gremlins and other goblins.

Hauterives★
25km/15.5mi N of Romans on the D 358.
The village of Hauterives, situated at the foot of a hillock bearing the ruins of the medieval castle, which once belonged to the lords of Clermont, has an unusual tourist attraction – the "Ideal Palace".

Palais Idéal★★
Jul–Aug 9.30am–7pm; Apr–Jun and Sept 9.30am–6.30pm; Feb–Mar and Oct–Nov 9.30am–5.30pm; Dec–Jan 9.30am–4.30pm. 25 and 31 Dec, 1 Jan and mid-end Jan.
€8 (children €5). 04 75 68 81 19. www.facteurcheval.com.
In the late 19C, Ferdinand Cheval, the local postman, began bringing home strangely shaped stones that he picked up on his route. Each evening he would add them to an unusual construction he was building in his garden, based on books and dreams, and possibly also inspired by the remains of petrified springs that were common in this area. Cheval continued his work when he retired, bringing sand and stones back home in a wheelbarrow. After 33 years of relentless labour, he finished his weird and wonderful "palace". He then spent the last 10 years of his life building his own grave in the cemetery, in the same style. He died in 1924.

Les Labyrinthes
3.5km/2.2mi from Hauterives. Follow D 51 towards Le Grand-Serre and turn left in St-Germain. Mid-Apr–Aug and Sat–Sun in Sept 11am–7pm. Oct–mid-Apr. €13 (child 3–14, €11.50). 04 75 68 96 27.
www.labyrinthes-hauterives.com.
Four large mazes occupying the top of a hill combine their network of paths and hedges to offer young visitors a thrilling treasure hunt. The Maison des Enfants, located in a shaded position, organises activities involving mosaics.

Albon
17km/10.5mi to the W of Hauterives by the D 51 and D 132.
Albon owes its existence to its counts, who progressively extended their domain from the 11C onwards, so creating Dauphiné. The Tour d'Albon is a link with the past and offers a lovely **panorama**★ over the Rhône valley.

Château de Mantaille
11km/7mi W of Hauterives by the D 147 and the D 132.
The ruins of the château stand on the side of the Bancel; it was here that Boson was crowned King of Burgundy in 879.

Postman Cheval's Palais Idéal, Hauterives

© Ludovic Maisant/hemis.fr

475

DISCOVERING VALENTINOIS AND THE LOWER DAUPHINÉ

🚗 DRIVING TOUR

LES COLLINES
44km/27mi. Allow 3h.

▶ Leave Romans to the NW by D 53.

St-Donat-sur-l'Herbasse
This old Drôme village is a popular haunt among music lovers. The 12C–16C **collegiate church** houses modern organs designed from plans made by the Silbermann Brothers (three keyboards, three sets of pipes).
Every year the church hosts a prestigious **Johann Sebastian Bach Festival** (℘04 75 45 10 29).

▶ Leave St-Donat on D 584 and head N for Bathernay.

Bathernay
This pretty village sits in the midst of the lush countryside. West of Bathernay a narrow road leads to the octagonal tower of **Ratières**.

▶ Take D 207 to the S, then D 53 for 1.3km/0.9mi; a path to the right will take you to the Chapelle St-Andéol.

Chapelle St-Andéol
The small chapel commands a superb **panorama** over the Isère valley, the Galaure Basin and Mont Pilat.

▶ A short, picturesque road to the S leads to Bren. Turn right to join the D 112. Turn left at the D 109.

Chantmerle-les-Blés
Leave the car in the square behind the post office. The footpath begins at the war memorial by the church.

🚶 The highlight of this small town is the view of the surrounding hills *(15mins walk from the church).*

ADDRESSES

🛏 STAY

Hôtel Karene – 455 rue du Soleil, Saint-Paul-les-Romans. ℘04 75 05 12 50. www.hotelkareneromans.com 36 rooms. Just five minutes by car from the city center, this comfortable hotel boasts a pool.

Hôtel L'Orée du Parc – 6 ave Gambetta. ℘04 75 70 26 12. www.hotel-oreeparc.com 16 rooms. This former private mansion in central Romans boasts Art déco influence and elegance.

🍴 EAT

Mandrin – 70 r. St-Nicolas. ℘04 75 02 93 55. www.lemandrin.com. Closed Sun eve, all day Mon, and Wed eve. Mandrin, the famous smuggler, found refuge in this house, dating from 1754. The tiled floor, wooden beams, timber-framing, studs and rounded stones give the restaurant a medieval atmosphere; it serves traditional cuisine.

St-Antoine-l'Abbaye★

Nestling in an undulation of the Chambaran plateau north of the River Isère is the old village of St-Antoine-l'Abbaye, dominated by an imposing Gothic abbey church.

THE ABBEY CHURCH
St Anthony's fire – In the 11C a nobleman from Vienne, Jocelyn de Châteauneuf, made a pilgrimage to the

- ▶ **Population:** 1 072.
- **Michelin Map:** 333: E-2.
- **Info:** Pl. Ferdinand-Gilibert, 38160 St-Antoine-l'Abbaye. ℘04 76 38 53 85. www.saint-antoine-labbaye.fr
- ▶ **Location:** 24km/15mi NE of Romans-sur-Isère.
- **Timing:** Allow a day to visit the abbey and the village.

ROMANS-SUR-ISÈRE

Saint-Antoine-l'Abbaye

Holy Land. On his return he brought back from Constantinople the bones of Anthony the Great, the original "desert father", who lived in the Upper Nile valley. In the Middle Ages this saint owed his popularity as much to the pig who was the daily companion of his hermetic life as to his battles with the devil.

The relics in the church of La Motte-St-Didier, which took the name of St-Antoine, were entrusted by the Bishop of Vienne to Benedictines from Montmajour Abbey. A first monastery was built. Not long after, in 1089, a dreadful epidemic broke out in Dauphiné – St Anthony's fire. It was a sort of gangrene which burnt away the limbs. The saint's relics drew a large crowd of sick and poor people; to help and care for them, a group of young nobles created the Brotherhood of Charity.

A powerful order – In the 13C the brothers managed to supplant the Benedictines. In 1297 the brotherhood became the Hospital Brothers of St Anthony; the Antonine monks founded hospices all over Europe.

The great abbey church of St-Antoine, which took from the 13C to the 15C to build, was visited by popes, emperors from Germany, and kings of France who came to kneel before the relics.

Abbey

Guided visits Apr–Oct daily except Mon and Tue. Nov–Mar, although the church is open all year. 04 76 36 44 46. www.saint-antoine-labbaye.fr.

The entrance to the abbey church is at the top of the village, through the 17C **main entrance gate** (Entrée d'Honneur), now the town hall (Hôtel de Ville), with its glazed mosaic tiles.

Musée de Saint-Antoine-l'Abbaye

Early Mar–Jun and Sept–mid-Nov daily except Tue 2–6pm; Jul–Aug daily except Tue 10.30am–12.30pm, 2:30–6:30pm. 1 May. 04 76 36 40 68. musees.isere.fr.

This museum, located in the monastery's old novitiate, contains works by Jean Vinay (1907-78), a landscape artist from Dauphiné, and thematic exhibitions by his friends from the Paris School, and exhibitions on the Middle Ages and the Antonine Order.

EXCURSIONS

Château de l'Arthaudière

7km/4.3mi to the S by the D 27B. Jul–Aug daily except Tue and Fri 3–7pm; Jun and Sept Sat–Sun 3–7pm. 04 76 38 63 88. www.chateau-arthaudiere.com.

DISCOVERING VALENTINOIS AND THE LOWER DAUPHINÉ

Built on the site of 13C house, the castle (16C–19C) has been altered many times. It now hosts temporary and permanent exhibits. Note the covered wells (18C) and the elegant lantern in the barn.

St-Marcellin
10km/6.2mi to the E on D 27, then D 20 on the right.
This town, where the last Viennese dauphin Humbert II set up his Parliament in the 14C, suffered greatly during the Wars of Religion: besieged twice by the Baron des Adrets, it was subsequently recovered by the Catholics in 1568.
The colourful Saturday market and annual fairs attract a great many locals from Bas-Grésivaudan. The area is known for its namesake soft, round cow's milk cheese. The **Promenade de Joud** affords pretty views of the Isère valley and the Royans, overlooked by the Vercors ramparts.

Chatte
8km/5mi to the SE on D 27.
The most interesting sight in this small village is its **Jardin Ferroviaire** (Apr–Jun and Sept Mon–Fri 2–7pm, Sat–Sun 10.30am–7pm; Jul–Aug daily 10am–7pm; Oct Sat–Sun 10.30am–6.30pm. €11.50 (child 3–12, €8). 04 76 38 54 55. www.jardin-ferroviaire.com) a miniature park complete with paths and 200 plant varieties, cut across by 1km/0.6mi of tiny tracks served by 30 trains. A charming outing for children and parents alike.

La Sône
6km/3.7mi to the S on D 20, then on the D 71.
This village stands in a lush, peaceful setting along the banks of the Isère.
Do not miss the **Jardin des Fontaines-Pétrifiantes** (May–mid-Oct: call or check site for hours. €9.20. 04 76 64 43 42. www.jardin-des-fontaines.com), where petrified water concretions have coated the surrounding relief and objects with glittering crystals. The leafy grounds, featuring around 15 000 plant species, are enhanced by a series of basins and small waterfalls.

The most picturesque way to visit the region is to take a **boat ride** (cruise with commentaries Apr–mid-Oct, check website for times and tariffs. 04 76 64 43 42. www.bateau-a-roue.com) on board the Royans-Vercors paddle-boat, which will enlighten you on the local fauna and flora lying at the foot of the Vercors.

Le Grand Séchoir★
Vinay: 26km/16.3mi E via the D 27 then the D1 092. Apr–Oct Tue–Sun 10am–6pm; Nov–Mar Tue–Sun 2–5.30pm. Jan, 1 May, 25 Dec. €4.50. 04 76 36 36 10. www.legrandsechoir.fr.
This great "drying" farm is dedicated to walnuts, the story of which is told from different angles, both traditional and mythical. The museum boasts a fine collection of nuts of the world and explanations of harvesting techniques.

Notre-Dame-de-l'Osier
26km/16.3mi E via the D 27, then the D 1092. Cross Vinay on the D 22, then turn right onto the D 201.
The present church, built in 1873, incorporates a mosaic of the 1649 miracle: Peter Port-Combet, peasant and Protestant, made the mosaic bleed before witnesses.

ADDRESSES

STAY

Chambre d'Hôte Les Voureys – *Les Voureys.* 04 76 36 41 65. www.les-voureys.fr. *3 rooms.* Three country-style rooms have been created in the old attic of this 150-year-old stone house. Meals are prepared from fresh farm ingredients, and are served in the owners' kitchen.

La Côte-St-André

This small town, a liqueur-producing centre built in a semicircle on a hillside above the Bièvre plain, is the birthplace of *Hector Berlioz (1803–69)* (*see Introduction above*). The Berlioz Festival is held every year during the second fortnight in August in the covered market and parish church of La Côte-St-André.

- **Population:** 5 118.
- **Michelin Map:** 333: E-5.
- **Info:** 5 Place Hector Berlioz. 04 74 20 61 43. www.tourisme-bievre-liers.fr.
- **Location:** NW of Grenoble via A 48.
- **Parking:** There are parking places in the centre.
- **Don't Miss:** The Château Louis XI and the Berlioz Museum.
- **Timing:** Allow 3hrs to walk around town and visit the museum.

SIGHTS

Musée Hector-Berlioz
Rue de la République.
10am–12.30pm, 1.30–6pm: Jul–Aug daily; rest of year daily except Tue.
1 Jan, 1 May and 25 Dec. 04 74 20 24 88. www.musee-hector-berlioz.fr.
This museum is housed in the composer's birthplace, a handsome residence built in the late 17C and restored in 1969.

Château Louis XI
Built in the 13C for Philip of Savoy on a fine defensive site, this castle was designed as both fortress and residence; it suffered extensive damage during the wars in the 16C but was rebuilt thereafter.

Musée des Liqueurs
Mid-Jul–Sept daily except Mon 3–6pm; rest of year Sun and public holidays 3–6pm. Jan–Feb, 14 Jul, 15 Aug, 25 Dec. 04 74 93 38 10. www.cherryrocher.com.
The Cherry Rocher company, which was set up in 1705 in a neo-Classical mansion, offers tours of its plant.
The museum contains a collection of old machinery (fruit press, stills, infusers).

EXCURSIONS

Château de Bressieux
8km/3mi S on D 71, then a narrow road to the left when you leave St-Siméon-de-Bressieux. In the centre of the village, when the road takes a bend, turn left into the small lane (15min on foot return).
Perched high on a promontory overlooking Bressieux village, the castle ruins make an attractive, picturesque sight.a

Marnans
18km/11.3mi to the S via the D 71, then the D 130, Viriville, and the D 156C.
Out in the wilds of the plateau of Chambaran, this humble village has a beautiful Romanesque church of considerable architectural merit.

Roybon
17km/10.6mi S on D 71.
This small town boasts a charming group of buildings with traditional façades characteristic of the area: carved clay and wood decorated with pebbles. This architectural heritage is enhanced by the remains of a medieval rampart.

Ruins of the Château de Bressieux

DISCOVERING VALENTINOIS AND THE LOWER DAUPHINÉ

Lac de Paladru★

Lake Paladru lies in a depression originally formed by a glacier. The lake, mainly supplied by rain and snow, has a tributary at its southern end; the Fure, which flows down to the River Isère. Its beautiful emerald waters form a lovely stretch 6km/4mi long which, during summer months, attracts many watersports enthusiasts and ramblers from Lyon and the Dauphiné region. Anglers will find a wide variety of fish to test their skills, including char and freshwater crayfish. The hillside farms overlooking the lake and Upper Bourbre valley will appeal to those interested in traditional rural architecture: these houses are remarkable for their imposing eaves, sometimes reaching over the barn almost right down to the ground. The walls are made of mud, sometimes combined with shingle.

- **Michelin Map:** 333: G-5.
- **Info:** 230 rue des Bains, 38850 Charavines. 04 76 93 17 60. www.paysvoironnais.info.
- **Location:** Just over 20km/12.5mi to the E of Côte-St-André.
- **Don't Miss:** Take a walk around the lake.
- **Timing:** Allow around 2 hours.

A BIT OF HISTORY

The discovery of a large number of piles emerging at low water level proves the existence of houses built directly on chalk shoals. The variety and abundance of the remains discovered as well as an analysis of pollen contained in the sediment have helped define the nature of the surrounding forest mantle and the daily activities of the inhabitants, who were mostly woodlanders.

"Les Baigneurs"

This farming village underwent two successive phases of occupation around 4 700 years ago, both connected with the Saône-Rhône civilisation. Axe handles, wooden spoons, flint stones, spindle-whorls and charred debris indicate the practice of several crafts as well as burn-beating after deforestation in preparation for cropping.

Colletière

This site to the south reveals a fortified village set up towards the end of the 10C, following a considerable drop in the level of the lake as a result of climate warming. The inhabitants were farmers, stock-breeders and fishermen. The discovery of riding equipment, lances and heavier weapons would indicate that there were knights with regular military duties tasked with protecting the community. This pre-feudal society was governed by laws concerning work and seems to have been more than able to provide for all its needs. The good condition of the dwellings has enabled specialists to reconstruct the originals with accuracy, using a model to represent the three buildings identified.

The lakeside environment has preserved numerous everyday objects, such as leather shoes, textiles, rare wooden musical instruments, games (a complete chess set) and even toy weapons.

AROUND THE LAKE

Musée Archéologique du Lac de Paladru

closed pending construction of new building.

This museum displays the finds of underwater archaeological excavations of the drowned Neolithic and medieval villages.

Tour of the Lake★

It is possible to walk all round the lake *(for details ask at the tourist office in Paladru)*. The Maison du Pays d'Art et d'Histoire de Paladru organises **heritage trails** *(information at the Musée du lac de Paladru in Charavines)*. Two scenic roads – D 50 and D 50D *(which become*

LAC DE PALADRU

Lac de Paladru

D 90) – encircle the lake (15km/9.5mi). They connect the lively resort of **Charavines** on the southern point of the lake to the village of **Paladru** at the other end.

Tour de Clermont

From Charavines, take the footpath along the Fure as far as the D 50 bridge, then the trail waymarked in yellow which goes uphill through fields. After the hamlet of La Grangière, take the path on the left up to the Tour de Clermont.

This 13C pentagonal keep is all that remains of the powerful stronghold of Clermont. The top of the tower has disappeared, and the doorway was knocked out after the original date of construction. This was the residence of one of the oldest families of the Dauphiné, which married into Burgundy to give rise to the Clermont-Tonnerre branch of the family.

EXCURSIONS

Château de Virieu★

7.5km/5mi NW on D 17. 2–6pm: Easter–Jun and Sept–Oct Sat–Sun and public holidays; Jul–Aug Tue–Sun. €8. 04 74 88 27 32. www.chateau-de-virieu.com.

The castle overlooking the Upper Bourbre valley dates from the 11C to 18C, and was restored at the beginning of the 20C; it still looks like a fortress.

Château de Pupetières

South of Virieu.

It was in the rustic setting of the Bourbre valley, at the Château de Pupetières, that Burgundy-born Alphonse de Lamartine (1790–1869), poet and statesman, composed, in 1819, his celebrated poem, *Le Vallon*, published the following year with his *Méditations poétiques*.

ADDRESSES

EAT

Hôtel les Bains – *345 r. Principale, 38850 Charavines (1km/0.6mi S of Lac de Paladru via D 50). 04 76 06 60 20. www.hoteldesbains-charavines.com.* This restaurant's appealing, old-fashioned decor – parquet, bistro furnishings, flowered plates – is most enjoyable. Traditional cuisine and a specialty of: *la friture*, tiny fish fried whole.

Crémieu ★

Crémieu sits in a narrow valley between fairly rugged hillsides and was once a fortress standing guard over one of the gateways into the Dauphiné region; it was also a busy trading centre. Among the local culinary specialities are *sabodets* (a variety of sausage) and *foyesse* (a type of cake).

WALKING TOUR

OLD QUARTER

▶ Start from Porte de la Loi, which was part of the 14C town walls. Go through Porte des Augustins.

Place de la Nation
The name of this square dates back to the French Revolution. In the NE corner is a lever-operated well built in 1823.

Hôtel de Ville
The town hall stands on place de la Nation and is housed in part of what was once an Augustinian friary founded in the 14C.
The former **cloisters** *(cloîtres)* are entered from place de la Nation through a beautiful 18C wrought-iron gate.

Église
This monastery chapel has undergone many changes between 1318 and 1791 and remains of architectural interest.

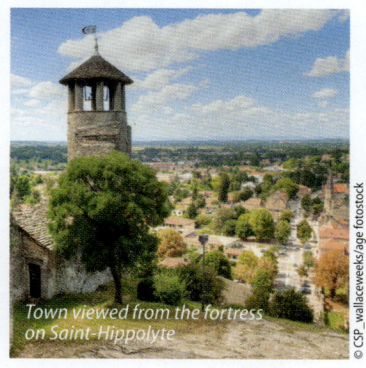

> ▶ **Population:** 3 408.
> ▶ **Michelin Map:** 333: E-3.
> ▶ **Info:** 9 Pl. de la Nation, Crémieu. ☎04 74 90 45 13. www.tourisme-cremieu.fr.
> ▶ **Location:** E of Lyon, and midway between the A 42 and A 43.
> ▶ **Parking:** There are a number of car parks around the edge of town, along the Cours Baron Raverat, for example, but limited parking in the centre.
> ▶ **Timing:** Half a day is sufficient; more if you take the tour.

▶ Take rue Porcherie to the market.

Halles ★
The covered market was built in the 15C. The roof covered in *lauzes* is supported at each end by a thick wall comprising three arches. At the end on the right are the stone troughs over which corn measures were fitted.

▶ Take rue Mulet then turn right onto rue du Four-Banal to Porte Neuve.

Fortified Gateways
Porte Neuve was built in the 16C; **Porte de Quirieu**, which has steps and a central gutter, dates from the 14C.

▶ Head along rue du Marché-Vieux.

On the right, at No. 14, note the 14C Window of the Three Hanged Men (Fenêtre des Trois Pendus).

▶ Carry on up montée St-Laurent.

Château Delphinal
This fortress on St-Laurent hill dates back to the 12C. On St-Hippolyte hill to the left are the remains of a 16C fortified Benedictine priory, including the old clock tower *(a footpath on the left leads to a viewing table)*.

Town viewed from the fortress on Saint-Hippolyte
© CSP_wallaceweeks/age fotostock

CRÉMIEU

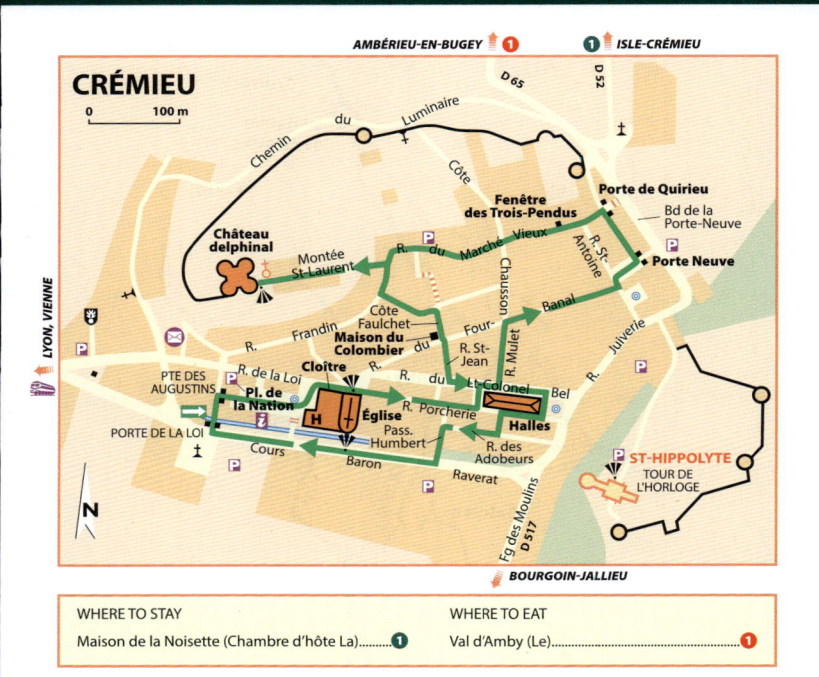

WHERE TO STAY	WHERE TO EAT
Maison de la Noisette (Chambre d'hôte La).........①	Val d'Amby (Le)...①

▶ Return down montée St-Laurent; turn right at bottom; left on côte Faulchet.

At the crossroads with rue du Four-Banal is a 16C house with mullioned windows, the **Maison du Colombier**.

▶ Go down rue St-Jean, rue du Lieutenant-Colonel-Bel and, after skirting the south-west corner of the covered market, rue des Adobeurs.

This street is lined with tiny low houses that used to contain craft workshops, including those of the town's tanners.

▶ Passage Humbert on the left leads to cours Baron-Ravenat.

🚗 DRIVING TOUR

ISLE CRÉMIEU: LAND OF STONE ROOFS
70km/44mi. Allow 5h.

With its cliffs, lakes, *lauze*-covered roofs, fields bordered by standing stones, and country houses, the Île Crémieu region is quite unlike anywhere else.

▶ Leave Crémieu on D 52 NE and follow signs to Optevoz.

As the road runs up the hill, there is a view of Lake Ry and, further up the slope, of the large, modern **Château de St-Julien**.

▶ Beyond the cool Optevoz basin, follow D 52 as far as Surbaix, then turn left on a pleasant little road (D 52B) which runs through a valley full of trees and meadows.

St-Baudille-de-la-Tour
This charming village contains an attractive 15C fortified house, known as the **Maison des Dames**, with a tower covered in *lauzes* and a porch decorated with a coat of arms; it is the headquarters of Roulottes Dauphiné *(see above)*.

LA LAUZE

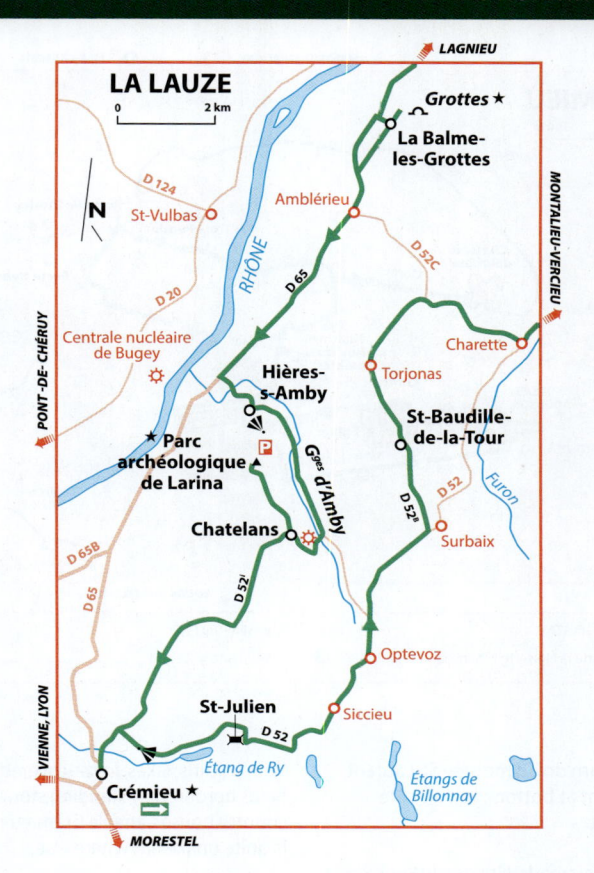

▶ Drive through Torjonas to D 65; turn right towards La Balme-les-Grottes.

La Balme-les-Grottes

Pleasant village known for its grottoes lying at the foot of a cliff marking the edge of the Île Crémieu plateau. Discovered during the Middle Ages, the **Grottes de la Balme**★ (*mid-Feb–Mar 1:30–6pm, Mar–Jun Mon–Fri 1.30–6pm, Sat–Sun and public holidays 10.30am–6pm; Jul–Aug daily 10.30am–6.30pm; Sept daily 1.30–6pm. €10 (child 4–11, €6.50) – prices reduced outside Jul–Aug. 04 74 90 63 76. www.grotteslabalme.com*) are said to have been used in the 18C by the infamous brigand Louis Mandrin and have been described as one of the "seven Wonders of Dauphiné".

The Lake Gallery skirts a series of small **pools**★★ forming terraces of waterfalls before reaching the underground torrent.

▶ Turn back along D 65 then take the first road on the left, to Hières-sur-Amby.

Hières-sur-Amby

This tiny village stands at the end of the Amby valley, at the foot of the Larina plateau. The former rectory is now the **Maison du Patrimoine** (*2–6pm: Oct–Mar Mon–Fri; Apr–Sept daily. 04 74 95 19 10. musee-larina-hieres.fr*), housing objects discovered during archaeological digs at Larina (*see below*) including bones, tools, coins and jewellery. It includes a model of a Merovingian farm. Models, videos and a display retrace the origins of the people living in Île Crémieu, with popular arts, crafts and traditions.

CRÉMIEU

▶ Drive through Hières-sur-Amby, turn left onto D 52A.

Gorges d'Amby
The river twists and turns between rocks covered with scrubby vegetation. There is a view of the 15C Brotel fortified house on the cliff.

▶ A narrow road (right), opposite an old cement works, crosses the River Amby and runs up a hill to Chatelans.

Chatelans
At the centre of the village is the **Musée de la Lauze** (*daily except Mon–Tue 9am–3pm*) which explains the traditional techniques in this region for cutting and fitting the stone slabs.

▶ In the centre of the village, turn right onto a narrow road that runs for 2.5km/1.5mi to the tip of the plateau.

Parc Archéologique de Larina★
The Larina site is bordered by cliffs overlooking the Rhône plain and Amby valley. The existence of human settlements on this site has been evidenced by objects dating from 5000 BCE. At the end of the Roman era and in the early days of the Dark Ages, two large farms existed in succession on this spot. The earlier one (4C and 5C) had a villa at its centre and included a number of farm buildings with stone foundations that are still clearly visible. From the 6C to 8C, a second farm developed around a large stonehouse.

EXCURSIONS
Morestel
21.8km/13.6mi E.
The lovely setting and exceptional luminosity here have attracted countless artists since the mid-19C, namely Corot, Daubigny and Turner; this has earned Morestel the nickname of "Painters' Town." **Auguste Ravier** (1814–95) spent the latter part of his life in Morestel. The D 517 road from Crémieu gives a delightful **view** of the village of Morestel, dominated by its Gothic church and the remains of a 12C square tower.

Maison Ravier
Wed–Sun 2–6pm, only for temporary exhibits (check site) *1 May.* €6. ℘04 74 80 06 80. www.maisonravier.fr.
This handsome residence was home to Auguste Ravier between 1867 and 1895. The house has been bought by the municipality and hosts art exhibitions.

Tour Médiévale
This former keep is all that remains of the 11C citadel overlooking the town. It offers lovely views of the region.

Parc d'Attractions Walibi Rhône-Alpes★
15km/9.5 mi S. Leave Morestel on N 75 towards Grenoble and in Veyrins turn left towards Les Avenières; D 40 on the right leads to the park (signposted). *Jul–Aug daily 10am–6pm/7pm; early Apr–Jun, Sat–Sun and public holidays 10am–5pm/6pm.* €34. ℘04 74 33 71 80. www.walibi-rhone-alpes.fr.
This is one of nine Walibi parks in Europe, found in Belgium, France and the Netherlands. The park is surrounded by lakes, with countless thrill rides and attractions; in summer, a water park opens as well.

ADDRESSES

STAY AND EAT

Chambre d'Hôte La Maison de la Noisette – La Prairie, 38460 Annoisin-Chatelans. ℘04 74 83 86 09. www.maison-noisette.com. *3 rooms.* A warm welcome awaits at this country house; rooms are cheerful, and in summer you might enjoy a barbecue.

Le Val d'Amby – Pl. de la République, 38118 Hières-sur-Amby. ℘04 74 82 42 67. www.hotel-levaldamby.com. *Restaurant closed Sun evening and all day Wed. 13 rooms.* This beautiful stone country house is on the village square. Café area and more comfortable, less noisy, dining room.

DISCOVERING VALENTINOIS AND THE LOWER DAUPHINÉ

Vienne ★★

Vienne, "perched like an altar on the buttresses of the noble Dauphiné", to quote a local poet, is a town of exceptional interest. In a delightful setting★ basking in sunlight reflected from the Rhône, a Gothic cathedral stands next to a Roman temple, while Romanesque cloisters and several ancient churches rub shoulders with an Antique theatre. The charm of "Vienne the Beautiful" of Roman times is enhanced by the charm of "Vienne the Holy", the Christian city. The flower-filled pedestrian precinct, along cours Brillier and around the Hôtel de Ville, is a popular place for a leisurely stroll. Two bridges connect Vienne to the west bank of the Rhône. The old suspension bridge is now used as a footbridge; the modern bridge (1949) has a remarkable central arch. A 15C humpbacked bridge spans the Gère.

- **Population:** 30 122.
- **Michelin Map:** 333: C-4.
- **Info:** 14 Cours Brillier, 38200 VIENNE. 04 74 53 80 30. www.vienne-tourisme.com.
- **Location:** Situated 38km/24ml to the S of Lyon, and 52km/32mi E of St Étienne.
- **Parking:** There are ample parking areas to the south of the town.
- **Don't Miss:** The important Gallo-Roman city of St-Romain-en-Gal; the cathedral of St Maurice, and the Temple of Augustus ad Livia.
- **Timing:** Allow half a day to explore Vienne; maybe an hour to visit St Romain.

A BIT OF HISTORY

Vienne the Beautiful – More than 50 years before Julius Caesar conquered Gaul, the stomping ground of the Allobroges tribe – of which Vienne became the capital in the 1C BCE – was subjugated by the Roman legions. In the absence of a more open site, the town was chosen for its geographical location which was easier to manage than that of Lyon as there was only one river to cross. Public monuments were erected at the foot of Mont Pipet, with private residences and trade and craft establishments on both banks. Vienne soon extended its suburbs beyond the Rhône to the present-day villages of Ste-Colombe and St-Romain-en-Gal. Drapers, leather workers and potters had flourishing businesses and the poet Martial described the town as "Vienne the Beautiful".

Joys and sorrows of "Greater Burgundy" – After the Western Roman Empire was dissolved in 476, and despite political confusion, Vienne remained a centre of artistic achievement: the construction of the church and necropolis of St-Pierre was continued; the foundations were laid for the abbey of St-André-le-Bas. The incessant in-fighting between the Carolingians for Charlemagne's heritage enabled Boson, Count of Vienne, Arles and Provence to proclaim himself "King of Burgundy" at Mantaille Castle in 879.

Vienne, the Holy City – As the distant Holy Roman Emperor only exercised nominal suzerainty, the temporal authority of the bishops, who were also the Counts of Viennois, held sway over the city and over an area of land on the east bank of the Rhône.

Around the abbey of St-André-le-Bas, which was at the height of its power, a large Jewish community plied a thriving trade. Two famous prelates sat on the throne of the "primate of the primates of the Gauls" – **Gui de Bourgogne** (1088–1119), crowned Pope in his own cathedral under the name of Calixtus II, and Jean de Bernin (1218–66), who directed the extensions to the cathedral of St-Maurice based on Gothic principles, ordered restoration of the Roman

Mosaics in the museum, St-Romain-en-Gal

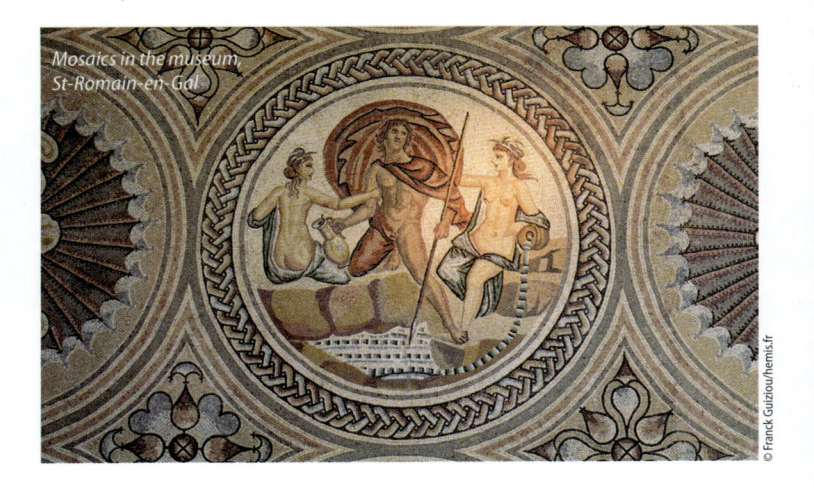

bridge over the Rhône, and built a hospital and the Château de la Bâtie.

Modern times – During the centuries of the Renaissance and the absolute monarchy, Vienne's decline offers a painful contrast with the prosperity of Lyon – commercial activity collapsed and the population dropped by one-fifth between 1650 and the beginning of the 18C. Even the bridge over the Rhône, swept away by flooding in 1651, was not rebuilt until the 19C. A certain industrial rebirth occurred once the Revolution had swept away the Ancien Régime.

ST-ROMAIN-EN-GAL

St-Romain-en-Gal and Ste-Colombe, on the west bank of the Rhône, are located in the Rhône administrative *département* whereas Vienne, opposite, is in the Isère *département*. In Ancient times, these three towns formed a single urban centre.

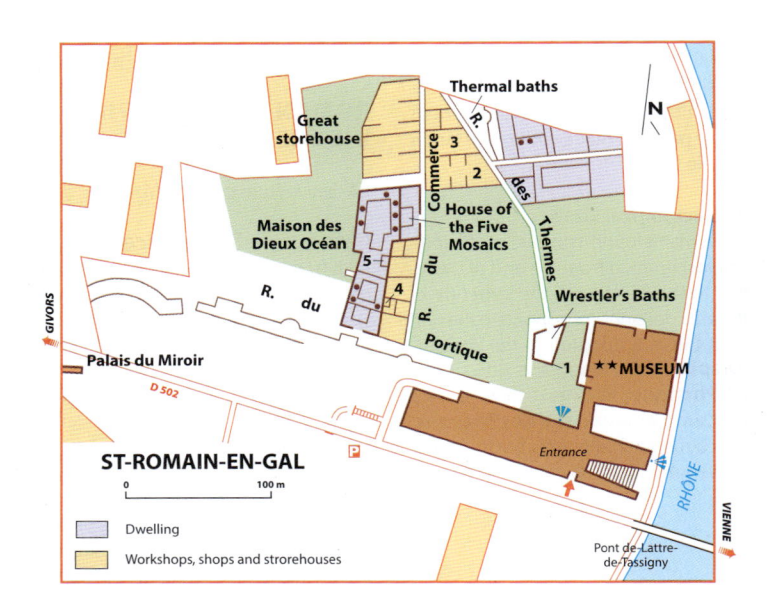

Gallo-Roman City of St-Romain-en-Gal★★

Excavations of the site since 1967 have unearthed an urban district including not only sumptuous villas but also businesses, workshops and *thermae* (hot baths).

Museum★

♿︎ ⏱ *Daily except Mon 10am–6pm (5pm Nov–Jan).* ⏱ *1 Jan, 1 May, 1 Nov, 25 Dec.* 👓 *€6 (no charge on 1st Sun of month).* ☏ *04 74 53 74 01.*
www.musees-gallo-romains.com.

This on-site museum was designed as a showcase presenting the archaeological site on the one hand and the Rhône and Vienne of today on the other. A staircase, situated just before the entrance, leads to a terrace offering a panoramic view of the town, the river and the excavations. The site includes a wealth of workshops and sumptuous residences, the most splendid of all being the **Maison des Dieux Océan** (House of the Ocean Gods).

The **Dieux Océan mosaic**★ invites visitors to discover works of art of the Gallo-Roman period. Vienne was a thriving city under Roman occupation; the Rhône, which played a key role in the town's prosperity, separated the city itself from the more residential district of St-Romain-en-Gal. The main assets of the site are the magnificent floor mosaics, which are as beautiful as the *opus sectile* pavings, made with much larger marble slabs.

Archaeological Site★

The remains found in the area so far indicate occupation from the end of the 1C BCE to the 3C, though the structure of the area does not correspond to the grid layout usually adopted by the Romans. A portico runs along the side of **rue du Portique**, from east to west. **Rue du Commerce** and **rue des Thermes**, which run approximately north–south, converge in the northern part of the site.

Dwellings

At the entrance to the site is the vast Maison des Dieux Océan; its southern entrance is its only connection with the outside. The vestibule had a mosaic floor depicting ocean gods with bearded heads and long flowing hair and marine motifs. To the north of the House of the Ocean Gods is the **House of the Five Mosaics**, named after the different mosaic floors discovered mainly in the peristyle, the *triclinium* and the reception room.

Northeast of the site, on the other side of rue des Thermes, is another residential area with **houses** as well as **baths** following a typically Roman arrangement: *hypocaust, caldarium* (hot room), *tepidarium* (warm room) and *frigidarium* (cold room).

SAINTE-COLOMBE

During Roman times, this suburb was filled with luxurious residences decorated with works of art and mosaics.

Tour Philippe-de-Valois

The tower was built next to the Rhône by Philippe de Valois in 1343, after Ste-Colombe became part of the royal domain.

👣 WALKING TOUR

ROMAN AND CHRISTIAN VIENNE★★

▶ Leave from place St-Maurice.

Cathédrale St-Maurice★★

Built from the 12C to 16C, the cathedral combines both Romanesque and Gothic styles. The patronage of St Maurice is a reminder of the veneration given to martyrs of the Theban Legion in the Burgundian kingdoms.

Doorways

The west front with its three doorways is adorned with fine Flamboyant ornamentation. Although the Wars of Religion deprived it of the statues decorating the niches of the engaged piers and

Temple of Augustus and Livia

tympana, the delightful decoration of the covings has fortunately remained intact.

The late-14C **south doorway** has two covings: the inner row depicts the prophets seated under canopies; the outer row has pairs of musician angels. The **central doorway**, with its cut-off gable, dates from the late 15C. It has three covings with sculptures which are to be read horizontally. The **north doorway**, from the second half of the 15C, is devoted to the Virgin.

Interior

The vast nave, with no transept, reflects a surprising harmony despite its construction over a period of four centuries. The far seven bays enclosing the Gothic nave are Romanesque. Reminiscent of Roman times, the piers are flanked with antique-style pilasters and fluted half-columns; this stage of construction, from the early 12C, is contemporary with or slightly later than the pontificate of Gui de Bourgogne. The four bays of the nave nearest the west front were built in the 15C in pure Gothic style, their engaged columns rising in an unbroken line to the base of the ribbing.

The **Romanesque capitals** form a decorative whole, closely inspired by Antiquity. They feature narrative scenes (right aisle) or whimsical subjects.

In the apse, on the right of the High Altar, stands the **mausoleum** of archbishops Arnaud de Montmorin and Henri-Oswald de La Tour d'Auvergne (1747), by **Michel-Ange Slodtz**; it is one of the finest 18C works in Dauphiné. A splendid Renaissance stained-glass window, the Adoration of the Magi, throws light from the east into the chancel from the right aisle. The stained-glass clerestory windows in the chancel date from the 16C; the central window depicts St Maurice, in armour, with St Peter.

The north aisle has interesting sculptures: between the sixth and seventh chapel, a large 13C bas-relief depicting the meeting of Herod and the Magi is striking for the very noble poses; an amusing detail is the two grotesque heads on either side of Herod, symbolizing his two-facedness – one, turned towards the kings, appears to listen to them attentively while the other, unseen by them, is laughing maliciously.

A covered passageway (north aisle) once connected the cathedral to the cloisters, which no longer exist.

▶ Leave the cathedral along the covered passageway (north aisle).

Outside, the decoration on the door of the north wall combines Romanesque and Gothic elements with Roman fragments. Beneath the pointed arch, delicate griffons and leaves decorate the lintel.

▶ Walk to place du Palais.

VIENNE

WHERE TO STAY

Bontemps (Camping)	❶
Gabetière (La)	❷
Pré Neuf (Chambre d'hôte Le)	❸

WHERE TO EAT

Chamade (La)	❶
Estancot (L')	❷
Medina (La)	❸

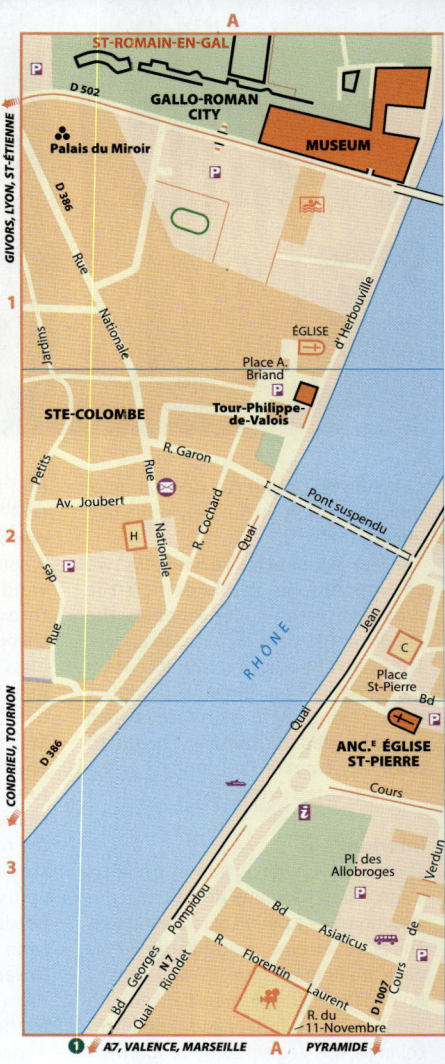

You will be taken aback by the beauty of the Roman temple standing in the centre of the square, pleasantly contrasting with the 18C façades of the houses framing place du Palais.

Temple of Augustus and Livia★★

This is a rectangular building of agreeable proportions. Its dimensions are approximately the same as those of the Maison Carrée, the well-known Roman temple in Nîmes. A row of six Corinthian columns supports the entablature on the façade and the sides; the carved ornamentation is better preserved on the north side. The rear part, which is the oldest, probably dates from the end of the 1C BCE.

The façade, facing east, overlooked the forum. It was rebuilt under the reign of Augustus. Its triangular pediment bore a bronze inscription to the glory of Augustus and Livia, his wife.

▶ Rue des Clercs leads to the church.

Église St-André-le-Bas★

Apart from the lower parts of the east end, the apse, a large part of the southern wall and a few later additions, the church mainly dates to the 12C. The large freestone gable wall provides an unusual effect. The decoration is remarkable, on the whole: piers and colonnettes on the twin openings, small festooned arches ending in consoles bearing expressive masks.

The Salle du Patrimoine (Heritage Gallery) hosts a **standing exhibition** on the theme "The Many Faces of Vienne".

◯ Walk into the southern courtyard flanked by the base of the bell-tower.

The first mask to be seen is poking out an enormous tongue. The nave was originally covered with timber framing; the restoration in 1152 consisted of raising and vaulting it, which required the construction of outside flying but-

DISCOVERING VALENTINOIS AND THE LOWER DAUPHINÉ

tresses and reinforcement of the walls by arches and piers.
The decoration of the fluted pilasters is attributed to Guillaume Martin who signed and dated his work (1152) on the base of the second pier from the right; the most beautiful capitals depict Samson overwhelming the Lion (second pier from the left).

▶ Leave the church through the north door.

Cloître St-André-le-Bas★
Daily except Mon. 1 Jan, 1 May and 11 Nov, 25 Dec. ☎04 74 85 50 42.
These small, trapezoidal cloisters date from the 12C. They have a series of blind arcades, resting alternately on twinned colonnettes and the piers marking the bays. The colonnettes in the south gallery show an element of fantasy: spiral or zigzag fluting, strings of beads or palm leaves with knotted stems.

▶ Take rue de la Table-Ronde to rue Marchande.

At No. 32, there is a beautiful portal with coving and a carved arch stone.

▶ Continue to rue des Orfèvres.

No. 11 has a 15C–16C inner courtyard whereas No. 9 has a beautiful Renaissance façade.

▶ Turn around and take rue du Collège on the right.

Église St-André-le-Haut
This church was once a Jesuit College chapel but was consecrated to St Louis in 1725.

Théâtre Romain★
The Roman theatre was abandoned from the time of Emperor Constantine, in the early 4. It was once one of the largest theatres in Roman Gaul; its diameter is greater than that of the Roman theatre at Orange in Provence and is only 1m less than that of the great theatre of Marcellus in Rome.

▶ Take rue des Célestes, then walk down montée St-Marcel to rue Victor-Hugo and the archaeological gardens.

Jardin Archéologique
A white-stone double archway is the only remaining part of a **portico**, thought in the past to be part of Roman baths; note the fine decorative frieze on the inside.
On the right of the portico is a wall which formed the northern side of a **theatre**.

▶ Take rue Chantelouve, then rue Ponsard to the Musée des Beaux-Arts.

Musée des Beaux-Arts et d'Archéologie
Daily except Mon; Apr–Oct 9.30am–6pm; Nov–Mar 1–5.30pm. 1 Jan, 1 May, 11 Nov, 25 Dec. €3.
☎04 74 78 71 04.
The Fine Arts and Archaeology Museum is housed in a 19C covered market and comprises several collections: prehistoric and Gallo-Roman antiquities; 18C French earthenware; paintings from the 17C and 18C European Schools and the Lyon, Vienne and Dauphiné Schools; and works by the Vienne sculptor, J Bernard (1866–1931).

▶ Cours Romestang, then boulevard de la République, lead to place St-Pierre.

ADDITIONAL SIGHTS
Ancienne Église St-Pierre★
The church of St-Pierre is the oldest building of Christian Vienne, dating to the 5C. The church was the burial place of the bishops of Vienne. St-Pierre, built outside the city walls, was to suffer from the devastations of the Saracens in about 725, followed by those of the Carolingian princes in 882.

Musée de l'Industrie Textile
4 rue Victor Faugier. ☎04 74 78 71 30.
Daily except Mon. €3.
About 30 machines, some of which still function, tell the story of the importance of the textile industry in Vienne since the 13C.

VIENNE

EXCURSIONS

Beauvoir-de-Marc
19km/12mi E. Leave Vienne on D 502. At La Détourbe turn left onto D 53B.
The small 11C–14C **church** with its painted ceiling stands on a hillside from the top of which there is a **panorama★** of the Viennois hills, dominated by the sombre mass of Mont Pilat.

St-Mamert
13km/8mi S. Leave Vienne on N 7 S and turn left onto D 131A.
The **Chapel of St-Mamert**, with its 11C belfry-wall and 17C restored interior, is built on a terrace of pebbles and offers a view of the Pilat mountain range.

Château de Septème
12km/7.5mi E on D 502 and D 75.
The 14C–16C castle is not far from Septème village. Overlooking the inner courtyard are Renaissance loggias on two storeys and a colonnaded gallery. The castle is surrounded by curtain walls that have kept many of their loopholes, and part of the watch-path.

ADDRESSES

STAY

Camping Bontemps – *38150 Vernioz (19km/12mi S of Vienne via N 7, D 131 and D 37). 04 74 57 83 52. www.camping-lebontemps.com. Open mid-Apr–Sept. Reservations recommended. 100 sites. Food service.* Tourism and sports are on this campground's programme, with horseback riding, mountain biking and swimming facilities.

Chambre d'Hôte Le Pré Neuf – *9 r. des Guillemottes. 04 74 31 70 11. http://aupreneuf.e-monsite.com. 3 rooms.* On the edge of town, this 19C house has a nice garden; the rooms are furnished with homely items.

La Gabetière – *269 Le Logis-Neuf, 38780 Estrablin. 04 74 58 01 31. www.la-gabetiere.com. 11 rooms.* A beautiful 16C mansion surrounded by a park. Swimming pool.

EAT

La Chamade – *24 r. Juiverie. 04 74 85 30 34. Closed Sun.* The decor of white walls, yellow tablecloths and indirect lighting is simple, the service efficient and the prices quite affordable.

L'Estancot – *4 r. de la Table-Ronde. 04 74 85 12 09. Closed Sun–Mon, Tues lunch.* Try *criques*, the delicious Ardéchois potato pancake, featured alongside vegetables, foie gras or prawns.

La Medina – *71 r. de Bourgogne. 04 74 53 51 35. www.restaurantmarocain-lamedina.fr. Closed Mon, Sun only on reservation.* Moroccan cuisine, decor and furnishings.

ON THE TOWN

Bar du Temple – *5 pl. du Gén.-de-Gaulle. 04 74 31 94 19. Daily except Sun and public holidays 7am–1am.* This is **the** café that everyone who's anyone in Vienne knows about. Its best feature is the superb terrace at the foot of the Temple d'Auguste et de Livie.

SHOPPING

Markets – On Saturday mornings, the streets of the city centre, from the banks of the Rhône to the Jardin de Cybèle, overflow with market stalls. This is the perfect time to shop for a few bottles of Côte-Rôtie, a delicious Côtes-du-Rhône wine made in the region.

THEATRE

Théâtre de Vienne – *4 r. Chantelouve. 04 74 85 00 05. http://theatredevienne.com.* Built in the early 18C, when Marivaux, Goldoni and Beaumarchais prevailed, this theatre exudes history and charm. Events of all genres are staged here, including drama, classical and pop music, dance, opera and children's shows.

INDEX

A

Abbatiale St-Austremoine, Issoire 247
Abbaye
 de Féniers 157
Abbaye de Sept-Fons............... 303
Abbaye Notre-Dame-des-Dombes ...361
Accessibility........................35
Agriculture.........................55
Aigueperse 267
Aiguèze........................... 447
Ainay-le-Château.................. 289
Air Travel..........................36
Albepierre-Bredons 181
Albon..............................475
Allanche 159
Allègre............................212
Ambert 238
Ambierle.......................... 384
Anglards-de-Salers.................183
Annonay...........................419
Antignac......................... 189
Antraigues-sur-Volane............ 432
Apcher.............................158
Apchon 186
Apollinaris, Sidonius.......... 60, 124
Arboretum de Balaine 280
Arbresle, L'....................... 377
Architecture 67
Ardèche Gorge, following.......... 446
Ardes-sur-Couze 156
Arlanc 241
Arronnes.......................... 306
Artense, L'........................153
Artonne 268
Aubenas..........................437
Aubière...........................111
Auriac-l'Église.....................159
Aurillac...........................165
Aurillac, Châtaigneraie and
 Monts du Cantal 162, 164, 186
Auvergne, Nature 84
Auvers........................... 202
Auzon 248
Avalanches 24
Aveize 377
Avenas............................374
Aven de la Forestière 450
Aven de Marzal.................... 444
Aven d'Orgnac 448
Avèze.............................152
Ayat-sur-Sioule..................... 270
Aydat.............................124

B

Bagnols........................ 155, 375
Balazuc........................... 438
Balcon des Templiers 445
Balme-les-Grottes, La 484
Banks..............................47
Banne d'Ordanche, La 150
Barjac............................ 449
Barrage
 de Bort 153
 de Grandval...................... 199
 de la Tache....................... 383
 d'Enchanet 168
 de St-Étienne-Cantalès................. 168
 de Villerest......................384
 du Rouchain 383
Basic Information 45
Basilique Notre-Dame-du-Port.......102
Basilique St-Julien, Brioude 215
Bassignac 189
Bastide-Puylaurent, La 440
Bathernay.........................476
Beauchastel...................... 425
Beaujeu...........................374
Beaujolais......................... 370
Beaujolais Wine 371
Beaumont.........................361
Beauvoir-de-Marc................. 493
Beauzac 410
Bed and Breakfast..................40
Bégude-de-Mazenc, La 460
Bellenaves 305
Belleville......................... 372
Belvédère
 de Commelle-Vernay................... 384
 de Gaud 443
 de la Cathédrale.................. 445
 de la Coutelle 445
 de la Madeleine 444
 de la Maladrerie.................. 445
 de la Sauveté 388
 de Mallet 199
 du Bois de Laoul 451
 du Colombier 447
 du Ranc-Pointu 447
 du Serrede Tourre 443
Belvédère de Veysset 161
Belvédères
 d'Autridge 443
 de Gournier...................... 443
Berlioz, Hector 466
Berry, Jean de 61
Bessat, Le 412
Besse-et-Saint-Anastaise 143

Besson	280
Bidon	444
Billom	254
Blesle	257
Boat travel	19
Boffres	426
Boitier, Le	375
Bort-les-Orgues	153
Boudes	250
Bouligneux	360
Bourbon L'Archambault	282
Bourbonnais	273
Bourboule, La	149
Bourg-Argental	412
Bourg-de-Péage	474
Bourg-en-Bresse	352
Bourget, Paul	124
Bourg-St-Andéol	450
Bouschet de Pranles, Le	430
Breakdowns (vehicle)	38
Bressolles	281
Brioude	215
Brugheas	299
Buellas	355
Buron	252
Burzet	433
Business Hours	45
Bus Travel	37
Butte de Montpensier	267
Butte d'Usson	249
Buxières-les-Mines	285

C

Calendar of Events	30
Camping	40
Car Rental	39
Cascade	
de Cornillou	160
de Faillitoux	178
de la Pisserotte	308
de la Roucolle	171
de la Vernière	151
de Liadouze	176
du Plat à Barbe	151
du pont d'Aptier	186
du Ray-Pic	433
du Sartre	187
Cathédrale Notre-Dame-de-l'Assomption	103
Cathédrale Notre-Dame, Le-Puy-en-Velay	206
Caving	22
Centre Montagnard Cap Guéry	134
Cérilly	290
Cervières	387
Ceyrat	111
Chaise-Dieu, La	242
Chalain-d'Uzore	395
Chalamont	361
Chalmazel	392
Chamalières	110
Chamaret	463
Chambéon	389
Chambles	407
Chambonas	439
Chambonie, La	392
Chambost-Allières	374
Champeix	146
Champs-sur-Tarentaine-Marchal	154
Chantelle	305
Chantmerle-les-Blés	476
Chapeauroux	224
Chapelle	
de la Font-Sainte	187
de Vassivière	138, 144
du Val-des-Nymphes	462
Notre-Dame-de-Laval	386
Notre-Dame-de-Montcham	454
St-Andéol	476
Ste-Marie-des-Chazes	222
Charnay	375
Charroux	304
Chartreuse de Port-Ste-Marie	272
Chas	255
Chastel-Merlhac	189
Chastreix	138
Château	
d'Alleuze	200
d'Anjony	191
d'Arginy	372
d'Aulteribe	236
d'Auzers	189
de Beauvoir	303
de Boulogne	433
de Branzac	190
de Bressieux	479
de Busséol	253
de Busset	298
de Chareil	305
de Chavaniac-Lafayette	219
de Chazeron	264
de Chouvigny	269
de Corcelles	373
de Cordès	136
de Cornillon	407
de Couzan	390
de Davayat	265
d'Effiat	268

495

INDEX

de Flèchères 358
de Fourchaud 280
de Goutelas 393
de la Bastie-d'Urfé 389
de l'Arthaudière 477
de la Vigne 188
de Lespinasse 217
de Mantaille 475
de Mauzun 256
de Messilhac 178
de Montgilbert 306
de Montmorin 255
de Murol 147
de Parentignat 249
de Paulhac 217
de Pesteils 179
de Pierre-Gourde (panorama) 427
de Pupetières 481
de Rochebaron 409
de Rochelambert 212
de Rochemaure 459
de Sédaiges 175
de Seganges 279
de Septème 493
d'Essalois 407
de St-Vidal 212
de Thoury 303
de Vachères 225
de Val 155
de Ventadour 436
de Villeneuve 251
de Virieu 481
de Vollore 238
du Cambon 190
du Chassan 199
d'Urfé 387
du Riau 280
Château de la Batisse 112
Château de Tournoël 115
Château d'Opme 111
Château et Jardins de la Chassaigne . 234
Châteaugay 116
Châteauneuf-les-Bains 270
Châteaux
d'eau de Philolaos 471
Chatelans 485
Châtel-de-Neuvre 280
Châtel-Guyon 264
Châtel-Montagne 308
Châtelperron 302
Châtillon 375
Châtillon-sur-Chalaronne 358
Chatte 478
Chaudes-Aigues 200

Chaudeyrolles 227
Chauriat 255
Chavroches 302
Chazay-d'Azergues 375
Cheire d'Aydat 121
Chemicals 55
Chénas 373
Chénelette 374
Chessy 375
Cheylade 187
Children, activities 27
Chilhac 219
Cinematograph 63
Cirque de Valcivières 240
Cirque du Falgoux 174
Clansayes 463
Classical Period 74
Claux, Le 187
Claveisolles 374
Clermont 99
Clermont Cathedral 73
Clermont-Ferrand 96
Clermont-Ferrand and monts Dôme ... 94
Coach Travel 37
Cognat 299
Col
de Cère 172
de la Chaumoune 159
de la Chavade 436
de la Croix de Bauzon 434
de la Croix-Morand 134
de la Croix-St-Robert 137
de Legal 175
de l'Escrinet 433
de Meyrand 435
des Supeyres 240
du Béal 237, 392
du Grand-Bois 406
Collandres 186
Coltines 197
Communications 45
Condat 160
Condrieu 413
Consulates 34
Cordieux 361
Corent 253
Costume 53
Côte-St-André, La 479
Coudes 252
Courpière 237
Couthon, Georges 63
Couvent d'Éveux 377
Credit and Debit Cards 47
Crémieua 482

Crest.	464	Côte Roannaise	382
Crest, Le	112	Couze Valleys, The	145
Crêt de la Perdrix	412	Crest Road	175
Crêt de l'Œillon	412	Dauphiné d'Auvergne	249
Crête de Blandine	434	Discovering La Limagne	267
Croix de Cheules	176	Former Mining Country	288
Croix-du-Sud, La	383	From the the Allier Gorges to the Deves	222
Crops	56	Gorges and Castles	269
Crozet, Le	382	Gorges de l'Alagnon	256
Cruas	431	Gorges de la Maronne	190
Cruises	20	Grangent Dam	407
Cunlhat	240	Haut-Allier and Sénouire Valley	217
Currency	46	Isle Crémieu: Land of Stone Roofs	483
Cusset	298	La Bresse	355
Customs	34	L'Artense	154
		Lauze Country	225
D		Lava Trail, The	124
d'Aurillac, Gerbert	65	La Voulte-sur-Rhône Round Tour	425
d'Auvergne, Henri de La Tour	65	Le Haut-Forez	397
Défilé de Donzère	454	Le Mont Mouchet	202
Dent de Rez	451	L'Enclave des Papes	464
Departmental tourist offices	33	Les Belvéderes	396
Désaignes	428	Les Boutieres	428
d'Estaing, Valéry Giscard	65	Les Collines	476
Dieulefit	460	Les Combrailles	263
Disabled Information	35	Les Margarides	235
Documents	37	Les Villages du Tricastin	462
Dombes, La	358	Livradois to the Dore	240
Domeyrat	220	Lyon Round Trip	377
Dompierre-sur-Veyle	360	Massif du Meygal and Pays des Sucs	429
Donzère	454	Medieval Towns	459
Dore-l'Église	241	Montagne and Haute Vallée de L'Ardeche	435
Drinking and Driving	38	Monts Dôme	115
Driving in France	37	Mountain Tour	374
Driving Tours	12	Northern Slopes	134
Along the Grandval Reservoir	199	Orgues de Bort	153
Alpine Pastures	156	Overlooking the Rhône	459
Approaching the Livradois	248	Pas de Peyrol	173
Around Vichy	298	Plateau des Gras	451
Beaujolais Vineyards	371	Plateau d'Orgnac	449
Belvédère de Veysset and Forêt de Maubert	161	Plateau du Coiron	430
Besbre Valley	302	Puy de Sancy	134
Bocage Bourbonnais	282	Puys Mountains	120
Bourbon Countryside	305	Queuille Meander	271
Canal de Berry	288	Rhue Gorge to Gentiane Country	160
Châteaux in the Bourbonnais Area	279	Route du Lioran	171
Chestnut Grove Country	169	Route Panoramique	442
Cheylade Valleysand Gentiane Country	186	Sancy Range, The	137
Churches of the Northern Plateaux	188	St-Étienne to Condrieu	412
Col de l'Escrinet	433	The Belvederes	406
Combraille Bourbonnais	285	The Cere to the Maronne	168
Corniche de L'Eyrieux	426	The Country South of Clermont	110
Corniche du Vivarais Cévenol	440	The Hills of Drôme	465

INDEX

    The Massif du Tanargue 434
    The Planeze 200
    Tour of the Lakes 360
    Upper Goul Valley and Carladès......... 178
    Val d'Allier 255
    Vallée de la Borne 212
    Vallée de la Jordanne................. 176
    Vallée de L'Ance....................... 409
    Vallée de L'Ander...................... 197
    Vallée de la Sianne 159
    Vallée de la Volane and Vallée
       de la Bourges 432
    Vallée de l'Onzon and Vallée de l'Aix 386
    Vallée du Sichon, La 306
    Via Col de Béal 390
    Via Col des Supeyres 393
    Villages du Vivarais Cévenol 439
    Volcanoes around Clermont 109
    Western Sologne Region 292
Driving TOurs
    Gorges Roannaises de la Loire 384
Drivng Tours
    Banks of the Saône.................... 346
    Castles and Wine-Growing Villages 252
    Défilés de L'Ardeche................... 438
    Eastern Sologne Region 290
    La Dore to Monts Forez................. 236
    Le Pays des Pierres-Dorées 375
    Livradois Chateaux..................... 255
Duchere, La 345

E

Ébreuil............................ 269
Écharmeaux, Les 374
Ecomusée de la Margaride, L'........ 202
Écomusée des Terrasses, à La
   Charayre 426
Economy........................... .54
Église
    d'Agonges 283
    d'Arlet 219
    d'Aubazat........................... 219
    d'Autry-Issards..................... 283
    de Biozat 304
    de Blassac 218
    de Bredons 181
    de Champdieu 394
    de Chanteuges..................... 219
    de Colamine-sous-Vodable......... 250
    de Colombier 288
    de Franchesse.................... 282
    de Job 237
    de Jou-sous-Monjou 178
    de Mailhat 249
    de Meillers....................283, 285
    de Peyrusses 219
    de Roffiac 197
    de St-Cirgues 219
    de St-Désiré 288
    de St-Illide 191
    de St-Menoux....................... 283
    de St-Pardoux..................... 138
    d'Étroussat 305
    du Vigean......................... 188
    d'Ygrande 283
    Notre-Dame-de-Prévenchère.......... 435
    Prieurale St-Pierre-et-St-Paul 284
    St-Hilaire-la-Croix 264
Égliseneuve-d'Entraigues..............159
Electricity 46
Embassies 34
Embassies and Consulates 33
Emergencies 46
Ennezat........................... 268
Entraygues.........................169
Entry Requirements 33
Éperon de Pourcheyrolles........... 435
Espaly-St-Marcel 212
Espinasse 200
Essertines-en-Châtelneuf............. 393
Estables, Les 226
Estivareilles 398
Étang de Pirot..................... 290
Étang de Saloup................... 292
Étang de St-Bonnet................. 291

F

Famous local figures.................64
Farges 146
Fay-sur-Lignon 428
Ferme aux Crocodiles, La 462
Ferme de Bourlatier 226
Ferme des Bois Noirs, La 241
Feurs 388
Firminy 406
Fishing 22
Fleurie 373
Flights 36
Flora and Fauna 89
Fontaine d'Amboise 99
Fontaine Viljot 290
Fontanges 175
Food and Drink....................57
Forest, Fernand 65
Forêt de l'Assise 308
Forêt de Maubert..................161
Forêt de Mazan 435
Forêt des Colettes 305

498

Forêt de Tronçais 289
Forêt du Meygal.................... 429
Fournols 241
French Words and Phrases 42
Freycenet-la-Tour 227
Frugières-le-Pin.................... 221
Funiculaire du Capucin 140
Futaie Colbert...................... 291

G

Gannat 304
Garde-Adhémar, La................. 462
Gentiane Express....................185
Gerbier-de-Jonc 226
Getting There and Getting Around 36
Givors 346
Glozel 306
Godivelle, La 158
Golf 23
Gorge de la Sainte-Baume 451
Gorges
    d'Amby 485
    d'Avèze........................ 152
    de Chouvigny.................. 269
    de la Borne 434
    de l'Alagnon 172
    de la Maronne 191
    de l'Ander..................... 197
    de l'Ardèche 442
    de la Rhue 160
    de la Truyère 198
    d'Enval 264
Gorges and Site de Montfermya......123
Gorges de Ceyrat....................111
Gorges de la Sioule 269
Gorges de la Truyère.................198
Gothic period 73
Gouffre d'Enfer......................412
Government 54
Grand Séchoir, à Vinay, Le........... 478
Grands-Murcins, Les............... 383
Grand Testavoyre................... 429
Gras 451
Gravières 440
Gregory of Tours 81
Grézieu-la-Varenne................. 378
Grézolles.......................... 388
Grignan........................... 461
Grillon 464
Grotte de la Madeleine 444, 445
Grotte des Fées 307
Grottes de Jonas 145
Grottes de Montbrun 430
Gué de la Chaux 308

Guizay, view 406

H

Hang-gliding.......................21
Hauterives.........................475
Health 34
Helicopters 21
Hérisson 288
Hières-sur-Amby 484
Highway Code 38
Hiking 23
History............................59
Hostels 40
Hostun 474
Hot-air balloons...................21
Hotels 39
Huriel............................ 288

I

Île de Grangent..................... 407
ILOA "Les Rives de Thiers"........... 235
Intendants 63
International Visitors 33
Introduction 51
Issoire 247

J

Jacquard...........................64
Jaligny............................ 302
Jarnioux 376
Jastres Panorama 438
Jaujac............................ 434
Jenzat 304

K

Karting 24
Know Before You Go.................32

L

Labastide-de-Virac 449
Labeaume 439
La Bourboule 149
La Bresse and La Dombes........... 350
Labyrinthes, Les....................475
Lac
    Chambon...................... 147
    Chauvet 138
    de Guéry...................... 134
    de la Landi................... 155
    de Lastioulles 155
    de Montcineyre 145
    d'Issarlès 225
    du Bouchet 223
    Pavin 144

INDEX

Servière 136
Lac d'Aydat 124
Lac de Paladru 480
La Chaise-Dieu 242
La Côte-St-André 479
La Dombes 358
Lamastre 428
Langeac 219
Language 52
Lapalisse 301
Lapeyrouse 361
La-Roche 385
Laroquebrou 168
L'Artense 153
Laussac 201
Lavaudieu 220
Lavoine 307
Lavoûte-Chilhac 218
Le Lioran 172
Le Monastier-sur-Gazeille .. 224, 225, 227
Le Mont-Dore 139
Lent 360
Léotoing 257
Le-Puy-en-Velay 205
Les Monts du Cantal 171
Les Vans 439
L'Hôpital-sous-Rochefort 386
Light aircraft and gliders 21
Limagne, Pays des Combrailles, Gorges de la Sioule 258
Lioran, Le 172
Lisseuil 270
Literature 81
Livradois-Forez Tourist Train 239
Londres, Albert 65
L'Oppidum des Côtes de Clermont .. 109
Lumière brothers 63
Luriecq 396
Lyon
    Fourvière Hill 324, 325, 327
    Getting Around 314
    Historic Textile Workers District ... 335
    Introduction 309
    La Croix-Rousse 335
    La Presqu'île and its Squares ... 328, 329, 331, 333
        Left Bank 340
        Le Plateau 339
        Musée des Beaux-Arts 330
        Musée des Tissus 334
        Outskirts 344
        Saint-Just Quarter 327
        St-Georges District 323
        St-Jean and St-Paul Districts ... 318
    The Montées 324
    The Part-Dieu District 341
    Touring the Town 314
    Vieux Lyon 318

M

Macintosh, Charles 98
Mail 46
Maison
    de Montagne 187
    des Fleurs d'Auvergne 134
Maisons du Parc 126
Malicorne 288
Mandailles 176
Manoir de Veygoux 264
Marcenat 158
Marcolès 169
Marcy 375
Marcy-L'Étoile 345
Mareugheol 251
Maringues 268
Marnans 479
Marols 397
Marquis de La Fayette 65
Marsac-en-Livradois 241
Marsat 116
Martinanches, Les 256
Massiac 197, 256
Massif du Sancy 133
Mauriac 188
Maurs 169
Mayres 436
Mazan-l'Abbaye 435
Mazerat-Aurouze 220
Maziaux et Bigorre 429
Méandre de Queuille 271
Media 52
Menat 270
Menet 187
Menu 41
Messager, André 65
Messeix 152
Metal working 54
Meysse 431
Mézenc Massif, The 227
Mézilhac 432
Michelin, André 65
Michelin brothers 99
Michelin, Édouard 65
Michelin Grand Prix 119
Microlights 21
Mineral Springs 85
Mirabel 430
Miremont 272

Miribel... 345
Moingt... 394
Monastere Royal de Brou... 352
Monastier-sur-Gazeille, Le . 224, 225, 227
Money... 46
Monistrol-d'Allier... 223
Monistrol-sur-Loire... 409
Montagne Bourbonnais... 306
Montagne de la Serre... 124
Montagny... 381
Montaigut-le-Blanc... 146
Montarcher... 397
Montbrison... 394, 395
Mont Brouilly... 373
Mont-Dore, Le... 139
Montélier... 471
Montélimar... 458
Montellier, Le... 361
Montet, Le... 285
Montferrand... 105
Montgolfier brothers... 64
Monthieux... 361
Montlosier Castle... 121
Montluçon... 286
Montmelas-St-Sorlin... 371
Mont Mézenc... 226
Monton... 112
Montpeyroux... 253
Montpezat-sous-Bauzon... 435
Montrevel-en-Bresse... 357
Montrond-les-Bains... 395
Montsalvy... 169
Monts Dôme... 117
Monts Dore, Artense and Cézallier... 127, 128
Monts du Cantal, Les... 171
Monts du Cézallier... 156
Monts du Forez... 390
Monts du Lyonnais... 377
Montségur-sur-Lauzon... 463
Montselgues... 441
Montuel... 364
Montverdun... 389
Morestel... 485
Motor Insurance... 37
Moudeyres... 227
Moulin de Vignal à Apinac... 398
Moulin, Jean... 66
Moulin Richard de Bas... 239
Moulins... 276
Mountain Biking... 22
Mourjou... 169
Mours-St-Eusèbe... 474
Moussages... 189

Mozac... 263
Mulatière, La... 345
Murat... 180
Murat-le-Quaire... 150
Musée
  de la Bresse... 355
  de la Mine de Saint-Pierre-la-Palud... 377
  distillerie de la Lavande, à Saint-Remèze 451
Musée d'Archéologie Bargoin... 108
Musée d'Art Roger-Quilliot... 109
Musée de l'Automobile
  Henri-Malartre... 346
Musée de l'École 1900... 240
Musée de Valence, Art et Archéologie 470
Musée du Canal de Berry... 288
Musée rural de la Sologne
  Bourbonnaise... 303
Mus'Energie, Ambert... 239
Muséum d'histoire naturelle Henri-Lecoq
  ... 108

N

Nadaillat... 124
Nature... 82
Nature Parks and Reserves... 20
Néris-les-Bains... 288
Neuilly-en-Donjon... 301
Neuville-sur-Saône... 346
Neyrac-les-Bains... 436
Noirétable... 387
Nonette... 249
Notre-Dame-d'Aiguebelle... 460
Notre-Dame-de-la-Neylière... 378
Notre-Dame-de-l'Osier... 478
Notre-Dame de Nièglès... 436
Notre-Dame-des-Neiges, trappe... 440
Notre-Dame-du-Château... 191
Novacelles... 241
Noyant-d'Allier... 285

O

Oingt... 376
Olliergues... 237
Olloix... 126
Orchards... 56
Orcival... 136
Outdoor Fun... 21

P

Paragliding... 21
Parc Archéologique de Larina... 485
Parc d'Attractions Walibi Rhône-Alpes 485
Parc des Oiseaux... 359

501

INDEX

Parc Européen du Volcanisme Vulcania....123
Parc Fenestre....150
Parc le Pal....303
Parc naturel régional des Volcans d'Auvergne....126
Parc Naturel Régional du Pilat....411
Parc Naturel Régional Livradois-Forez 230
Parc Salva Terra à Haute-Rivoire....377
Parc Zoologique et d'Attractions Touroparc....373
Parking Regulations....38
Pascal, Blaise....65, 81, 97, 118
Pas de Cère....171
Pas de Peyrol....174
Pays de Thiers and Livradois-Forez....228
Payzac....440
Pébrac....219
Pélussin....413
Pérouges....362
Perrier....250
Pétanque....456
Pets, travelling with....35
Pic de Chenavari....459
Pic du Capucin....141
Pierre Charbonnière....308
Pierre-sur-Haute....392
Pilat, Le....410
Place de Jaude....99
Plaine du Forez....388
Plantay, Le....361
Plateau d'Ally....217
Plateau de Chanturgue....109
Plateau de Gergovie....111
Plateau de la Danse....407
Plateau de la Verrerie....382
Pleaux....184
Plomb du Cantal....172
Poët-Laval, Le....460
Polignac....213
Polminhac....171
Pommiers....386
Pompidou, Georges....65
Pont-d'Arc....443
Pont de Tréboul....201
Pont-de-Vaux....356
Pont-de-Veyle....355
Pont-du-Château....255
Pontgibaud....123
Population....52
Pouilly-lès-Feurs....389
Pourchères....433
Prades....223
Prades, Les....158

Privas....430
Public Holidays....48
Puy
   de Bessolles....148
   de la Tache....141
   de Mazeyres....146
   de Montchal....144
   du Roc....308
   d'Usson....249
   d'Ysson....250
   Ferrand....144
   Griou....173
   Mary....174
   Saint-Romain....253
   St-Ambroise....302
   St-Mary....188
   Violent....175
Puy Basin, The....206
Puy Chopine....122
Puy de Dôme, Le....117, 118
Puy de Gravenoire....121
Puy de la Vache....121
Puy de Pariou....122
Puygiron....459

R

Rail Travel....36
Regional Parks....399
Regional tourist offices....32
Region Today, The....52
Registration Papers (vehicle)....37
Renaison....383
Renaux, Eugène....119
Rental Cars....39
Resistance Movement....66
Rhône Valley, Nature....82
Rhues, The....161
Richerenches....464
Riding Tours....24
Riom....260
Riom-ès-Montagnes....185
Roanne....381
Roc Courlande....138
Rochecolombe....438
Rocher
   de Borbes....235
   de Carlat....179
   de la Volpie....237
   de Rochefort....383
   de Ronesque....179
   de Sampzon....439
   des Pendus....178
   Saint-Vincent....307
Rocher de l'Aigle....138

Rochetaillée 412
Roche Vendeix 151
Rock-climbing 25
Roffiac. 196
Rolle, Michel 65
Romanèche-Thorins. 373
Romanesque period. 68
Romans-sur-Isère. 472
Rond de Buffévent 291
Rond de la Cave 291
Rond de Meneser. 292
Ronzières 250
Royat 112
Roybon 479
Rozier-Côtes-d'Aurec 397
Rudez 176
Ruins of Rochebonne. 428
Ruoms. 439
Ruynes-en-Margeride 202

S

Saignes 189
Sail-sous-Couzan. 390
Saint-André-de-Bâgé. 356
Saint-Cernin 190
Saint-Cirgues-en-Montagne 435
Saint-Clément. 307
Saint-Cyr-sur-Menthon 355
Sainte-Colombe. 488
Saint-Front. 429
Saint-Hilaire-Cusson-la-Valmitte 397
Saint-Jean-Soleymieux 397
Saint-Laurent-les-Bains. 440
Saint-Montan 451
Saint-Nizier-de-Fornas. 397
Saint-Pal-de-Chalencon 398
Saint-Symphorien-sur-Coise 378
Saint-Trivier-de-Courtes 357
Salelles, Les 440
Salers. 182
Salles-Arbuissonnas-en-Beaujolais . . .371
Sandrans 360
Sarcouy, Le Grand 122
Saugues 222
Saurier. 146
Sauvain. 393
Sauvetat, La. 253
Sauviat 237
Sauxillanges 249
Savigny 377
Sceautres 430
Sea Travel. 36
Serre de Pepeyrier. 427
Signal de St-Bonnet 371

Signal du Luguet 158
Singles. 152
Site de Cotteughes et Preydefont 187
Site de la Chapelle Ste-Madeleine . . . 257
Site des Hurlevents 298
Site du Château d'Alleuze 197
Skiing. 25
Smoking. 48
Sône, La 478
Source du Dôme 300
Sources Pétrifiantes de Gimeaux. 265
Souvigny 284
Speed limits. 38
Sport 52
St-Agrève 428
St-Alyre-ès-Montagne 158
St-Amand-Roche-Savine. 240
St-Amour-Bellevue 374
St-André-d'Apchon 382
St-Anthème. 393
St-Antoine-l'Abbaye. 476
St-Arcons-d'Allier. 219
STAY
St-Baudille-de-la-Tour 483
St-Bonnet-le-Château 396
St-Bonnet-Tronçais 292
St-Chamant 190
St-Chamond 406
St-Christophe-d'Allier 224
St-Clément. 428
St-Dier-d'Auvergne. 256
St-Donat-sur-l'Herbasse 476
Stebbing Oak 291
Ste-Croix-en-Jarez. 413
Ste-Eulalie 226
St-Étienne 401
St-Étienne and Le Pilat. 399, 400
St-Étienne-de-Choimeil 186
St-Étienne-de-Vicq 299
Stevenson, Louis 225
St-Floret 146
St-Flour. 194
St-Flour, Sanflorain and Margeride
   du Cantal. 192
St-Germain-Laval. 386, 387
St-Germain-Lembron. 251
St-Germain-l'Herm 241
St-Gervais-d'Auvergne. 271
St-Gervazy 257
St-Haon. 224
St-Haon-le-Châtel 384
St-Ilpize. 218
St-Jacques-des-Blats. 172
St-Jean-de-Pourcharesse 440

503

INDEX

St-Jean-des-Vignes 375
St-Julien 371
St-Julien-Chapteuil 429
St-Julien-du-Serre 433
St-Julien-le-Roux 426
St-Just-St-Rambert 407
St-Laurent-du-Pape 425
St-Laurent-Rochefort 387
St-Mamert 493
St-Marcel-de-Félines 385
St-Marcellin 478
St-Martin-d'Ardèche 447
St-Martin-Valmeroux 190
St-Maurice-de-Gourdans 364
St-Maurice-sur-Loire 385
St-Michel-d'Aiguilhe, Le Puy-en-Velay 211
St-Myon 268
St-Nectaire 129
St-Nizier-d'Azergues 374
St-Nizier-le-Désert 361
Stock breeding 56
St-Paul-de-Varax 360
St-Paulien 213
St-Paul-Trois-Châteaux 462
St-Pierre-Eynac 429
St-Pierre-le-Déchausselat 440
St-Pierreville 425
St-Pourçain-sur-Sioule 296
St-Préjet-d'Allier 224
St-Rémy-sur-Durolle 235
St-Restitut 463
St-Romain-en-Gal 487
St-Romain-le-Puy 395
St-Saturnin 124
St-Sauves-d'Auvergne 152
St-Sauveur-de-Montagut 425
St-Victor-sur-Loire 408
St-Vincent-de-Barrès 431
St-Yorre 298
Super-Besse 144
Super-Lioran 172
Sury-le-Comtal 396
Suze-la-Rousse 463

T

Taulignan 460
Taxes 47
Tazenat 264
Telephone 45
Temple du Fival 425
Ternand 376
Ternant 122
Ternay 346
Terrasse, La 374

Textiles 54
Theizé 375
Themed Tours 17
Thiers 231
Thiers Cutlery 231
Thiézac 178
Thimonnier 65
Thines 441
Thueyts 436
Thuret 268
Time 48
Timeline 59
Tolls 38
Toulon-sur-Allier 280
Tour-d'Auvergne, La 138
Tour de la Clauze 222
Tourist Offices 32
Tourist trains 19
Tournemire 191
Tourzel-Ronzières 250
Traditional Rural Housing 78
Traditions in the Auvergne 53
Train Travel 36
Trévoux 359
Triptych by the Master of Moulins . . . 277
Trizac 187

U

Ucel 433
Usine de Pied-de-Borne 440
Ussel-d'Allier 305
Usson-en-Forez 398

V

Vague de l'Amitié, La 368
Val d'Allier and Alagnon 245, 246
Valence 468
Valette, La 389
Valgorge 435
Vallée
   de Chaudefour 137
   de d'Eyrieux 424
   de la Credogne 306
   de la Jordanne 176
   des Rouets 235
   des Saints 250
   du Mars 175
   du Sailhant 197, 198
Val Legat, Le 240
Vallon-en-Sully 288
Vallon-Pont-d'Arc 443
Valréas 464
Vals-les-Bains 432
Vandeins 355

Vans, Les	439
Vaulx-en-Velin	344
Vaux-en-Beaujolais	371
Veauce	305
Veauche	378
Vernoux-en-Vivarais	426
Viaduc de Garabit	199
Viaduc des Fades	271
Vichy	293
Vichy government	63
Vichy Government	295
Vichy Springs	297
Vic-le-Comte	252
Vic-sur-Cère	177, 179
Vieille-Brioude	217
Vienne	486
Vignes, Les	282
Villars-les-Dombes	360
Villedieu	196, 197
Villefranche-sur-Saône	367
Villeneuve	251
Villeneuve-les-Cerfs	268
Villerest	384
Villeurbanne and the East	344
Villié-Morgon	373
Vineyards	56
Visan	464
Viviers	452
Vogüé	438
Volcanoes of the Auvergne	86
Vollore-Montagne	237
Volvic	114
Vonnas	355
Voulte-sur-Rhône, La	425

W

Walking	23
Wars of Religion	62
Watersports	26
Weather Forecast	17
Websites	26, 32
What to See and Do	21
When to Go	17
Where to Eat	40
Where to Stay	39
Wine-tasting	18

Y

Ydes-Bourg	189
Yronde	252
Yssingeaux	429
Yzeure	279

INDEX

STAY

Ambert	241, 244
Aurillac	170
Aven d'Orgnac	450
Beaujolais	376
Bort-les-Orgues	155
Bourbon L'Archambault	283
Brioude	220, 221
Clermont-Ferrand	113
Crémieu	485
Fôret de Tronçais	292
Gorges de la Sioule	272
Grignan	463
Issoire	251
La Bourboule	152
La Dombes	361
Lapalisse	303
Le Pilat	413
Lyon	347
Massif du Sancy	138
Montbrison	396
Monts Dôme	116, 123
Monts du Lyonnais	378
Murat	181
Pérouges	364
Roanne	385
Romans-sur-Isère	476
Royat	113
Salers	184
St-Antoine-l'Abbaye	478
St-Bonnet-le-Château	398
St-Étienne	408
St-Flour	198
St-Nectaire	132
Thiers	238
Vals-les-Bains	436
Vienne	493
Villefranche-sur-Saône	369
Viviers	454

EAT

Ambert	241
Aurillac	170
Aven d'Orgnac	450, 451
Beaujolais	376
Besse-et-St-Anastaise	148, 152
Clermont-Ferrand	113
Gorges de l'Ardeche	447
Grignan	463
Issoire	251
La Dombes	361
Lapalisse	303
Le Pilat	413
Les Vans	442
Lyon	347
Montélimar	461
Montluçon	289
Monts Dôme	116, 123
Monts du Forez	394
Monts du Lyonnais	378
Moulins	281
Murat	181
Privas	432
Riom	265, 266
Roanne	385
Romans-sur-Isère	476
Salers	185, 187
St-Bonnet-le-Château	398
St-Étienne	408
St-Flour	198, 201
St-Nectaire	132, 142
Thiers	238
Valence	471
Vals-les-Bains	436
Vichy	300
Vienne	493
Villefranche-sur-Saône	369
Viviers	454

MAPS AND PLANS

THEMATIC MAPS
Driving Tours . . . . .Inside front cover
Principal Sights . . . . .Inside back cover
Volcanoes of Auvergne 88
Metro map. 510-511

MAPS AND PLANS

Clermont-Ferrand and Monts Dôme
Clermont-Ferrand and Monts Dôme. 95
Vieux Clermont 98
Clermont-Ferrand. 100-101
Cathédrale Notre-Dame 104
Old Montferrand 106
Around Clermont-Ferrand 109
Dôme Mountains. 120
Lava Route. 125

Monts Dore, Artense and Cézallier
Monts Dore, Artense and Cézallier 128
Château de Murol 131
Massif du Sancy 135
Hikes around Mont-Dore 140
The Couze Valleys 145
Randonnées 150
Discovering the Artense 154
From Cézallier to the Sianne 157
Rhue Gorge to Gentiane Country. 161

Aurillac, Châtaigneraie and Monts du Cantal
Aurillac, Châtaigneraie and
    Monts du Cantal. 162-163
Aurillac. 167
The Cantal Mountains 172-173
Salers. 184
Gorges de la Maronne 191

St-Flour, Sanflorain and Margeride du Cantal
St-Flour, Sanflorain and Margeride
    du Cantal. 193
St-Flour. 195
Gorges of the Truyère 200-201

Velay and Brivadois
Velay and Brivadois. 204
Cathédral Notre-Dame 207
Le Puy-en-Velay 209
St-Julian's Basilica 216
Churches of the Haut Allier 218
Gorges from the Allier to the
    Devès Mountains 223

Thiers and the Livradois-Forez
Thiers and the Livradois-Forez 229
Thiers. 232
The Forez Mountains 236
Abbey Church of St-Robert 243

Val d'Allier and Alagnon
Val d'Allier and Alagnon 246

Limagne, Pays des Combrailles and Gorges de la Sioule
Limagne, Pays des Combrailles and
    Gorges de la Sioule 259
Riom 261
Gorges of the Sioule. 271

Bourbonnais
Bourbonnais 274-275
Cathédrale Notre-Dame 277
Moulins. 278
Montluçon. 287
Tronçais Forest 291
Vichy 294
Around Vichy 299
The Bourbonnais Mountains 307

Lyon
Lyon. 310-311
Lyon Metro Map. 315
Vieux-Lyon Fourvière. 319
La Presqu'île 329
La Croix-Rousse 336-337
Left Bank 342-343

Bresse and the Dombes
Bresse and the Dombes. 351
Pérouges 363

Beaujolais and the Monts du Lyonnais
Beaujolais and the Monts du Lyonnais. . . 366
Villefranche-sur-Saône 368
Beaujolais. 372

Roannais and Le Forez
Roannais and Le Forez. 380
Foothills and Gorges of the Roanne area . 383
The Forez Mountains 391

St-Étienne and Le Pilat
St-Étienne and Le Pilat. 400
St-Étienne 404-405

The Ardèche
The Upper Vivarais and Le Velay 414-415
The Lower Vivarais 416-417

The Upper Vivarais and Le Velay
Annonay. 420
Corniche de l'Eyrieux 425

The Lower Vivarais
Massif du Tanargue. 434
The Gorges of the Ardèche 444-445
Viviers 453

Drôme Provençale and the Préalpes Drômoises
Drôme Provençale and the
    Préalpes Drômoises. 457

Valentinois and the Lower Dauphiné
Valentinois and the Lower Dauphiné 467
Valence. 469
Romans-sur-Isère 474
Crémieu 483
La Lauze 484
St-Romain-en-Gal 487
Vienne 490-491

MAP LEGEND

★★★ Worth a special journey
★★ Worth a detour
★ Interesting

Tourism

	Sightseeing route with departure point indicated	AZ B	Map co-ordinates locating sights
	Ecclesiastical building		Tourist information
	Synagogue – Mosque		Historic house, castle – Ruins
	Building (with main entrance)		Dam – Factory or power station
	Statue, small building		Fort – Cave
	Wayside cross		Prehistoric site
	Fountain		Viewing table – View
	Fortified walls – Tower – Gate		Miscellaneous sight

Recreation

	Racecourse		Waymarked footpath
	Skating rink		Outdoor leisure park/centre
	Outdoor, indoor swimming pool		Theme/Amusement park
	Marina, moorings		Wildlife/Safari park, zoo
	Mountain refuge hut		Gardens, park, arboretum
	Overhead cable-car		Aviary, bird sanctuary
	Tourist or steam railway		

Additional symbols

	Motorway (unclassified)		Post office – Telephone centre
	Junction: complete, limited		Covered market
	Pedestrian street		Barracks
	Unsuitable for traffic, street subject to restrictions		Swing bridge
	Steps – Footpath		Quarry – Mine
	Railway – Coach station		Ferry (river and lake crossings)
	Funicular – Rack-railway		Ferry services: Passengers and cars
	Tram – Metro, underground		Foot passengers only
Bert (R.)...	Main shopping street	③	Access route number common to MICHELIN maps and town plans

Abbreviations and special symbols

A	Agricultural office (Chambre d'agriculture)	P	Local authority offices (Préfecture, sous-préfecture)
C	Chamber of commerce (Chambre de commerce)	POL.	Police station (Police)
H	Town hall (Hôtel de ville)		Police station (Gendarmerie)
J	Law courts (Palais de justice)	T	Theatre (Théâtre)
M	Museum (Musée)	U	University (Université)
		a	Hotel
			Park and Ride

COMPANION PUBLICATIONS

MICHELIN

travelguide.michelin.com
www.viamichelin.com

MAPS
Regional and local Maps

Motorists who plan ahead will always have the appropriate maps at hand. Michelin products complement each of the sites listed in *The Green Guide*; map references are given to help you find your location on our range of maps.

♦ The regional maps at a scale of 1 : 200 000 **nos 519, 522, 523 and 526**, which cover the main roads and secondary roads, include useful indications for finding tourist attractions. In addition to identifying the nature of the road ways, the maps show castles, churches and other religious edifices, scenic view points, megalithic monuments, swimming beaches on lakes and rivers, swimming pools, golf courses, race-courses, air fields, and more.

♦ The local maps maps at a scale of 1:150 000 and 1:175 000 are the latest maps in our collection. They include useful symbols for identifying tourist attractions, town plans and an index. The map diagram below indicates which maps you need to travel in Auvergne and the Rhône Valley.

Road Map

Remember to travel with the latest edition of the **map of France no 721** (1 : 1 000 000), which gives an overall view of the region, and the main access roads that connect it to the rest of France. Convenient Atlas formats (spiral, hard cover and "mini") are also available.

ROUTE PLANNING

Michelin is pleased to offer a route planning service at **www.viamichelin.com**.

Personalised route plans, comprehensive maps, addresses of hotels and restaurants featured in *The Red Guides* and practical and tourist information.

YOUR OPINION IS ESSENTIAL TO IMPROVING OUR PRODUCTS

Help us by answering the questionnaire on our website:
satisfaction.michelin.com

LYON METRO MAP

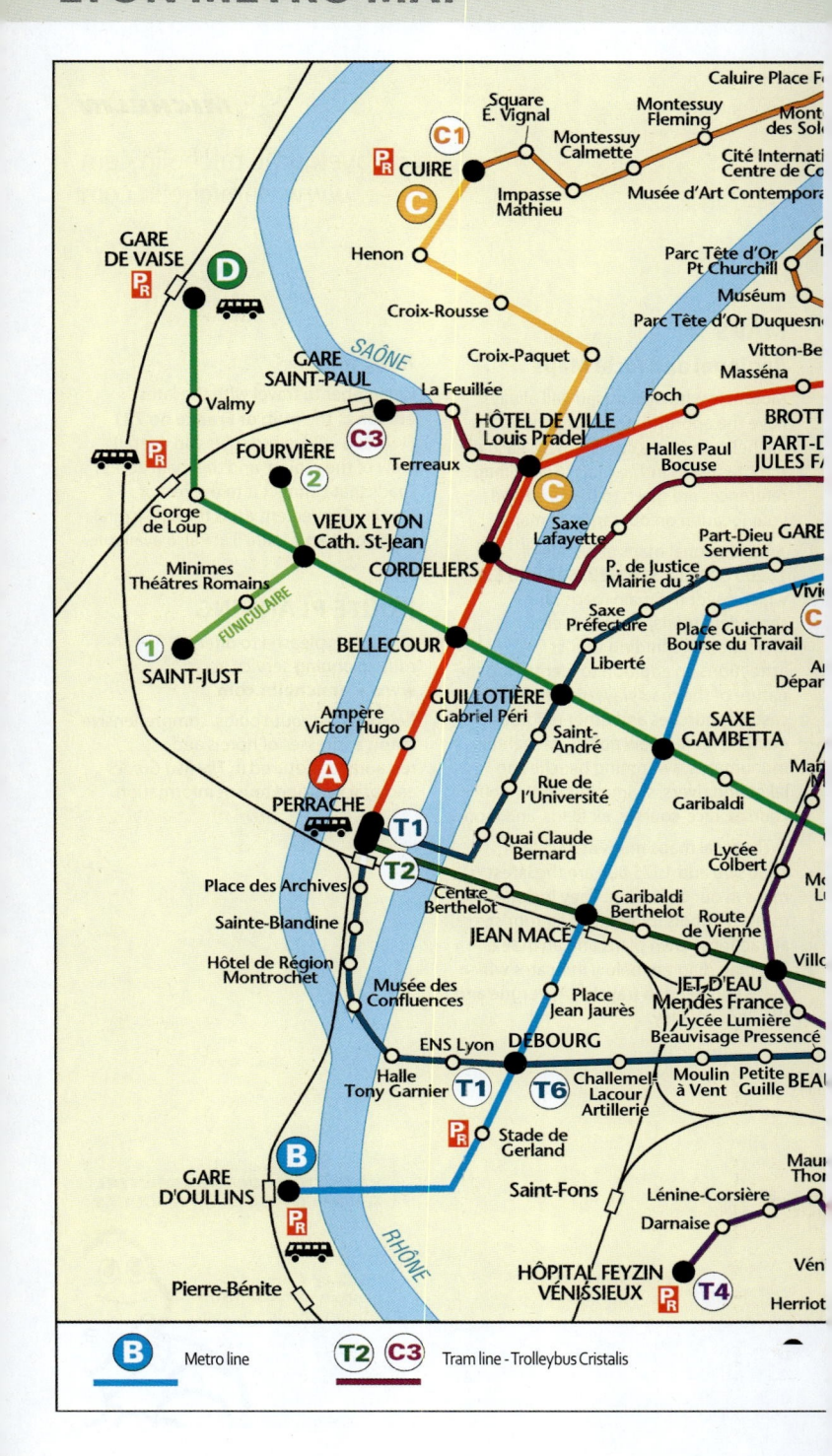

511

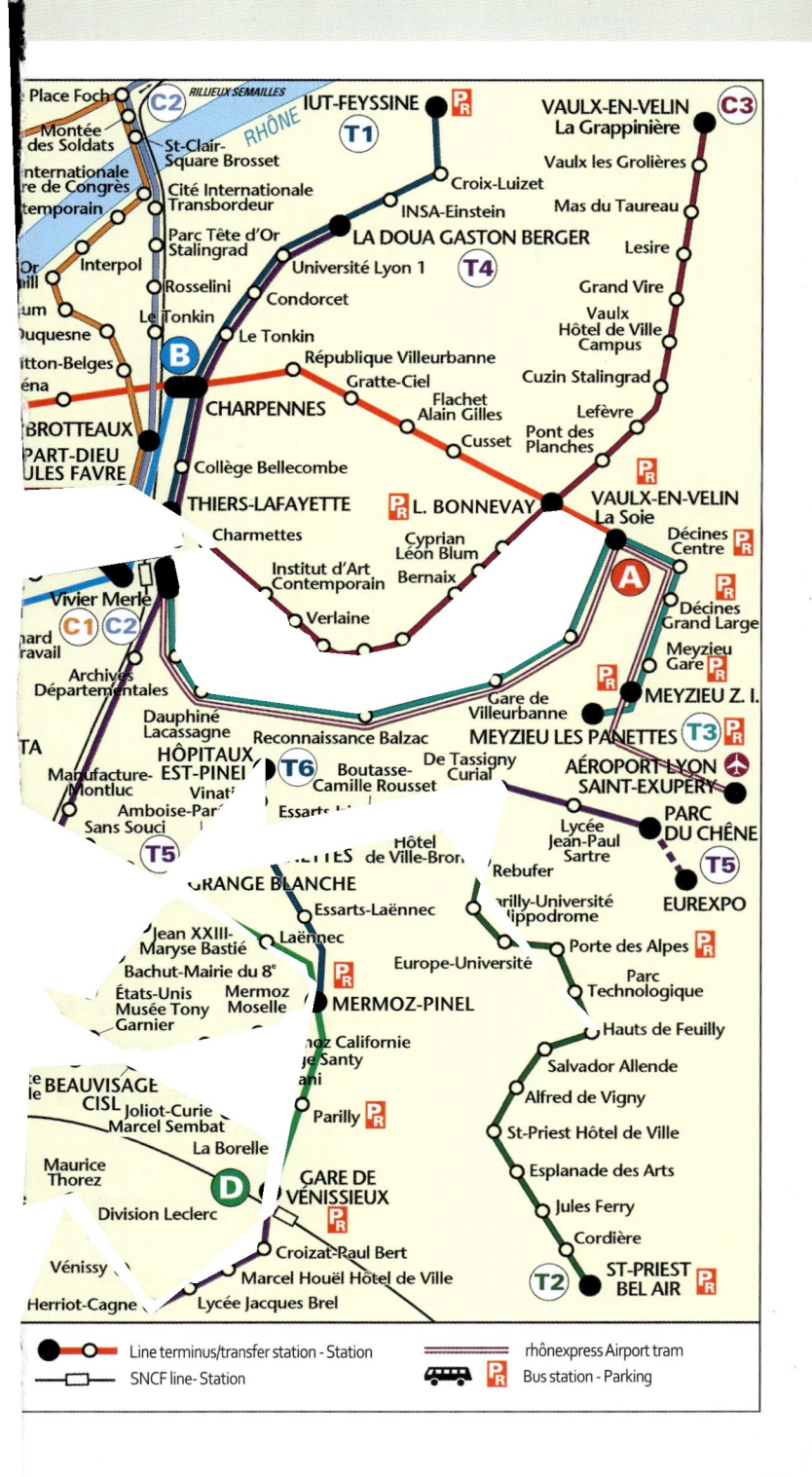

MICHELIN

Michelin Travel Partner

Société par actions simplifiées au capital de 15 044 940 EUR
27 cours de l'Ile Seguin - 92100 Boulogne Billancourt (France)
R.C.S. Nanterre 433 677 721

No part of this publication may be reproduced in any form
without the prior permission of the publisher.

© Michelin Travel Partner
ISBN 978-2-067243-20-0
Printed: March 2020
Printed and bound in France : Imprimerie CHIRAT, 42540 Saint-Just-la-Pendue - N° 202003.0189

Although the information in this guide was believed by the authors and publisher to be accurate and current at the time of publication, they cannot accept responsibility for any inconvenience, loss, or injury sustained by any person relying on information or advice contained in this guide. Things change over time and travellers should take steps to verify and confirm information, especially time-sensitive information related to prices, hours of operation, and availability.